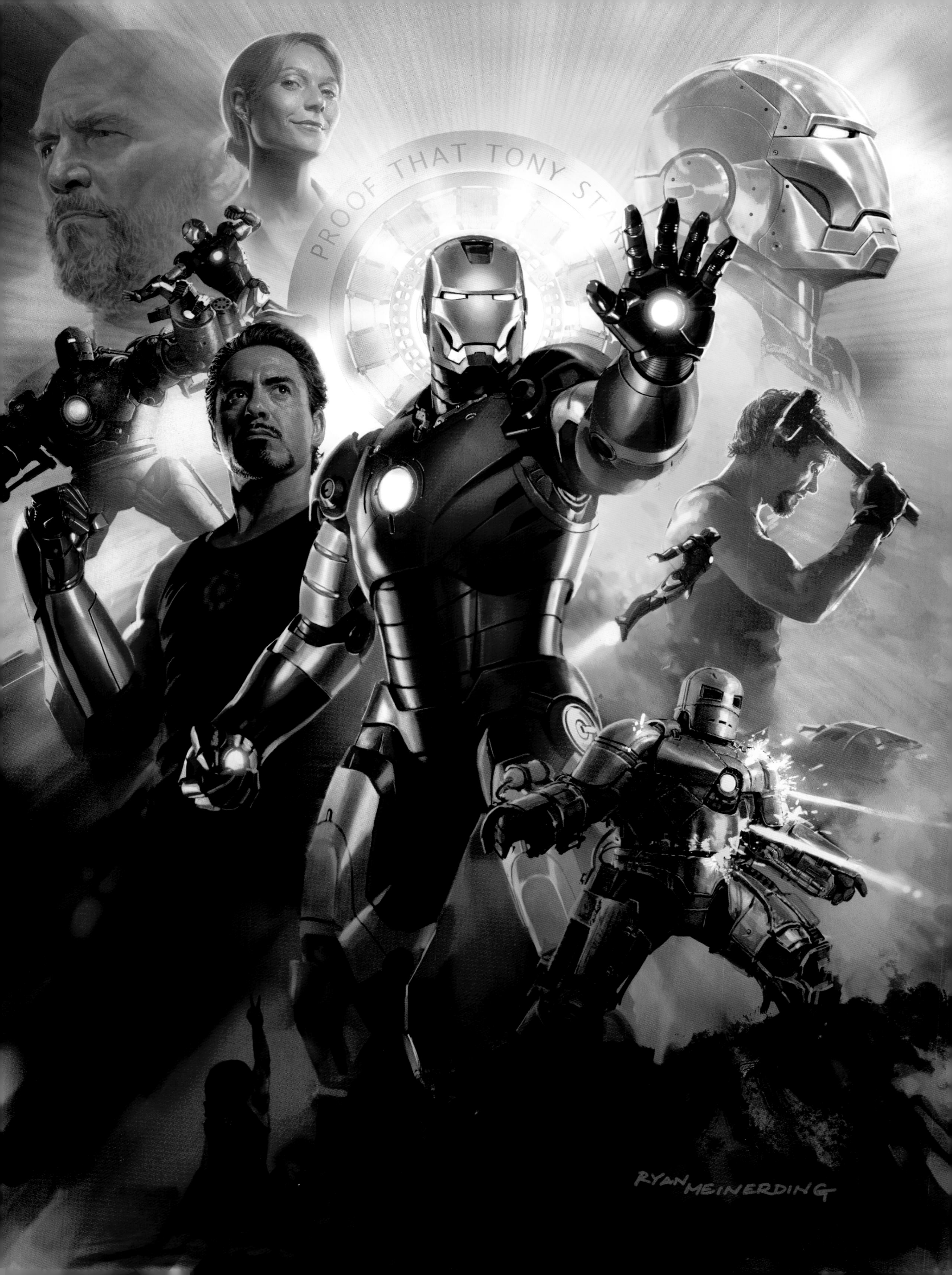
PROOF THAT TONY STARK
RYAN MEINERDING

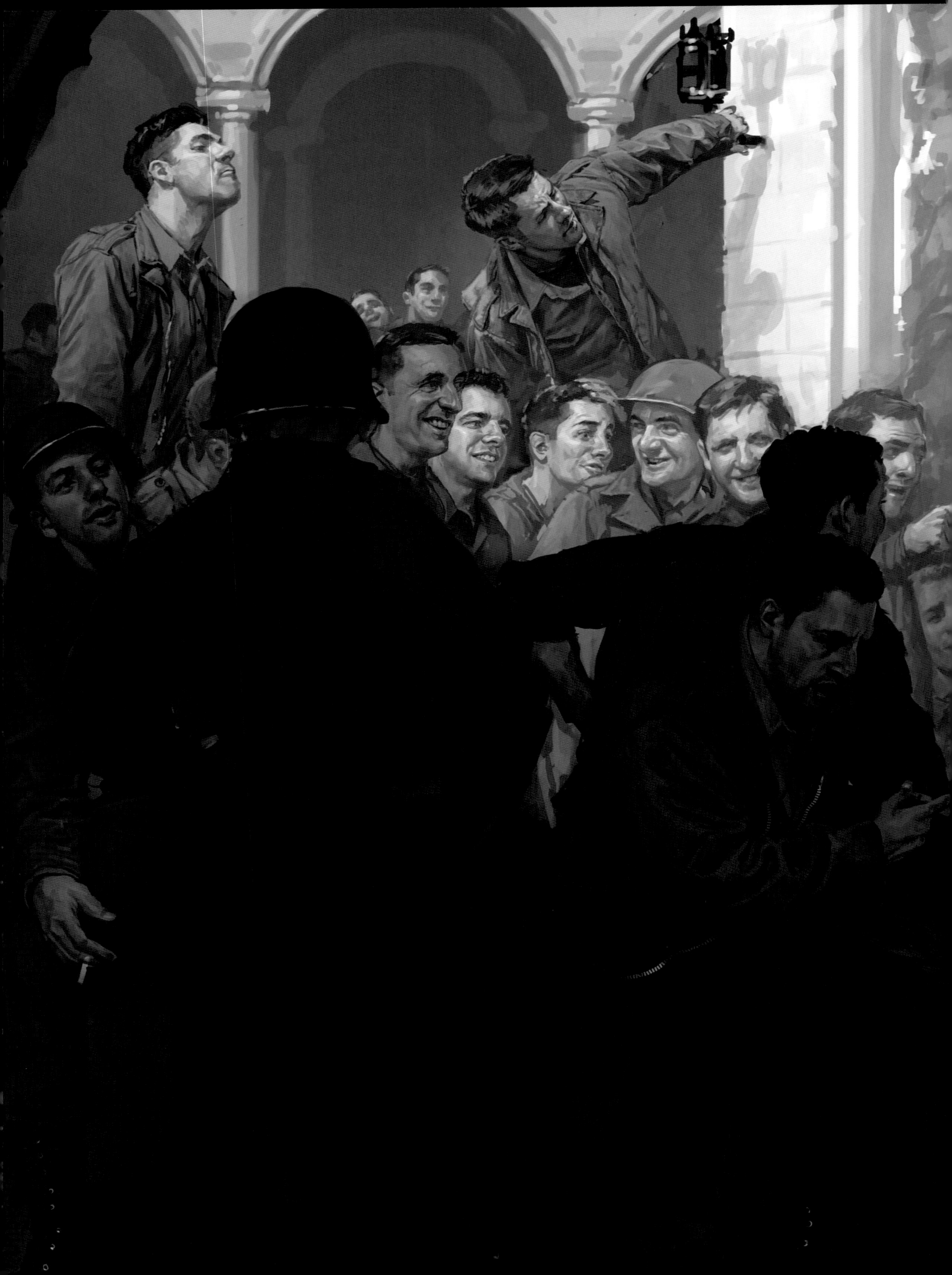

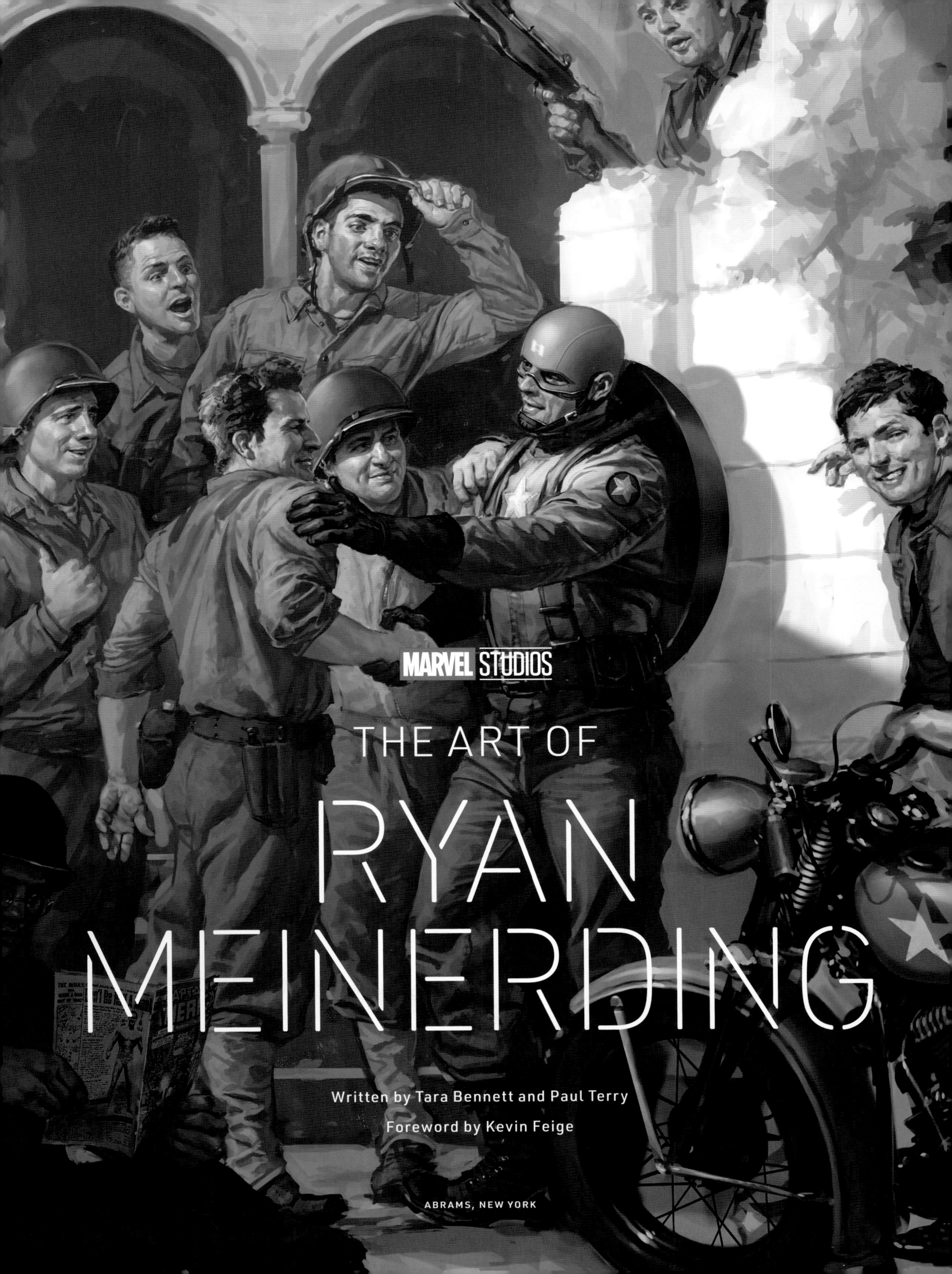

MARVEL STUDIOS

THE ART OF RYAN MEINERDING

Written by Tara Bennett and Paul Terry

Foreword by Kevin Feige

ABRAMS, NEW YORK

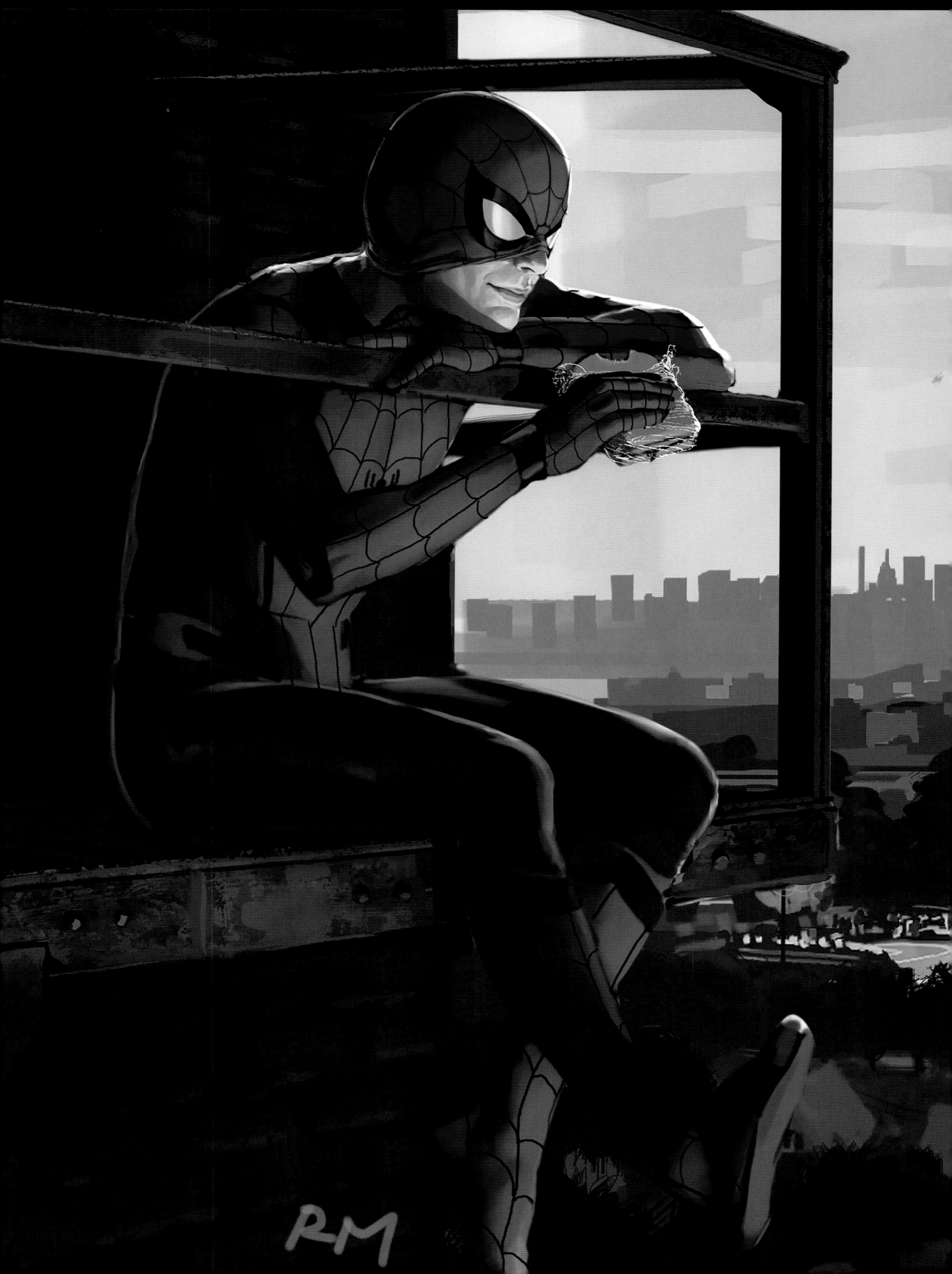
RM

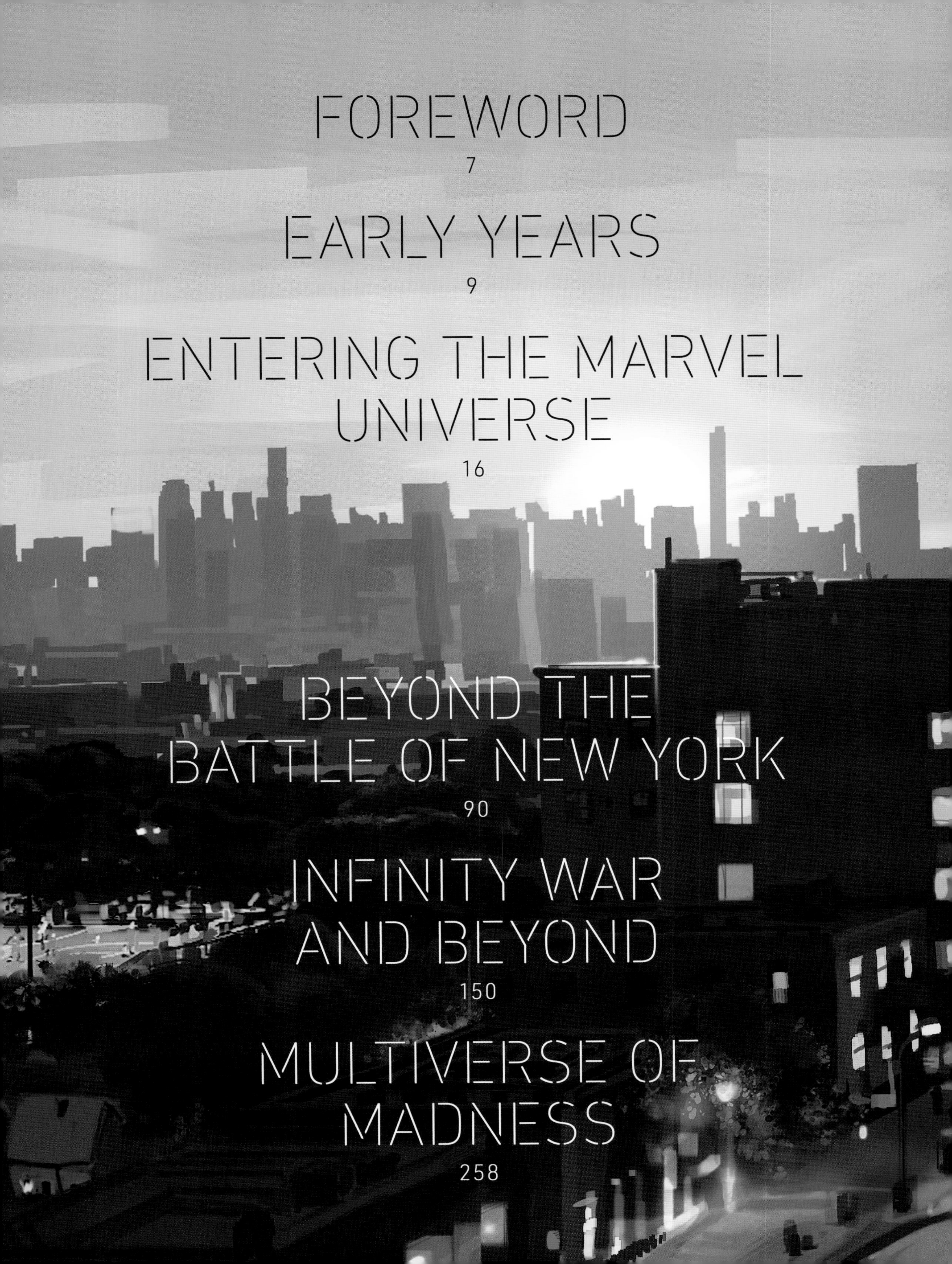

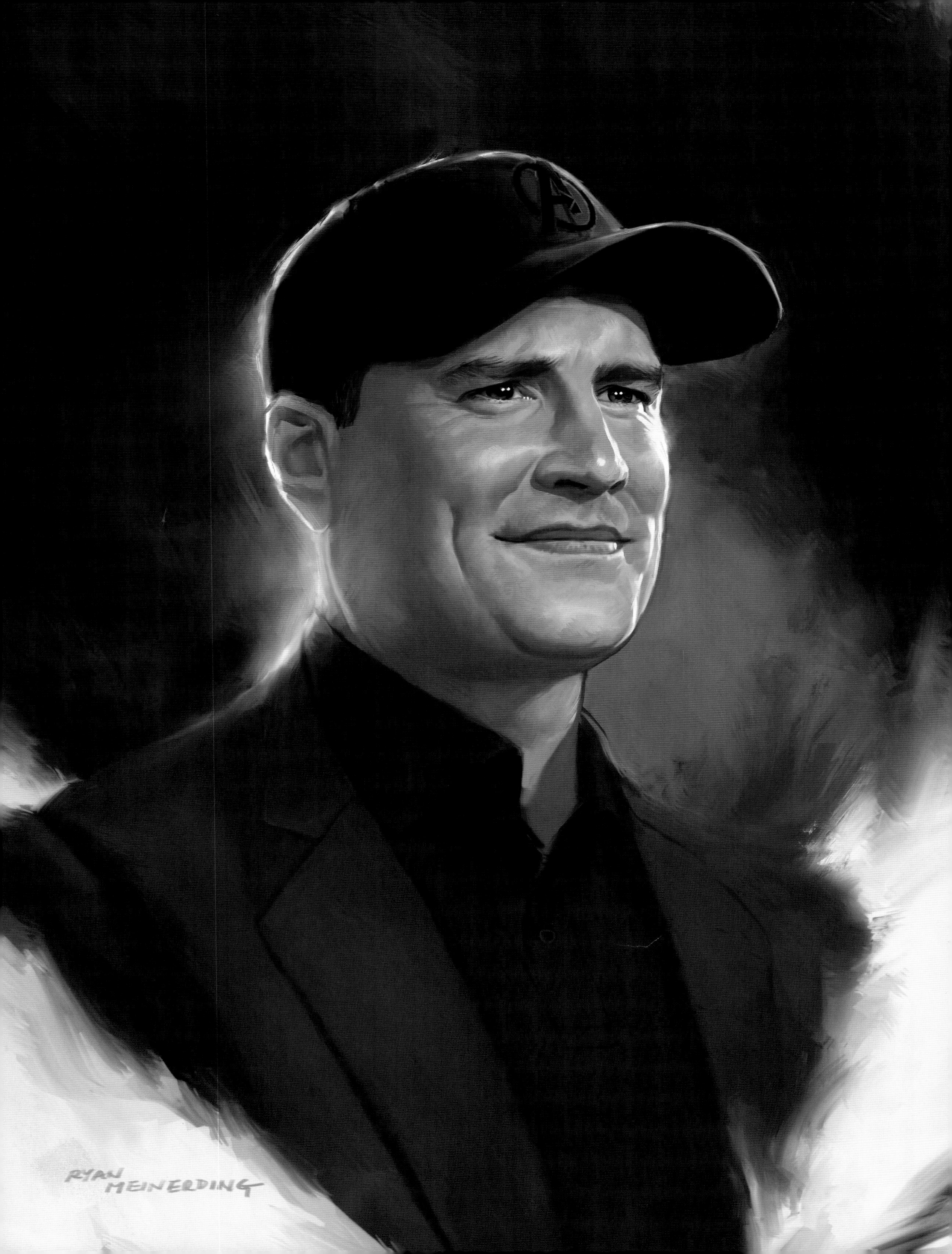
RYAN
MEINERDING

FOREWORD

By Kevin Feige

Ryan Meinerding is a humble genius who pours his passion about the work *into* the work. And he's not just a great visual artist. He's a great *storyteller*.

Since way back on *Iron Man*, this has remained the most impressive thing about Ryan. It's not just that he can envision the translation from the comic page to the movie screen. He's an *idea* machine. Marvel is the House of Ideas. And he's right at the front door of that. It's impossible to truly convey how important Ryan is to Marvel Studios and its success.

Back on the development of *Iron Man*, after Jon Favreau asked him to take an artistic run at some things, Ryan quickly came up with unforgettable images. These included the black-and-white illustrations of Tony Stark working underneath an Iron Man suit in his garage, with the jukebox in the background, and the first test-flight moment with the boot thrusters. I can still remember how those images were transformative for that film. Just looking at them, it was like, "Oh . . . here it is. *This* is the movie." Like the best concept artists in history, Ryan creates key frames that encourage us to make the movies.

Not long after *Iron Man*, while we were having a brainstorming meeting in our first Marvel Studios offices—shared with a kite company—we had comic art up on the wall for visual ideas for what would become our first Thor movie. Next to those we had a couple images Ryan had started for the first Captain America movie. And every time we brought a filmmaker in to talk about our Norse god adventure, they kept turning and pointing to Ryan's Captain America illustrations.

These are just a handful of early examples of the impact Ryan and his artwork have had on other artists, filmmakers, storytellers, Marvel Studios, the MCU, and its audience.

I grew up reading making-of books about *Star Wars* and saw how Ralph McQuarrie was the first person that ever put the images from George Lucas's imagination onto paper. And all those McQuarrie images have become classic pieces of artwork. At Marvel Studios, we, of course, have the benefit of the comics. So we weren't visually starting from nothing. But comics have had many different interpretations over the decades. Because Ryan loves these characters, he is able to interpret *all* of that material through his hand, his imagination, and his heart. Ryan draws them as *he* sees

them. Putting all that passion onto a page—before we put that passion onto a screen—is an integral part of the translation from the comic page to the screen. And it's the reason why our Marvel Studios logo starts with comic pages, script pages, then Ryan's artwork, and *then* the live-action footage. You see how big those Ryan images are in that logo? That tells you the importance of what he does for us.

Most artists are freelancers who go from project to project. And Ryan did that for the first few Marvel Studios movies. But it fast became clear he was so much a part of the visual language of the MCU that we asked him if he was interested in coming in-house full-time and leading the team that became the Visual Development department. Thankfully for you, he was more than willing to do that. Over the years, that's really where he's been able to thrive beyond just being a concept artist, moving into other realms of storytelling and really helping lead the charge when Marvel Studios entered animation—stretching a whole other artistic muscle he had.

One of my favorite Ryan Meinerding moments was our initial Peter Parker MCU conversation. The instant I first came to him saying, "I think we're going to be able to use Spider-Man. . . . What would *you* do with Spidey?" Right off the top of his head, one of the very first ideas he had was to make the eyes in the suit move mechanically to convey emotion. That was such a brilliant idea. It mimicked the way comic book artists, panel to panel, would cheat the eyes slightly to express how Spider-Man was feeling.

Another favorite moment was when I went to Ryan to say, "You have an hour. I need you to draw a secret character for the tag to *Guardians of the Galaxy*. But use the comic as the inspiration, not the movie." He goes, "Who?" I said, "Howard." Ryan turned around and looked up at me. "The *duck*?!"

One of my most loved pieces by Ryan—which I have hanging in my house—is the poster art he did for the Marvel Studios art exhibition in Paris, France. I think it's one of my favorites because being in an art gallery in Paris emphasizes what Ryan Meinerding's work is: It is *art*. It deserves to be seen—not just as it translates into our films and shows—but as art, in and of itself, to be displayed for everyone to see and enjoy. So, with that spirit in mind, I am thrilled we now have this celebration of the *art* of Ryan Meinerding.

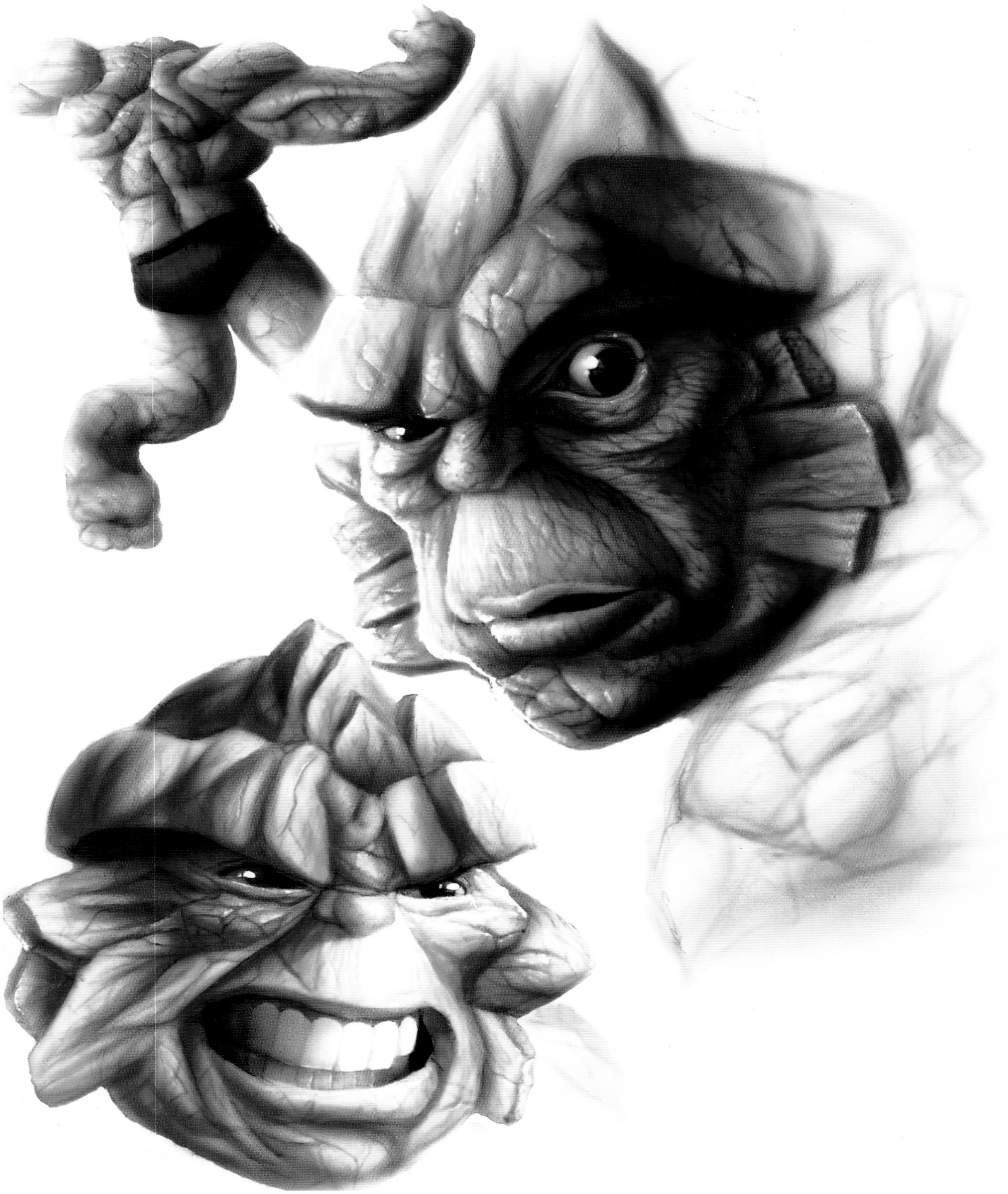

always begins with a solitary experience, toiling to capture the right facial expression or dynamism on the page. That individual place of creation is the shared experience of every artist. Often, it's that lonely pursuit of perfection that compels them to stay with an image until it's right. In the world of comic book art, the Jack Kirbys, the Jim Lees, the Todd McFarlanes—to name just a few—sketched, composed, and ultimately shared with the world what have since become indelible representations of modern storytelling's greatest comic book Super Heroes. Their work has altered forever how observers "see" seminal characters in sequential art. And perhaps even more consequential is how they've inspired further generations to make magic with their pencils, markers, or digital pens.

Ryan Meinerding is a member of that further generation of artists who looked to the greats making comic book art and pored over their work to fuel his own artistic passion. As a Midwestern kid in a family with no connection to publishing or film, he forged his own path to follow in the footsteps of his artistic heroes. Learning his craft through industrial design, character design, and eventually concept work, Meinerding approached his own craft with a journeyman's work ethic and an undeterred dedication to making his art better. Eventually, his ambitions aligned with opportunity. In 2007, director Jon Favreau sought Meinerding's visual eye to help him first develop a John Carter of Mars film, and then Marvel Studios' first self-made production, *Iron Man*.

Two decades later, Meinerding's art is now synonymous with how audiences around the world perceive Marvel Studios' version of the Marvel Comics roster of Super Heroes. It's his character designs that established the Marvel Cinematic Universe's iconic looks for Iron Man, Captain America, Black Panther, Spider-Man, and so many more. It's his key frame studies of those Super Heroes in action together that have become the bedrock images that entire film sequences were built around, from *Iron Man* to the most recent Marvel Studios releases. And if you tour the Marvel Studios offices at the Walt Disney Studios lot in Burbank, California, it's Meinerding's art that adorns the exteriors of their array of conference rooms. The studio's foundational characters cover full walls, capturing the MCU Super Heroes at their best, all rendered by Meinerding with startling detail, energy, and realism.

Today, Meinerding remains the humble artist in residence at Marvel Studios. As their Head of Visual Development, he continues to create seminal images that become memorable sequences in their films and television shows, as well as guiding a gifted department of visual artists. His art is already inspiring the next generation of artists who look to his work to ignite their own.

Every artist has that moment where something inspires them to take a crayon or a pencil in hand and just draw. Ryan Meinerding, the younger son of mother and father Ann and Wes of North Canton, Ohio, can still cite his earliest artistic inspirations as the comic strips of Jim Davis's *Garfield* and Peyo's *The Smurfs*. And with them came his Saturday ritual of dressing up in his Spider-Man Underoos to watch the morning block of animated cartoons with his older brother, Wes. An instant favorite: *Spider-Man and His Amazing Friends*.

As the siblings grew, Wes graduated to comic books and brought his little brother along with him. "He'd go around our hometown, finding where there were actually comic book stores," Meinerding remembers. "So, I started buying *Wolverine* and some *X-Men* comics." From that new medium he started to copy and draw characters like Captain America or Spider-Man. Intent on trying to capture Super Heroes with fidelity, as Meinerding got better, he pushed himself to reproduce his favorite characters with heightened realism.

The Meinerding boys were raised in a household that encouraged their creative endeavors. Young Ryan remembers observing his mother's passion for painting and crafting all year long.

"I look back at my childhood and the craft projects she would put together, the decorations she would do, the Advent calendars that she would make by hand—I just thought everybody's life was like that," he reminisces. "She had a desire to create art in general. But also, I think for her kids, she wanted to make a nice, wonderful childhood. To have special things that we would hang up at Halloween and Christmas

OPPOSITE At the age of sixteen, Ryan Meinerding drew this interpretation of the Fantastic Four member, The Thing.

On his father's side, Meinerding remembers the influence of his grandfather, who managed an assembly line at Ford Motors doing tool and die work. Meinerding's father spent a lot of time at his father's development project—a community he was instrumental in forming after he retired—and watched him build the roads and infrastructure to turn the lots into sellable property.

Inside his grandfather's machine shop, Ryan was eyewitness to his grandfather's concepts that were tinkered with until he could take them to market. "He developed a bike light that was so rudimentary that he could sell it to the Amish," he shares. "He ended up developing one of the first mulching blades, which he ended up getting a patent for and licensing out."

"My grandpa was always coming up with ideas, and my dad was always trying to help him get those ideas made," he continues. "So whereas neither of my parents were in a creative field necessarily, I felt like I was around people always trying to make things, always wanting to build stuff, always spending time doing something creative. I was inspired by things my dad did, I remember wanting a car bed when I was a kid, but we couldn't afford to get one, so my father built me one based on my favorite concept car out of plywood and my mother painted it."

Meinerding carried that mindset into his own illustration skills, which he honed through grade and middle school. By the time he hit high school, he was primarily working in colored pencils. It was around that time that he discovered artist Todd McFarlane's Spider-Man work.

Deeply inspired, he purposefully studied and mimicked McFarlane's hyper-detailed style. "I ended up being heavily influenced by him, creating comic book characters and trying things that were literally rip-offs of what he was doing in *Amazing Spider-Man* at the time." Meinerding also found himself drawn to the nineties era-defining work of Jim Lee's *X-Men* and Alex Ross's *Marvels*.

Continuing to hone his own skills, Meinerding's drawing talent was recognized by his high school art teacher, Ty Palmer. It was through him that he was introduced to the world of airbrushes and compressors. "I figured out how to use an airbrush in a way that's not like T-shirt airbrushing but felt more like how illustrators would use it. From that I was able to get to some realistic stuff pretty early in my art career."

With a new tool to up his game, Meinerding says his focus became twofold: achieving realism but also figuring out the rudiments of great design. "Making it look real became a part of not only the visual but the problem-solving inside the image," he explains. "I think that's fundamentally why I also enjoyed commercial art more than fine art. I like *ideas* I like concepts. I like the idea of basing an amazing visual on an amazing concept."

When he was sixteen, Meinerding attended a small Canton, Ohio, comic convention with his brother, and it surprisingly led to his first paid comic book work. A local entrepreneur was trying to start his own comic book imprint and needed artists to make covers, and he was tasked with attempting to create very Jack Kirby—esque drawings. "This was the first time I'd ever gotten paid to do art outside of a couple portraits for people," he says. "And this was the first version of me working in comics." The comics job never went anywhere of note, but Meinerding remembers drafting an image of The Thing (see page 8) around the same time that incorporated his early explorations of realistic skin. "I was interested in The Thing because his skin was so cracked and I was trying to make that feel really tangible and rough," he details. It was an image that showed progression in his skills, and one he kept in his portfolio.

The experience with the comic book spurred Meinerding to apply his inherent work ethic toward pursuing art as a potential career. In high school, he put a portfolio of his art together so he could cold-call businesses in the area for summer work. Literally flipping through the phone book, he sought out advertising agencies around town. Then, with the help of his brother, who drove him to various companies, Meinerding says he would just show up with his portfolio and ask if anybody would be willing to look at his work. One Akron, Ohio, advertising agency gave the budding artist a test—and fifty bucks—to illustrate an ad for a system of interlocking landscaping bricks that earned him some early appreciation.

However, due to his age and high school workload, Meinerding was limited in what he could commit his time and attention to. But, he says, by shopping his work around so early, he was exposed to great feedback and the professional "yes" way ahead of many of his peers. And he discovered the people in the field who were willing to talk to him about his work, and even hire him for some minor jobs. "I was realizing that I *could* get work like this," he says of that time.

Despite dipping his toe into those professional waters, Meinerding admits he didn't seriously consider applying to art schools after high school. "In my experience, 'art' was me sitting down and drawing things. When I went to class I would get critiques." The implication of an abundance of theory with little doing didn't sit well with him. "I thought i

LEFT Acrylic painting of resort hotel, done during high school

were to go [to an art school], I'm gonna waste money and not be able to get a job. So the plan for me after high school was going to a liberal arts school. I'll take art classes, but I'll probably be a business major or something." With that mindset, he applied to Ohio State, University of Michigan, Syracuse University, and Notre Dame . . . and was then accepted at all four schools.

For context, at that time, Pixar's *Toy Story* had just been released in theaters, and Meinerding was playing the PC game *Myst*. Both rocked his world in terms of opening his mind toward pursuing studies in computer-generated graphics. "It seemed like a way of doing something that was artistically minded but it also felt like you still did it for a company that would pay you, and that was on the commercial side of things." With that field of study top of mind, Meinerding matriculated at Notre Dame as an art major.

In the Notre Dame Art Department, Meinerding was mentored by professors who recognized his talent and propensity toward analytic design. He was then encouraged to meet with the university's industrial design teachers.

"In my own brain, I was never going to be the painter that changed the world," he says with clarity. "I didn't even know what industrial design was, but I met Professor Paul Down and took some classes. The idea of basically combining art with a lot of the stuff that my grandpa did made a lot of sense to me. And so, the home that I had at Notre Dame was really in the industrial design department, learning the basic design philosophy of approaching problems, problem-solving, coming up with options, and looking at a problem from as many angles as possible."

Meinerding threw himself into the program and, as a self-proclaimed introvert, admits he became the embodiment of the clichéd artist who observed his peers going out on Friday and Saturday nights while he would stay working in the art building both nights. A regret for some, but not to Meinerding, who says he can connect that dedication to a marked maturing of his skills and techniques.

"I feel like when artists are successful in their career, it's because they're mostly incredibly hardworking," he observes. "But the thing they get credited for is their talent. It's almost like if you're an artist and you're credited with being hardworking, it's a knock to your talent in some ways. All the successful commercial artists I know are some of the most hardworking people I've *ever* met in my life, in a way that other people that are not in creative fields wouldn't even understand. If you talk to somebody that has a regular nine-to-five job and say, 'I gotta work until three in the morning four days a week, and then I gotta work both days on the weekend,' they're just like, '*What?*' It's not something to even consider because it's so far out of their realm. But that's what my entire college experience was: everyone else was having a college experience, with me being in the art building."

In keeping with that ethos, Meinerding secured an internship at Hasbro Interactive leading up to his senior year. While there, his goal was to over-deliver and impress his supervisors. It was his experience there, around professional product design, as well as his existing love for comic art that inspired him to focus on character design for his final thesis project. He designed his own comic book featuring

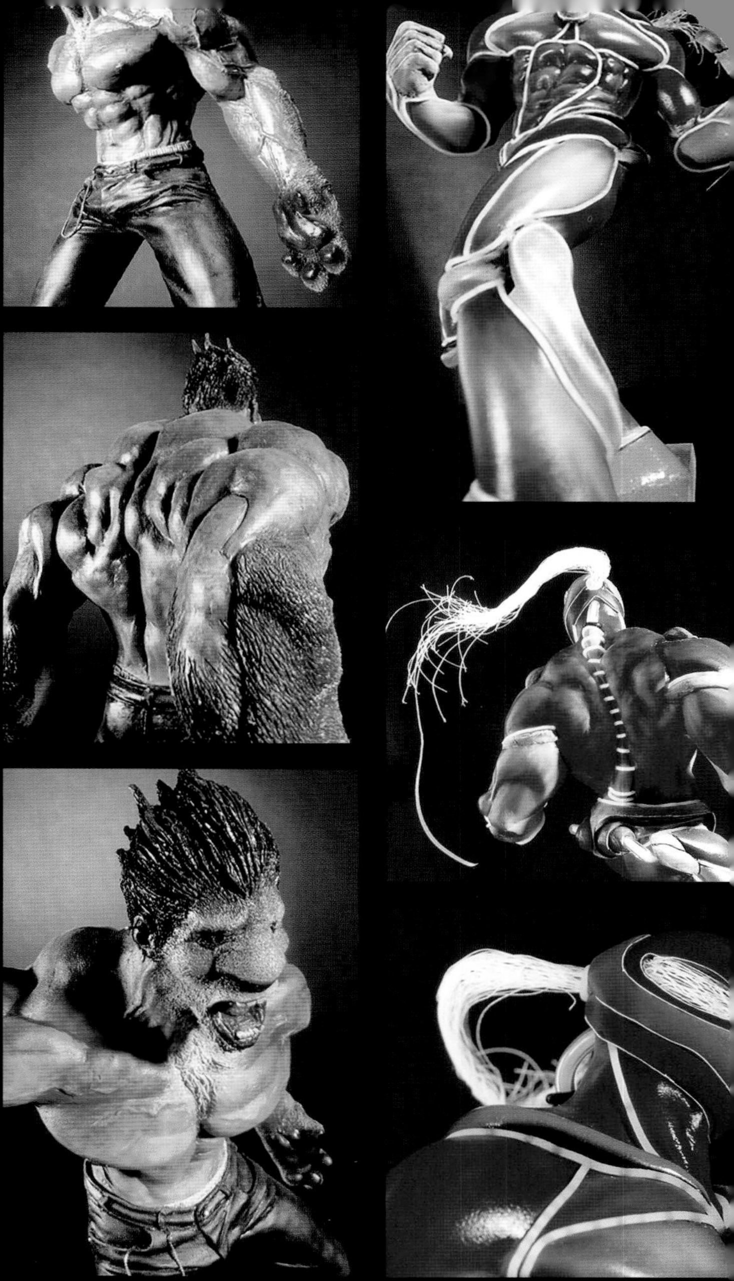

ABOVE Sculpted characters from Ryan Meinerding's final thesis—his own original comic book idea.

original characters, then sculpted them and presented retail toy packaging for the concept's line of toys. His success in both the internship and his graduation thesis secured him a full-time job at Hasbro Interactive upon graduation, and his professional life started in earnest.

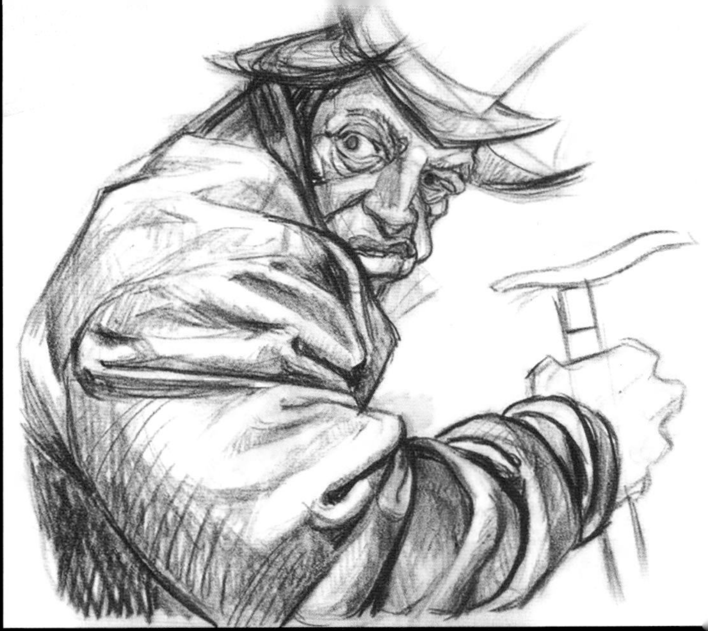

A CAREER BEGINS

The job had Meinerding relocating to Boston, Massachusetts, to work at the Hasbro Interactive home office. It was there he had his first experiences working in earnest on huge brands from Atari to Tonka, and even their own venerable in-house titles like *Monopoly* and *Scrabble*. Despite the fun products, Meinerding remembers it as a very corporate environment, with a lot of older employees. As it turns out, six months after his start date, the entire Hasbro Interactive division was downsized. Meinerding was out of a job, with no resources to easily replace it.

However, a web boom was happening around him. Start-ups and tech-savvy businesses were taking off, and Meinerding was contacted by a friend to join his company, Inforte, based in Chicago. A software implementation company, they were interested in expanding into design. Meinerding became the first hire in their newly christened design department. Now working with executives and designers much closer to his age, he found himself more at home at his day job.

Introduced to the world of pitching clients design concepts, Meinerding's work impressed major companies like PlayStation, who hired him via Inforte to make the websites for their games releasing on playstation.com. "I did *MediEvil*, *Wild Arms 2*, and *The Legend of Dragoon*. Then the biggest title I did was *Twisted Metal: Black*. It was a fun time," he reflects. "I was getting to work on big brands, and it wasn't just corporate stuff. I was trying to be as cutting edge as I could be—learning Flash and coding—trying to work all of that together into design that was fun." Eventually, he found himself hitting a wall in terms of gaining skills for his bigger goals, so he quit and moved back to Ohio to reorient his attention toward art school.

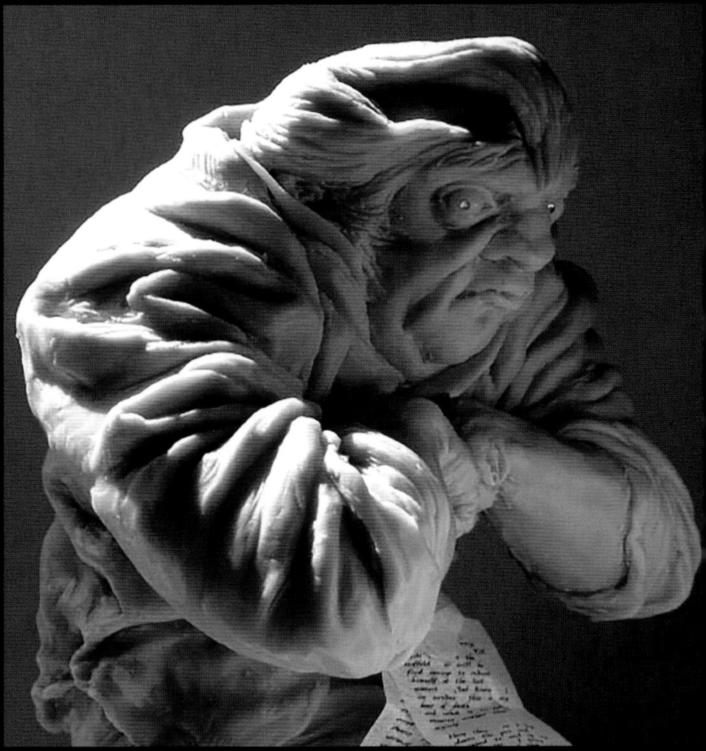

BACK TO SCHOOL

Having worked in corporate design, Meinerding found himself wrestling with pursuing a path favoring animation or returning to an art school where he could continue to improve his overall design and illustration skills. He was split between ArtCenter in Pasadena for their design department and Sheridan College in Ontario, Canada, for their animation program. After visiting both, he made the call for ArtCenter. He packed up once again to go west . . . still uncertain, but resolute in pursuing a second bachelor of fine arts.

"I drove cross-country with my dad in my Escort wagon," he says. "The only things that I brought were what I packed into the car: a folding desk, a computer, and an air mattress. And I kept that air mattress for about two years because I didn't think I was going to make it. I didn't think I was going be able to exist in California," he admits. "I thought, *I'm not gonna buy a bunch of crap out here because I'm just gonna end up putting everything back in the car and driving home*. So a lot of it was down to looking at the options in front of me, looking at what other people were doing, trying to understand the paths that they were on, and if I'm gonna be as efficient as possible with my time, what can I learn?"

"I didn't really care about graduating, as it was really just about gaining skills and building networks with people," he says of his mentality at the time. "One of the coolest things about ArtCenter is if you're [considered] hardworking and talented, the professors will generally allow you to sit in on their classes. Or if a teacher is also running a figure-drawing workshop, they won't have a problem with you joining. So I ended up spending every moment I had at ArtCenter trying to be as efficient as possible."

Meinerding remembers living very lean off his work savings, taking freelance jobs from his professional contacts, and existing in cheap housing. "I would essentially go to ArtCenter for a term, take a term off, freelance, and then go back," he says of how he paid for his schooling the second time around. He was able to stay out of debt maintaining that cycle, as well as winning a series of accruing end-of-term scholarship shows that kept his tuition covered.

ArtCenter is an intensely competitive program, and Meinerding remembers that period as entirely dedicated to building his skills. Initially focused on becoming an animation character designer, he redoubled his efforts on figure drawing and learning about story and storytelling, as well as character design and illustration. "I was at Borders [bookstore] every weekend trying to find something new to read, to learn something else, as well as going to my classes," he details. "But ArtCenter didn't have a real entertainment program back then, so it was a lot of me trying to piece together what I felt I needed to learn at a place where there were a lot of talented students."

He eventually found a mentor in Dallas Goode, a former CG modeler turner professor. "I showed him my portfolio and told him where I was trying to go. He let me get into one of his independent study classes. We would meet up on a Saturday to go see movies and talk about them, which was exactly what I needed; somebody that was actually willing to deconstruct the construction of stories and storytelling with me."

While studying, Meinerding also reconnected with his lifelong appreciation for the illustrations of Norman Rockwell. The Americana illustrator whose cover work is synonymous with the heyday of *The Saturday Evening Post* magazine impressed Meinerding for his ability to tell such rich story in a painted image. "Whenever I was trying to make art from when I was a kid onward, I think his work was always something I was trying to lean into, because it was a singular image that was hugely evocative that made you feel something and told a story," says the artist. "And it was mostly in the characters where the story was being told."

But while at ArtCenter, Meinerding came to grasp that modern editorial illustration was a dying art, and even animation design was too niche to be a viable path to a sustainable career. "I realized that Carter Goodrich, Peter de Sève, Buck Lewis, and Nico Marlet were the people that did the design for every single Pixar, DreamWorks, and Blue Sky movie," he reflects. "There were so few people at a high level contributing to what the characters looked like, so it was a huge realization. And that was honestly one of the times where I pivoted because I thought, *I don't think I can bank on myself being one of those four people in the industry.* It sounds idiotic to try and put all of my eggs in that basket."

Meinerding reassessed the creative landscape and noticed that video games were making leaps and bounds when it came to realistic illustration. "It was a viable option. And then, I always wanted to get into live-action movies," he adds. "But I never really thought of that as being a viable option outside of seeing the *Star Wars* art books." However, being located in California meant proximity to professionals in both fields. So he went back to his days of cold-calling with his portfolio, this time at conventions and game developers' conferences.

"I was *that* guy," he laughs. "Just shoving my portfolio in front of people's faces. I would look at name tags and if it said 'Art Director' on it, I would be like, 'Hey, dude! Can you talk a minute?' I was more forward then than I ever was any other time."

During one show, he showed his portfolio to Paul Topolos, a matte painter at Pixar Animation. "He was nice enough to look at it and give me some pointers and feedback. But there was a guy that was working the convention, oddly enough, who also looked over my shoulder. He heard Paul being complimentary to me and wanted to see it."

A producer at Midway Games, he invited Meinerding to interview at their San Diego studio. There, he met the art

THIS SPREAD Character designs for Dr. Jekyll and Mr. Hyde for a school project while at ArtCenter

director and was hired as a freelancer to do concept pieces for games in development. He was eventually placed onto *Gauntlet Seven Sorrows* and threw himself into the work. "I would put so much detail in each one of these characters," he remembers. "It would take me three days to finish one character. And they were paying me two hundred dollars per character. I was working thirteen-, fourteen-, fifteen-, sixteen-hour days. And they liked the level of detail, even though it was a PlayStation 2 game," he says, sighing. "They ended up using the stuff I was doing for marketing and for the character select screens. But that's how I actually got the portfolio that got me hired with Iain McCaig."

THE INTERVIEW THAT CHANGED EVERYTHING

An illustrator who worked on films like *Star Wars*: Episode I *The Phantom Menace*, McCaig was an industry hero to Meinerding. So much so that Meinerding attended certain conferences in order to hear him speak. "After one of his talks, I handed him my portfolio. He was very kind and encouraging. During his talk, he had said that he takes on an apprentice every few years. So I got him alone and asked, 'How can I become your apprentice, because I would love to learn from you.' He said, 'It's very simple. I have a Jedi test. I'm gonna ask you to do a self-portrait, and I'm looking for something very specific. But I'm not going to tell you what I'm looking for.'" Then, McCaig gave Meinerding his personal email and his home phone.

"This is the artist I looked up to the most," he continues. "He's the best version of what a concept artist is supposed to be. Because he's not only talented—he inspires everyone with his attitude, with the way he talks, with helping people find their way forward in their own careers and their lives. So I do the work. I emailed it to him. And I didn't hear back."

Undeterred, Meinerding called, but no one answered. So he called again. And again. The call always went straight to voicemail. "I called enough times that his wife answered," he laughs. From that, he resubmitted and waited again. "And then, when I was at a cousin's wedding—I remember this very specifically—Iain called me back. I was shaking because he was very complimentary. But basically he said, 'Thank you for sending it. It's really amazing. It might be the best one anyone's ever sent me. But I'm not taking an apprentice on this year. I'm so sorry.'"

It was a gutting moment despite the encouraging words. "A *huge* bummer," he admits.

The only thing Meinerding could do was go back to ArtCenter and continue looking for more inroads into the business.

Emboldened, he asked a friend who took classes with concept artist Bill Perkins for an introduction and got an invitation to Perkins's workshop. Meinerding brought his portfolio along. Impressed, Perkins shared that—remarkably—he was actually working with McCaig at a startup concept design studio called Ninth Ray. "He said he thought Iain would like my work. I had a whole portfolio of these fantasy characters, and they were working on a Viking movie." Not long after, Meinerding met once more with McCaig, who looked at his portfolio and hired him on the spot. "He also remembered me from my drawing, so it ended up paying off in a good way."

HELLO, HOLLYWOOD

Meinerding suddenly found himself in his first full-time job working in a field he always dreamed about. "I'm working with Iain McCaig, who is my hero," he says. "Ryan Church, who is one of the premiere concept artists in the business. Stephen Platt, whose *Moon Knight* comics I had grown up reading and was now a storyboard artist. Bill Perkins, who's an animation legend."

His first project was for a Viking movie that would eventually become the 2008 film *Outlander*. "Iain brought the director, Howard McCain, over to tell me what they were looking for, and I start working. This is a Monday," he clarifies. "Then they tell me, 'We're gonna have a presentation on Friday,' and ask me how many character designs I can have done by then. And I'm like, 'I'll try and get five characters for you.'"

"The first day, I get through two black-and-white character designs and I'm feeling really good about myself," he continues. "Iain brought the director over on Tuesday morning to look at it. And he basically says they are are all wrong. So Tuesday I do three characters in a day. And the same thing happens."

"This is not working out. It's Wednesday. And I don't have anything for Friday," he remembers of his panic. "Ryan Church is acting as the art director and asks me what I'm gonna have for Friday. We had looked through the script, and there's about twenty-six characters in the whole movie. Iain said that maybe he would do half and then I would do half. So between Wednesday at noon and Friday morning, I didn't sleep. And I got through twenty-five designs."

"We were pasting up boards twenty minutes before the meeting," he continues. "I filled three huge foam-core boards with designs. And we showed the first one. The director walked over, and he liked a couple of them. But then he saw the two other boards. He walked over to them and was like, 'Oh, that one's great! These two are great. These are great!' So that was my first week trial by fire. Over the course of that time, with the ones that were rejected, I probably did about forty designs in a week."

Meinerding stayed with the team to complete the work on *Outlander*. They then disbanded briefly before they were reassembled to work on the concept designs for director Jon Favreau's John Carter of Mars film. "That's where I first met Jon Favreau, which is the direct lineage of how I got onto *Iron Man*."

OPPOSITE Meinerding standing with a screen-used Mark I suit from *Iron Man*, based on his concept design, at Legacy Effects.

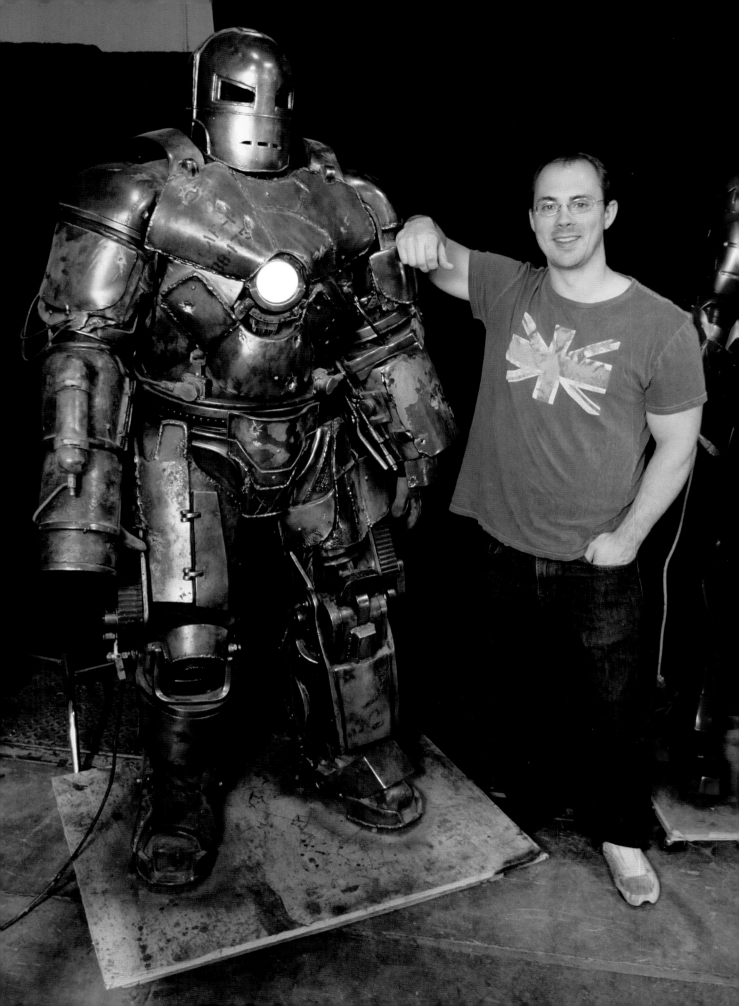

ENTERING THE MARVEL UNIVERSE

In 2005, Meinerding was working with Ninth Ray and McCaig on contract jobs like developing visuals for a Las Vegas stage show and a national truck commercial. He also found himself back in video games, developing concept art for PlayStation's *God of War 2* under Director of Visual Development Charlie Wen. And then Ninth Ray's McCaig, Ryan Church, Phil Saunders, Dave Krentz, Stephen Platt, and Meinerding were asked to develop *John Carter* for director Jon Favreau.

"It was the first time I had actually been working with a real big-name director," Meinerding remembers. "It felt like this was my one shot."

A big proponent of using concept art to flesh out the visuals of his films, Favreau was particularly focused on figuring out the practicalities of meshing both practical and visual effects for *John Carter*. "He was very supportive and very engaging," Meinerding notes. "He was a good communicator and talked about what he liked and what he didn't like. I felt very fortunate to be there and to be working with a group of people that were fantastic, and that Jon was welcoming of having somebody like me in there."

For *John Carter*, Meinerding was tasked with drawing key frames for the first time. Instead of the static character images or landscape studies that often define concept art, key frames are dynamic drawings of "key" moments in the script. Sometimes they capture complex action set pieces or primary characters meeting for the first time, or even high-concept visual effects sequences. But they require the artist to fully realize a scene and convey the energy and emotion of the moment.

"I had no experience doing anything like that," Meinerding says with candor. "I had done a couple frames like that for a color class at ArtCenter, but I didn't have experience storyboarding other than just *really* basic storyboards."

But Meinerding's initial attempts ended up being in alignment with Favreau's expectations. "I was doing key frames that Jon was absolutely loving. So what I learned at a high level was that people are usually looking to be inspired at those early stages of a project," he explains. "If you can give them something that's capturing 70 percent of what they were talking about, they're probably going to be excited about what they're seeing."

The team worked for an intense period of long days in order to deliver materials for Favreau to show to Paramount Studios, which owned the rights to the Edgar Rice Burroughs books. Of that time, Meinerding remembers little sleep, long commutes with McCaig to Favreau's Santa Monica office

and seven-day work weeks. But then, in 2006, Paramount declined to renew their rights to John Carter, which effectively killed the project. It was a huge disappointment.

But the collaboration between the artists and director ending up bearing fruit, just on a different project. In that same year, Favreau agreed to direct the first independently produced Marvel Studios film, *Iron Man*. Favreau asked McCaig to invite any of the Ninth Ray artists who were on *John Carter* to work for him on this title. For various reasons, only Saunders, Platt, and Meinerding accepted the offer. Together, they went to meet with the fledgling Marvel Studios creative team, including *Iron Man* producers Jeremy Latcham, Louis D'Esposito, and Kevin Feige. Meinerding remembers going out to lunch with his fellow artists after, where one of them posed to him: "If this whole thing takes off, can you imagine *just* working on Super Hero movies for the next ten years?"

"I know he was saying it as a negative, but I was like, 'That sounds amazing. How could that be a *bad* thing?' My heart was more into anything that had to do with Marvel and Super Heroes than probably any other gig," he says.

Meinerding formally came on board *Iron Man* in May 2006, joining Saunders, Platt, and other artists he admired deeply, like Adi Granov, Rodolfo Dimaggio, David Lowry, and Eric Ramsey. From the top, there were three Iron Man suits and the Crimson Dynamo—which became Iron Monger—to design. Starting later than some of his peers, Meinerding looked at what Saunders and Granov had already developed for the hero Iron Man suit and decided to pivot to Stark's rougher first-pass suits.

"The idea of the first of something, or somebody building out of desperation—there's actually a lot of story that goes into that, as opposed to just the main hero look," he says of where his mind was at the time. "That's all stuff that I really loved."

Concurrently, Meinerding returned to key frame compositions, pursuing an early Favreau key frame idea of Tony Stark's rough RT sticking out of his chest while attached to a car battery. "I focused on showing the emotional response of Tony waking up," Meinerding says of his approach. "It wasn't only designing the suit but was finding that language that [implies] this needs to look awful, but still cool enough to be Iron Man." Pleased with the outcome, Favreau assigned him more key frame moments like the cave escape and when Stark is building an Iron Man suit in his garage.

Meinerding also pitched his own key frames studies, like a black-and-white image of Stark working underneath the

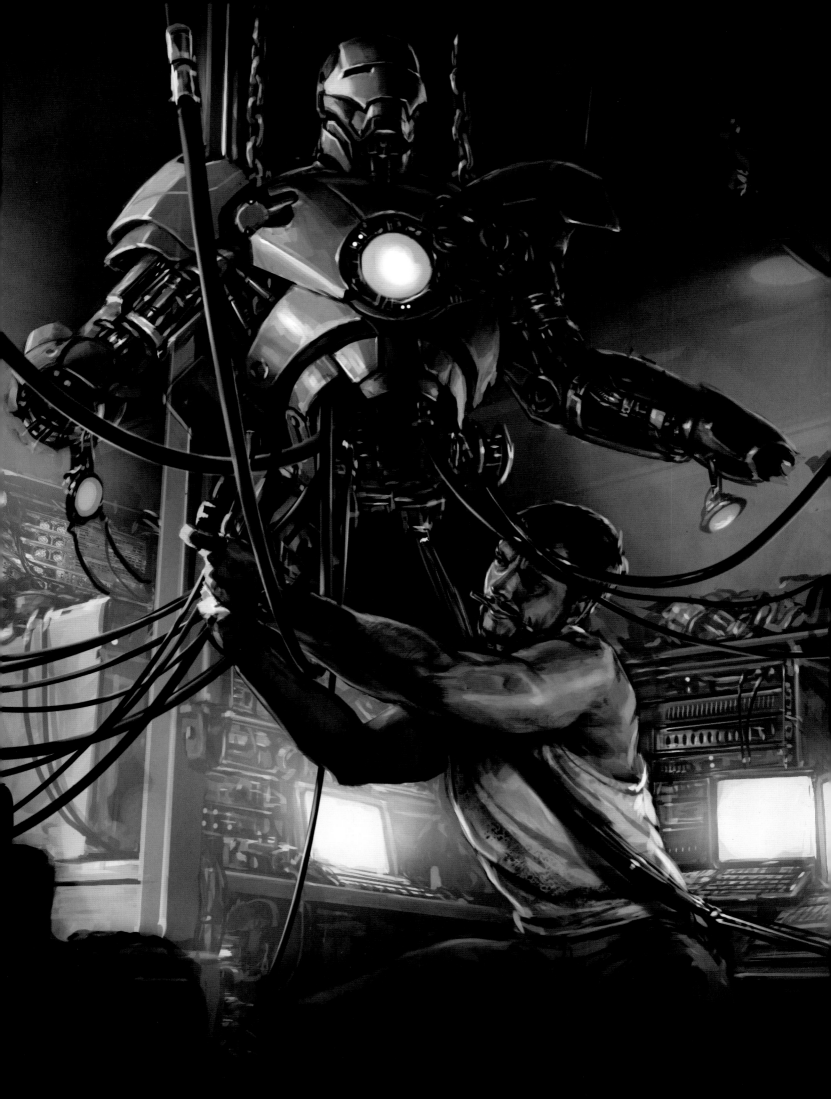

suit's half-made torso. Inspired by Granov's actual *Iron Man* comic cover art, plus his personal memories of working inside his grandfather's machine shop, Meinerding says he was compelled to take a more real and grounded approach.

"It was a little bit more of a drill-press-and-band-saw feeling, with keyboards and plastic see-through covers on them, which was stuff that I felt I had an understanding of," he details. "And Jon seemed to respond to that."

He calls that beginning period of creativity at Marvel Studios "electric" because of the spirit of unbridled potential and the egoless atmosphere of just making cool stuff together. Meinerding says, "I got to work with people like Adi and Phil, who are just as passionate, as excited, and wanting to deliver as much as I did."

And their individual skills complemented one another. I had more 3D modeling experience than both Phil and Adi. But Phil had the car-design experience. And then Adi really had the comic cover polish that he brings to everything he does, as well as many other things, including a really clean design sense," he explains. "We were all willing to help each other make our work better." They bonded further over multiple all-nighters working with the Stan Winston Studios digital team in Van Nuys for their big presentation for Marvel.

Of that time, Meinerding also remembers the sanctity of the Friday creative meetings where Favreau tasked the different departments to show off that week's work to everyone. They would all pack into the huge Marvel Studios conference room and present. On one Friday, he remembers revealing his Mark I designs to Favreau and producer Avi Arad. "I remember the one that ended up getting picked, with Avi going, 'I think this looks pretty cool.' And Jon being like, 'I think so, too.' And I was just like, 'So that's the design?'"

He says he was astounded a decision of that importance wasn't made behind closed doors. "It was my first movie in a room where my work is being reviewed by the head of a studio and the director," he says. "That direct of a line of communication, but also hierarchy, was fantastic. It felt like you were connected and part of the magic. You felt like you could make something and then have people look at it."

Another seminal design lesson came when the legendary Stan Winston reviewed one of his suit designs and conveyed a concern about the shoulder structure. "I said, 'Go to the next slide, because I had elucidated how it would work.' And then he was like, "Oh yeah, that'll be fine." It reinforced to Meinerding the goal of not only accomplishing "one amazing illustration," but putting enough thought into a design that you can either speak to how you got there or speak to how it works.

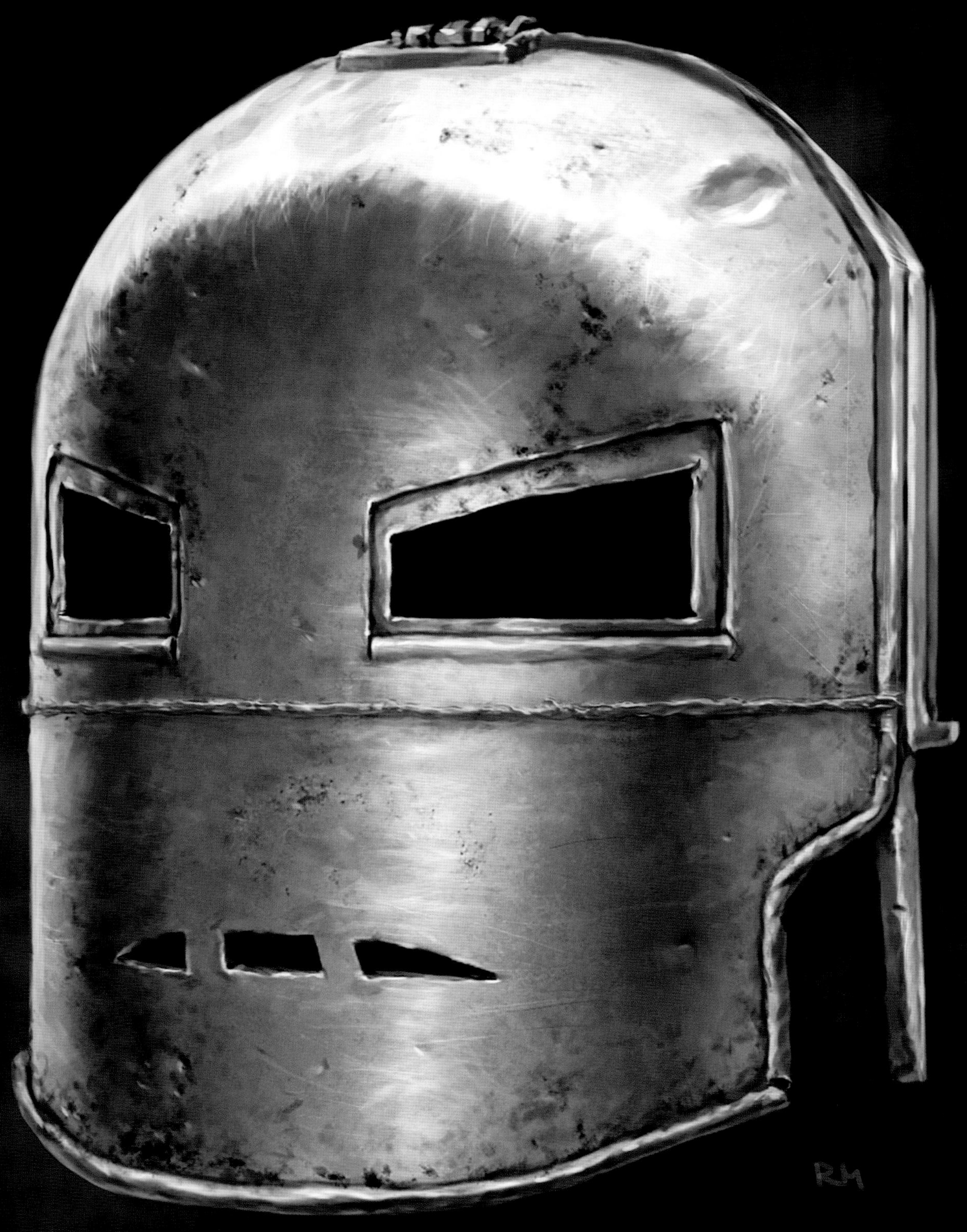

THIS AND FOLLOWING TWO SPREADS "In terms of concept design, the Mark I has a lot of story baked into it," explains Meinerding. "Because it is what [Tony Stark] designed in a cave with no time—he could only armor the front. So all the machine parts are showing in the back." Although relatively unseen at first glance, there are layers upon layers of storytelling within the Mark I design, showing how Stark used scraps from his own company's weapons. Meinerding continues: "I put these huge belt drives that spin and actually drive the legs. And I liked that type of idea—exposing the mechanics of the suit and showing how it works by putting it on the *outside* and trying to find a way to do that without making it feel simple and toylike. The aesthetic where Marvel Studios started was based in trying to find a reality that felt heightened but also achievable."

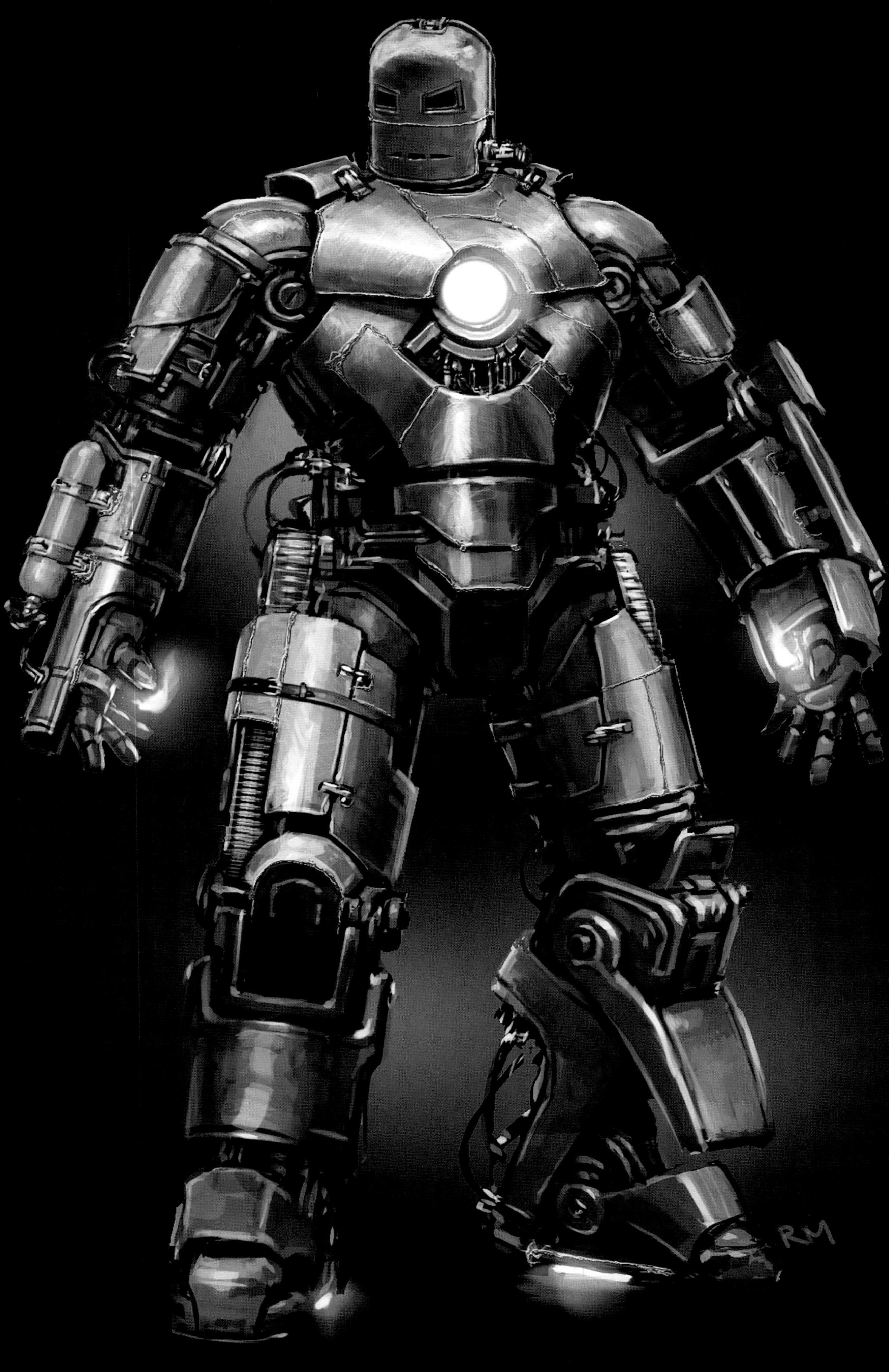
RM

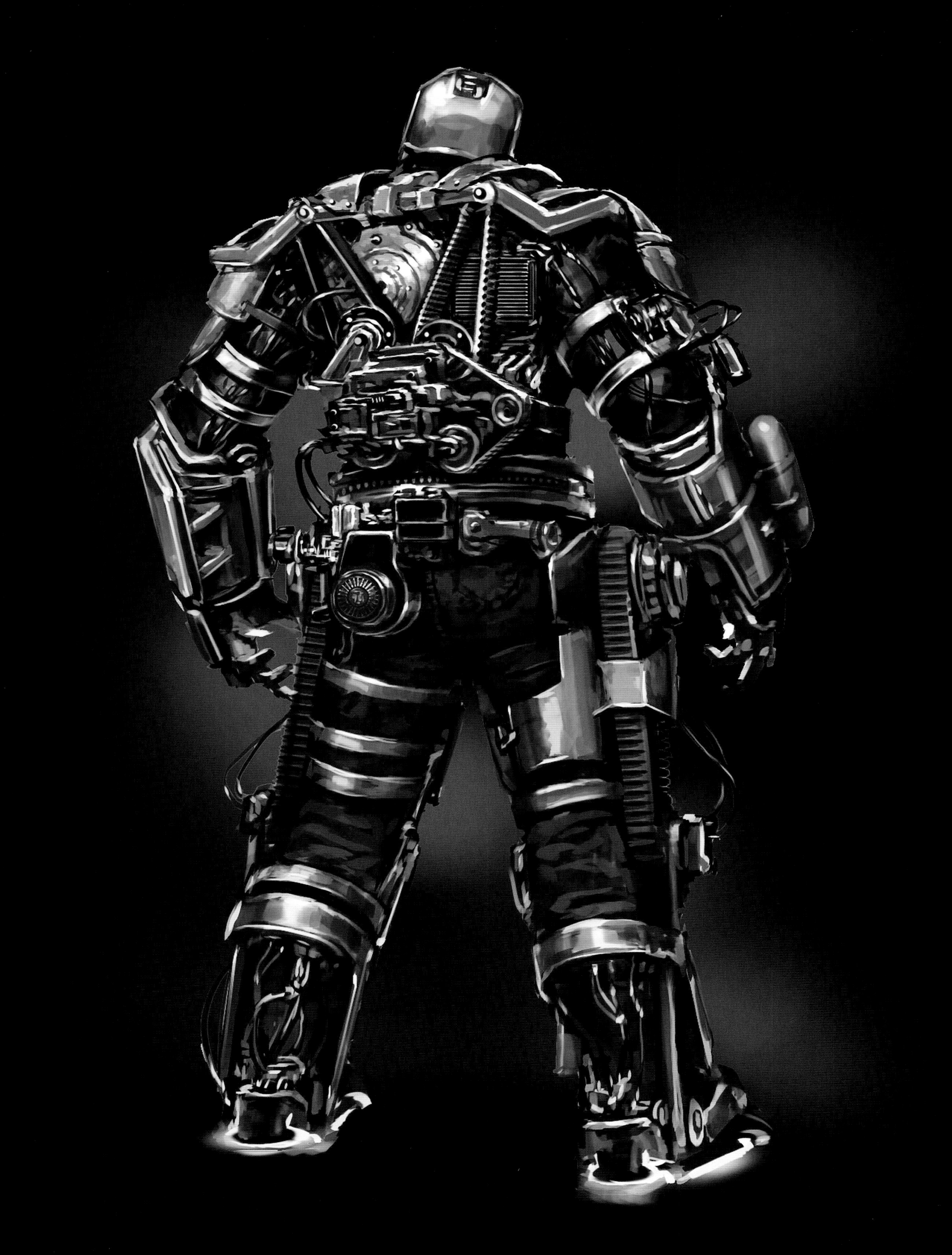

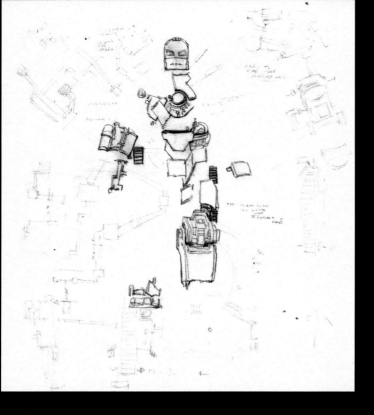

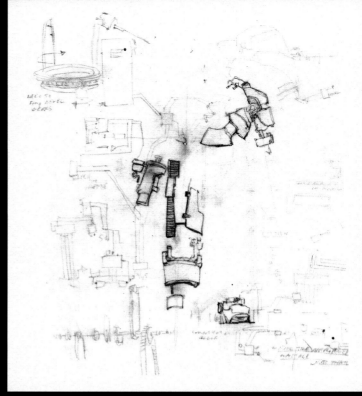

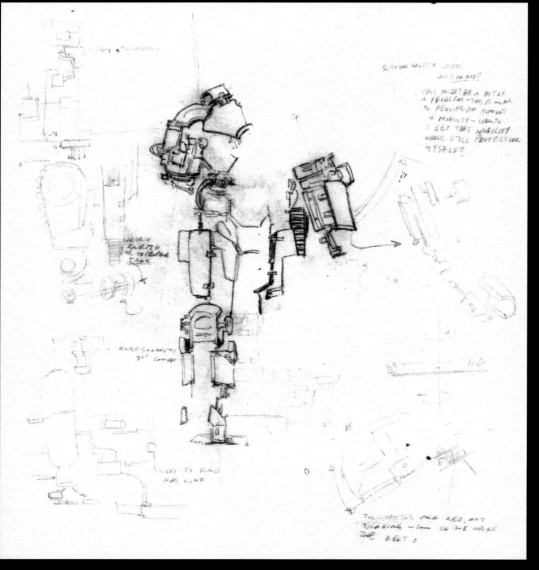

In coming up with all the
intricate Mark I "blueprints"
that Tony Stark draws in the
cave, Meinerding's degree in—
and love for—industrial design
was crucial. "The aesthetic
that everyone was responding
to was definitely one that felt
solid and realistic," he says.
In one of the more stressful
challenges working on the film,
Meinerding needed to come
up with all of the drawings on
these pages for shooting that
would occur *the following day*.

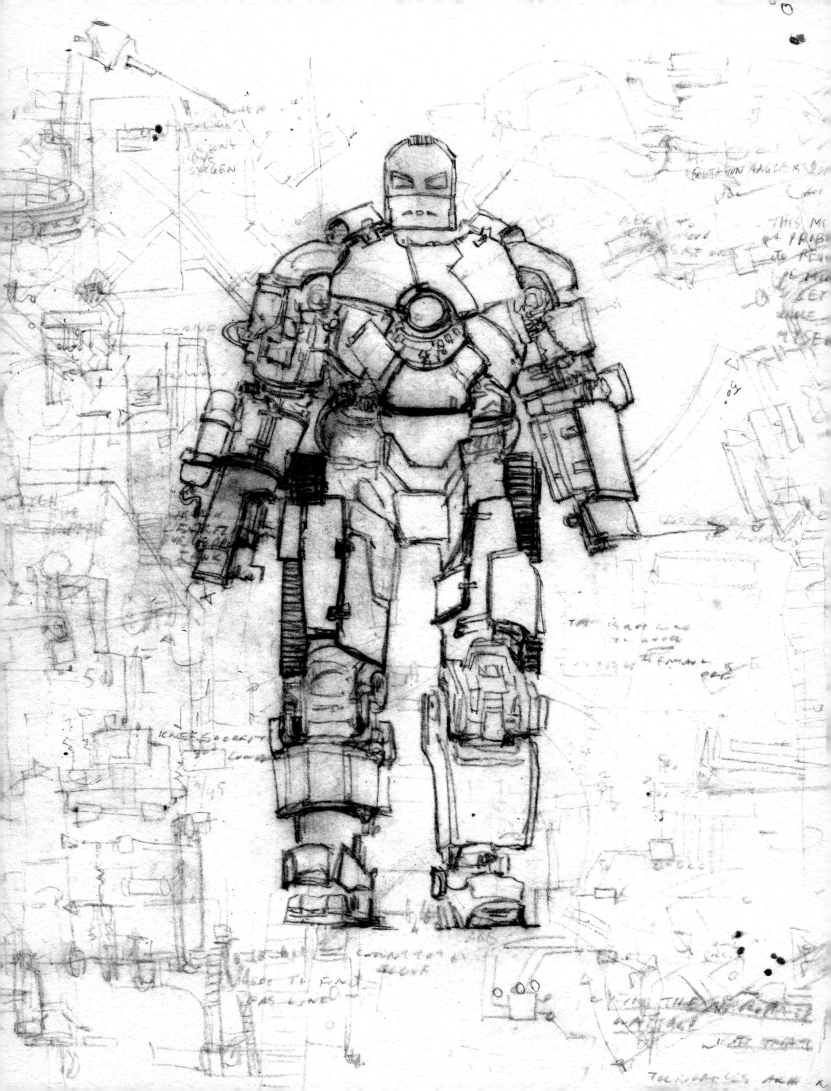

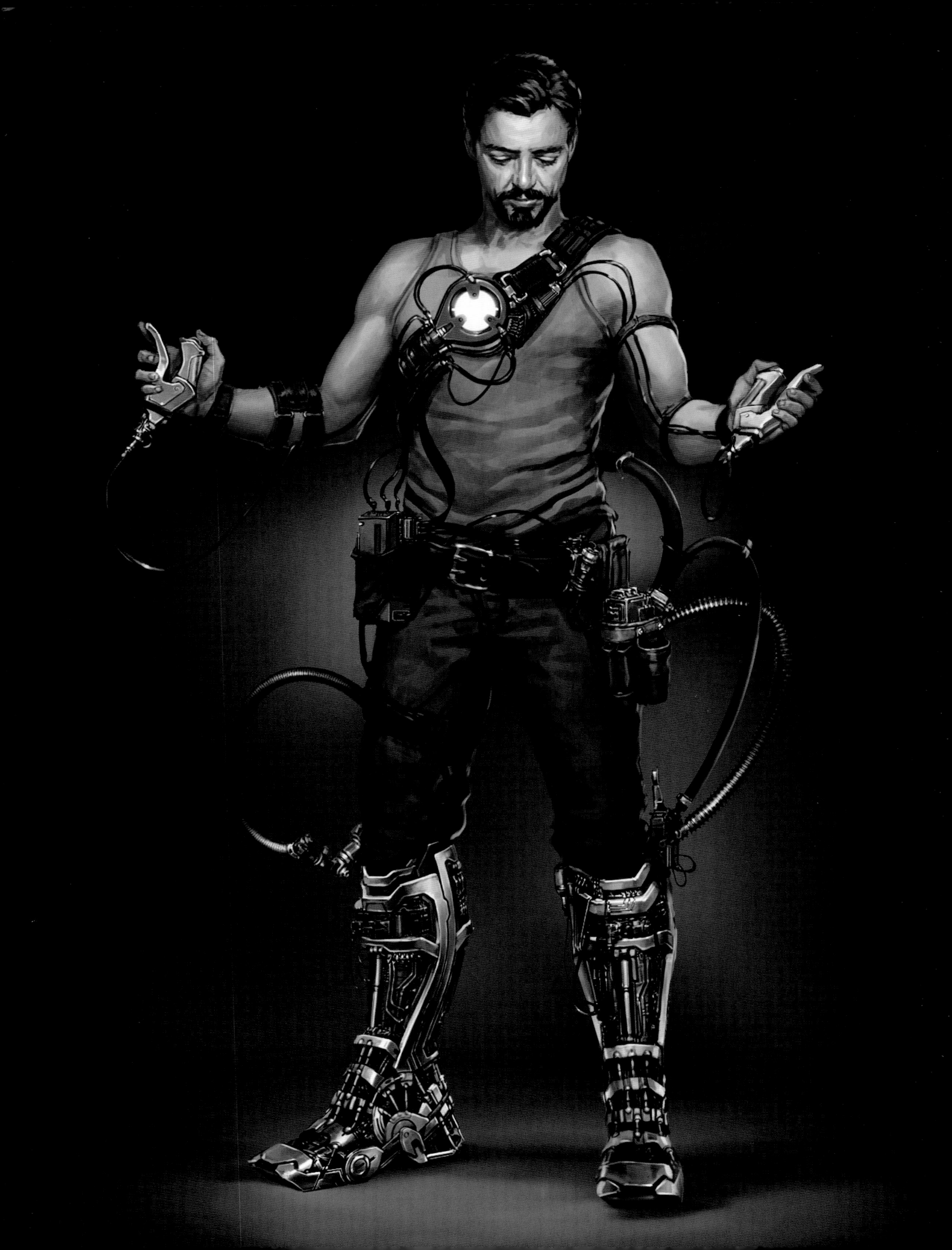

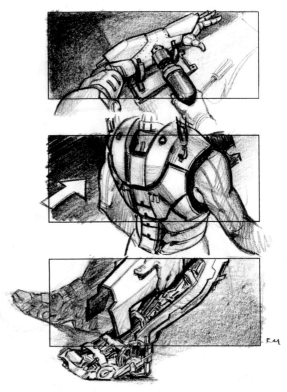

Meinerding pitched the idea of the "boot test" sequence to *Iron Man* director Jon Favreau. One of the artist's main inspirations for the key frame was the casting of Robert Downey Jr. The thought of Downey Jr. performing as Tony Stark hovering in the experimental rocket boots and reacting to what's happening with a surprised look on his face, "and the fact that he's got all of these *precious collectibles* all around him," felt to Meinerding like a perfect visual representation of Stark's personality. He adds, "It's one of my favorite things I got to work on."

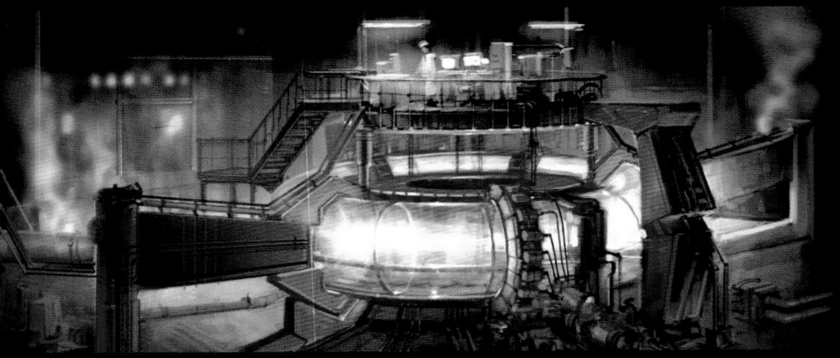

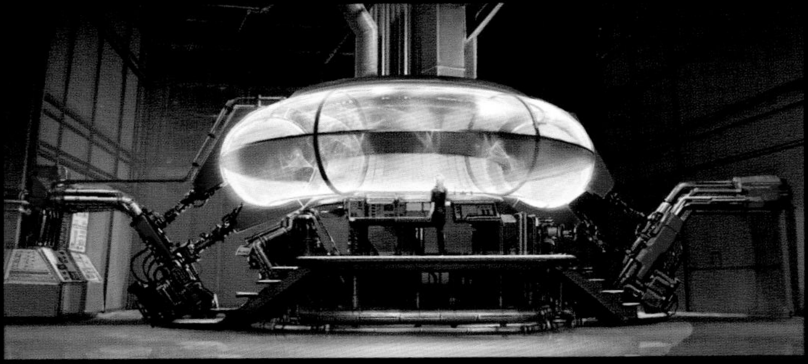

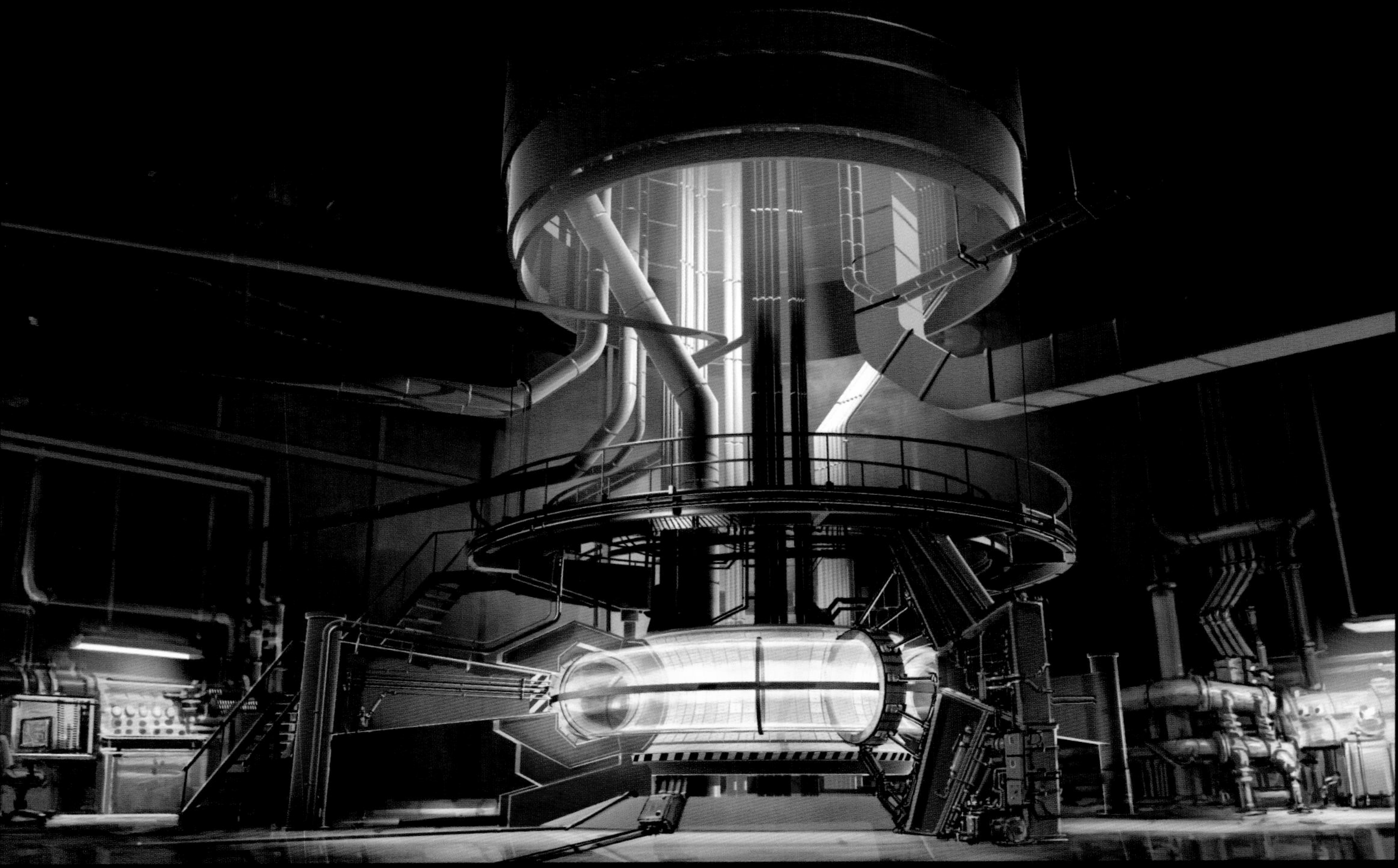

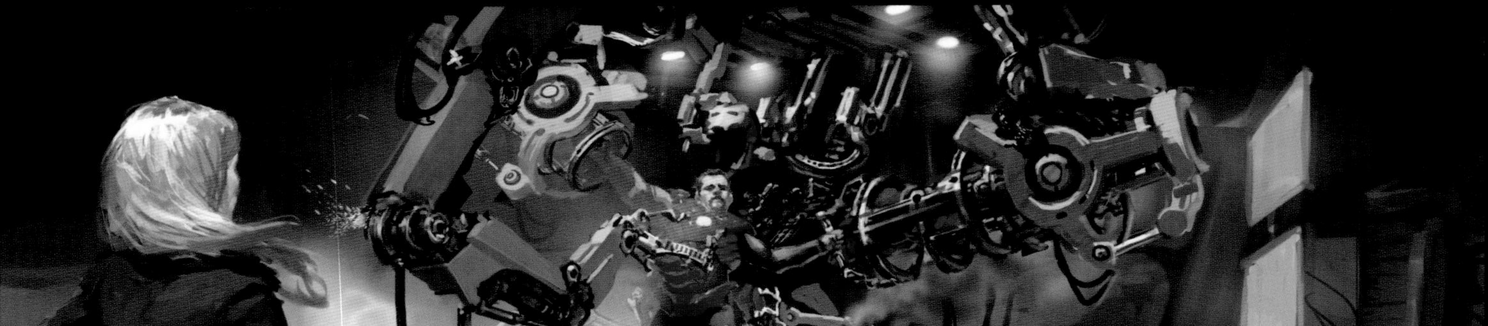

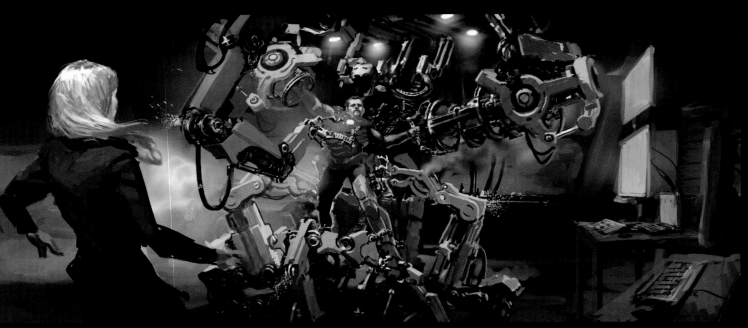

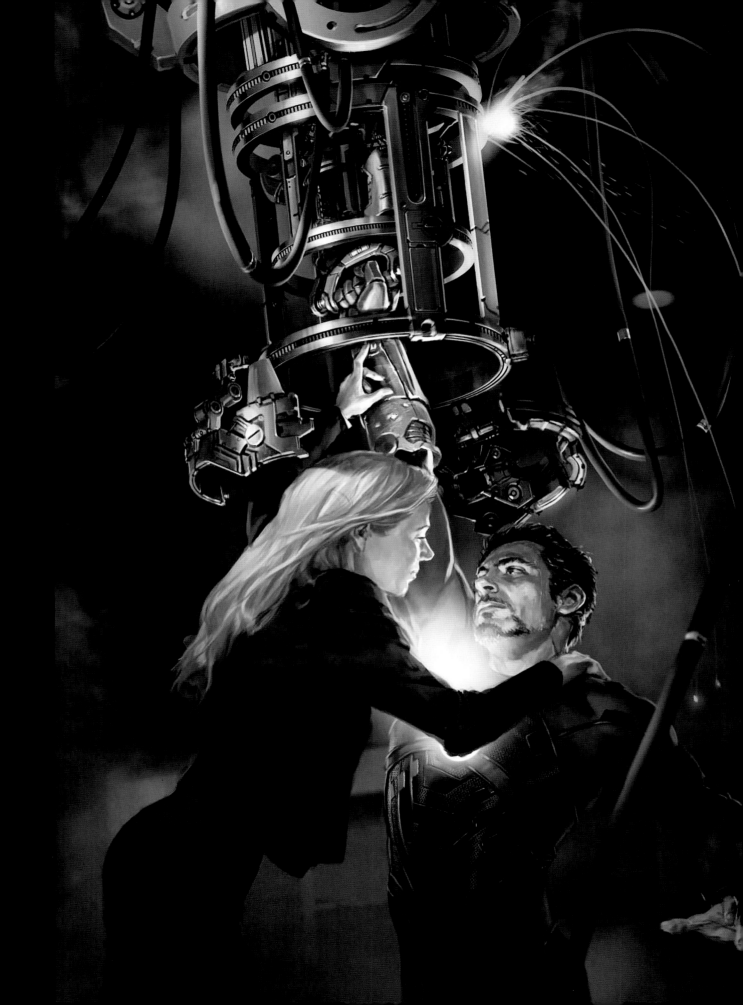

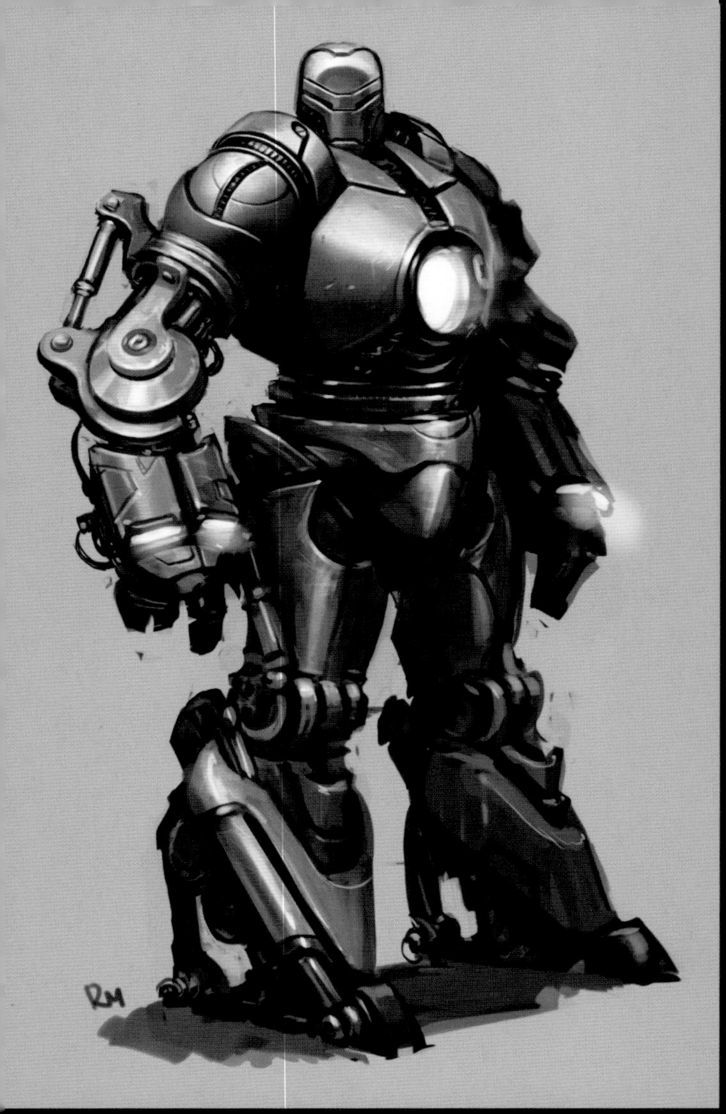
RM

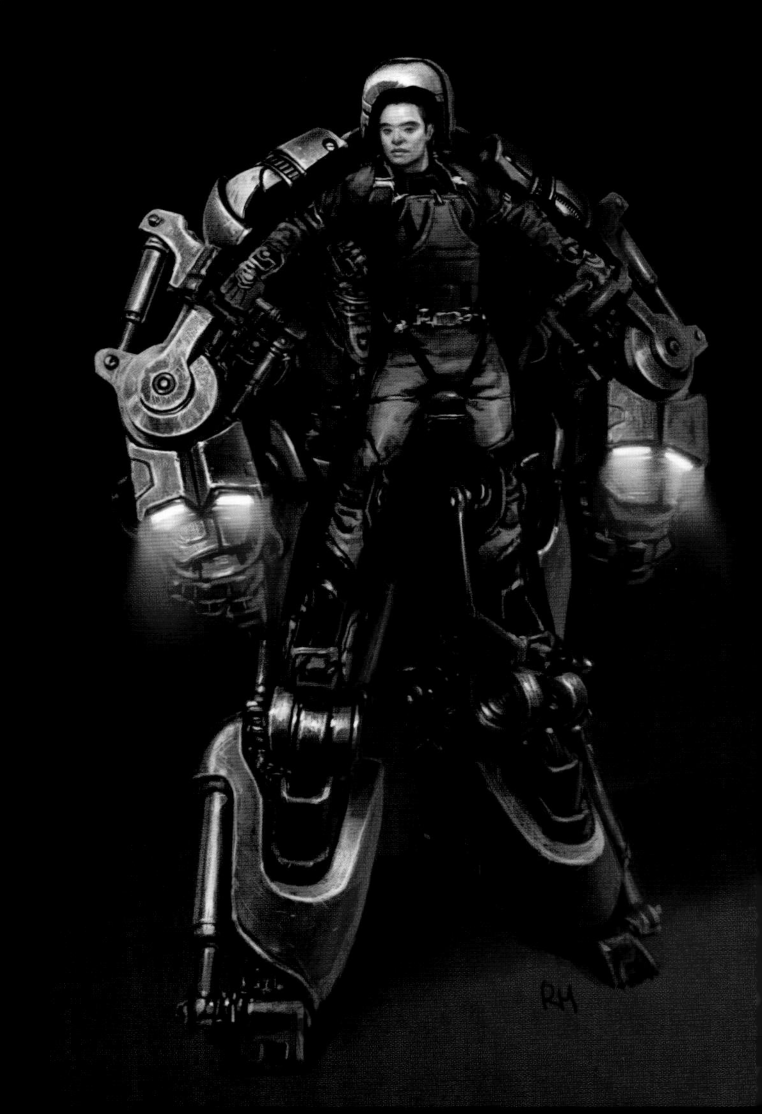
RM

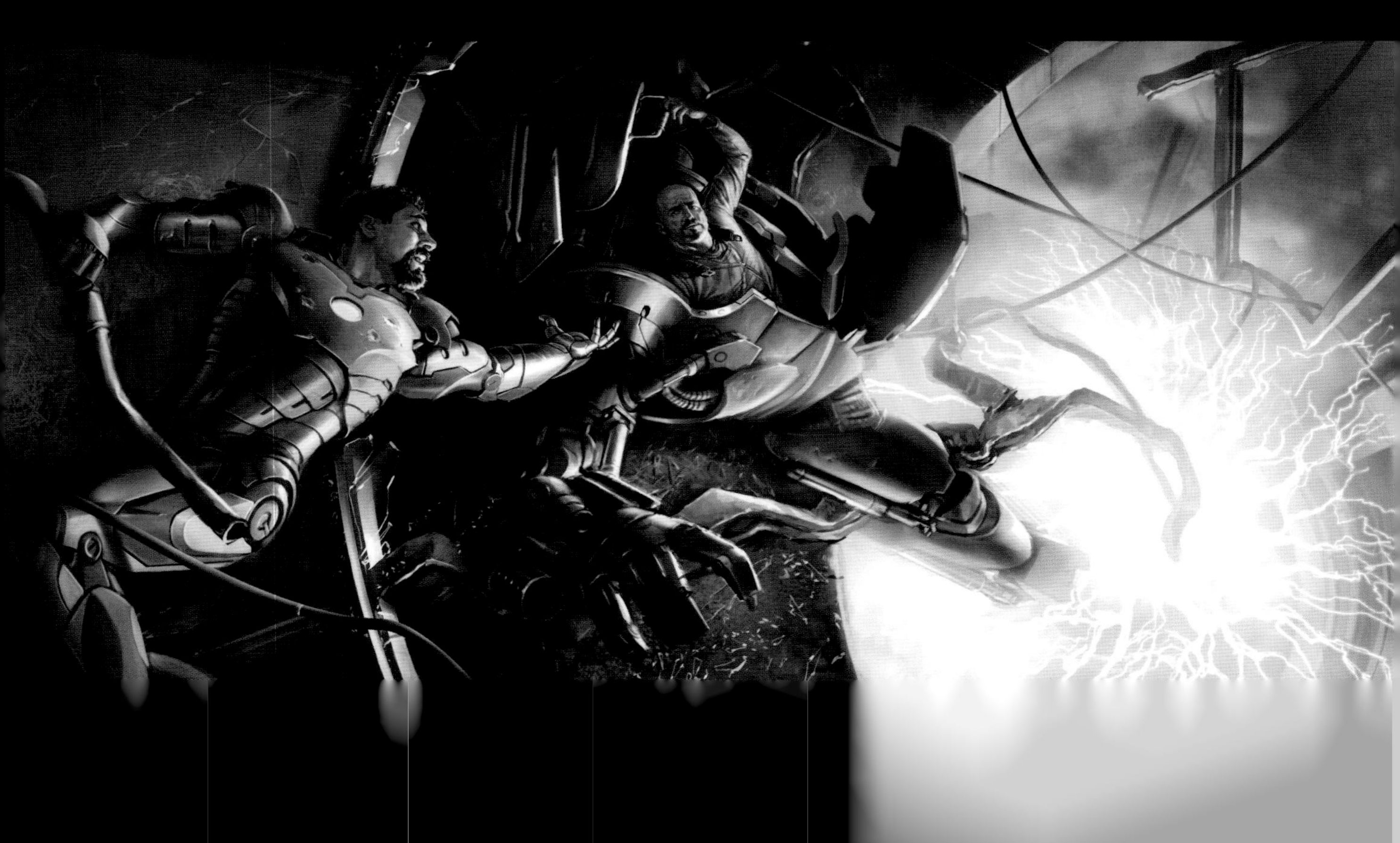

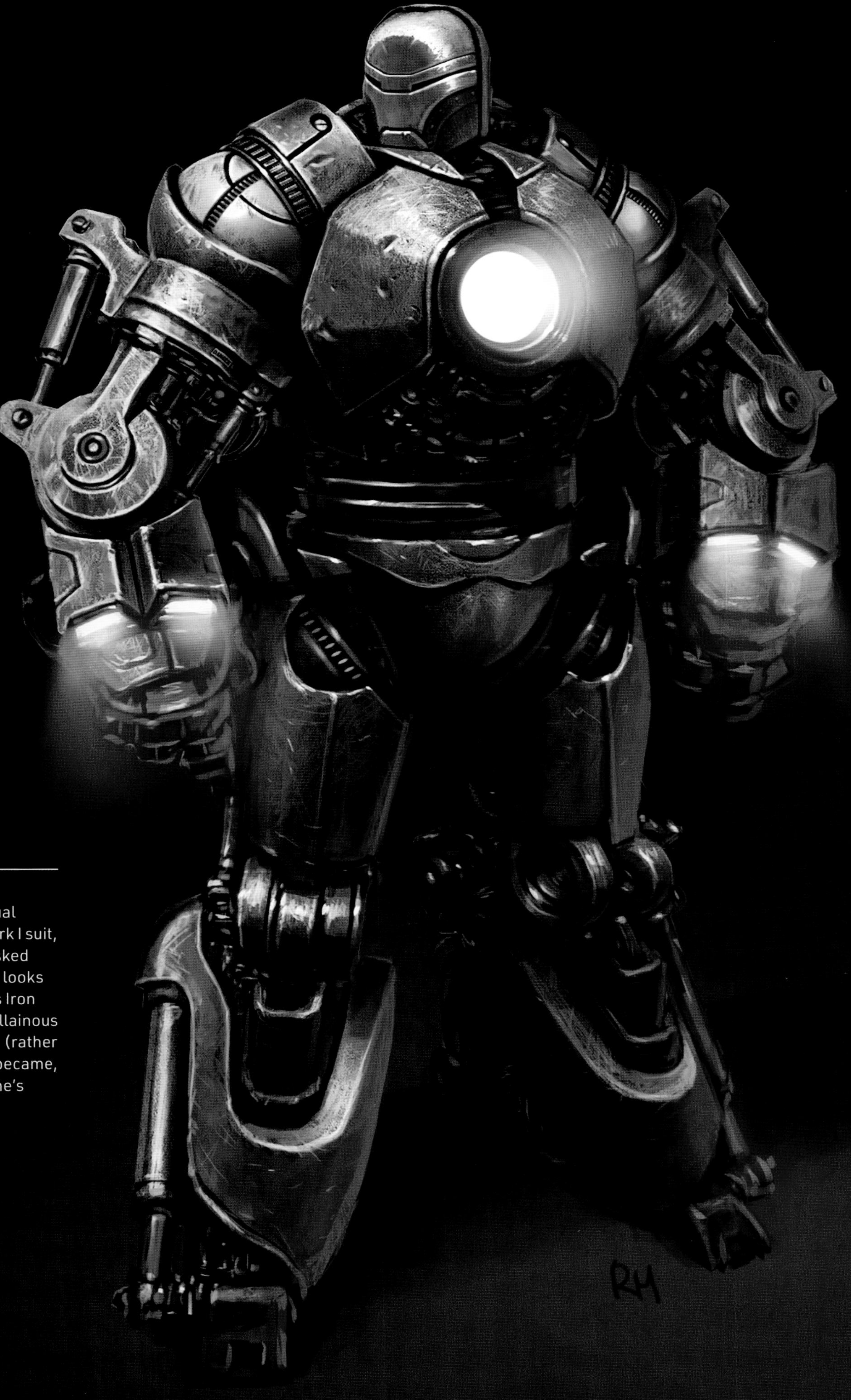
RM

While he worked on visual development for the Mark I suit, Meinerding was also tasked with exploring potential looks for Crimson Dynamo. As Iron Man's counterpoint, a villainous suit was initially needed (rather than what it eventually became, which was Obadiah Stane's Iron Monger armor).

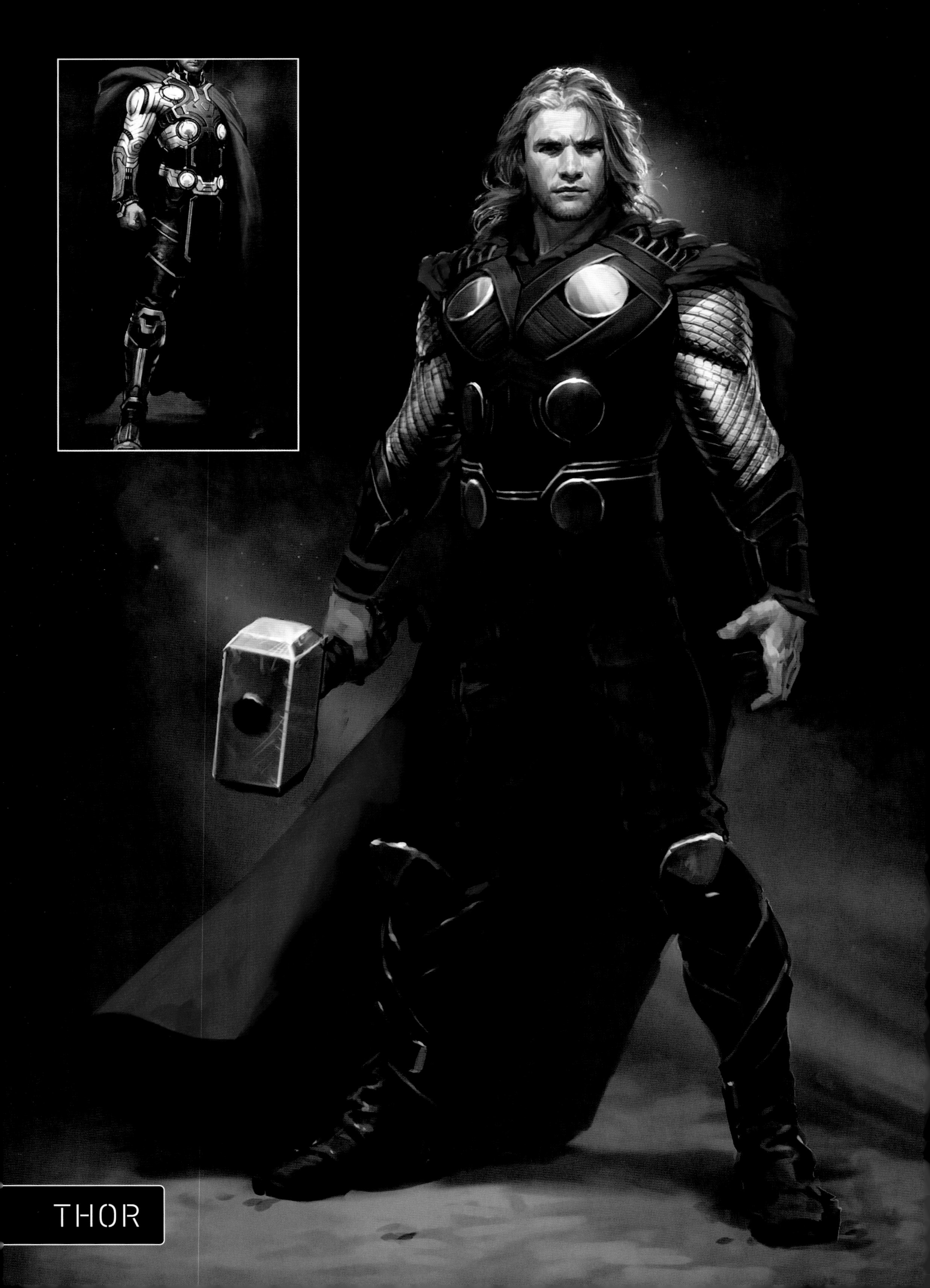

THOR

These three Ryan Meinerding studies were done during pre-production on *Thor*. (Before doing these, Meinerding was still a freelance artist; he briefly left the Marvel Studios offices to create concept art for Zack Synder's *Watchmen*.) They were created over a two-week period of long-lead exploration, during which time *Thor* was being developed as a Viking-era period film. Around this time, Meinerding recommended Charlie Wen to take the lead on the visual development of *Thor* while he pivoted to focus on *Captain America: The First Avenger*.

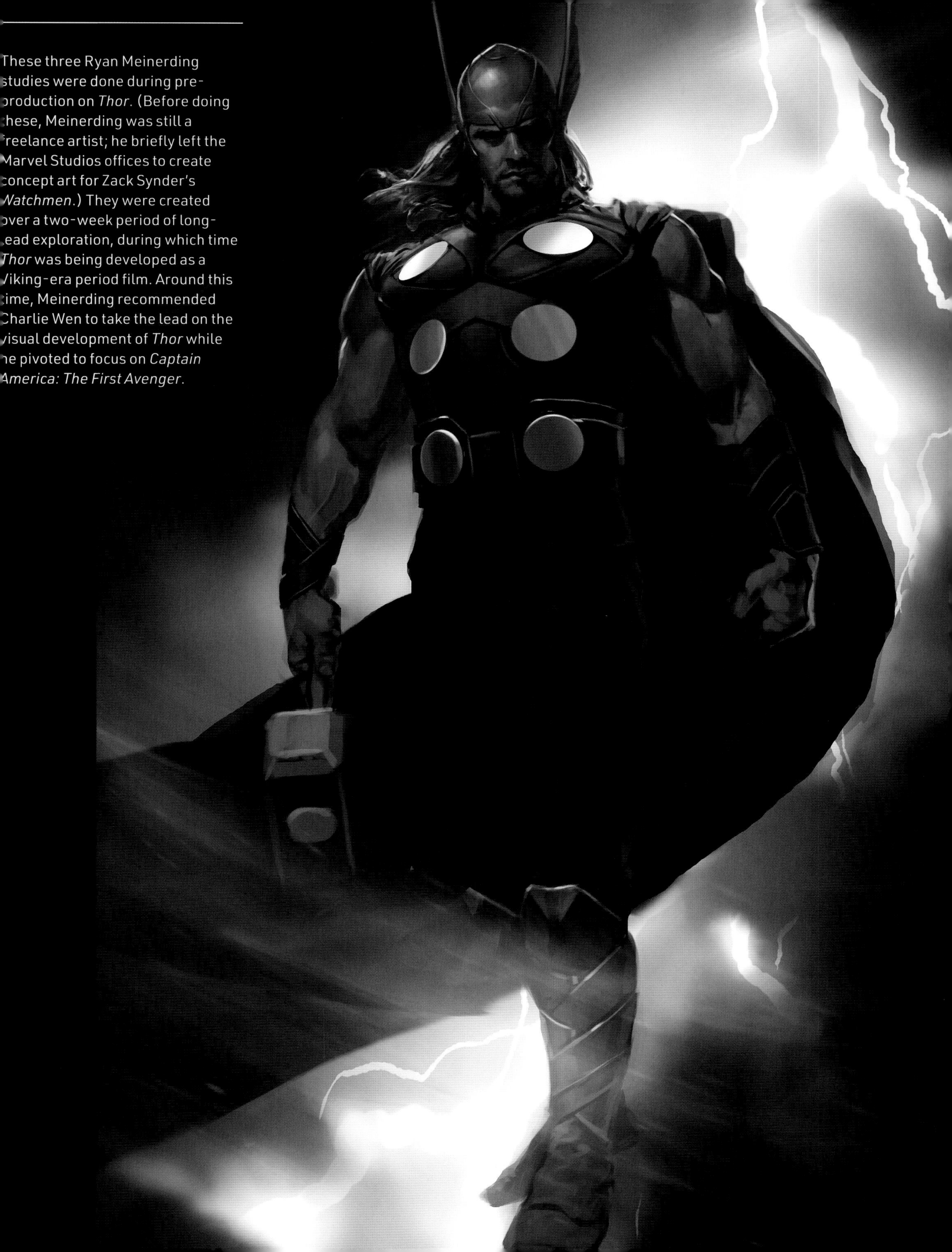

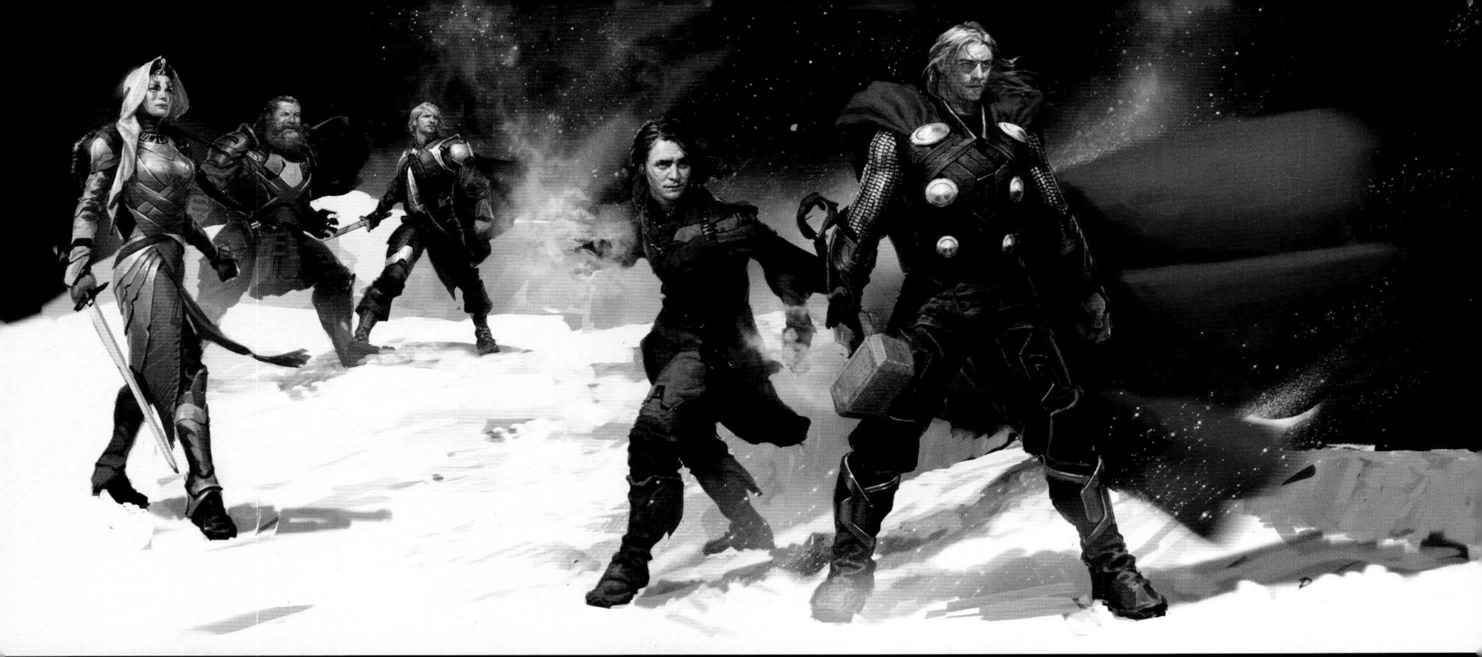

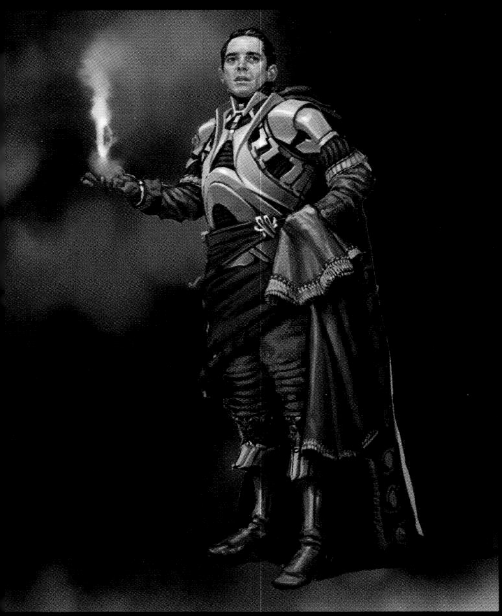

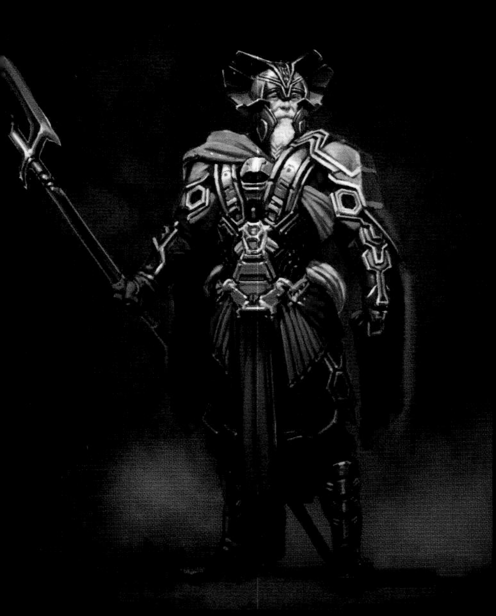

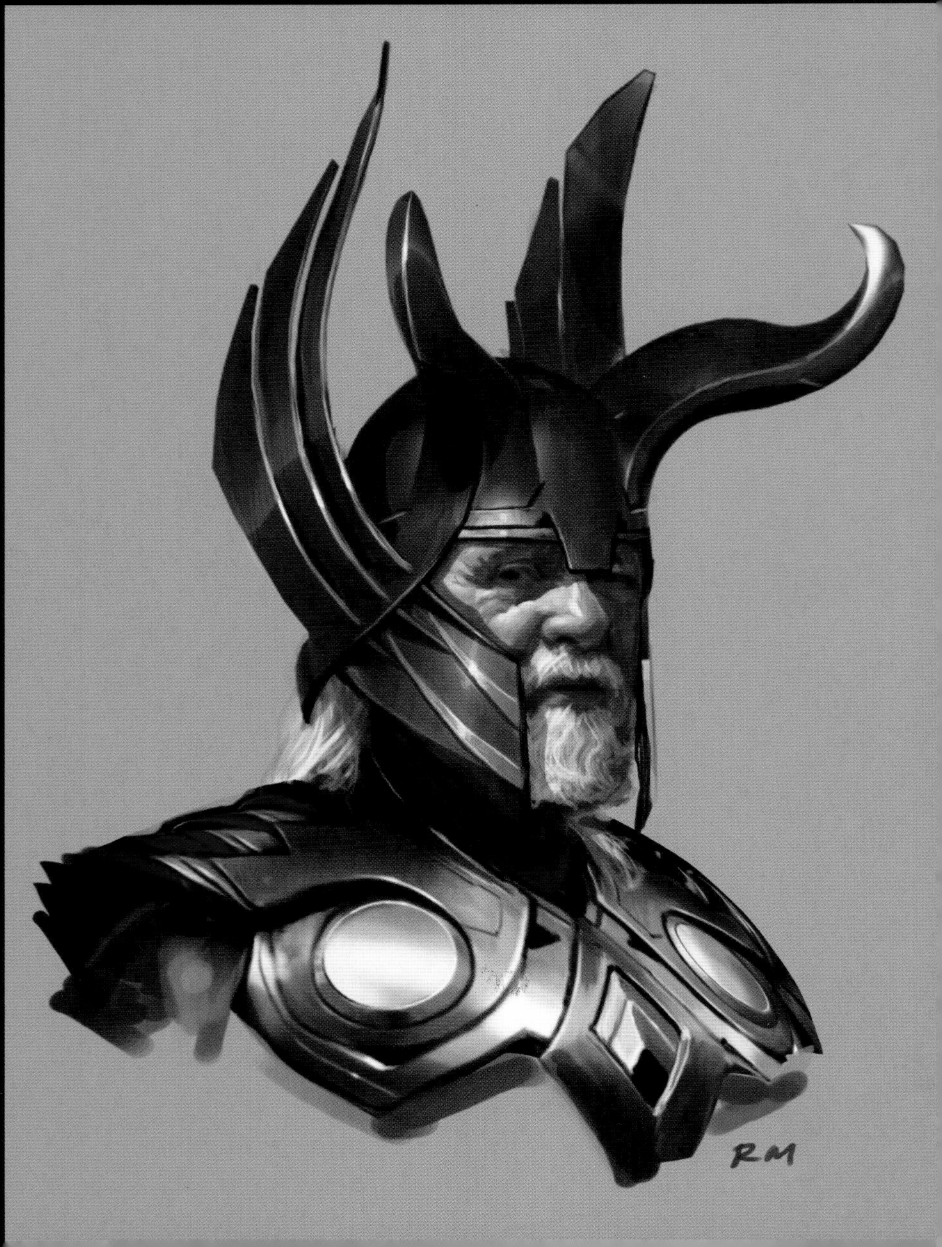
RM

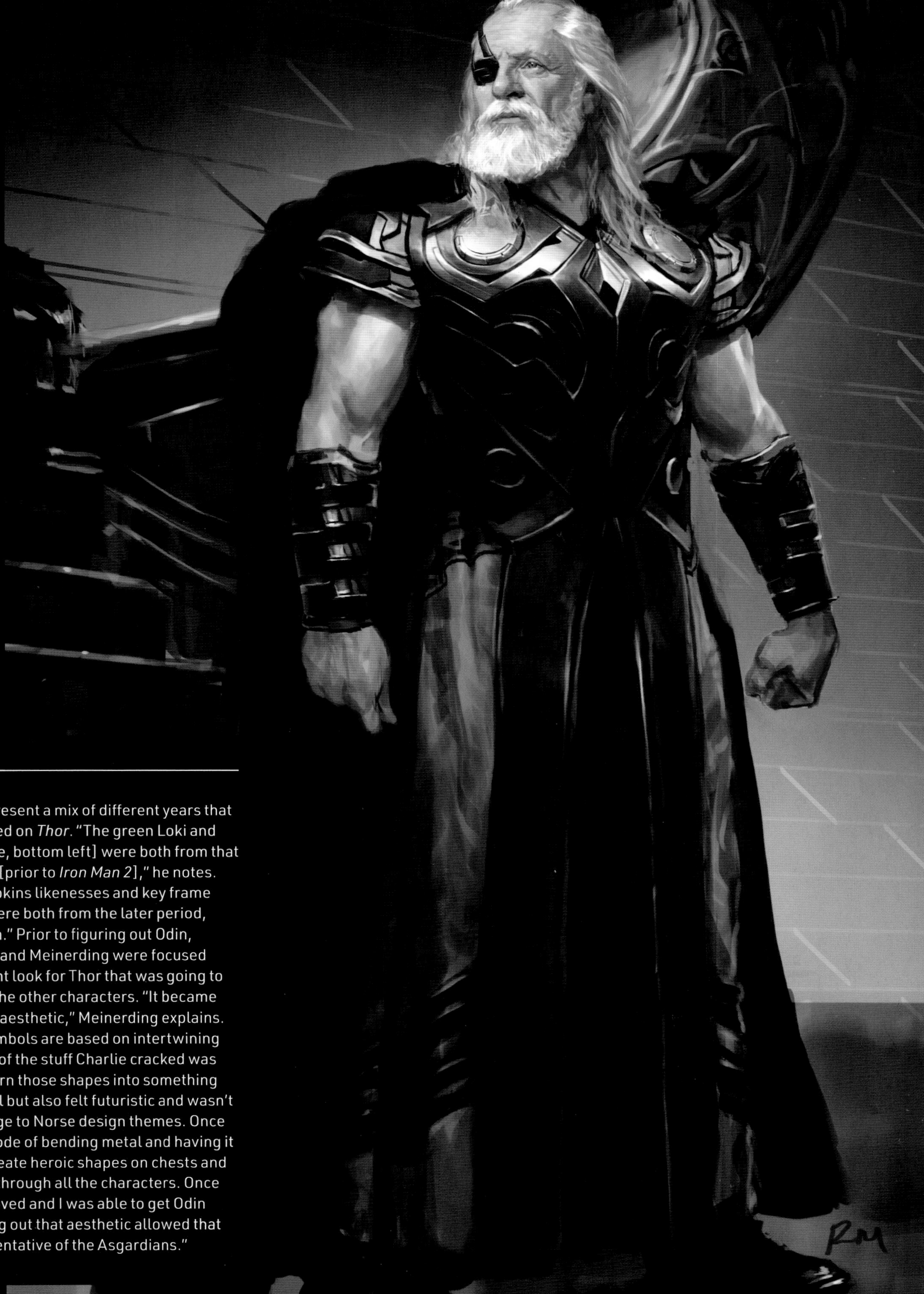
RM

These pieces represent a mix of different years that Meinerding worked on *Thor*. "The green Loki and the Odin [opposite, bottom left] were both from that very early period [prior to *Iron Man 2*]," he notes. "The Anthony Hopkins likenesses and key frame [opposite, top] were both from the later period, during production." Prior to figuring out Odin, both Charlie Wen and Meinerding were focused on finding the right look for Thor that was going to filter through all the other characters. "It became this sort of armor aesthetic," Meinerding explains. "A lot of Norse symbols are based on intertwining shapes. And a lot of the stuff Charlie cracked was finding ways to turn those shapes into something that felt like metal but also felt futuristic and wasn't just paying homage to Norse design themes. Once he cracked that code of bending metal and having it intertwine and create heroic shapes on chests and things, it filtered through all the characters. Once he got Thor approved and I was able to get Odin approved, figuring out that aesthetic allowed that look to be representative of the Asgardians."

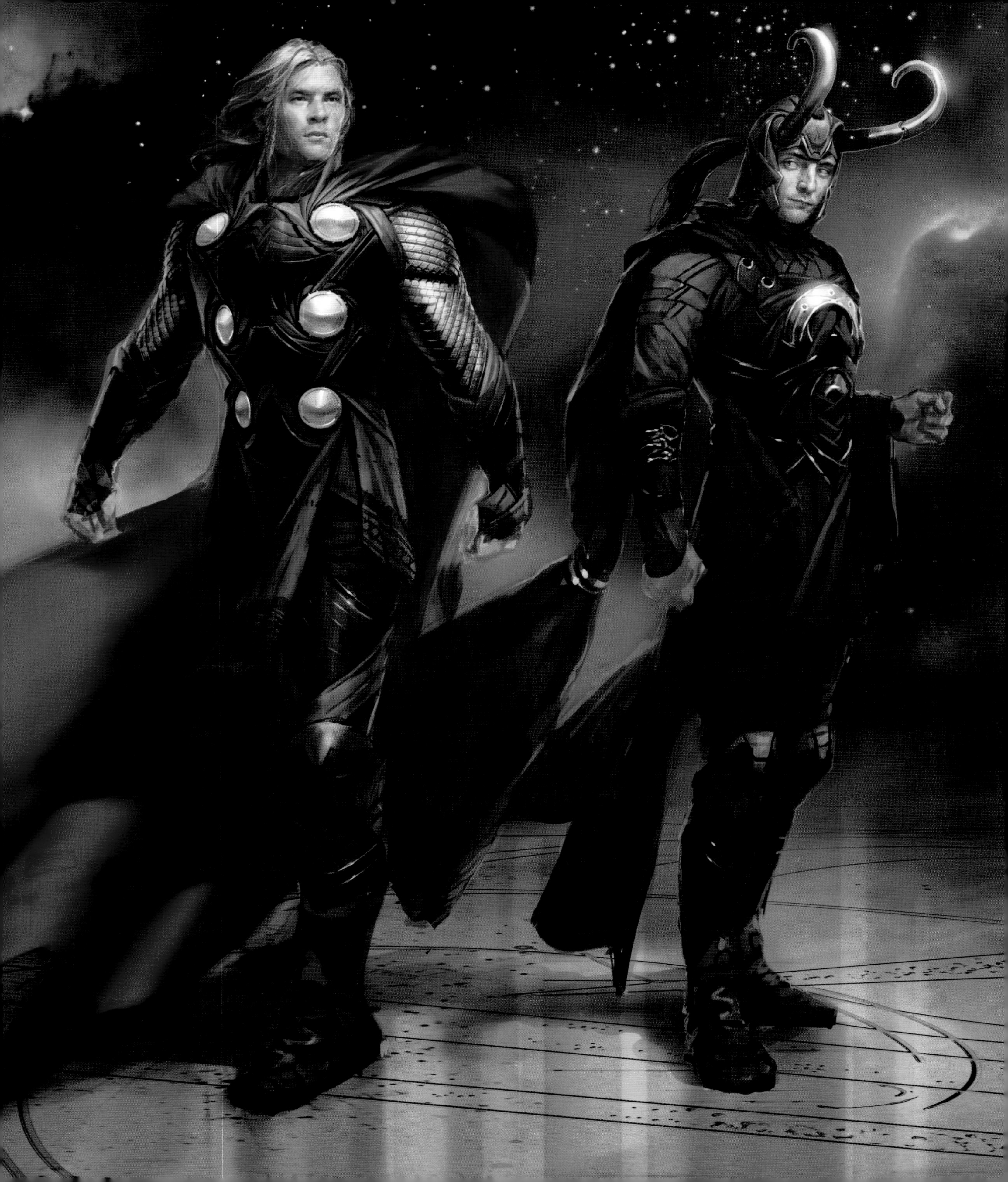

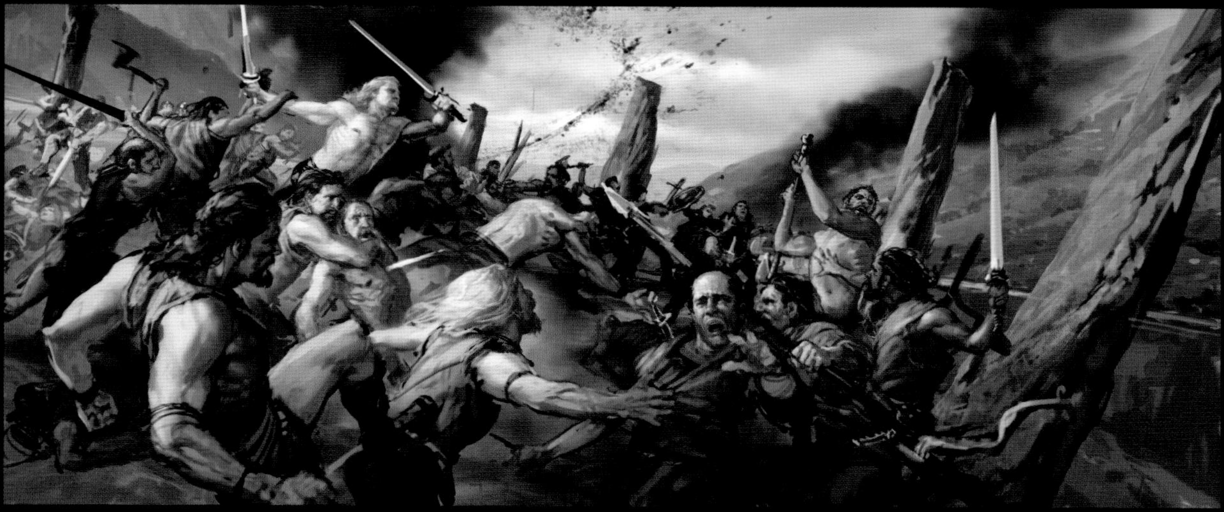

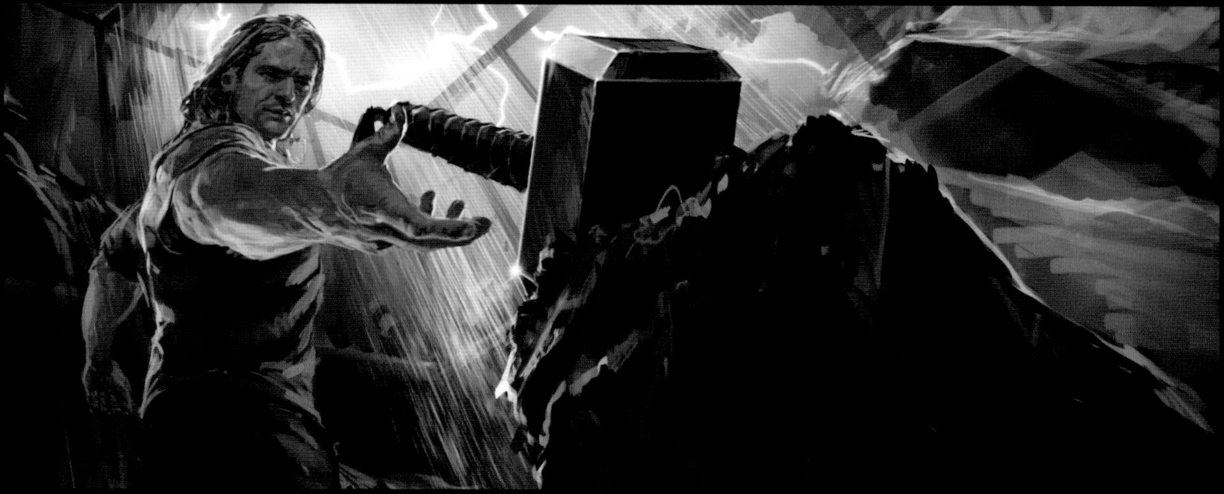

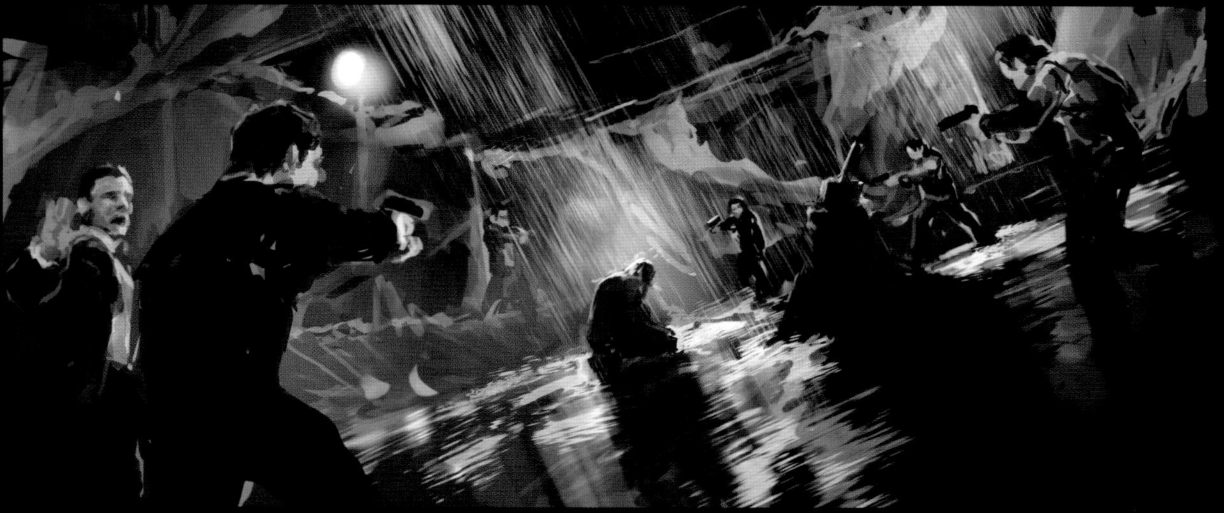

On his preference for working in black and white for early visual development art, Meinerding explains, "The challenge for me with color is, I'm venturing into a world where I have to make everything look real. Which, strictly speaking, isn't true. But it's the way my brain works. If I put color in something, I have to spend all the time making sure somebody doesn't think it looks artificial, fake, or that the color is bad. If I'm just doing it in black and white, it's enough of an abstraction that people can really enjoy the frame, and I can spend the time detailing it. It becomes an exercise in 'what needs to get solved' as opposed to 'how finished is something?' With black and white, I'm able to focus on what feels like it needs solving."

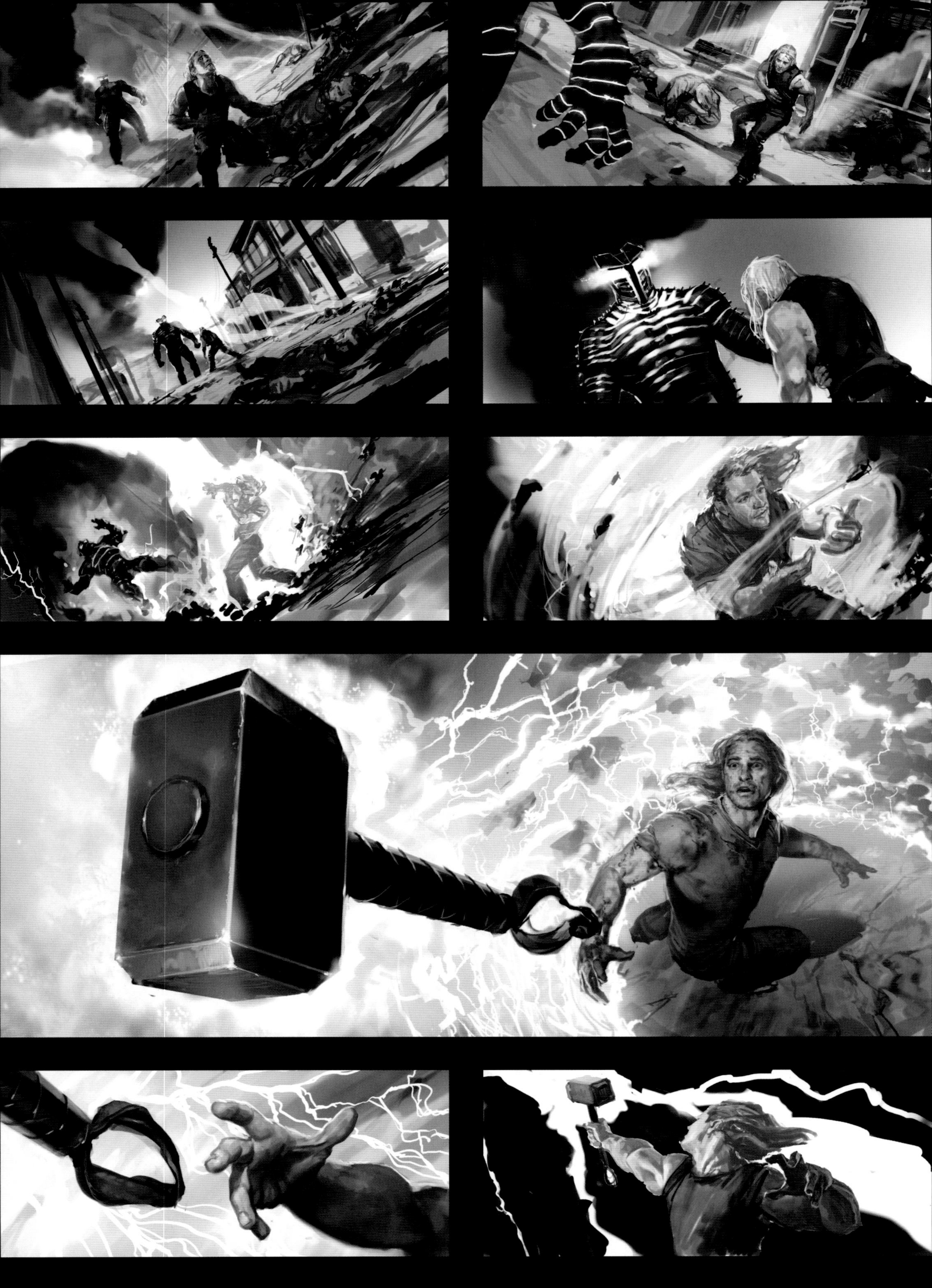

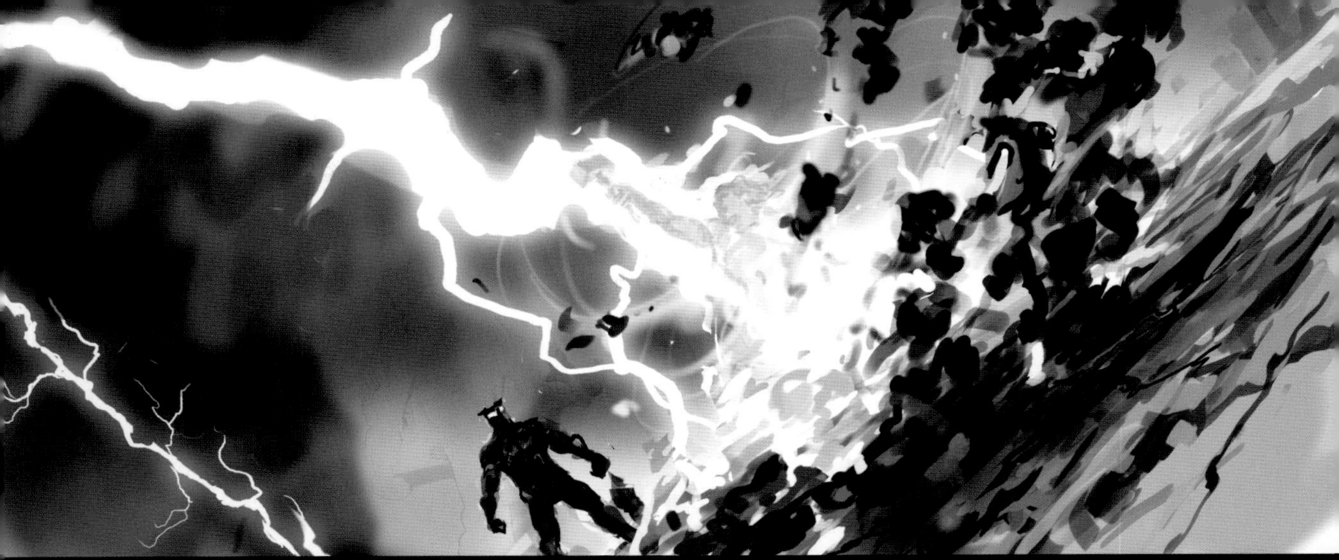

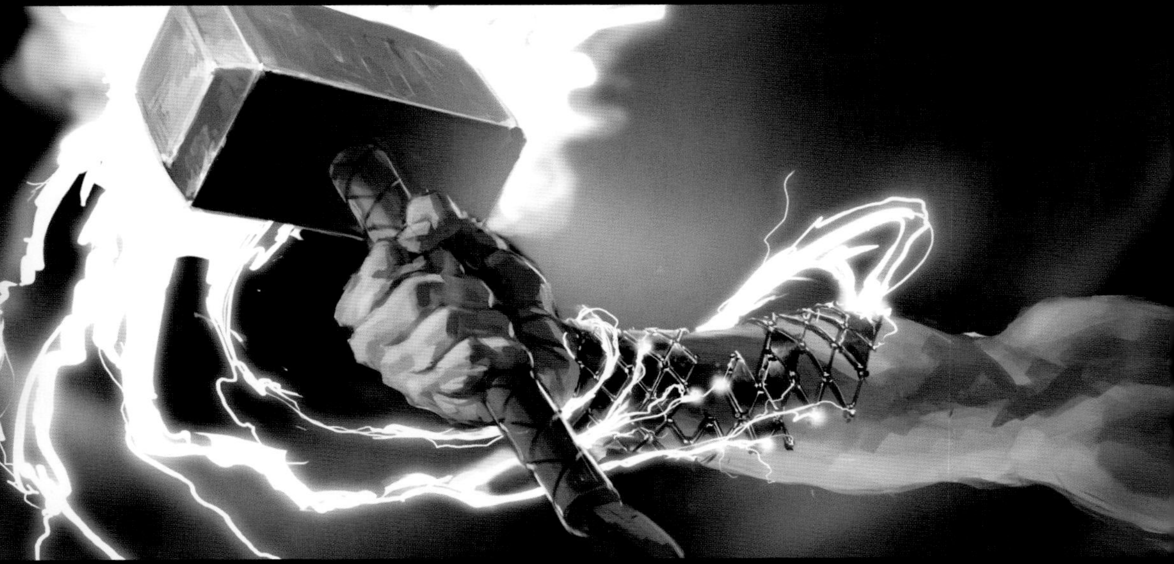

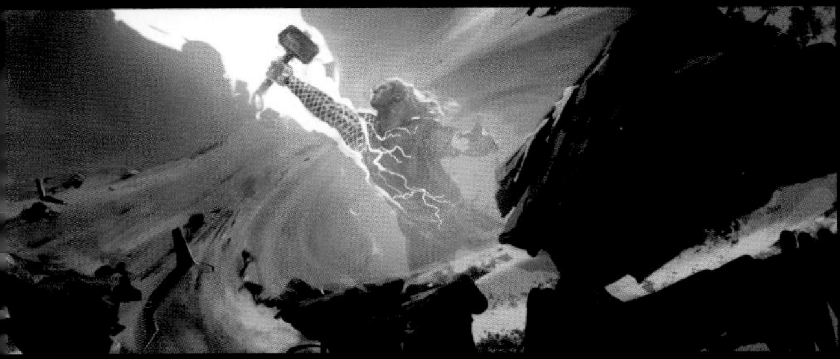

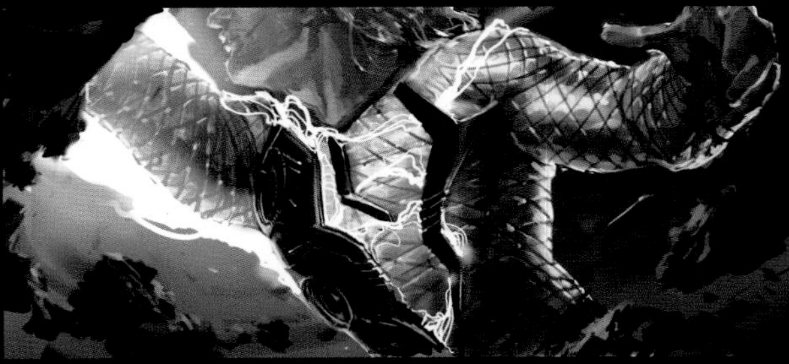

This immediately recognizable sequence with the Destroyer was pitched by Meinerding to *Thor* director Kenneth Branagh. "I worked pretty hard on this," shares Meinerding. "I was in the art department and was tasked with doing key frames for important moments, and then some character and/or costume design as well. This [sequence] was super challenging. I was breaking the moments—really the *sub*-moments— into basically seeing this experience through Thor's eyes instead of through Jane's."

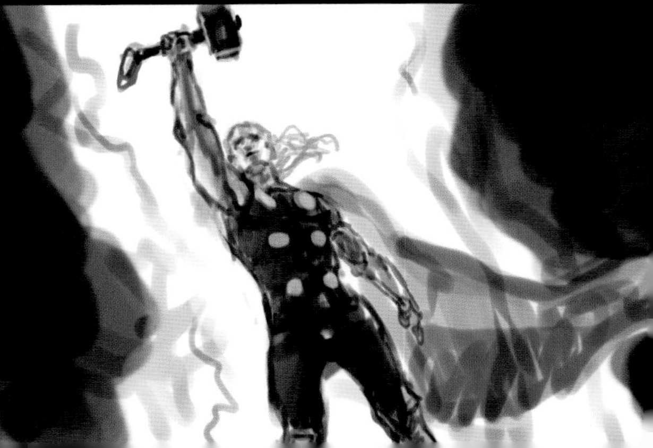

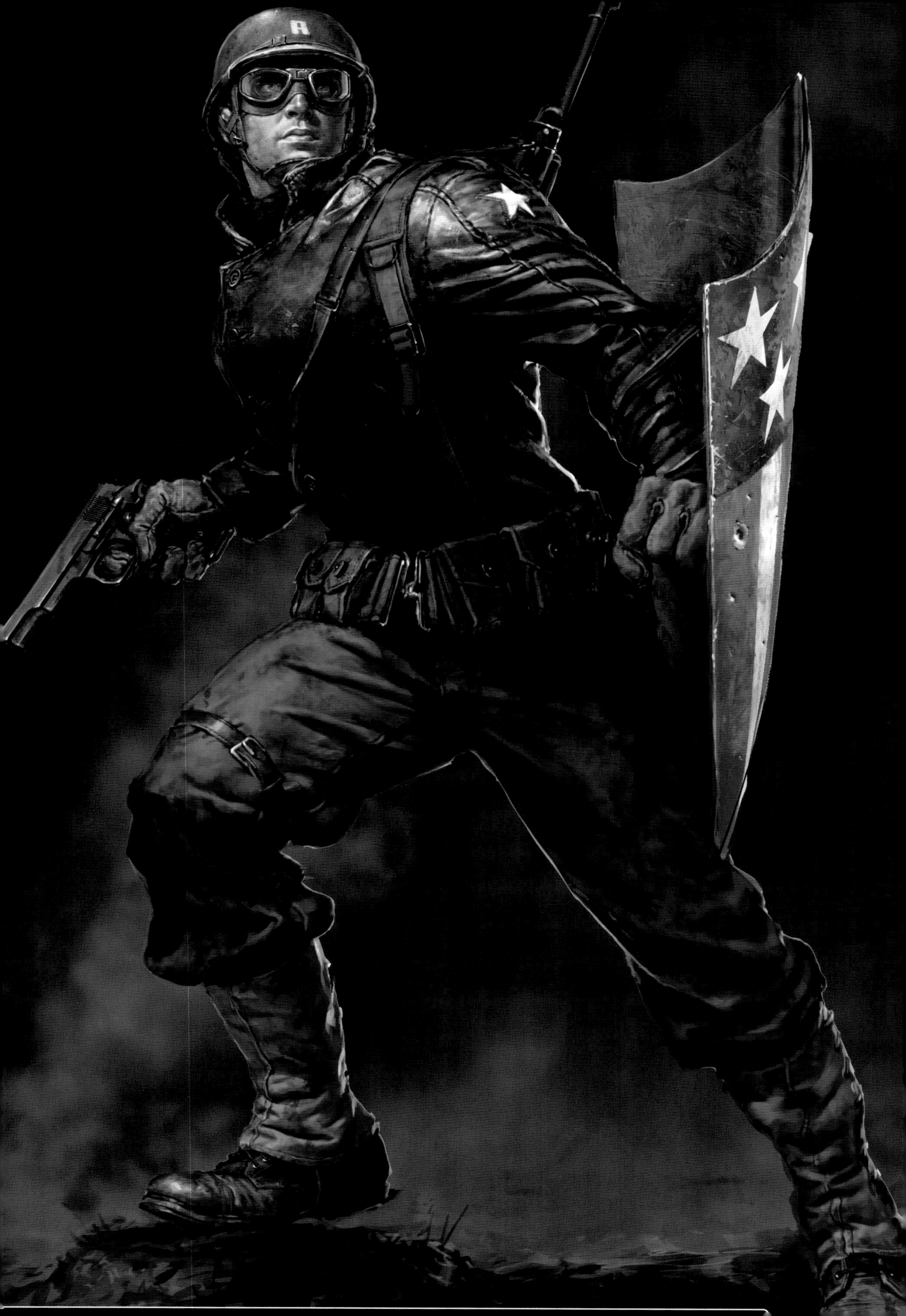

As *Iron Man* and *The Incredible Hulk* shifted into postproduction, the design work wound down and Meinerding was approached by *Watchmen* costume designer Michael Wilkinson to join his design team. Kevin Feige asked Meinerding if he'd like to stay and work on long-lead designs for *Thor*, but the lure of Alan Moore and Dave Gibbons's seminal graphic novel adaptation wasn't something he felt he could pass up. However, it was made clear that the door would remain open for Meinerding to return whenever he was ready.

A few months later, Marvel Studios' Unit Production Manager Louis D'Esposito called to request Meinerding come back, which he did. Unbeknownst to Meinerding at the time, Feige and the producers were worried about losing his talents, so they asked him to come back a year before actual preproduction was planned to start on either *Thor* or *Captain America*. D'Esposito pitched him the idea of their intention to launch a full-time Marvel Studios design team, including storyboard and concept design work. It was a huge departure from how most studios operated, and one that had a lot of appeal for Meinerding.

Still a freelancer, Meinerding started work in earnest on *Captain America*, beginning with a piece inspired by Kevin Maguire's *Adventures of Captain America* series. Initial studies oriented around World War II–era drawings, including USO outfits and a main hero costume. There were also early ideas around the look of Red Skull and Hydra.

Feige also requested key frames featuring evocative images from the period. "The first drawing I did of Captain America with a metal shield was in a propaganda poster," he remembers. "And that black-and-white [key frame] I did of Cap and the troops together [see page 42] took me two and a half weeks."

Meinerding says in the early days of the studio's formation, he had the luxury of time, so he took advantage of it to really interpret these Marvel characters in new ways. "One of the great things about Marvel comics is that there's such a wealth of understanding about each character that if you take the time to take all that in, it can affect you in a lot of different ways," he explains. "With Cap, we had, like, seventy years of comics to understand him and to look at him, which then sparks an idea of what could be a way of representing him? It's all there, so I can ask, 'What is the thing that's integral to these characters I'm working on? What is the thing that if I don't create *this* image, the filmmakers might not see it as a component of the character?'"

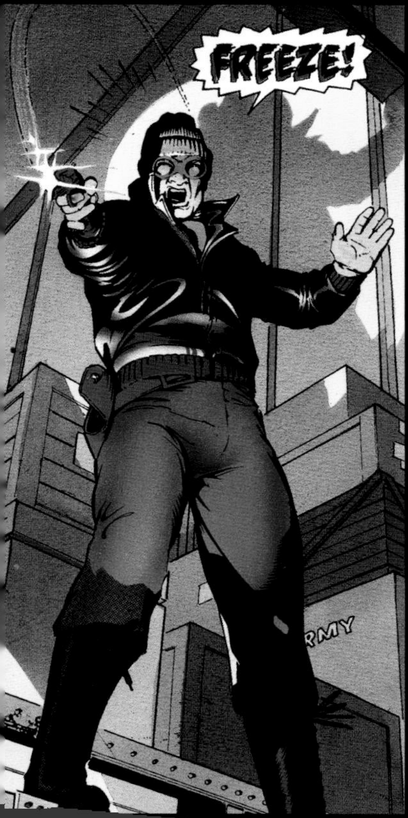
FREEZE!

LEFT Panel from *Captain America: First Flight of The Eagle* (1991) #1, written by Fabian Micieza, pencils by Kevin Maguire, inks by Joe Rubinstein, color by Paul Mounts

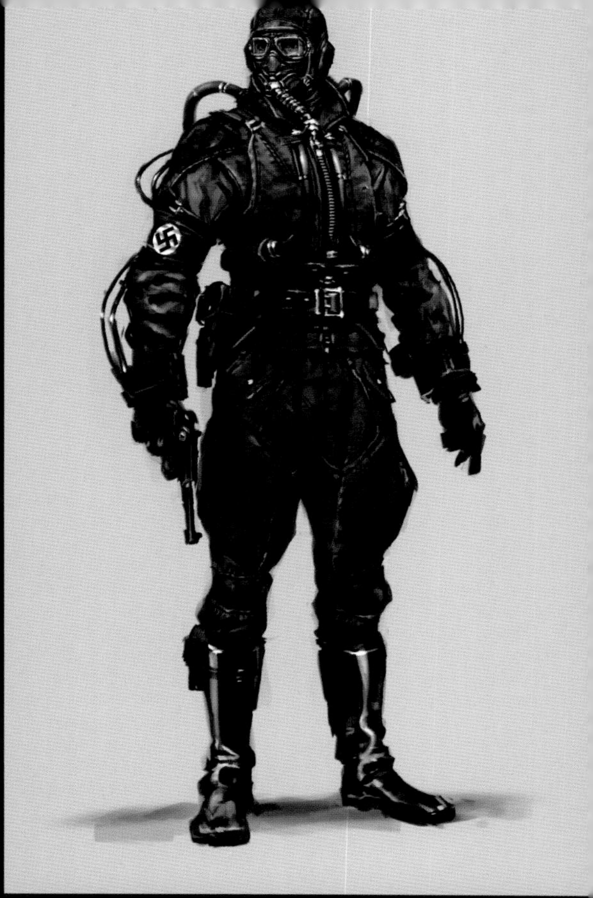

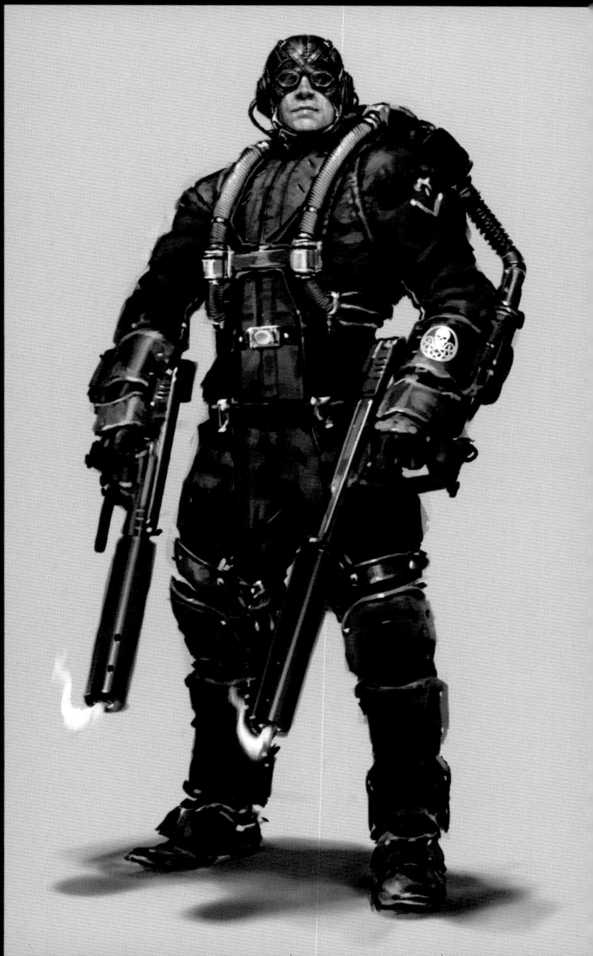

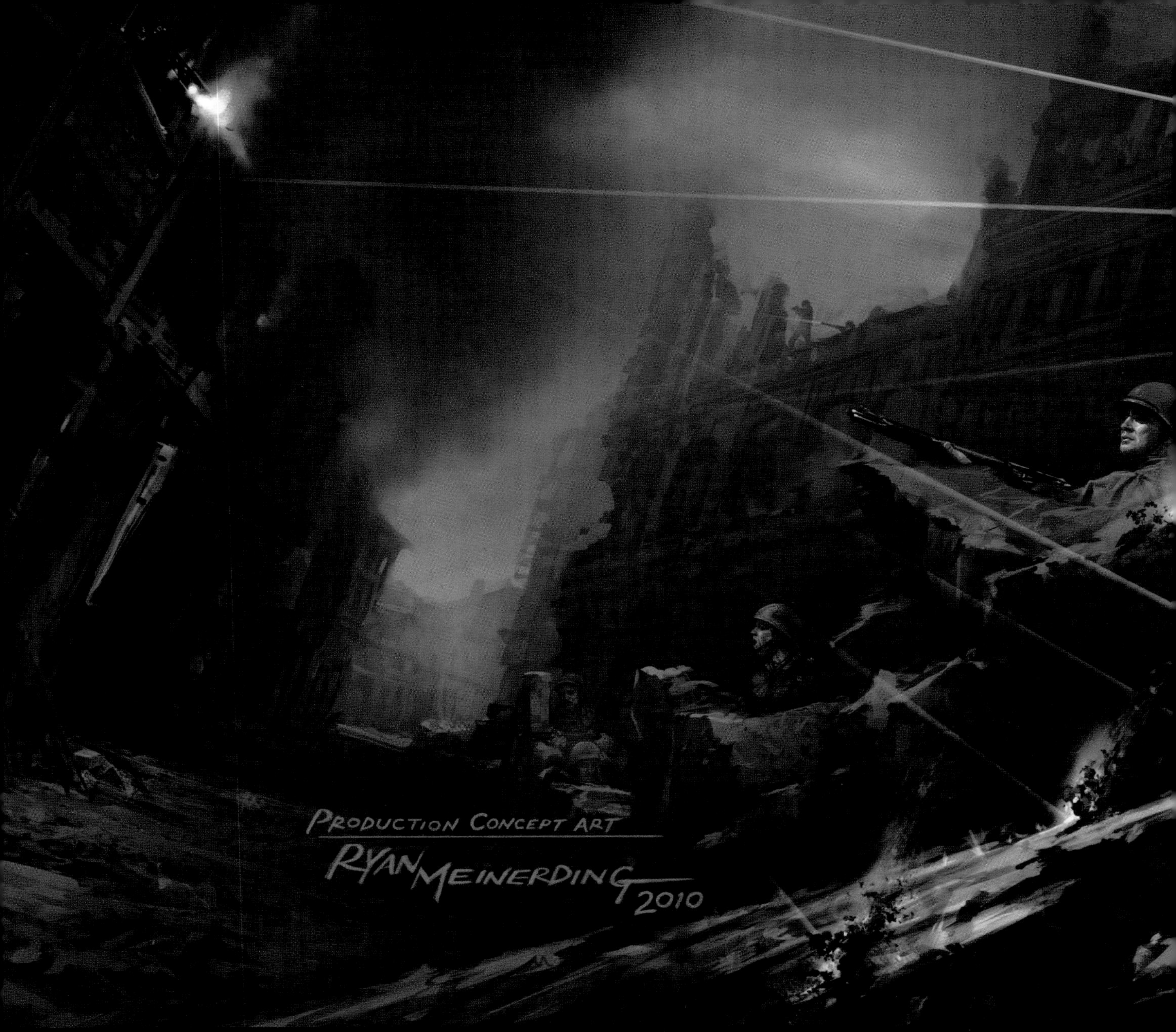
PRODUCTION CONCEPT ART
RYAN MEINERDING 2010

THIS AND FOLLOWING TWO SPREADS Meinerding created these pieces during the three months he was left on his own to draw and explore his "early pass" ideas for *Captain America: The First Avenger*. They are a perfect example of an aspect that Kevin Feige admires about Meinerding—Feige feels his art and storytelling echo that of legendary *Star Wars* concept artist Ralph McQuarrie. Humbled by the comparison, Meinerding says of Feige, "I think one of the things he loves so much about McQuarrie's artwork is that it does feel like those frames sprung from his imagination, down to the details, the emotion, the design, the setting, and the composition, all at once." During his time left alone to conjure up *Captain America* art, Meinerding admits, "I was full of anxiety. I was freaking out because they paid me for three months' worth of work. . . . What if nobody liked this stuff? But I did get to do a lot of things I really wanted to do. I felt like the stuff I was working on was good to explore."

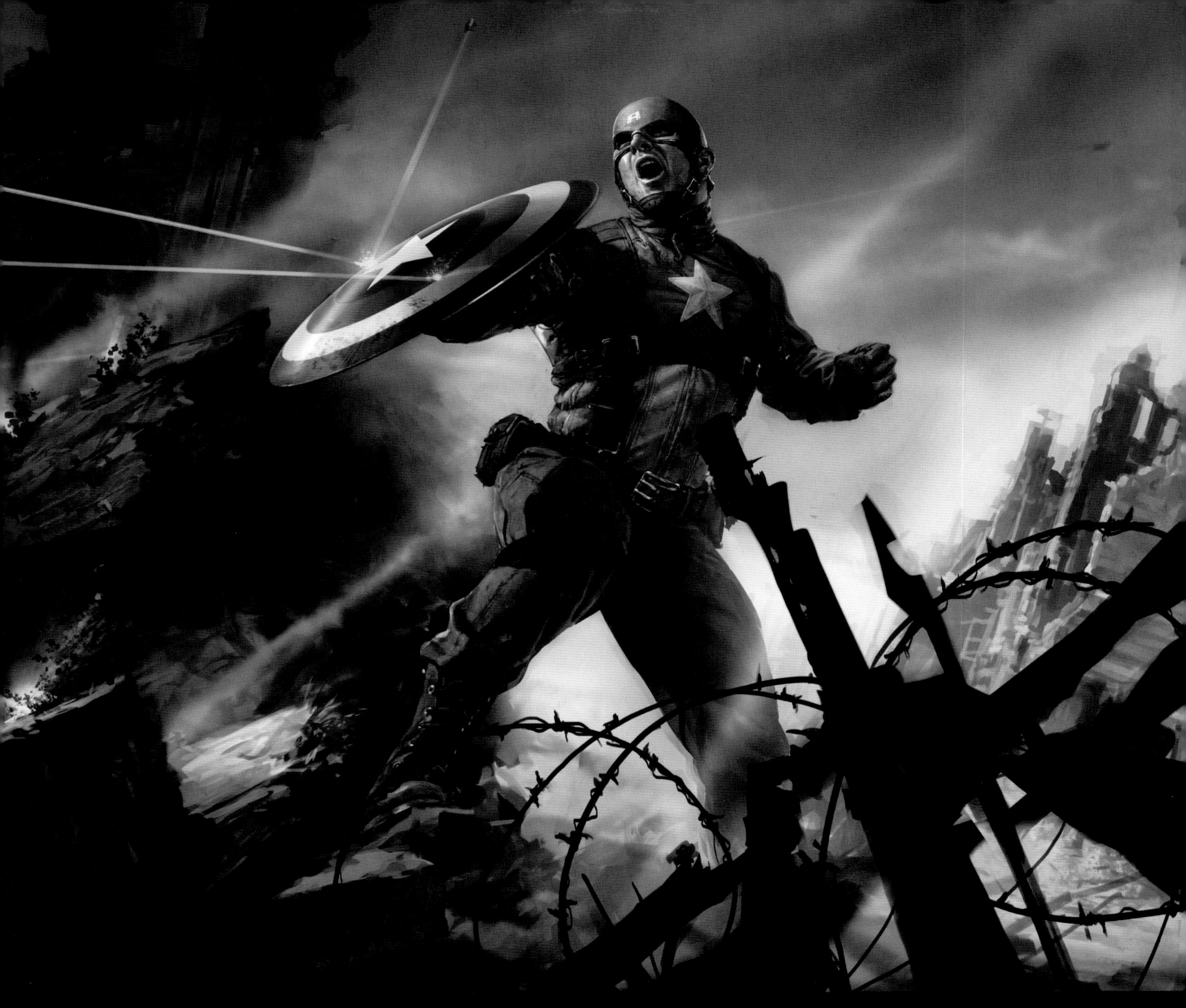

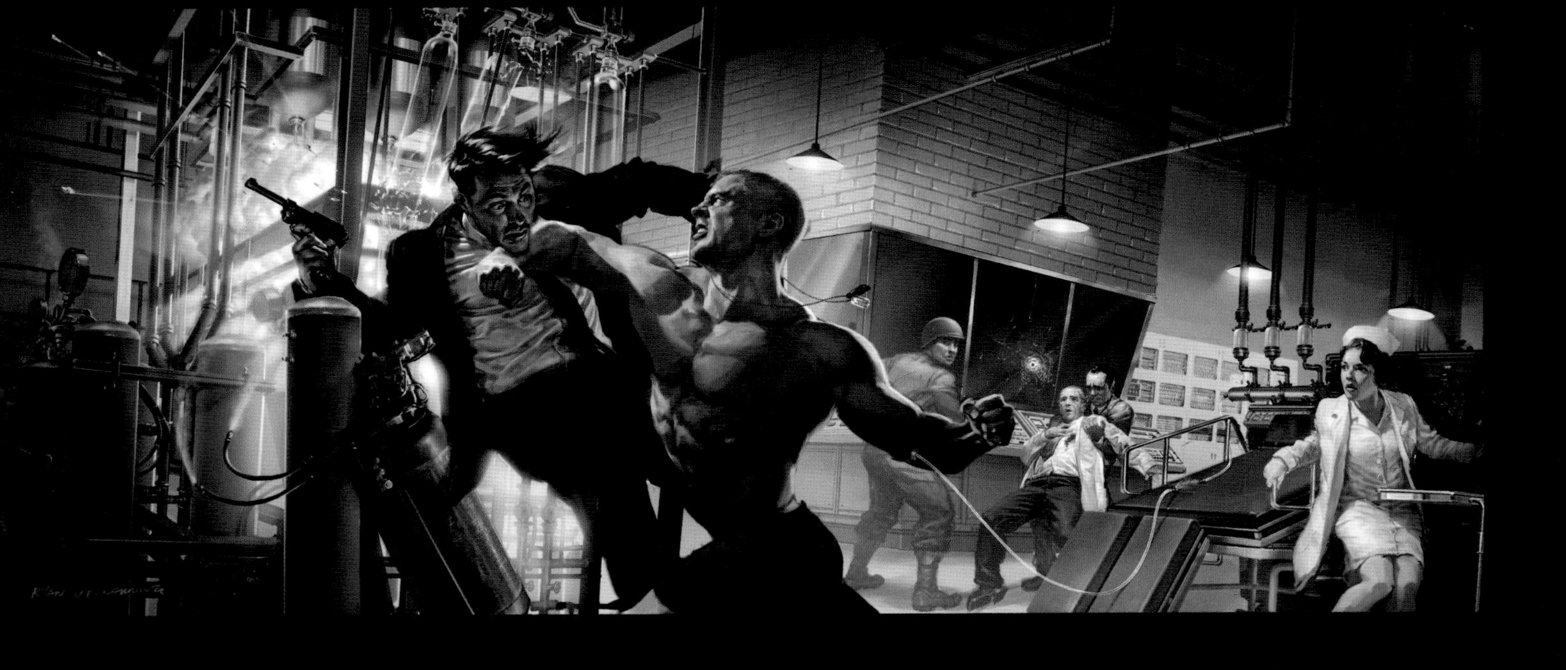

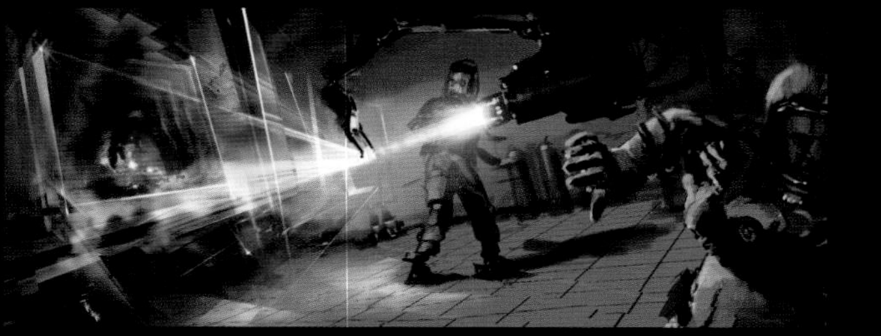

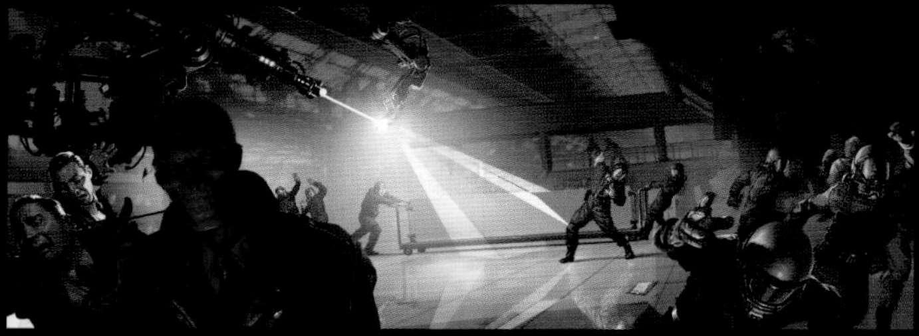

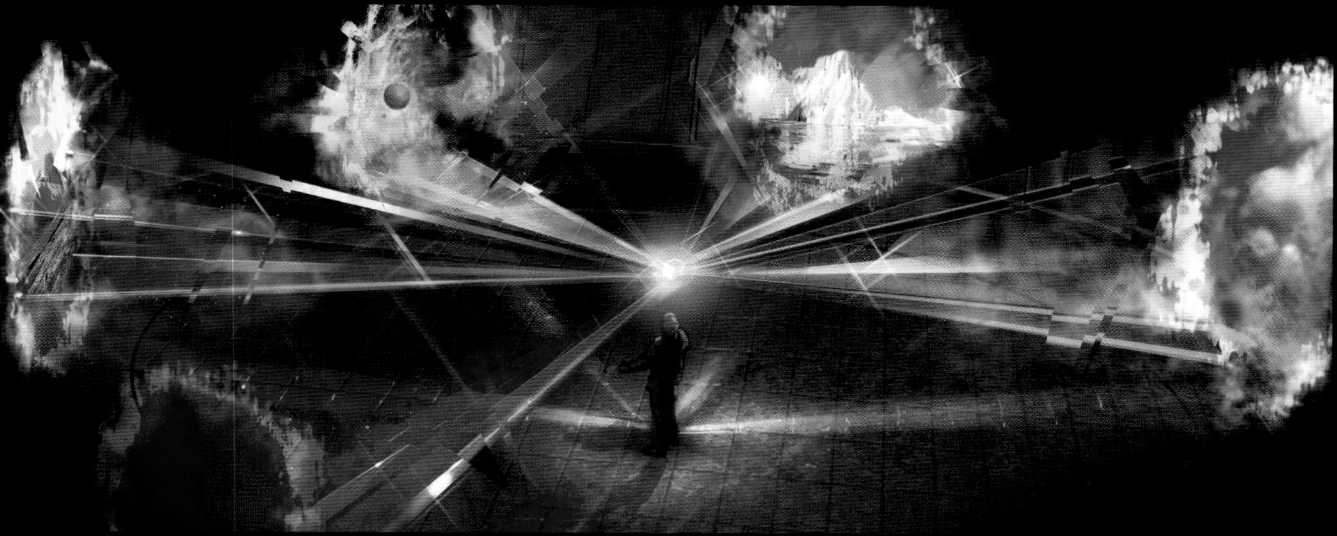

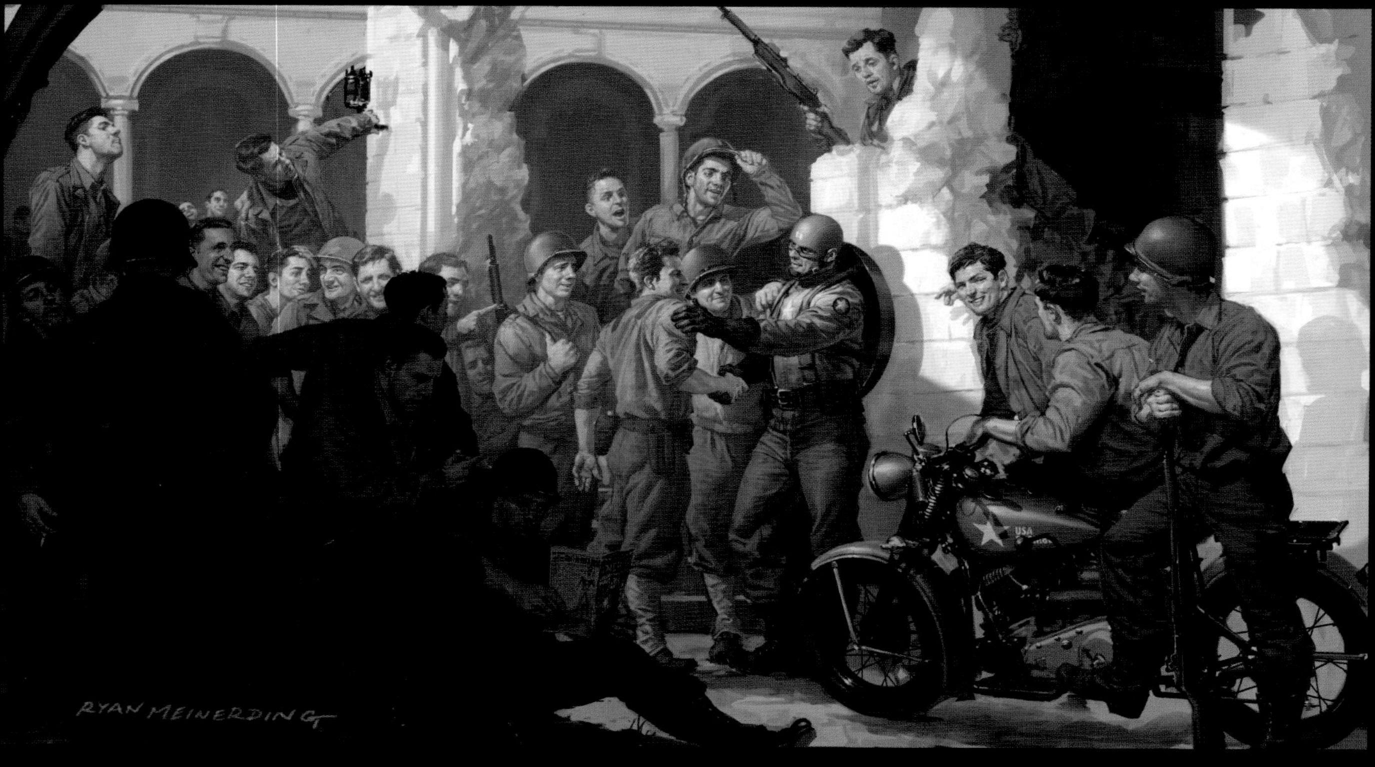
RYAN MEINERDING

"This frame [above] is hugely important because it shows Cap being a normal guy," says Meinerding. "He's not a Super Hero in the classic sense. He's not flying above everybody. He understands what all these soldiers are going through. It highlights him caring about them. And it showcases something about his character that, if I was just doing action shots, I would never attempt. That kind of understanding and thought process, it's almost like you'd have to push all the other things away that you know a production might need in order to make space for an image you know is important, conceptual, and integral to the character."

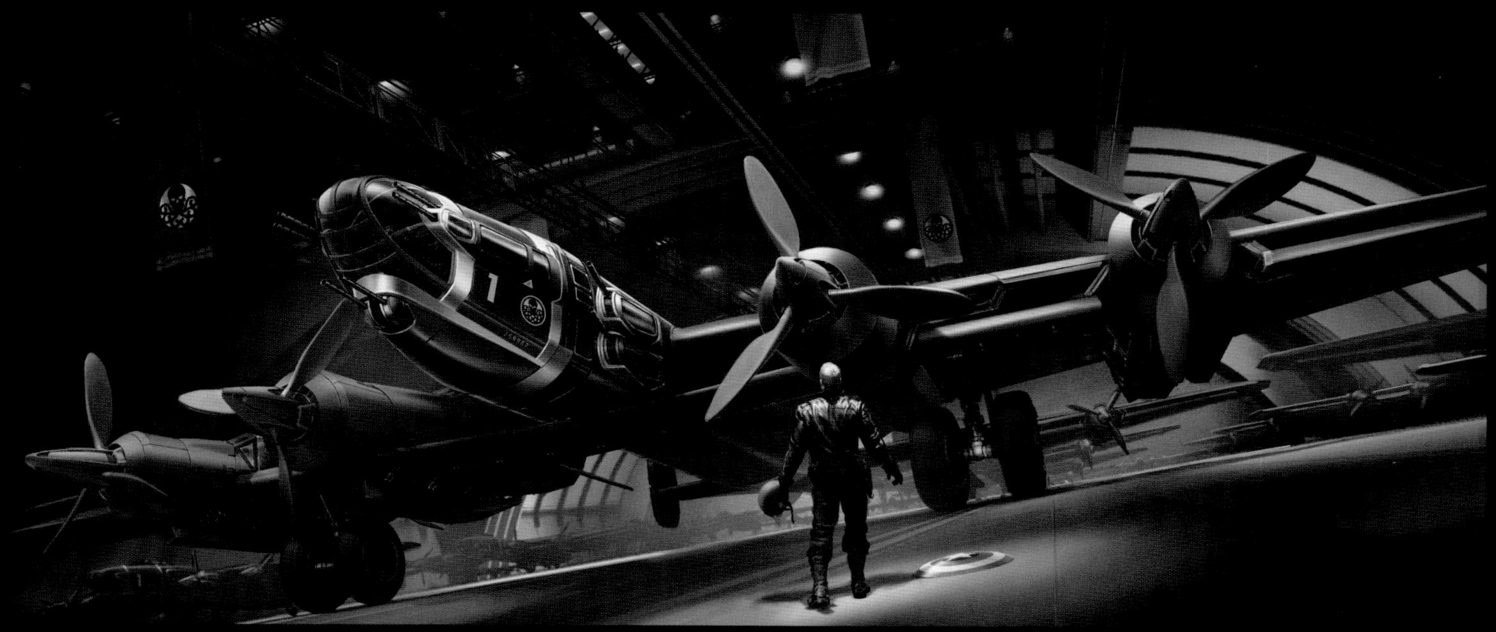

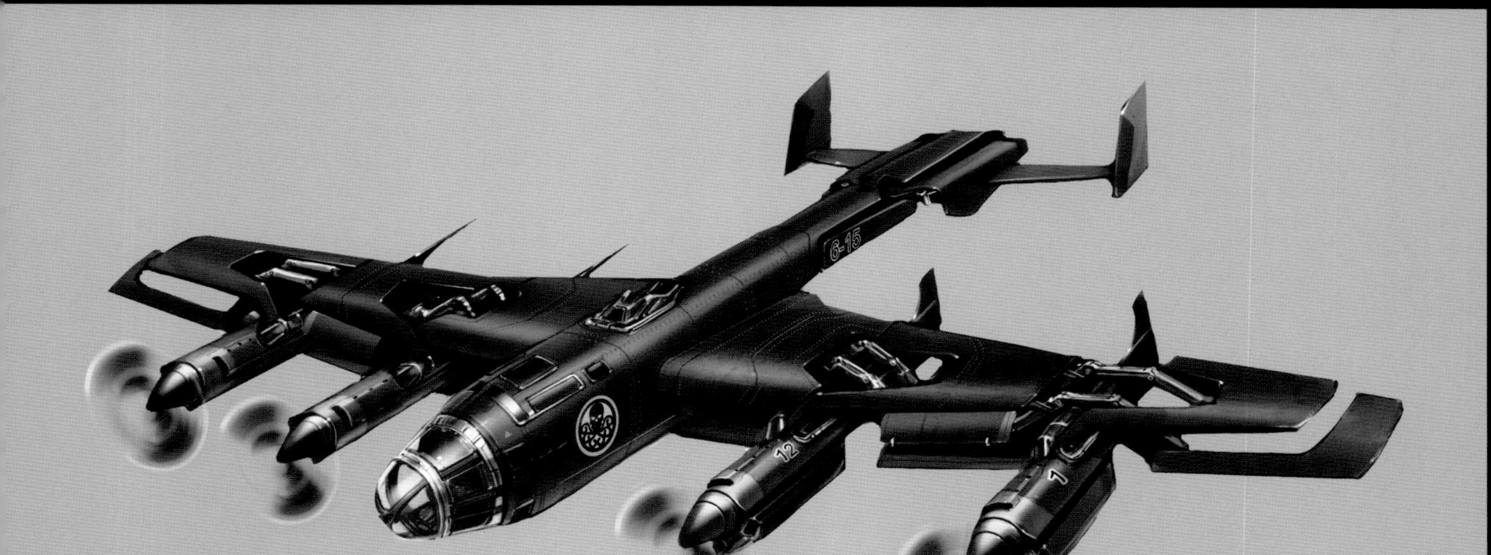

6-15
12
1

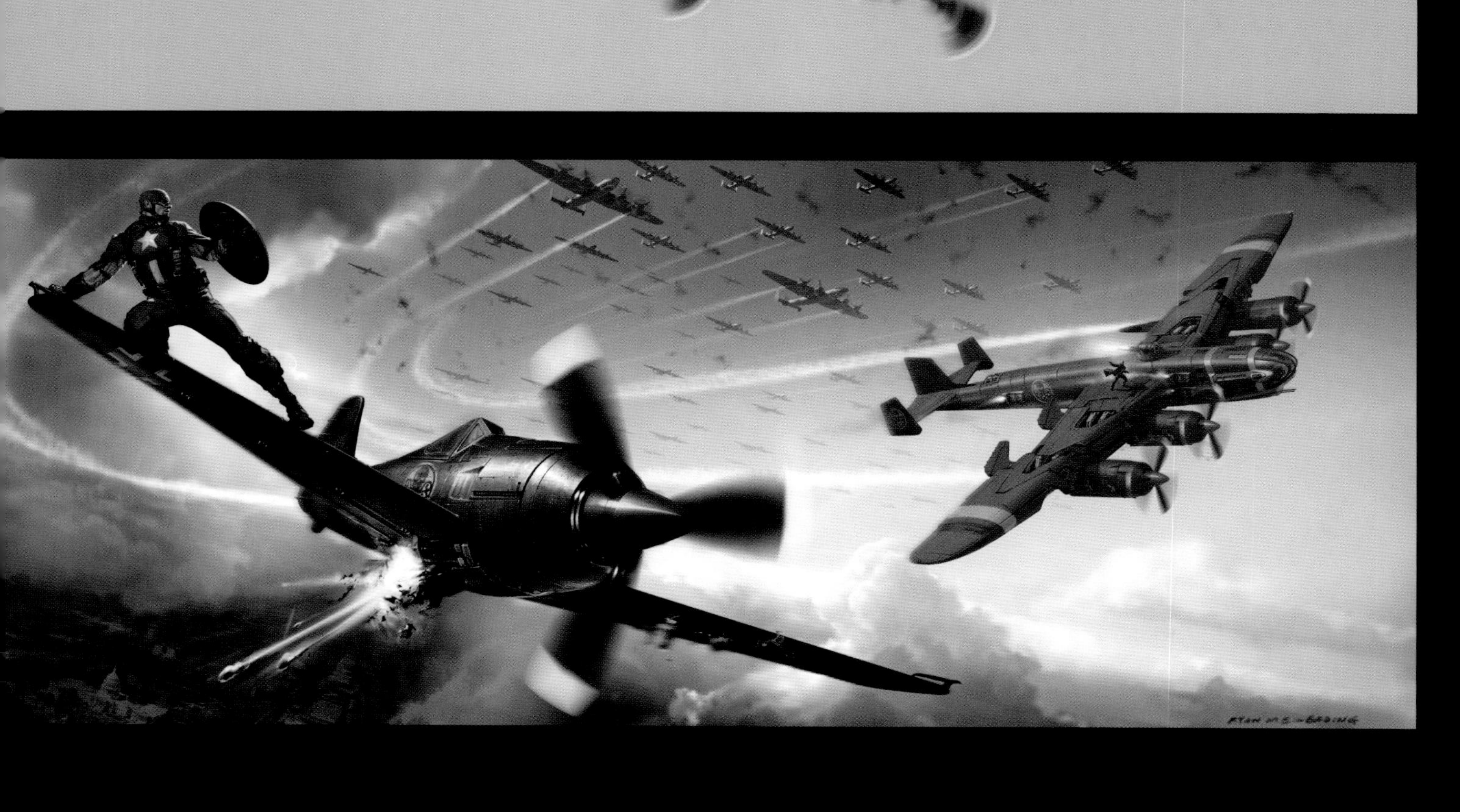

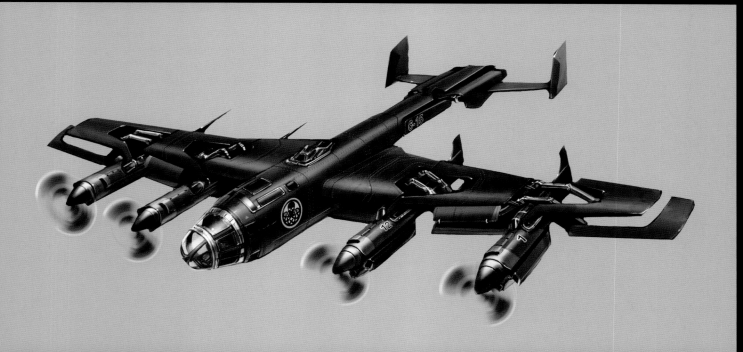

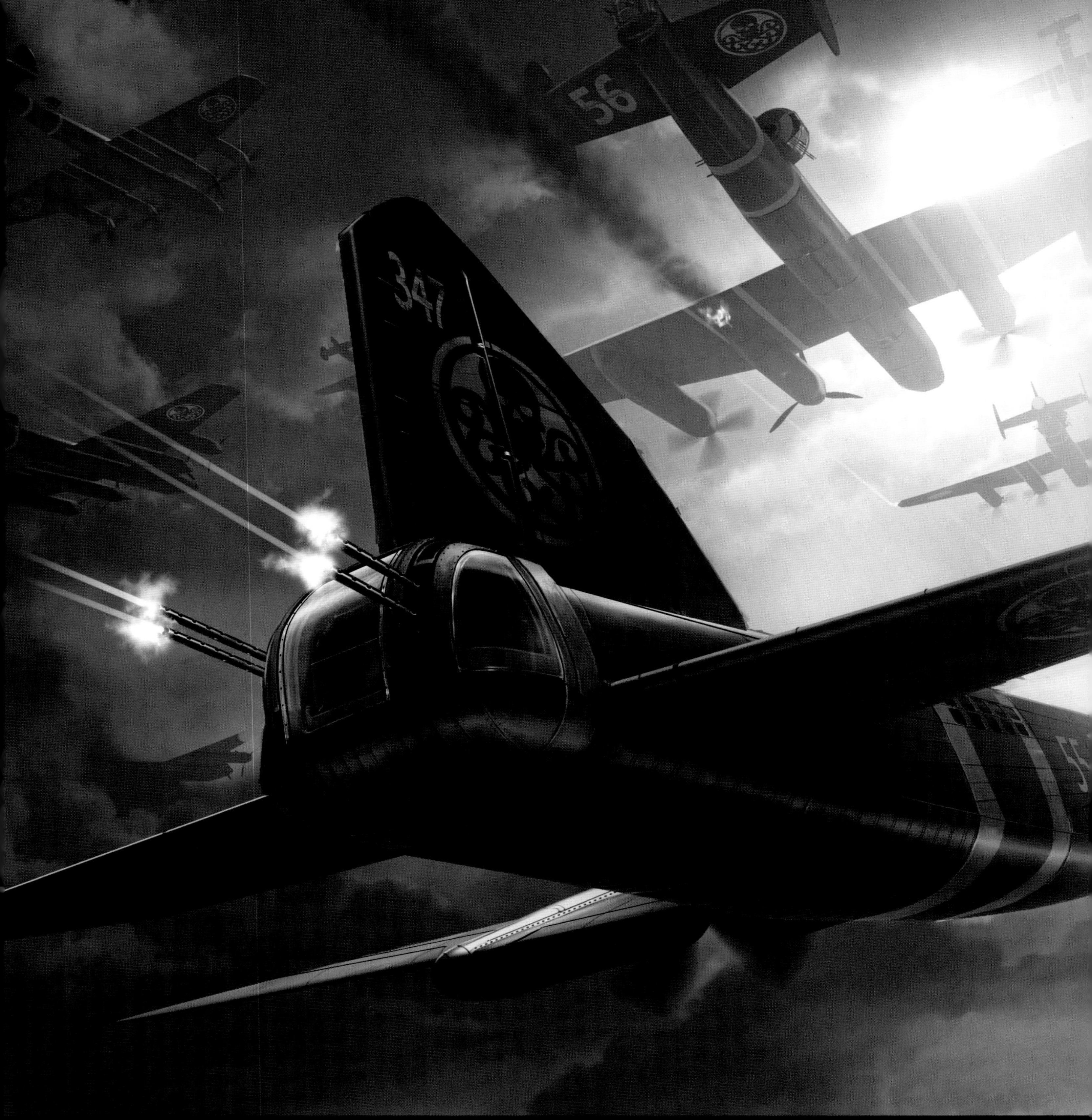
56
347

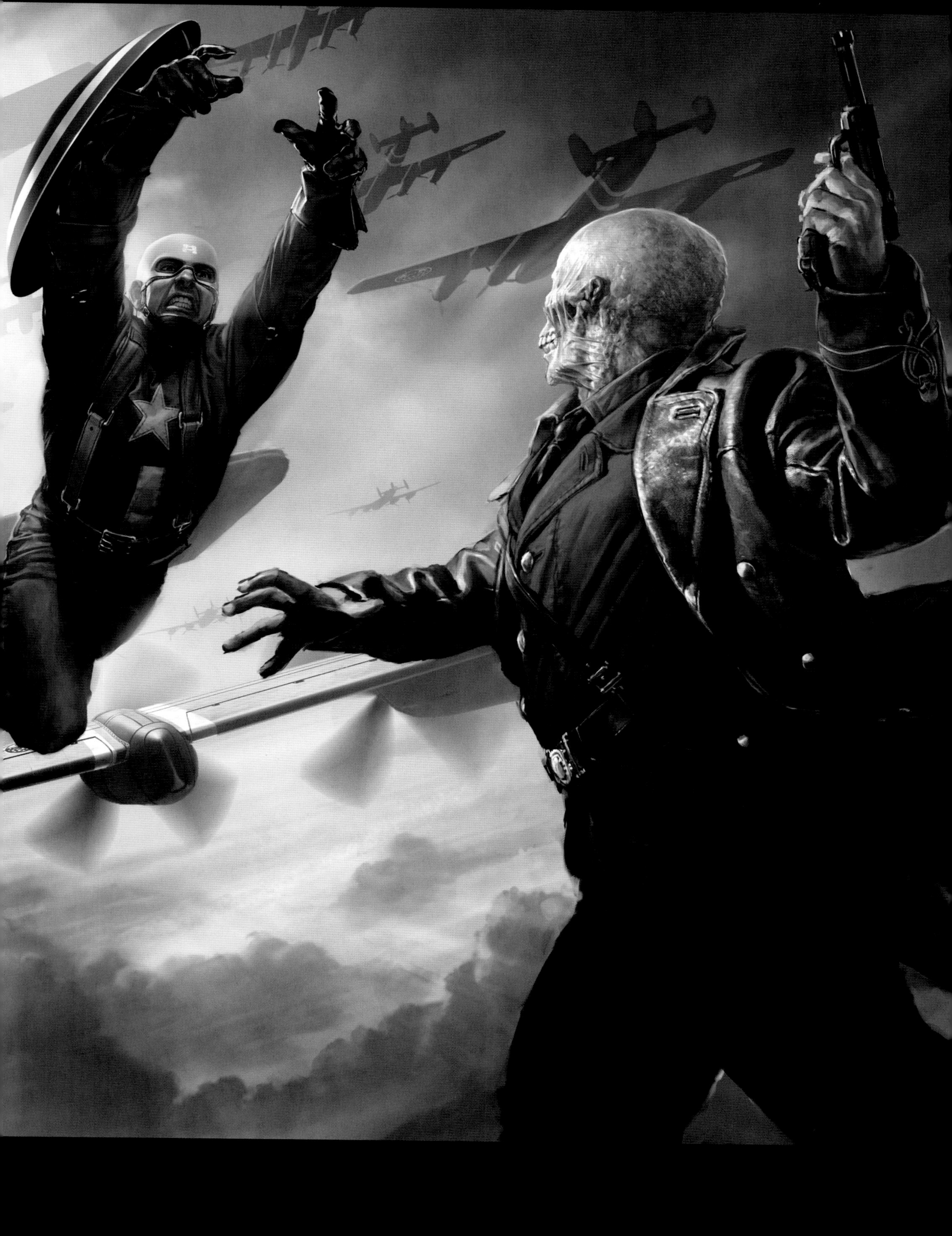

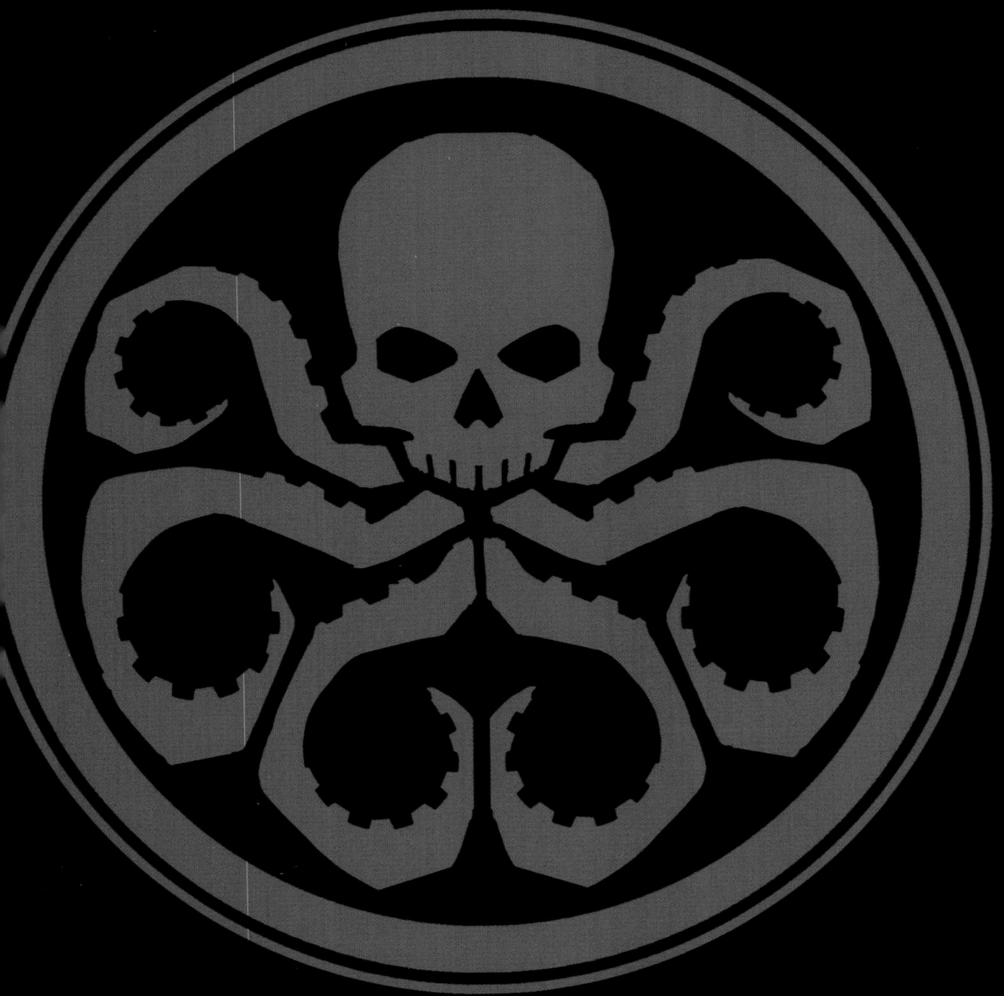

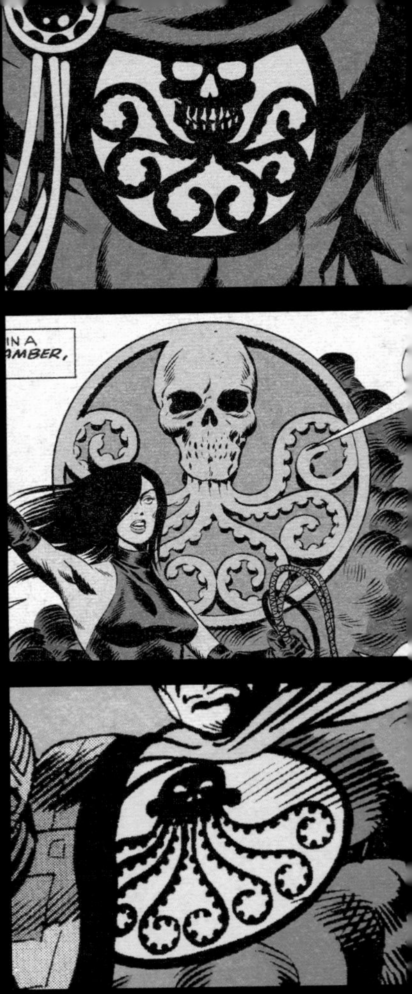

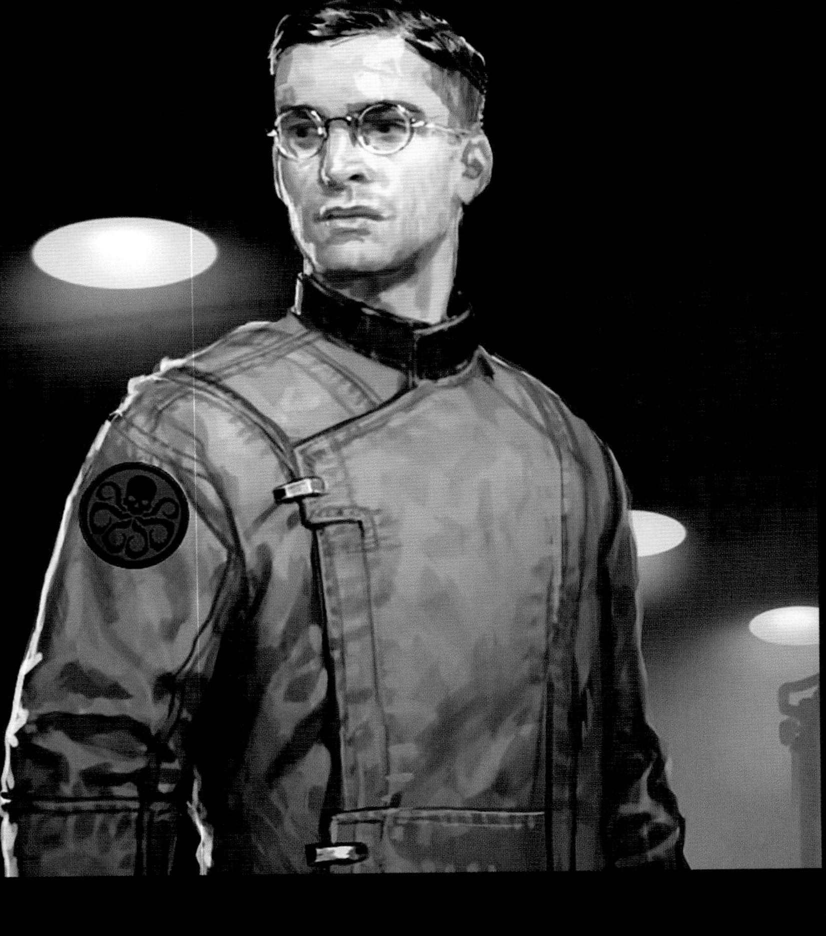

Left to his own devices for that initial exploration period for *The First Avenger*, Meinerding chose what to work on purely based on where ideas and inspiration led him on a day-to-day basis. "I didn't have a list they gave me that I needed to check off," he says. "So the reality of that period of time on those early projects is that it was a pretty free-form stream of consciousness: I might do a character design, I could do a whole new key frame, I could choose to show this moment with Red Skull or this moment with Cap. What does it *feel* like? How do you do *ten* images and make it *feel* like a whole movie? And what are you gonna have to accomplish? It's some of the work I'm most proud of."

ABOVE LEFT Meinerding's design for the Hydra logo

ABOVE RIGHT Previous incarnations of the Hydra logo from (top to bottom) *Stange Tales* (1967) #156; *Captain America* (1969) #111; and *Nick Fury: Agent of S.H.I.E.L.D.* (1992) #34

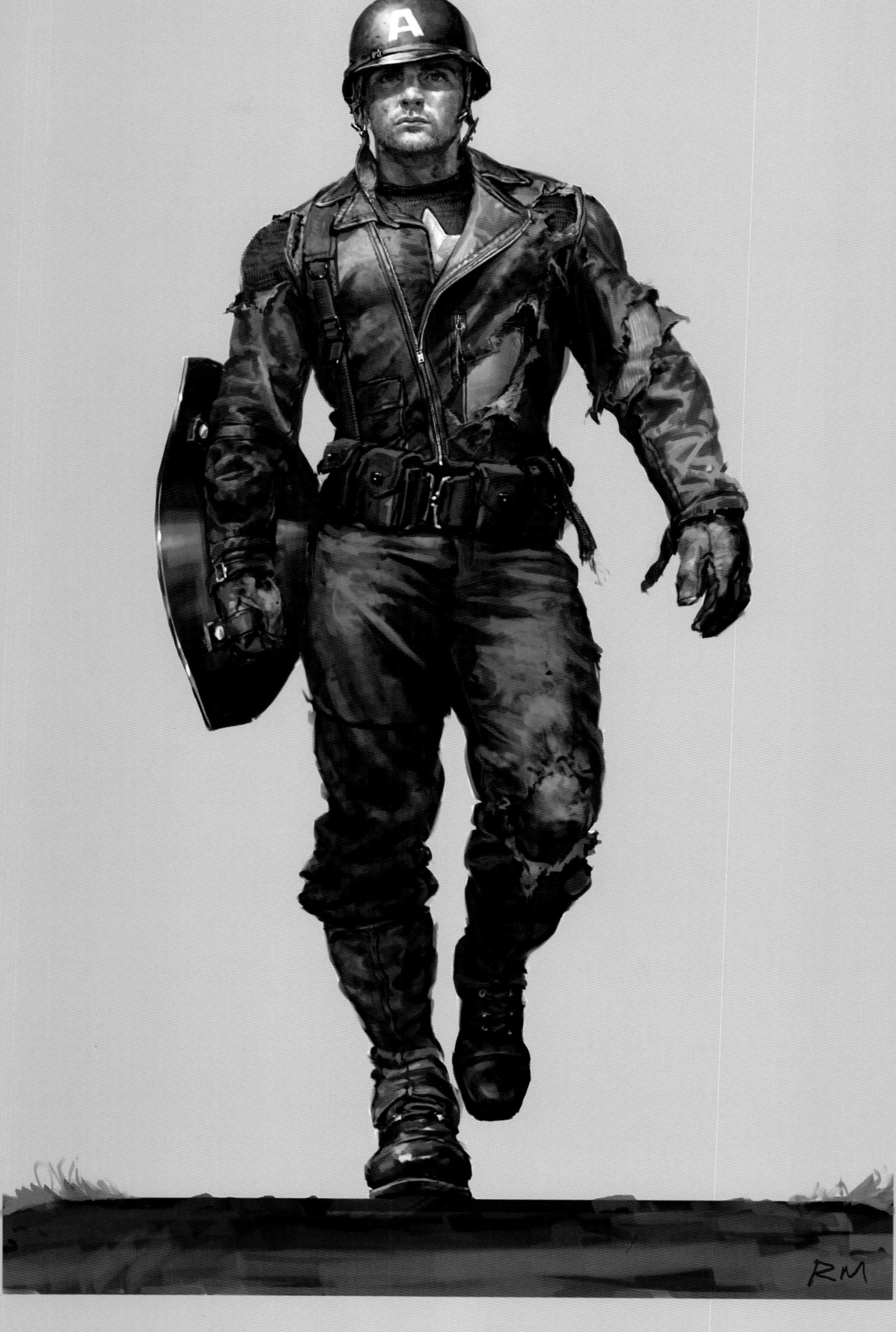
A
RM

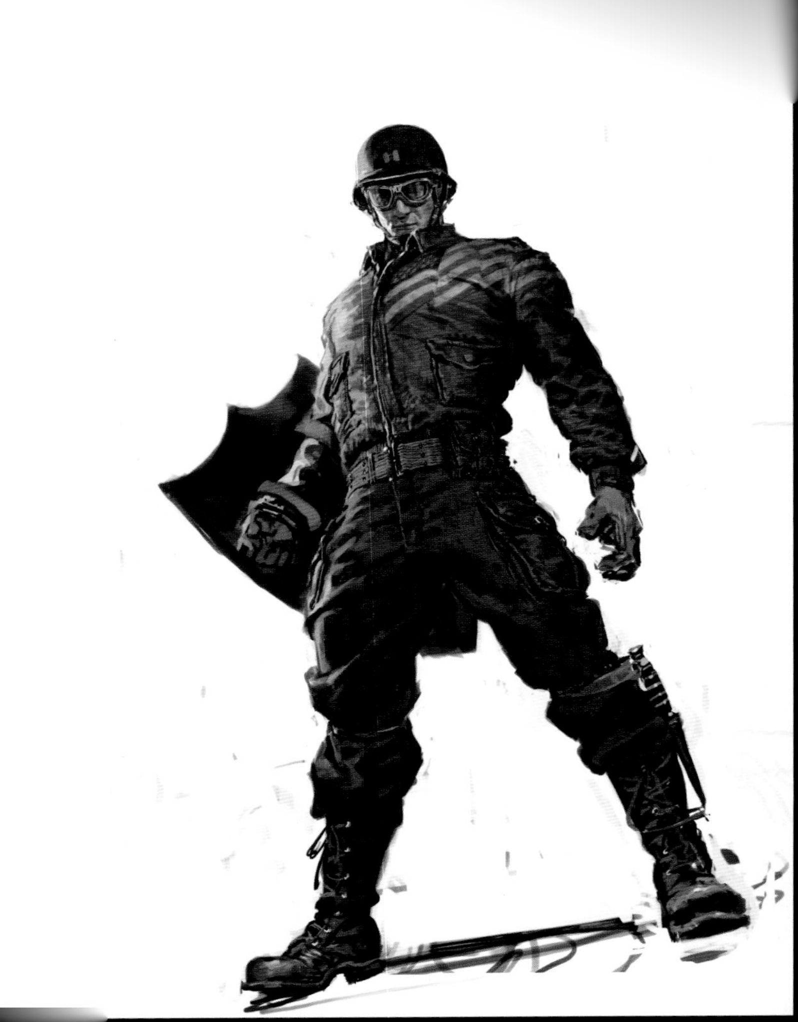

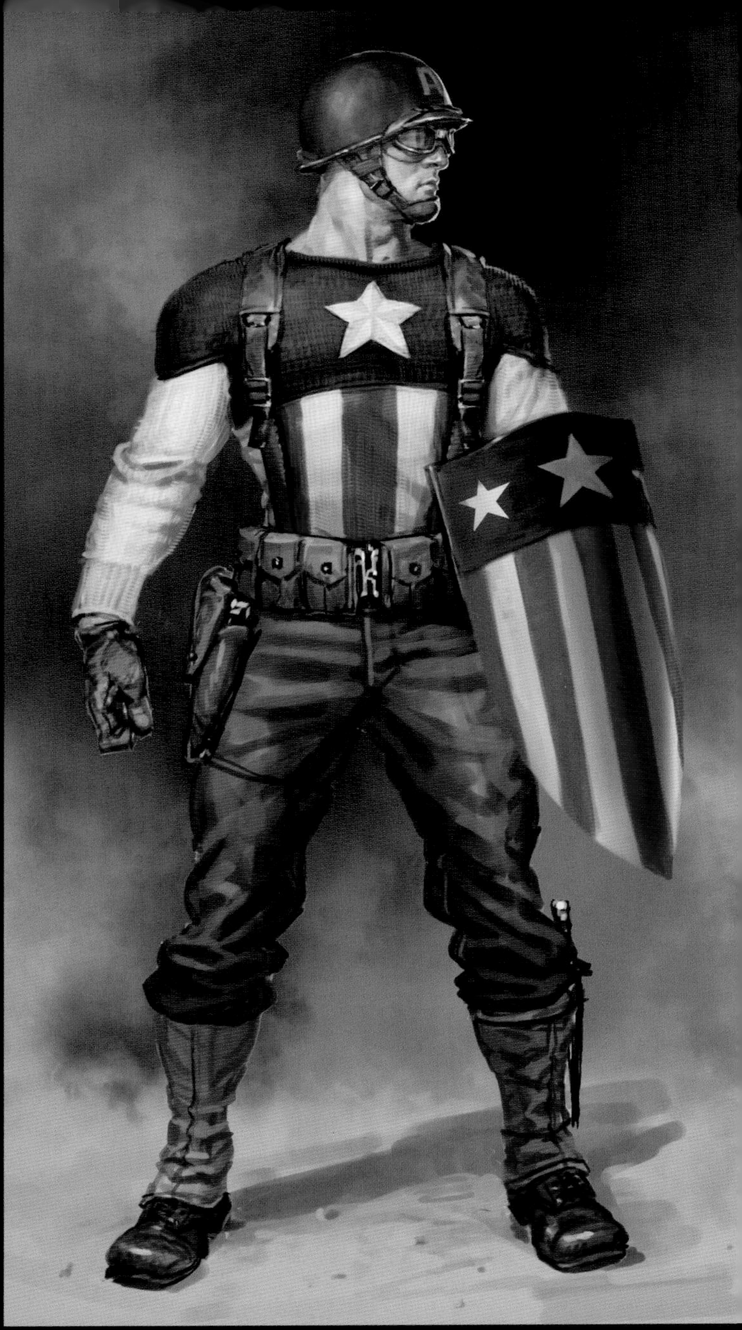

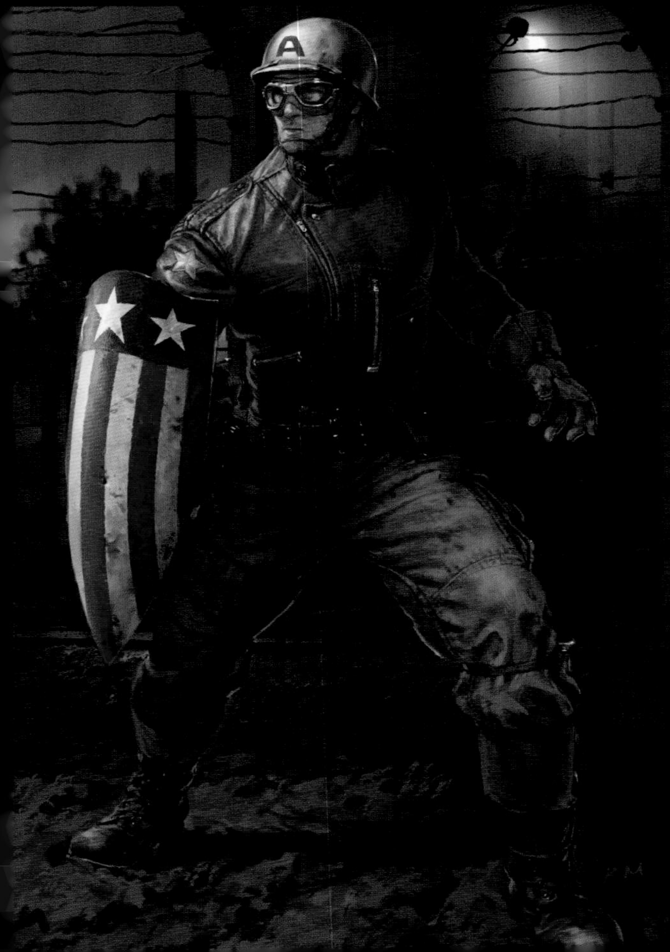

When it was decided that *Captain America: The First Avenger* would be shot in the UK, Meinerding traveled there, too. "I was in England for three months. I met my wife there on that production," says the artist. "I also started working directly with the costumers and the people making the costumes. My skill set on *Captain America* was really about the overall look and aesthetic and doing my best to work in a costume department, which I'd never done before. I was out of my depth in many respects. But it was also in a comfort zone, at least with the aesthetic and the painting and design work I'd done."

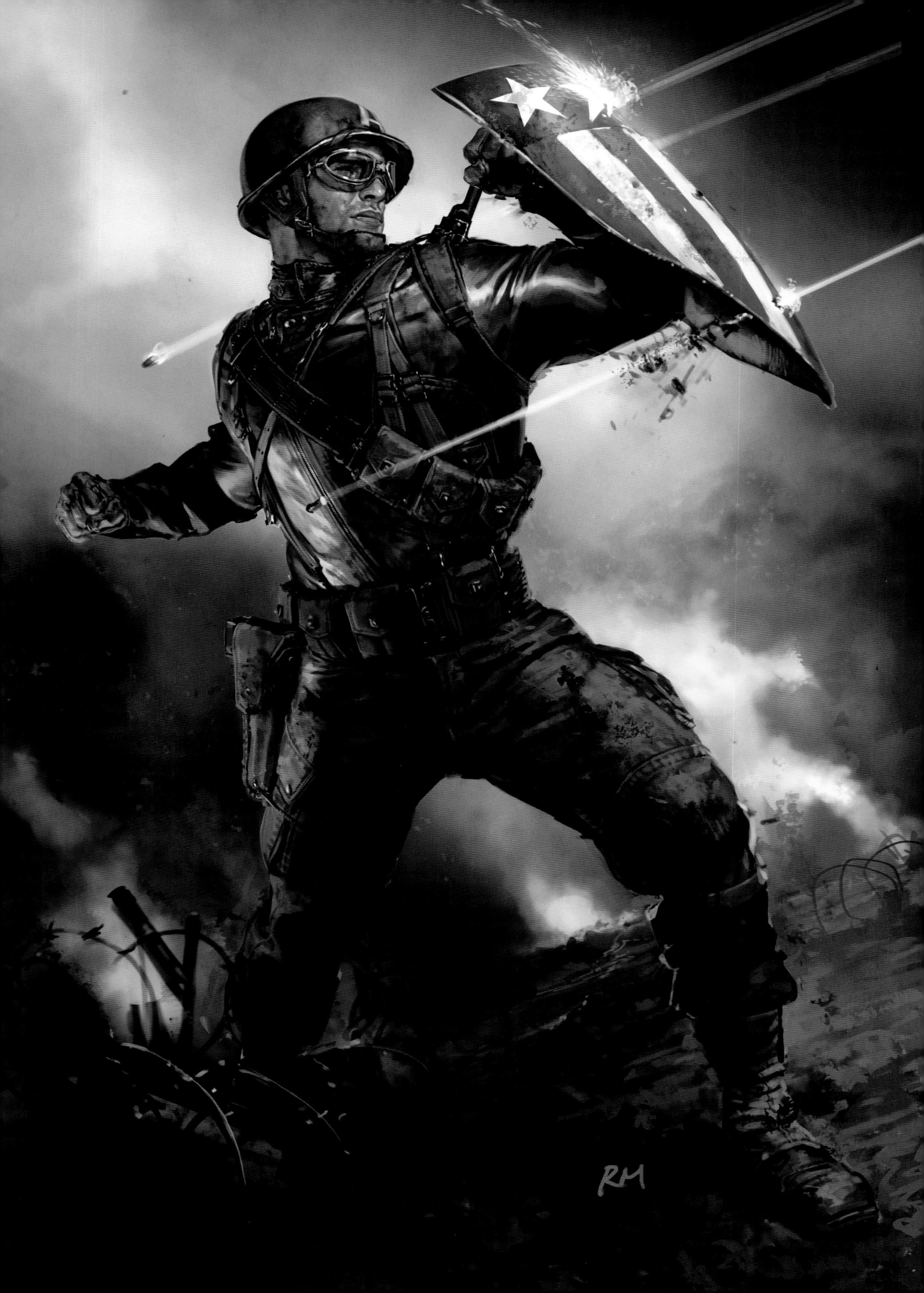
RM

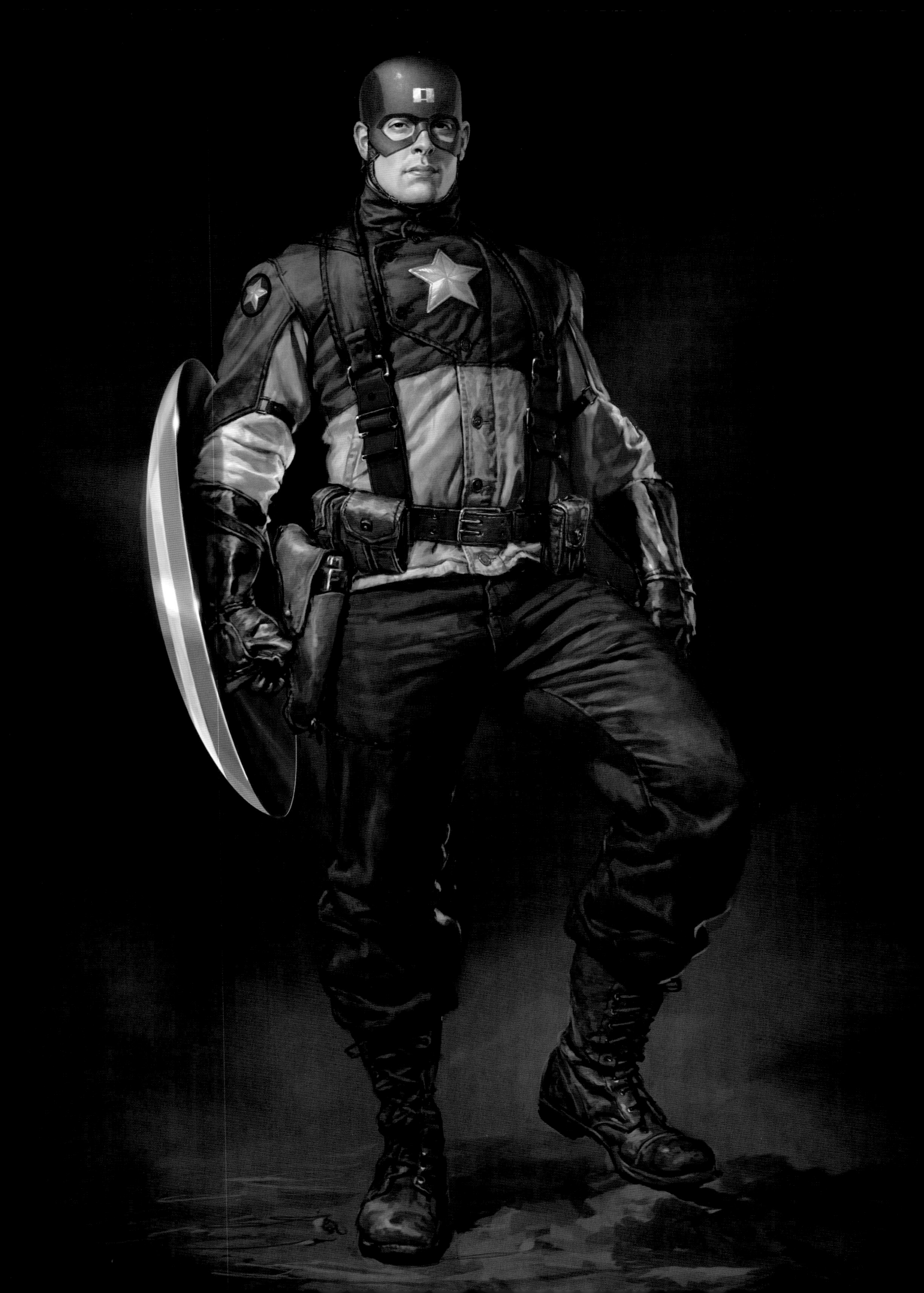

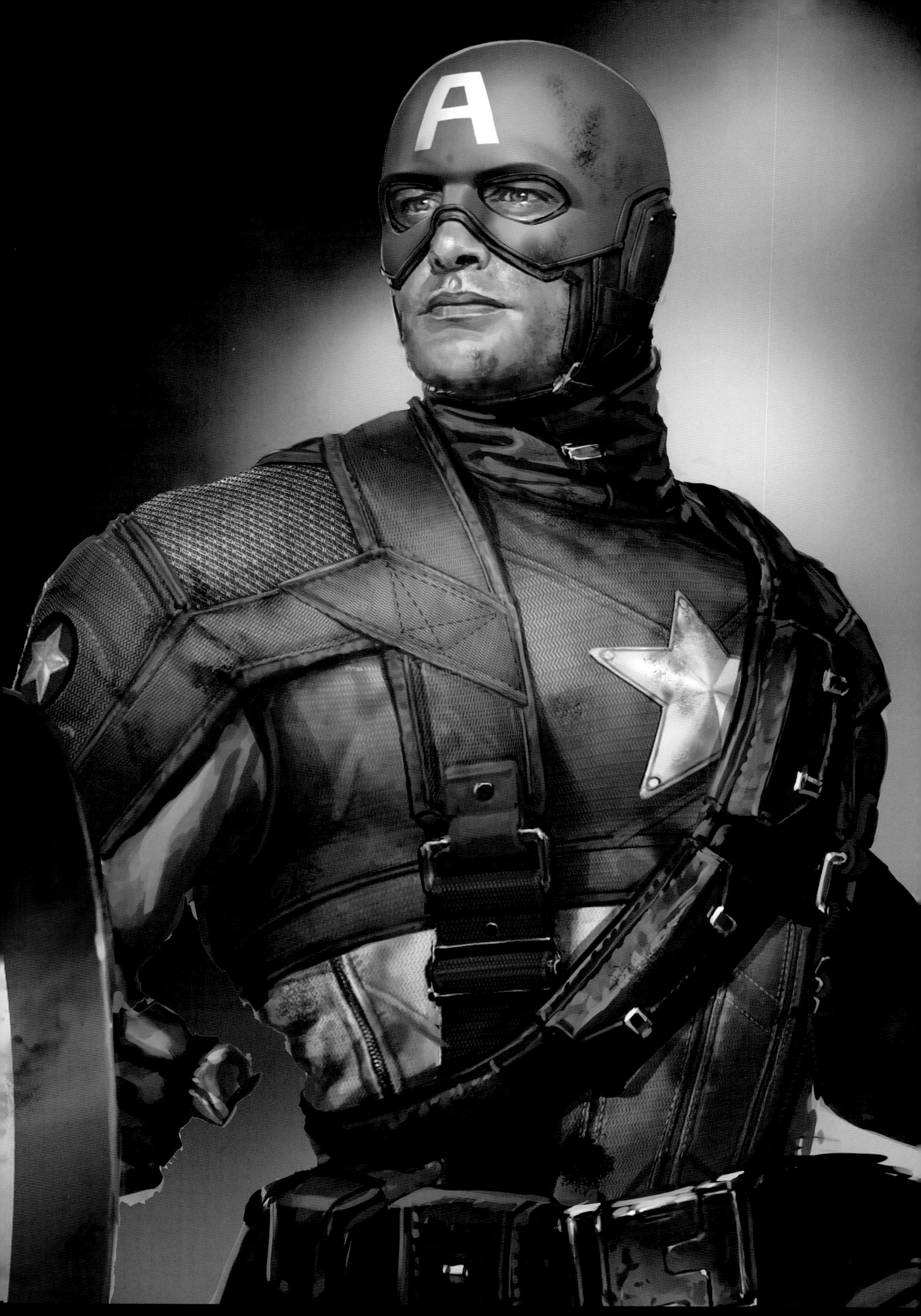

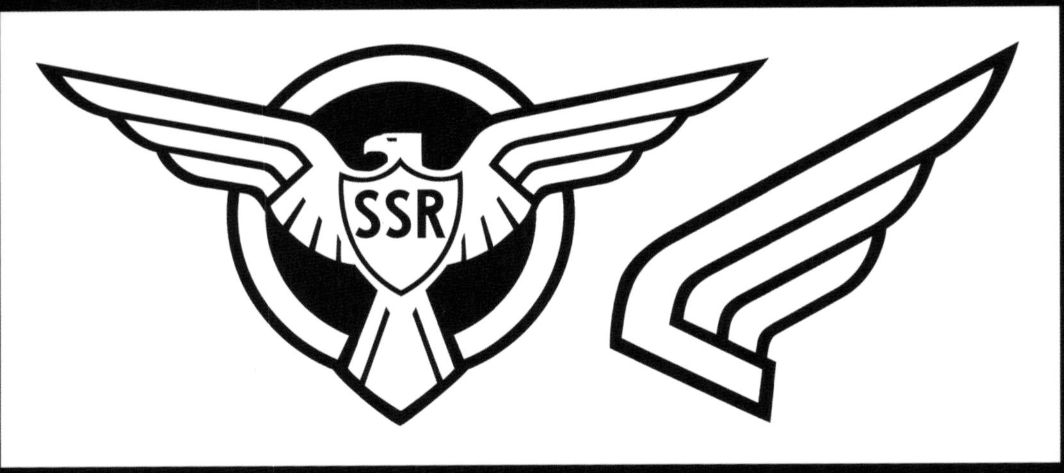
SSR

Meinerding also des
the various logos an
insignias needed fo
Captain America: Th
First Avenger. Prese
here is a collection c
studies to determine
final fonts and form

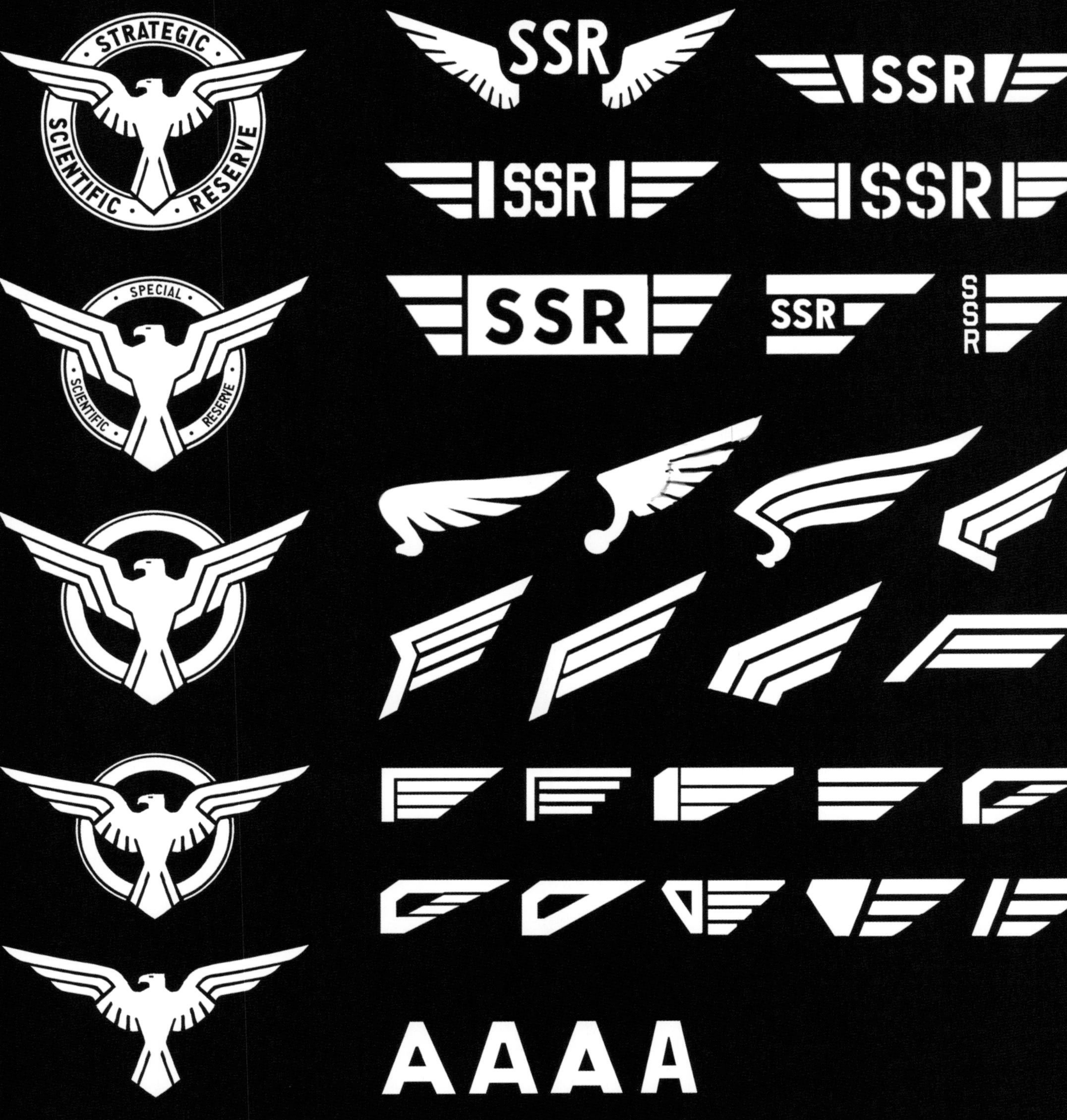
STRATEGIC
SCIENTIFIC
RESERVE
SSR
SSR
SSR
SSR
SSR
SSR
SSR
SPECIAL
SCIENTIFIC
RESERVE
AAAA

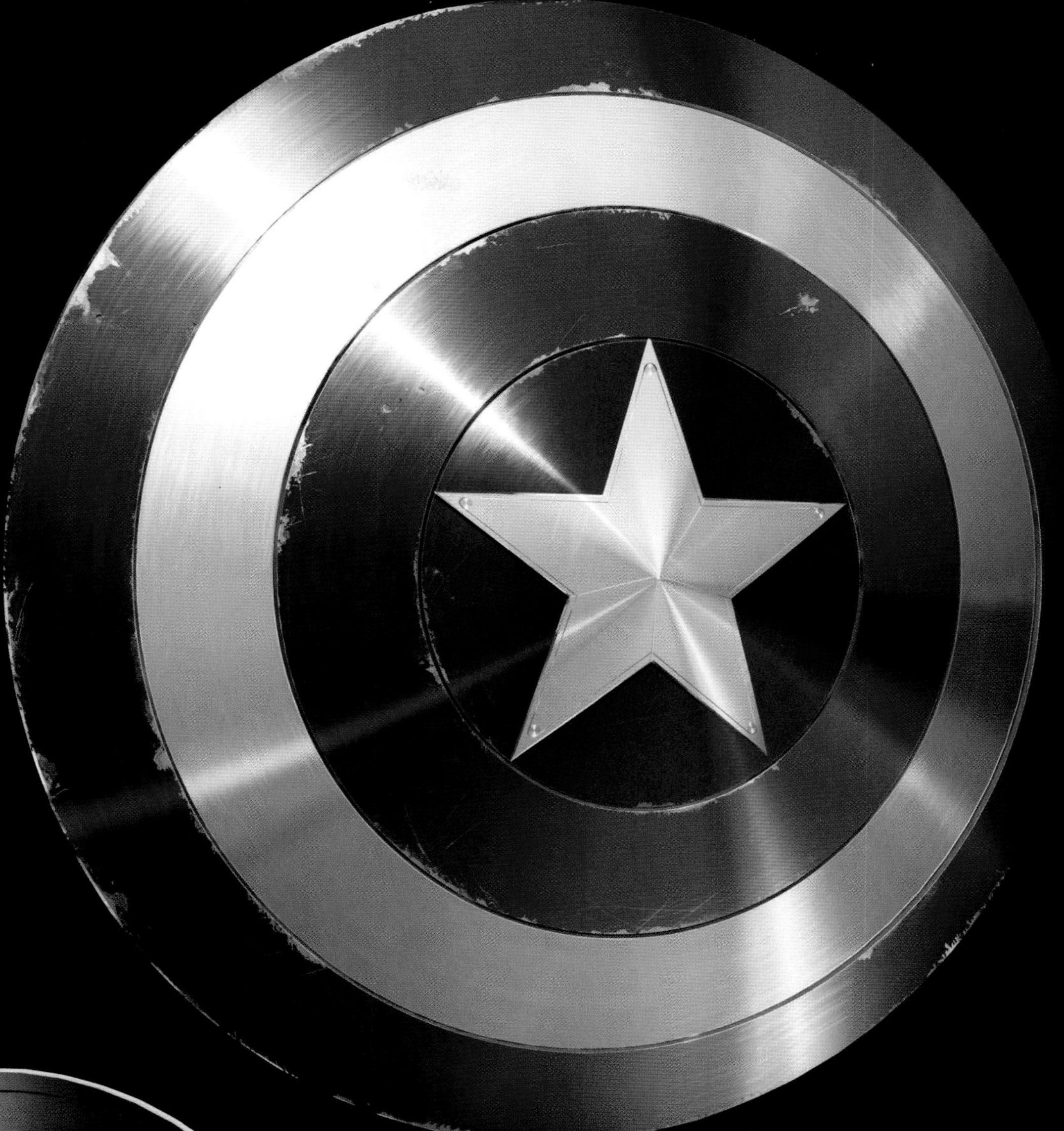

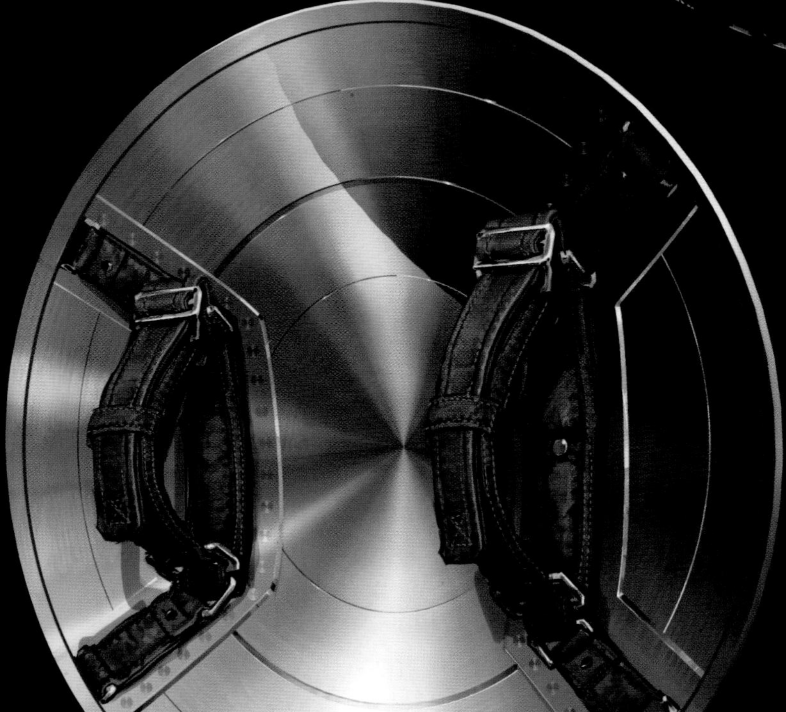

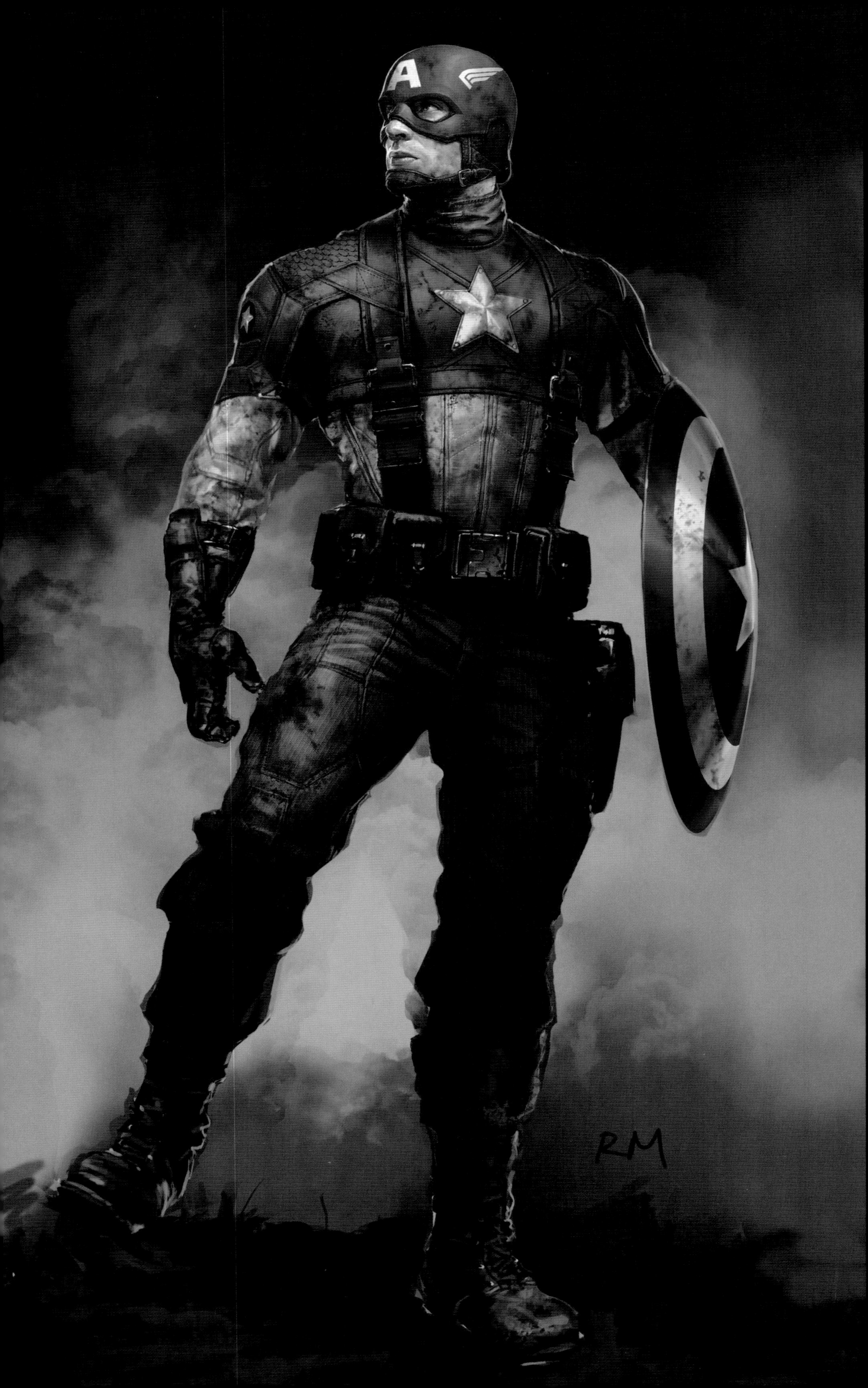
RM

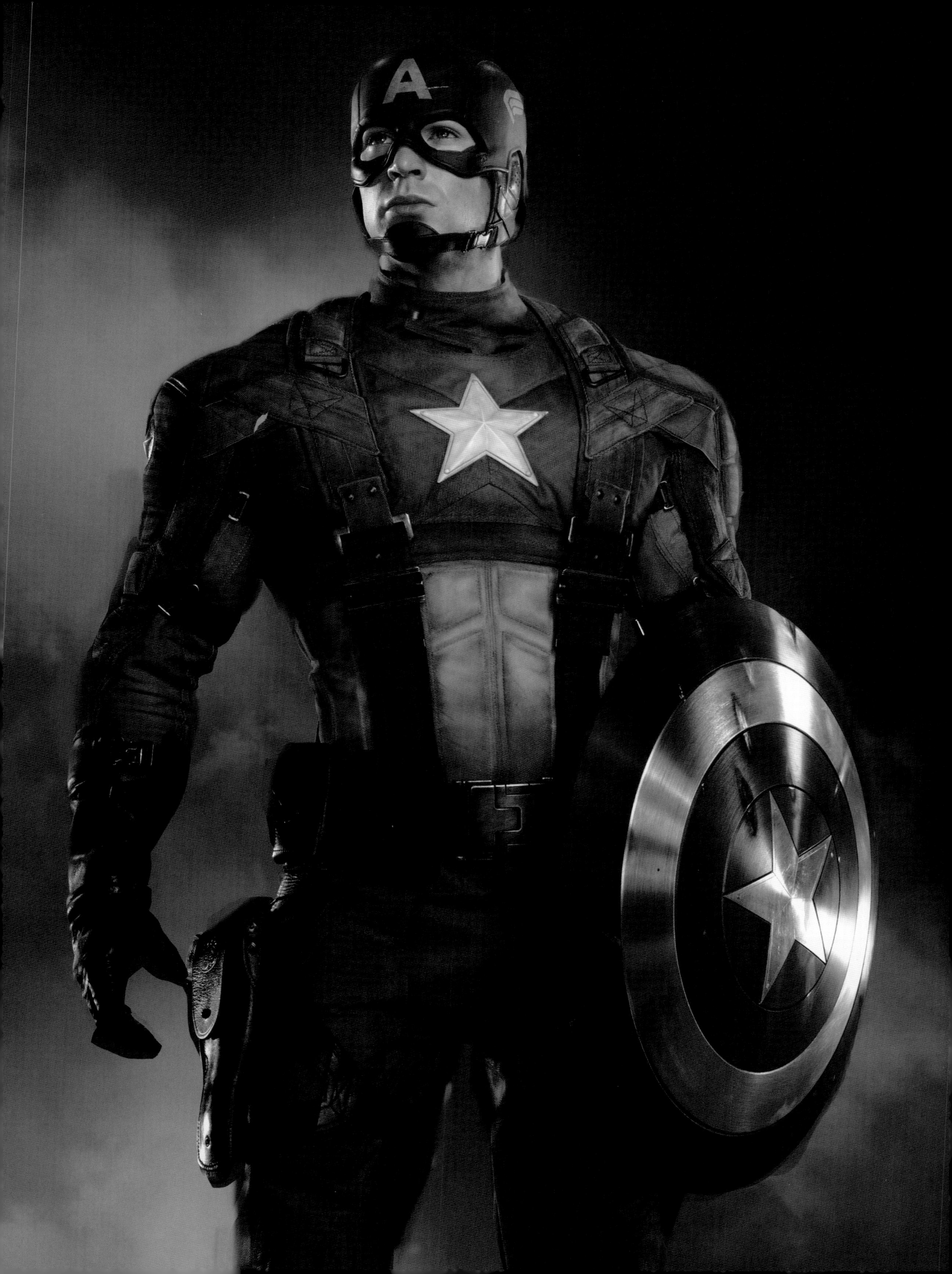

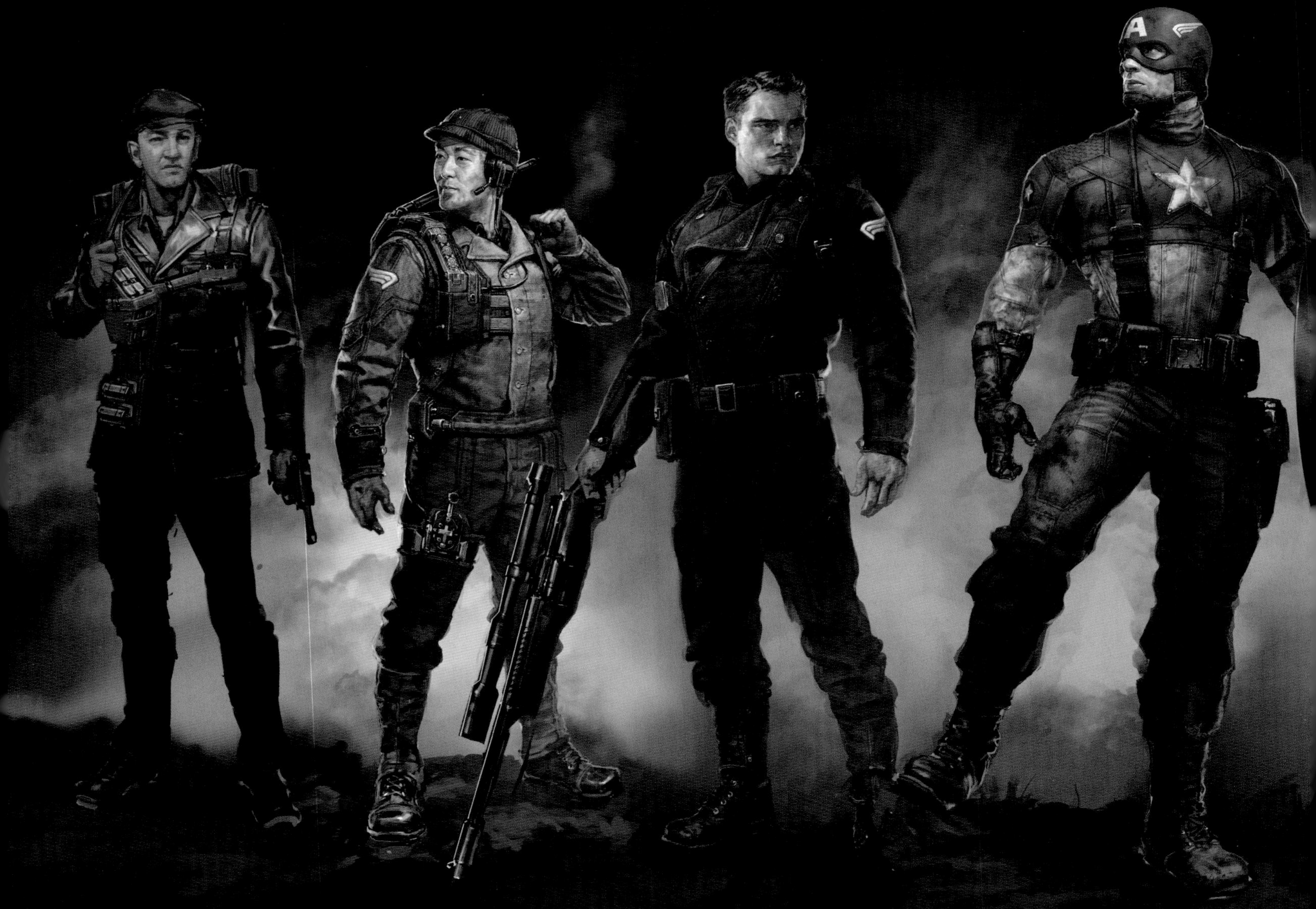

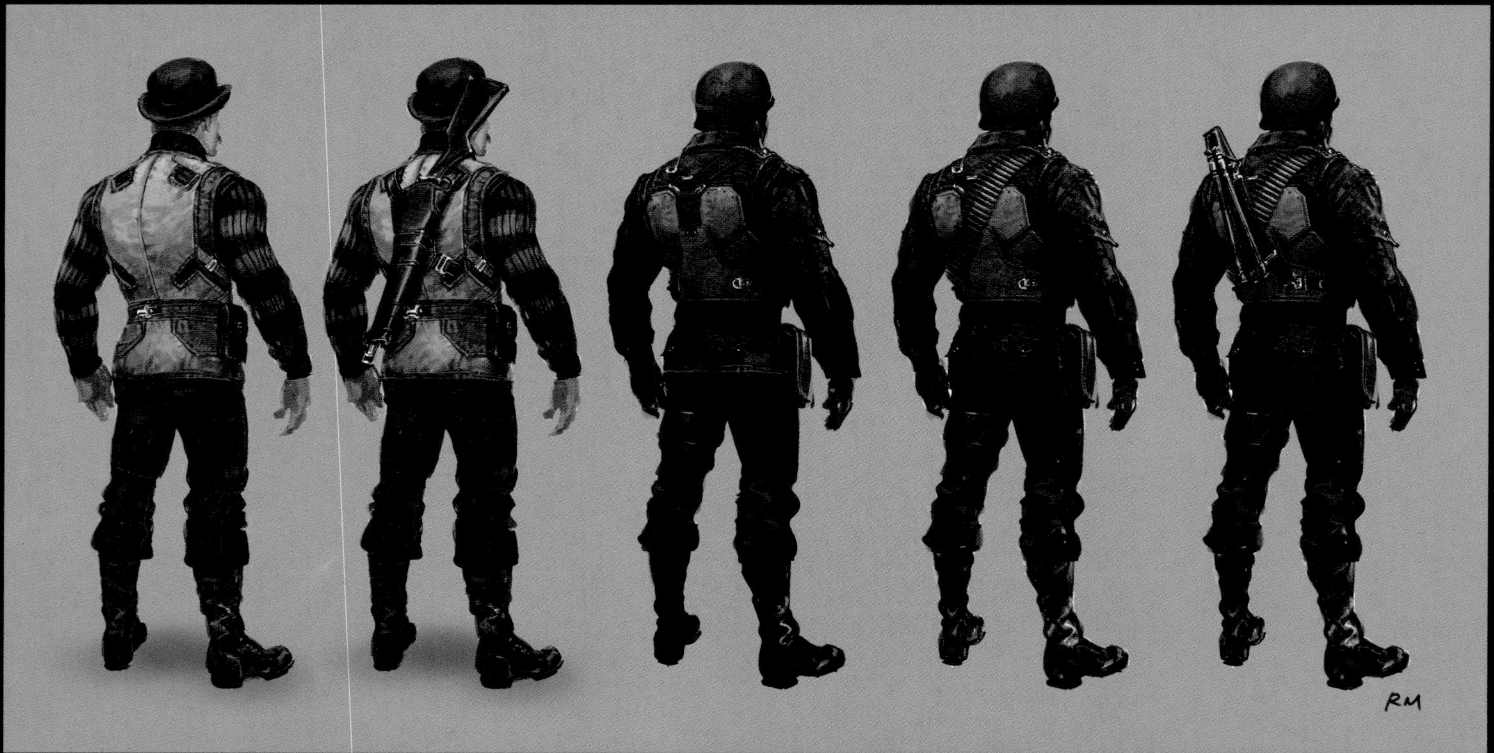
RM

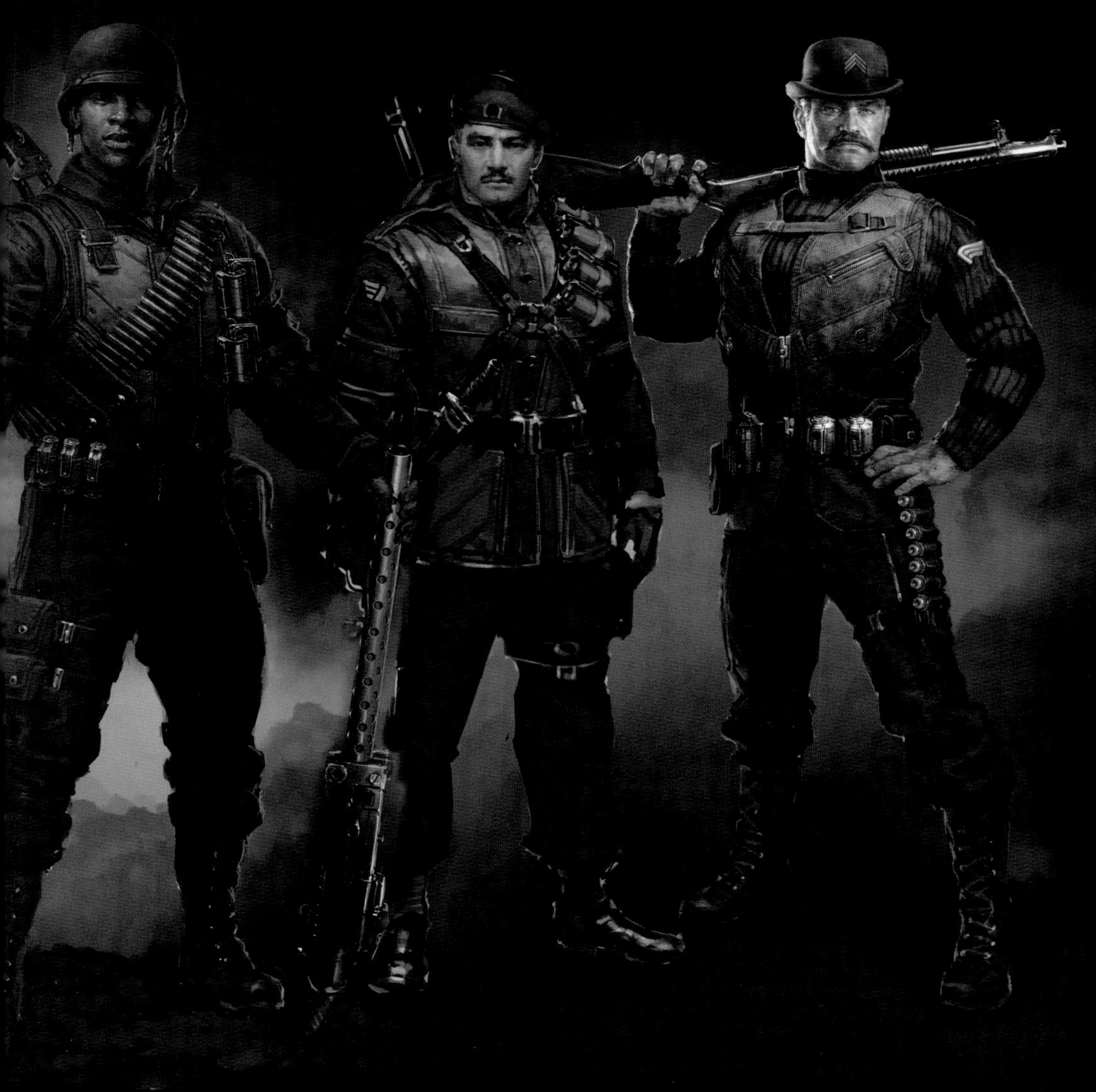

PREVIOUS SPREAD The final costume design for Chris Evans's Steve Rogers in *Captain America: The First Avenger*, brought to life by costume designer Anna B. Sheppard and her UK team. The photograph on the right, to which Meinerding applied smoke and other effects, emphasizes the photorealism of his digital concept art creation (on the left).

THIS SPREAD Prior to *Captain America* moving to England, as Charlie Wen was working on art ideas for the Red Skull and the villains, Meinerding focused on Cap and the Howling Commandos.

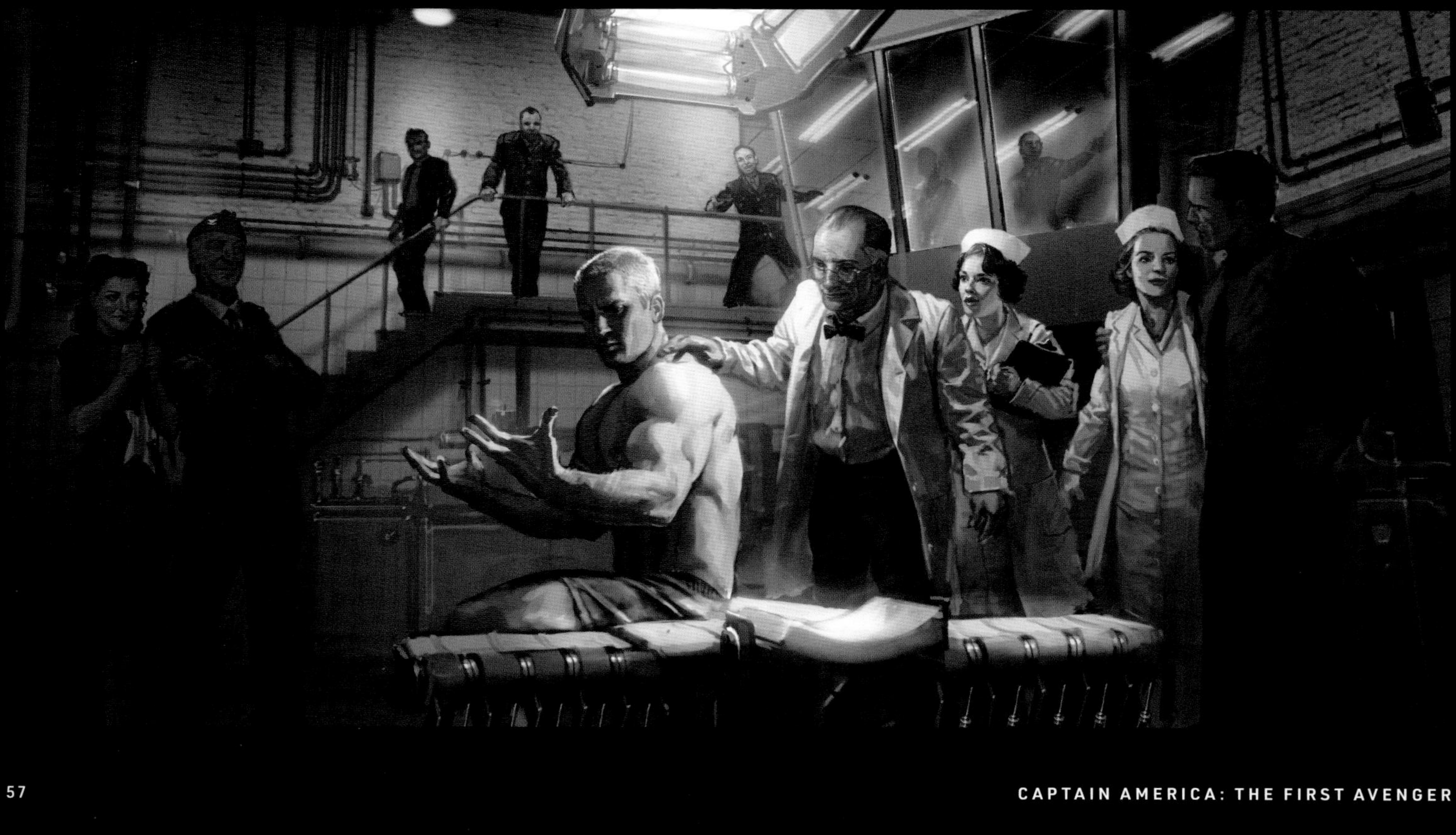

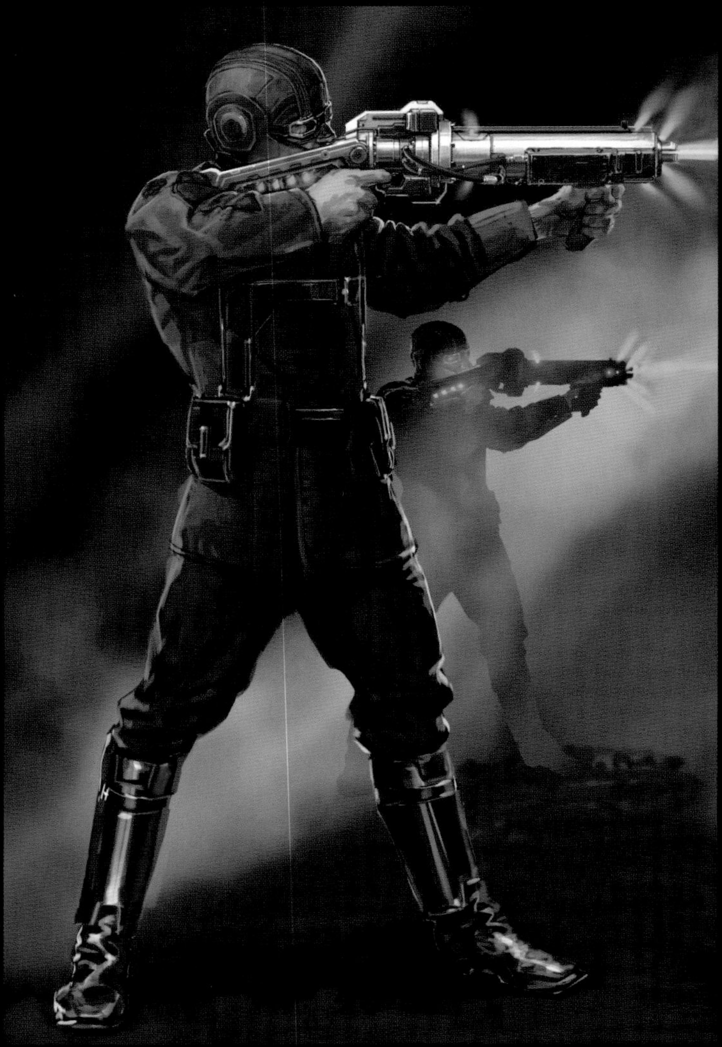

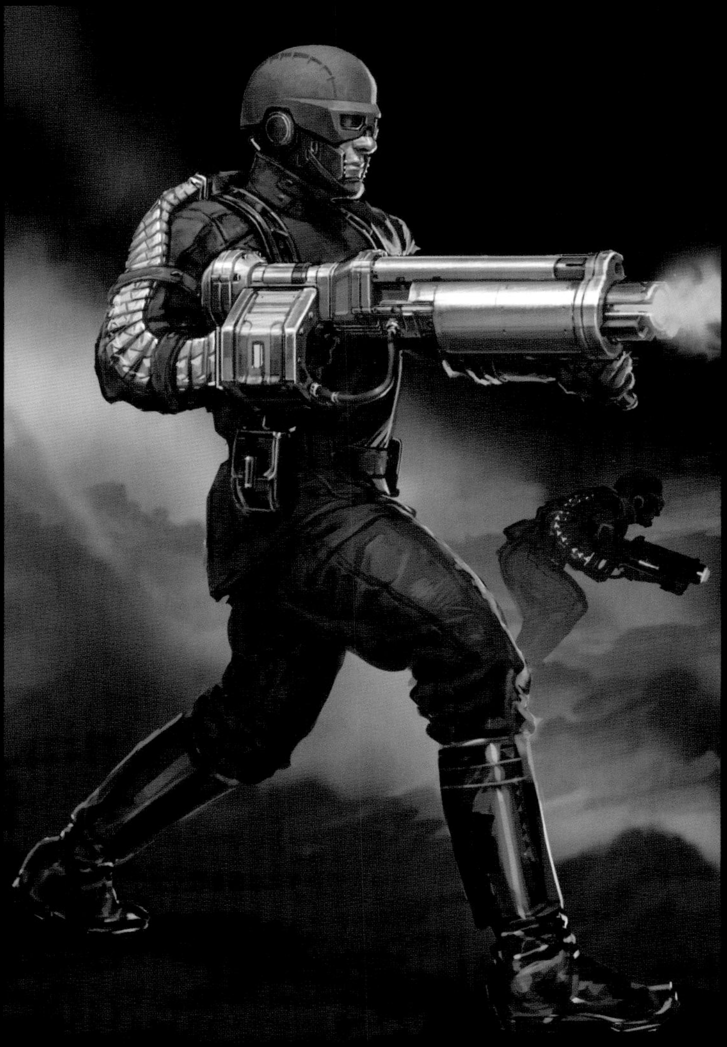

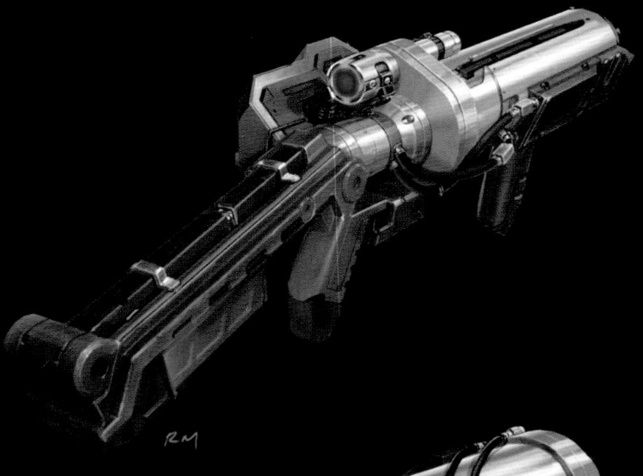
RM

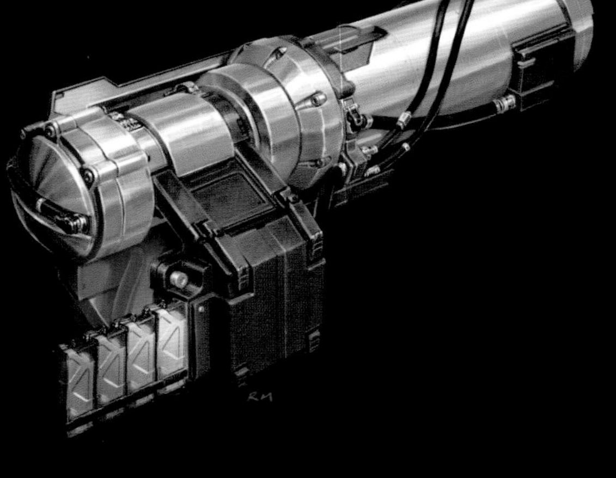
RM

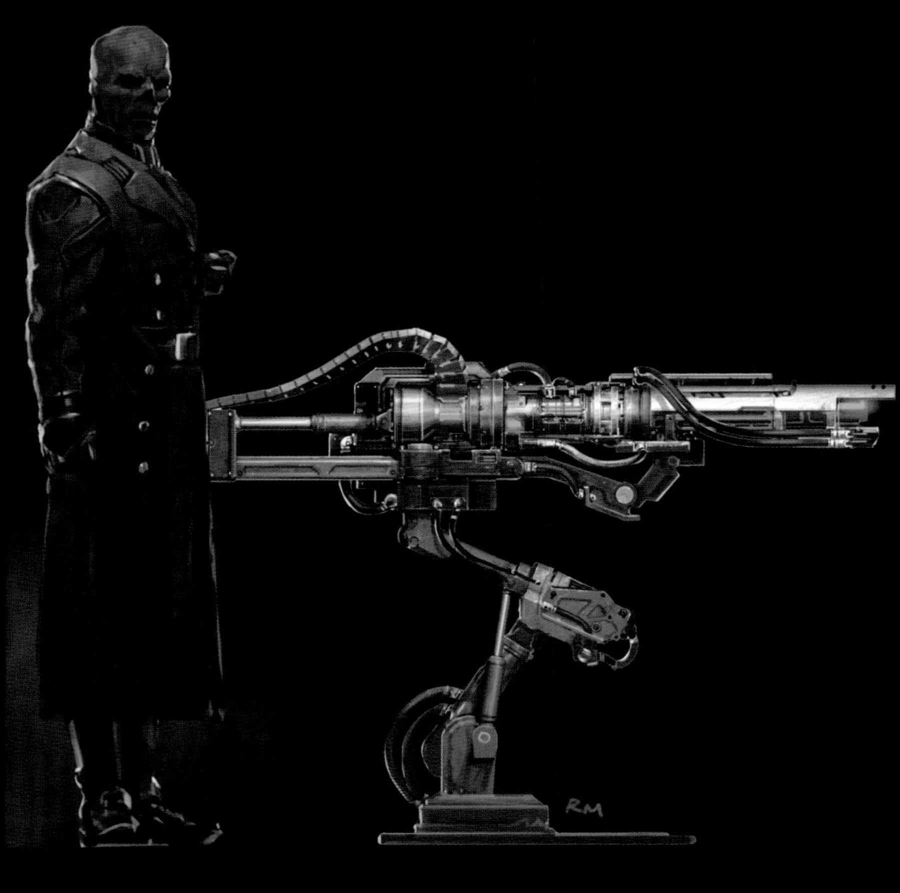
RM

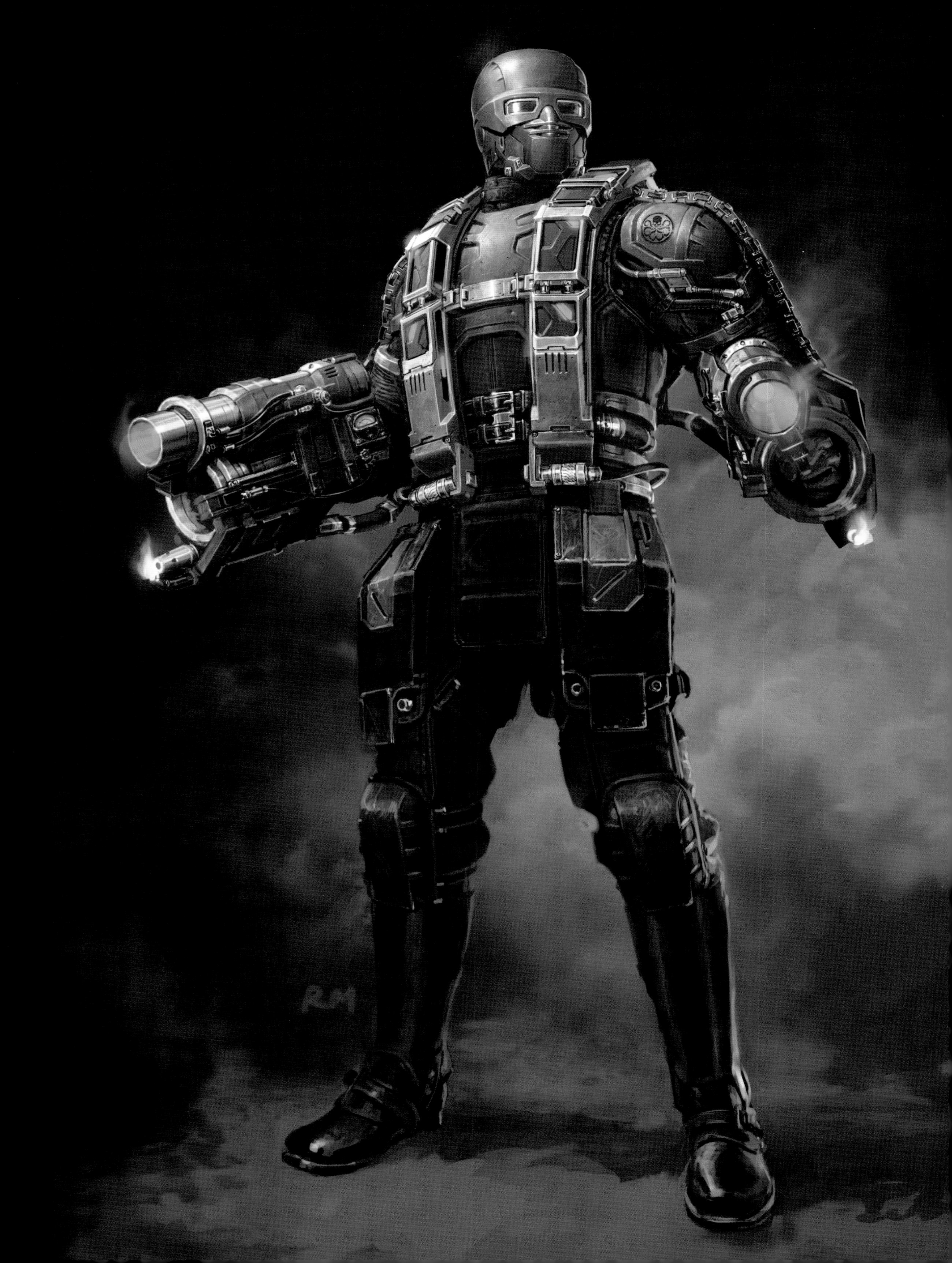

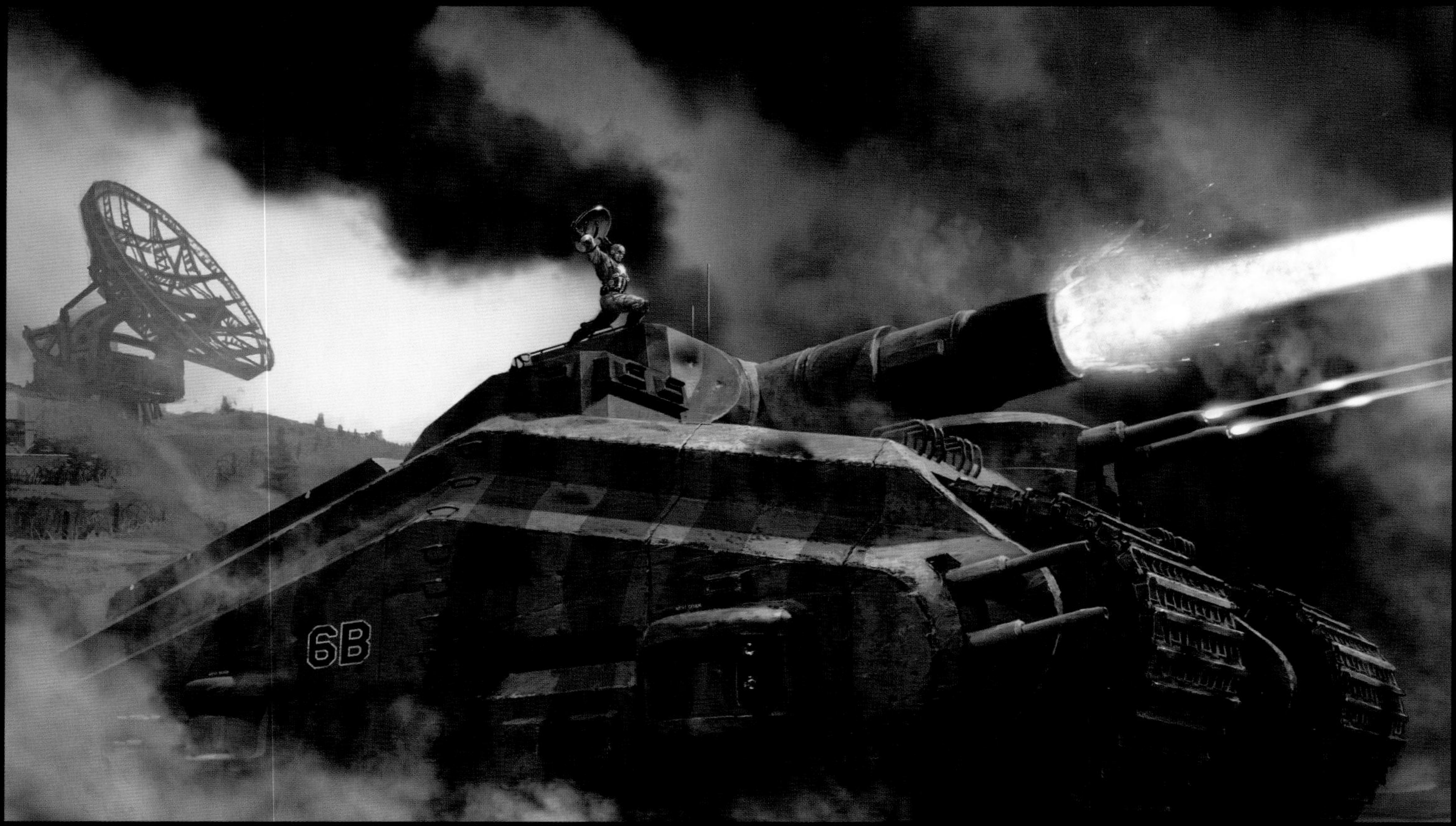
6B

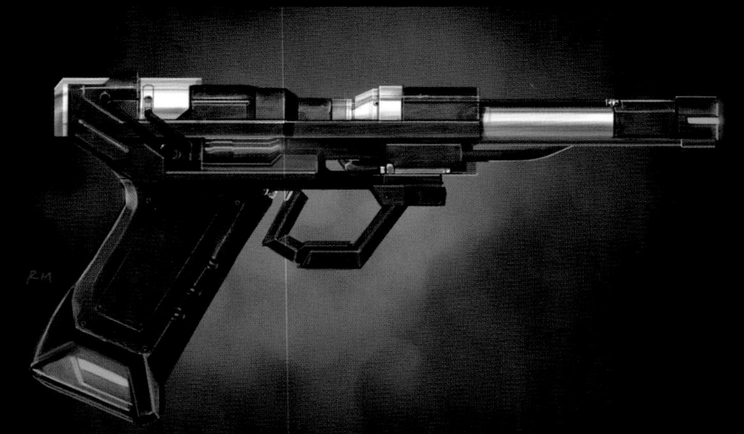
RM

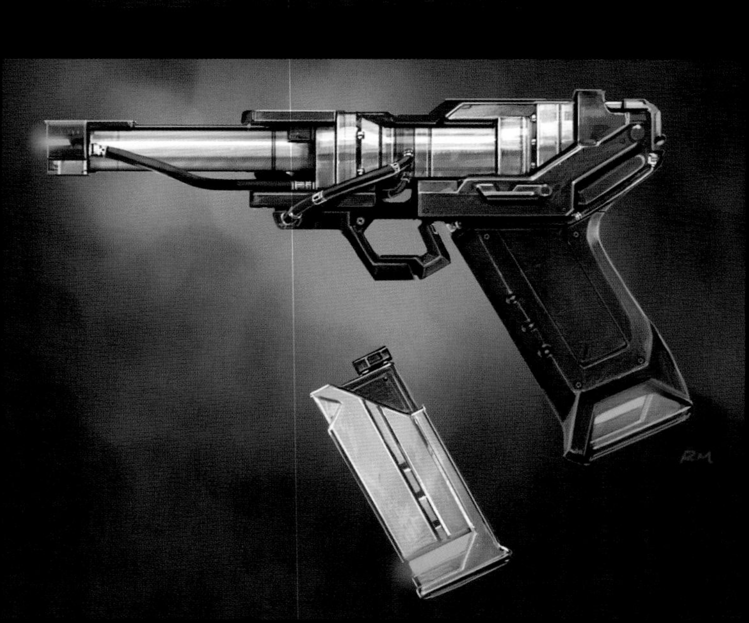
RM

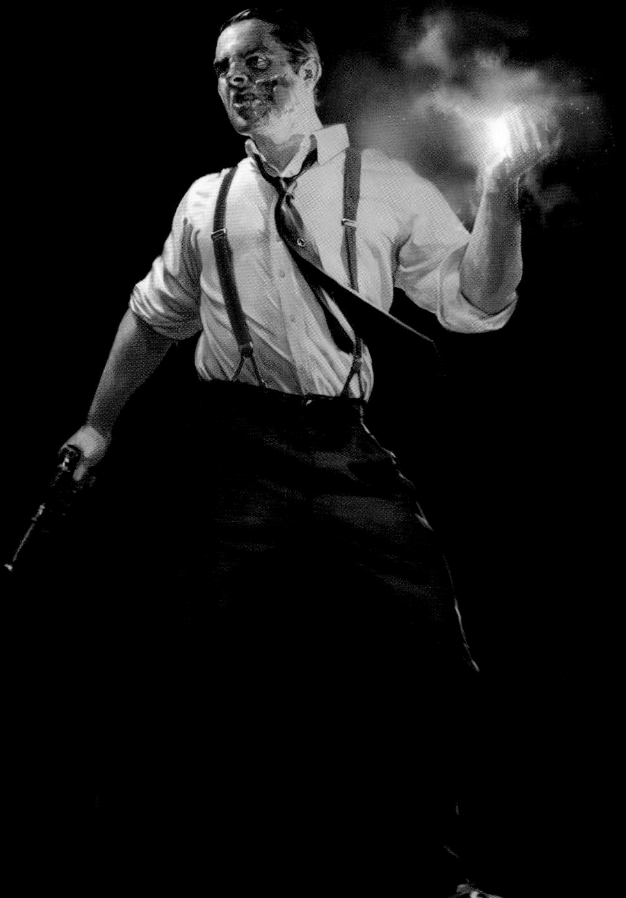

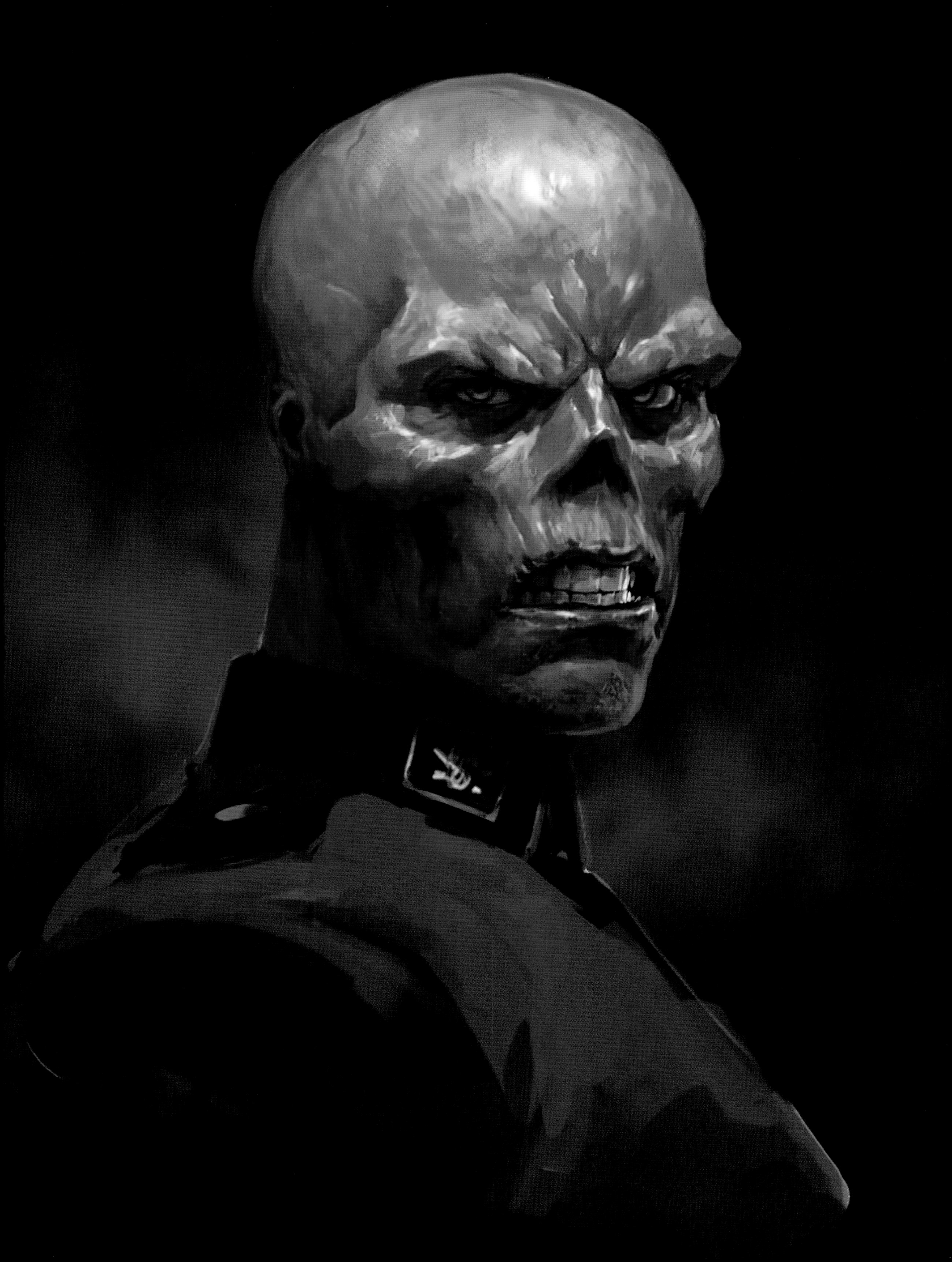

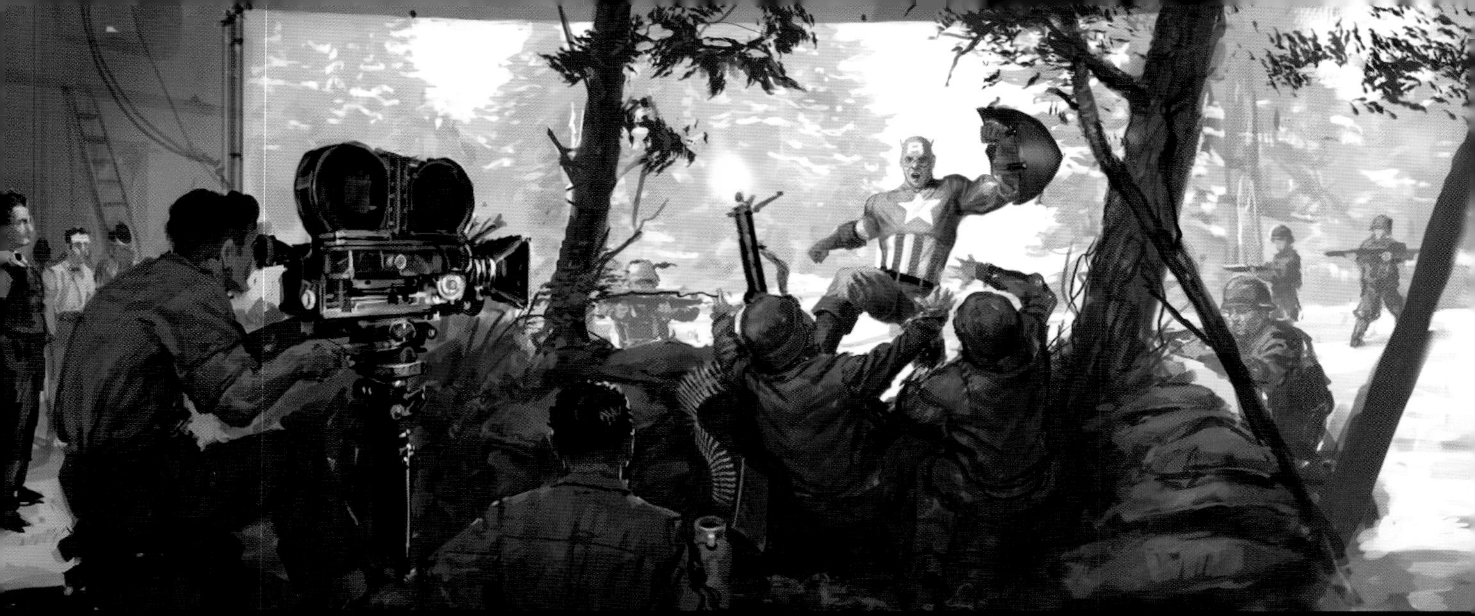

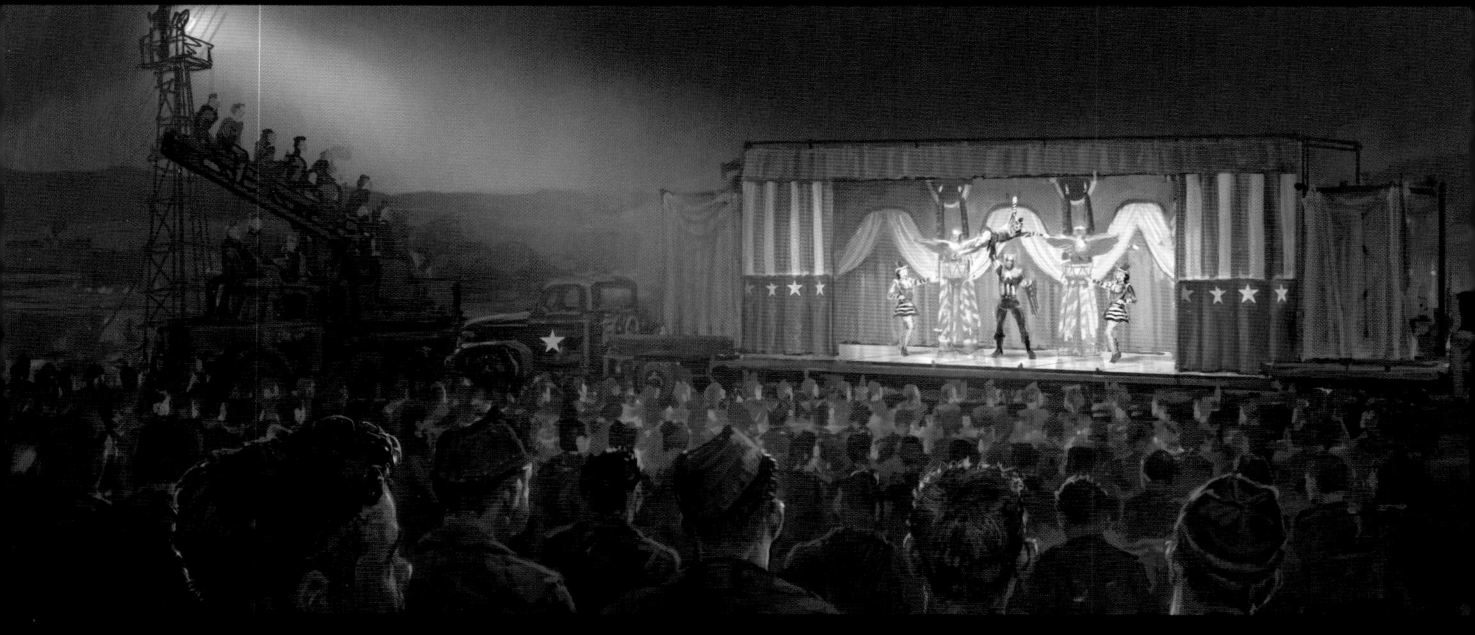

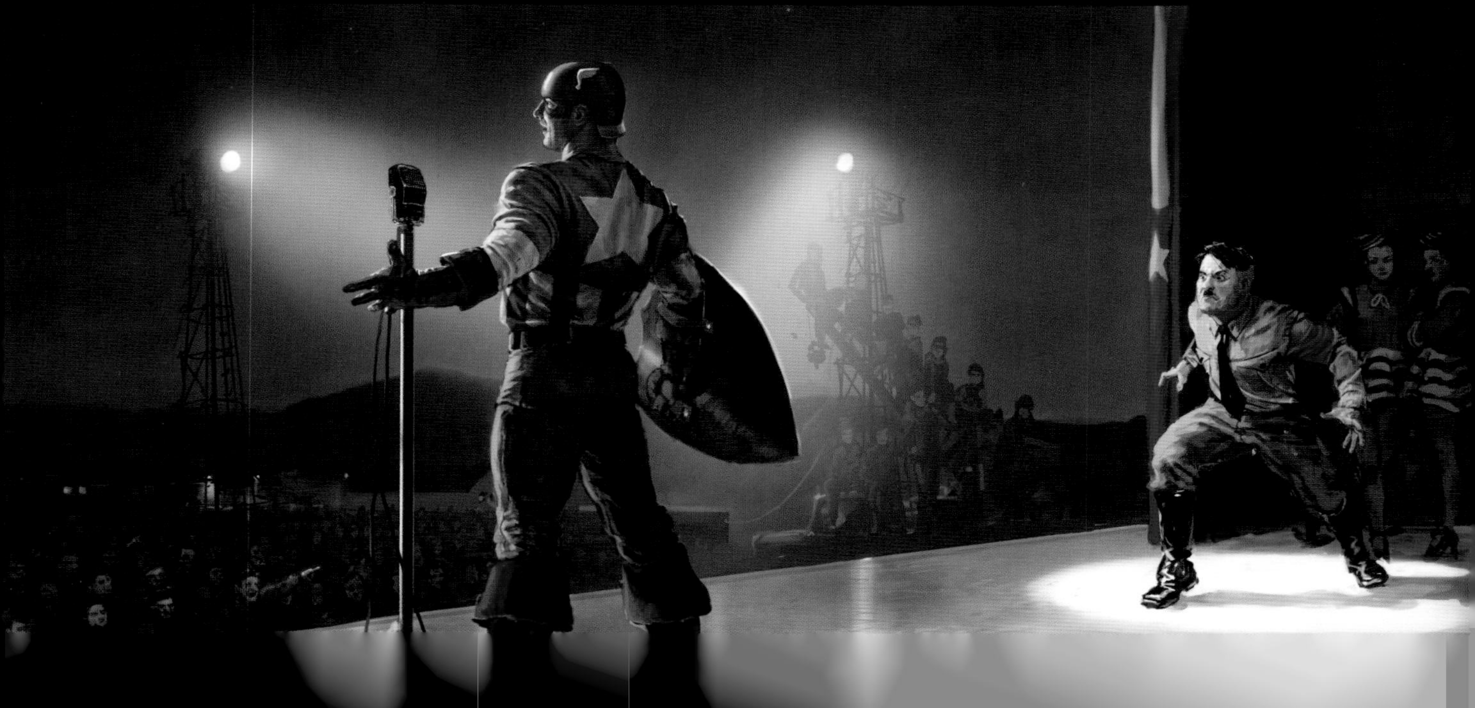

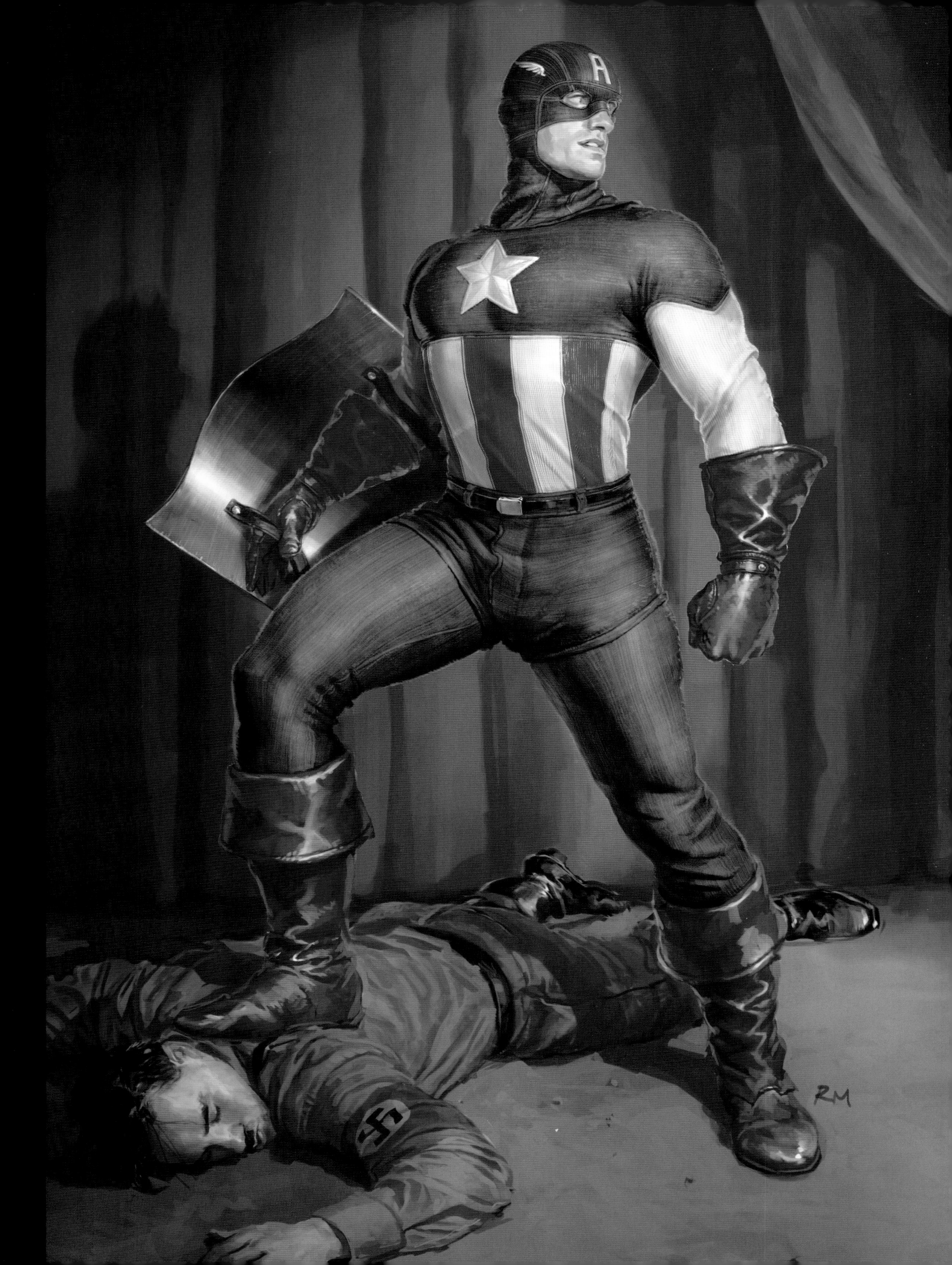
RM

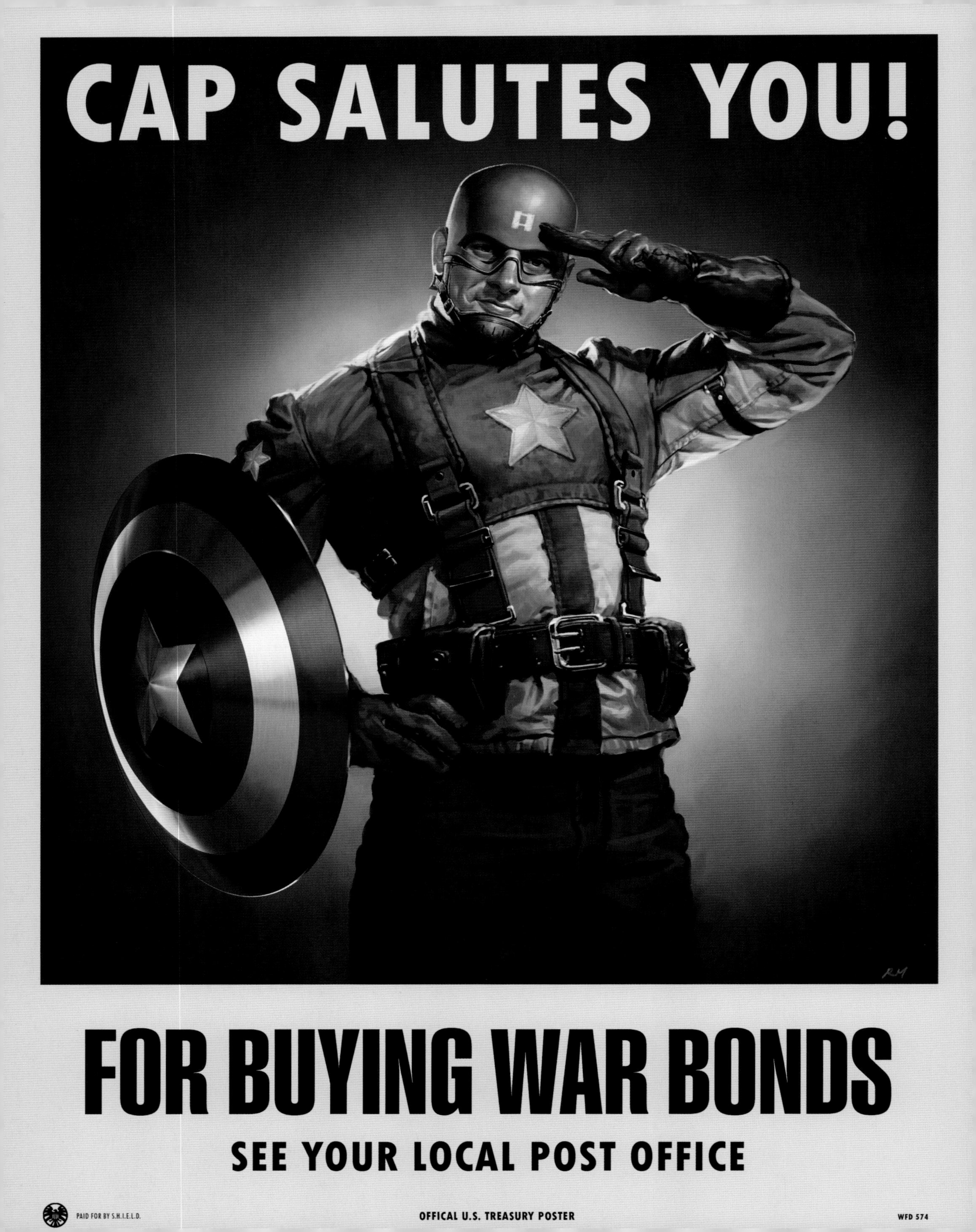
CAP SALUTES YOU!
FOR BUYING WAR BONDS
SEE YOUR LOCAL POST OFFICE
PAID FOR BY S.H.I.E.L.D.
OFFICAL U.S. TREASURY POSTER
WFD 574

CAP SALUTES YOU!

FOR BUYING WAR BONDS
SEE YOUR LOCAL POST OFFICE

WFD 574

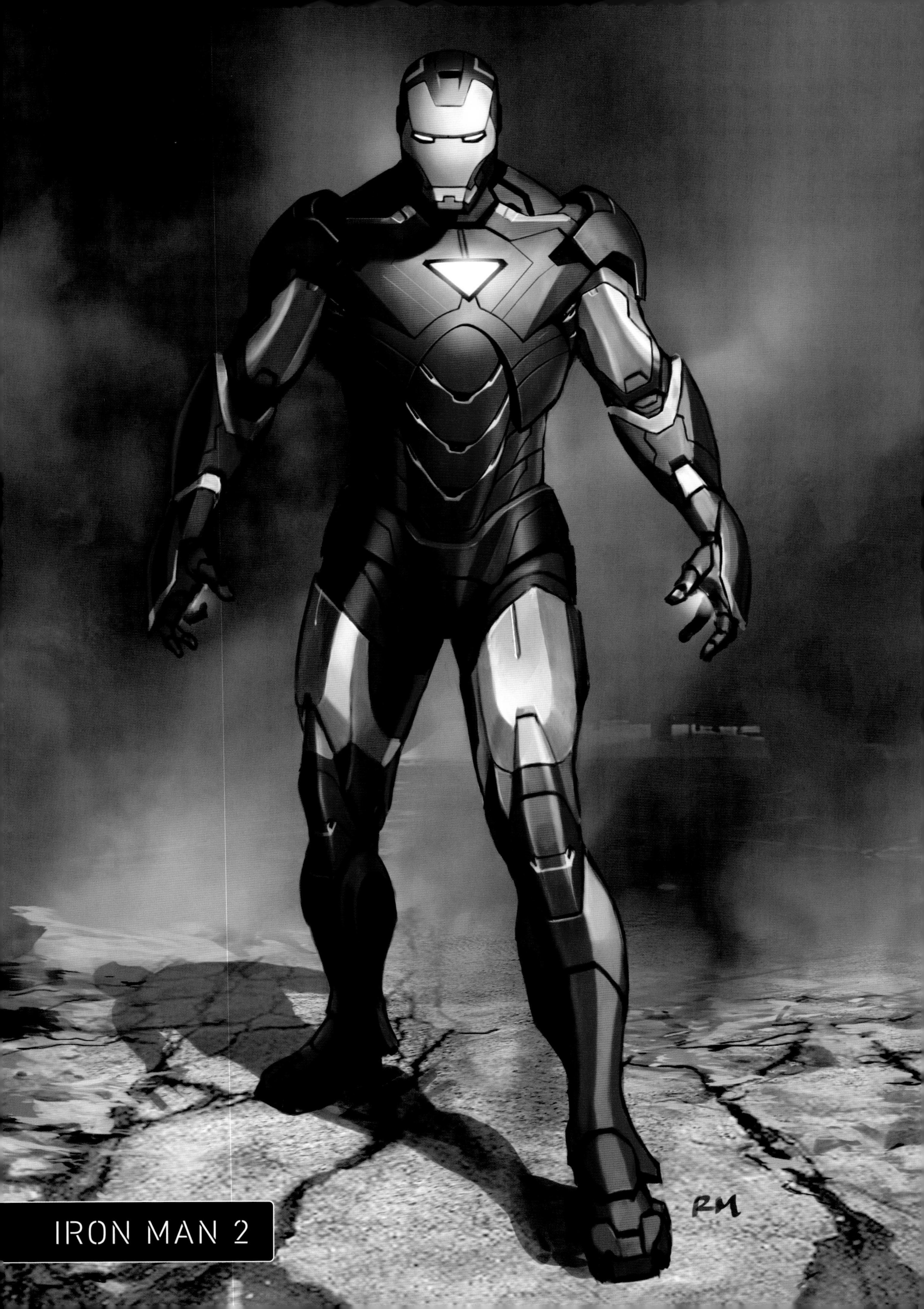
RM

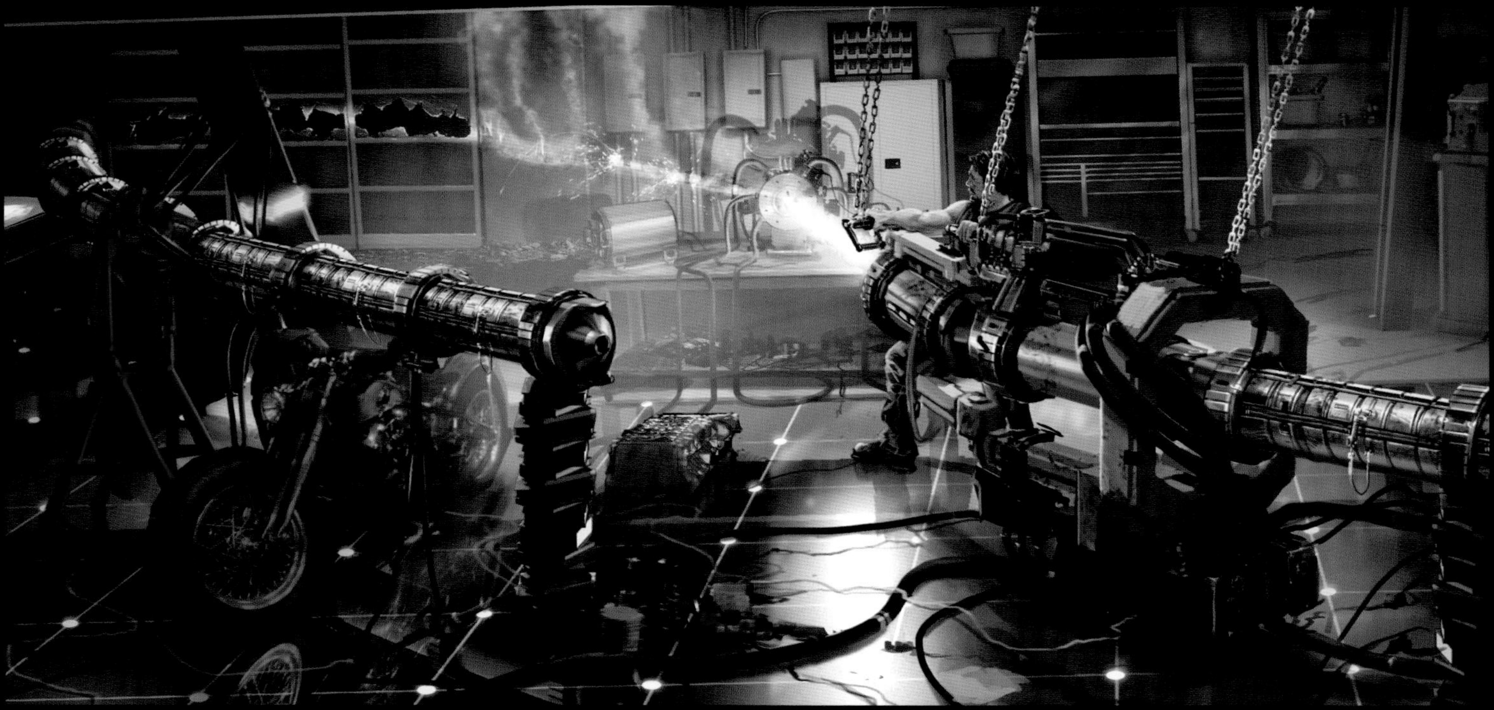

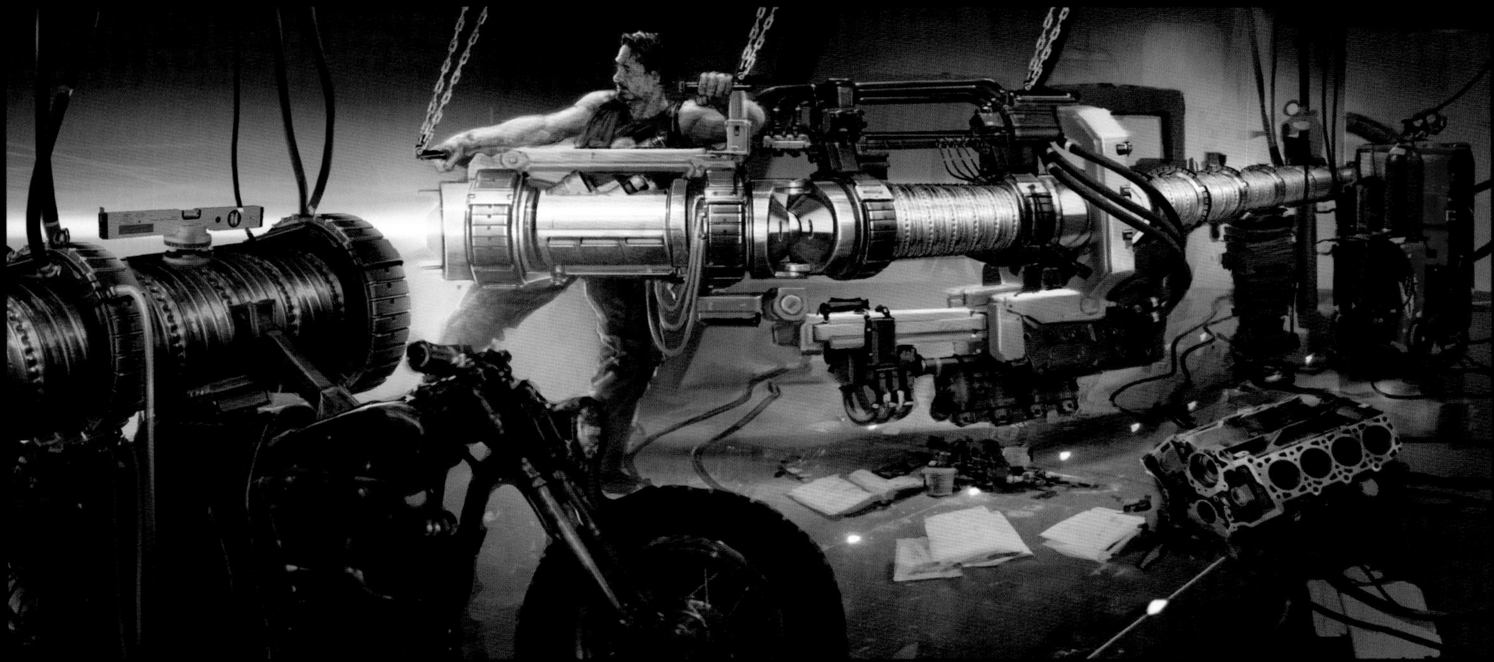

OPPOSITE Looking back at Tony Stark's second MCU outing, Meinerding remembers, "It felt like there was a *lot* of pressure on my shoulders. And *all* of it felt different. The work that I had done on *Iron Man* was a ton of key frame work—suggesting ideas—plus rougher versions of suits or costumes. For *Iron Man 2*, the idea of trying to do a really refined, high-tolerance suit design, where the forms are important—but the surface catches light and creates reflections in a way that's beautiful—was a big challenge. So the Mark IV and VI [suits] were me definitely stepping outside my comfort zone." While working closely with artist Adi Granov, in addition to three new Iron Man suits (including the Mark VI, pictured here), Meinerding had to design a War Machine suit, Whiplash, and all of the Hammer drones. Noting the process from sketch to screen, he says, "After designs were approved by director Jon Favreau and Marvel Studios, they would go to Legacy Effects for 3D modeling and fabrication. Then those models would go on to visual effects."

ABOVE While developing the idea of the particle accelerator scene, Jon Favreau and the Marvel Studios producers really wanted to get Tony Stark to reprise his "blacksmith" moment from *Iron Man*. "The idea of building this thing was trying to tap into how closed off and cloistered he is," adds Meinerding. "He's using just stuff he has around the house, and he's *destroying* the house—that was a huge part of it. But also, the image of him sticking a wrench in the handle and being able to turn it was something they were very interested in."

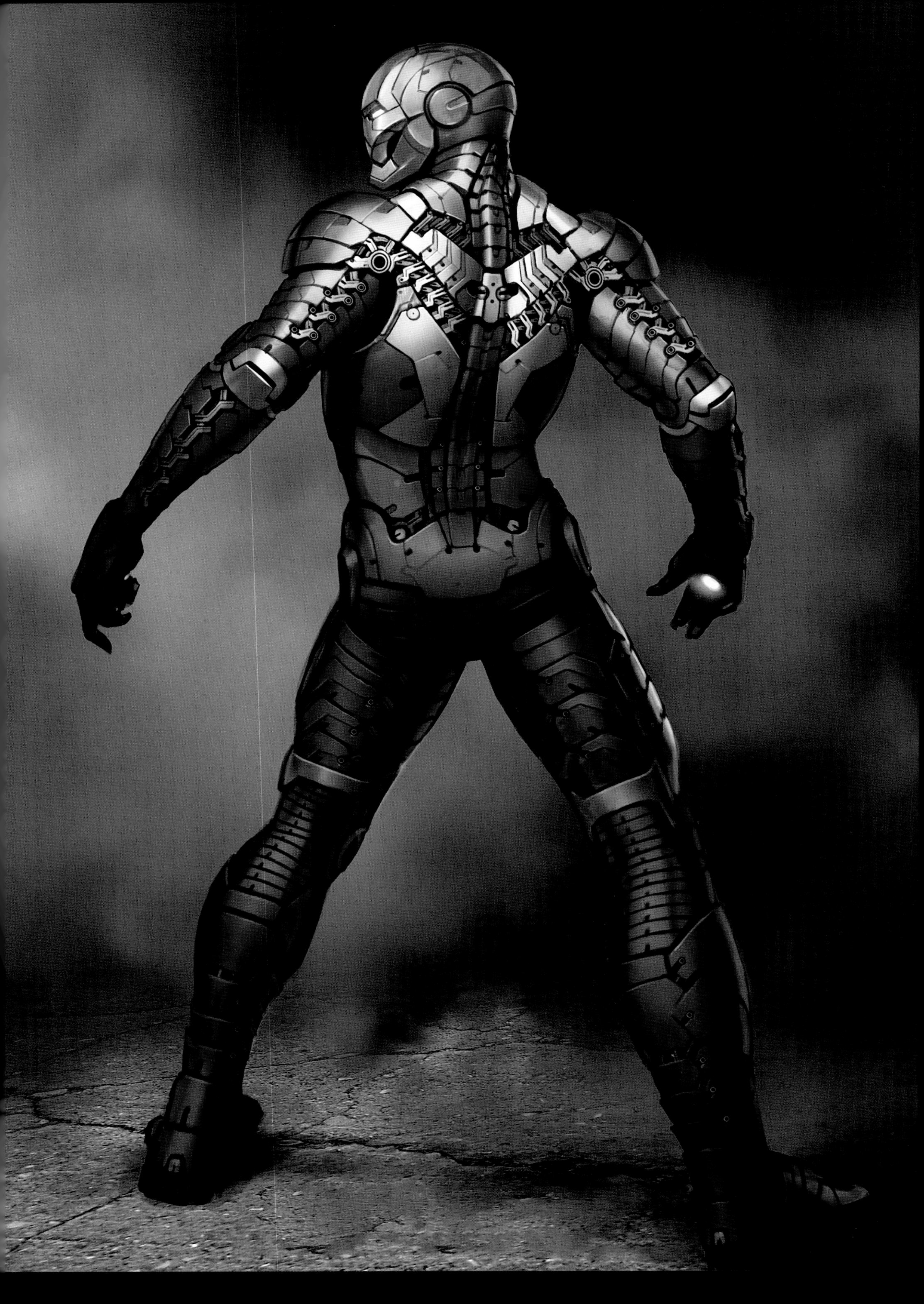

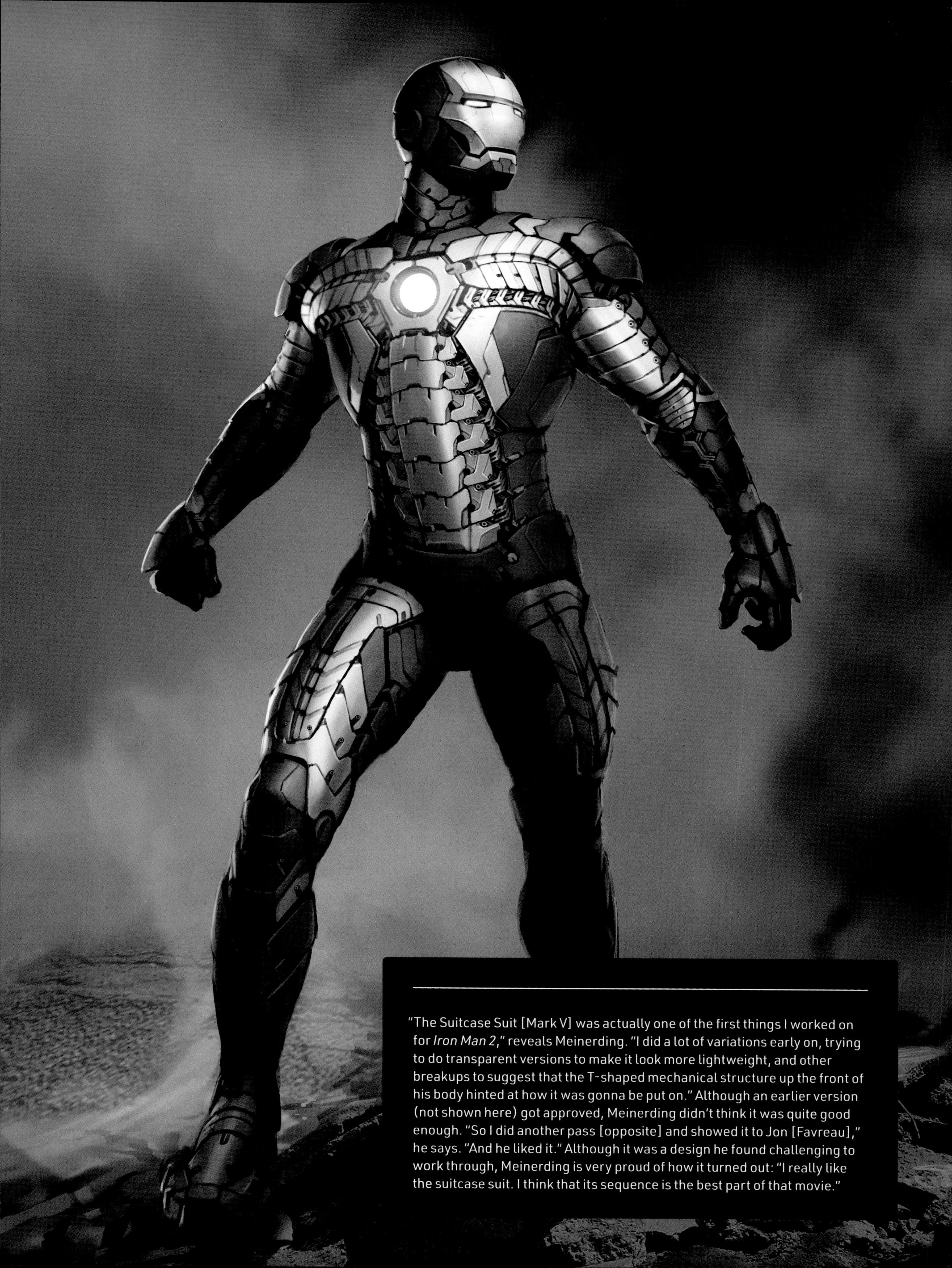

"The Suitcase Suit [Mark V] was actually one of the first things I worked on for *Iron Man 2*," reveals Meinerding. "I did a lot of variations early on, trying to do transparent versions to make it look more lightweight, and other breakups to suggest that the T-shaped mechanical structure up the front of his body hinted at how it was gonna be put on." Although an earlier version (not shown here) got approved, Meinerding didn't think it was quite good enough. "So I did another pass [opposite] and showed it to Jon [Favreau]," he says. "And he liked it." Although it was a design he found challenging to work through, Meinerding is very proud of how it turned out: "I really like the suitcase suit. I think that its sequence is the best part of that movie."

Ivan Vanko's "lab" required a different vibe to Tony Stark's. "Trying to get that across was a lot of fun," says Meinerding. "Vanko didn't have a lot of space, so he created like a loft area using servers. Some thought it looked too much like Tony's workshop, so we did the same idea but without servers, and more of a sitting space [bottom]."

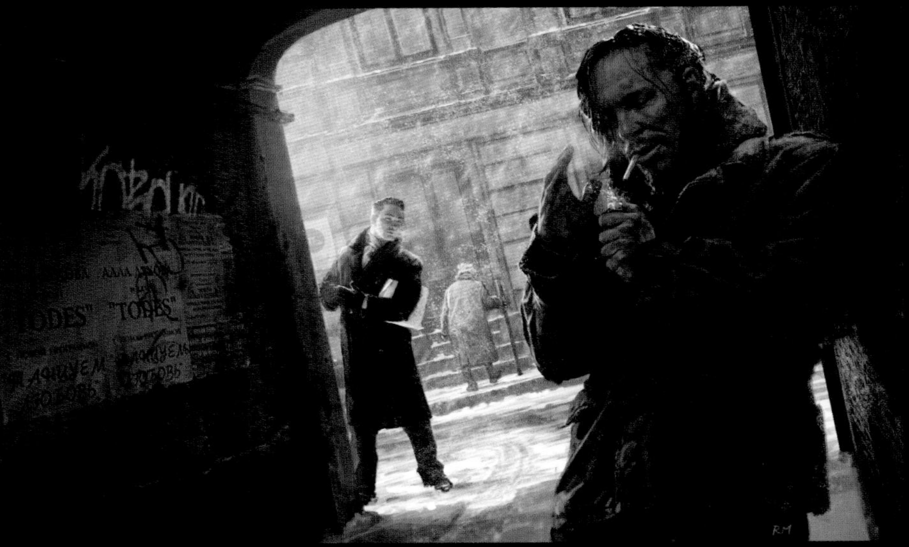

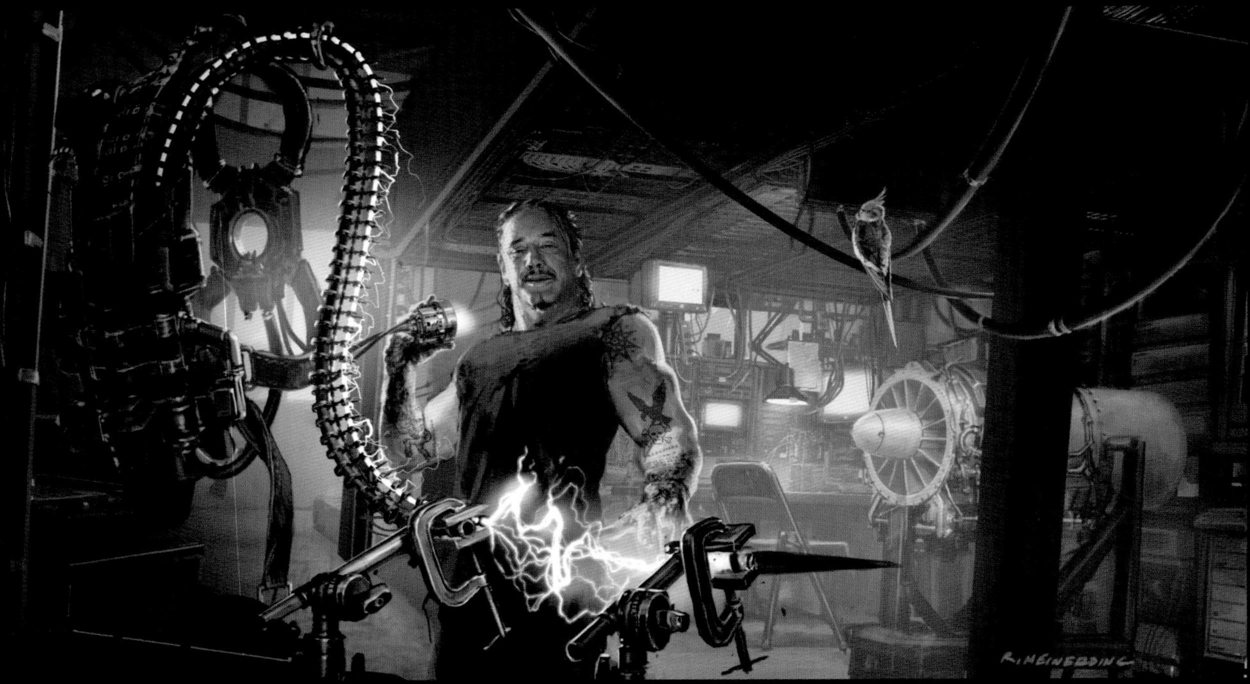

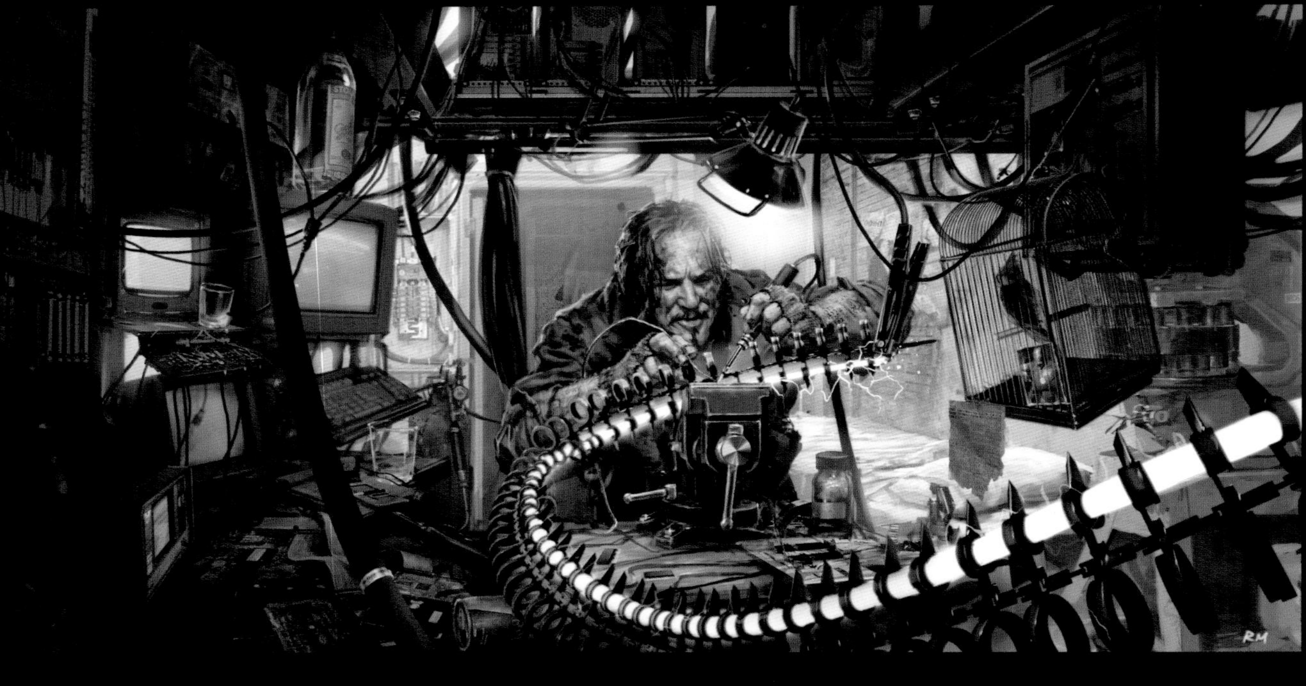

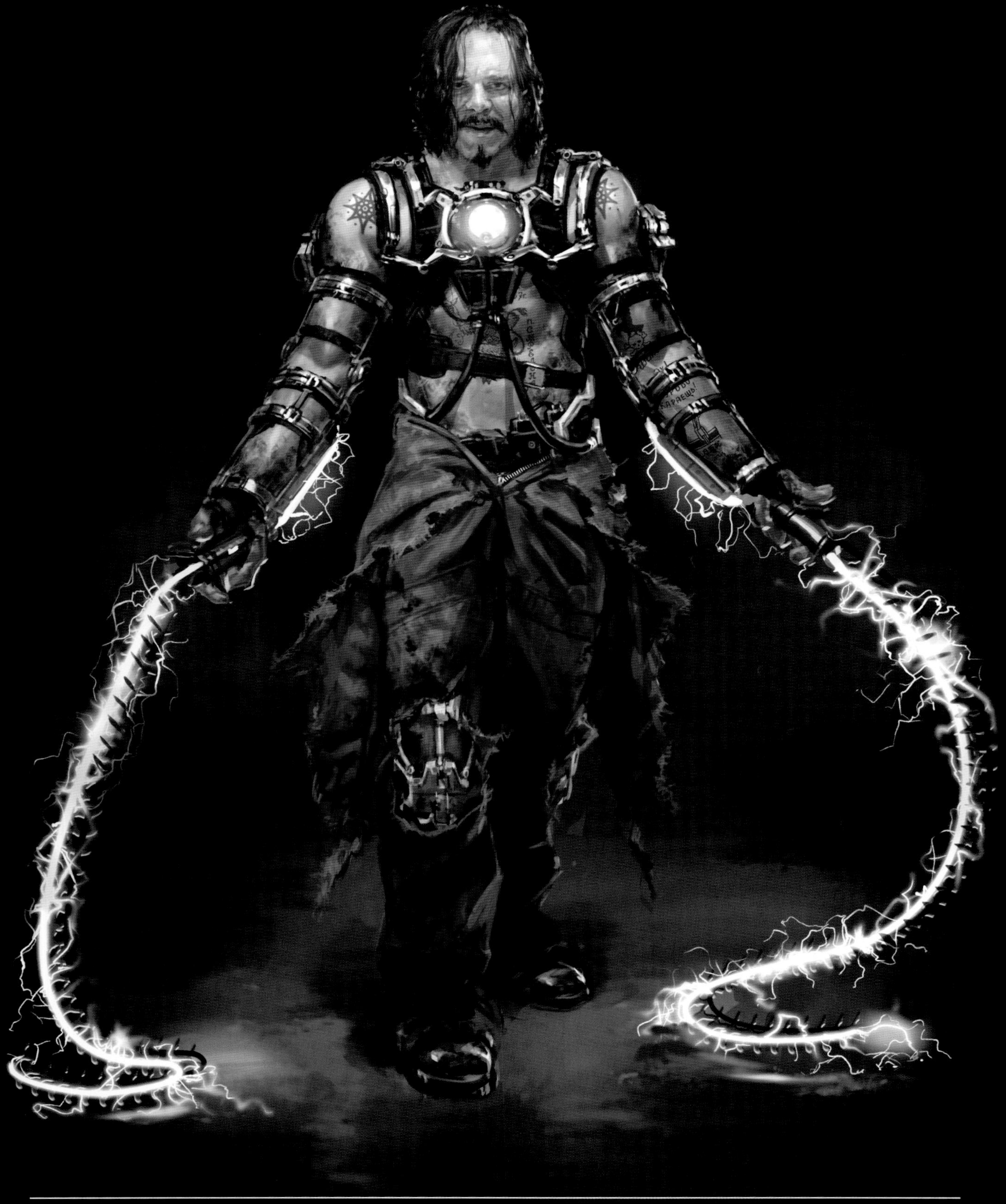

Because the filmmakers wanted actor Mickey Rourke to play Ivan Vanko in *Iron Man 2*, Meinerding explains, "I did this image to incorporate what I had done with the design with Mickey's likeness to get him interested in the project." Much of the concept art was based on technology that was left in the Marvel Studios office from Stan Winston. "A telemetry suit is a puppeteering rig," continues the artist. "The performer would be in it, controlling another character somewhere else, using these sort of stainless steel or milled aluminum structures. That became the basis for what Whiplash was. I had done details on the whips as well—all kinds of segmentation for how electricity is filtered through it. That ended up in the movie, which I think are some of the coolest shots. Like when Whiplash walks in slow motion, whips the whip, and it has an arc of electricity that hits at some parts of the track."

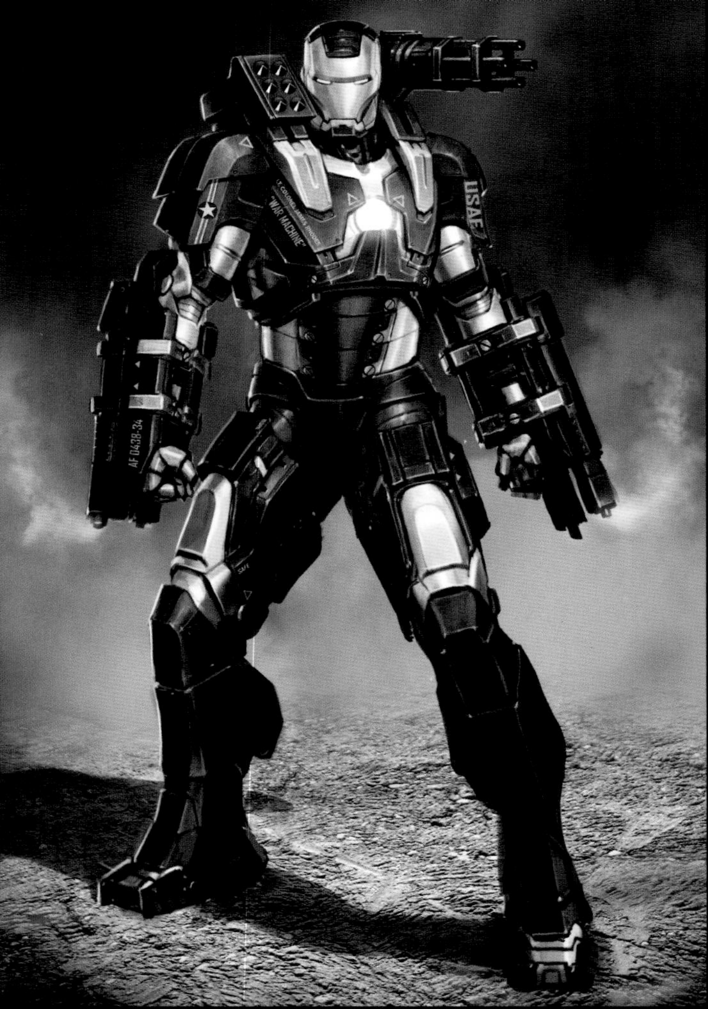
USAF
"WAR MACHINE"
AF 0438-34
SAFE

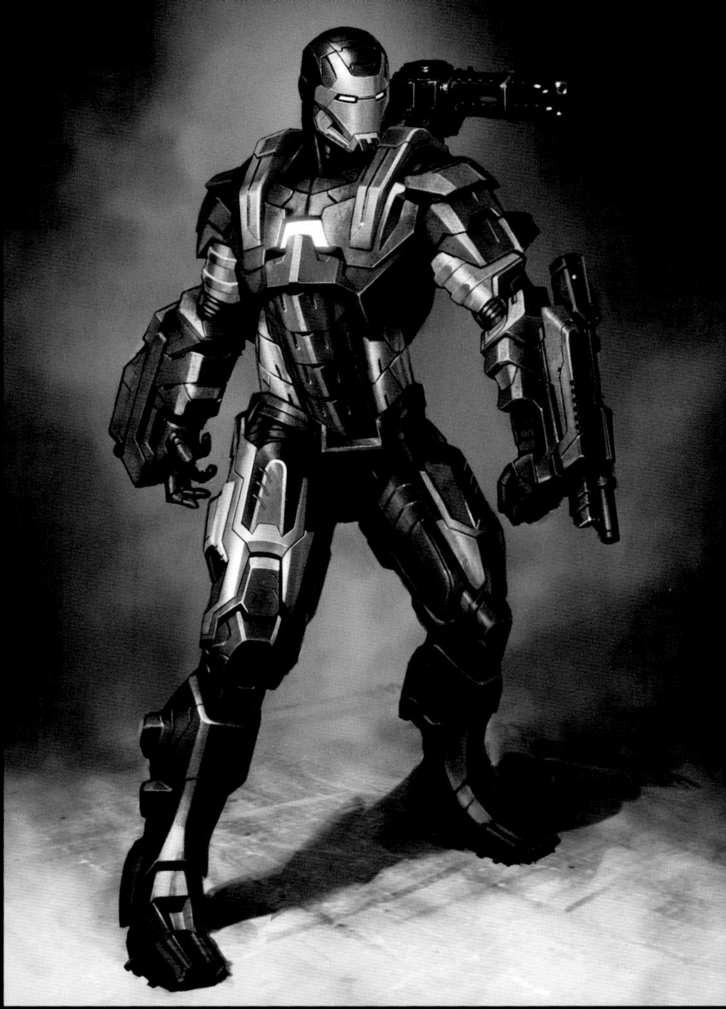

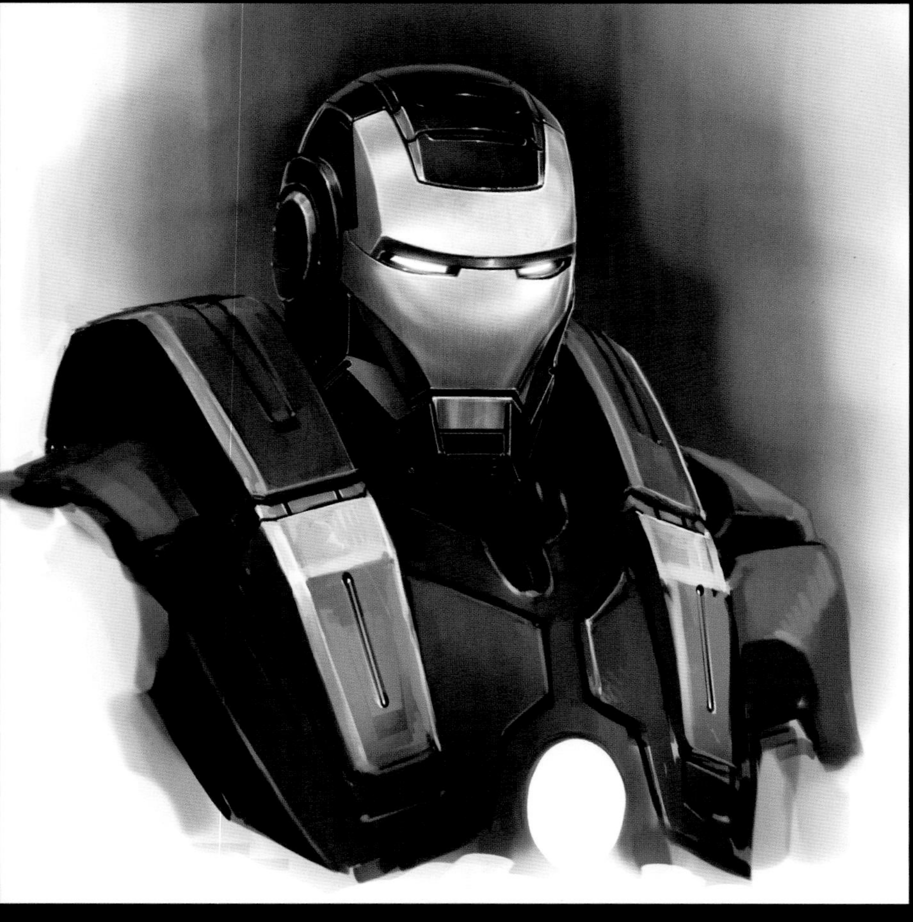

The roots of *Iron Man 2*'s War Machine look extend back to the first film. "Phil Saunders had done some cool designs for where Tony was gonna essentially upgrade his armor for the final battle," says Meinerding. "It was heavier duty, and it was red and gold. But he also realized he'd essentially just designed a War Machine suit. So [for the sequel] we had sort of a Phil starting point. But I did a couple designs for this. And Adi Granov did designs on War Machine, too. The idea was that the Mark II is still very visible underneath whatever Justin Hammer had added on [left]. Layering the storytelling is fun when you're starting with something that was Tony's and then Justin's adding stuff."

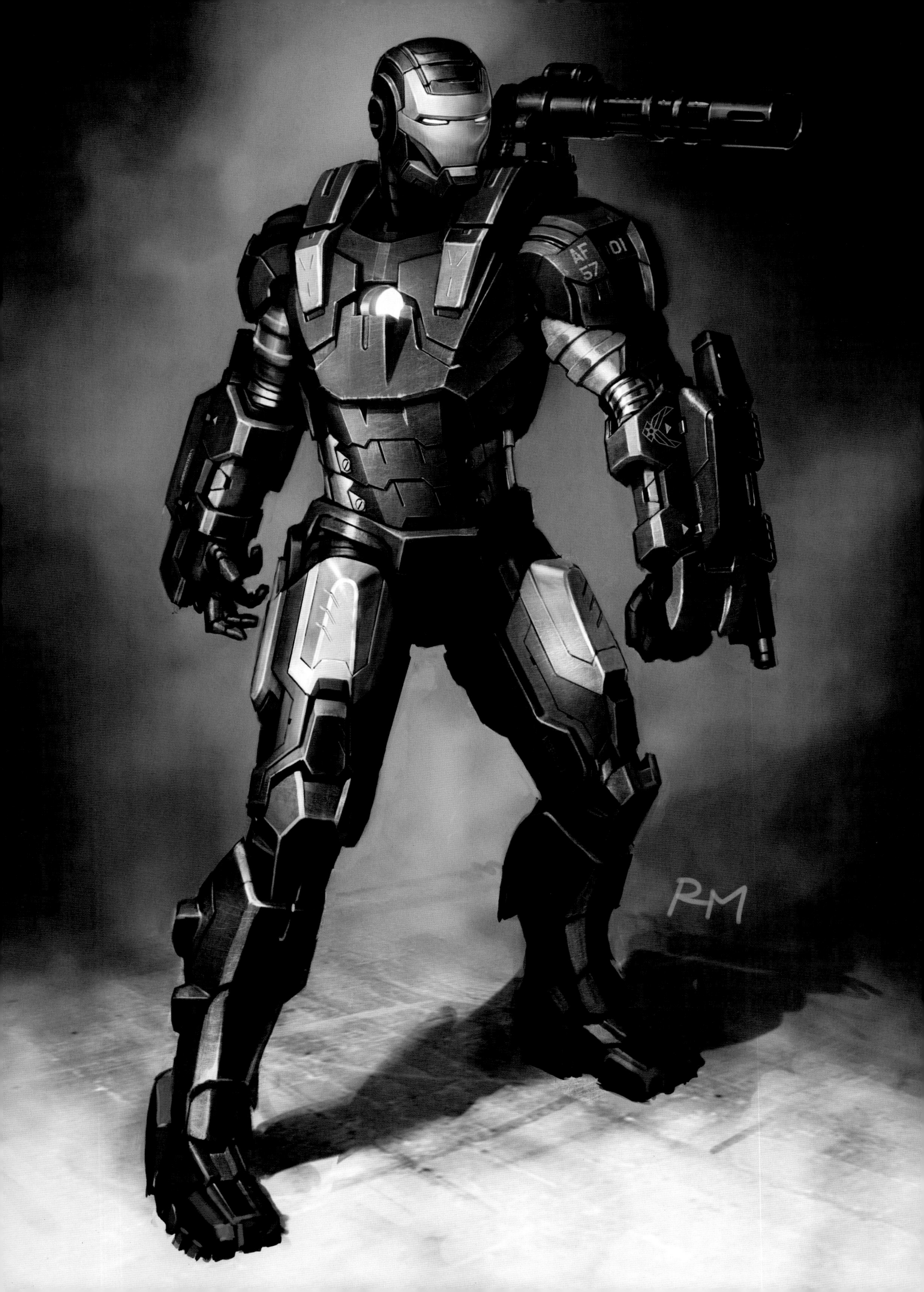
RM

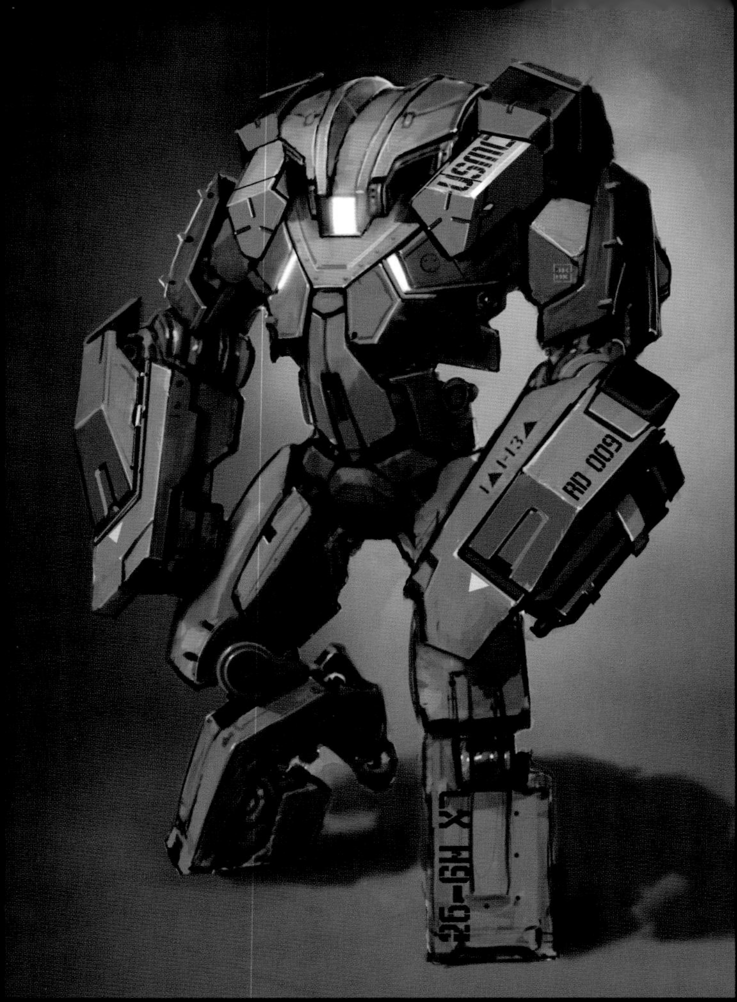
USMC
RD 009
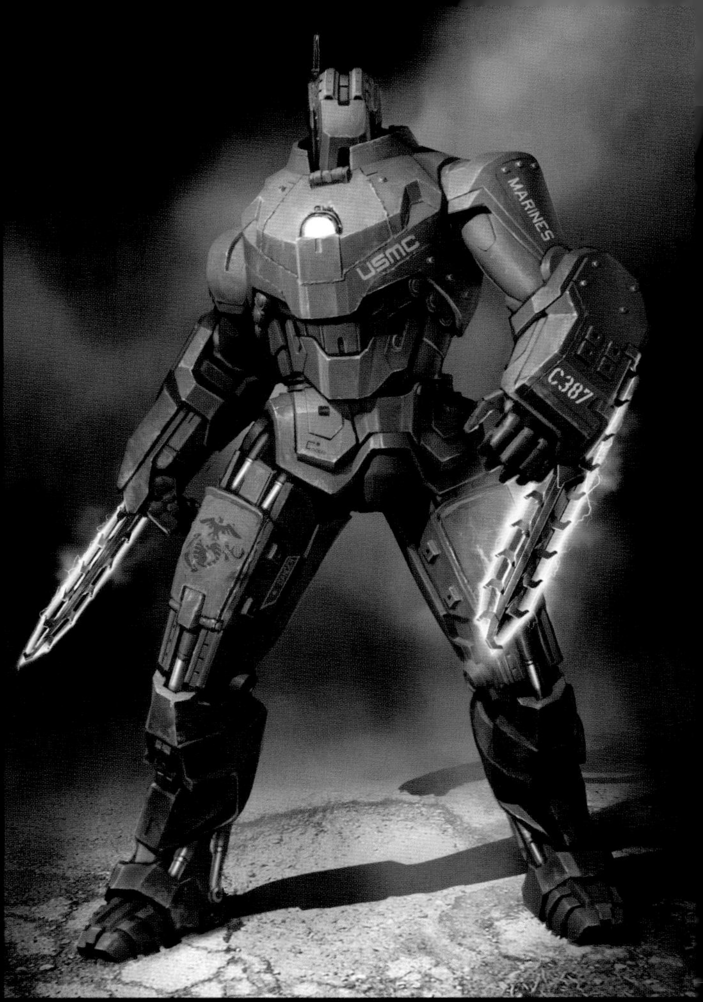
USMC
MARINES
C387
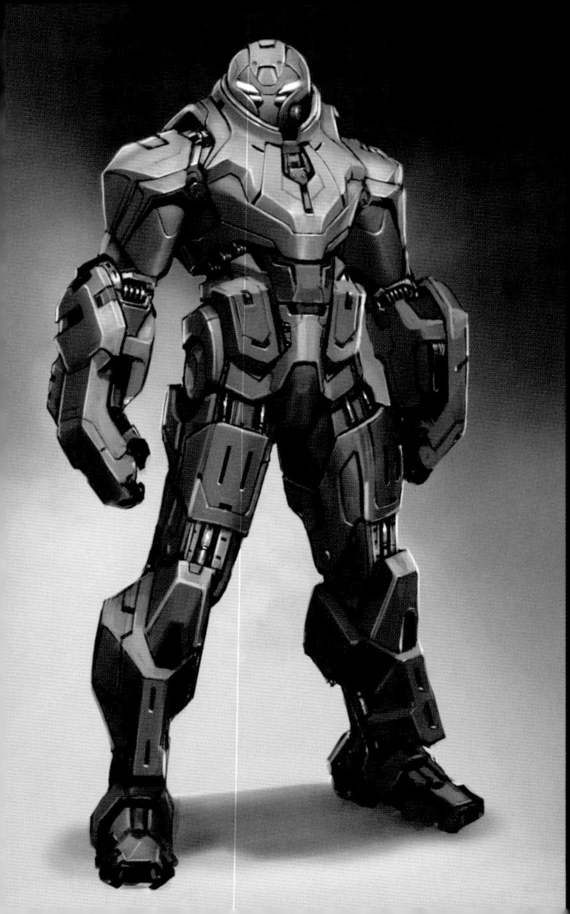
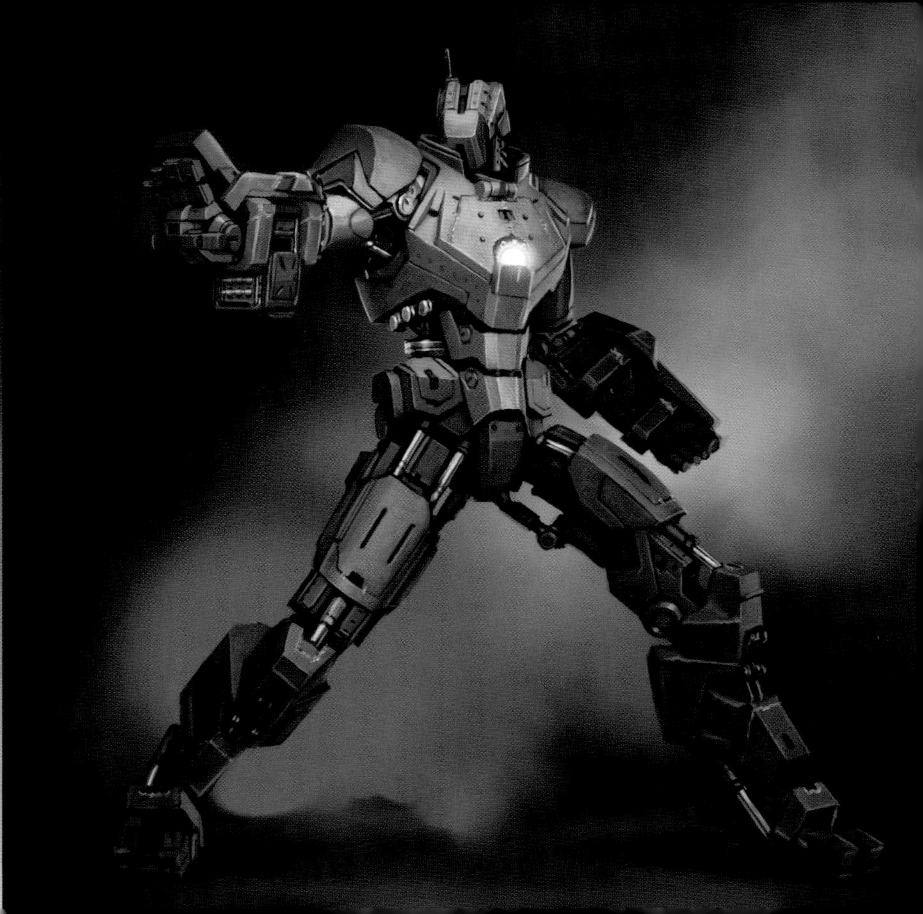

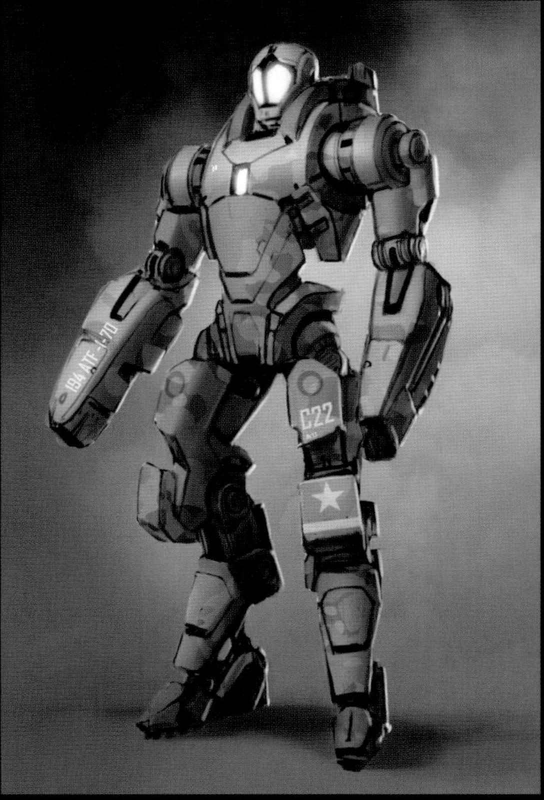
C22

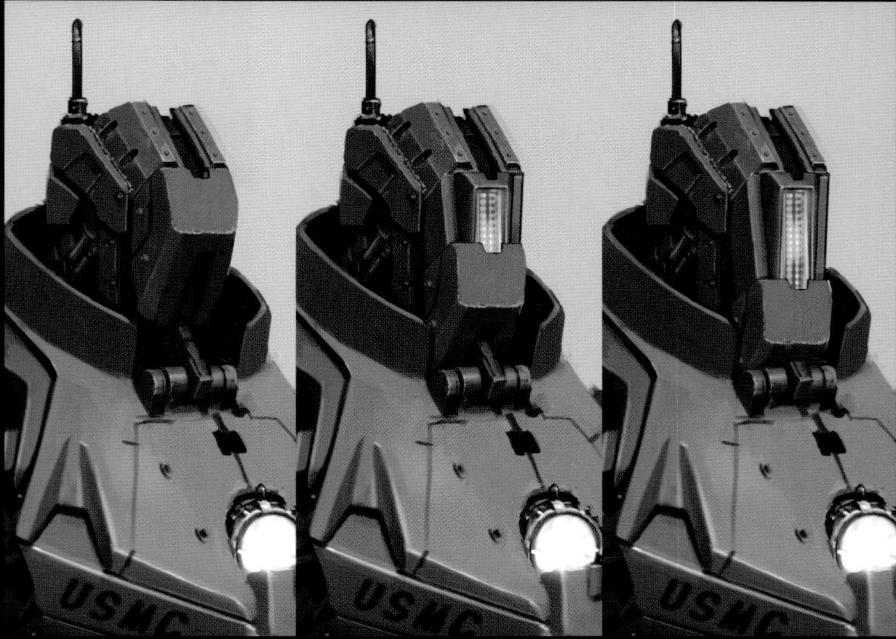
USMC
USMC
USMC

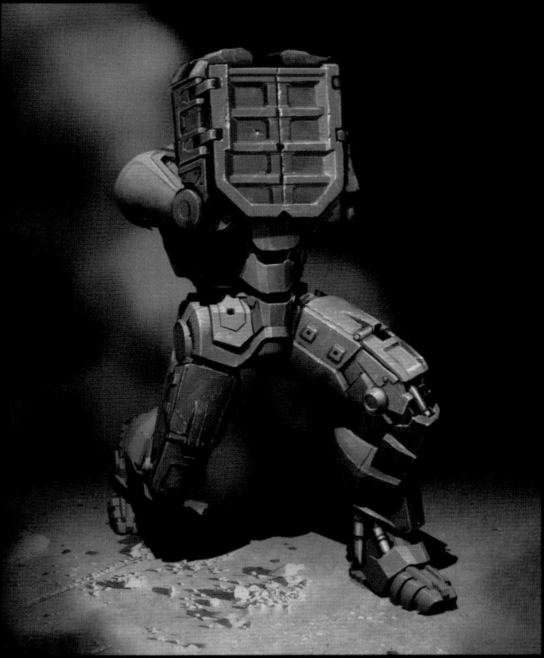

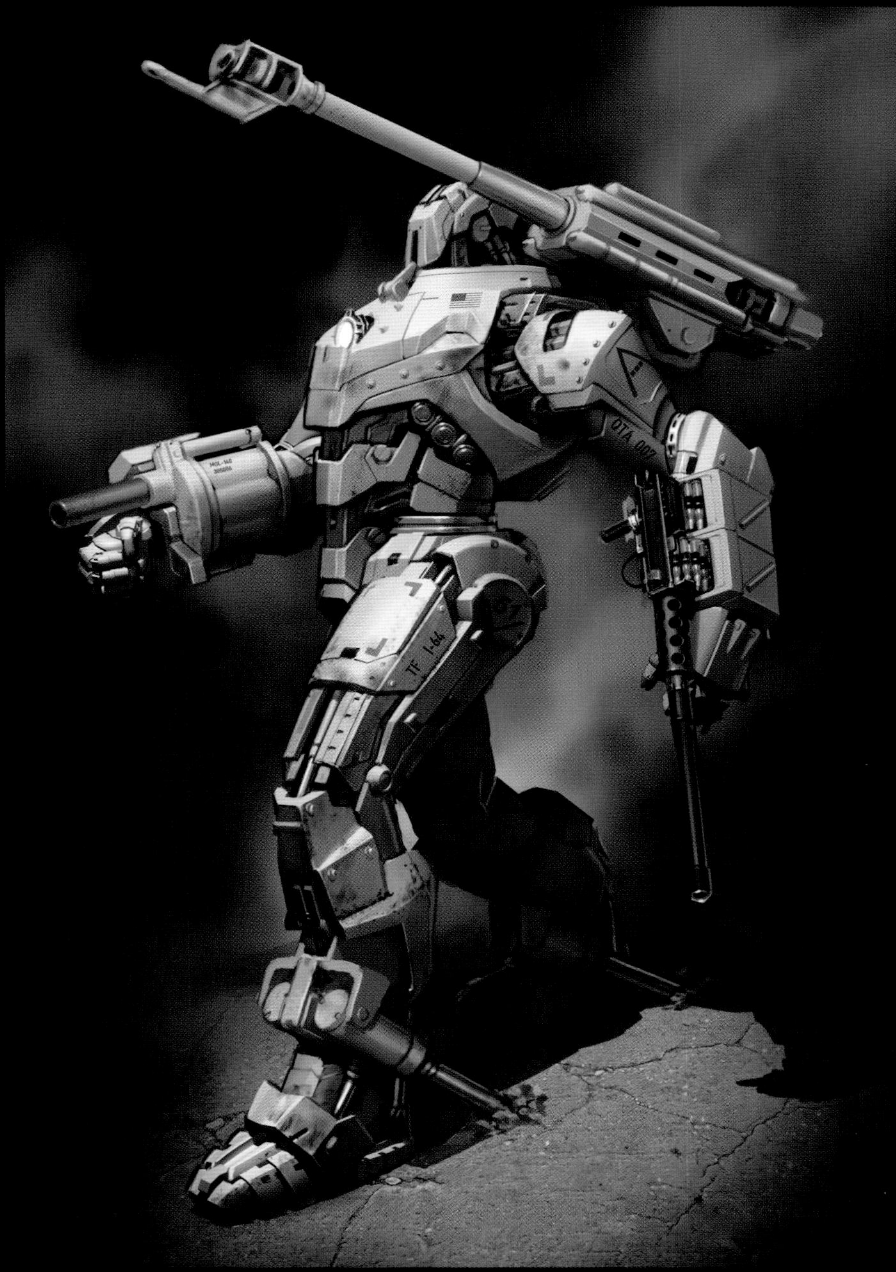
TF 1-64

Coming up with all of the different drones was an additional design challenge for Meinerding and Adi Granov, simply because they didn't have the volume of people required to model them. "So I ended up having to model a bit of them also," says the artist. "But I think doing designs for militarized robotics is a fun thing to do. And to try and take sort of a base drawing that we had and find a way for it to work for the different branches of the military was cool."

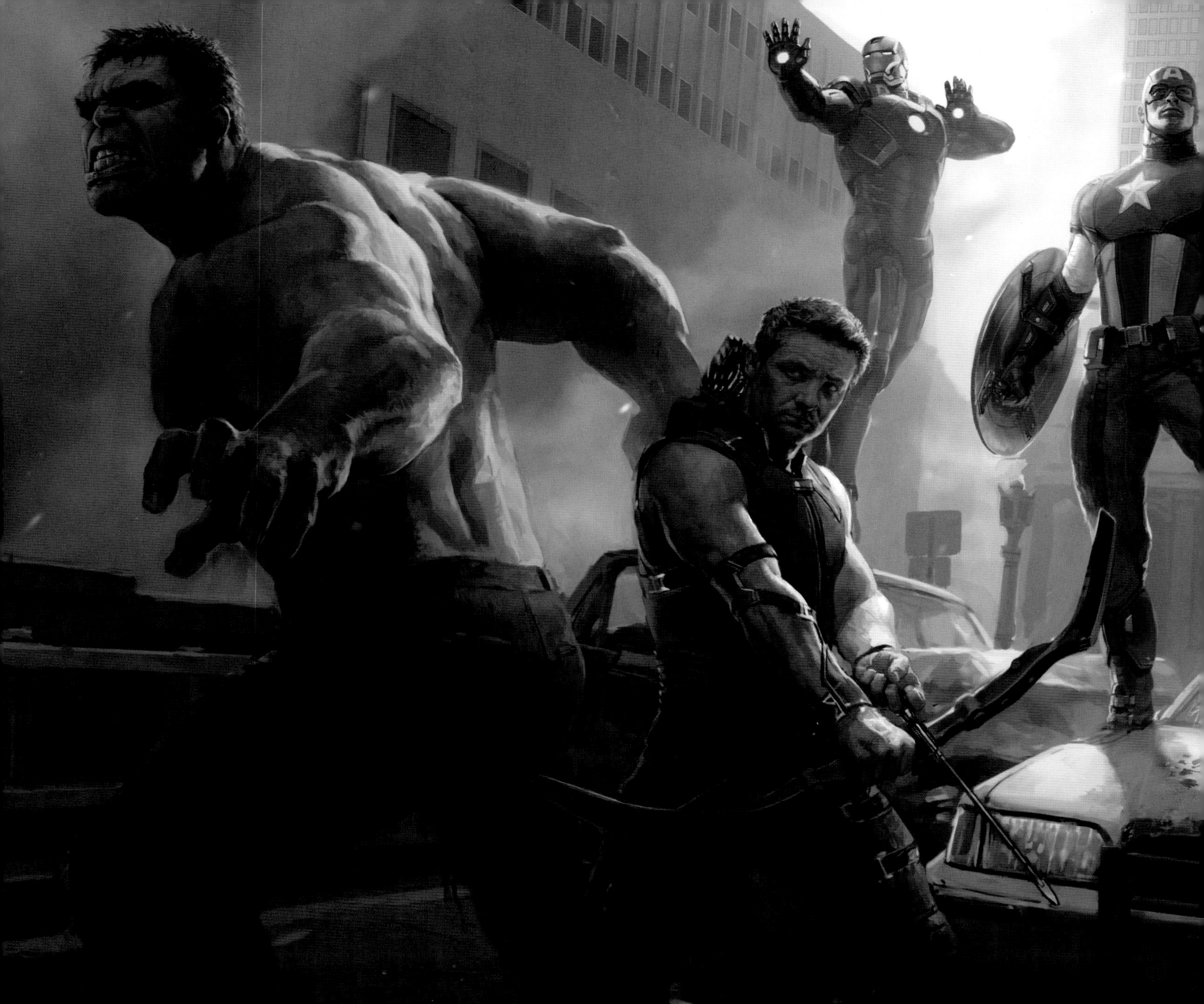

When *Iron Man 2* went into preproduction, Meinerding and Adi Granov returned to assist Favreau in further developing Tony Stark and his ever-evolving suits. A challenging production on all counts, Meinerding took on the mantle of unofficial art director, working with returning production designer J. Michael Riva. But the concept team was feeling the departure of Phil Saunders, who hadn't returned, and Stan Winston, who passed away between the first two *Iron Man* films. Exhausted by the end of production, Meinerding took a month-long break to mentally refresh. His return reunited him with former boss Charlie Wen, who had been hired to develop *Thor.* Together, they shared the title of Co-Supervisors of Visual Development.

"I think by the end of *Iron Man 2,* I had a degree of trust from [producers] Kevin [Feige] and Louis [D'Esposito] and Jeremy [Latcham]," he says. "I felt like I had worked very hard on *Captain America* and had designed quite a lot of that show," he says. Being on location also afforded him new perspectives and opportunities to problem-solve through design as needed during the film's production.

At the end of *Cap*, Meinerding returned to the Marvel Studios home offices and dove into developing *Marvel's The Avengers* for producer Jeremy Latcham and director Joss Whedon. "*Avengers* was bigger than any film we'd ever done before," he says of its scope and the expectations riding on its success. They hired more permanent artists to help explore character and concept design work that was supervised by Meinerding and Wen.

"There were times when concept art could be used as a conceptual tool and a development tool that would allow people to understand the movie they wanted to make," he says of their department's evolving function. "After the first *Avengers*, concept art became more of a preproduction and production tool. It was about finishing what [the filmmakers] already knew they wanted or designing what they knew that they wanted."

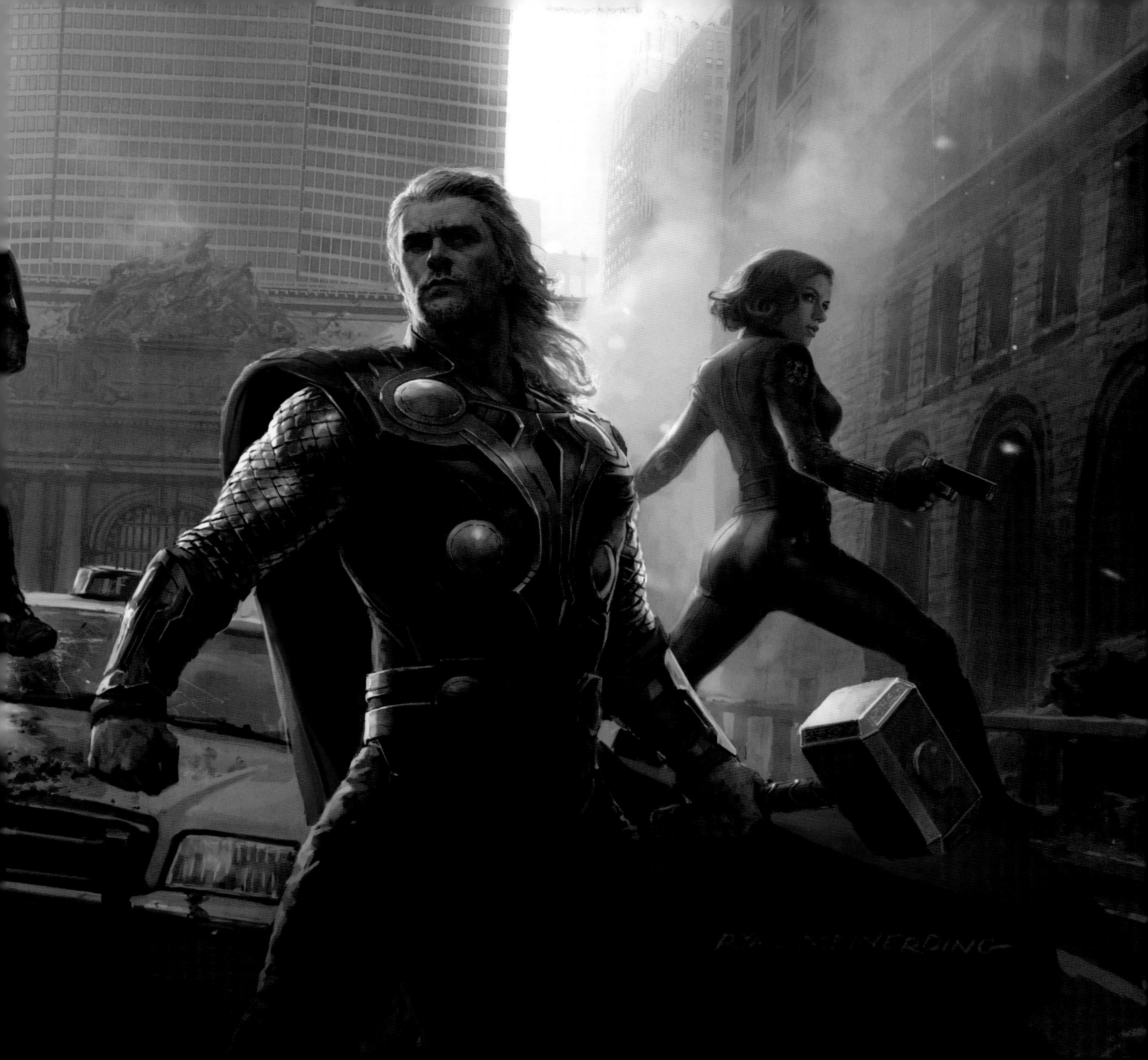

ABOVE While Ryan Meinerding was busy finishing up his work in England on *Captain America: The First Avenger*, the Visual Development team—now including Andy Park, Rodney Fuentebella, and Jackson Sze—was expanding to prepare for Phase One's finale—*Marvel's The Avengers*. "We knew this was gonna be a bigger movie than we had done before, so we needed to hire more people and get started as early as we could," says Meinerding, who flew straight from the *Cap* set back to Marvel Studios' operation in California's Manhattan Beach without missing a beat. "There was a lot of concern about the characters being unified enough," the artist continues. "The production designer, James Chinlund, brought up that at least three characters have red on them—four if you count Hawkeye, who is kind of a red. Black Widow's hair can roughly fall in that category as well. So when I did this key frame of them all standing together, the only pitch I had was getting the characters that have some [visible] red in there, but also allow the lighting to unify them. Essentially, if you're backlighting them—and then throw the additional hit of yellow in there—you can make them all standing together feel a little bit more real. But this was more of an inspiration piece than a specific guide."

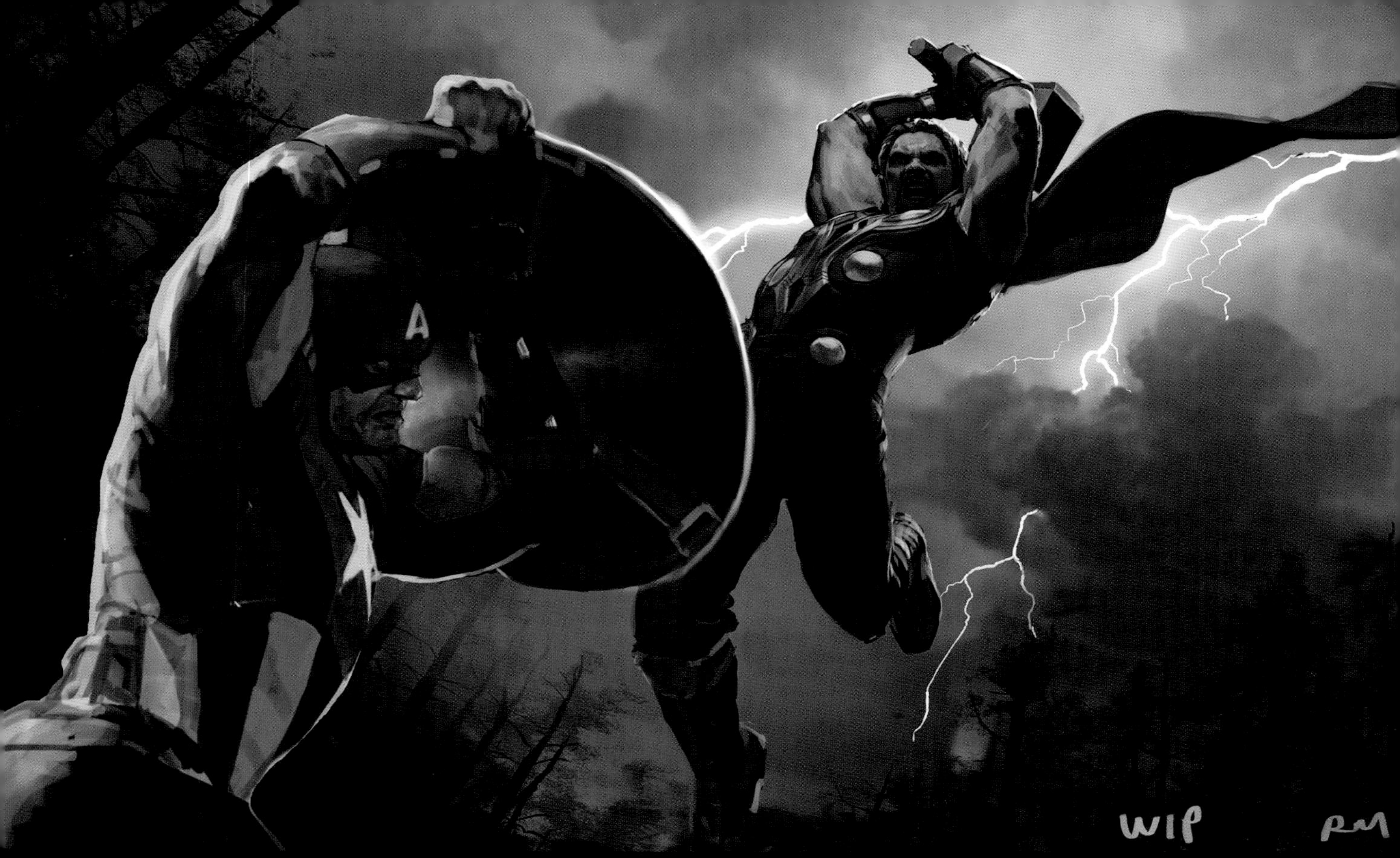
WIP
RM
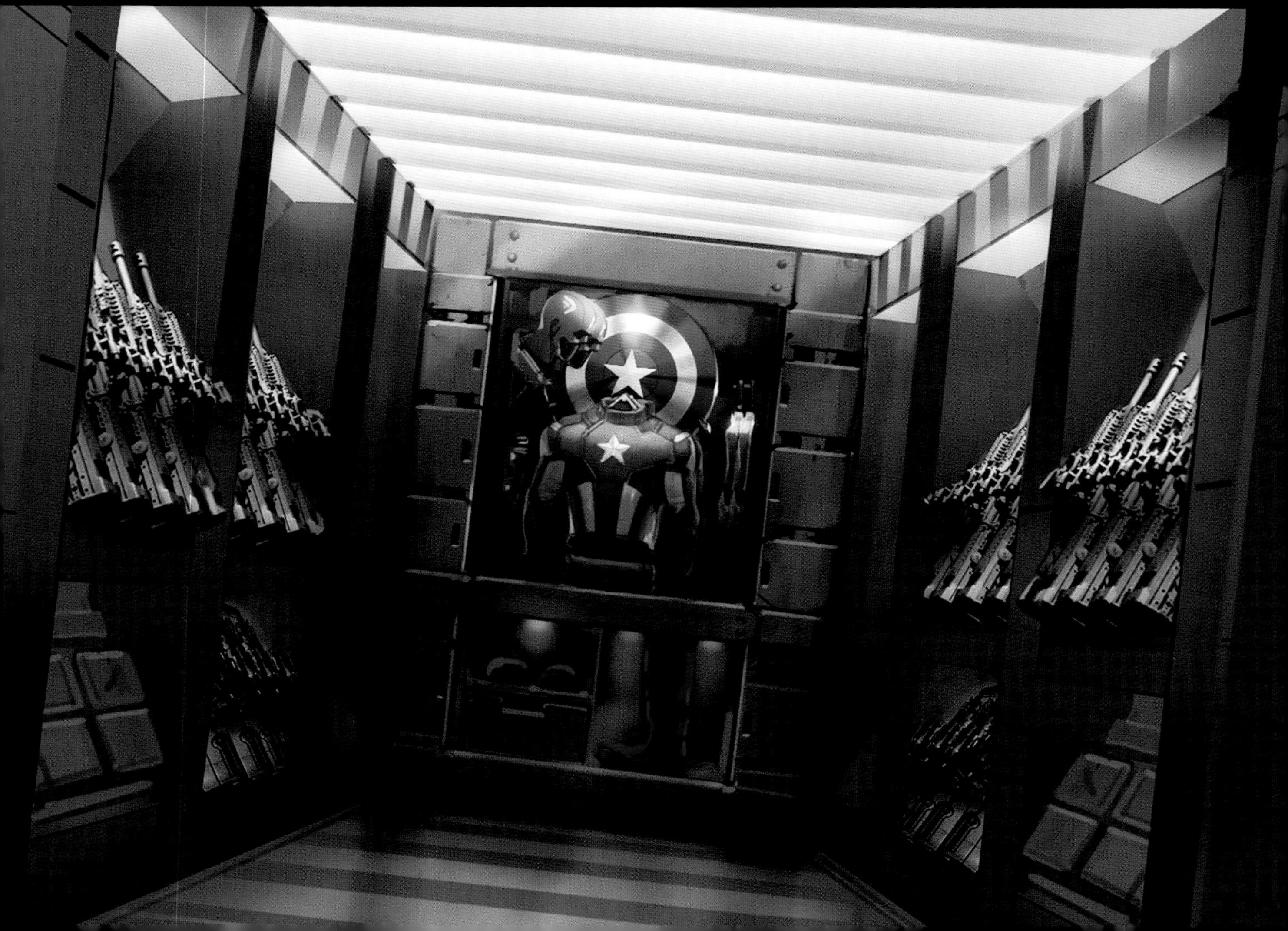

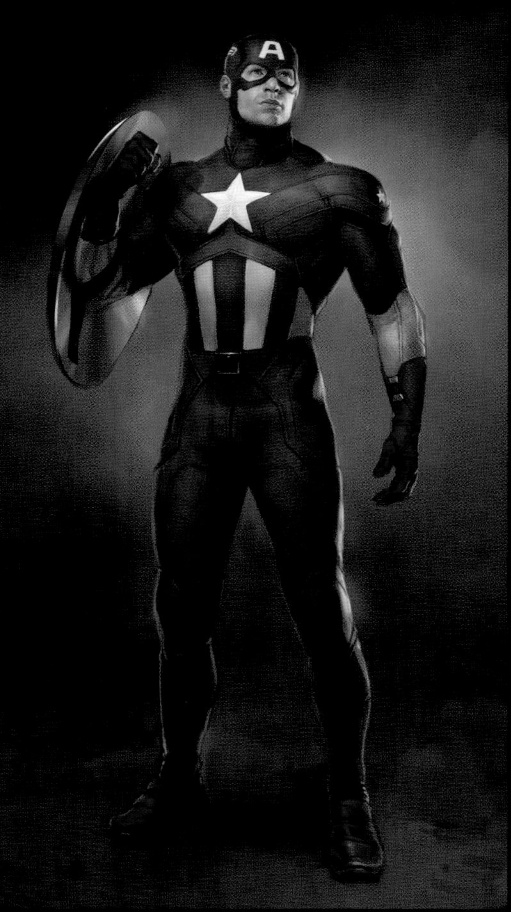

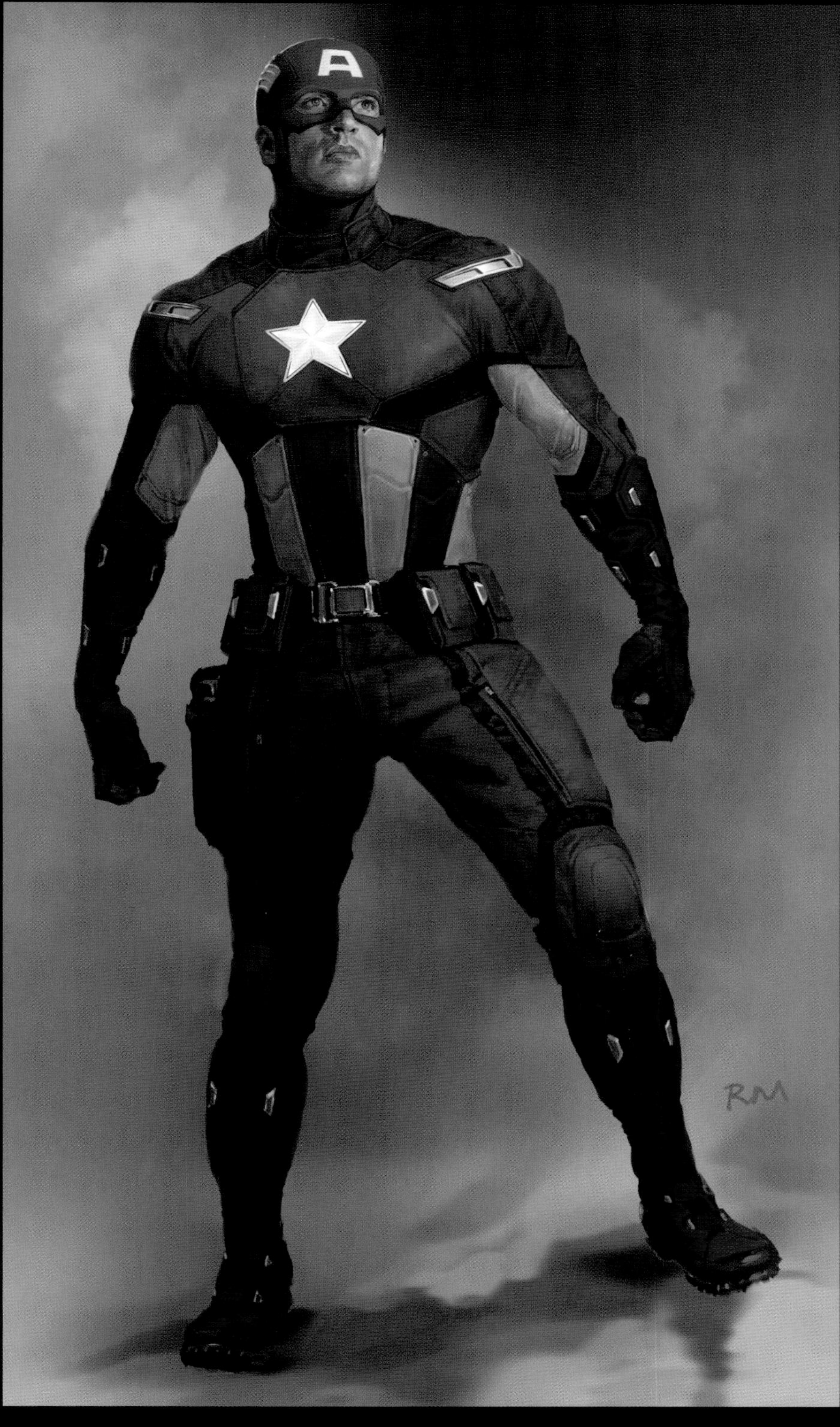
RM

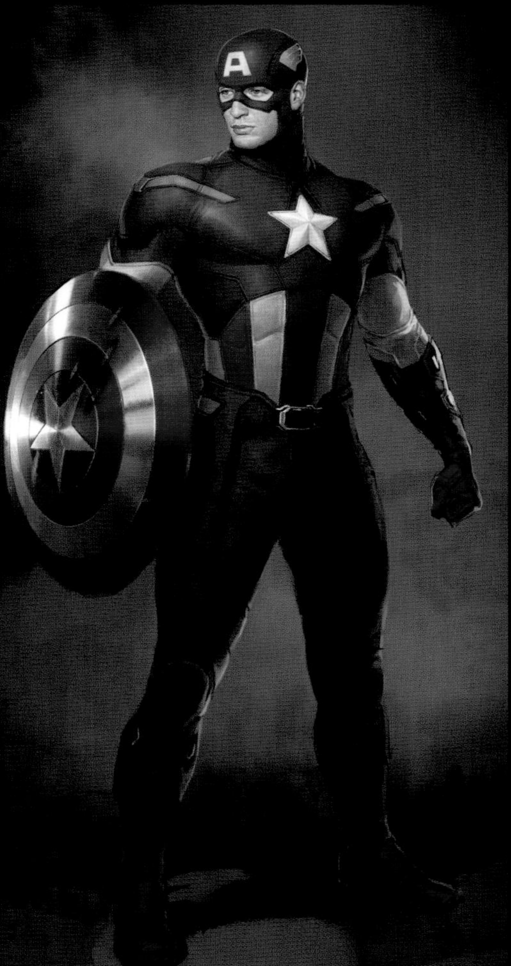

"On *Marvel's The Avengers*, the amount of people I was overseeing had gone up by a *lot*," says Meinerding. "I was art directing, doing design work and paintings, as well as putting the presentations together, taking all the notes in the meetings, and then giving them to the artists. . . . This was the first project where all of that meant my drawing time took a big hit. This is the only movie where other people have actually worked on designing Captain America, just because I was so worried about not having time to explore enough ideas. Andy [Park] did a take, and Charlie [Wen] did a couple." Additionally, Phil Saunders and Adi Granov worked on artwork, as did Justin Sweet and Josh Nizzi for a period of time.

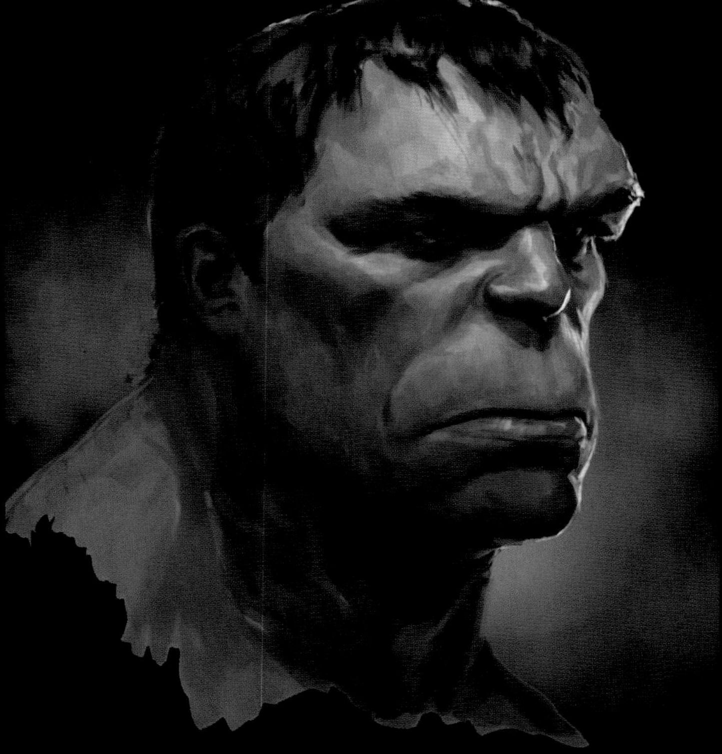

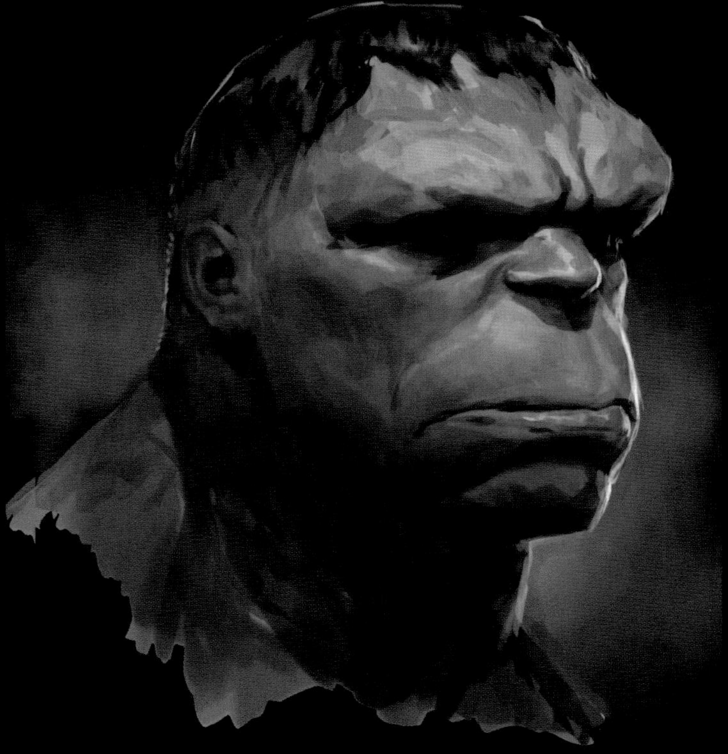

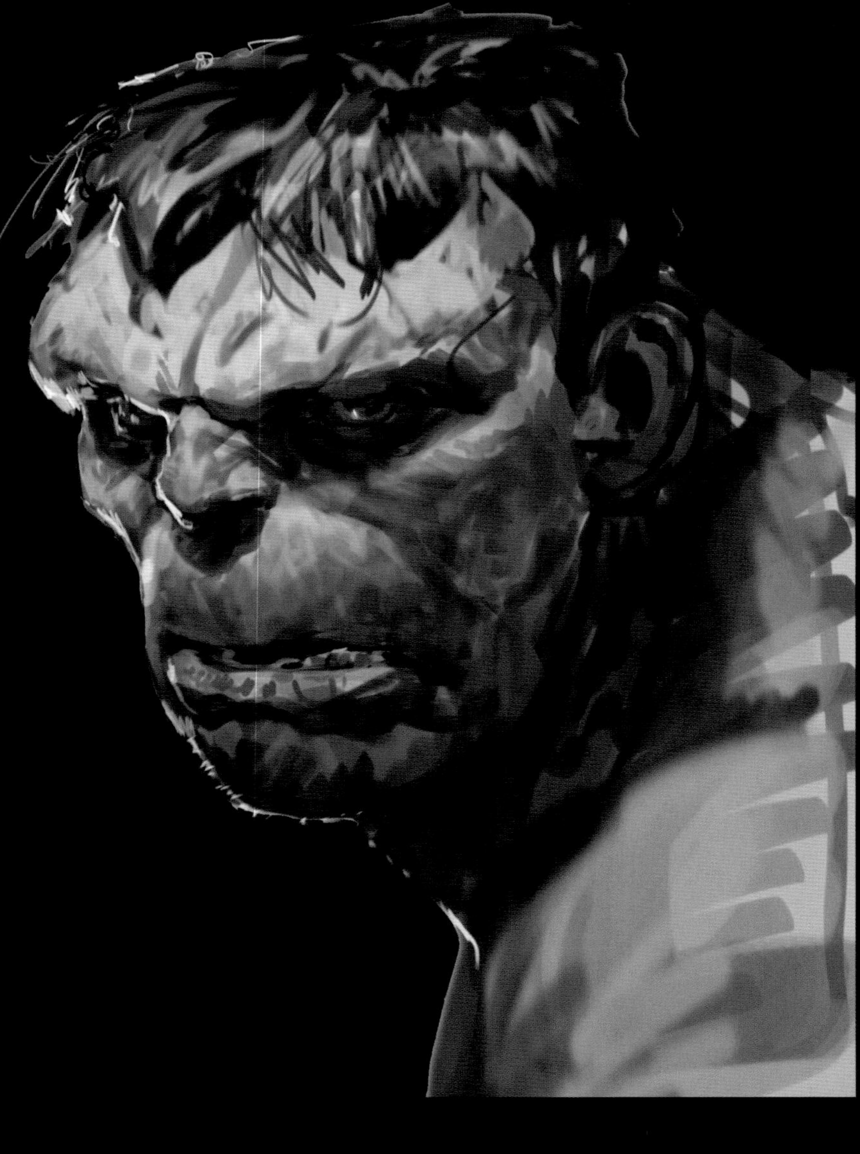

The first character Meinerding and his Visual Development team focused on for *Marvel's The Avengers* was the Hulk. "The picture on the left is my first drawing that got shown in a presentation to director Joss Whedon," says Meinerding. "I was learning [art software] ZBrush to try and sculpt the Hulk in 3D so I could do his face. Charlie [Wen] was sculpting the body. Essentially, that's how it worked out. Charlie designed the body and I did the head. We ended up merging them together and creating a maquette [opposite, far right]." But there was one very specific thing that Meinerding pitched for the Hulk. "I was excited about making the Hulk a *monster*, using Mark [Ruffalo] as the reference point. A lot of the time, we get into challenges with designs when we don't know what the archetype of the character is. Whenever you're trying to make the Hulk equal parts hero and monster, you can't find it. I pitched the idea of making him primarily a monster. But having Ruffalo's face be a huge component of the design also meant we were always gonna be able to fall back on something that *wasn't* a monster—you were able to see to the hero within the creature."

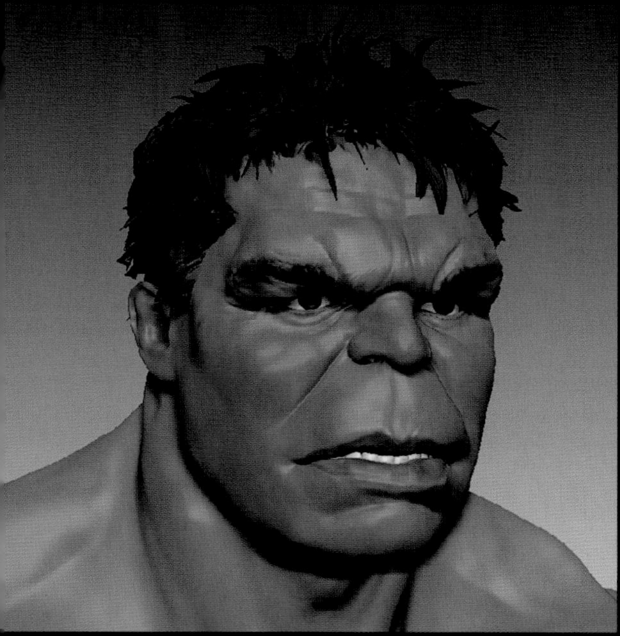
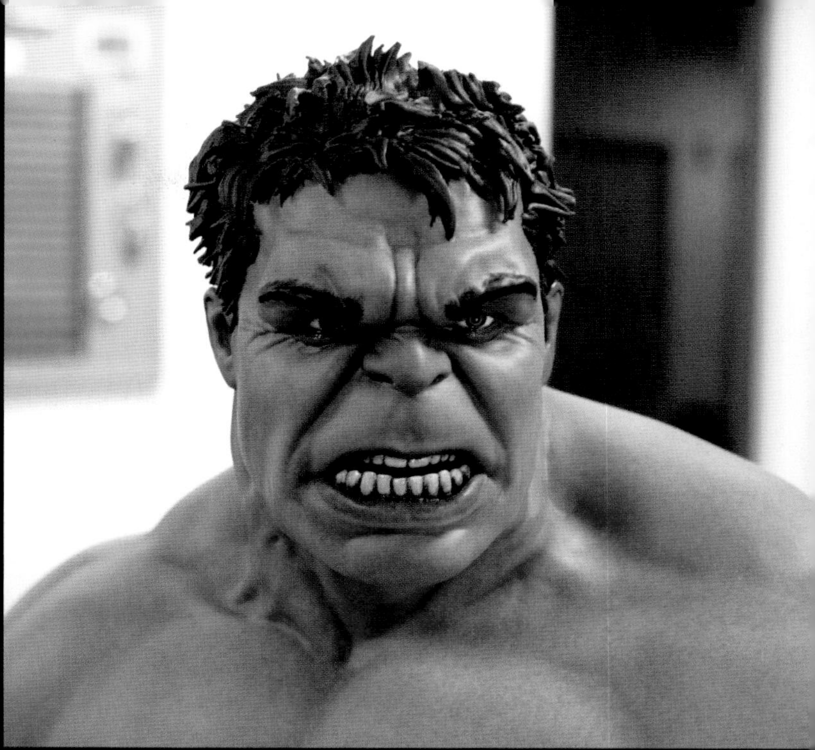
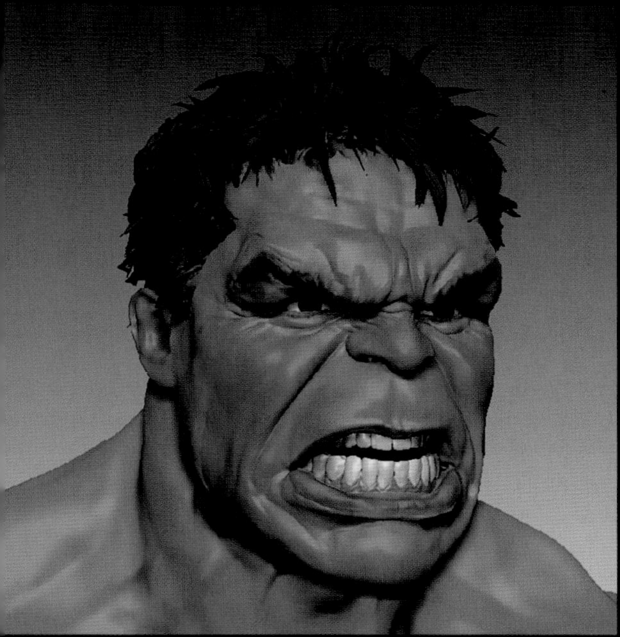
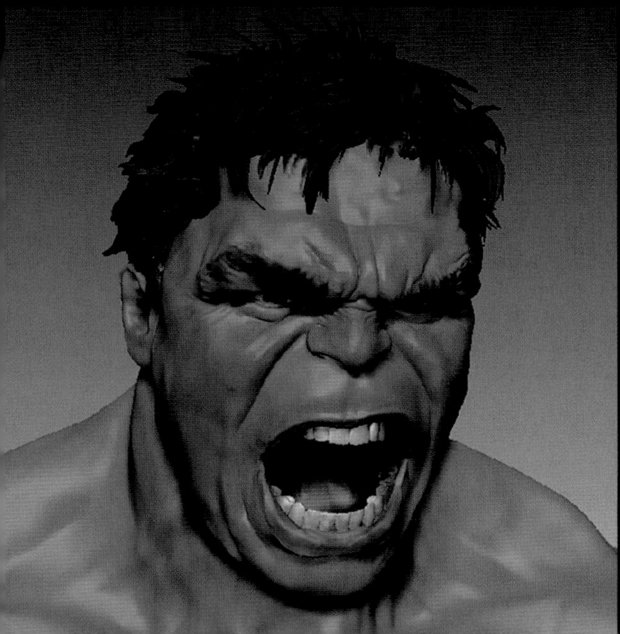
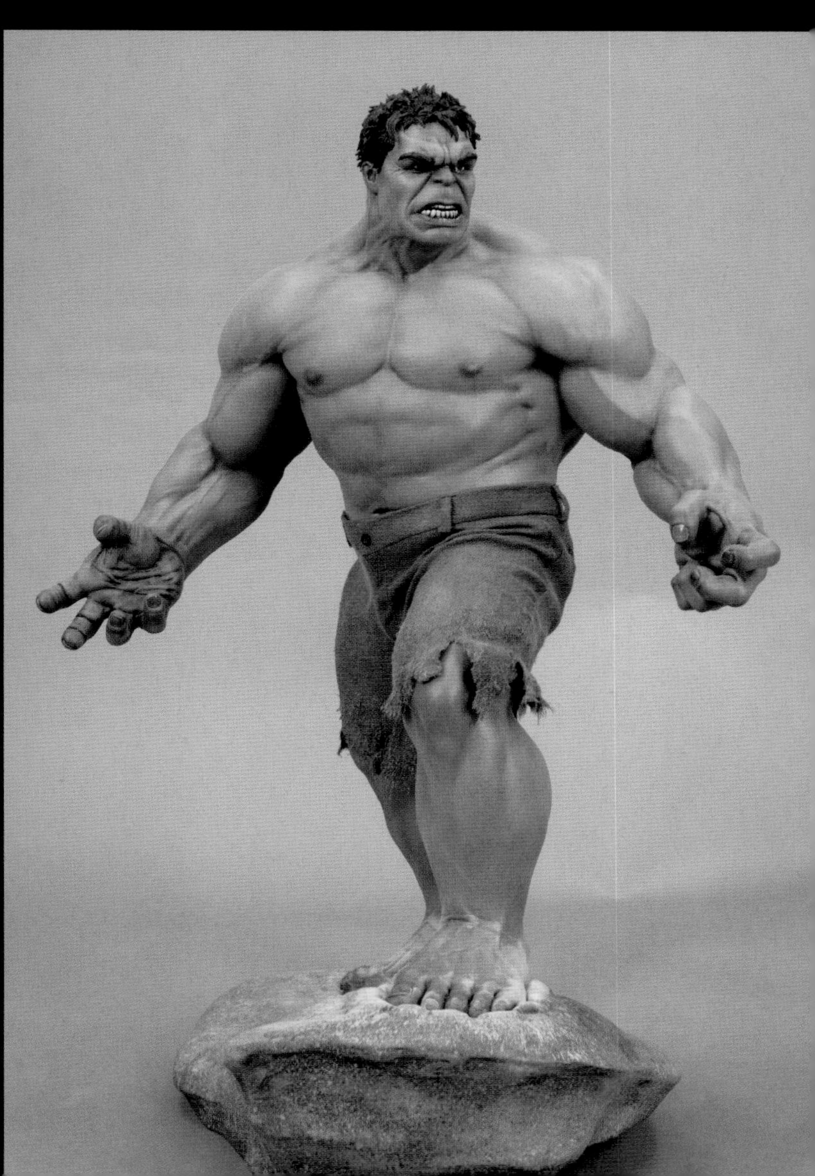

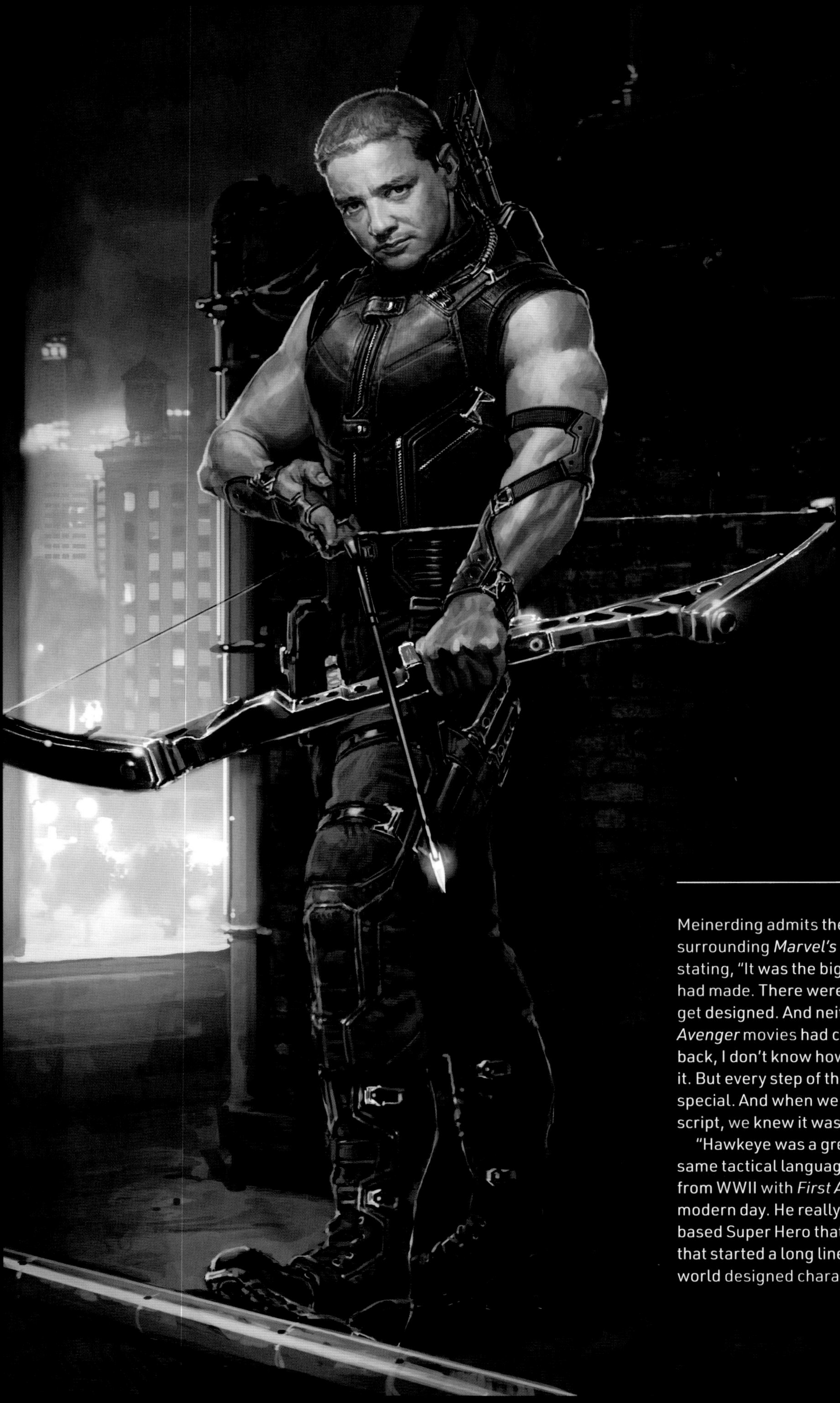

Meinerding admits the amount of anxiety surrounding *Marvel's The Avengers* was high, stating, "It was the biggest gamble the studio had made. There were a *lot* of characters to get designed. And neither *Thor* nor *The First Avenger* movies had come out yet. Looking back, I don't know how Kevin Feige kept doing it. But every step of the way felt like something special. And when we read the [*Avengers*] script, we knew it was gonna work.

"Hawkeye was a great chance to take the same tactical language we were working on from WWII with *First Avenger* and bring it into modern day. He really was the first tactical-based Super Hero that we did in the MCU, and that started a long line of compelling, real-world designed characters."

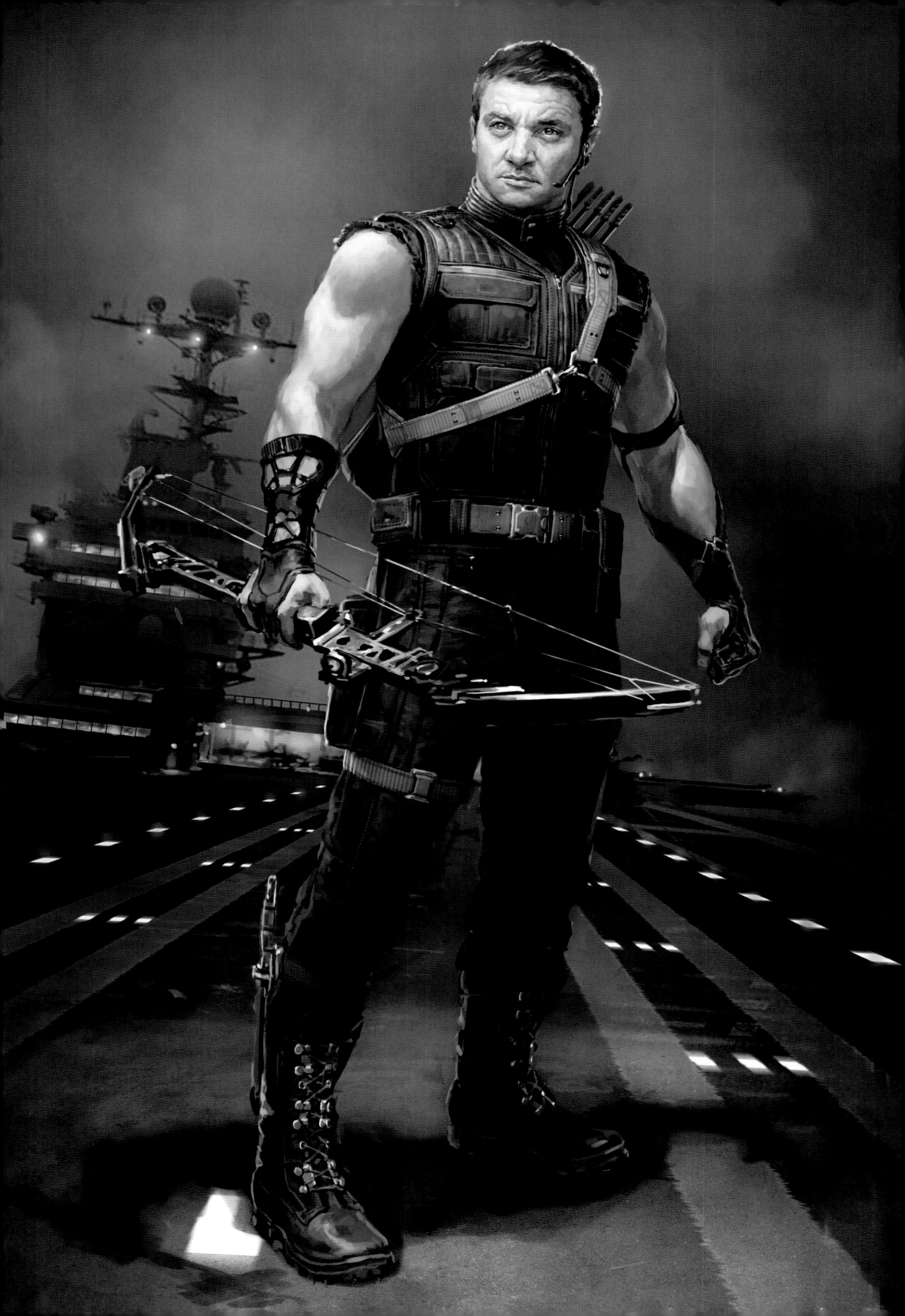

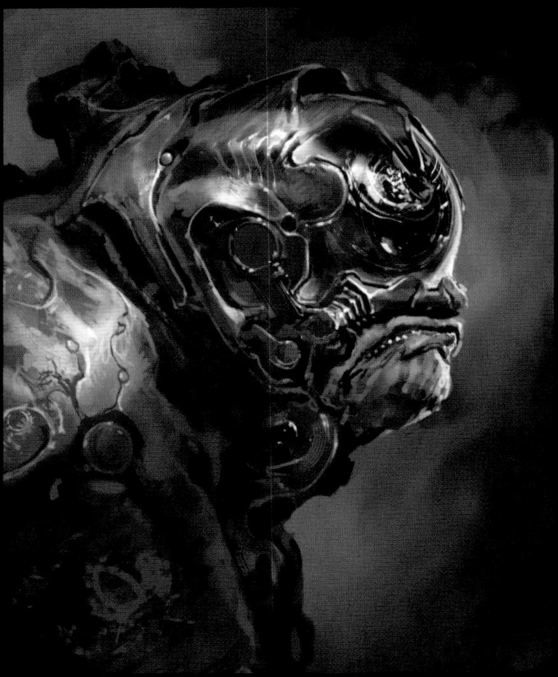

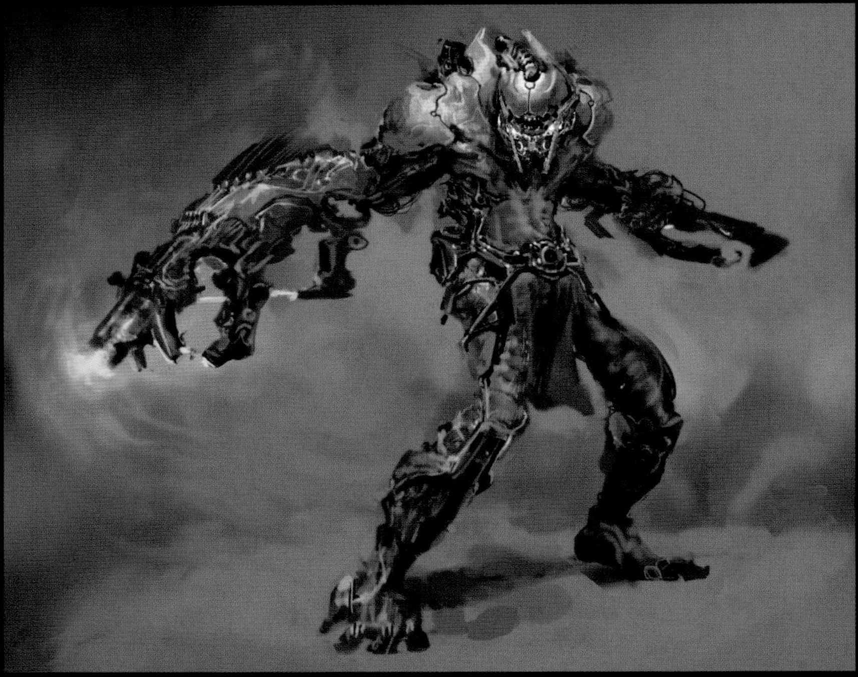

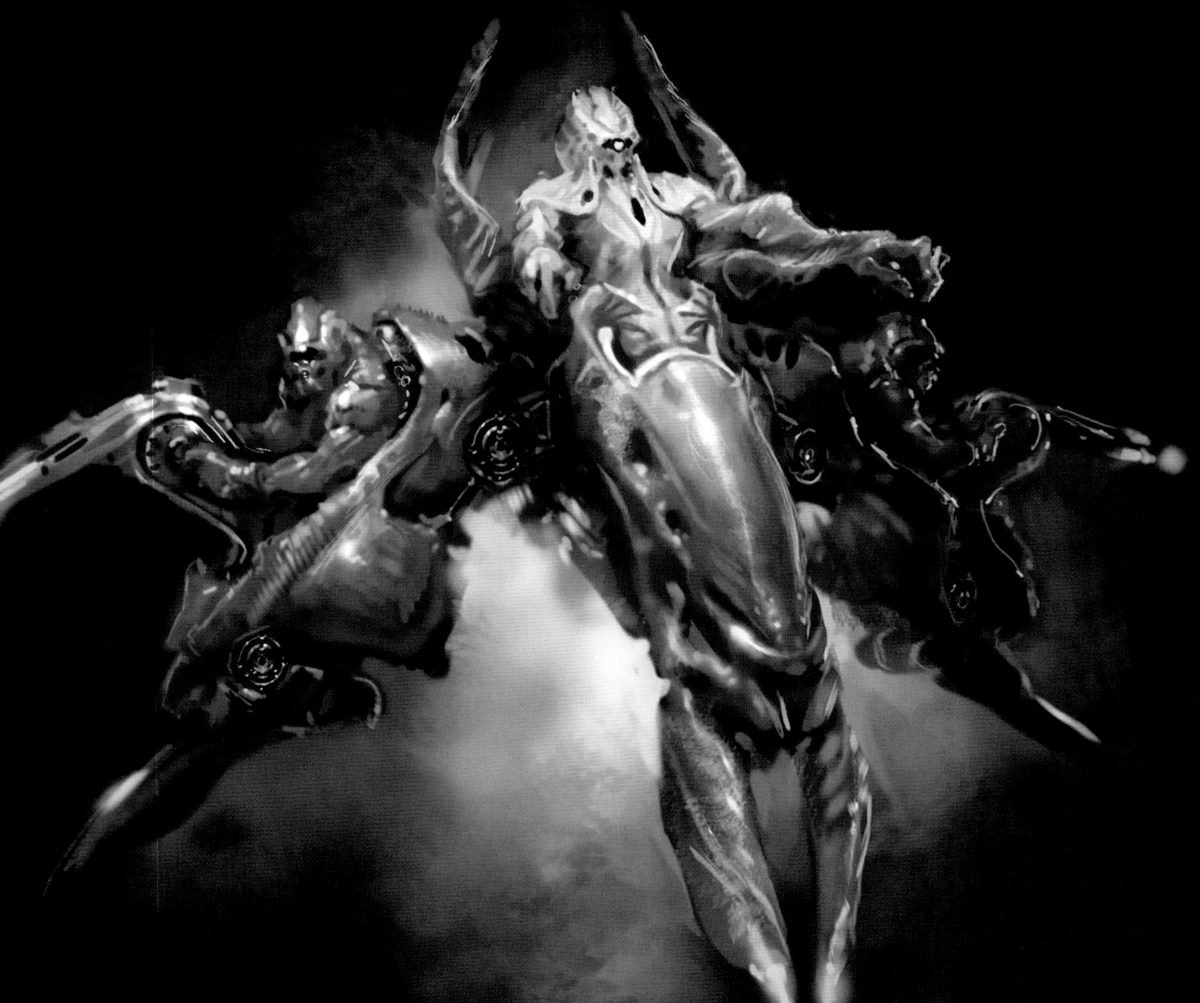

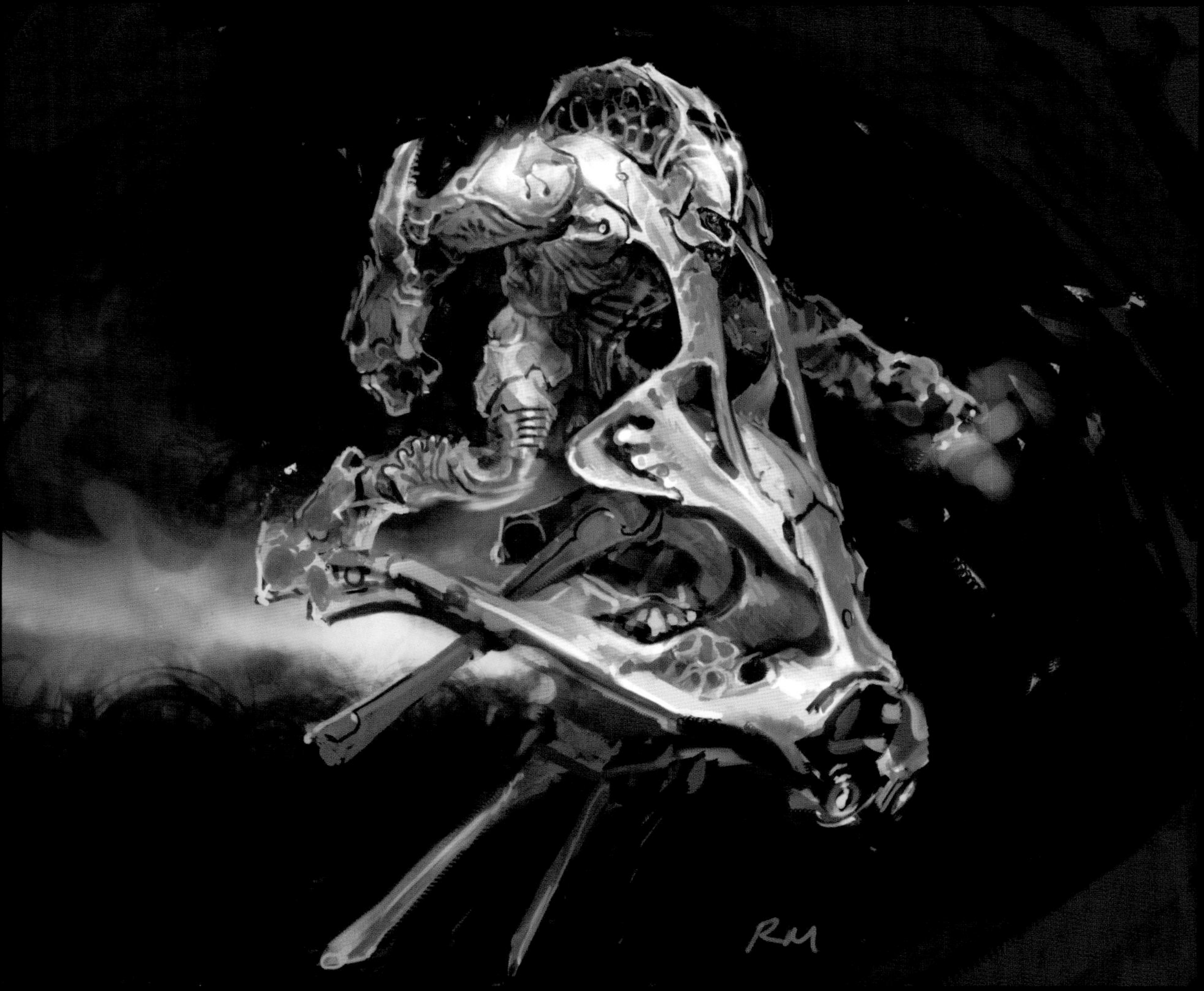
RM

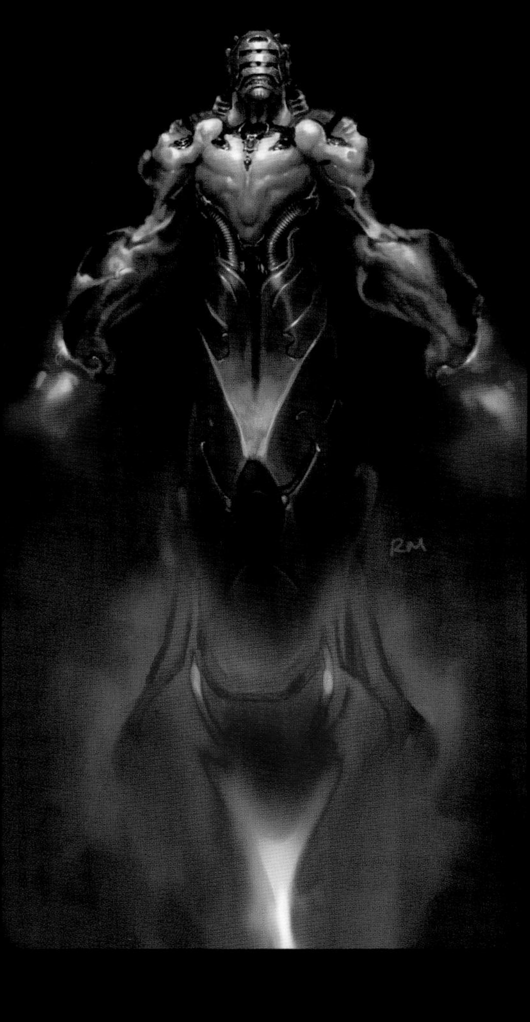
RM

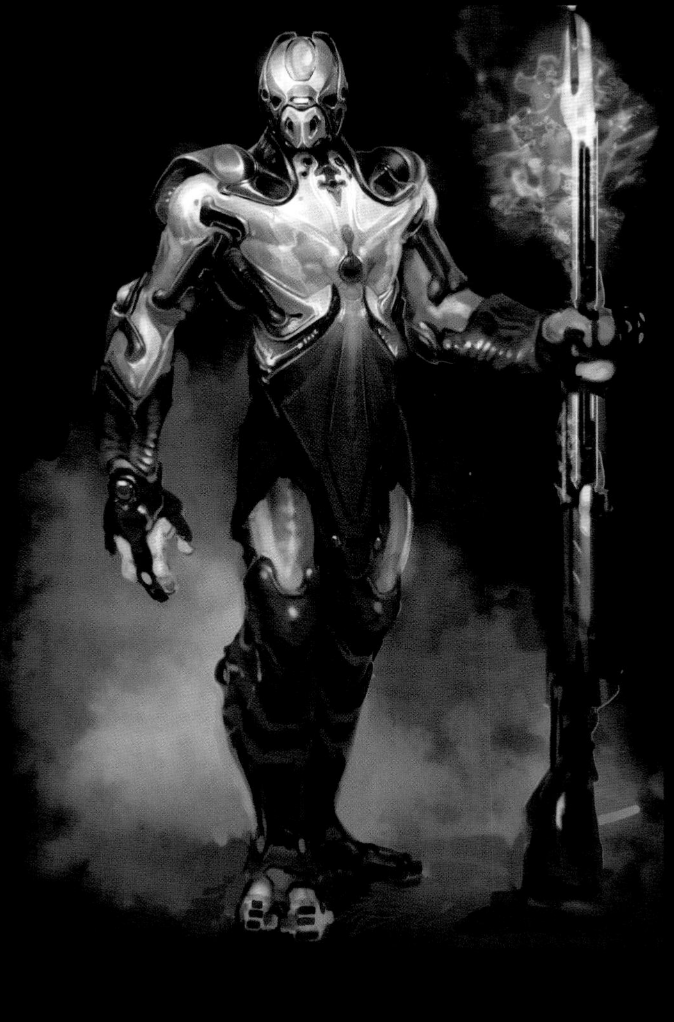

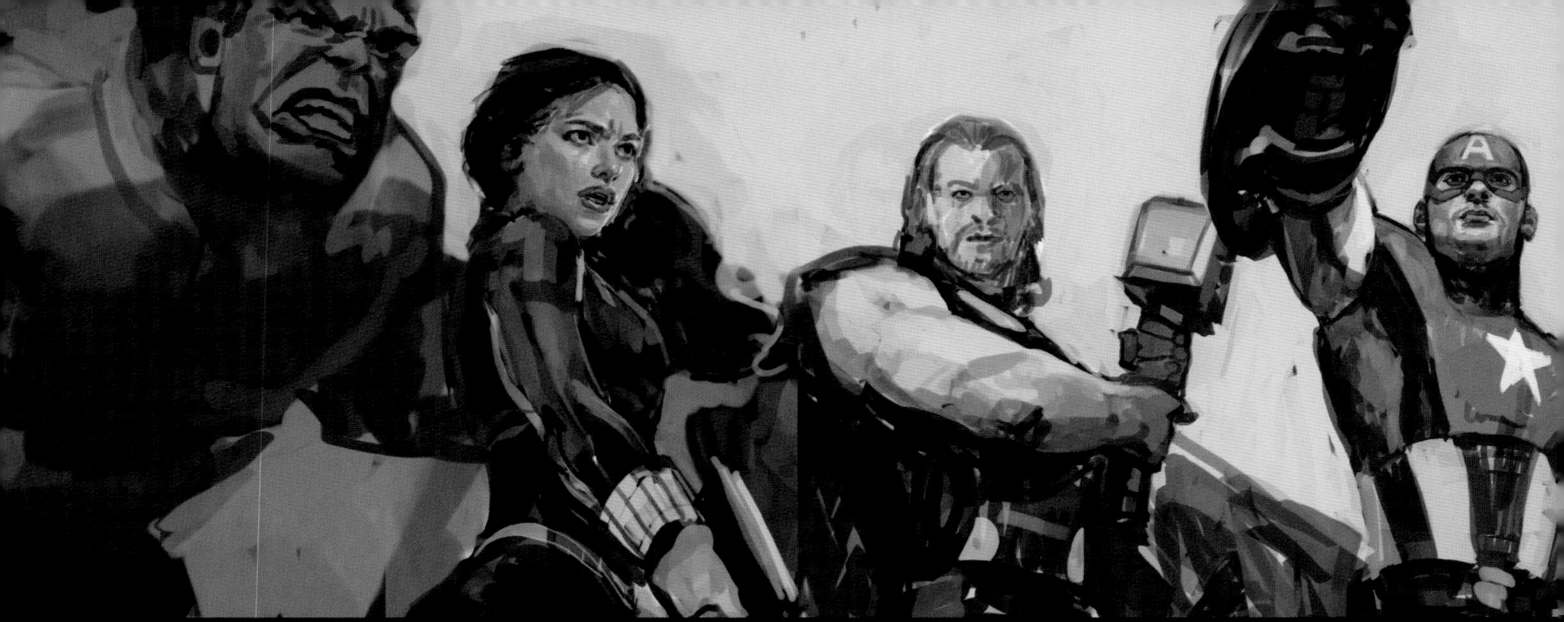

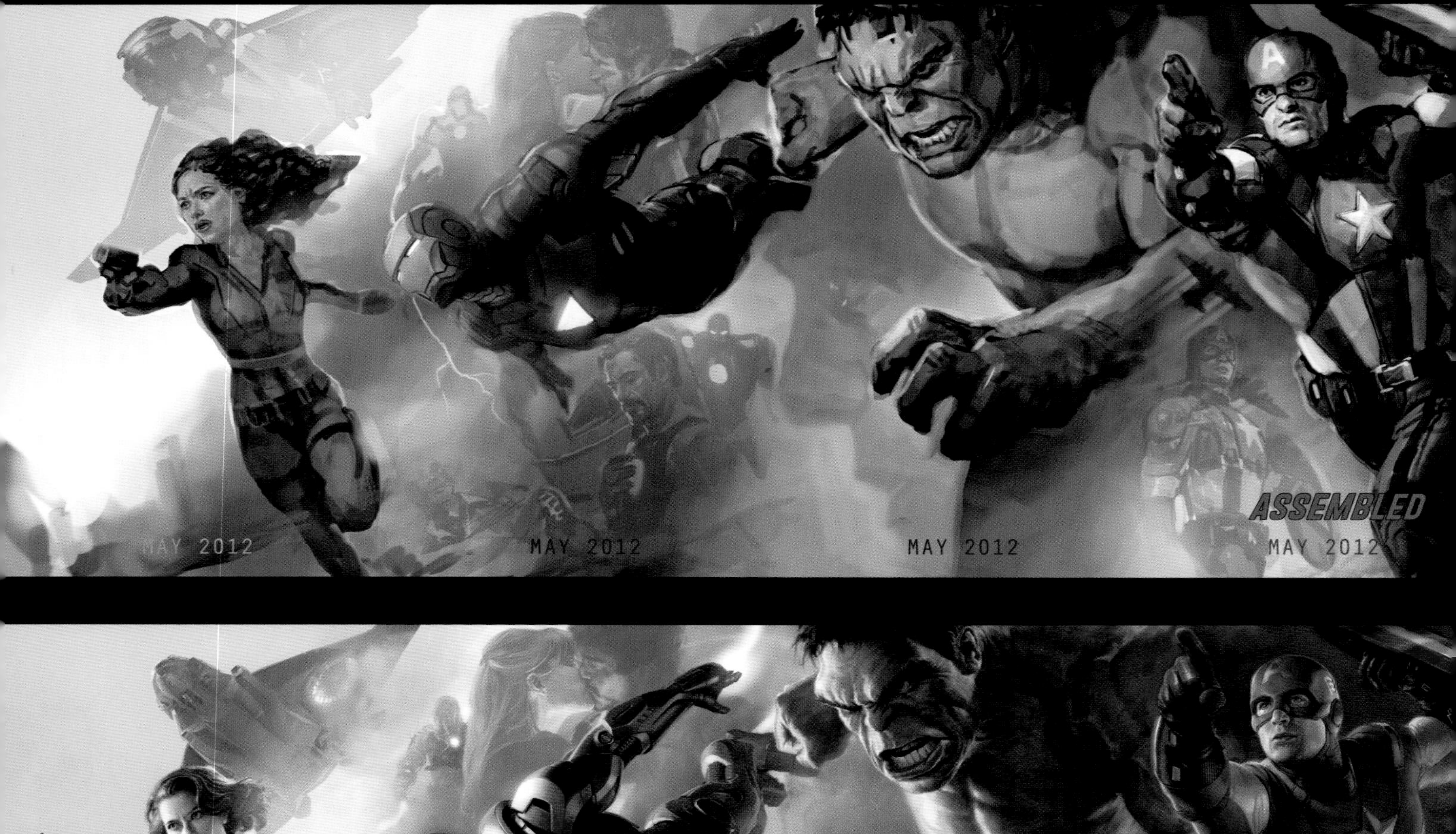

MAY 2012
MAY 2012
MAY 2012
ASSEMBLED
MAY 2012

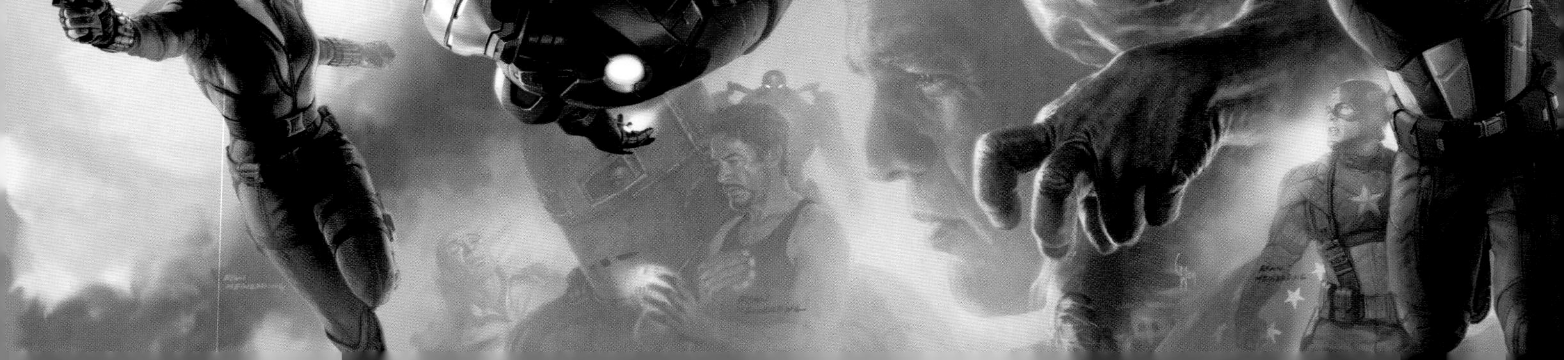

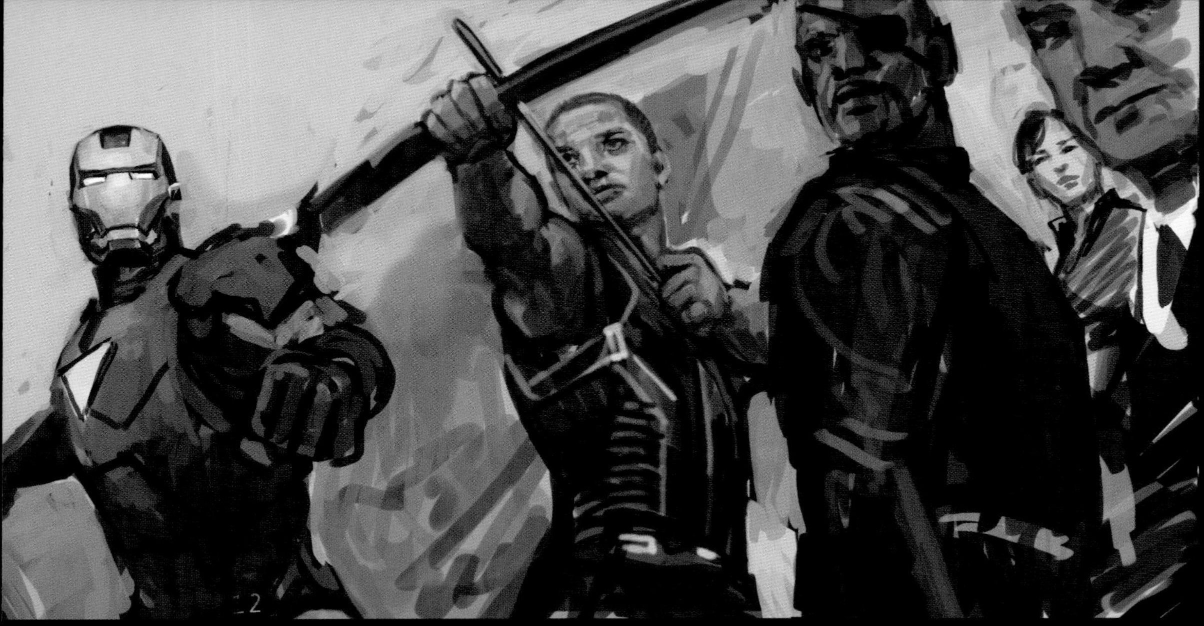

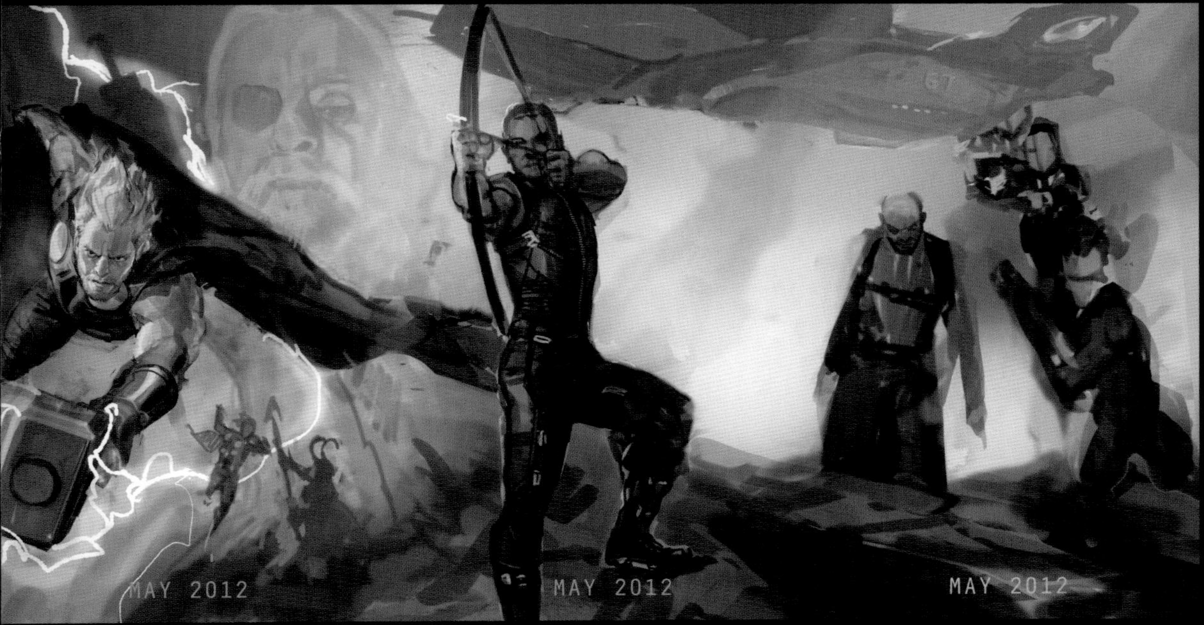
MAY 2012
MAY 2012
MAY 2012

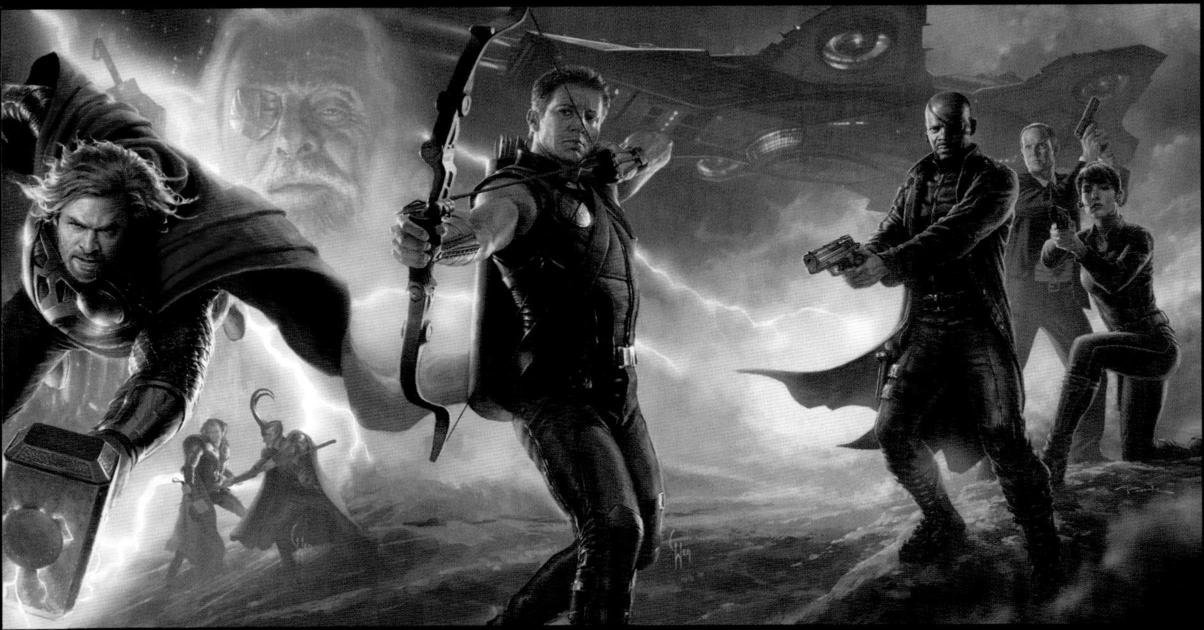

LEFT Working off of Meinerding's comp (center), Charlie Wen completed Hulk, Thor, and Hawkeye while Andy Park completed Nick Fury, Agent Colson, and Maria Hill.

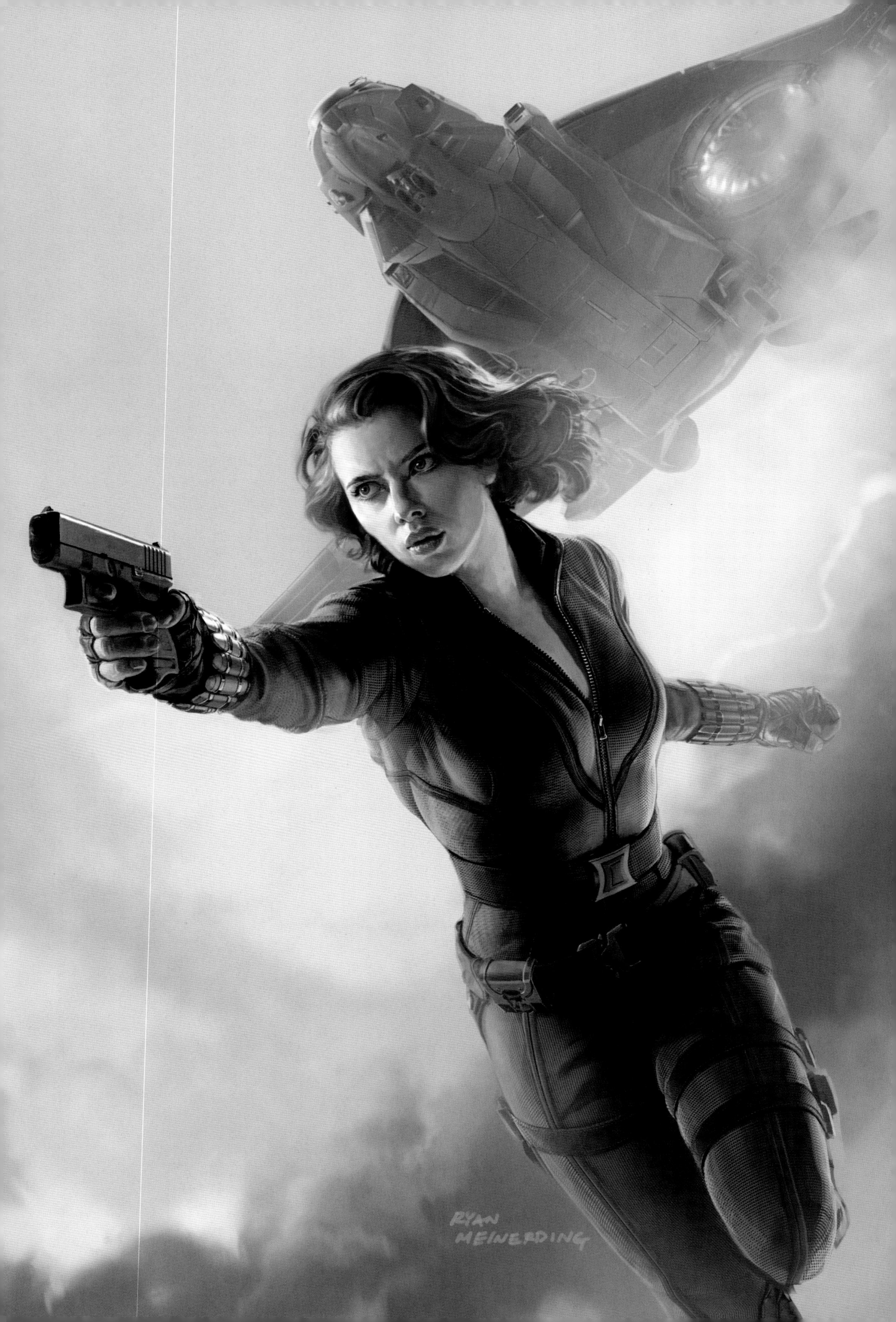
RYAN
MEINERDING

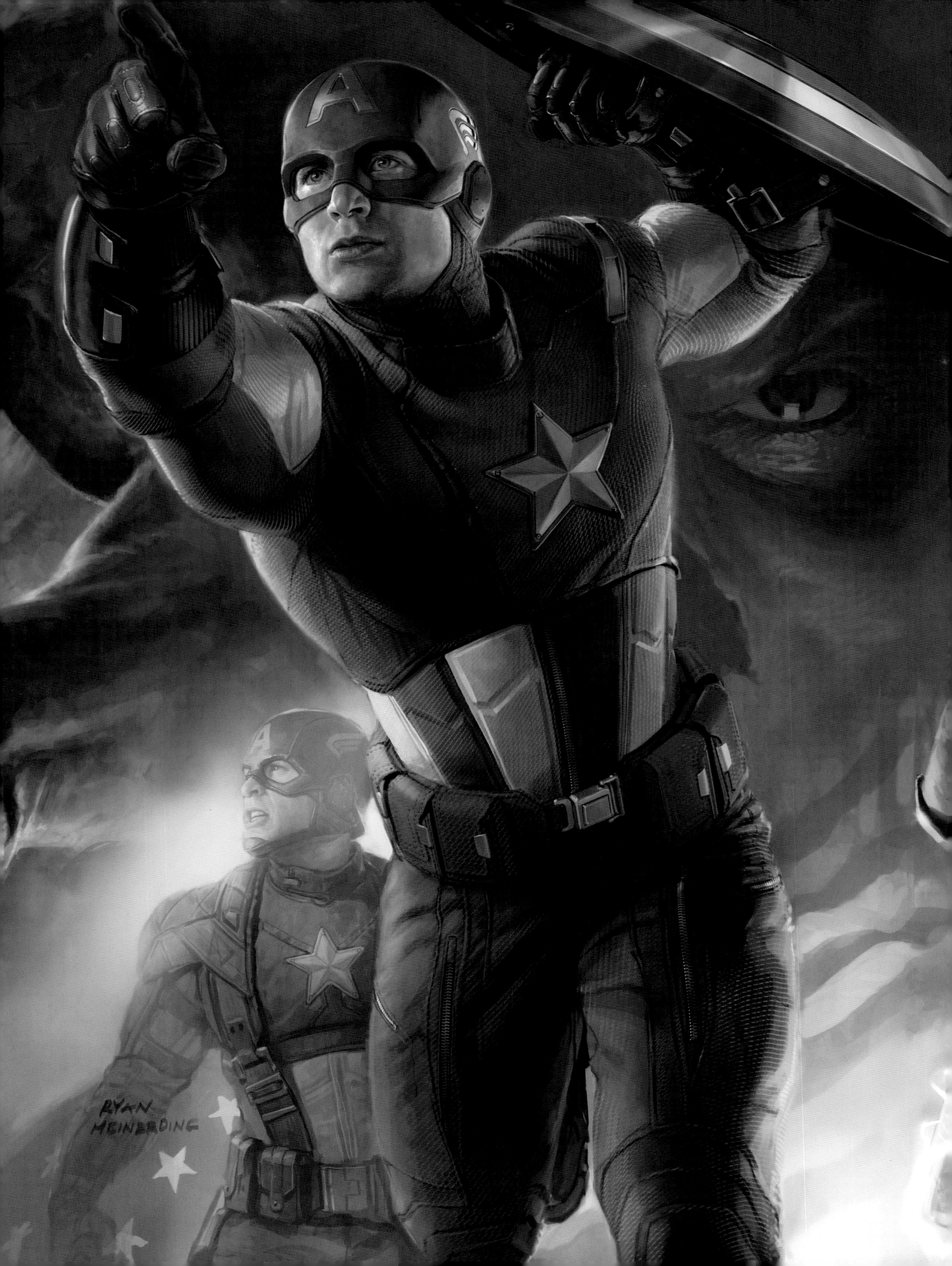
RYAN
MEINERDING

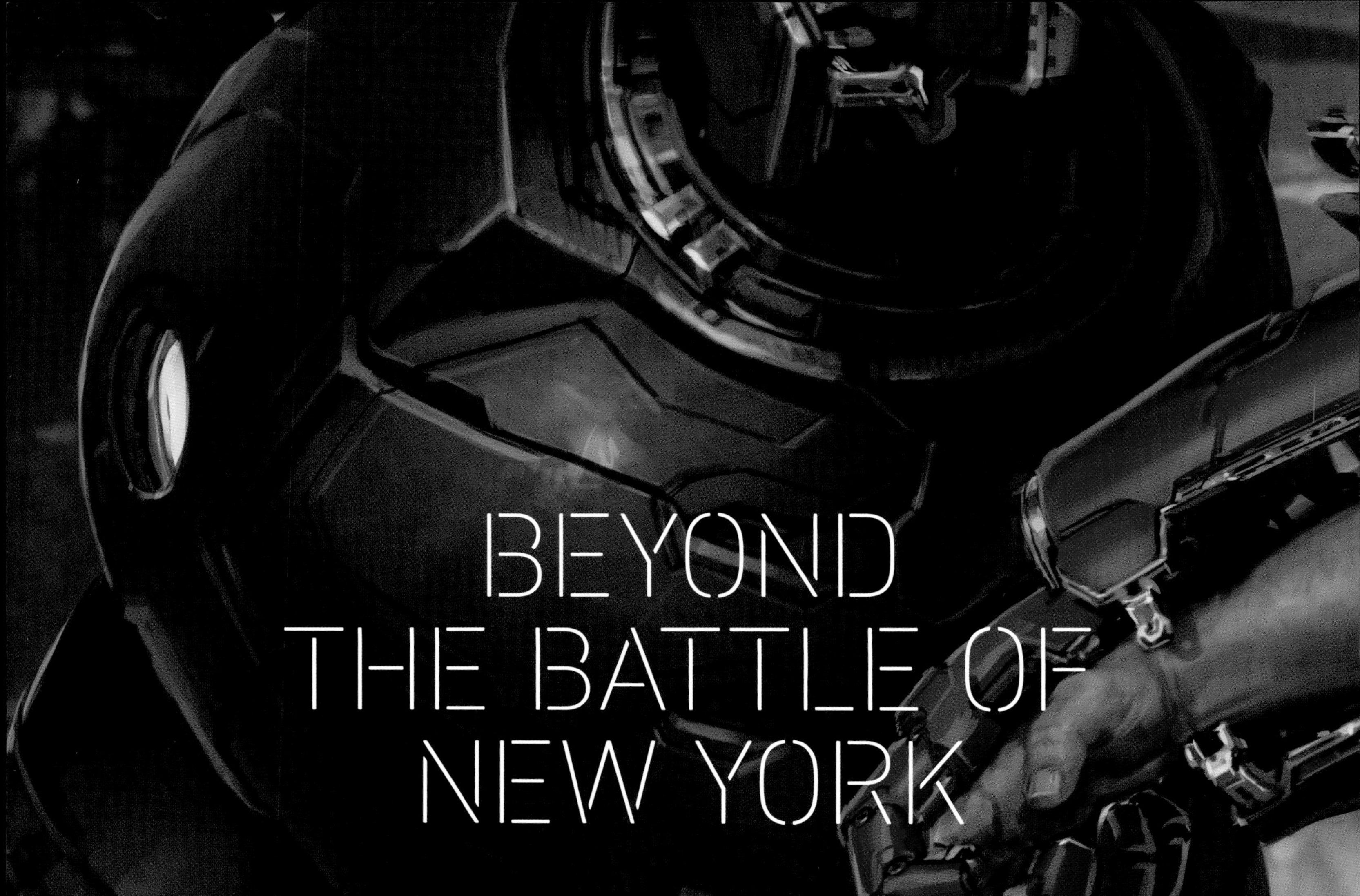

BEYOND THE BATTLE OF NEW YORK

Marvel's The Avengers was a critical, audience, and box office phenomenon. Internally, its success was also definitive proof that all of the design efforts led by Meinerding and the visual development artists to make sure the characters could exist together in a cohesive visual universe worked. It was a watershed moment for Visual Development and spurred the studio's ambition to add more realms and characters into the Marvel Cinematic Universe, which meant an increase in design work for Meinerding and Wen.

With new directors and screenwriters coming into the Marvel Studios fold, Meinerding says it became part of their introduction to understand what in-house visual development was, because it didn't exist in this fashion at other studios. "I don't know if there's another team like ours within Marvel Studios where we're so helpful at an early stage of the project, and where we're also relied upon for most of production or most of preproduction," he explains. "There are things that our group does that helps the productions in important ways, like figuring out what a character does. And hopefully, we get that done early so it can filter to visual effects and costume. Key frames also help Kevin understand and sell the movie; the same with the directors."

After *Avengers*, Meinerding returned to the world of Tony Stark in *Iron Man 3*, continuing his long history with the character. For this movie, which had more disparate characters than ever, he was often associated with development of the more grounded, Earth-based characters. "I was working on the stuff that was probably more rooted in the actual reference of the comics and trying to reinterpret and reimagine them for the story world," he explains.

"From *Avengers* onward, this place had more interesting work to do than I have capacity to accomplish," he says. "Coming up with the most effective use of my time is basically how I spend my time." As the planned film slate grew, Meinerding says he had to let the development of interesting new characters, and even his association to certain sequels, go to his talented colleagues.

With an ever-renewing slate of upcoming movies, Meinerding admits listening to his artistic gut would often determine his choices. "If I feel like I'm super inspired to do something, that's usually when I'll take [a film] on, because the best work will come out of me. Hopefully, the work will be the most inspiring to other people as well," he says. "And Kevin, obviously, has strong viewpoints on some of those things. He'll tell me very specifically that he wants to see this or he wants to see that. Obviously, that's a very easy organizing principle of what I should be working on, too."

As *Avengers: Age of Ultron* then came into development, the number of characters and set pieces meant that Meinerding and Wen decided to split the massive workload to create a feasible division of labor.

"I had voiced an interest in working on Hulkbuster and Vision, while he was going to design Ultron," he explains. "But we also wanted to give each other enough space to do takes on other things. As such, director Joss Whedon ultimately chose Meinerding's design for Ultron's head, while Wen and Phil Saunders designed a body that Joss and Kevin approved.

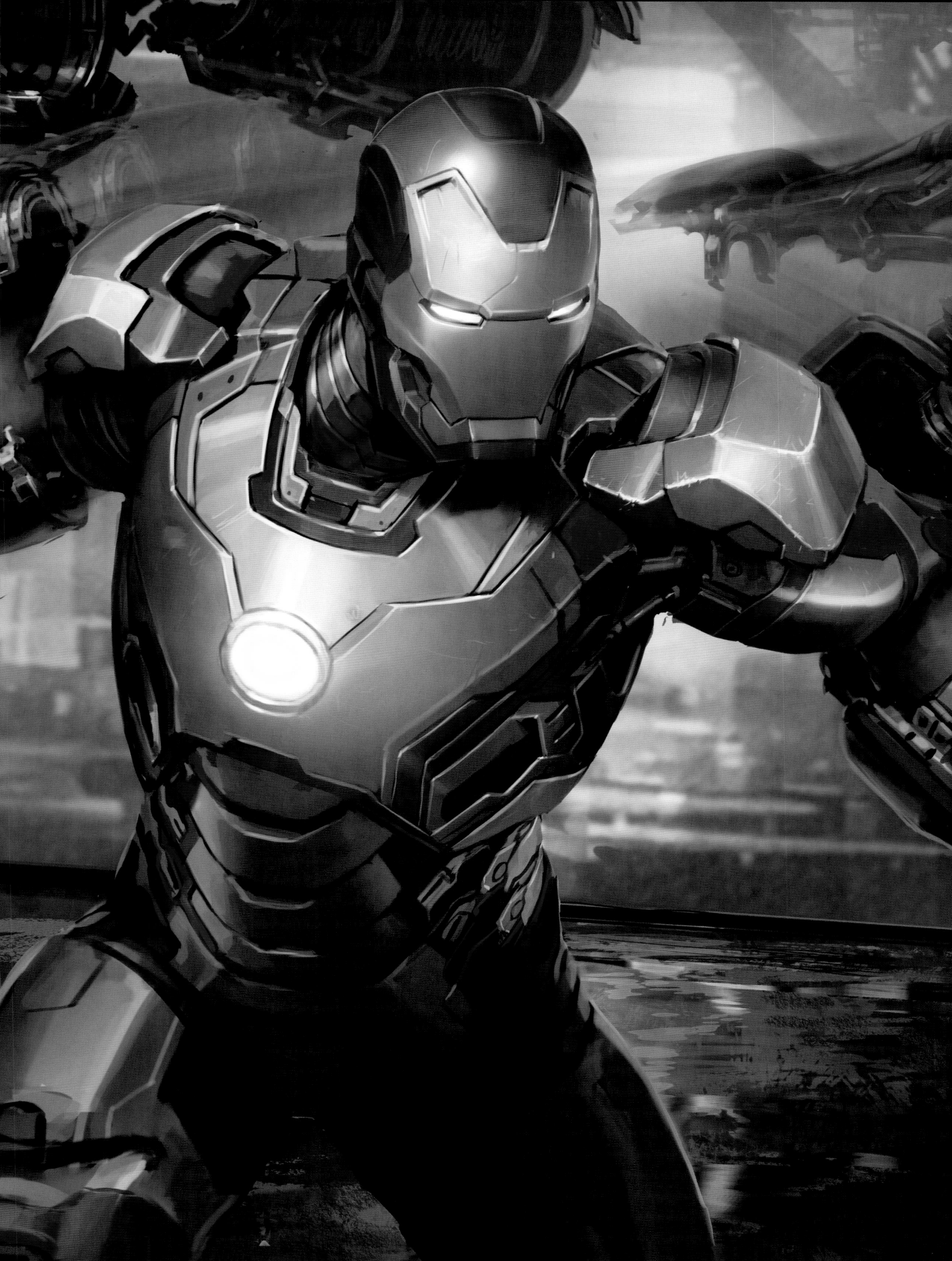

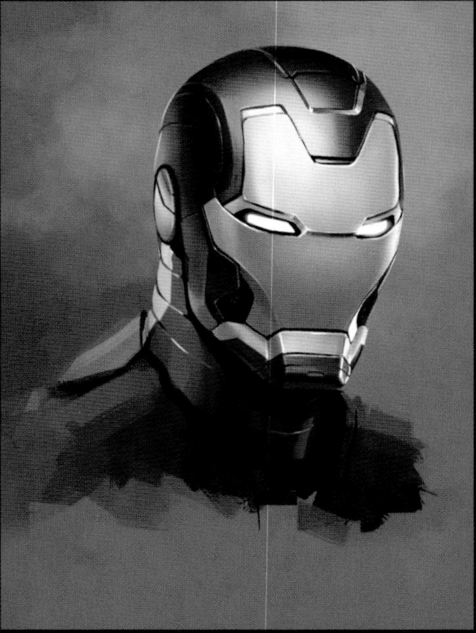

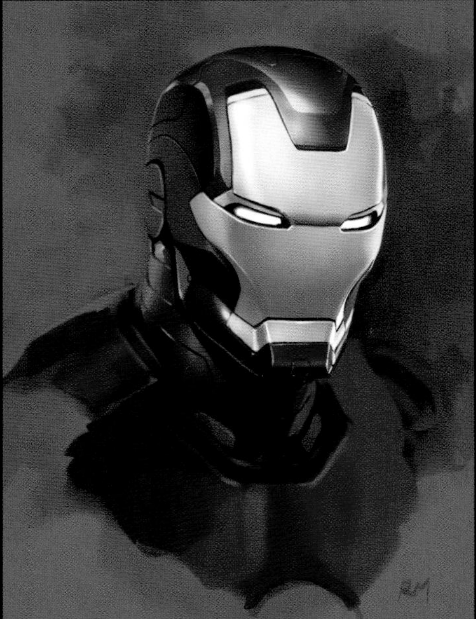
RM

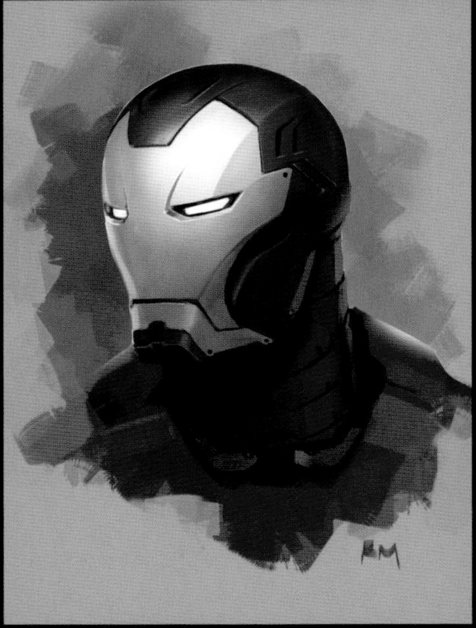
RM

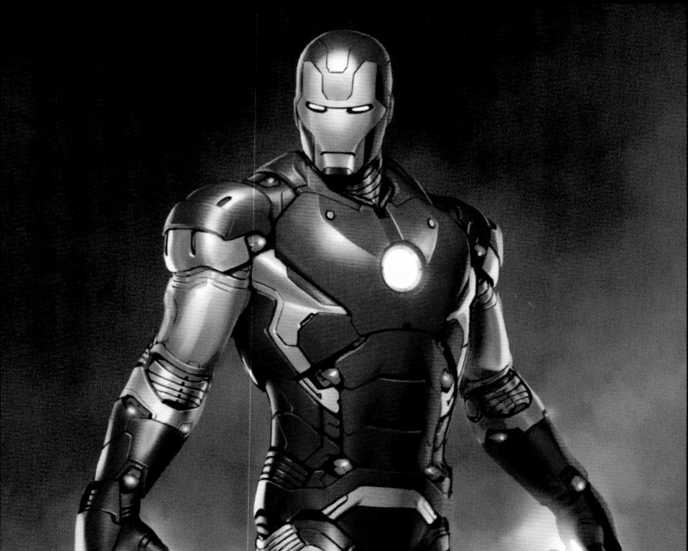
RM

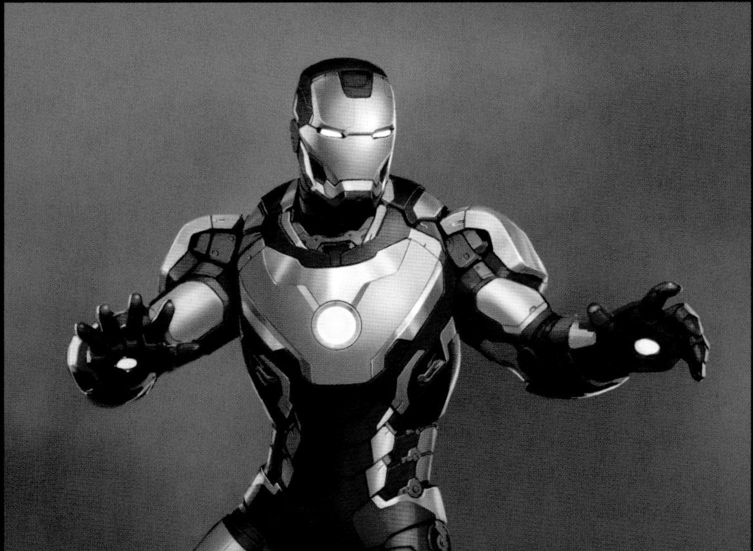

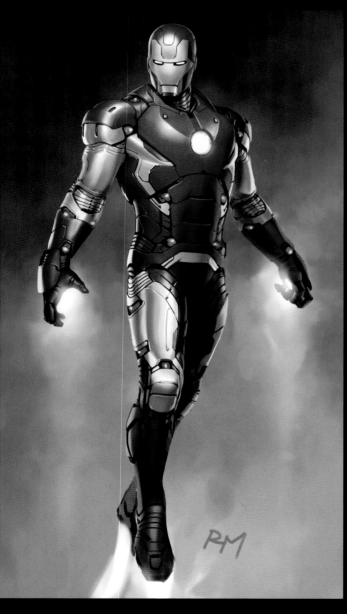

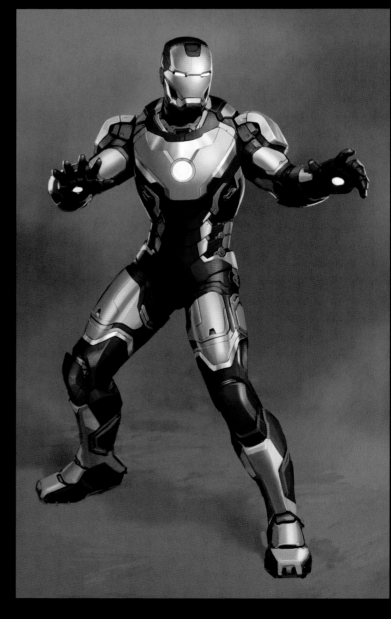

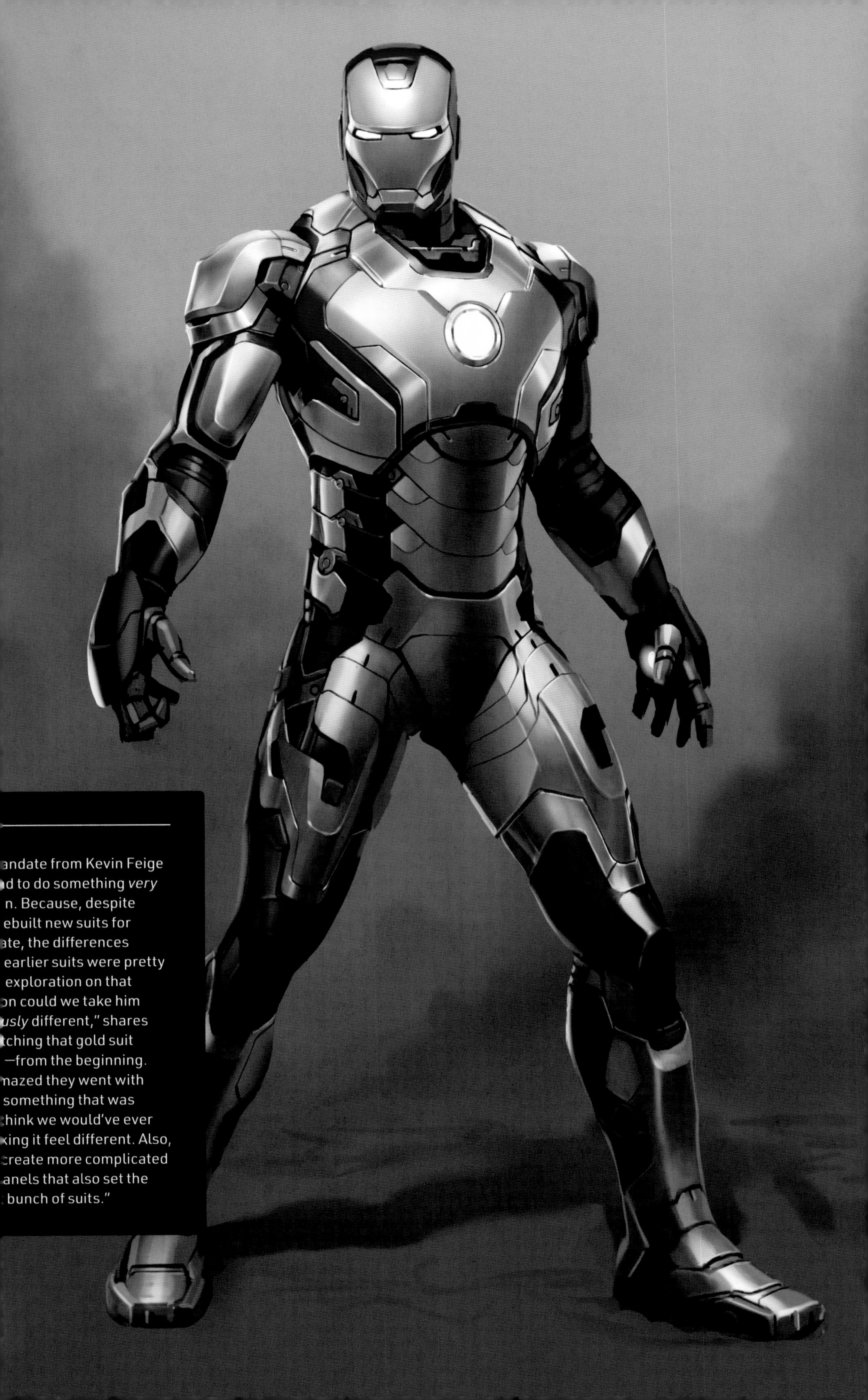

andate from Kevin Feige
d to do something *very*
n. Because, despite
ebuilt new suits for
ate, the differences
earlier suits were pretty
exploration on that
on could we take him
usly different," shares
tching that gold suit
—from the beginning.
mazed they went with
something that was
hink we would've ever
king it feel different. Also,
create more complicated
anels that also set the
bunch of suits."

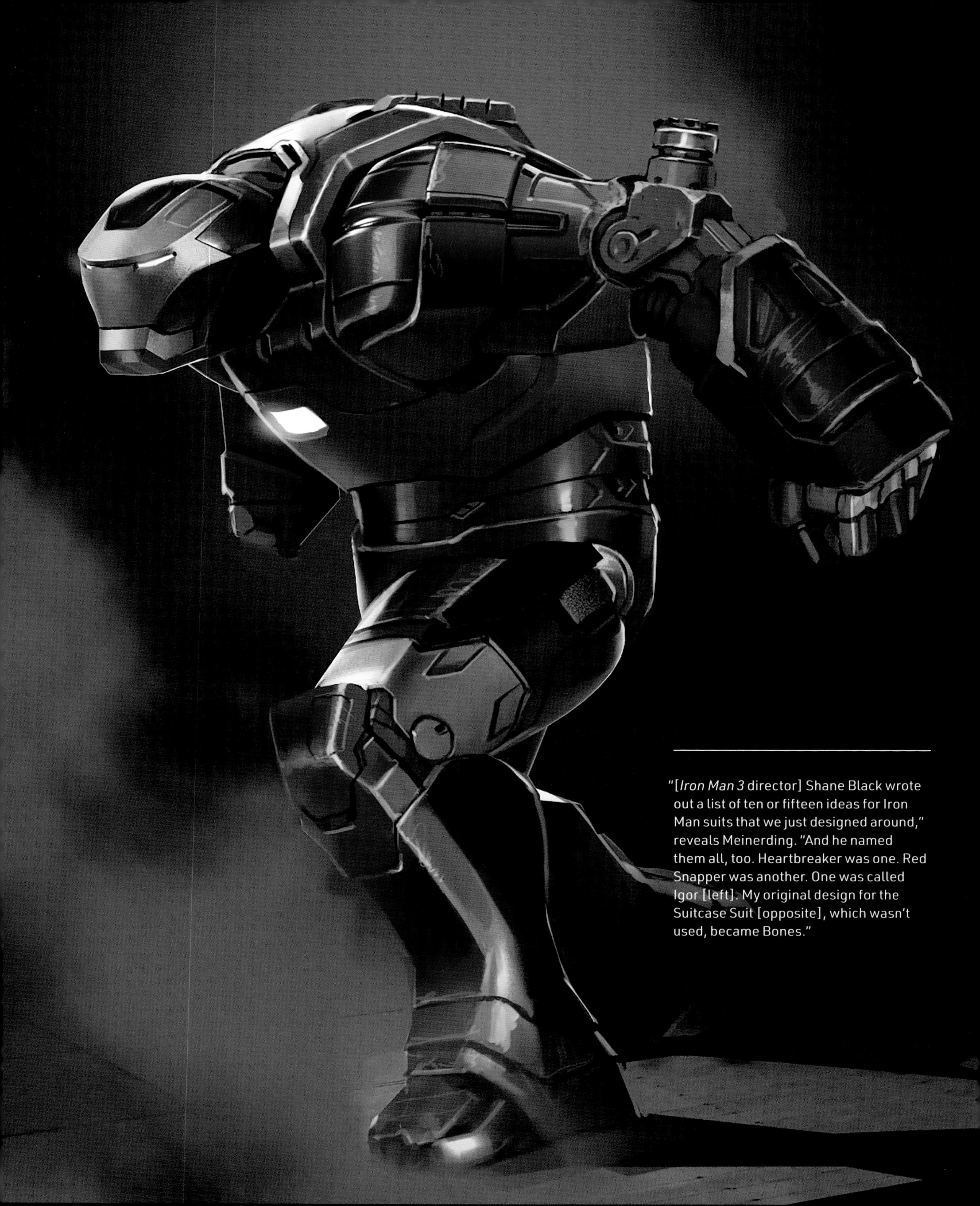

"[*Iron Man 3* director] Shane Black wrote out a list of ten or fifteen ideas for Iron Man suits that we just designed around," reveals Meinerding. "And he named them all, too. Heartbreaker was one. Red Snapper was another. One was called Igor [left]. My original design for the Suitcase Suit [opposite], which wasn't used, became Bones."

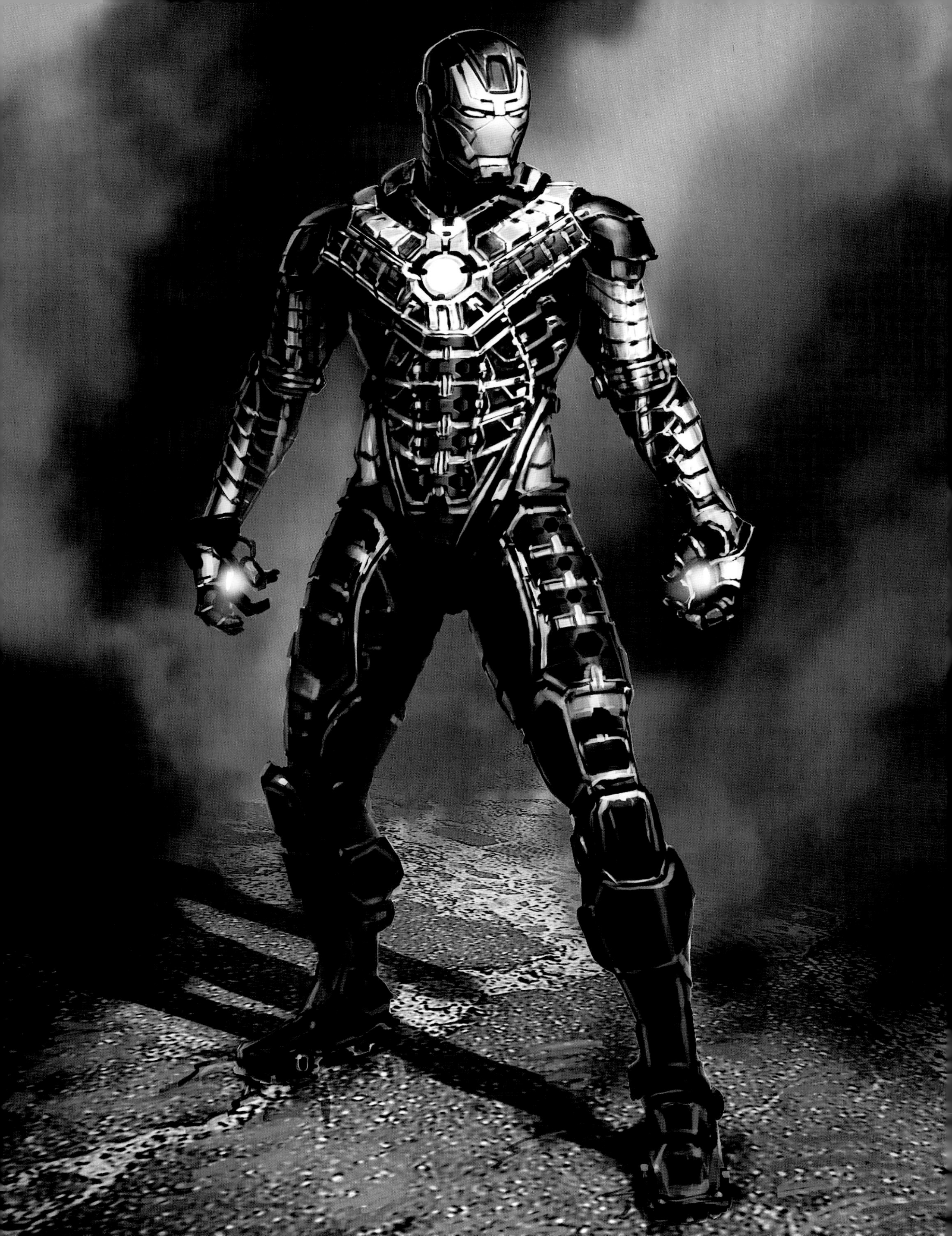

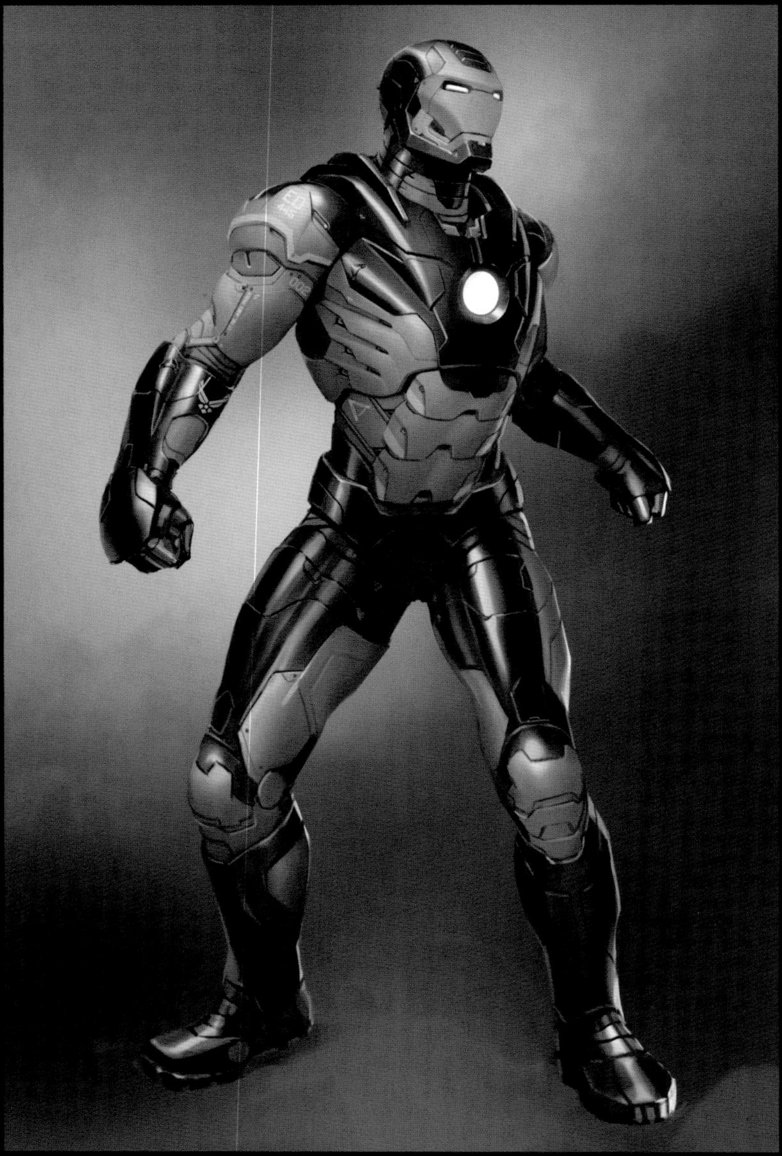

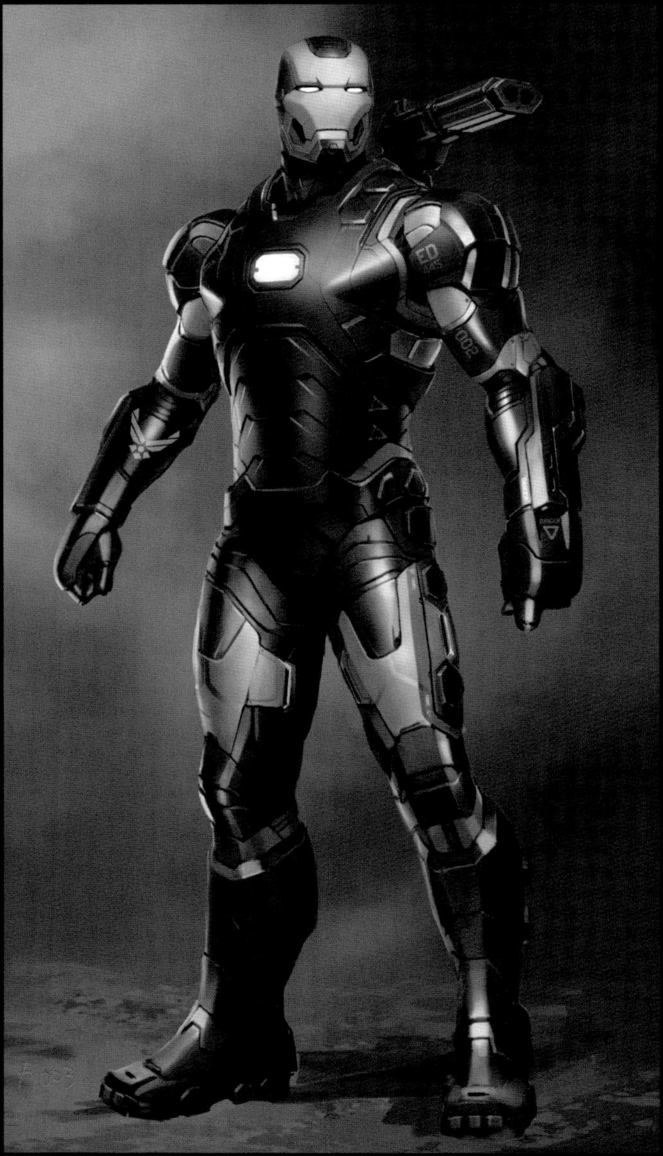

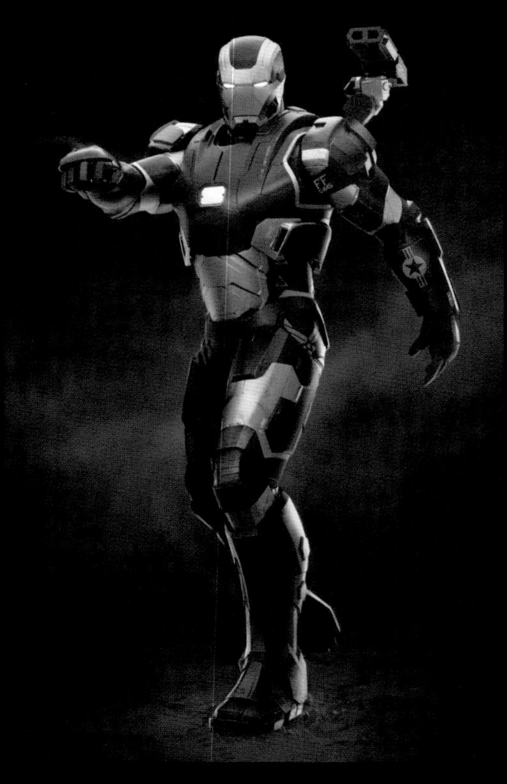

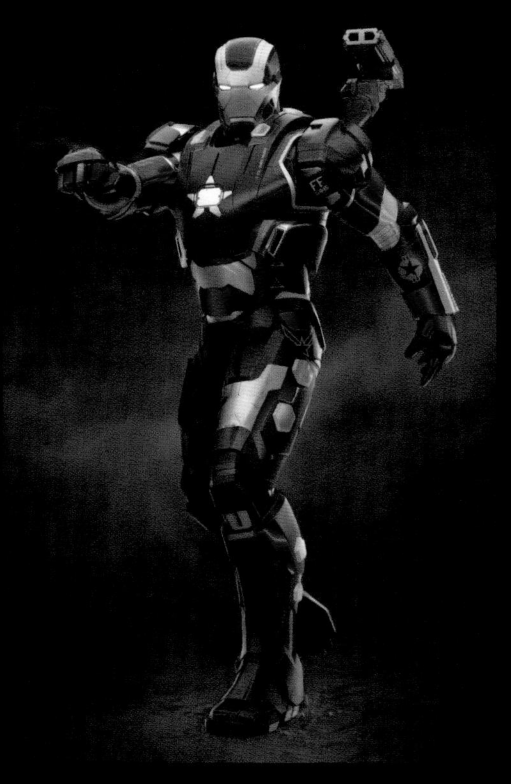

LEFT War Machine and Iron Patriot armor based on 3D models by Josh Herman

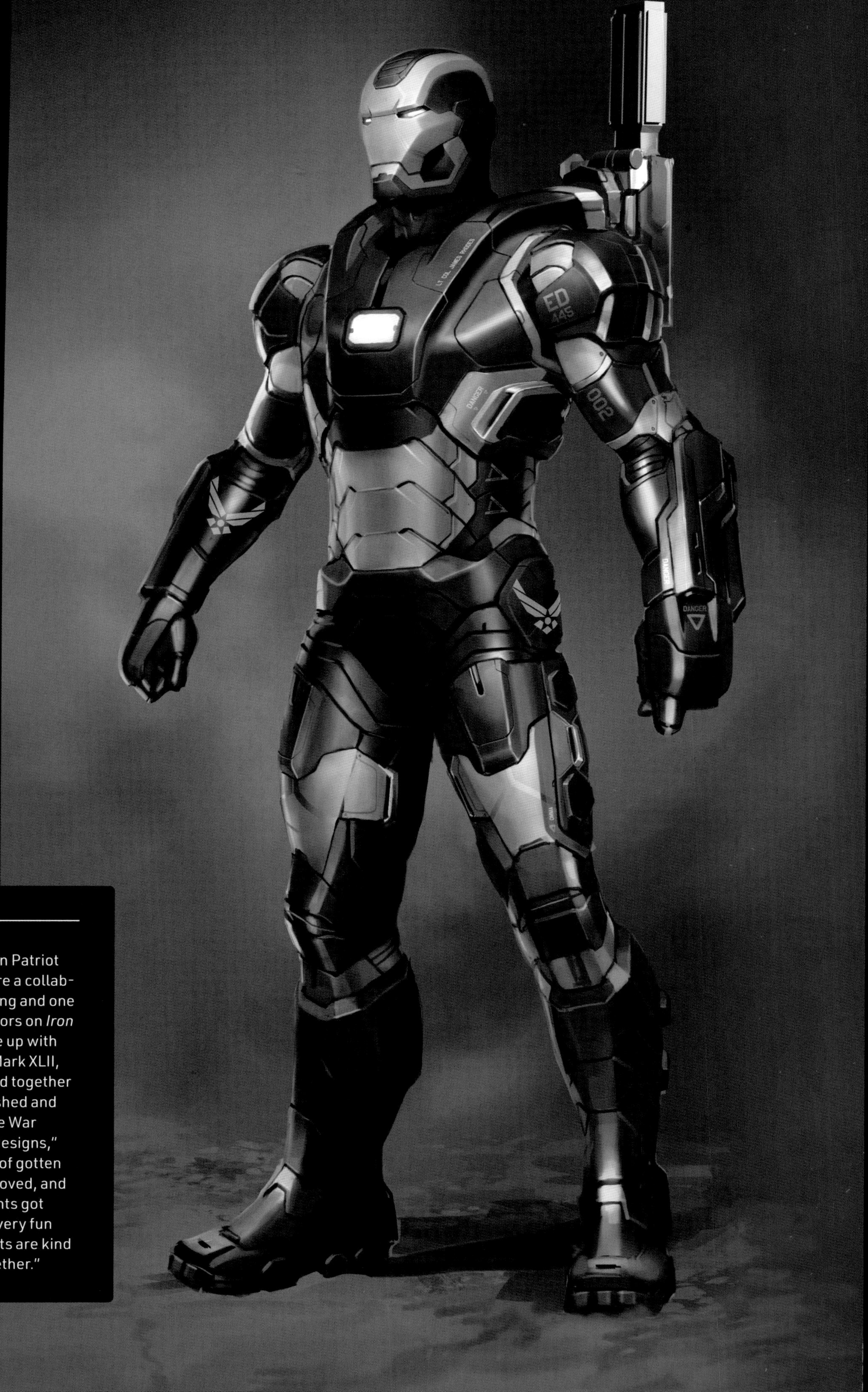
ED
445
DANGER

The final War Machine/Iron Patriot designs for *Iron Man 3* were a collaboration between Meinerding and one of his Stark suit collaborators on *Iron Man*. "Although I had come up with the original image of the Mark XLII, Phil Saunders and I worked together to get it approved and finished and did the same thing with the War Machine and Iron Patriot designs," says Meinerding. "I'd kind of gotten the original direction approved, and then some of Phil's elements got combined with it. It was a very fun project, because those suits are kind of a mix of us working together."

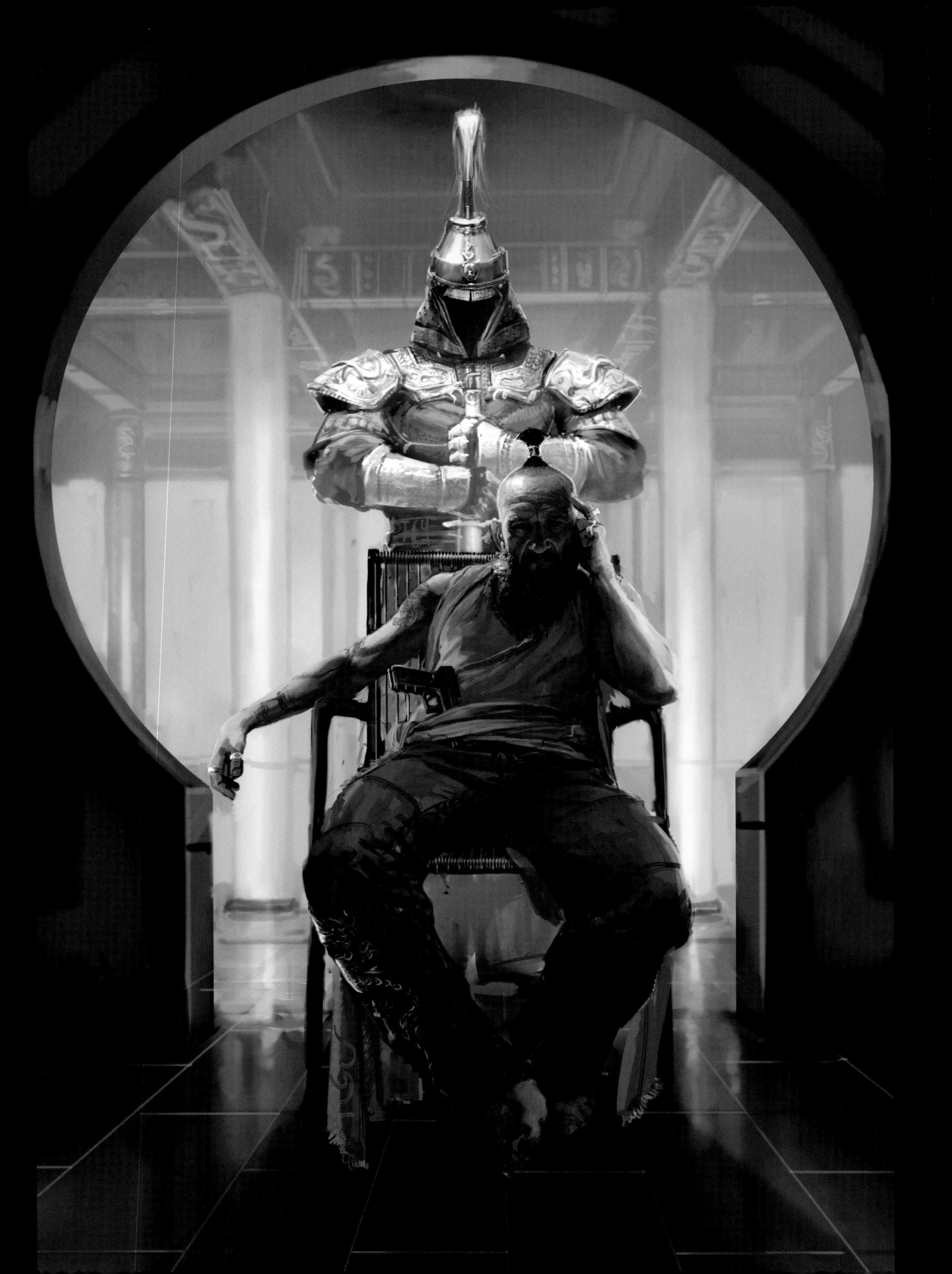

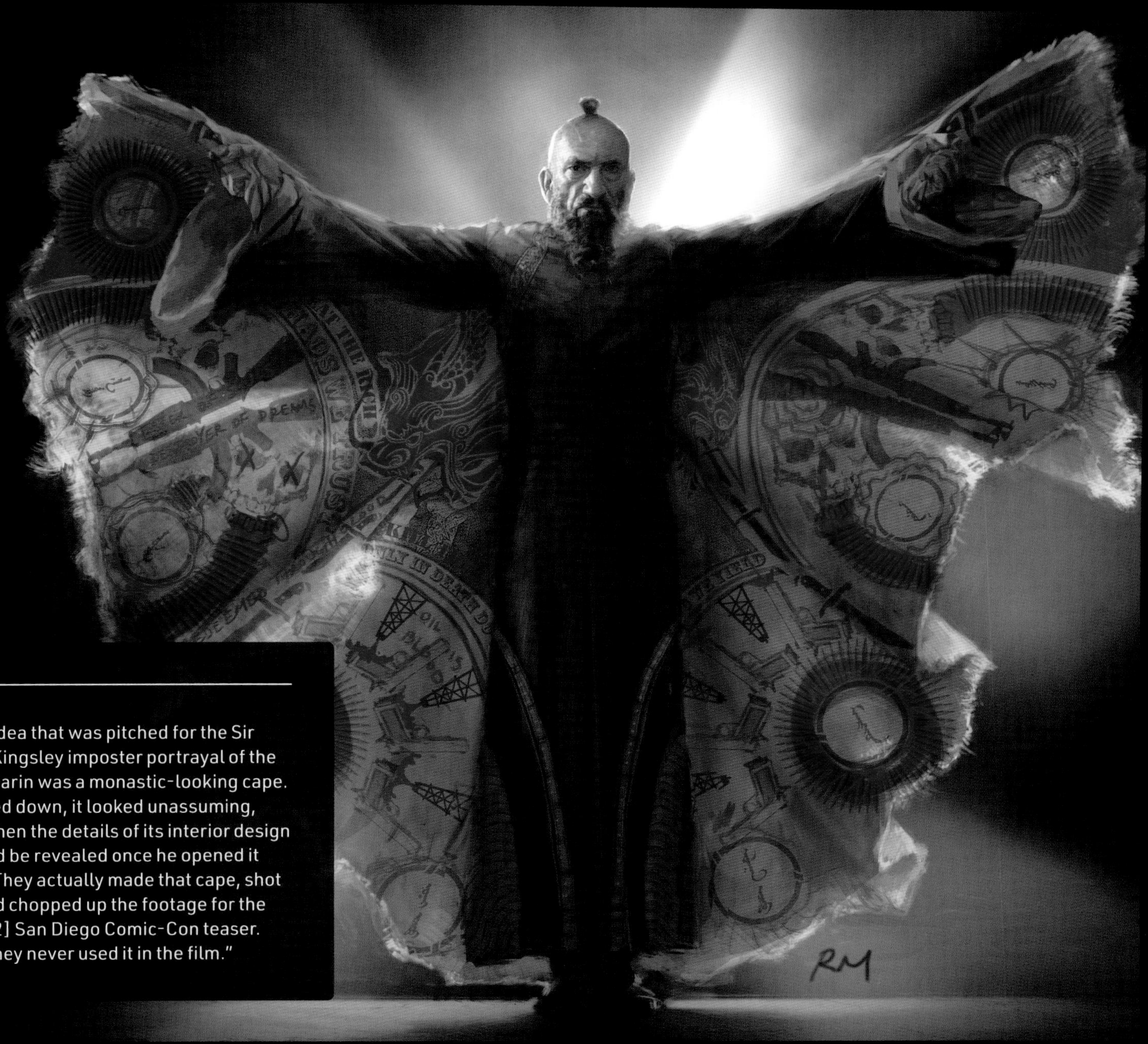

One idea that was pitched for the Sir Ben Kingsley imposter portrayal of the Mandarin was a monastic-looking cape. Folded down, it looked unassuming, and then the details of its interior design would be revealed once he opened it up. "They actually made that cape, shot it, and chopped up the footage for the [2012] San Diego Comic-Con teaser. But they never used it in the film."

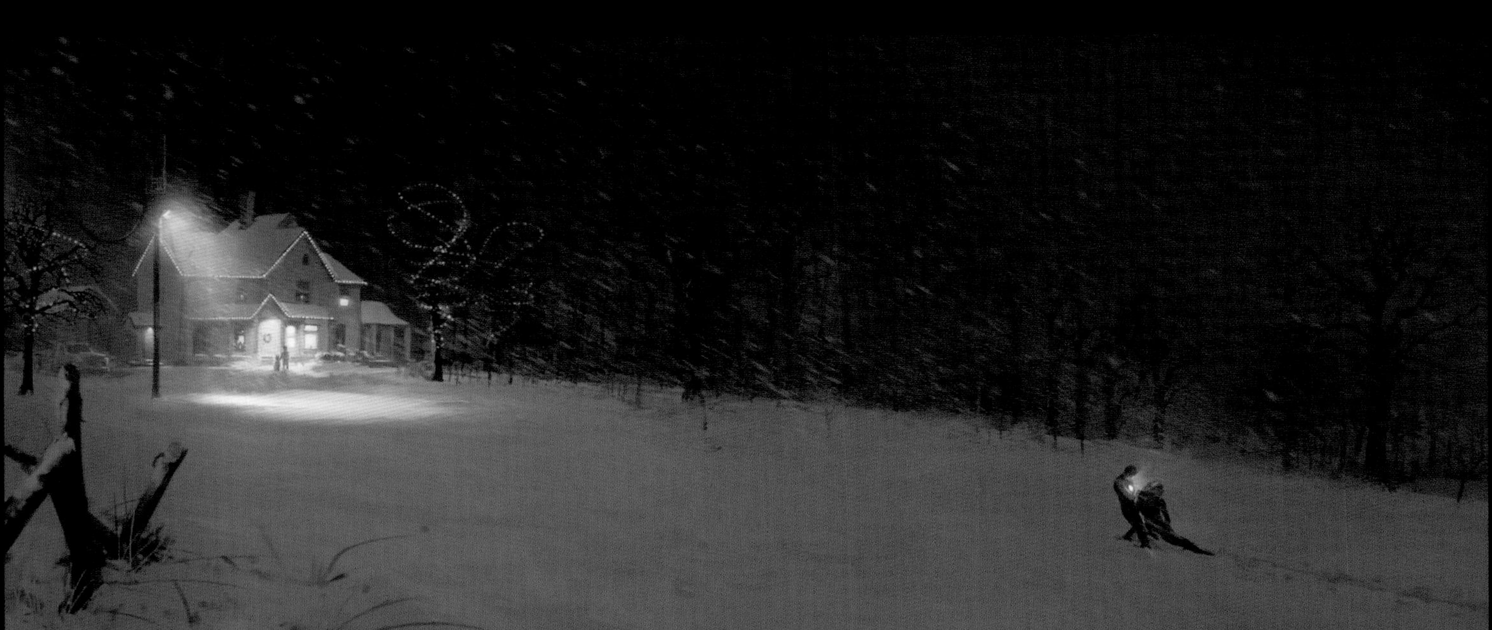

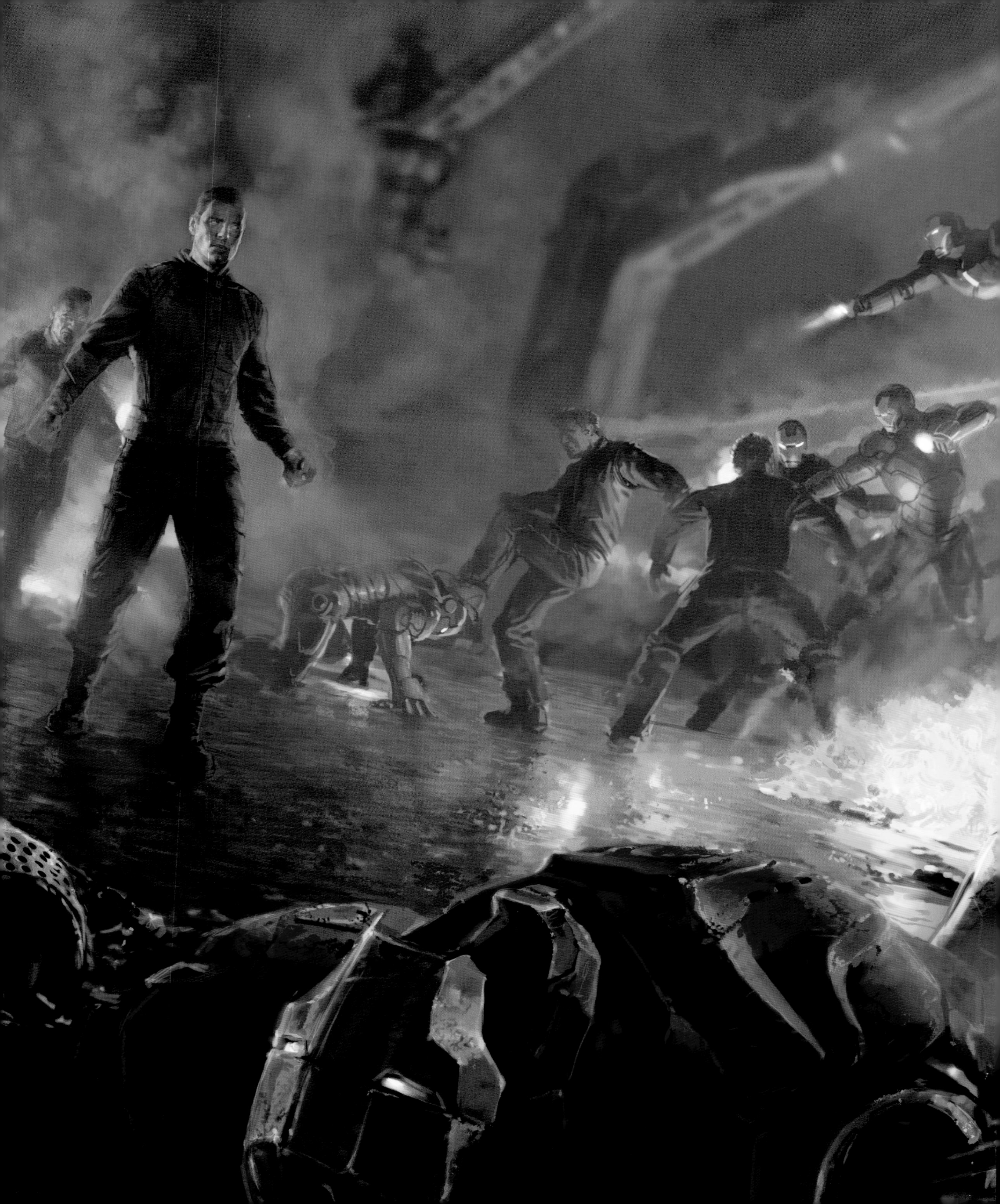

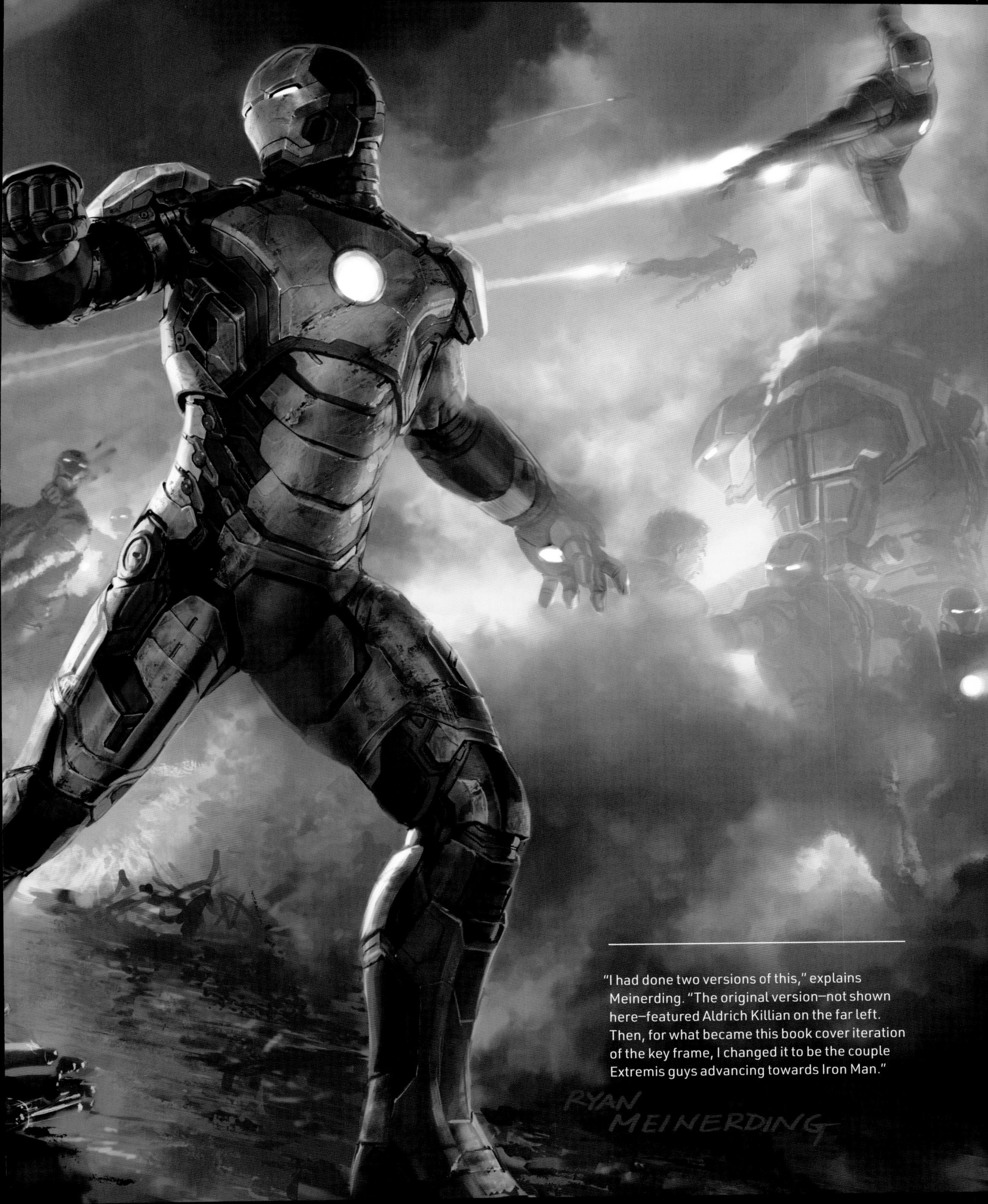
RYAN MEINERDING

"I had done two versions of this," explains Meinerding. "The original version—not shown here—featured Aldrich Killian on the far left. Then, for what became this book cover iteration of the key frame, I changed it to be the couple Extremis guys advancing towards Iron Man."

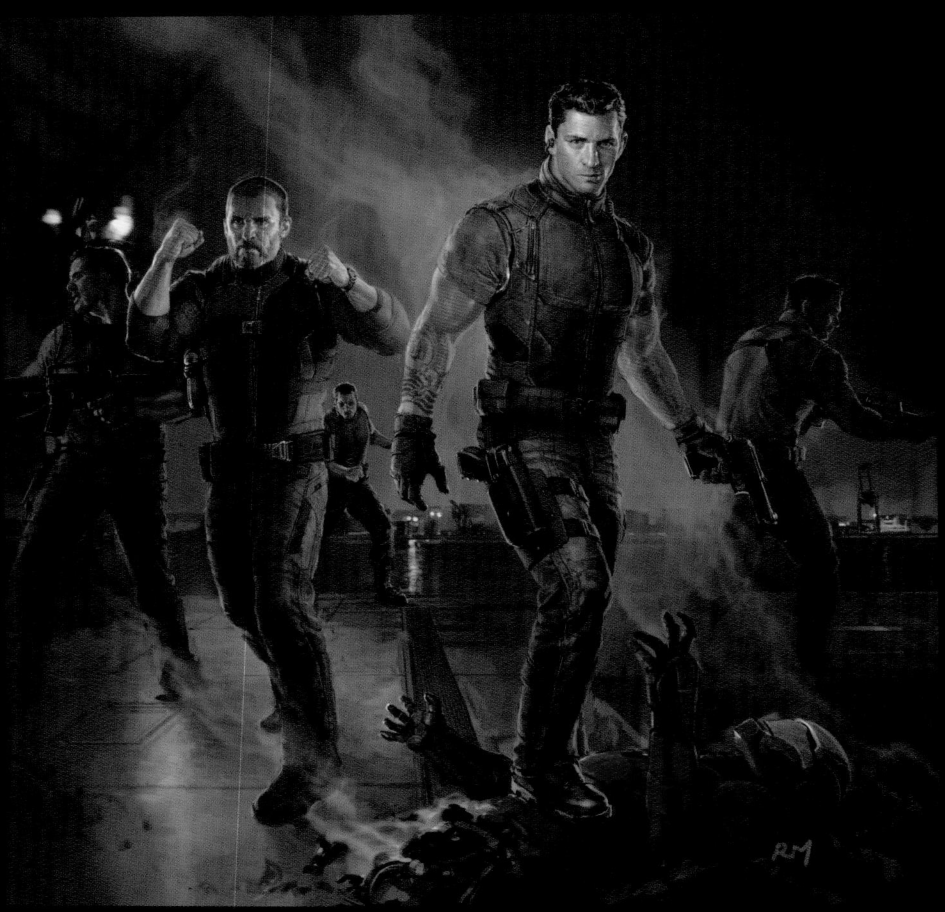
RM

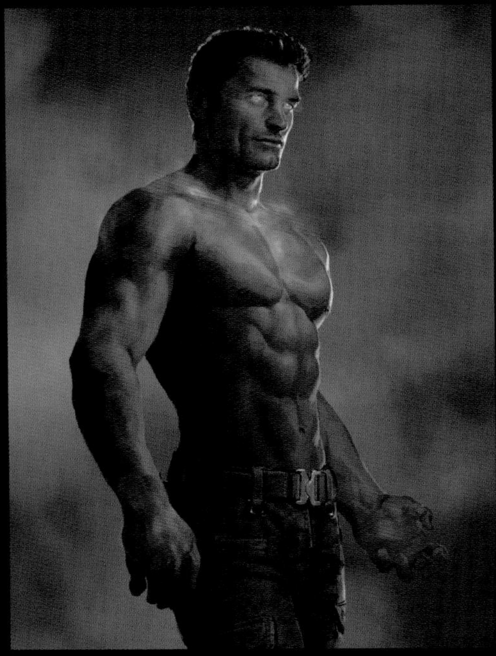

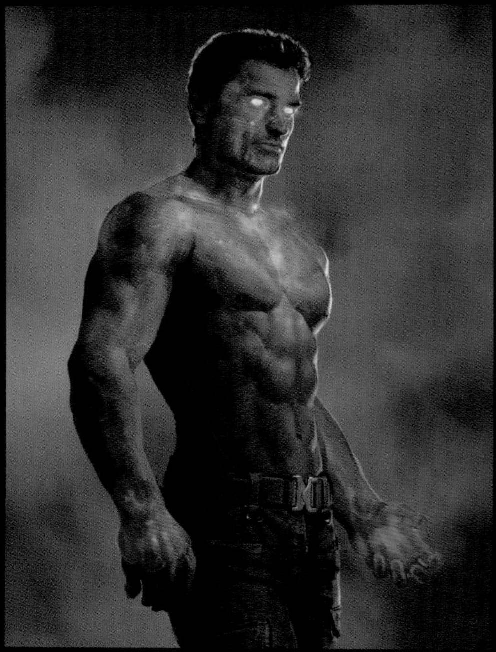

Kevin Feige asked for Meinerding and his Visual Development team to make exploring the Extremis effect a priority for *Iron Man 3*. "We spent weeks and weeks trying to do something that was different than glowing effects, and it was a challenge," admits Meinerding. After developing multiple variations of characters getting a limb cut off and then being able to grow it back with and without bioluminescence, the subcutaneous glowing effects became the agreed path forward.

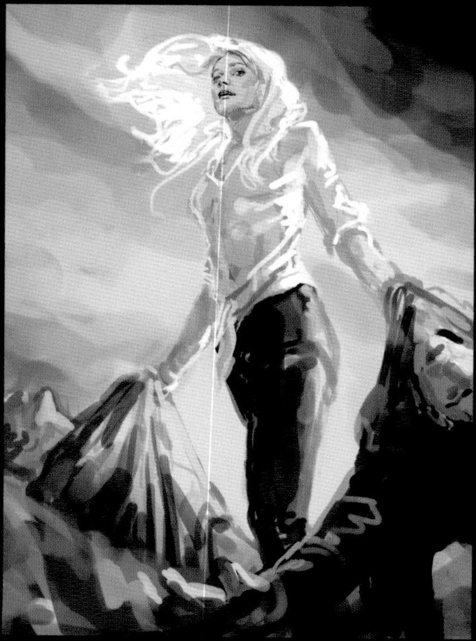

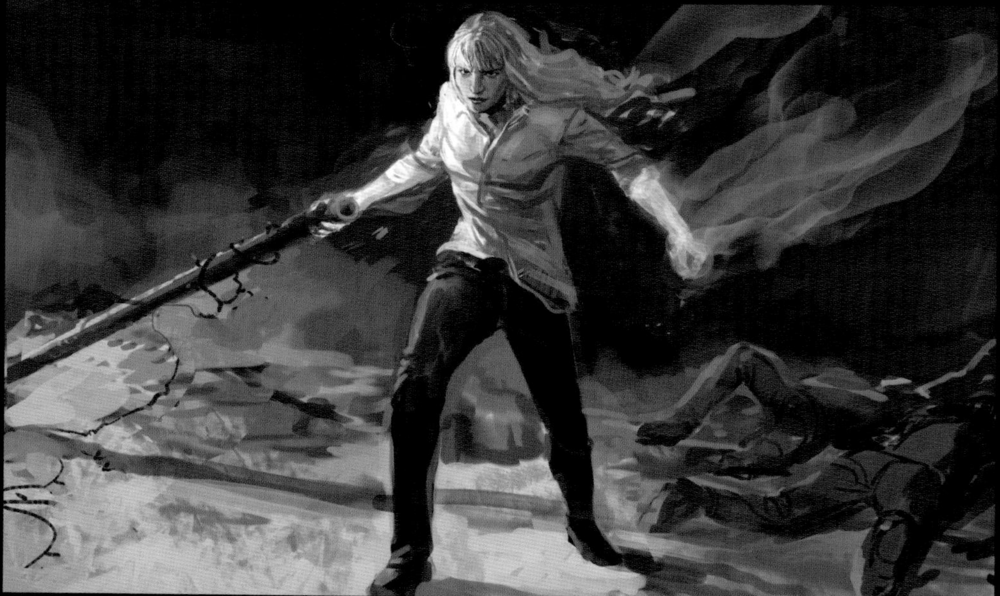

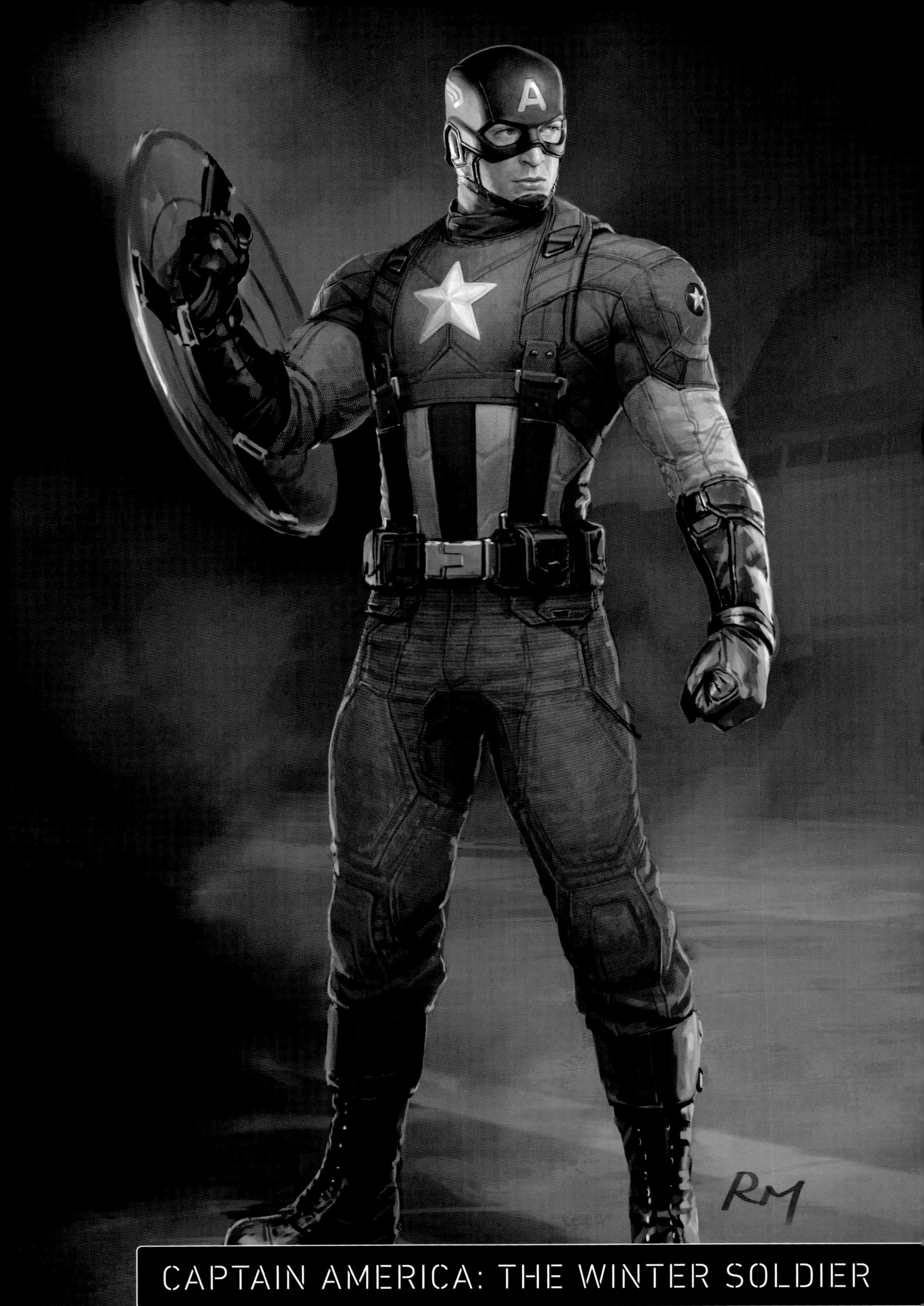
RM

CAPTAIN AMERICA: THE WINTER SOLDIER

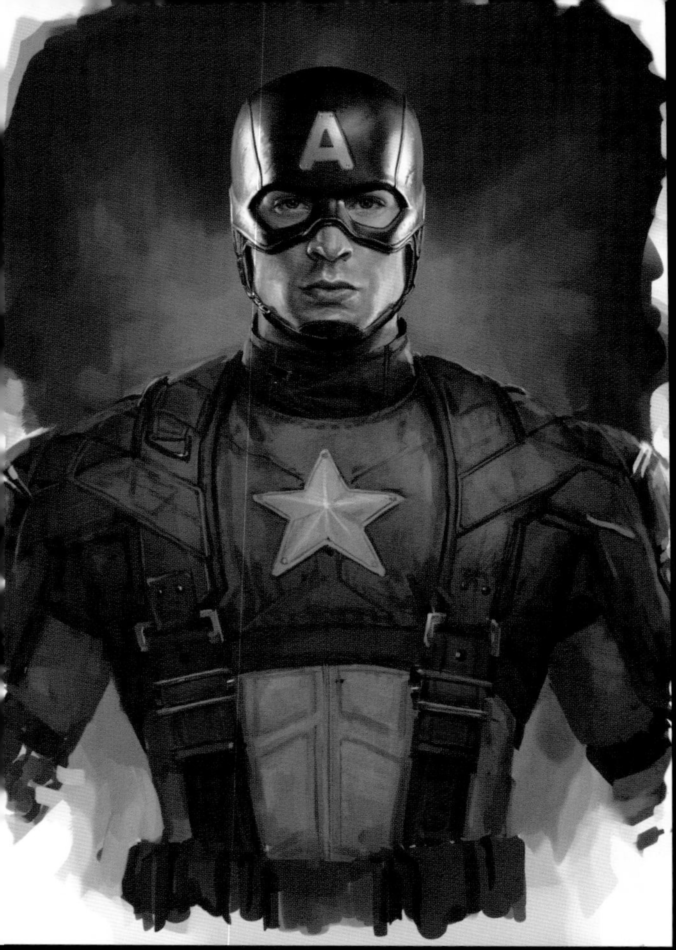
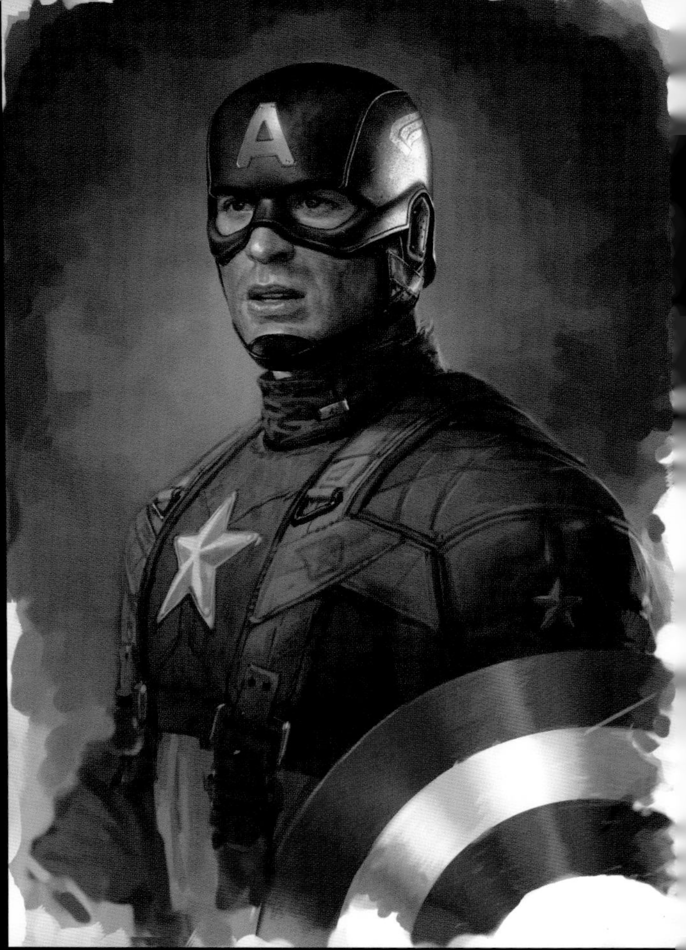
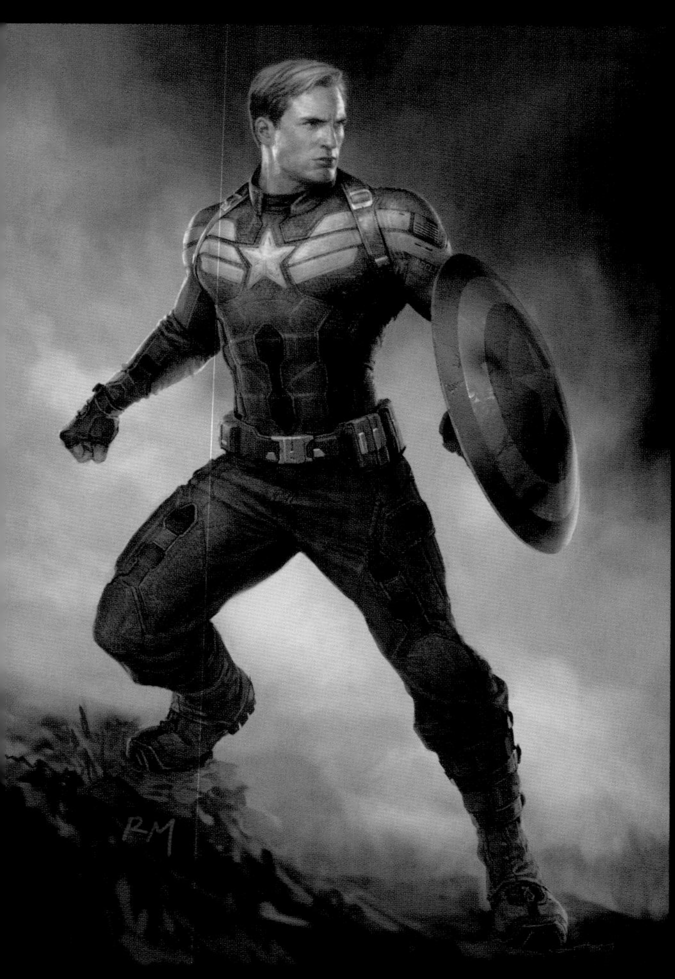
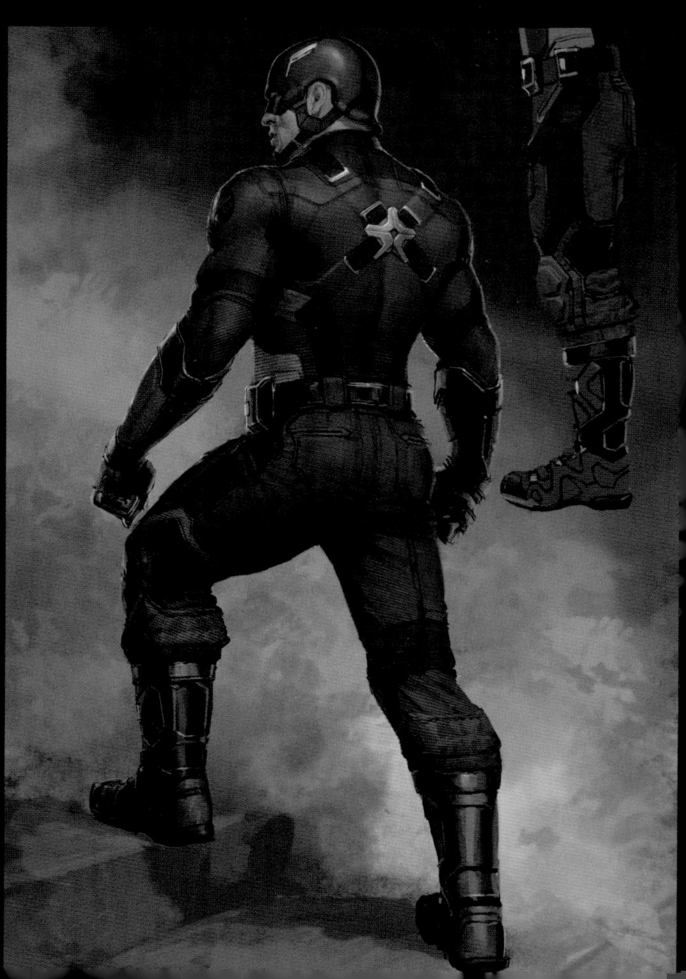

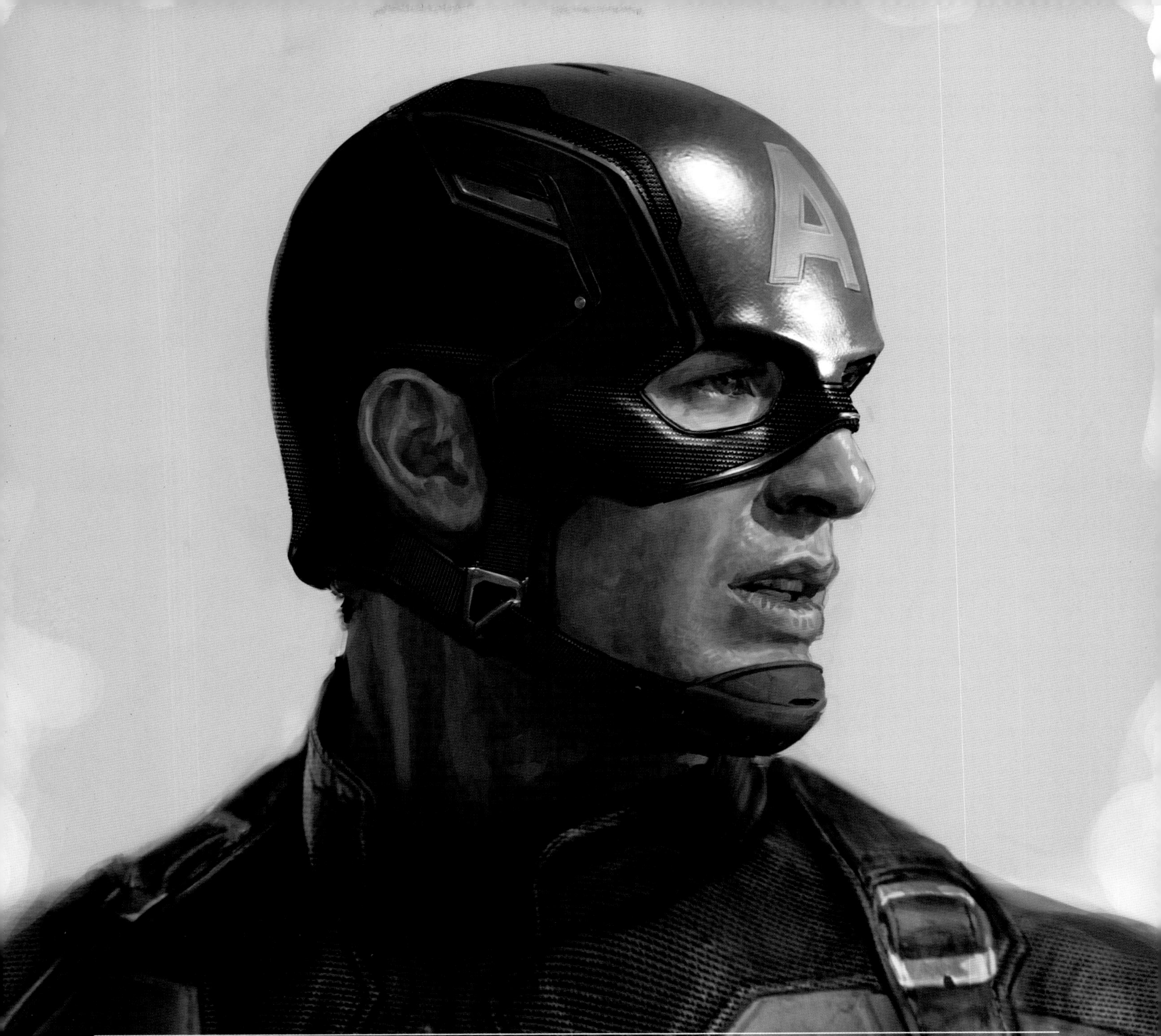

When *Captain America: The Winter Soldier*'s producer Nate Moore told Ryan Meinerding they wanted to give Steve Rogers the super soldier "Stealth Suit" from the Marvel comics (designed by Marko Djurdjević), the artist was excited—but also worried. "It's a cool costume, but it doesn't have a cowl or helmet, and I knew we could improve on the helmet from *Marvel's The Avengers*," says Meinerding. Kevin Feige agreed that it needed a redesign. "That was the biggest challenge for me. I was supremely motivated to get the helmet right."

In the first presentation meeting, Meinerding's suit design—from the neck down—was approved. But there was originally an additional Cap costume for the film. Meinerding shares, "The back view [opposite, bottom right] was for an alternate suit that was cut from that movie. When Cap came back from the Lemurian Star mission and was in the Triskelion, he was gonna have this updated Avengers suit. So originally, he was not in the stealth suit at all times."

To explore ideas for the new helmet, Meinerding took a fresh approach: "It was the first time I had taken to doing head designs from two angles at once, so people could see a three-quarter and a front view at the same time. We were rendering it from multiple angles in 3D to allow Kevin and everybody to see stuff as exhaustively as possible." Part of Meinerding's breakthrough was figuring out that the helmet needed to have a break in the hard surface—where the wing details rest, a cut line goes up and hinges, so it closes snugly around Chris Evans's head. "Adam Ross was instrumental in modeling the helmet in 3D during this process," details Meinerding. "We are fortunate enough to work with the best people in the industry, and Adam is one of those people. We ended up with a design that stayed the same for the rest of Steve Rogers's appearances in the MCU. Thankfully, it paid off."

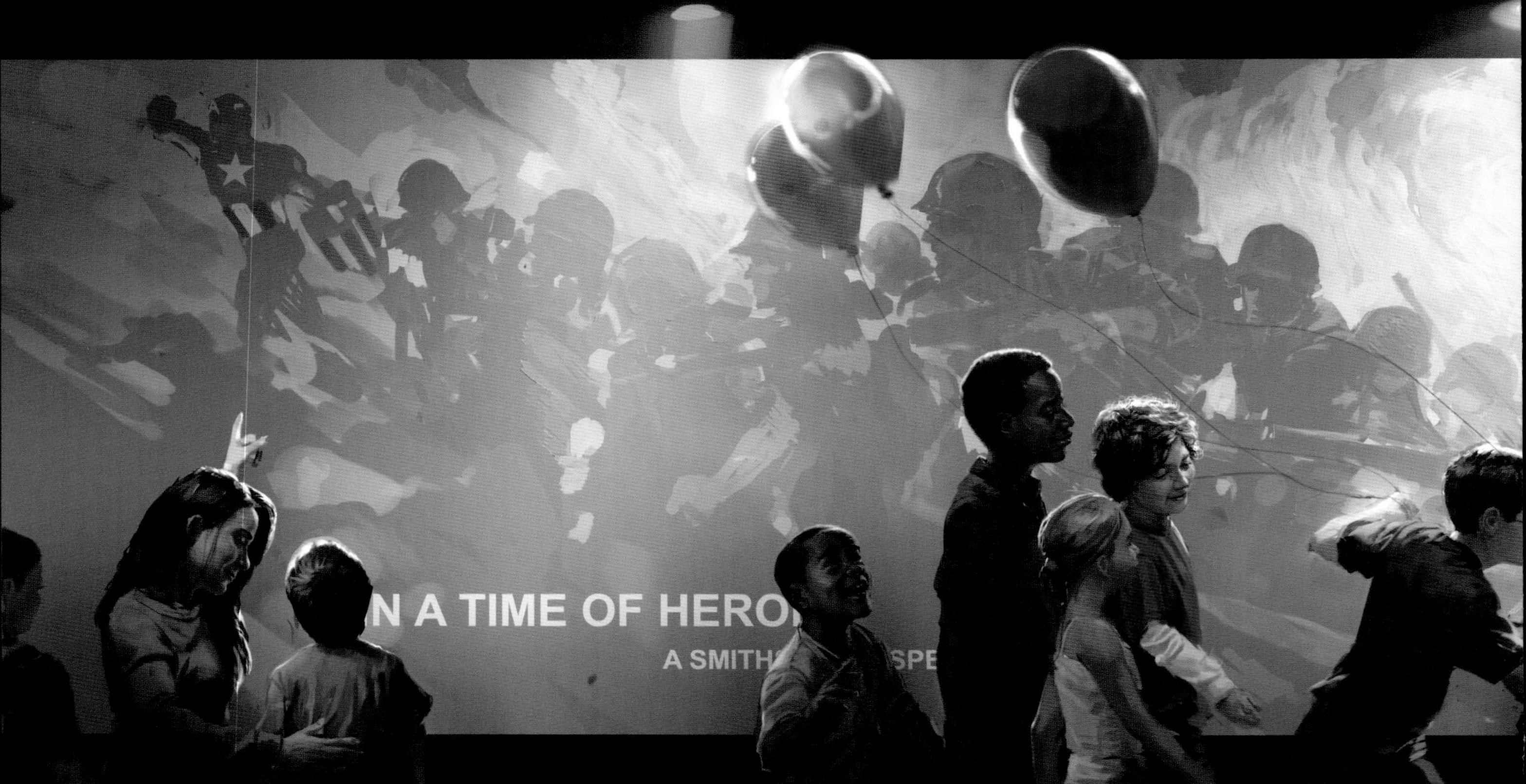
N A TIME OF HERO
A SMITH SPE

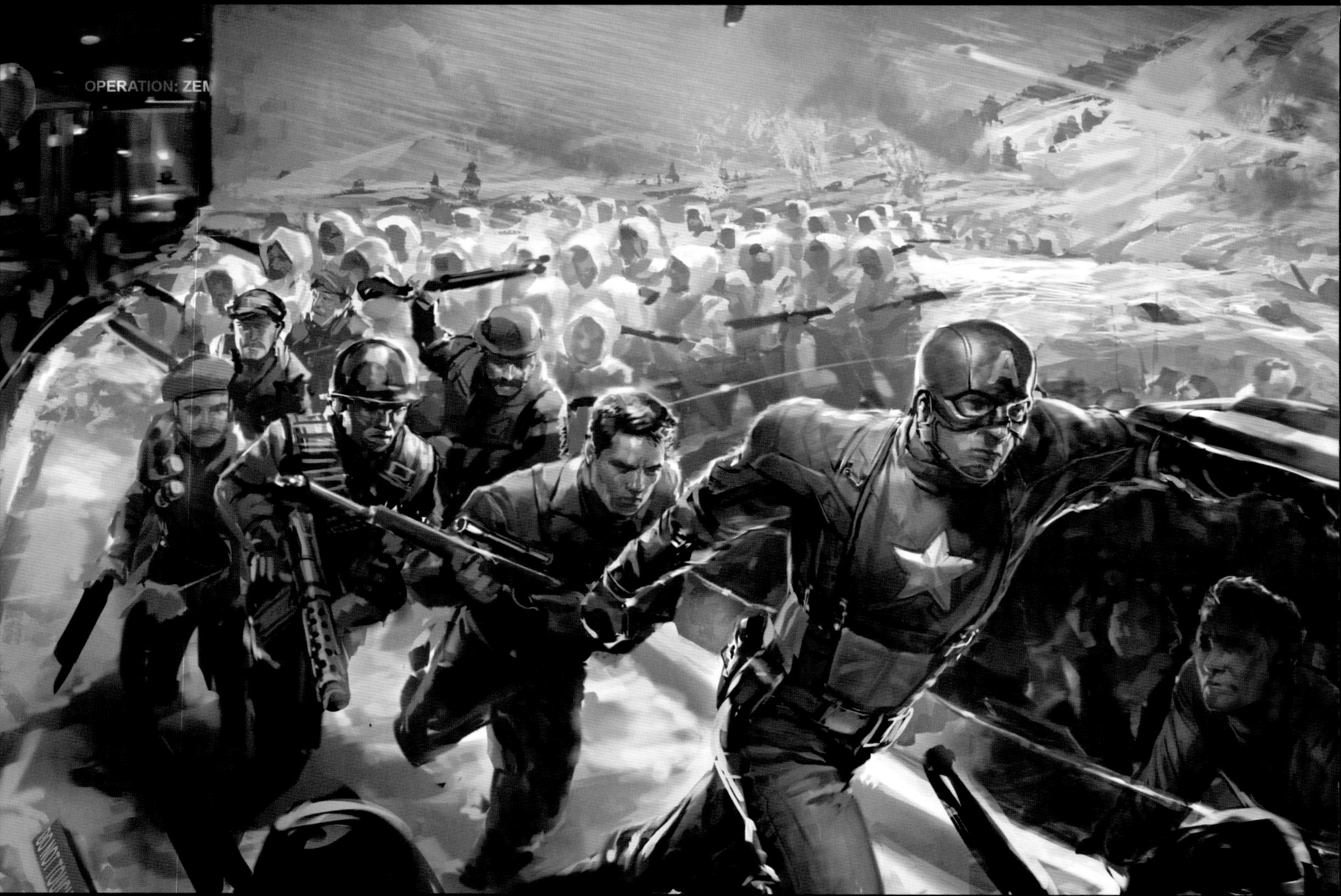
OPERATION: ZEM

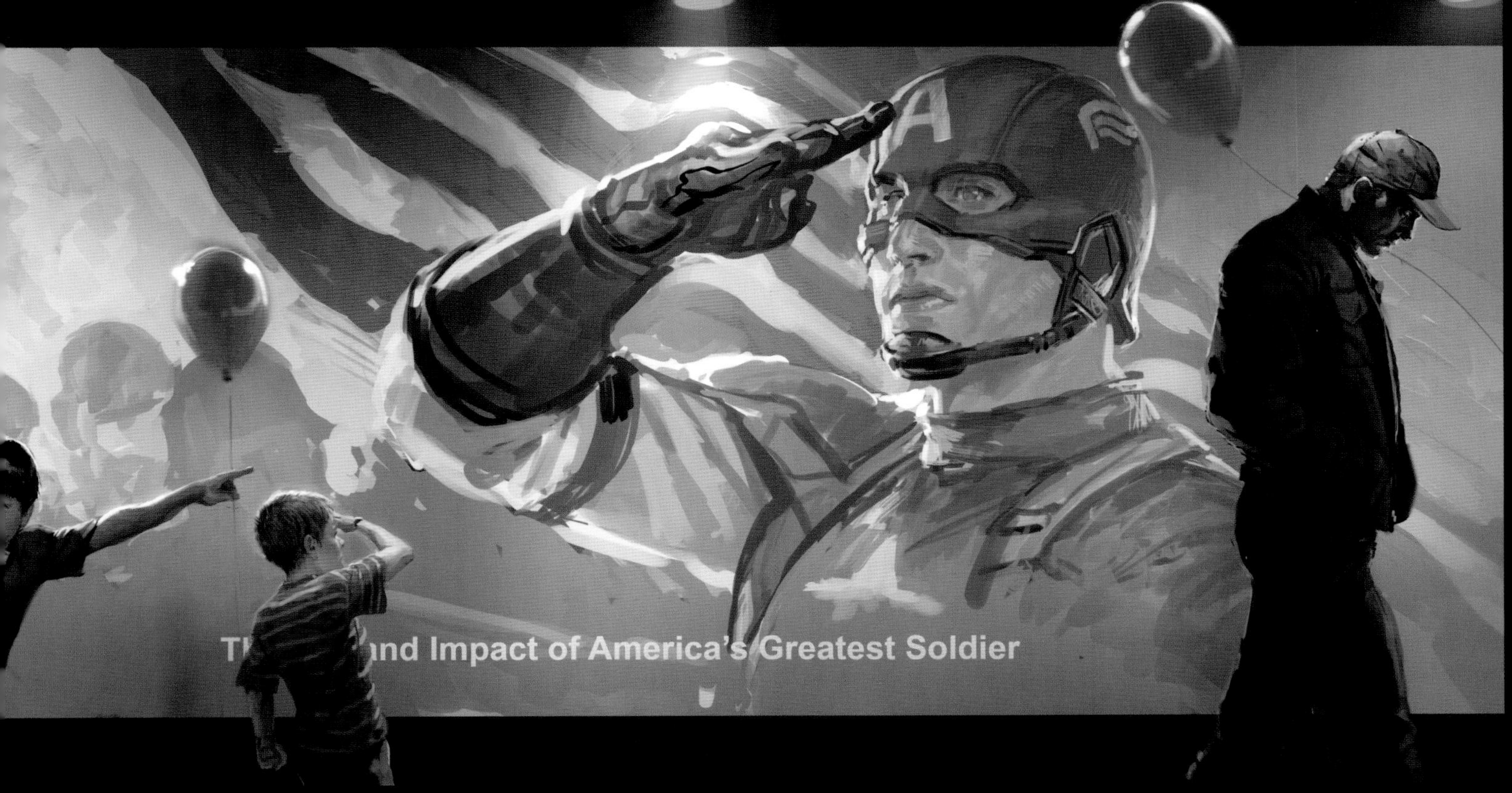
and Impact of America's Greatest Soldier

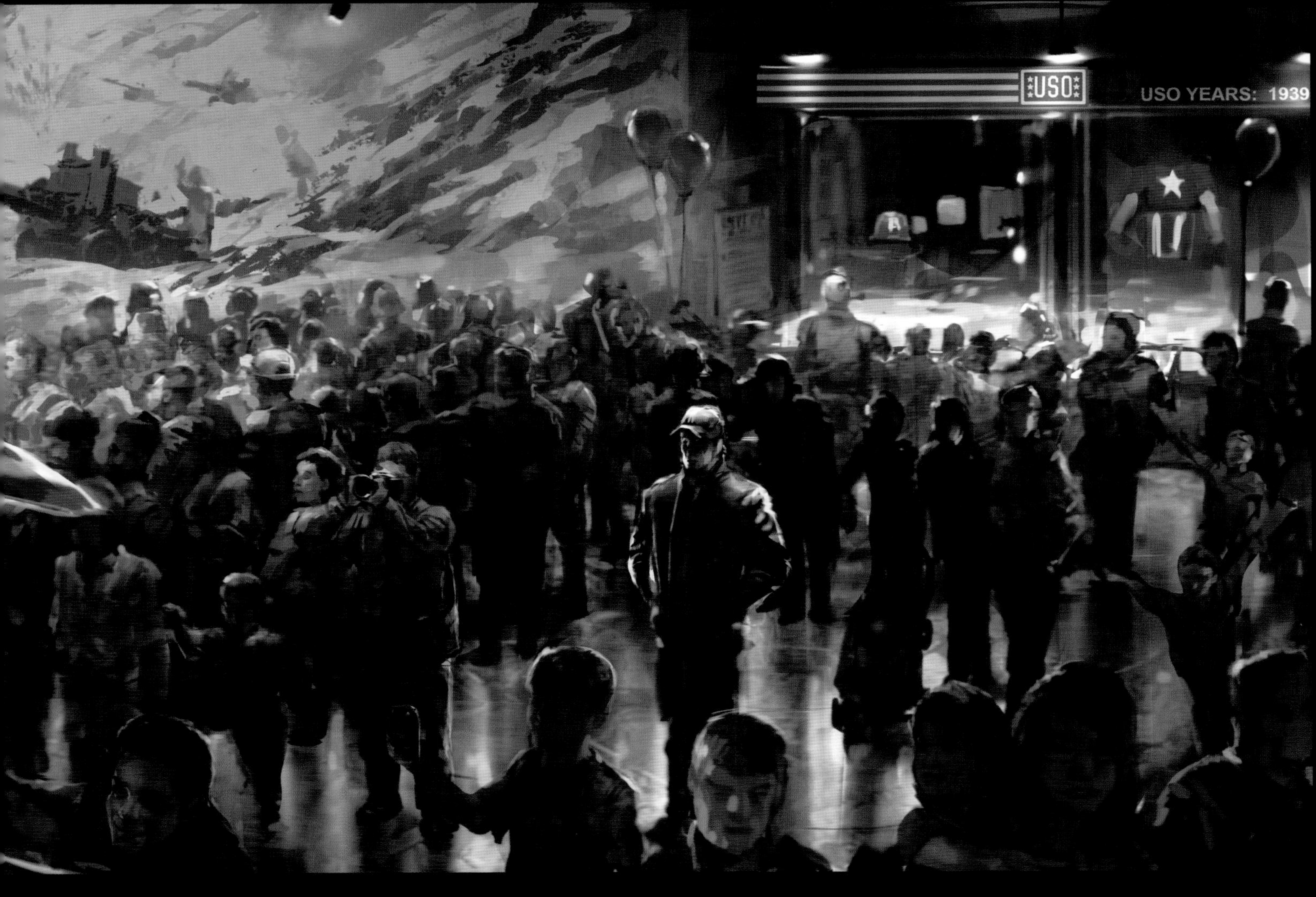
USO
USO YEARS: 1939

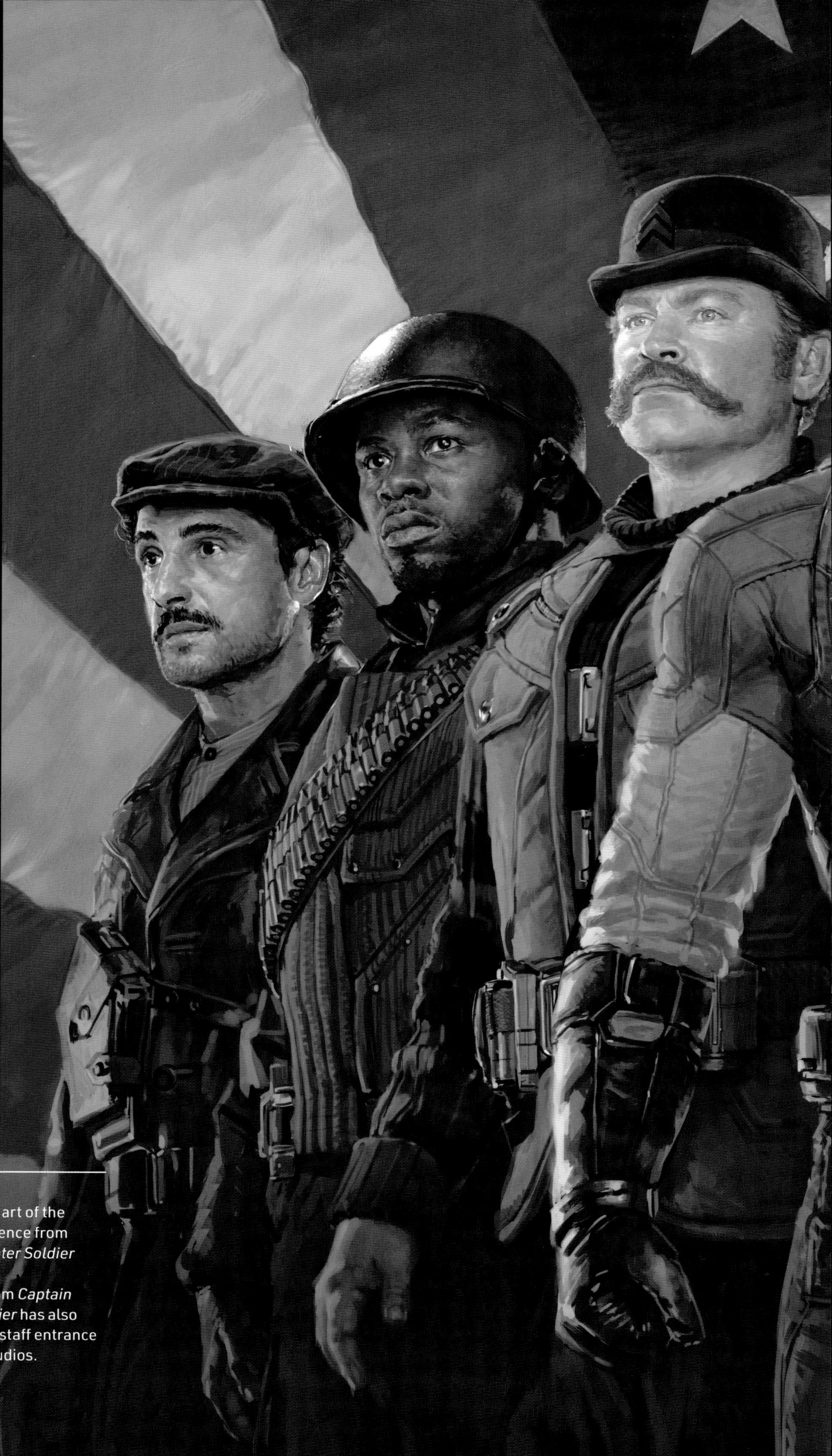

PREVIOUS SPREAD Concept art of the Smithsonian exhibit sequence from *Captain America: The Winter Soldier*

THIS SPREAD The mural from *Captain America: The Winter Soldier* has also been immortalized in the staff entrance elevator bay of Marvel Studios.

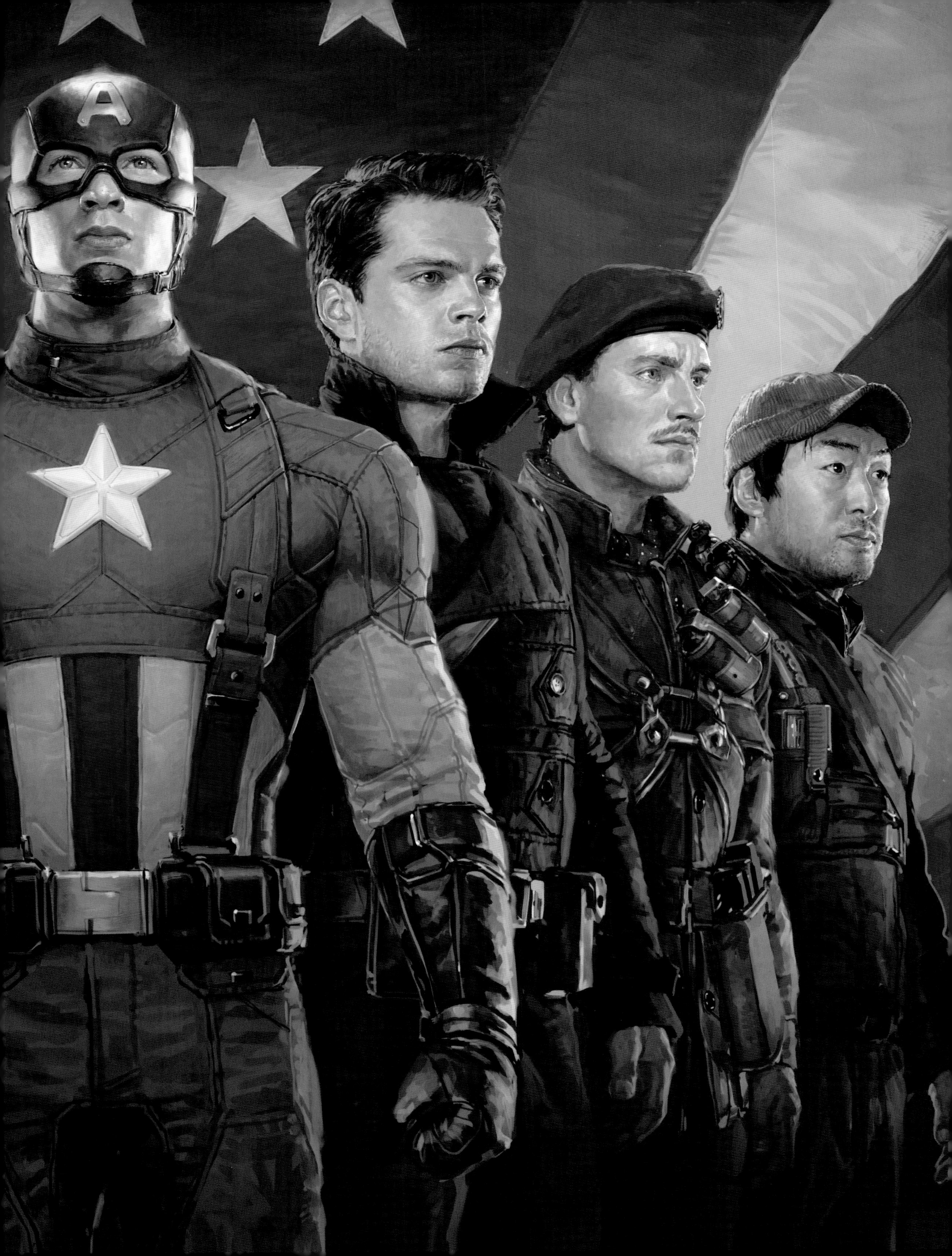

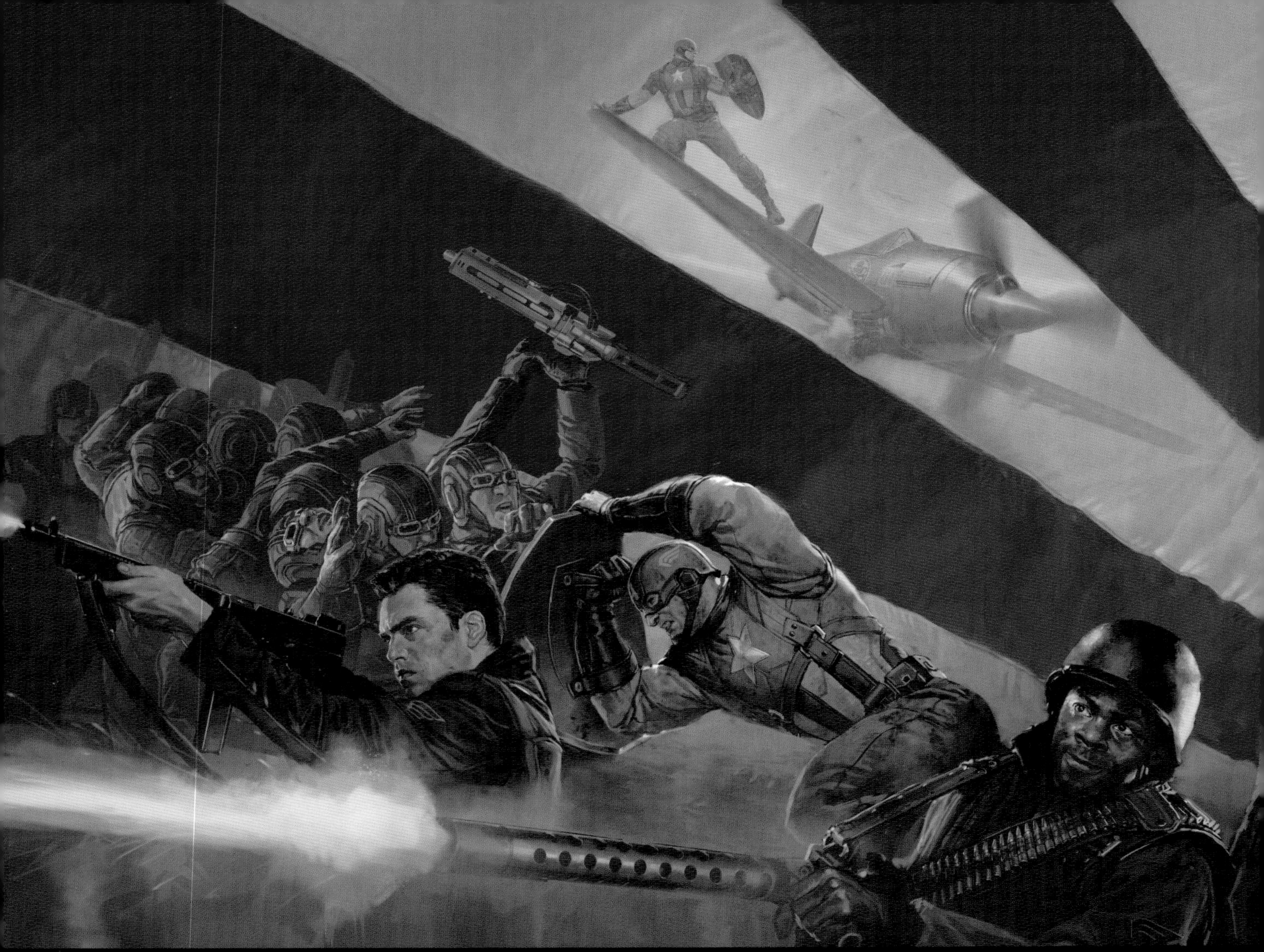

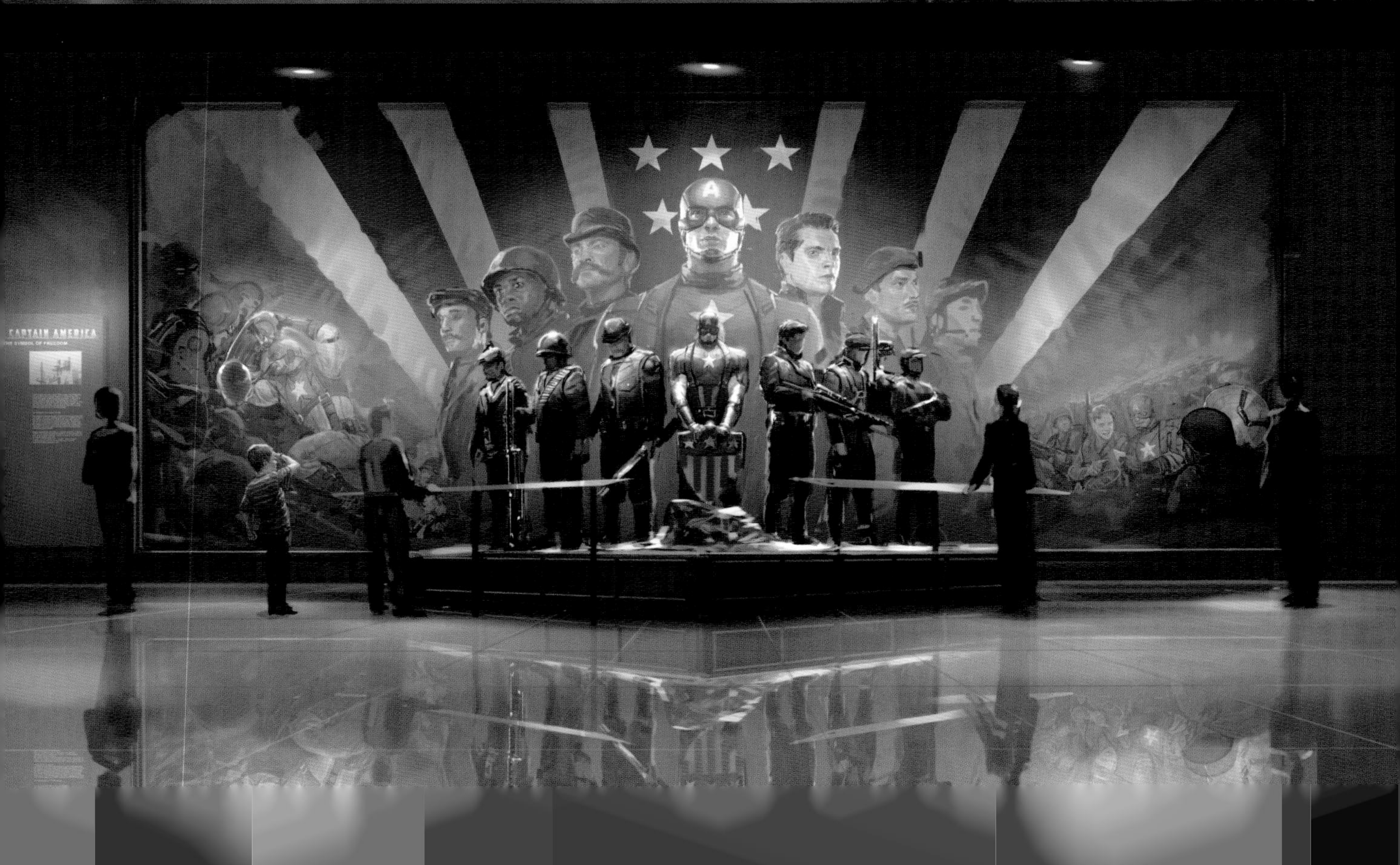
CAPTAIN AMERICA
THE SYMBOL OF FREEDOM

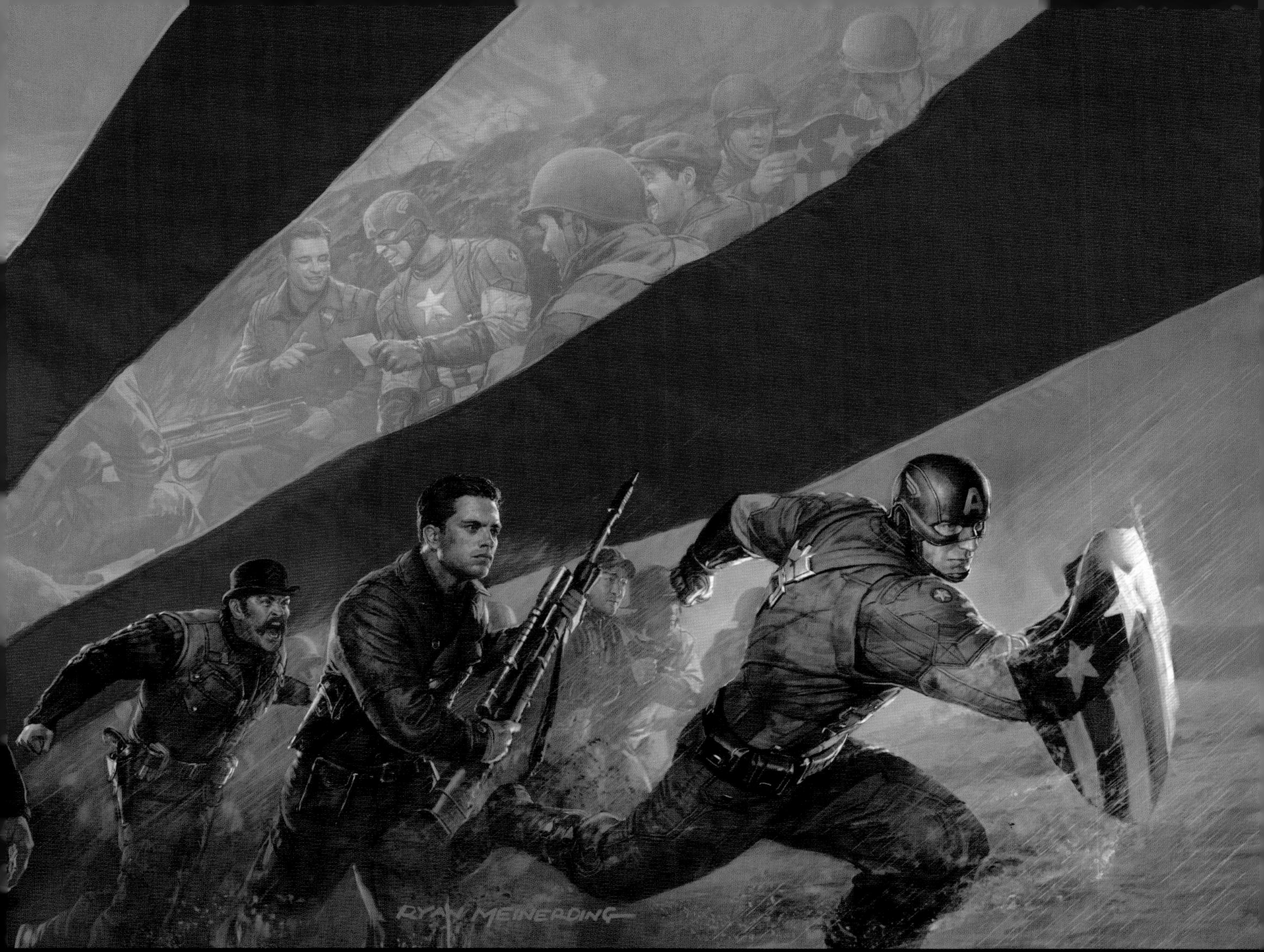
RYAN MEINERDING

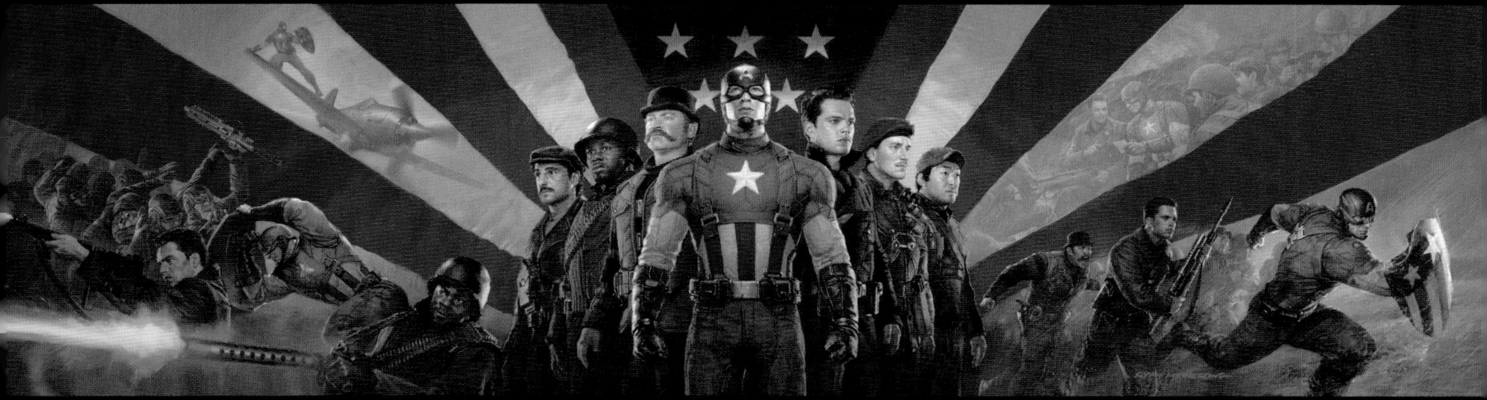

Ryan Meinerding and Kevin Feige share a love for Washington, D.C.'s Smithsonian museums. Meinerding visited them during a seventh grade school trip, and they were very impactful to the young artist. "The notion of doing this kind of work for *The Winter Soldier* was cool to me because I got to essentially design the space as well as paint the murals," he says. "Plus, there was also the connection I had to working on *The First Avenger* and on Cap in the World War II era." The sequence was filmed inside a real museum in Cleveland, where directors Anthony and Joe Russo were filming *The Winter Soldier*. Being originally from Ohio, Meinerding used the opportunity for a very memorable family visit: "I took my wife and my parents to the set, and they got to be there and see the murals up close for the day's shooting. That was super cool."

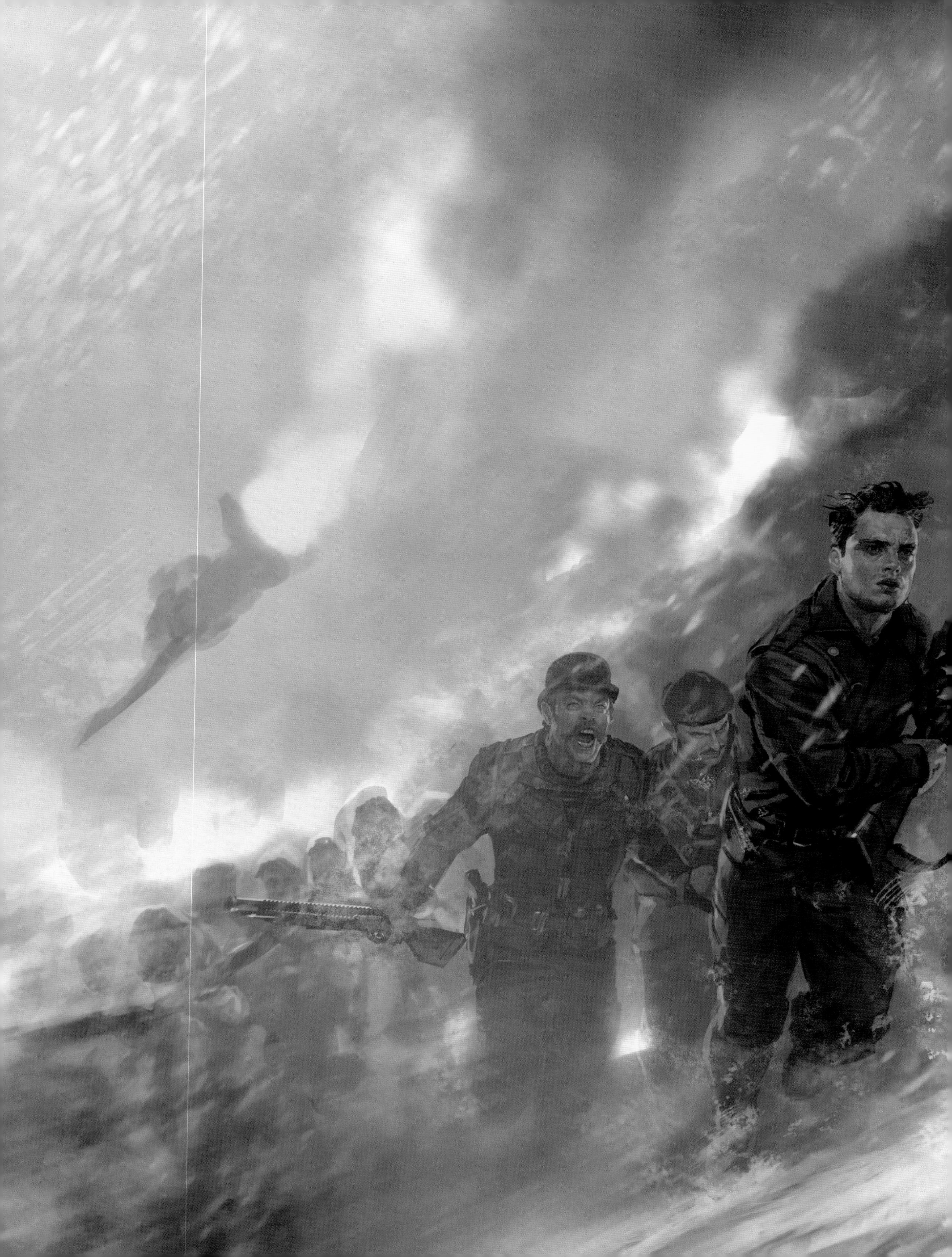

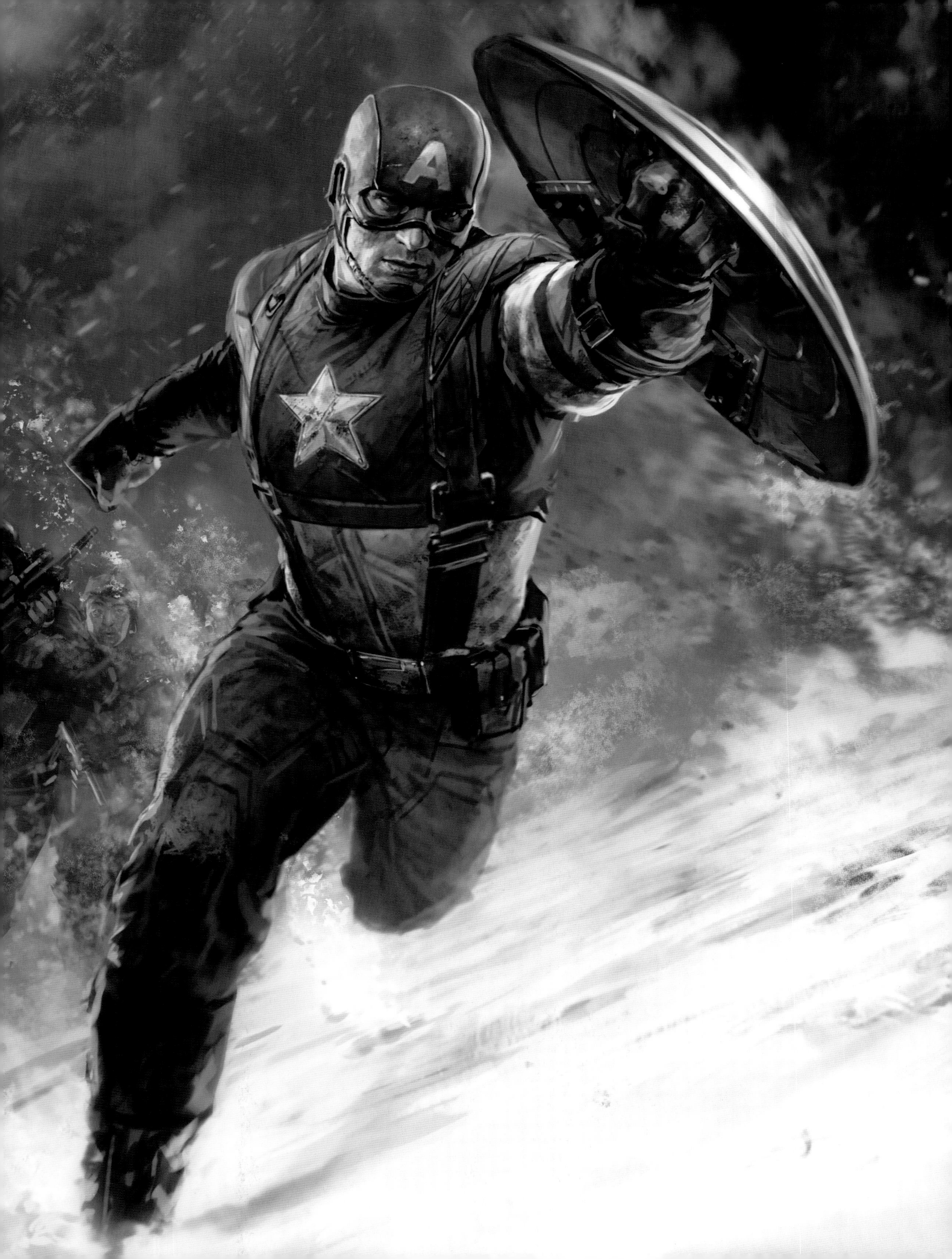

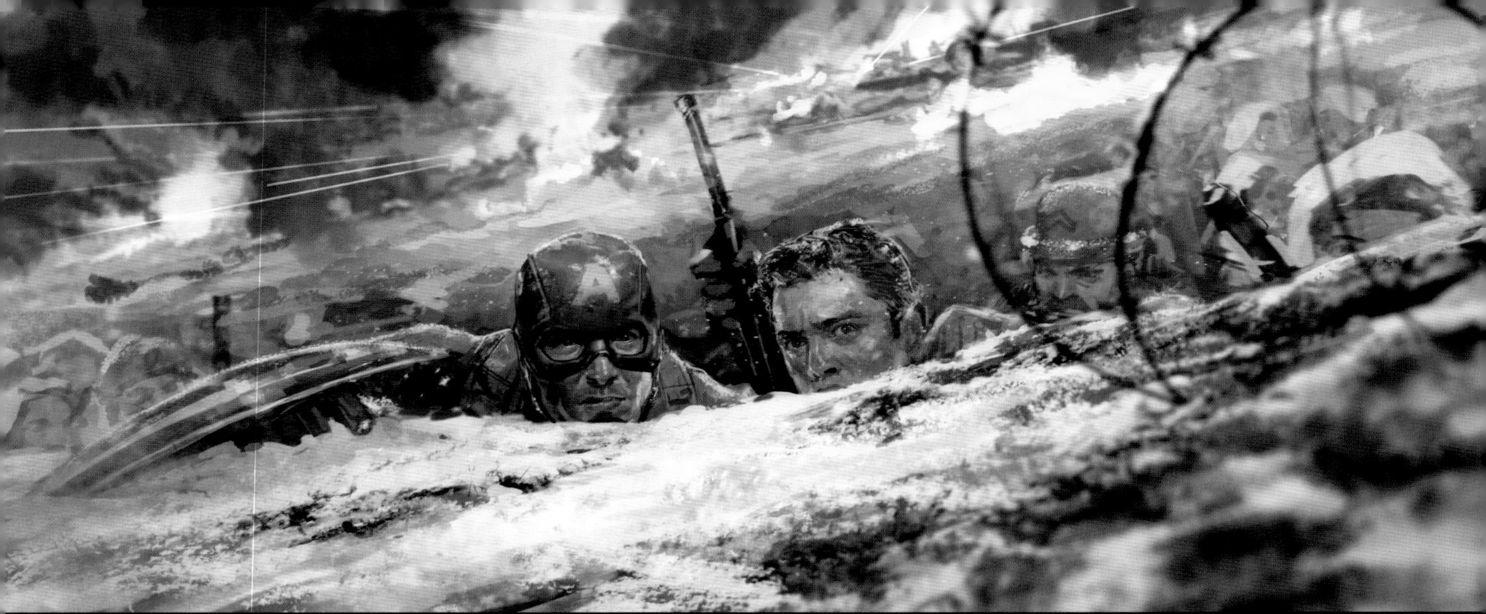

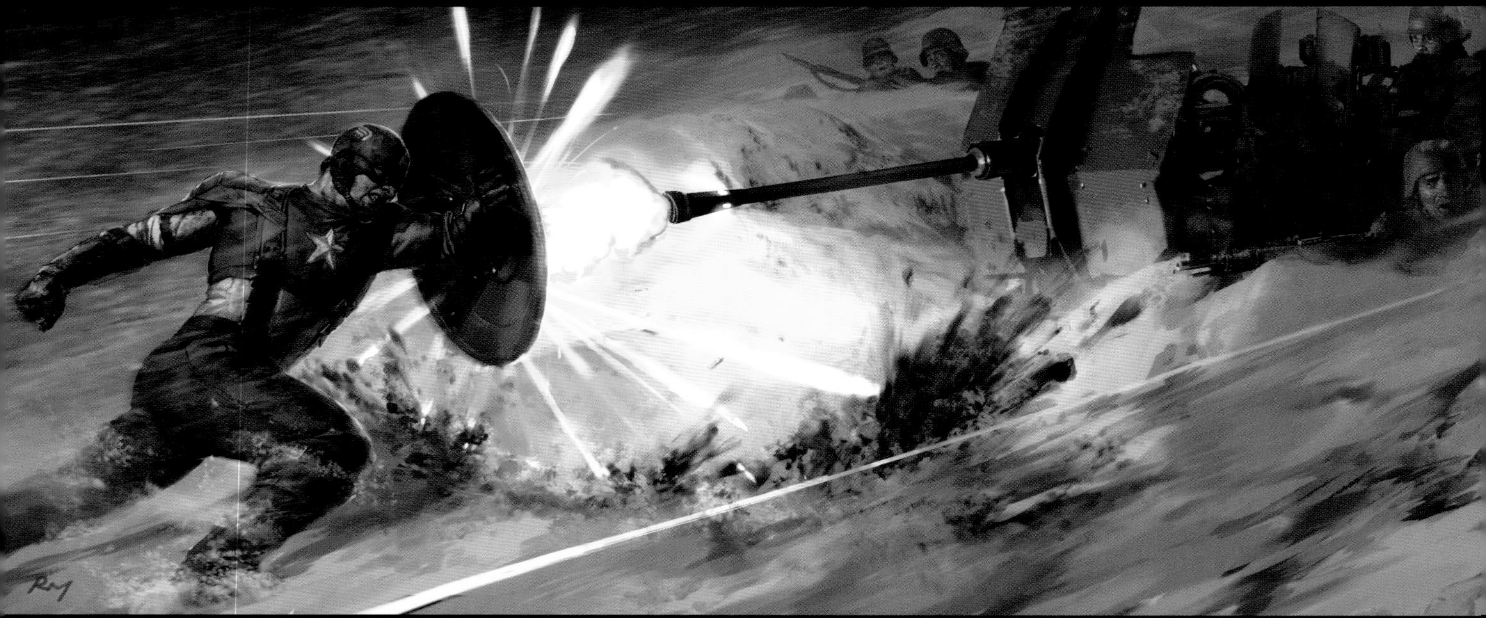

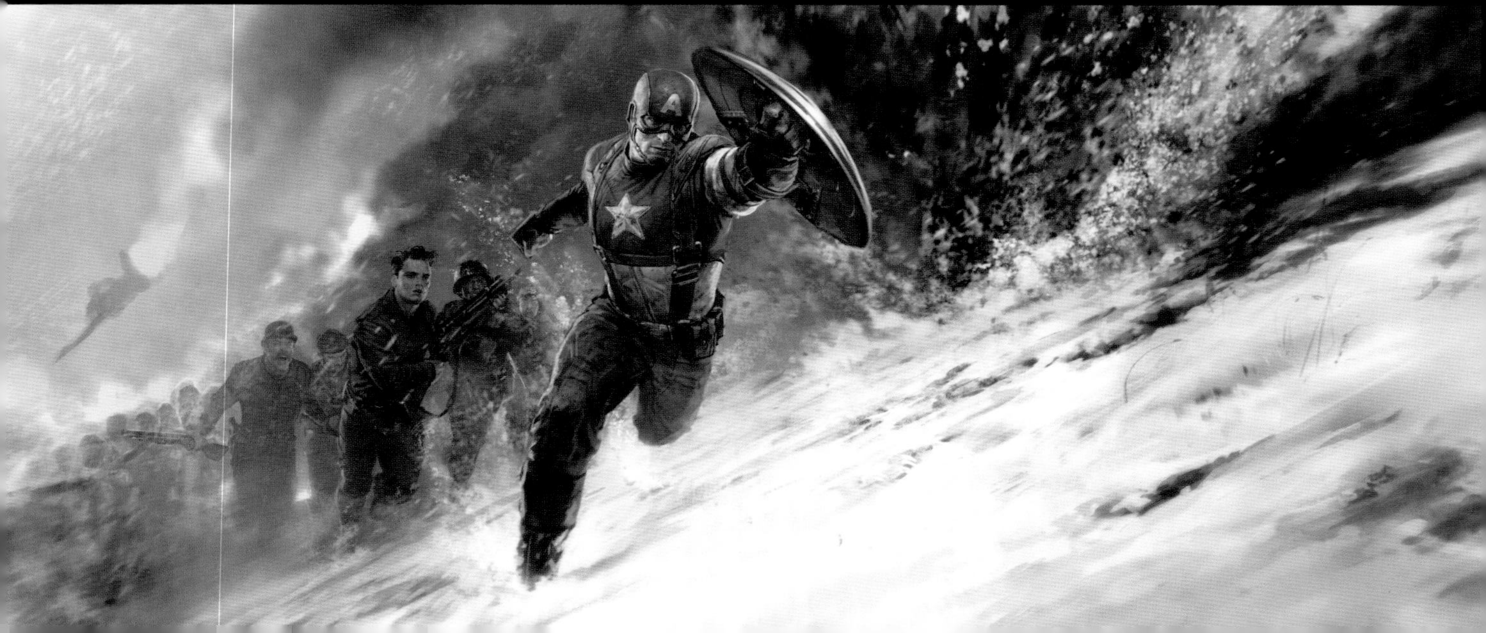

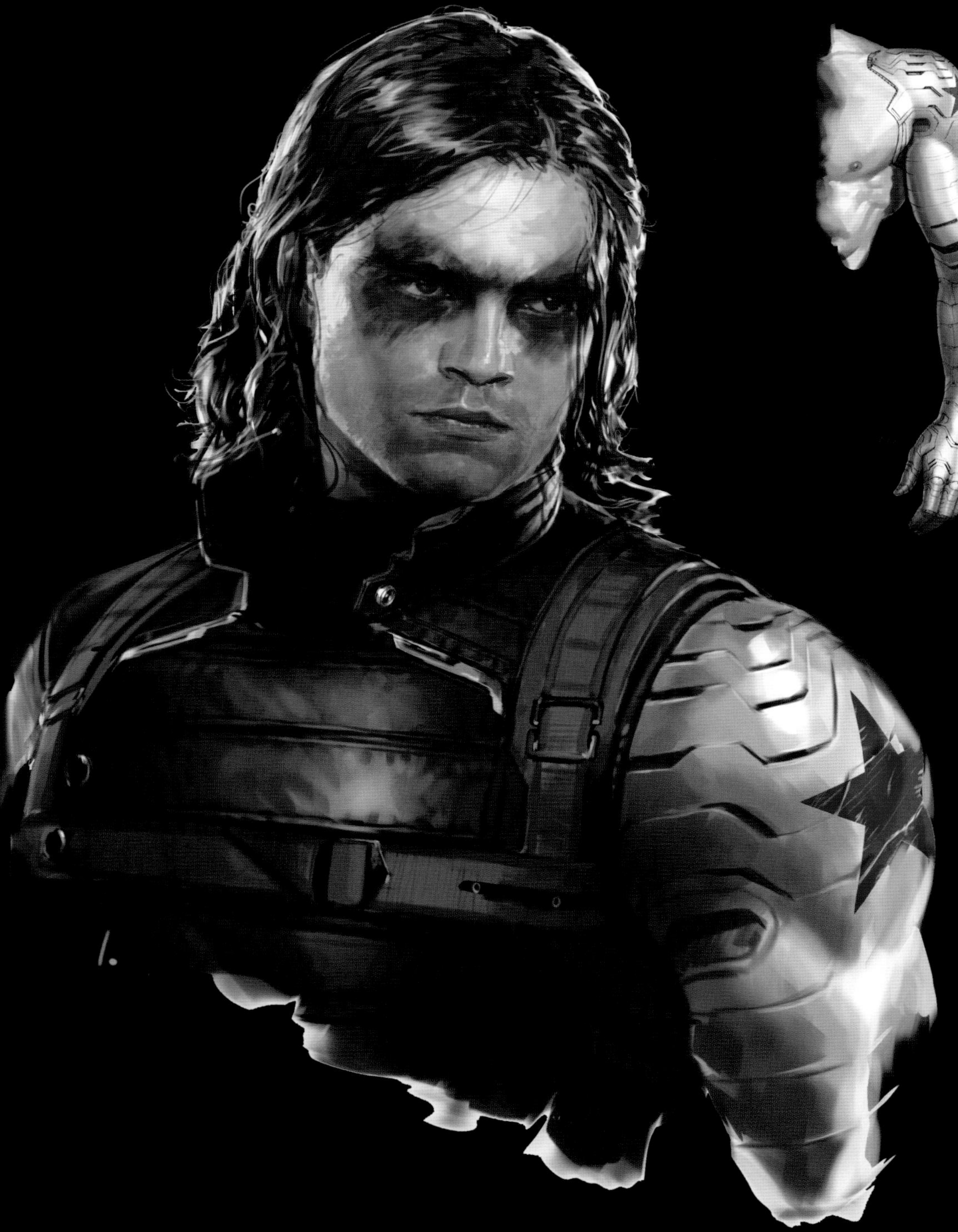

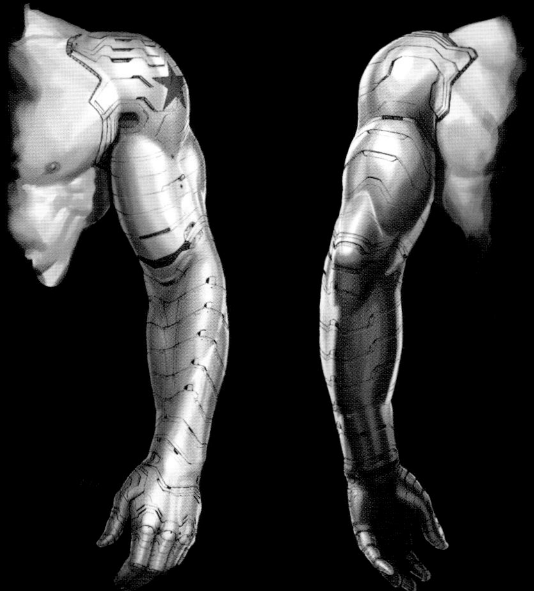

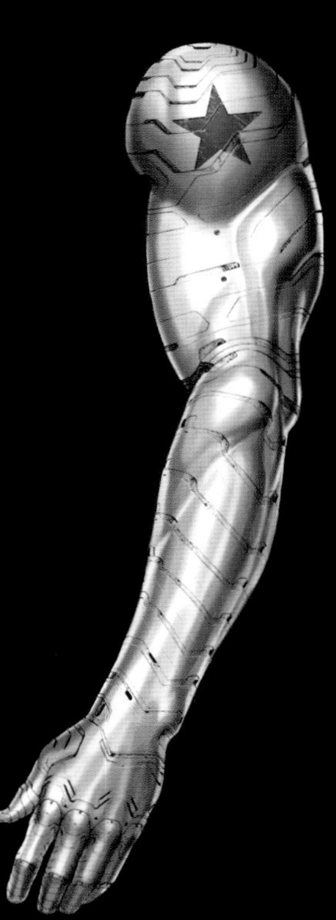

OPPOSITE These key frames were created by Meinerding for what was the original—and then cut—idea for the opening of *The Winter Soldier*. "This was a dream sequence of Cap remembering a battle with the Howling Commandos," says Meinerding. Notably, this image is used for the Captain America flip in the Marvel Studios main title logo sequence.

THIS PAGE Meinerding's initial design idea for Bucky Barnes/the Winter Soldier's mechanical arm was very different. "I wanted to make it look kind of coarse. That's where I started," he explains. "Pretty soon afterward, I just moved toward a design [above] that was more classically 'Marvel Comics.' One of those things that's quintessential Marvel, even outside of Winter Soldier, is the concept of the metal arm with the lines on it. It was a fun thing to try and accomplish." The directors, the Russo brothers, wanted to put the Winter Soldier in dark tactical gear to heighten the extremely villainous component of him in the first half of the movie. "It was an interesting experience because we were trying to come up with costume stages to gradually expose his true identity," details Meinerding. "The face mask and goggles, and then the mask and eye makeup, and the hairstyle—I was trying to give them enough ingredients so they could figure out the sequencing of how his look was revealed."

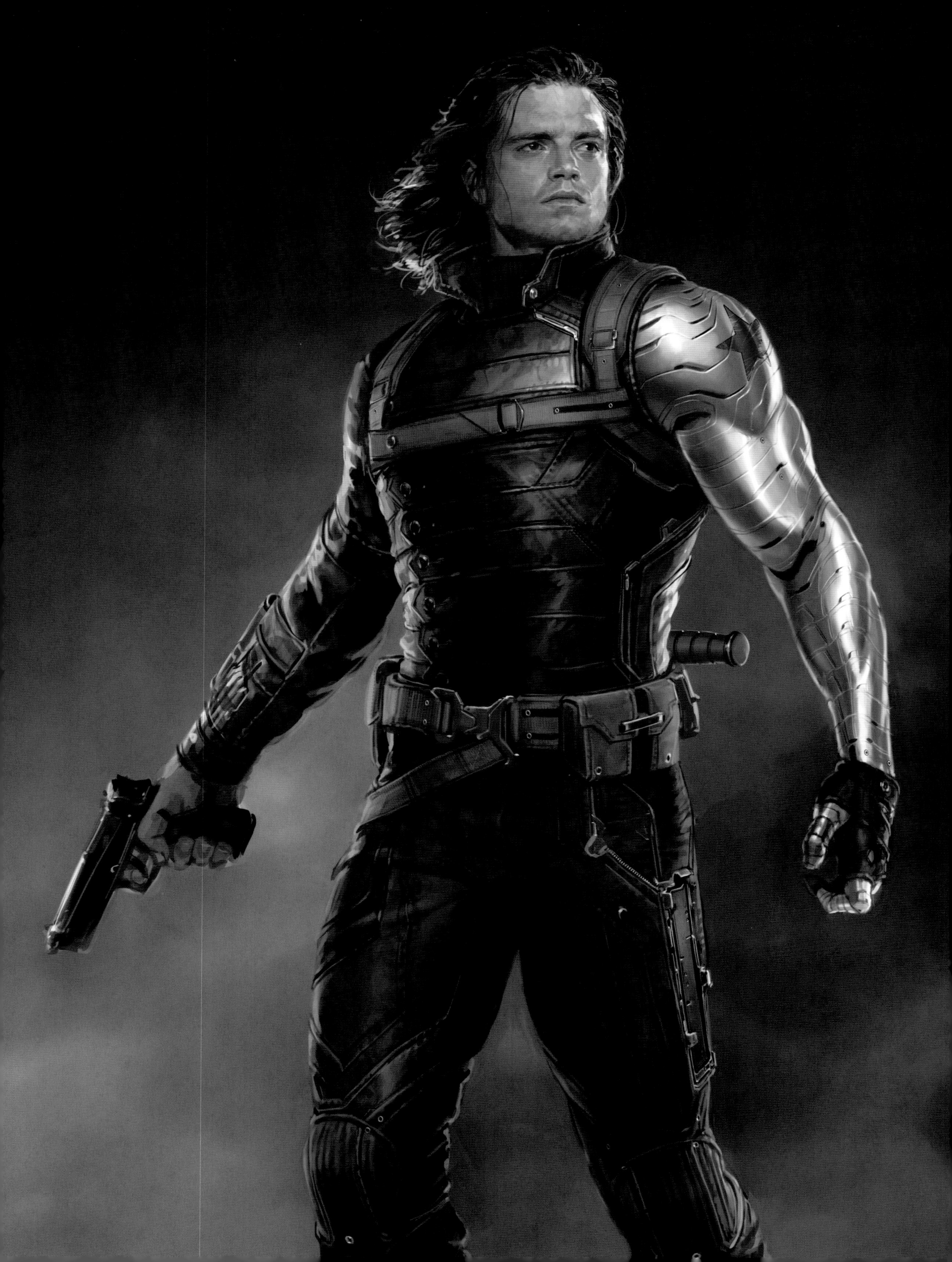

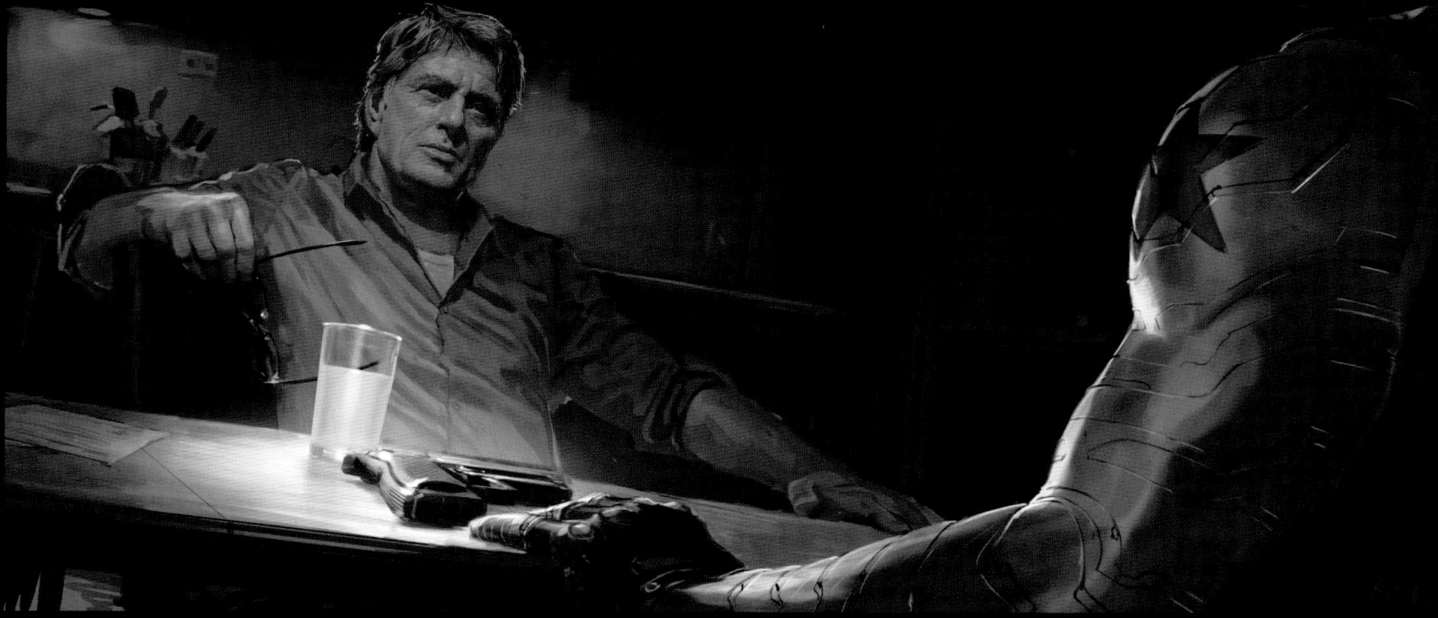

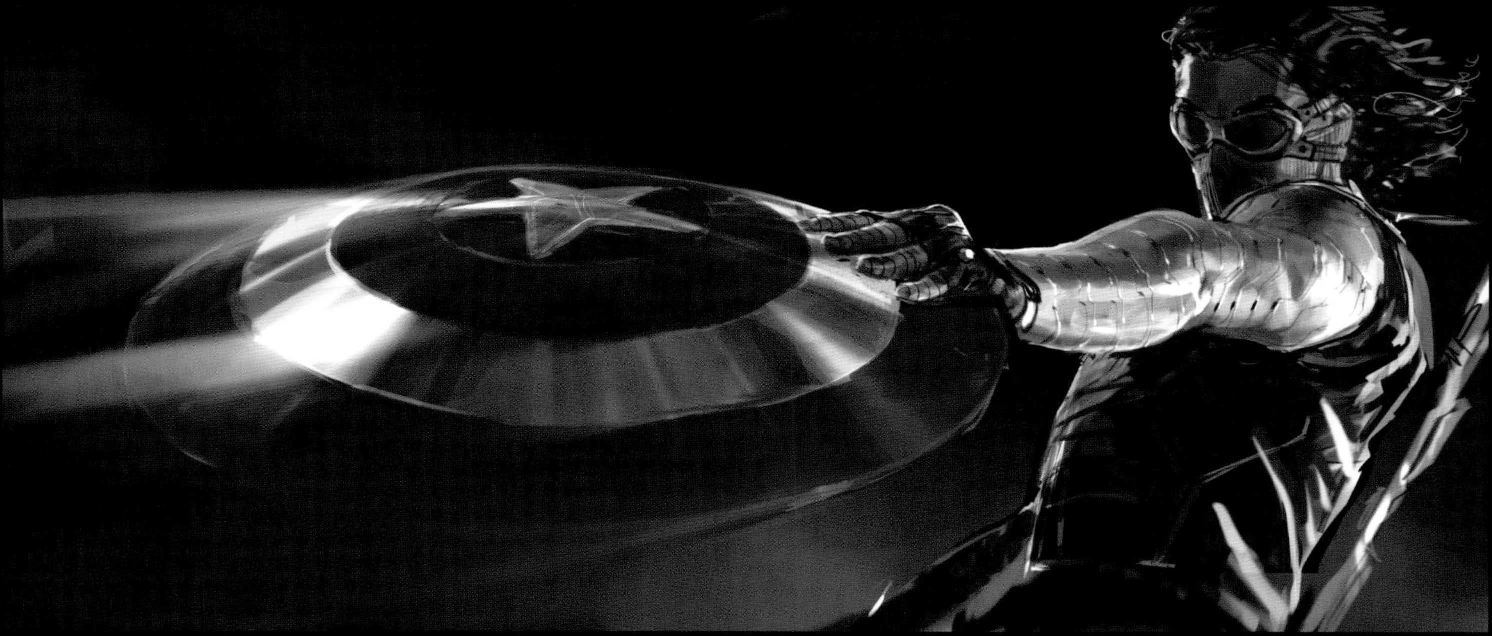

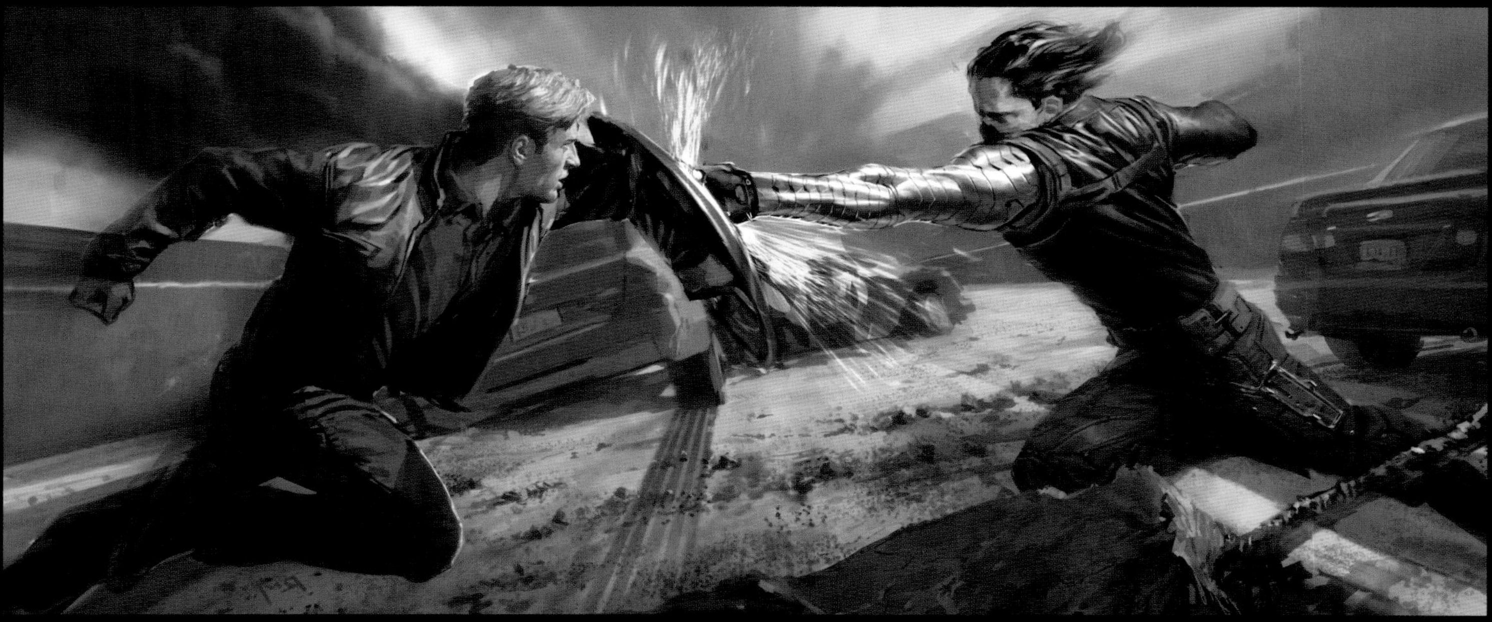

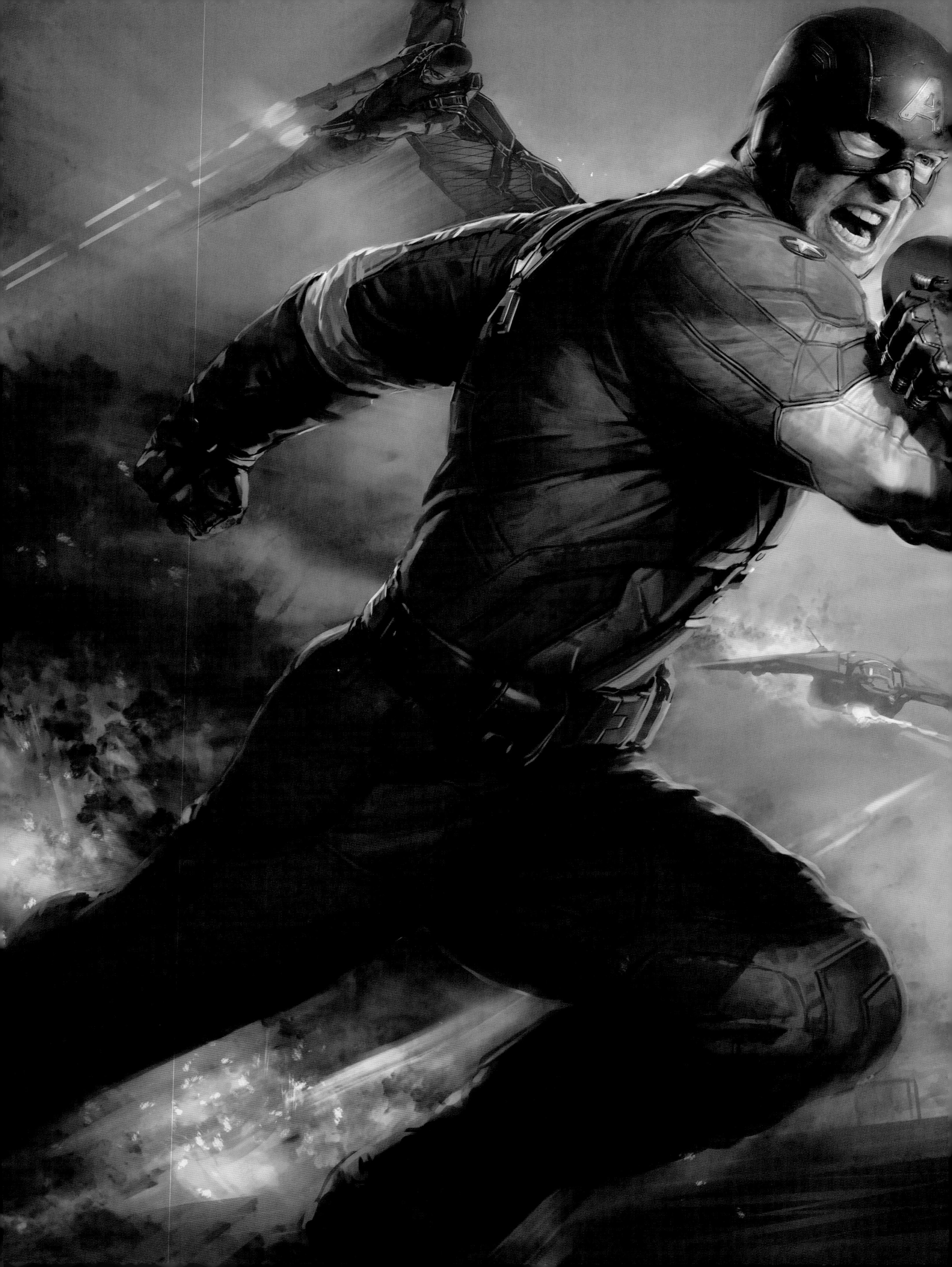

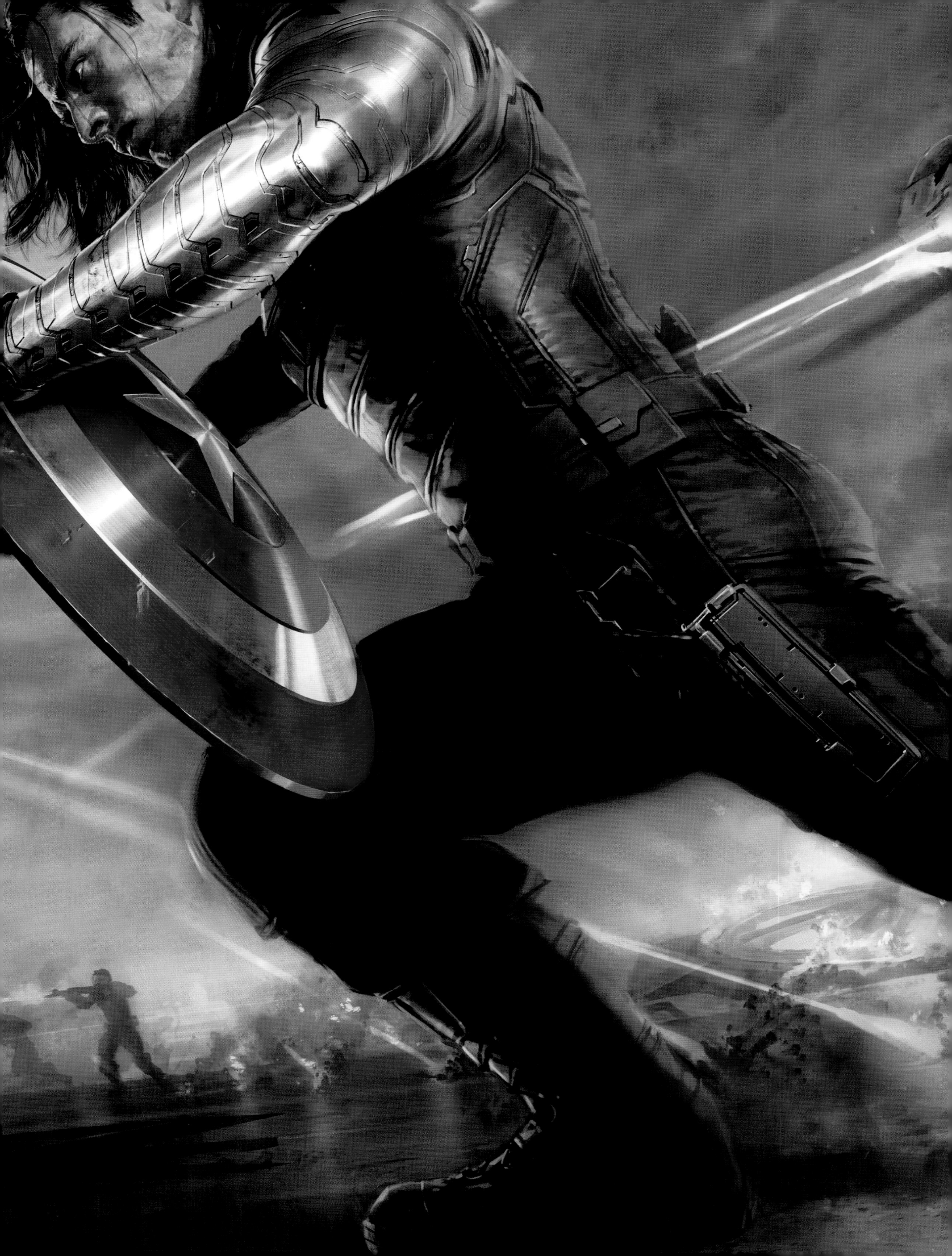

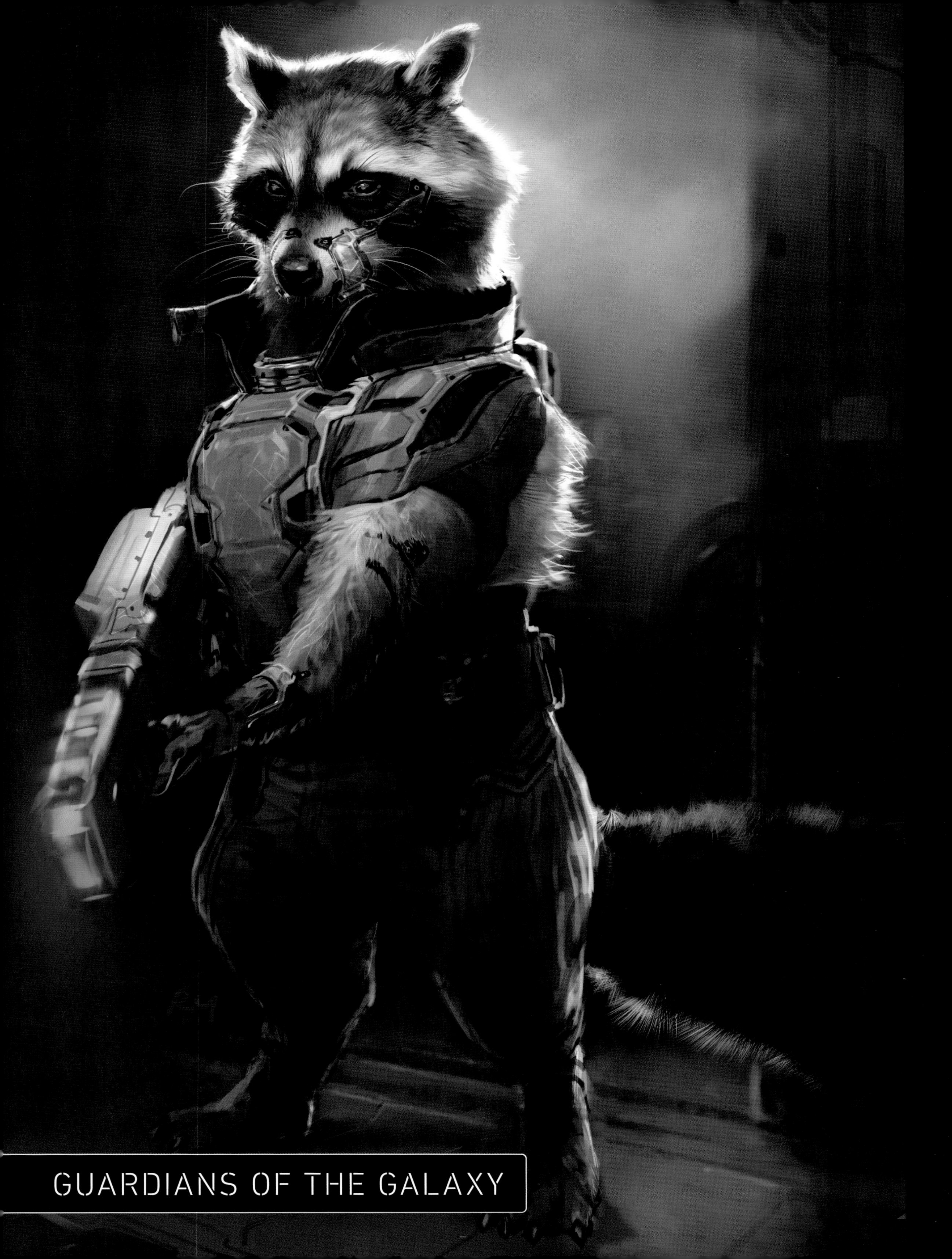

GUARDIANS OF THE GALAXY

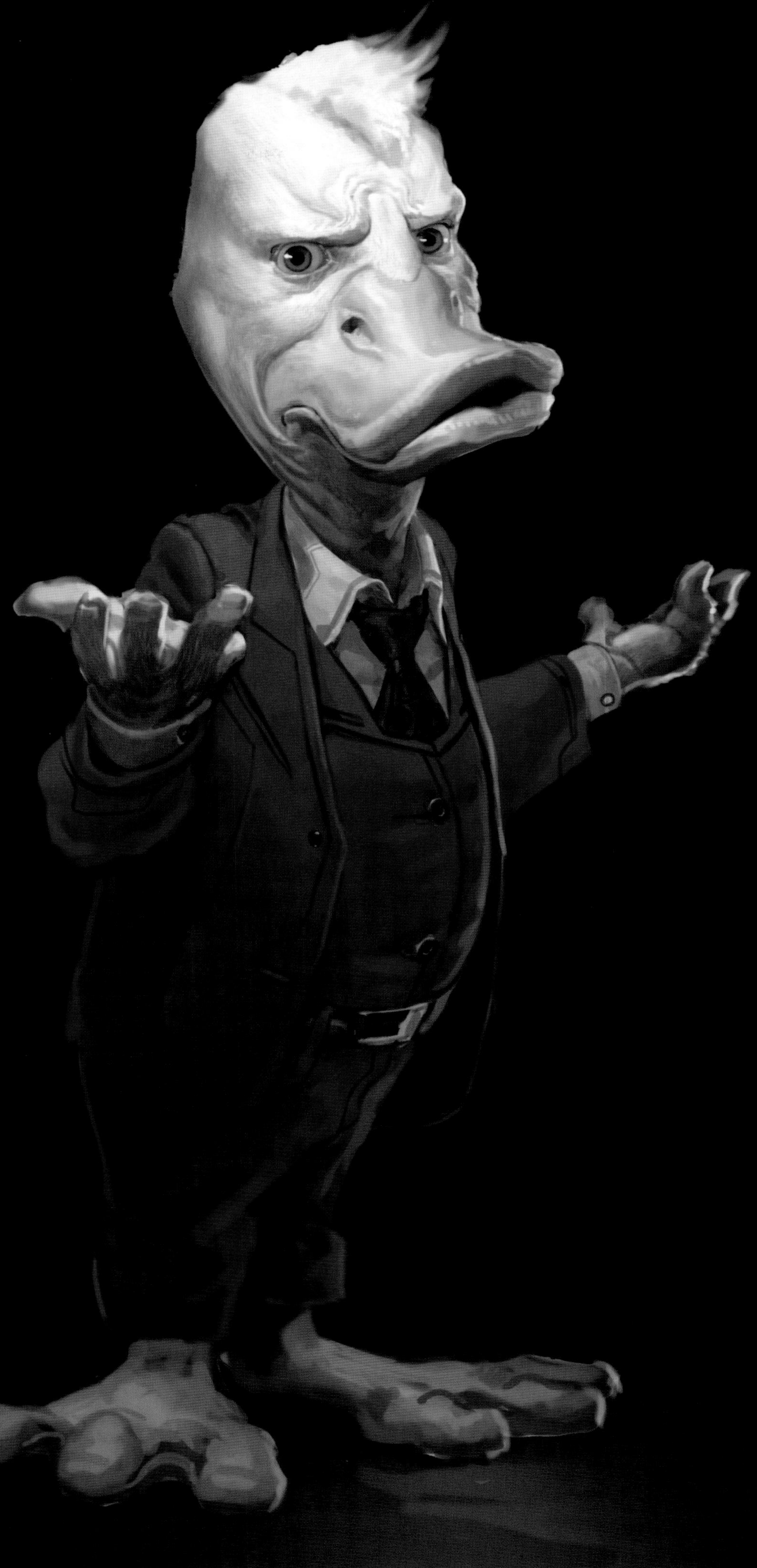

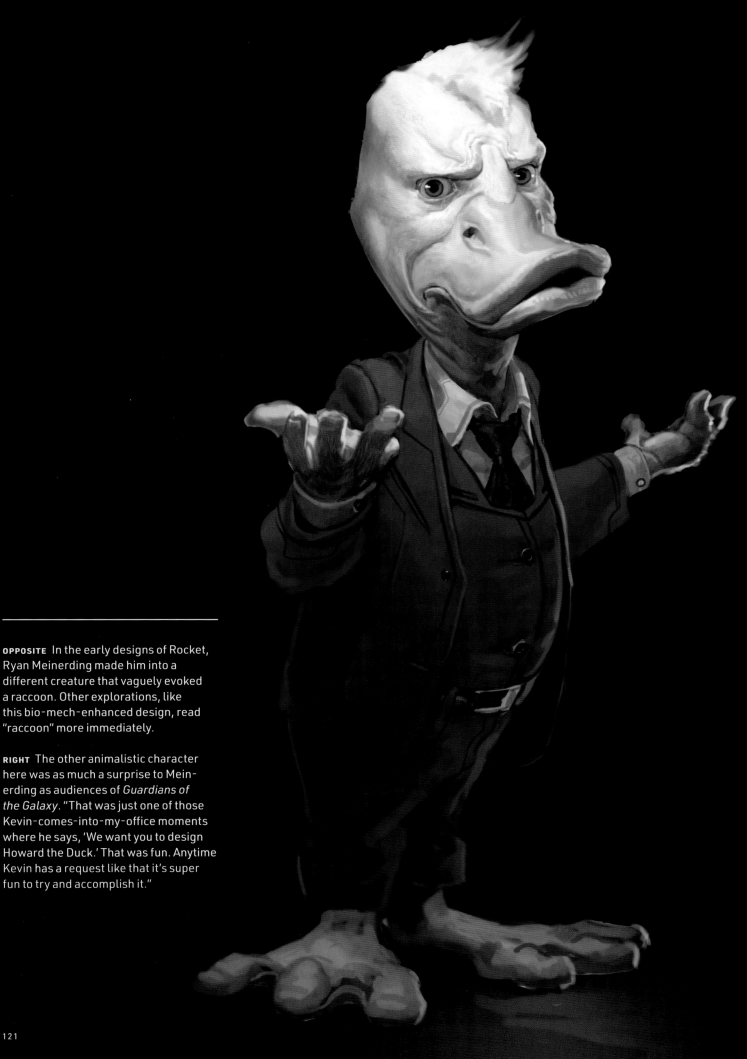

OPPOSITE In the early designs of Rocket, Ryan Meinerding made him into a different creature that vaguely evoked a raccoon. Other explorations, like this bio-mech-enhanced design, read "raccoon" more immediately.

RIGHT The other animalistic character here was as much a surprise to Meinerding as audiences of *Guardians of the Galaxy*. "That was just one of those Kevin-comes-into-my-office moments where he says, 'We want you to design Howard the Duck.' That was fun. Anytime Kevin has a request like that it's super fun to try and accomplish it."

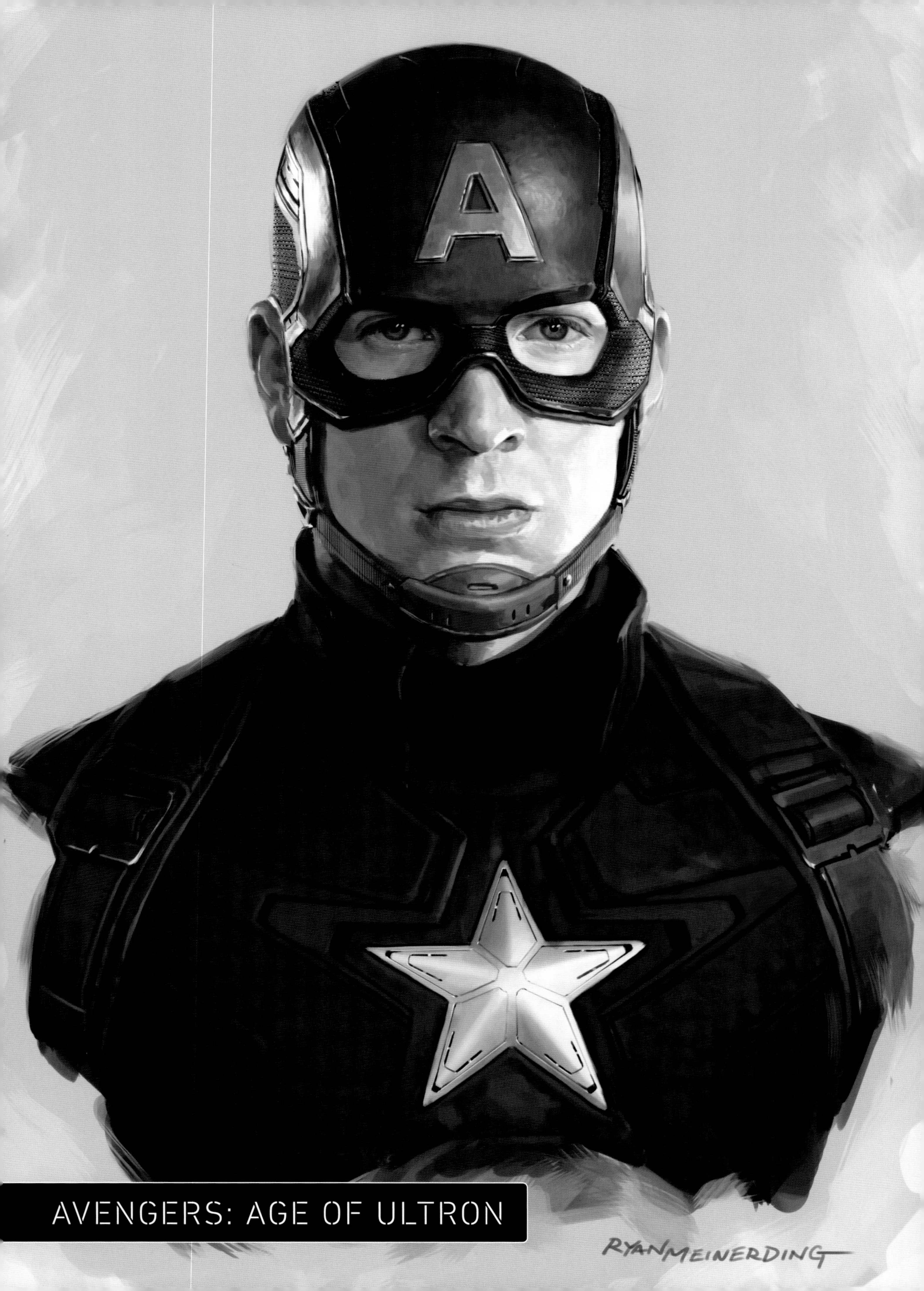
RYANMEINERDING

AVENGERS: AGE OF ULTRON

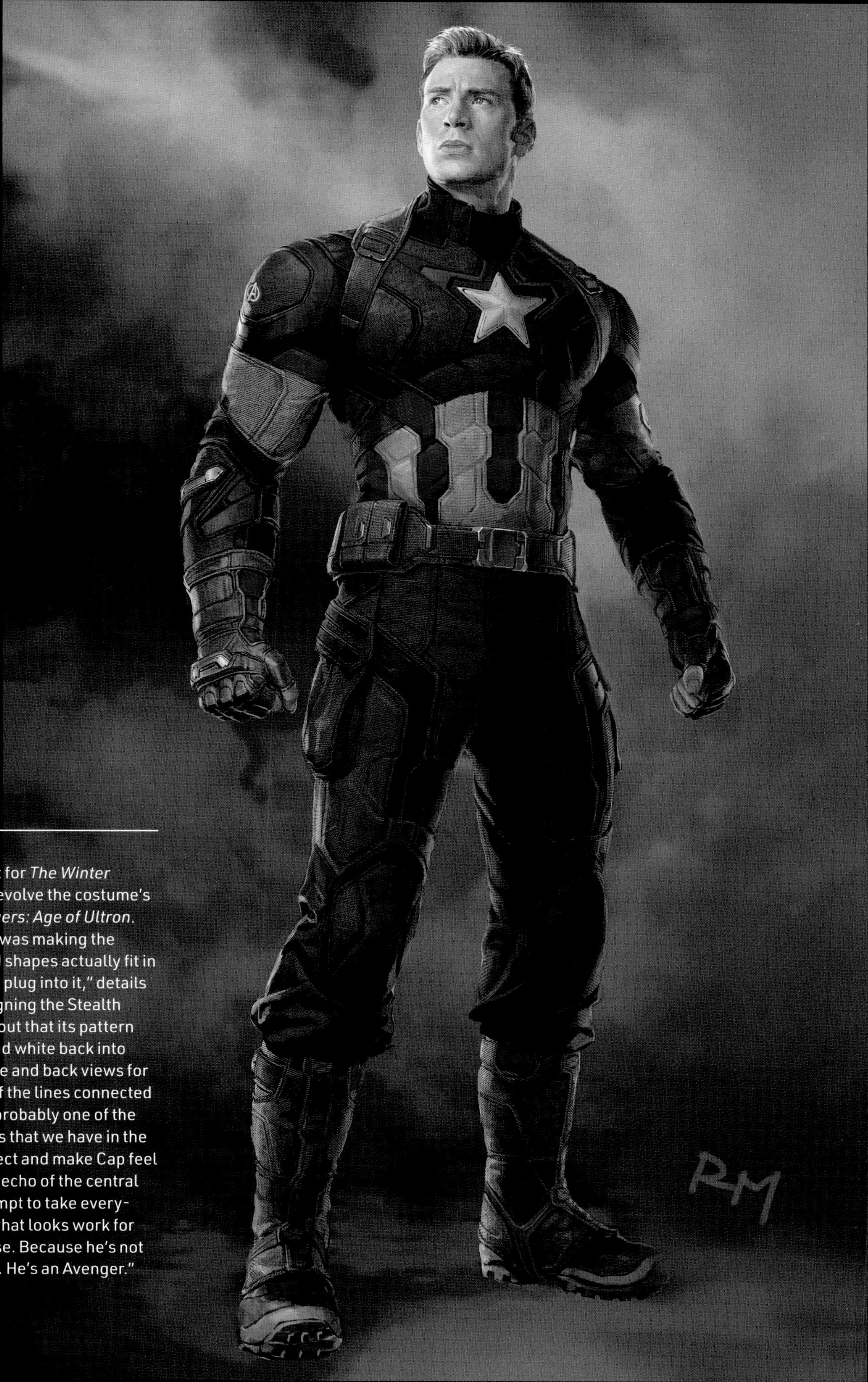
RM

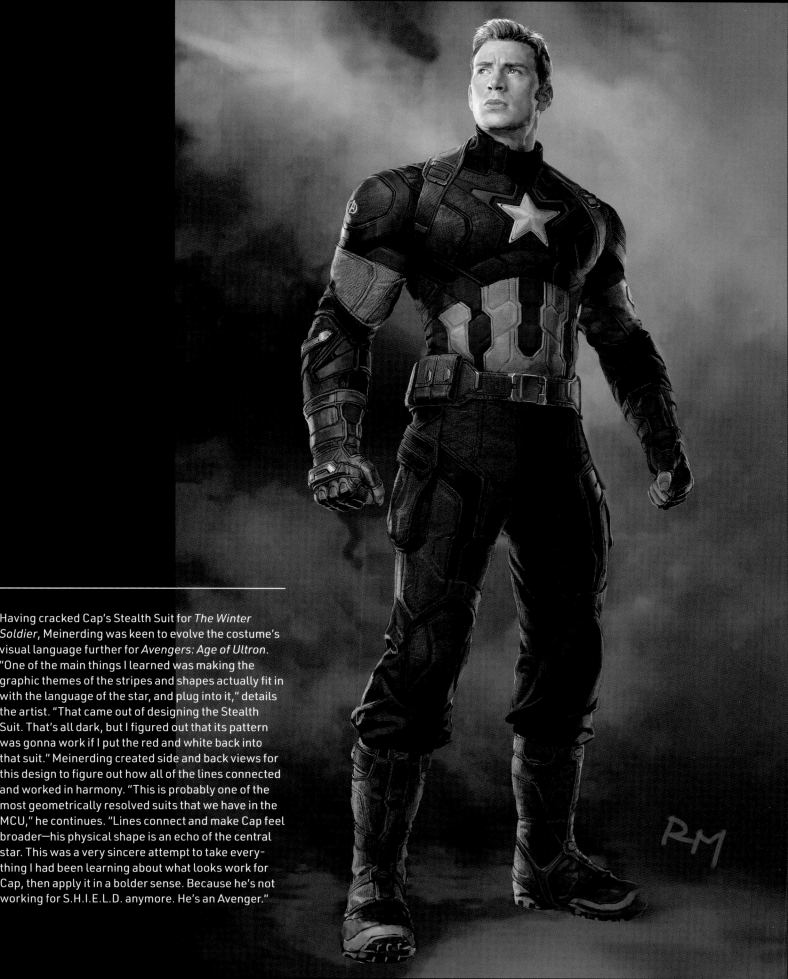

Having cracked Cap's Stealth Suit for *The Winter Soldier*, Meinerding was keen to evolve the costume's visual language further for *Avengers: Age of Ultron*. "One of the main things I learned was making the graphic themes of the stripes and shapes actually fit in with the language of the star, and plug into it," details the artist. "That came out of designing the Stealth Suit. That's all dark, but I figured out that its pattern was gonna work if I put the red and white back into that suit." Meinerding created side and back views for this design to figure out how all of the lines connected and worked in harmony. "This is probably one of the most geometrically resolved suits that we have in the MCU," he continues. "Lines connect and make Cap feel broader—his physical shape is an echo of the central star. This was a very sincere attempt to take everything I had been learning about what looks work for Cap, then apply it in a bolder sense. Because he's not working for S.H.I.E.L.D. anymore. He's an Avenger."

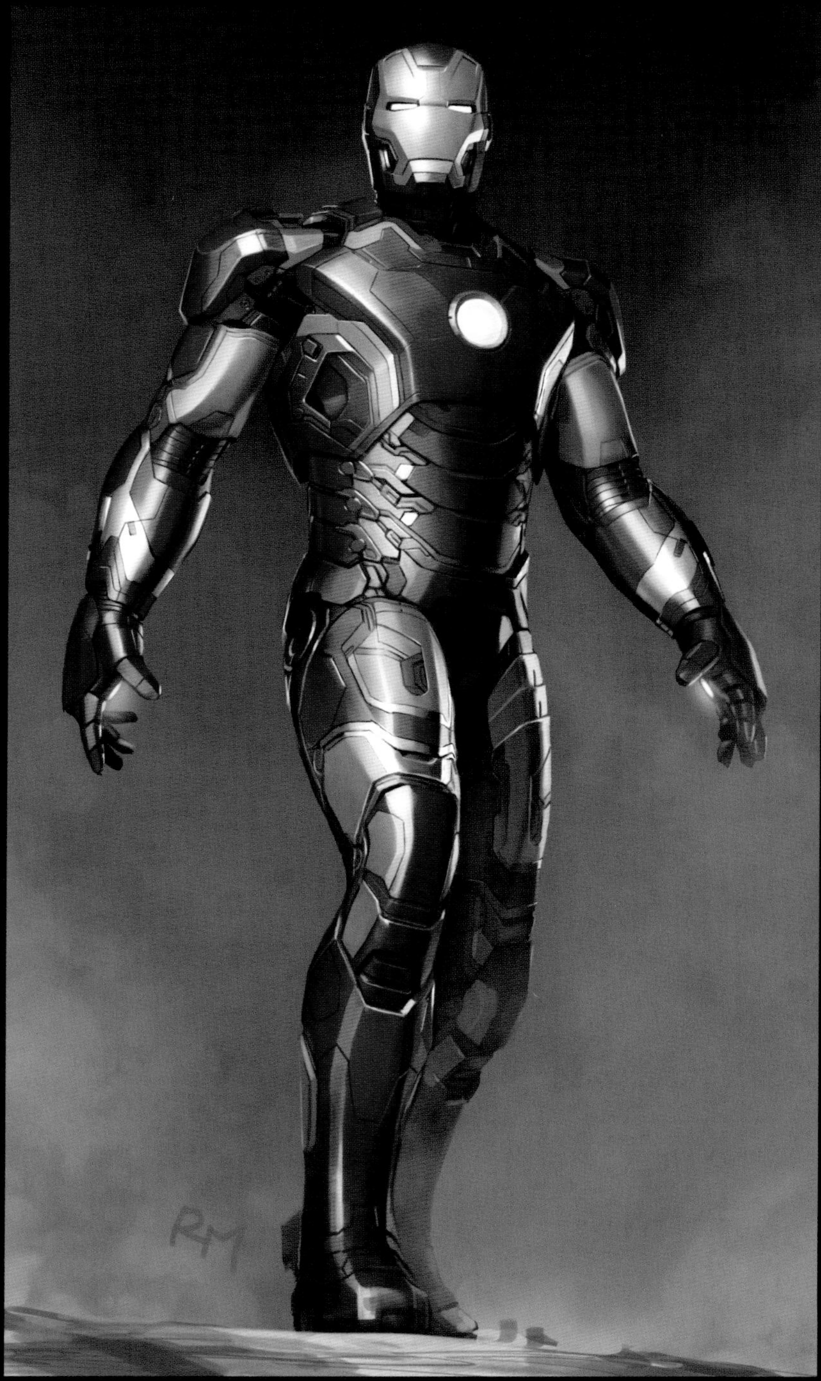

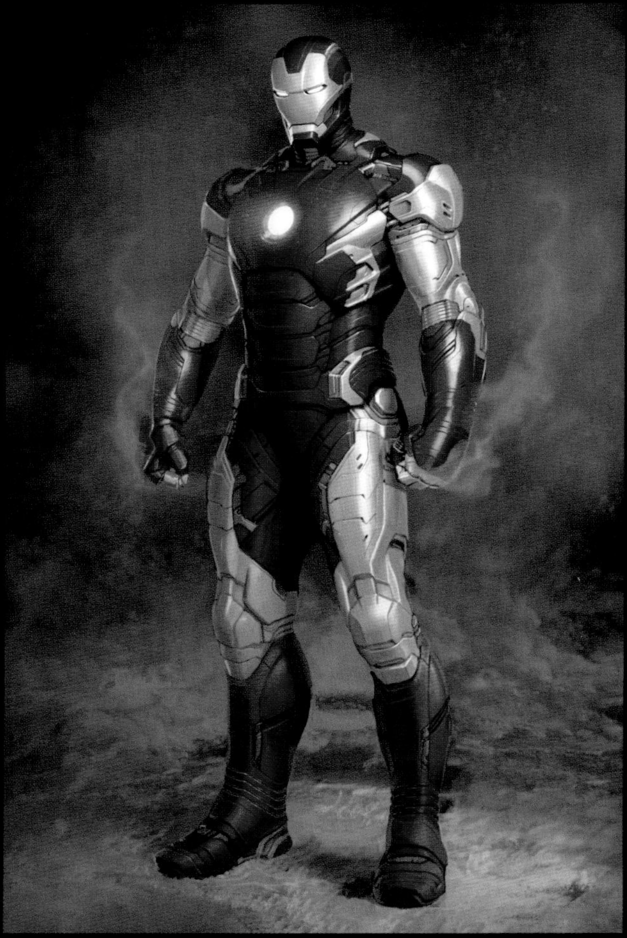

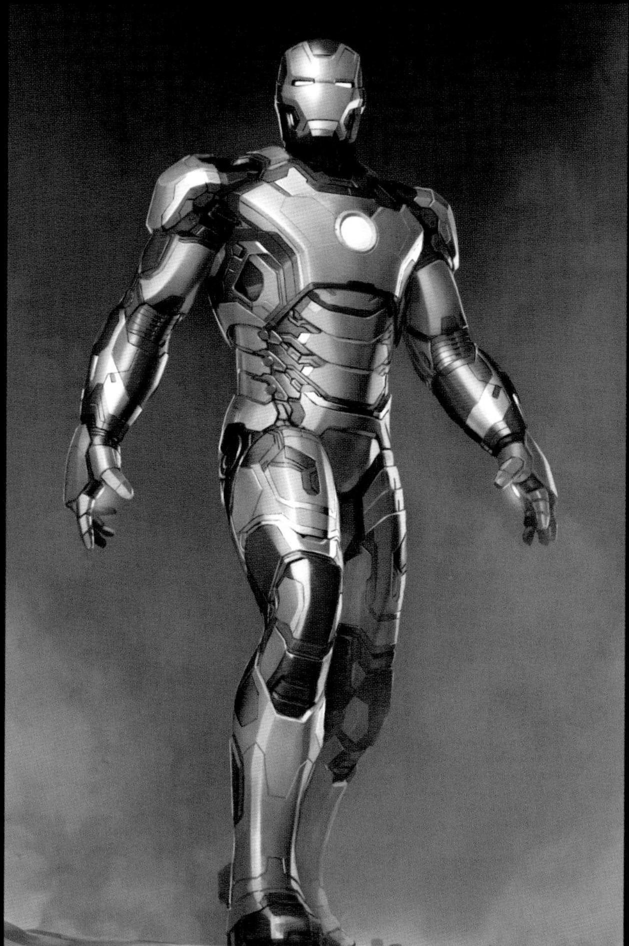

The creative exploration that led Ryan Meinerding to Cap's look for *Age of Ultron* ended up influencing his approach to future Stark tech as well. "It was sort of the culmination for me, realizing on some level that designing Iron Man suits is the same thing," he explains. "When you come up with a Repulsor Transmitter shape, that chest shape really defines the visual aesthetics of what the rest of the suit is. If you say, 'How do you get a star or light on a guy's chest to not look silly?' The answer is, you design the whole suit for the star or light to plug into."

ABOVE The Mark XLIII: ostensibly a red-recolored version of the Mark XLII

OPPOSITE Bruce Banner/the Hulk concept art for *Age of Ultron*, debuting the character's Stark-created stretchy pants

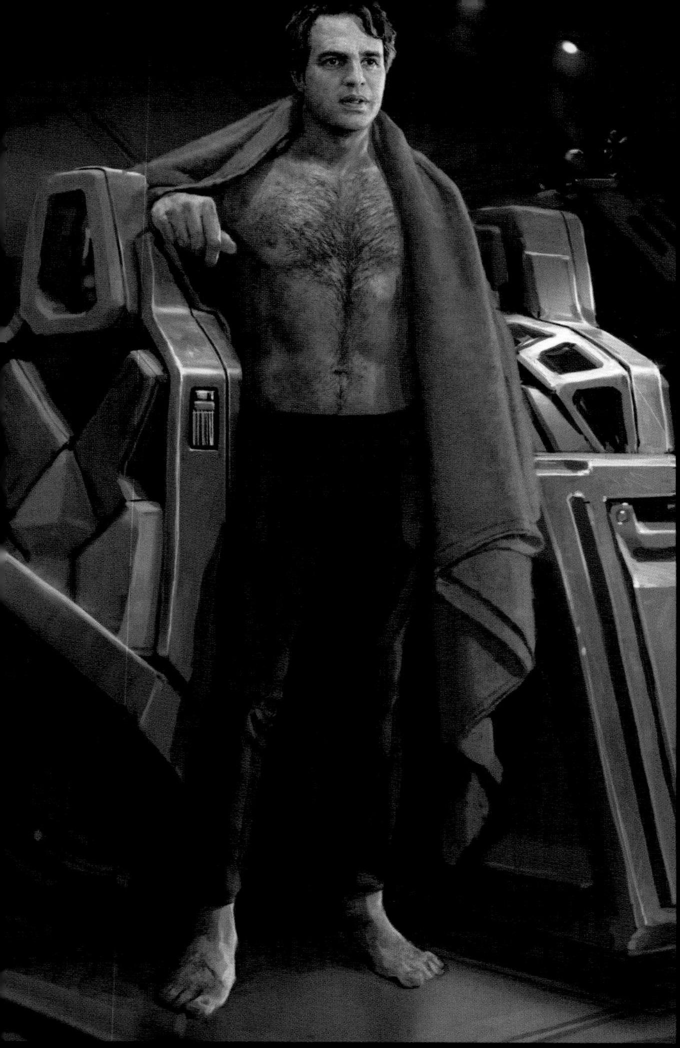

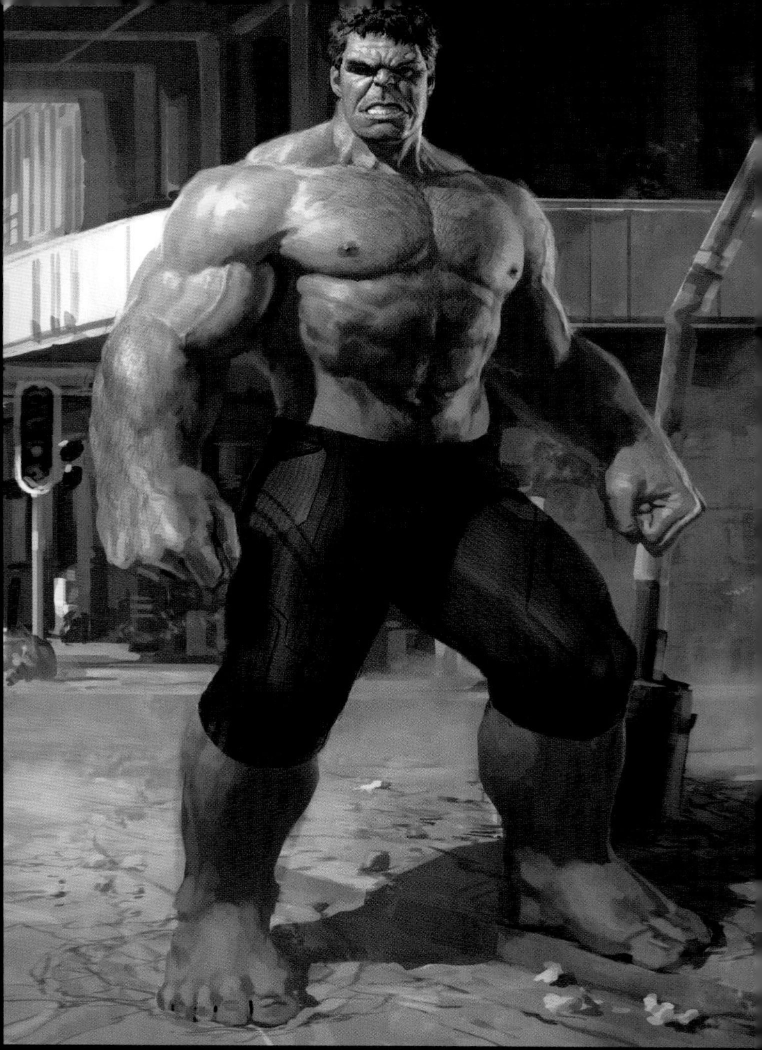

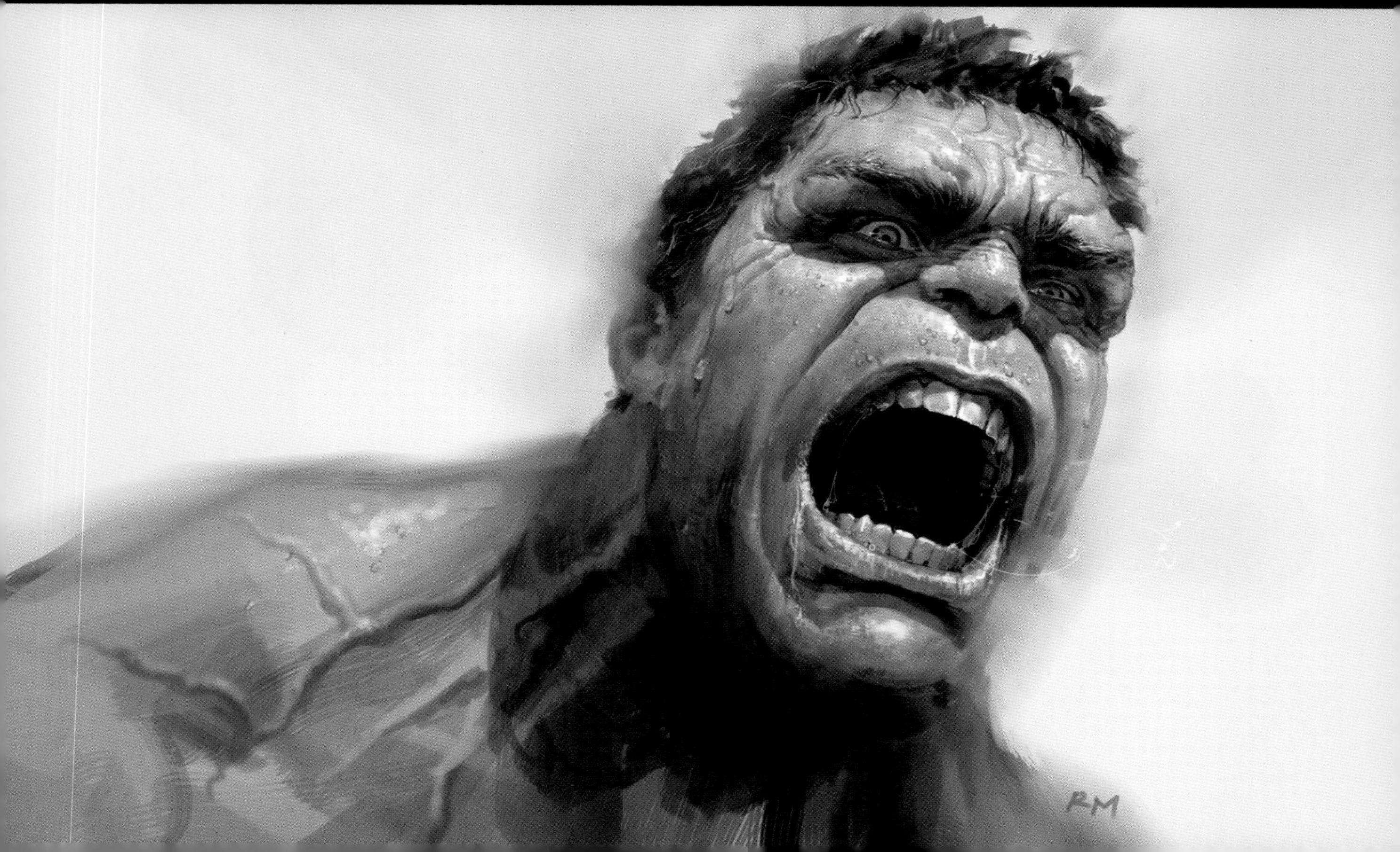
RM

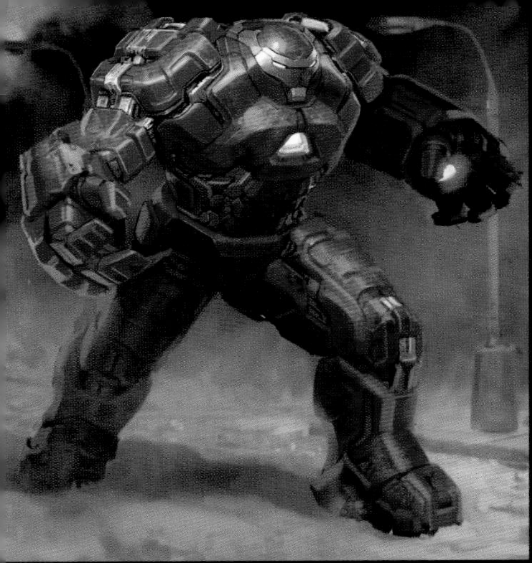

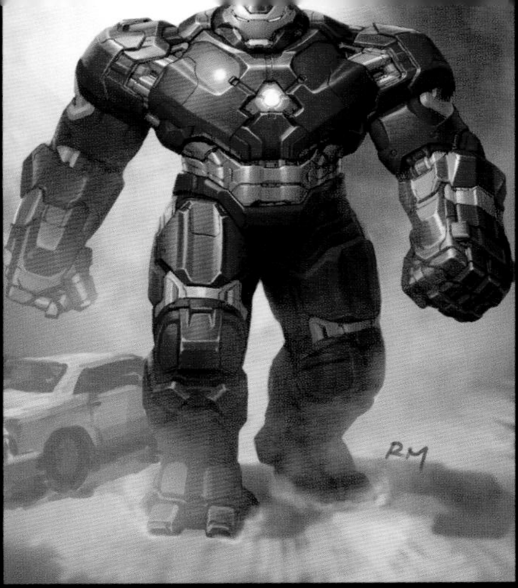
RM

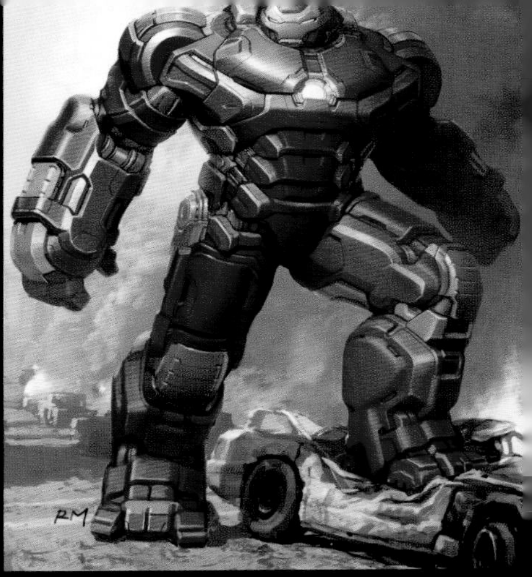
RM

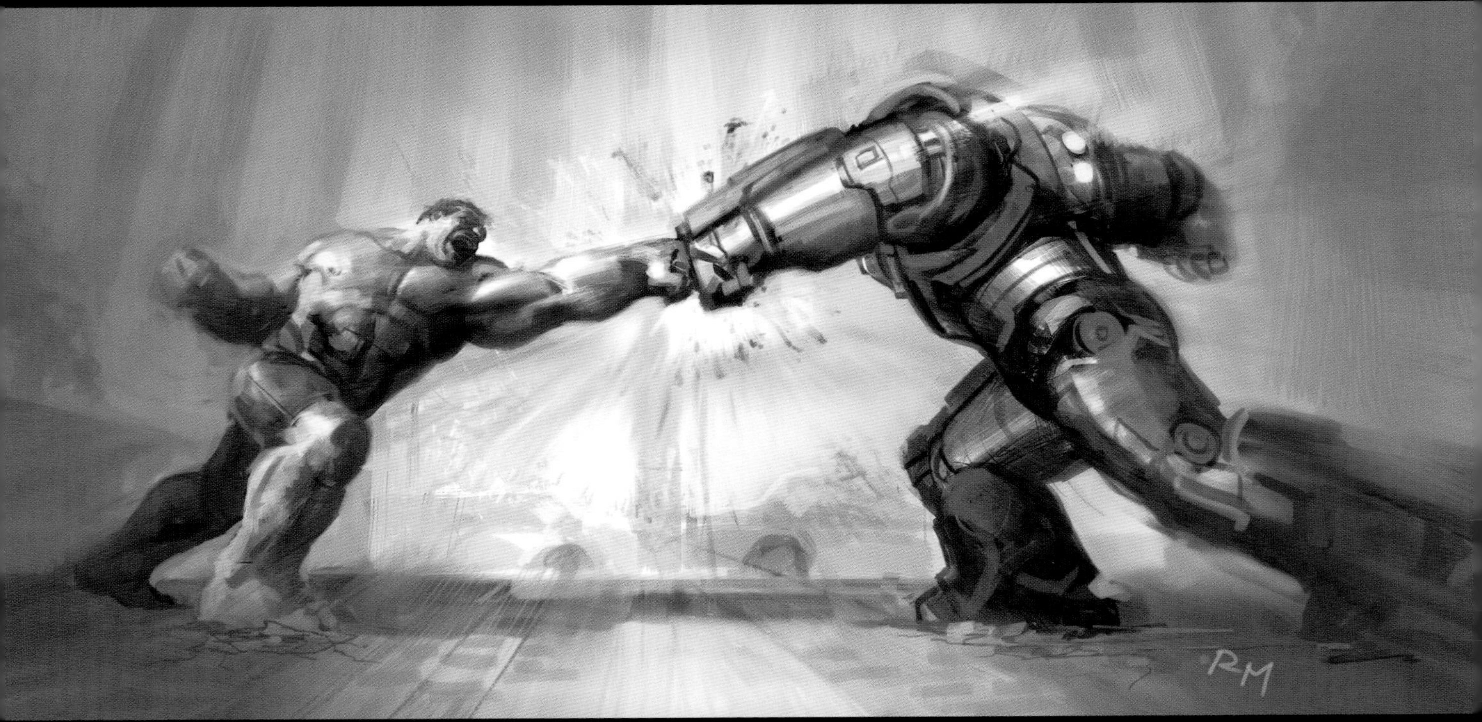
RM

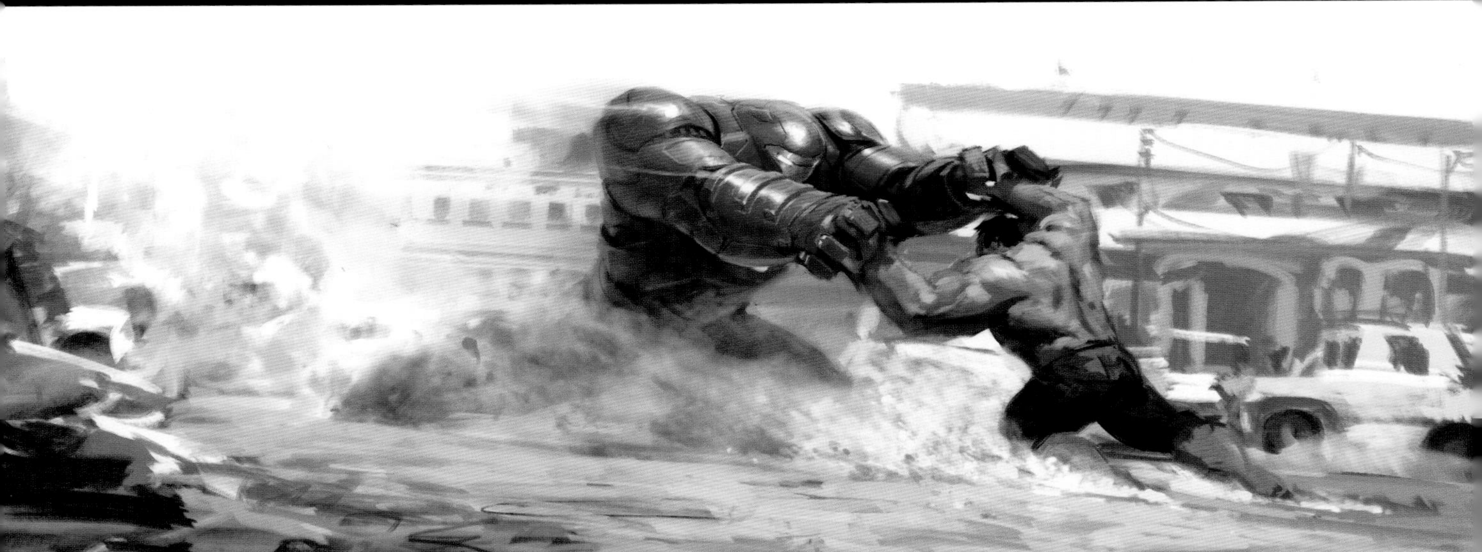

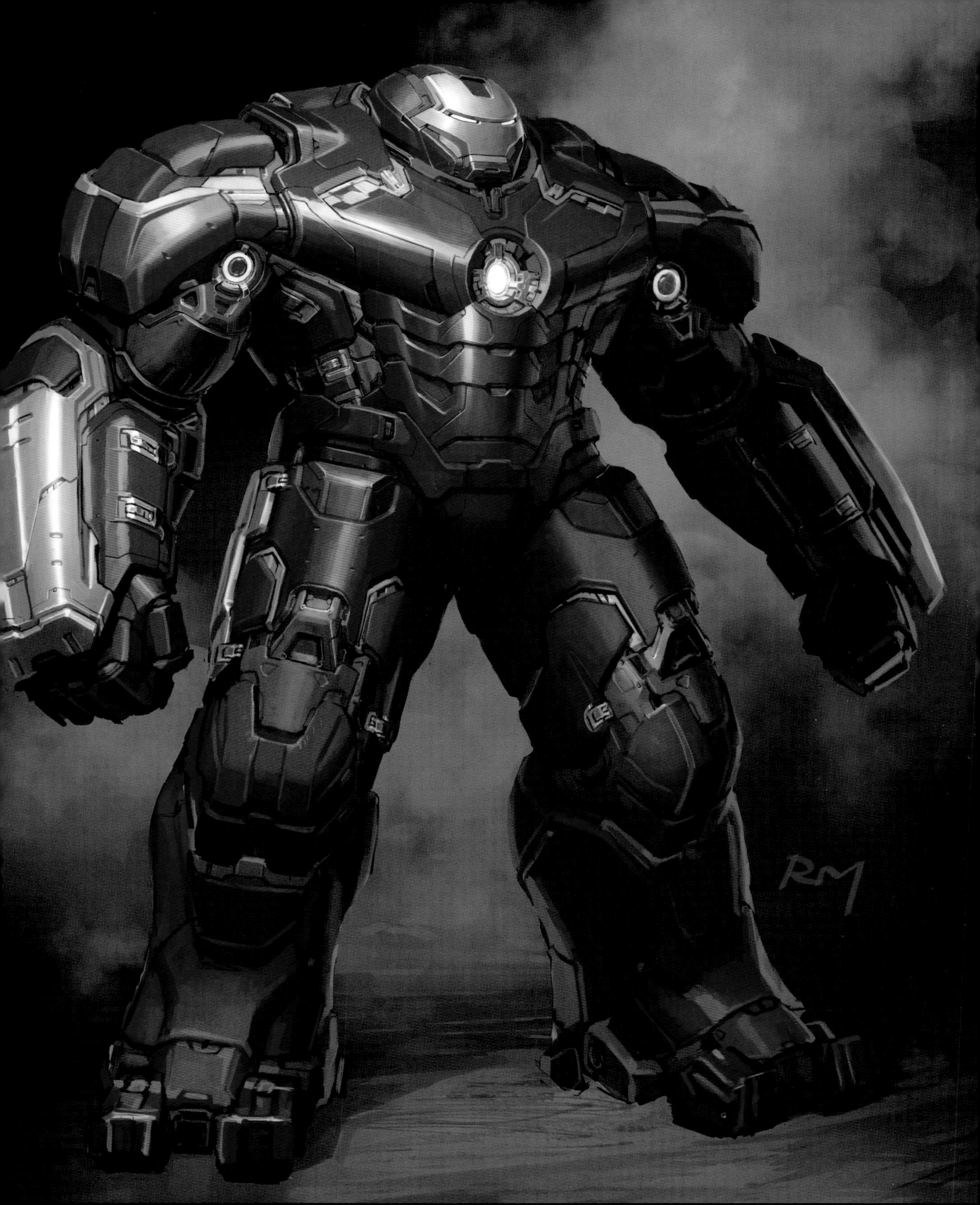
RM

s point in the MCU, Meinerding and his team had ssfully designed a number of iterations of Iron Man, in America, and Thor. Therefore, on *Age of Ultron*, brand-new, pivotal visuals were the most important complish: Ultron, Vision, and the "Hulkbuster" (the XLIV, which the Mark XLIII nestled inside in order to pilot). For the latter, Meinerding's concern was to make sure it didn't look cartoony. Some of the interior, hyper-detailed ideas Meinerding pitched included devious defense mechanisms: "If Hulk was ripping apart the panels, Tony had surprises underneath, like turning saw blades, self-healing mechanisms, or force fields."

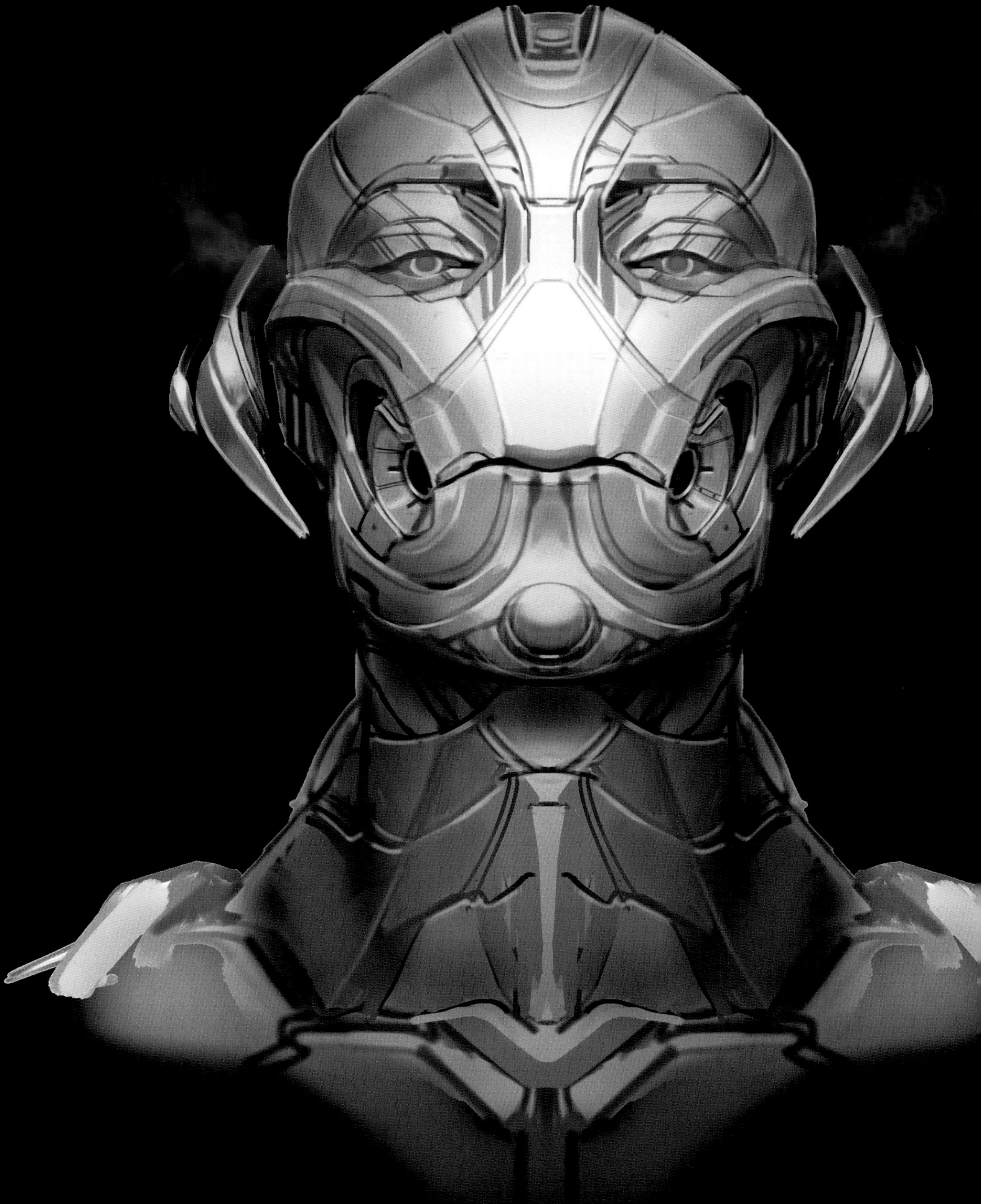

Similar to when Meinerding figured out the best look of Hulk's face very early on in the visual development process for *Marvel's The Avengers*, returning director Joss Whedon fell in love with the artist's initial swing at the face of *Age of Ultron*'s titular villain. "The very first image I did was a portrait [above] that I ended up pasting on a body [page 131]. Joss really liked that head," says Meinerdi For the all-important sake of exploring other ideas, M erding and the Visual Development team embarked or a long, multi-face design journey to try out other style Ultimately, the final design of Ultron's face came all th way back to Meinerding's first idea.

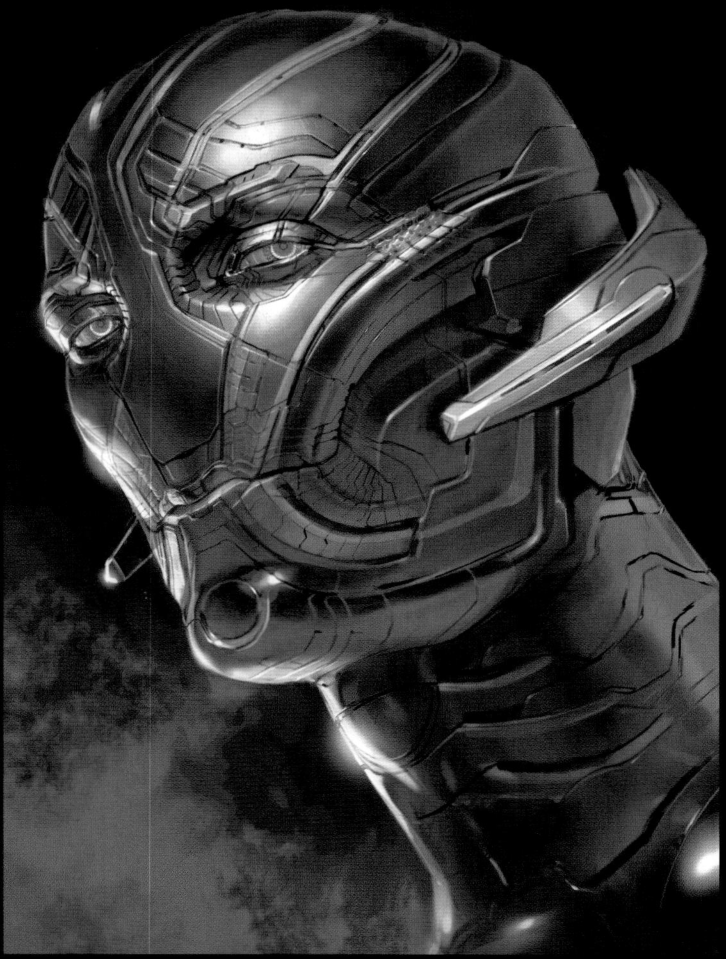
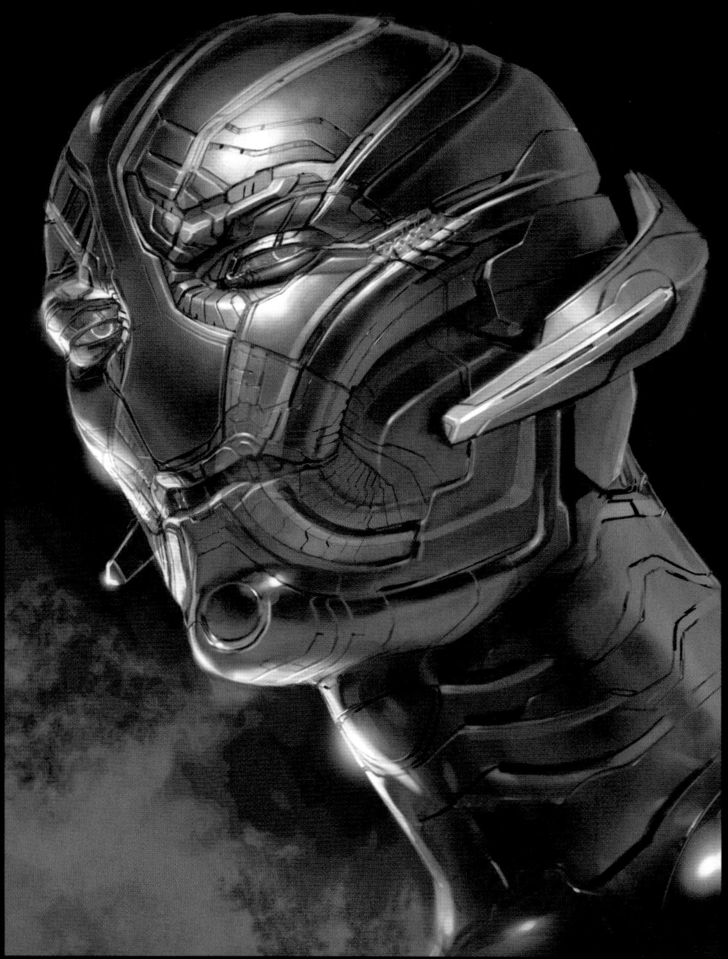
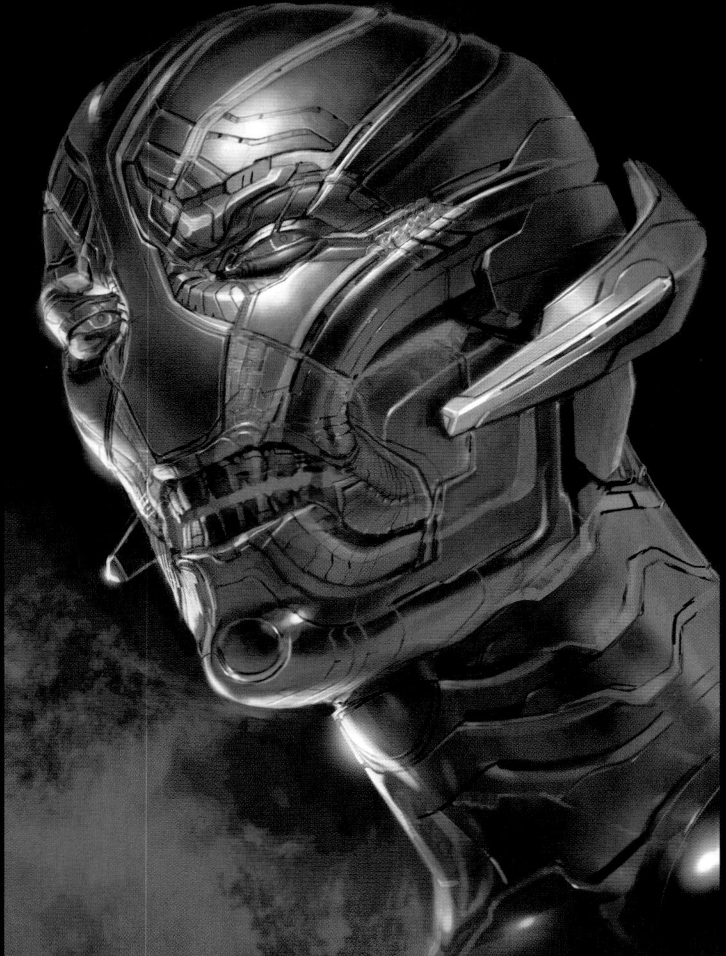
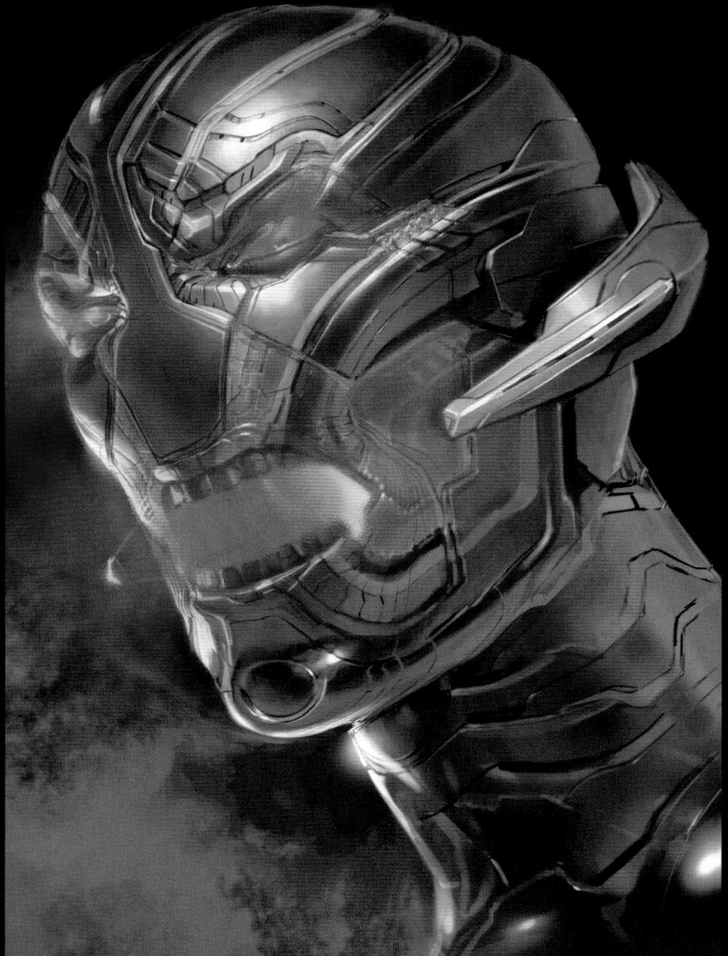

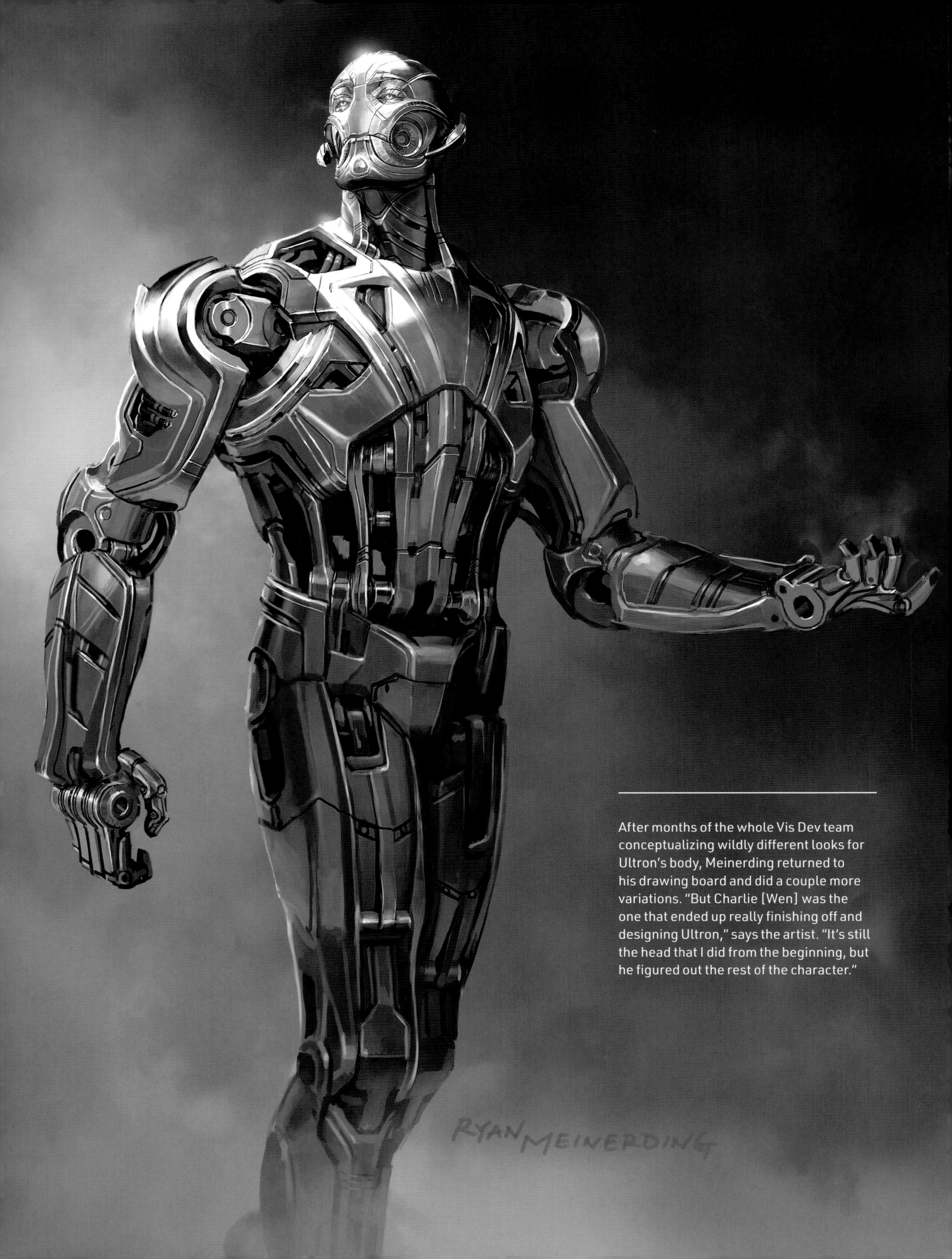
RYAN MEINERDING

After months of the whole Vis Dev team conceptualizing wildly different looks for Ultron's body, Meinerding returned to his drawing board and did a couple more variations. "But Charlie [Wen] was the one that ended up really finishing off and designing Ultron," says the artist. "It's still the head that I did from the beginning, but he figured out the rest of the character."

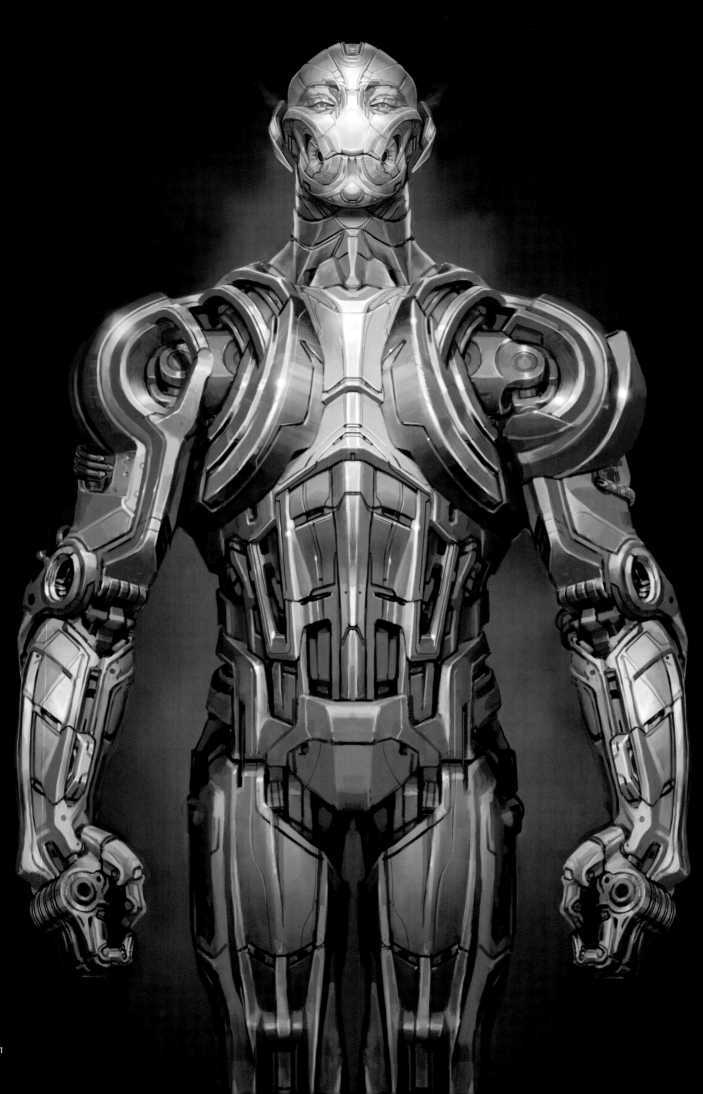

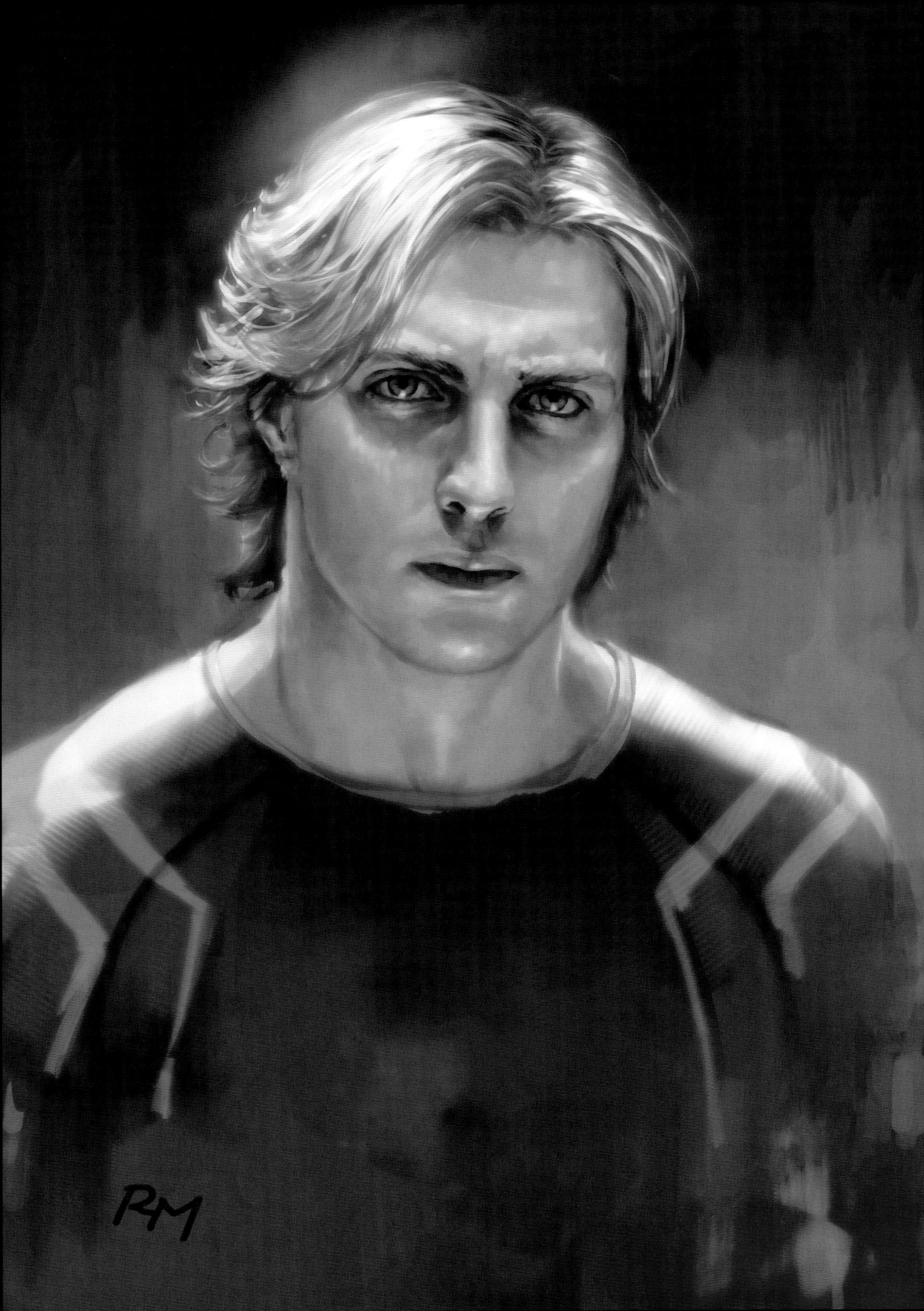
RM

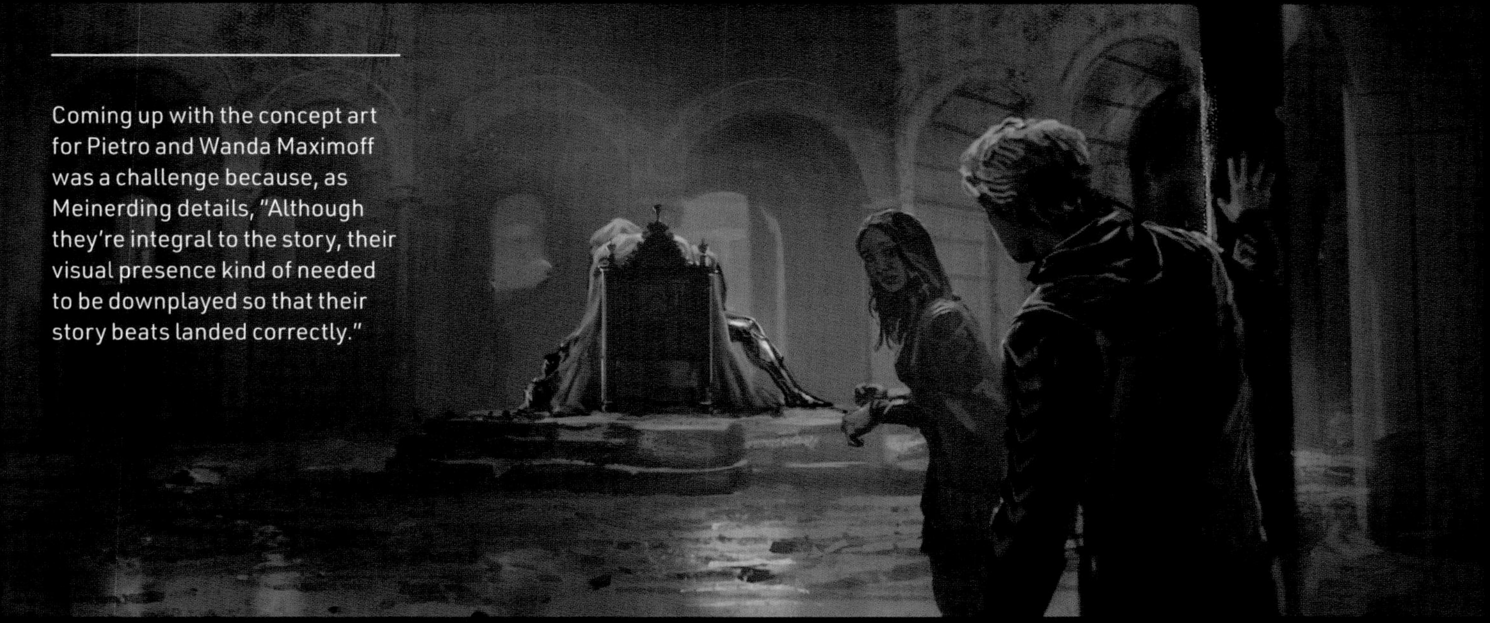

Coming up with the concept art for Pietro and Wanda Maximoff was a challenge because, as Meinerding details, "Although they're integral to the story, their visual presence kind of needed to be downplayed so that their story beats landed correctly."

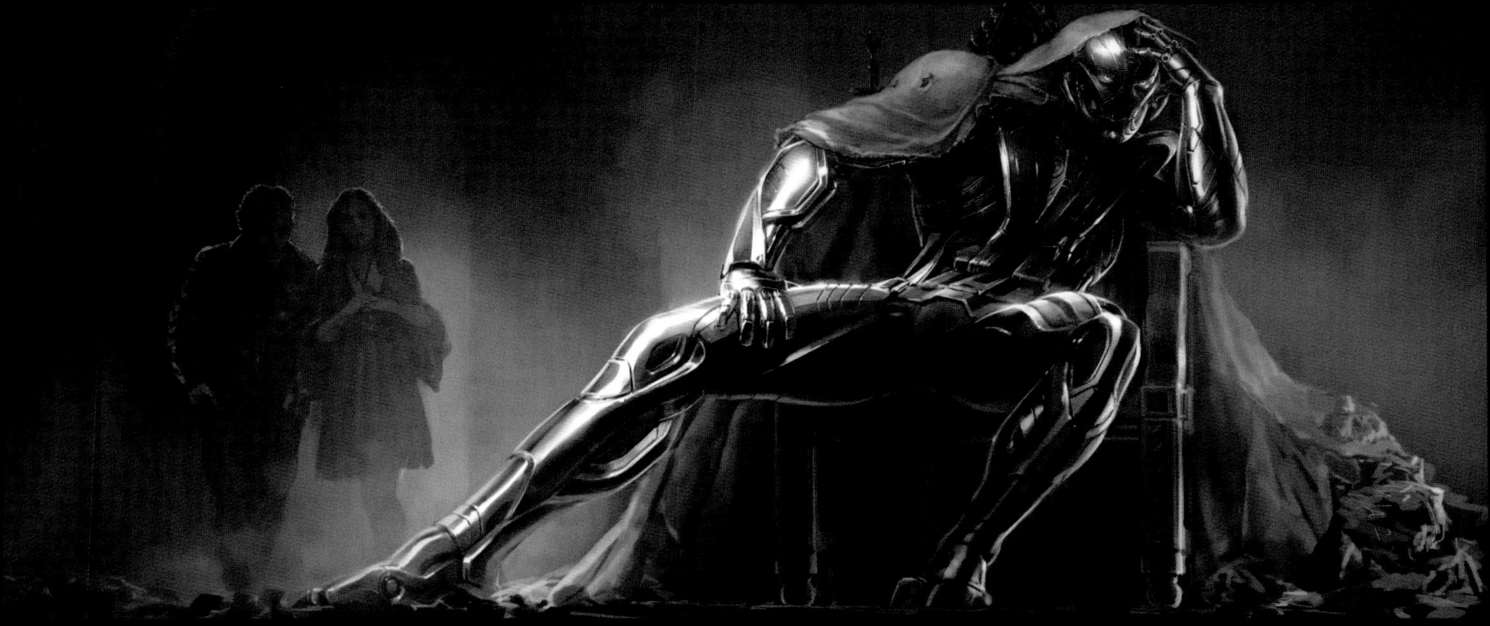

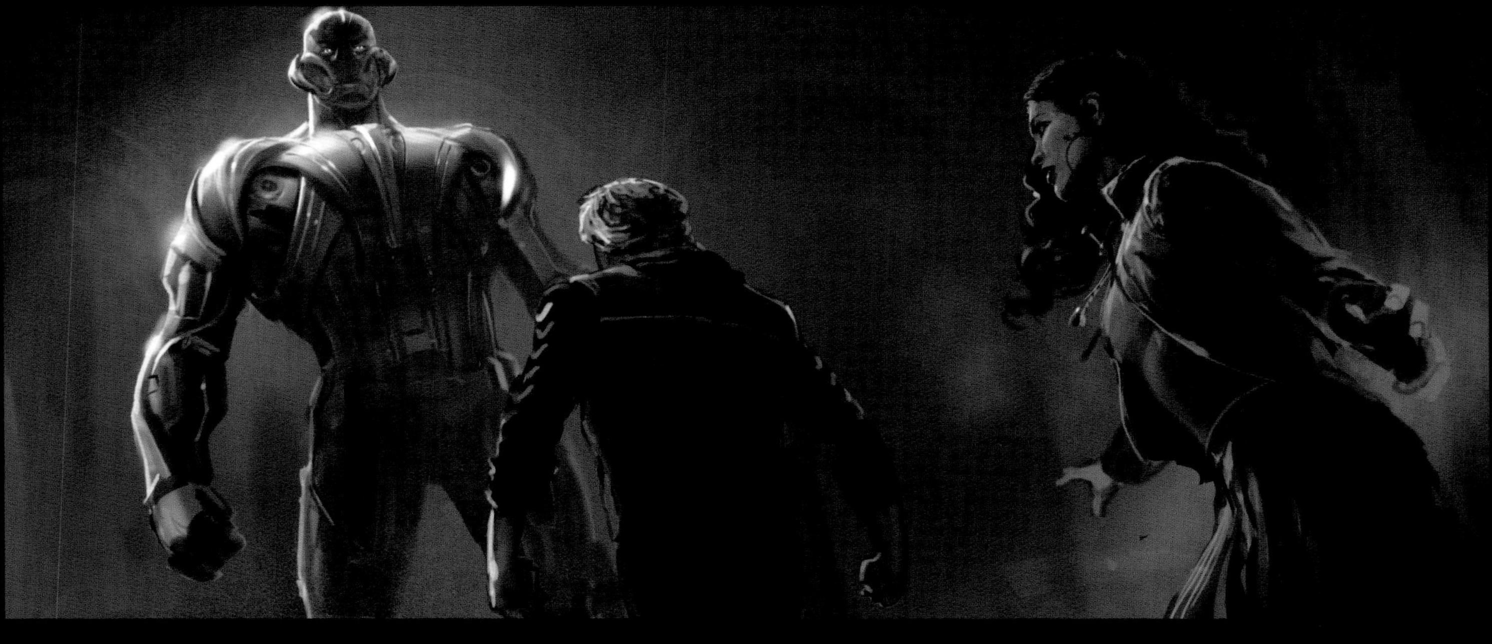

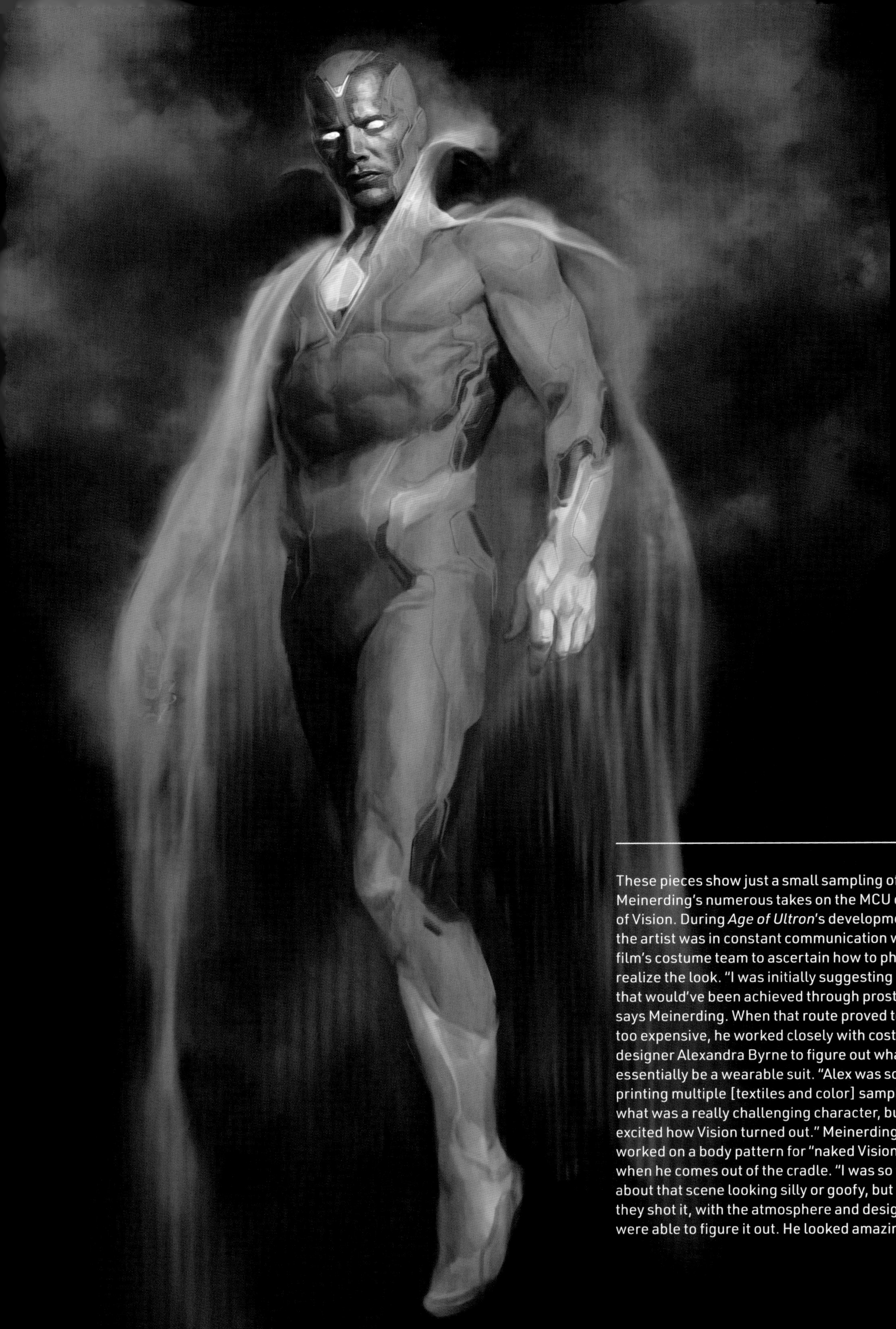

These pieces show just a small sampling of Meinerding's numerous takes on the MCU debut of Vision. During *Age of Ultron*'s development, the artist was in constant communication with the film's costume team to ascertain how to physically realize the look. "I was initially suggesting ideas that would've been achieved through prosthetics," says Meinerding. When that route proved to be too expensive, he worked closely with costume designer Alexandra Byrne to figure out what would essentially be a wearable suit. "Alex was screen-printing multiple [textiles and color] samples for what was a really challenging character, but I was excited how Vision turned out." Meinerding also worked on a body pattern for "naked Vision," for when he comes out of the cradle. "I was so worried about that scene looking silly or goofy, but the way they shot it, with the atmosphere and design, they were able to figure it out. He looked amazing."

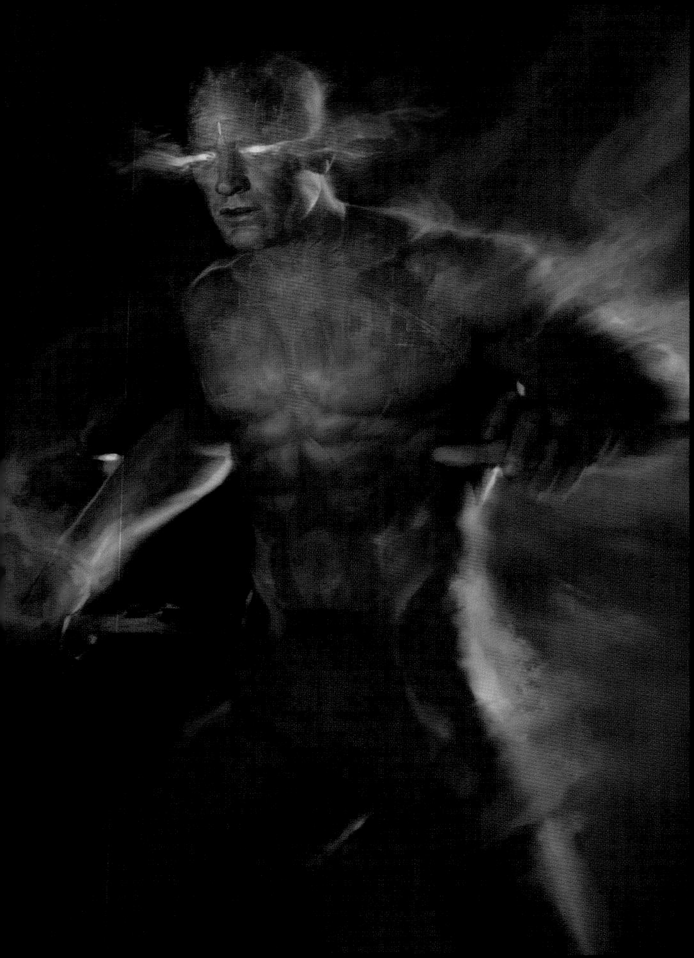
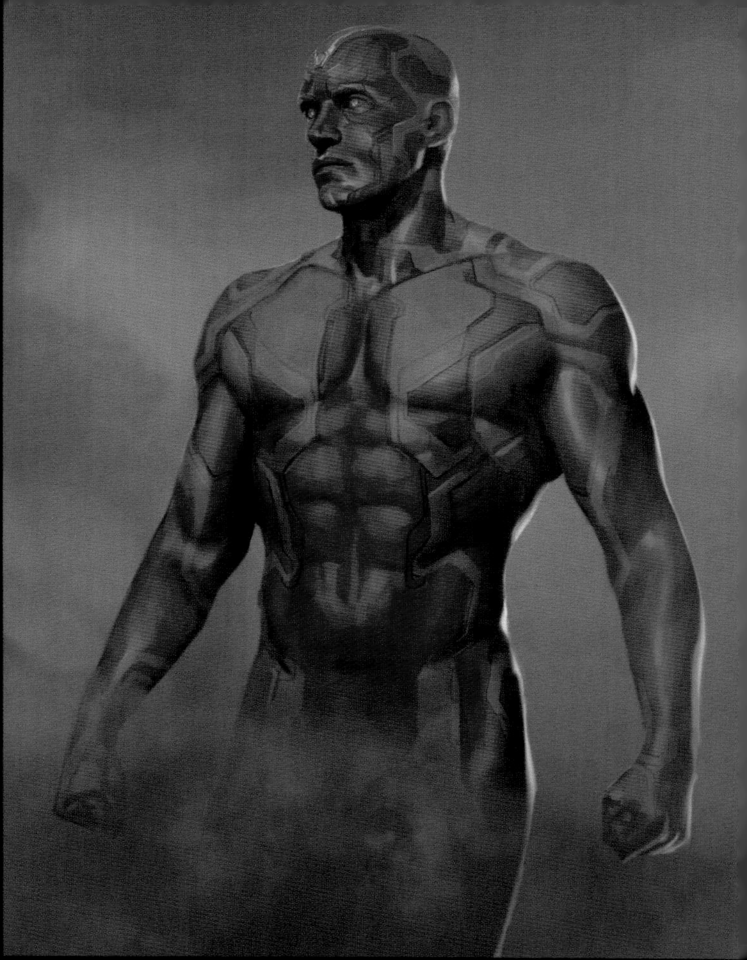
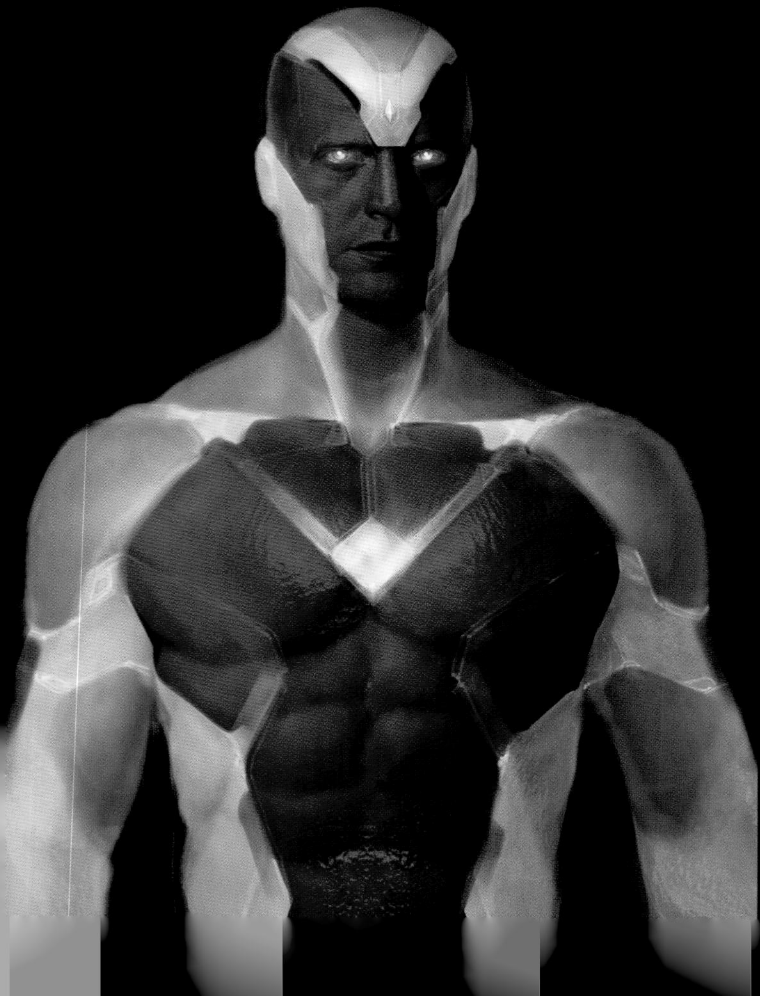
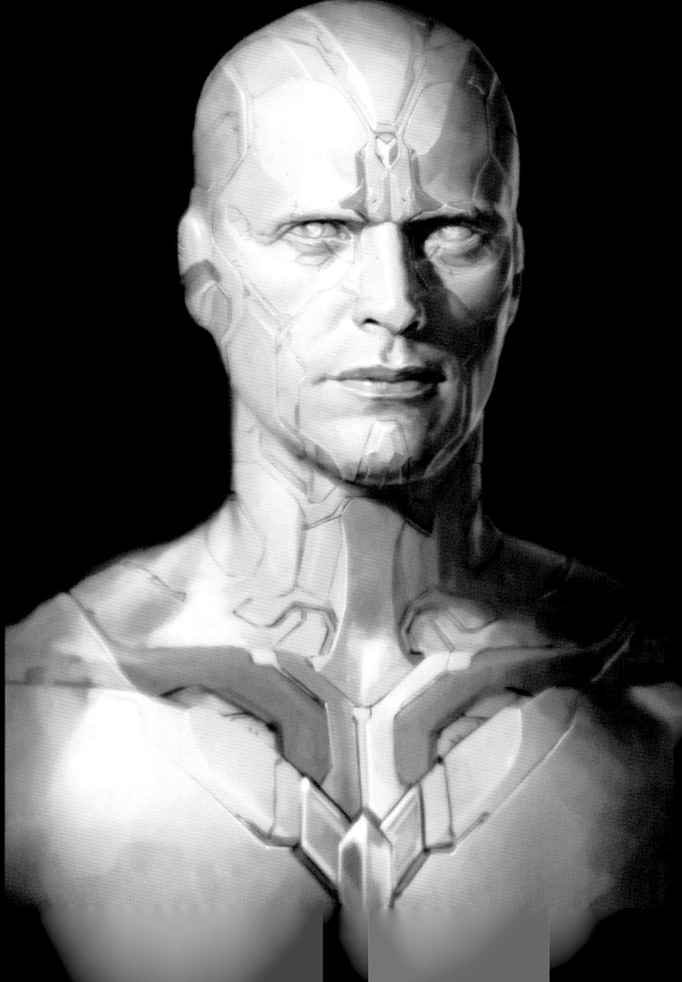

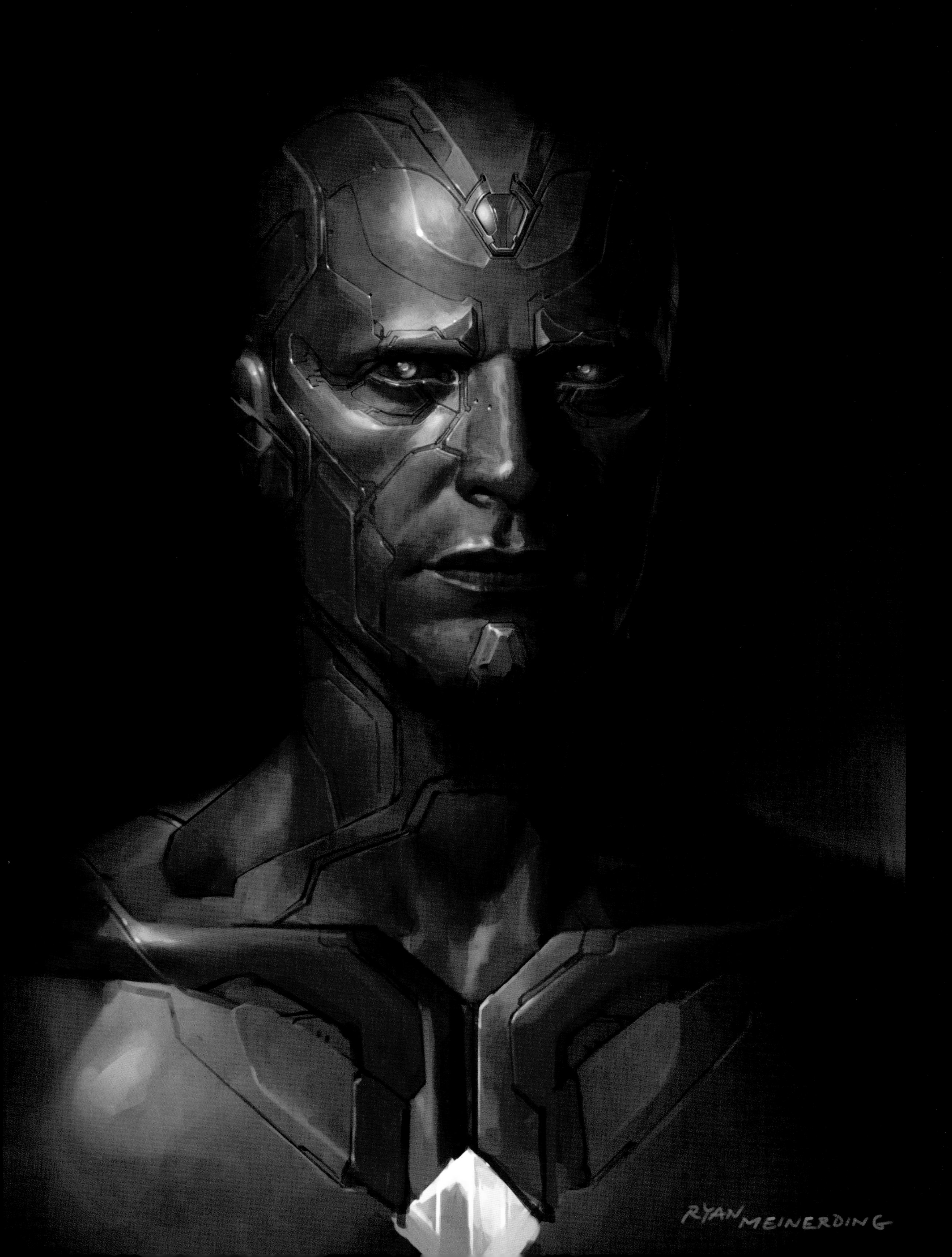
RYAN MEINERDING

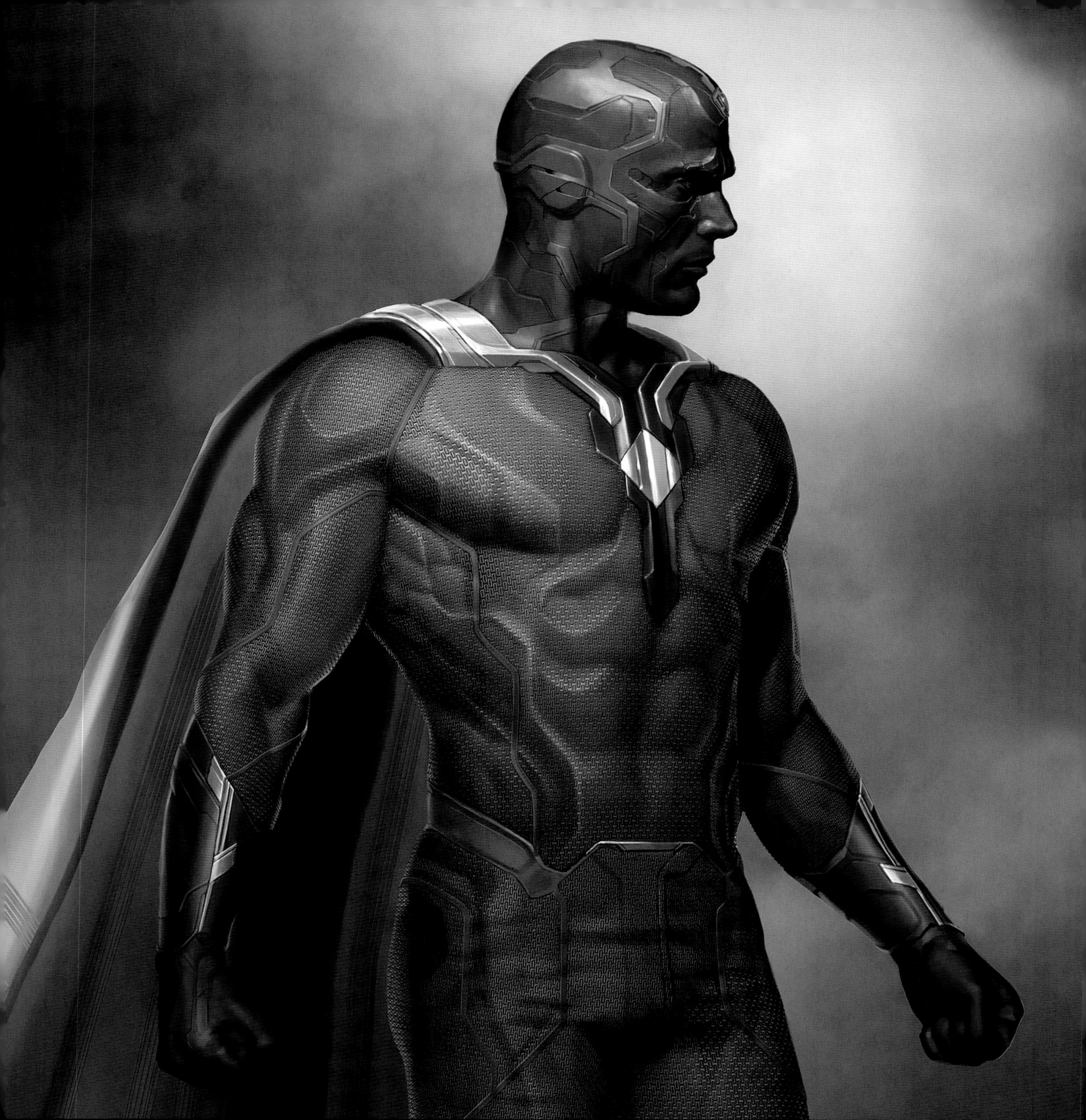

Meinerding took what he learned by refining Cap's suit designs by growing out of the chest star, and so, he says, "You can see the same sort of echoing and concentric things coming off how the Mind Stone fits into this design. Also, because Vision is always meant to be an empathetic character, baking in these brow shapes means he's always gonna look like he's got an upturned, worried brow. With the added visual effects, they modulate that stuff. But those are things that I try to do. The intent is there. Also—and this isn't visible from this angle—in the back of Vision's head there's actually the design of Ultron's face. It's like, no matter what happens, Ultron was always going to be a part of him."

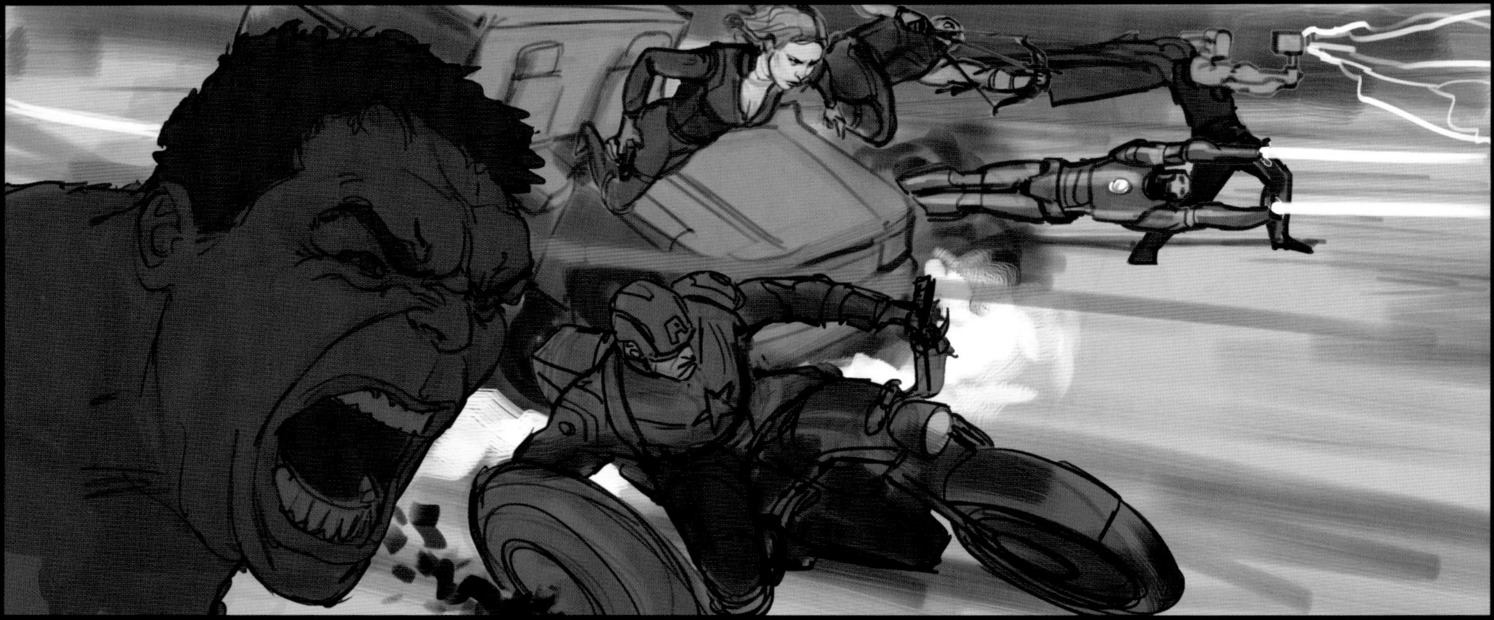

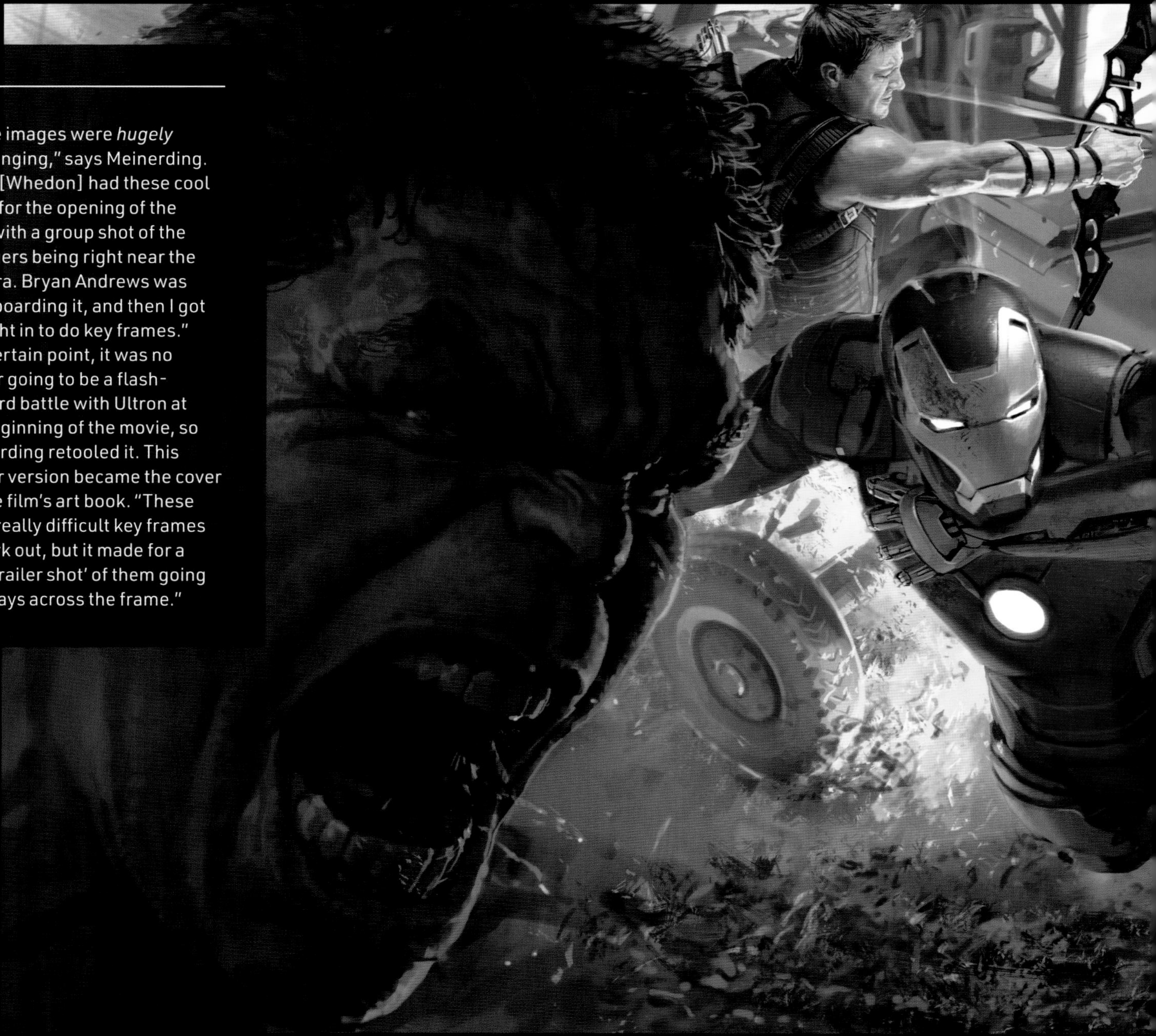

"These images were *hugely* challenging," says Meinerding. "Joss [Whedon] had these cool ideas for the opening of the film, with a group shot of the Avengers being right near the camera. Bryan Andrews was storyboarding it, and then I got brought in to do key frames." At a certain point, it was no longer going to be a flash-forward battle with Ultron at the beginning of the movie, so Meinerding retooled it. This earlier version became the cover for the film's art book. "These were really difficult key frames to work out, but it made for a cool 'trailer shot' of them going sideways across the frame."

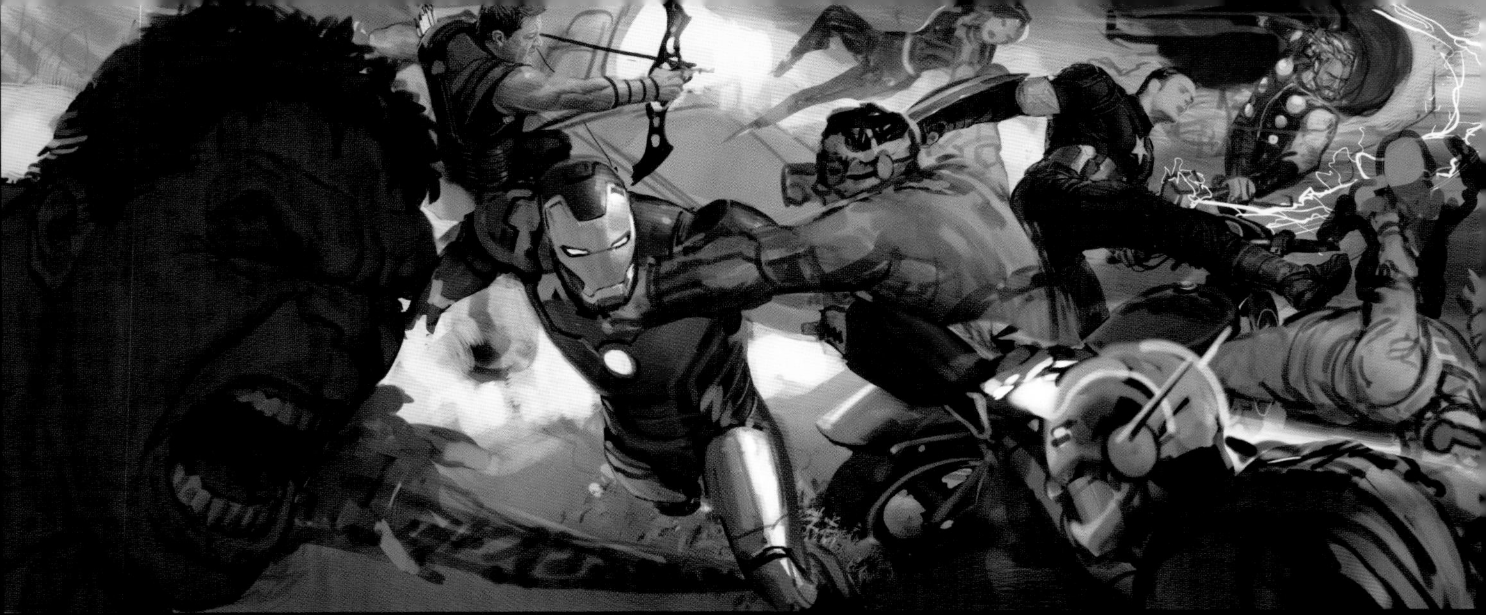

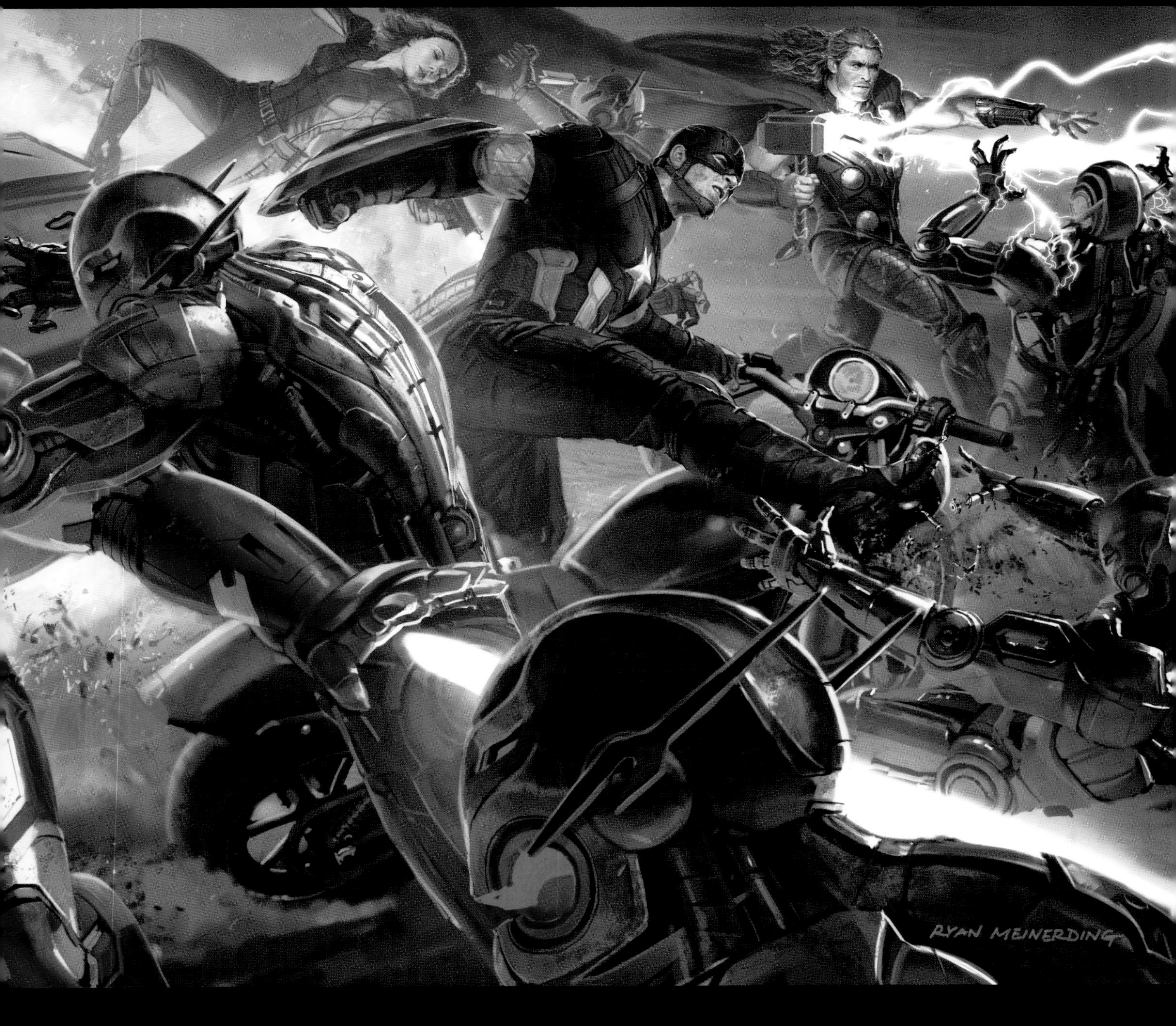
RYAN MEINERDING

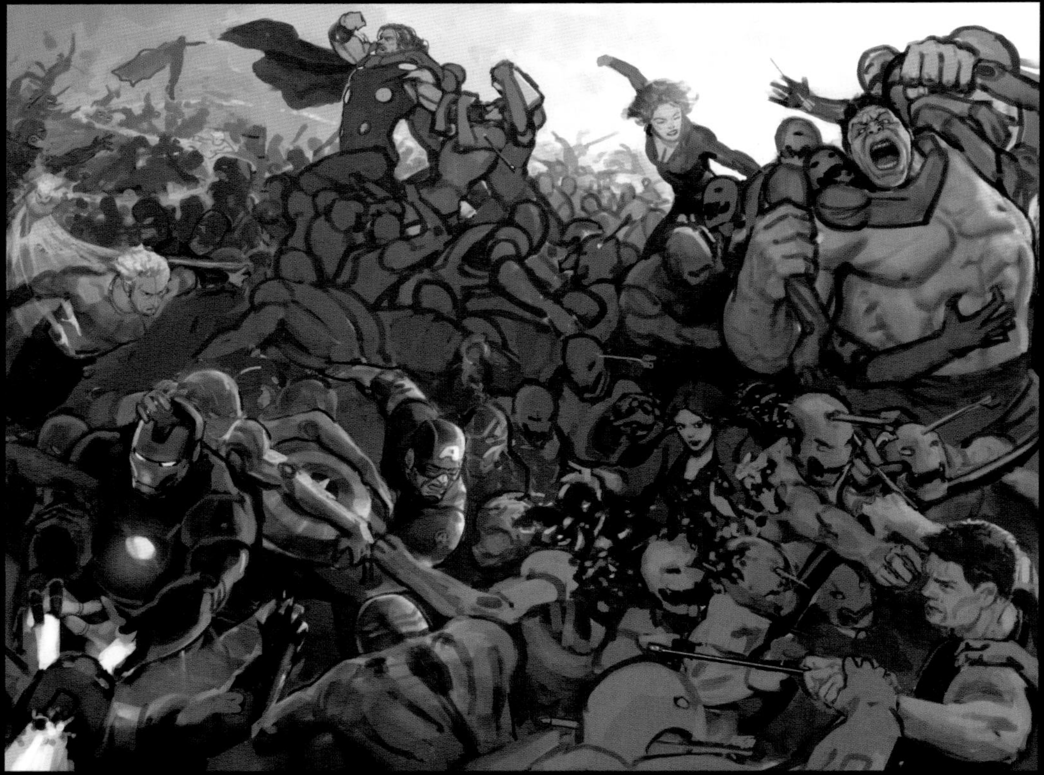

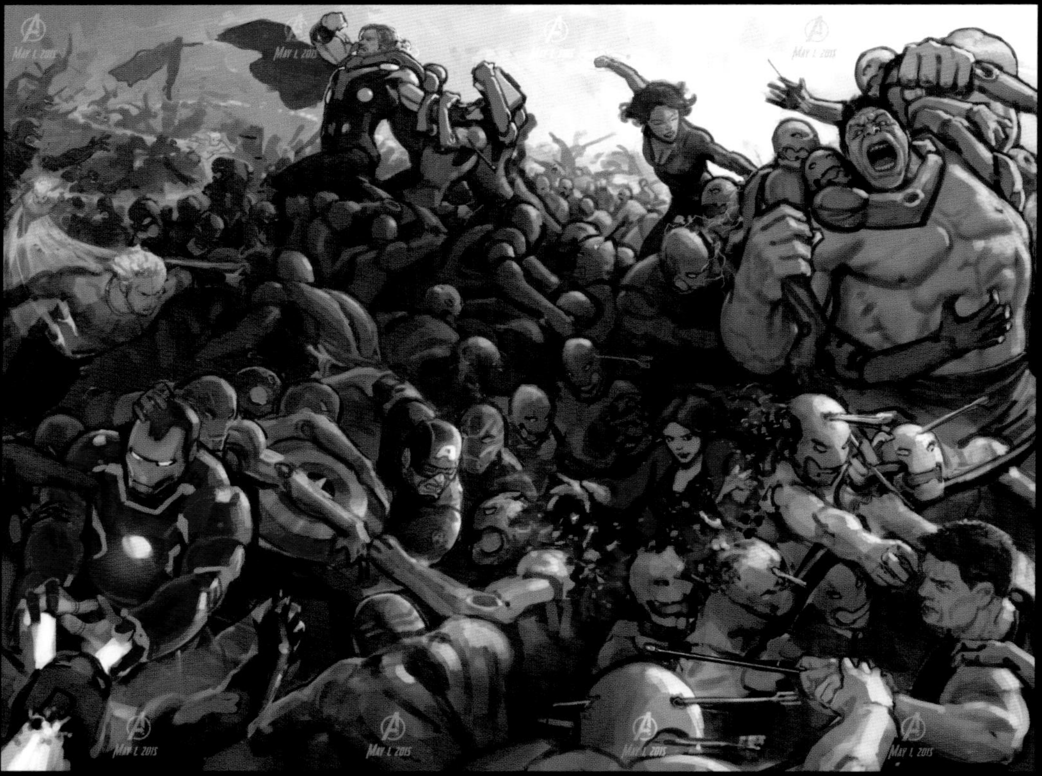
MAY 1, 2015

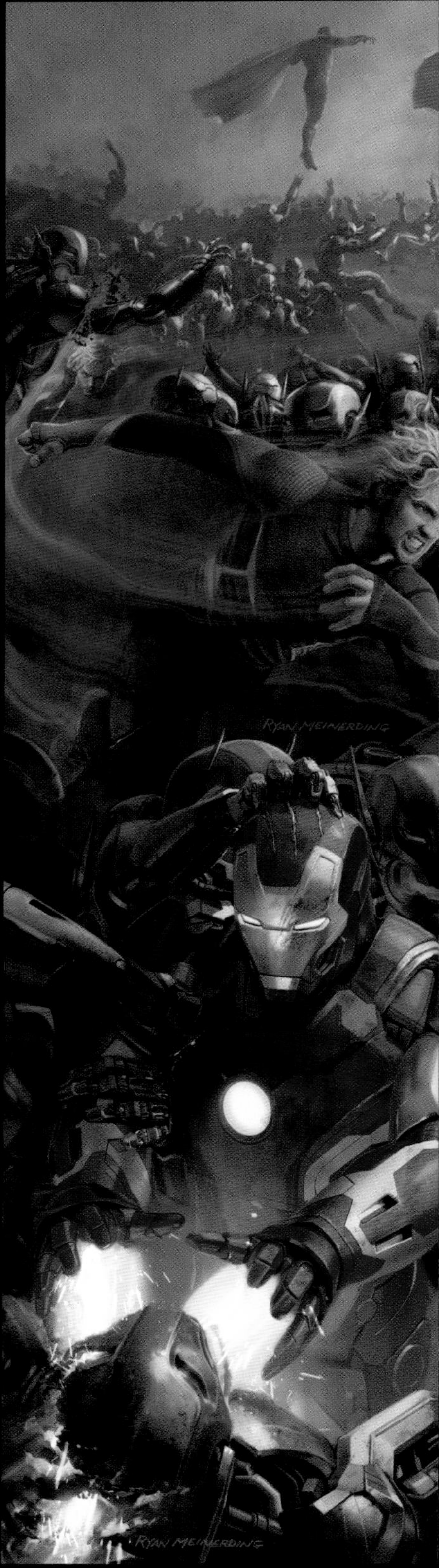
RYAN MEINERDING
RYAN MEINERDING

Several films in, Marvel Studios had grown a reputation for doing exclusive San Diego Comic-Con posters. Adi Granov crafted an *Iron Man* print. Ryan Meinerding did one for *Captain America: The First Avenger*. And Charlie Wen's art was used to promote *Thor*. But a question mark hung over what to do for *Avengers: Age of Ultron*. "I came up with the idea of doing an interconnected poster," shares Meinerding. "Charlie [Wen] and I both did a bunch of comps for what that could be. Kevin [Feige] picked one of mine. That became the image Charlie, Andy [Park], and I would collaborate on. But the movie was still in production, so we didn't really know what it was gonna look like. I just assumed there was gonna be some kind of zombie-like wave of Ultron robots at some point. The chaos of

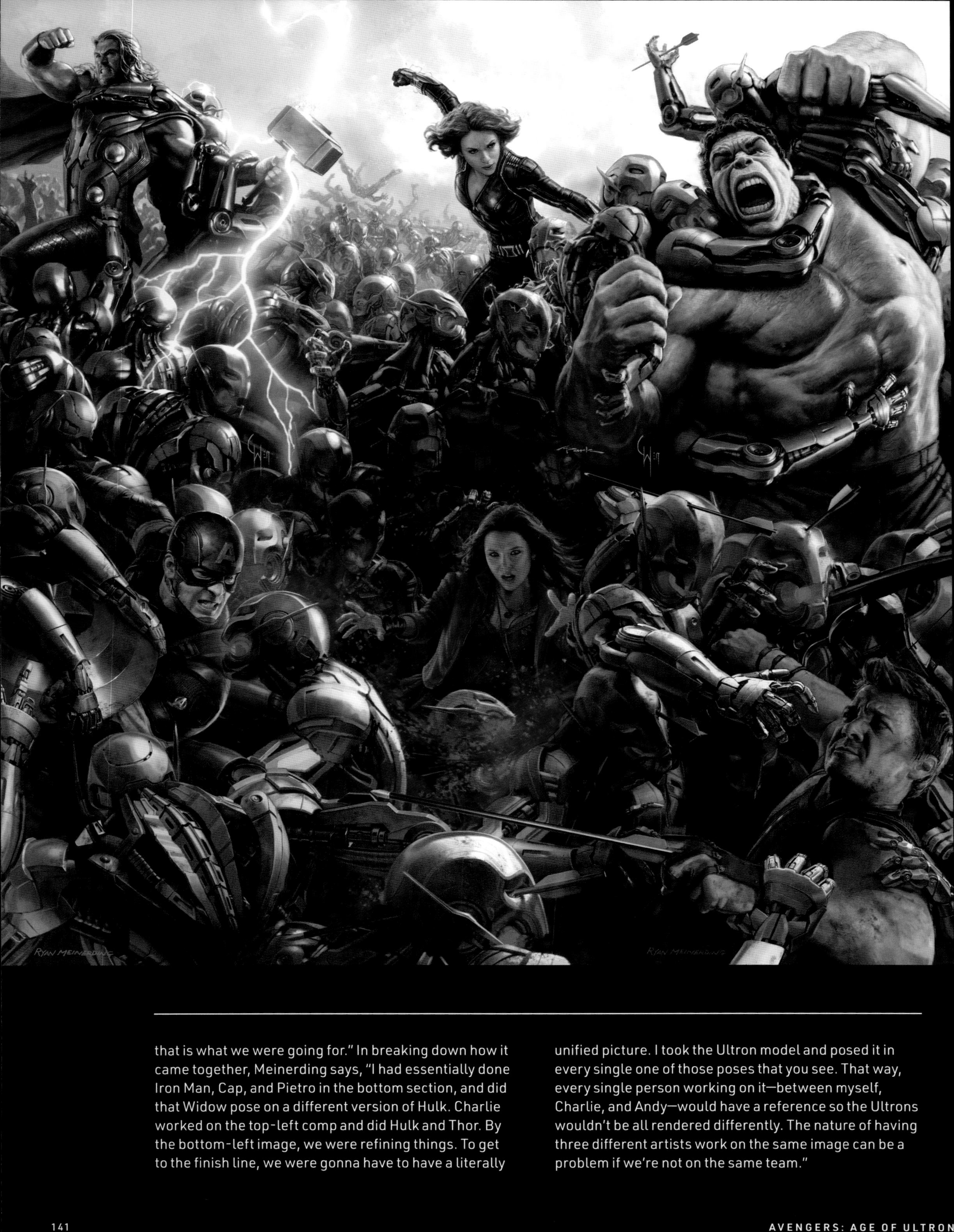
RYAN MEINERDING
RYAN MEINERDING

that is what we were going for." In breaking down how it came together, Meinerding says, "I had essentially done Iron Man, Cap, and Pietro in the bottom section, and did that Widow pose on a different version of Hulk. Charlie worked on the top-left comp and did Hulk and Thor. By the bottom-left image, we were refining things. To get to the finish line, we were gonna have to have a literally unified picture. I took the Ultron model and posed it in every single one of those poses that you see. That way, every single person working on it—between myself, Charlie, and Andy—would have a reference so the Ultrons wouldn't be all rendered differently. The nature of having three different artists work on the same image can be a problem if we're not on the same team."

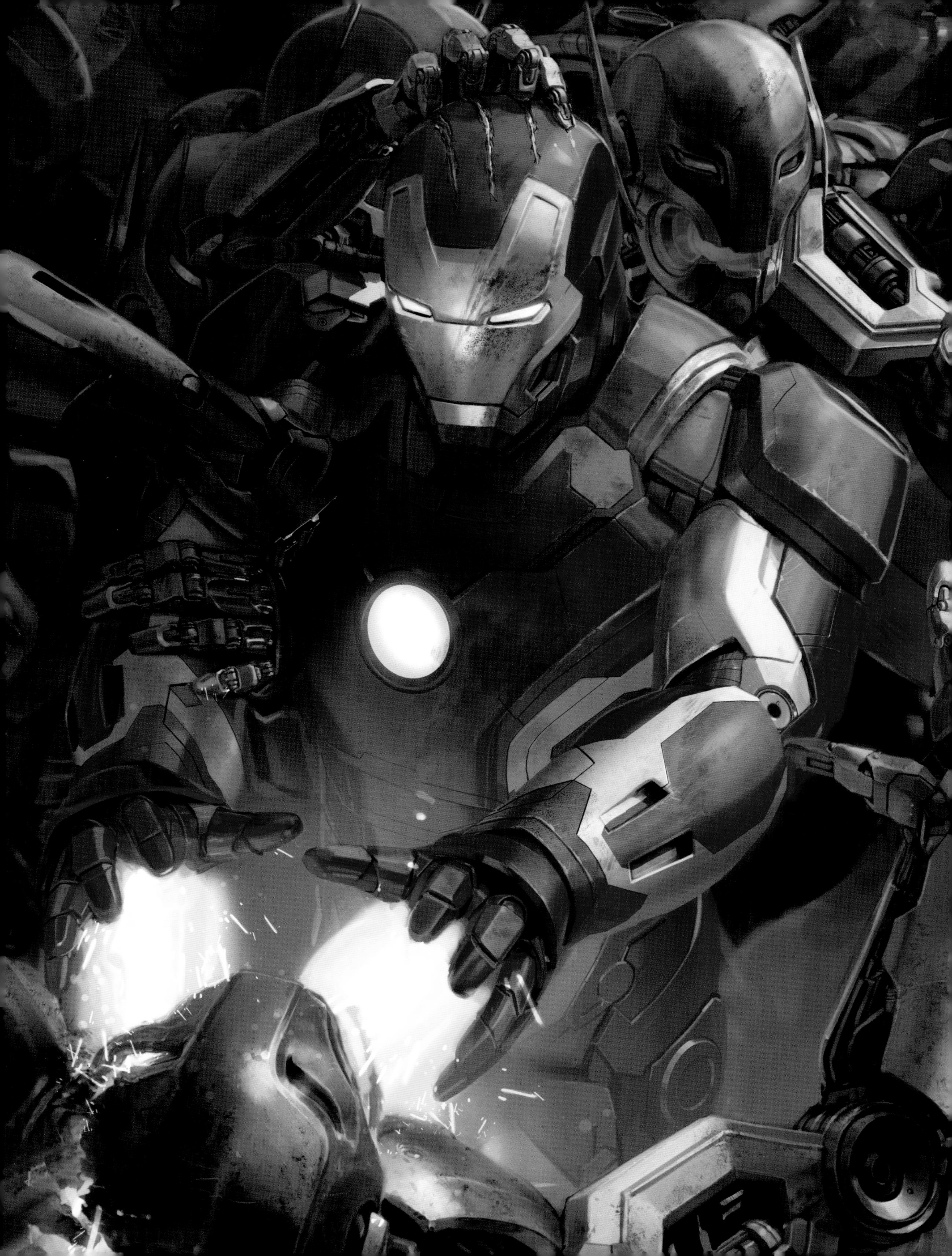

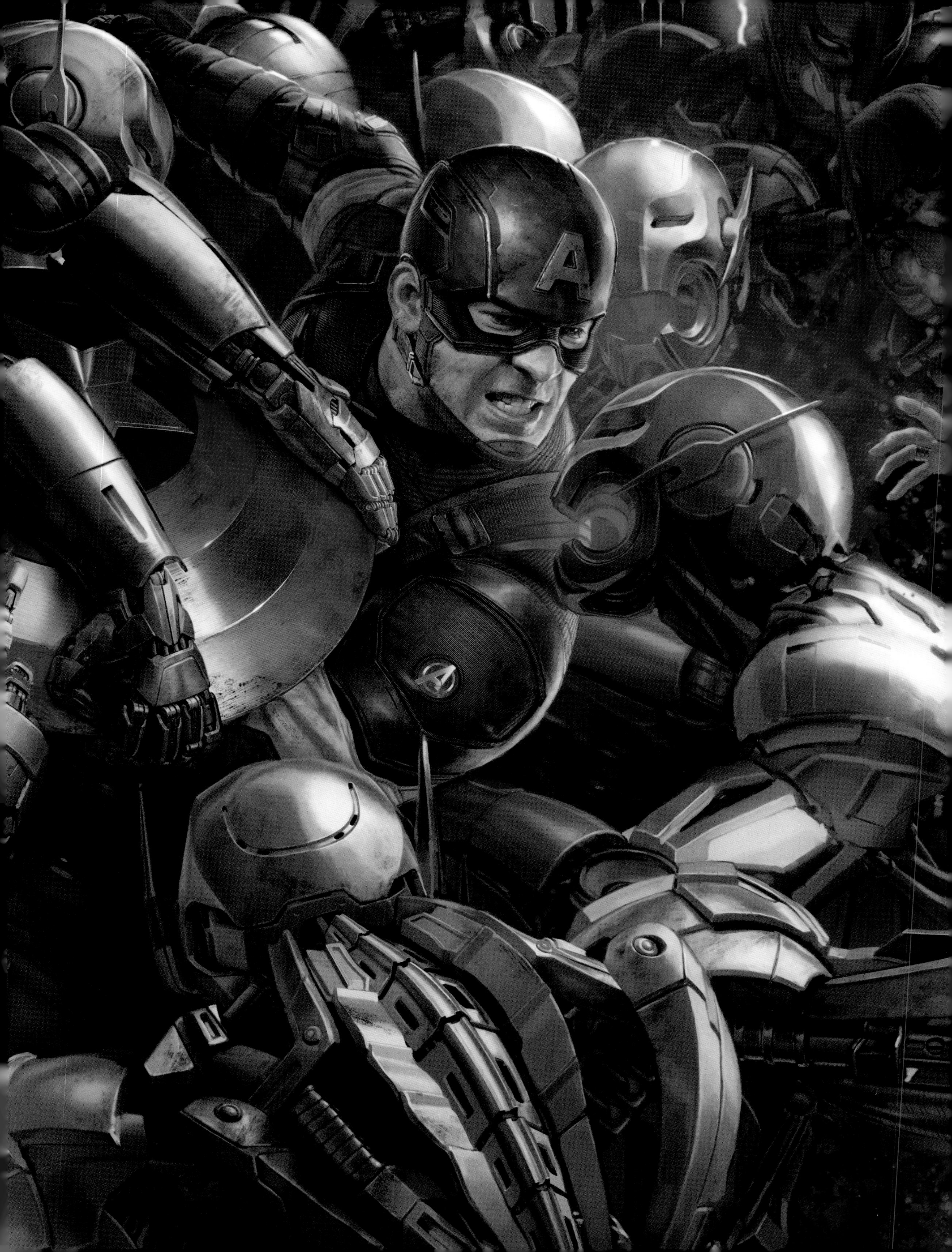

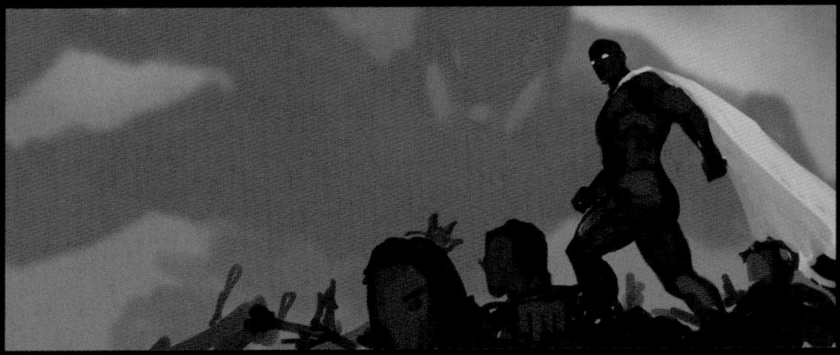

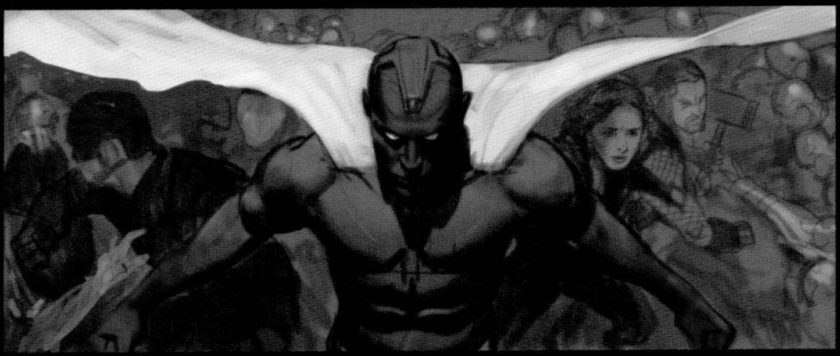

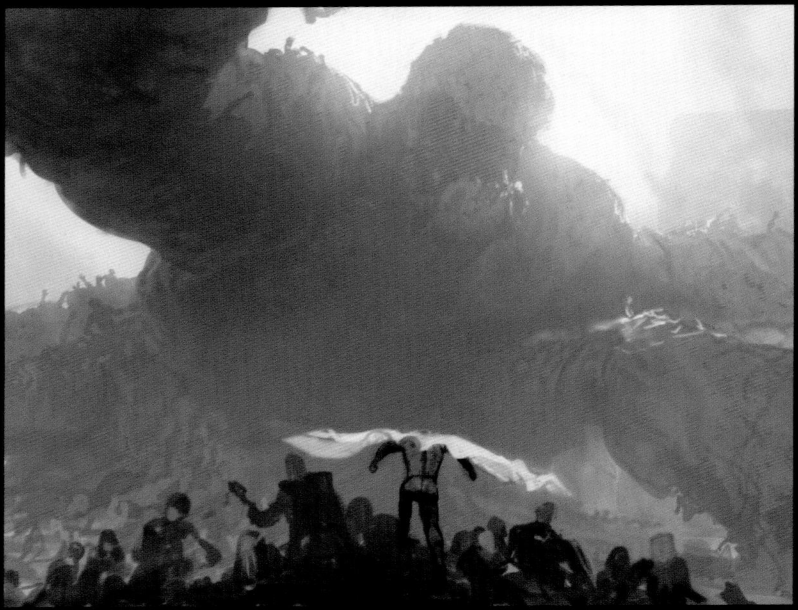

"Part of what I do at Marvel Studios, shown here, is pitch sequences," says Meinerding. "For these pages, I was trying to help out with ways of making Vision cool, because he's an empathetic character. People are supposed to feel for him, but they don't often get to see him being as heroic as possible." This art was for the idea of a "Mega Ultron" attacking Earth's Mightiest Heroes. "I just loved the idea of Vision not knowing who the Avengers really are and still saying, 'Get behind me,'" says the artist. "Then you get that second shot where he's facing off, does this massive blast out of the Mind Stone, and faints afterward. And then for that wave of Ultrons, Vision just leans in and eviscerates them, which I thought would be a cool thing."

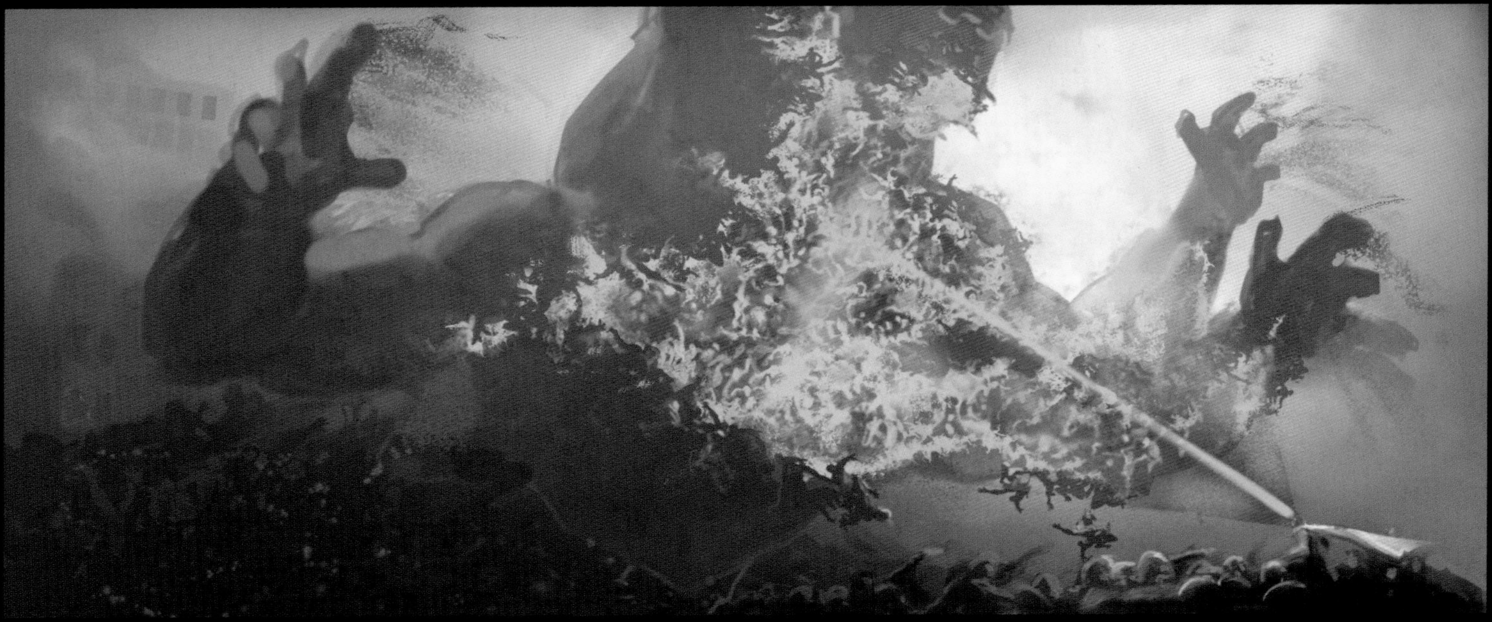

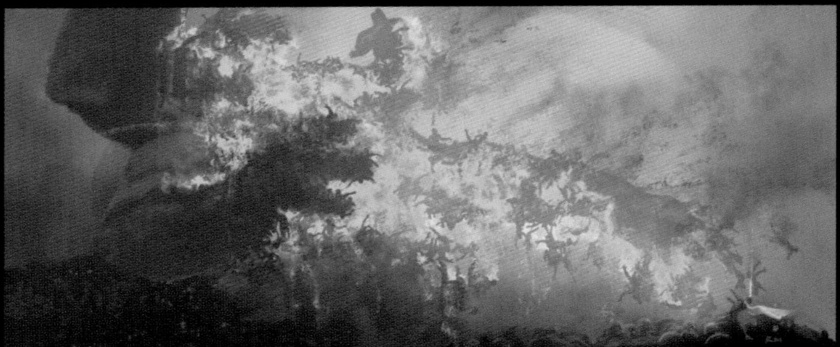

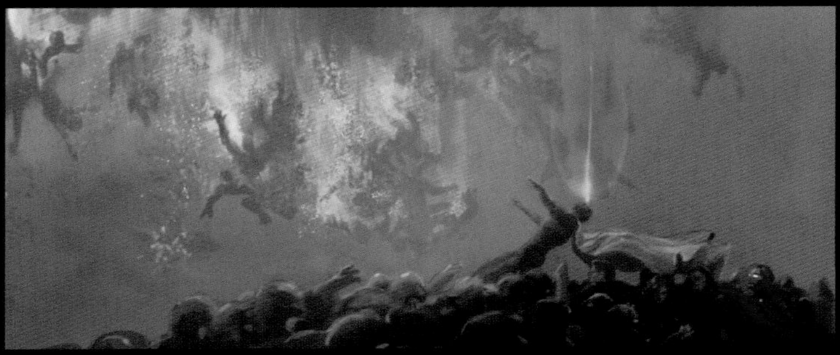

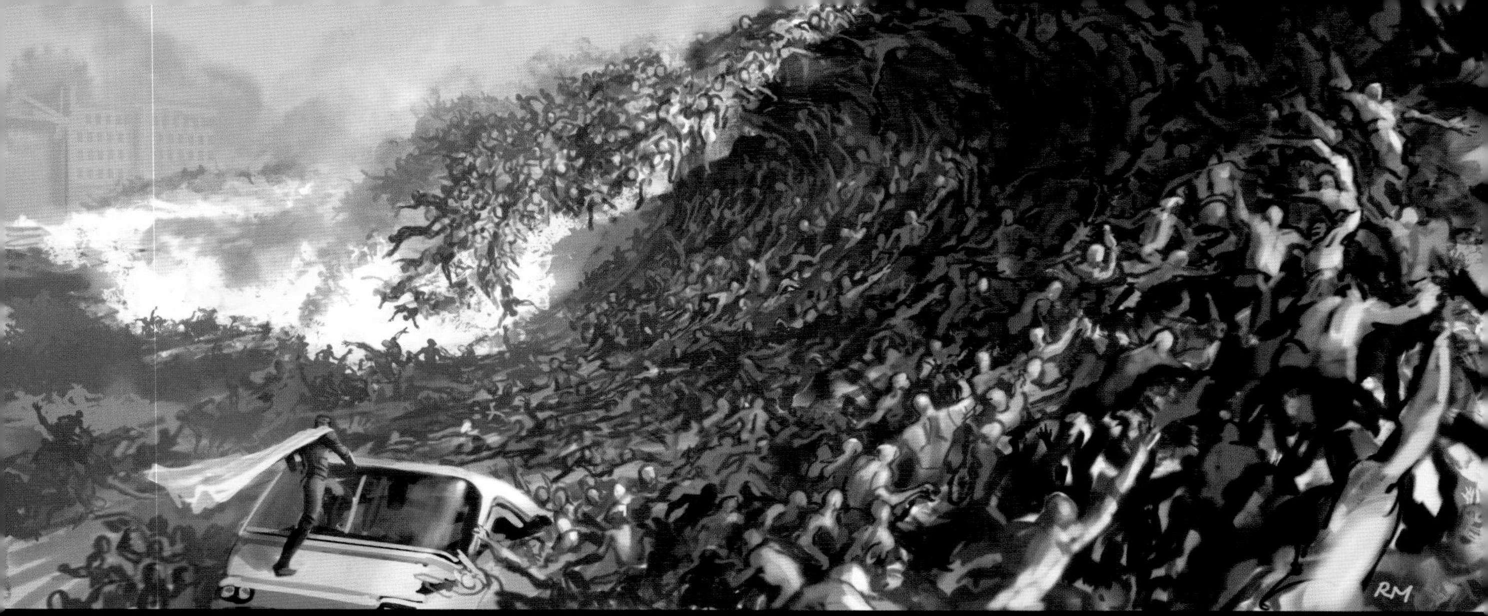
RM

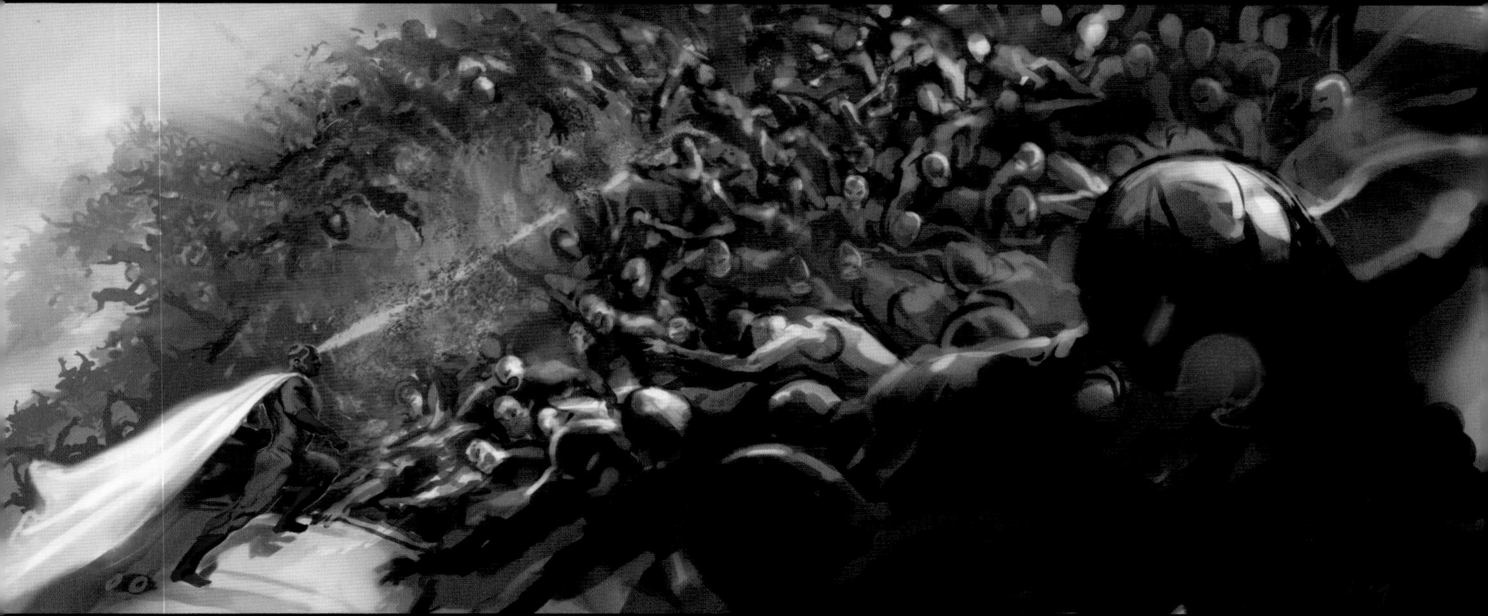

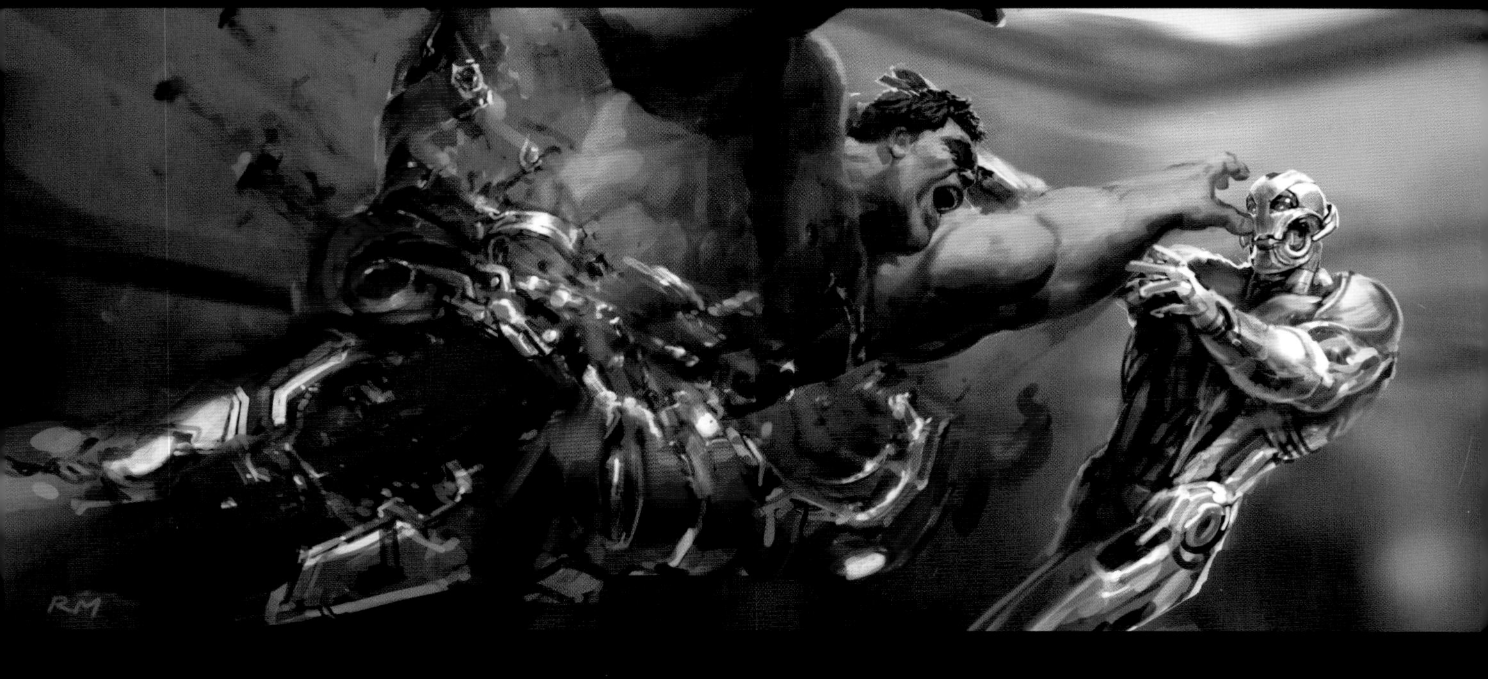
RM

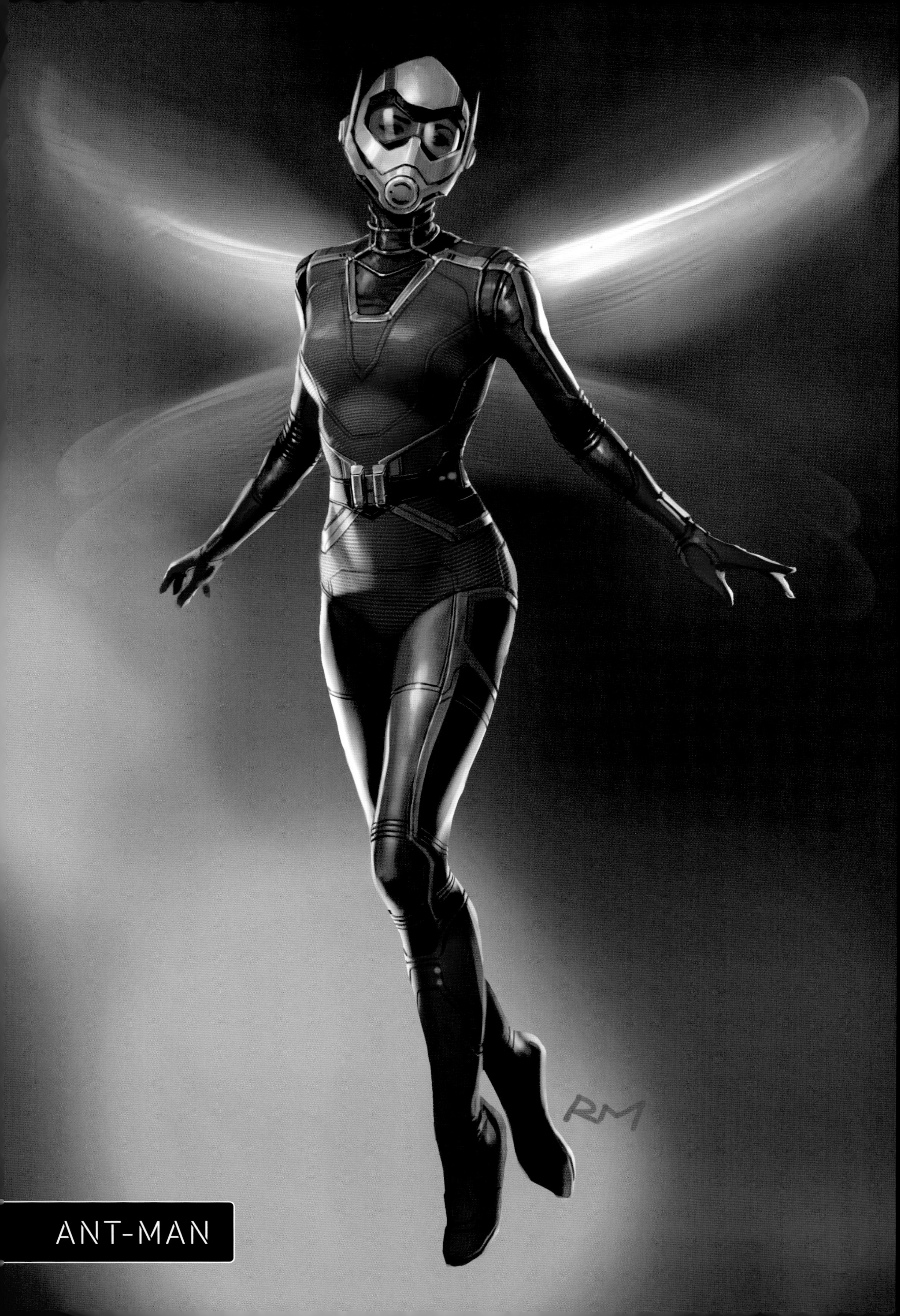
RM

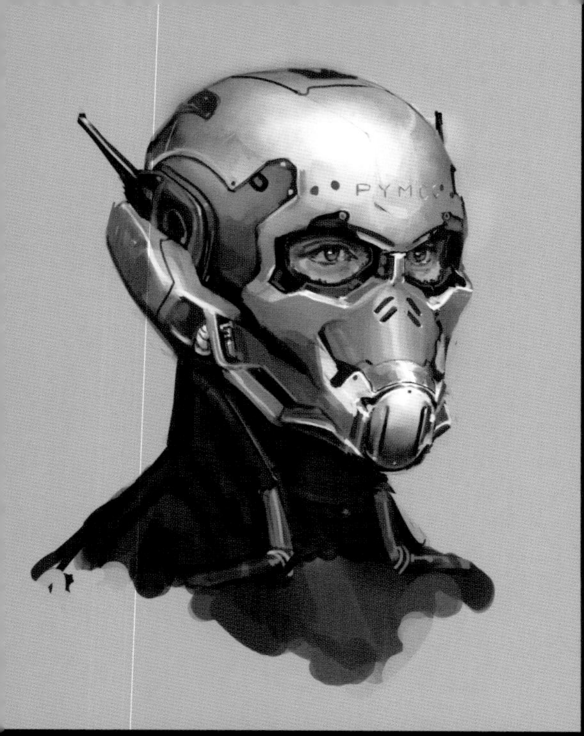

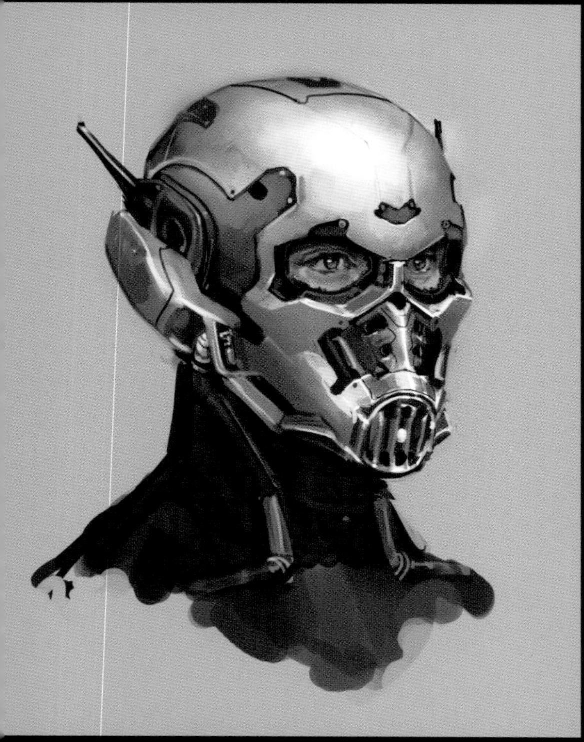

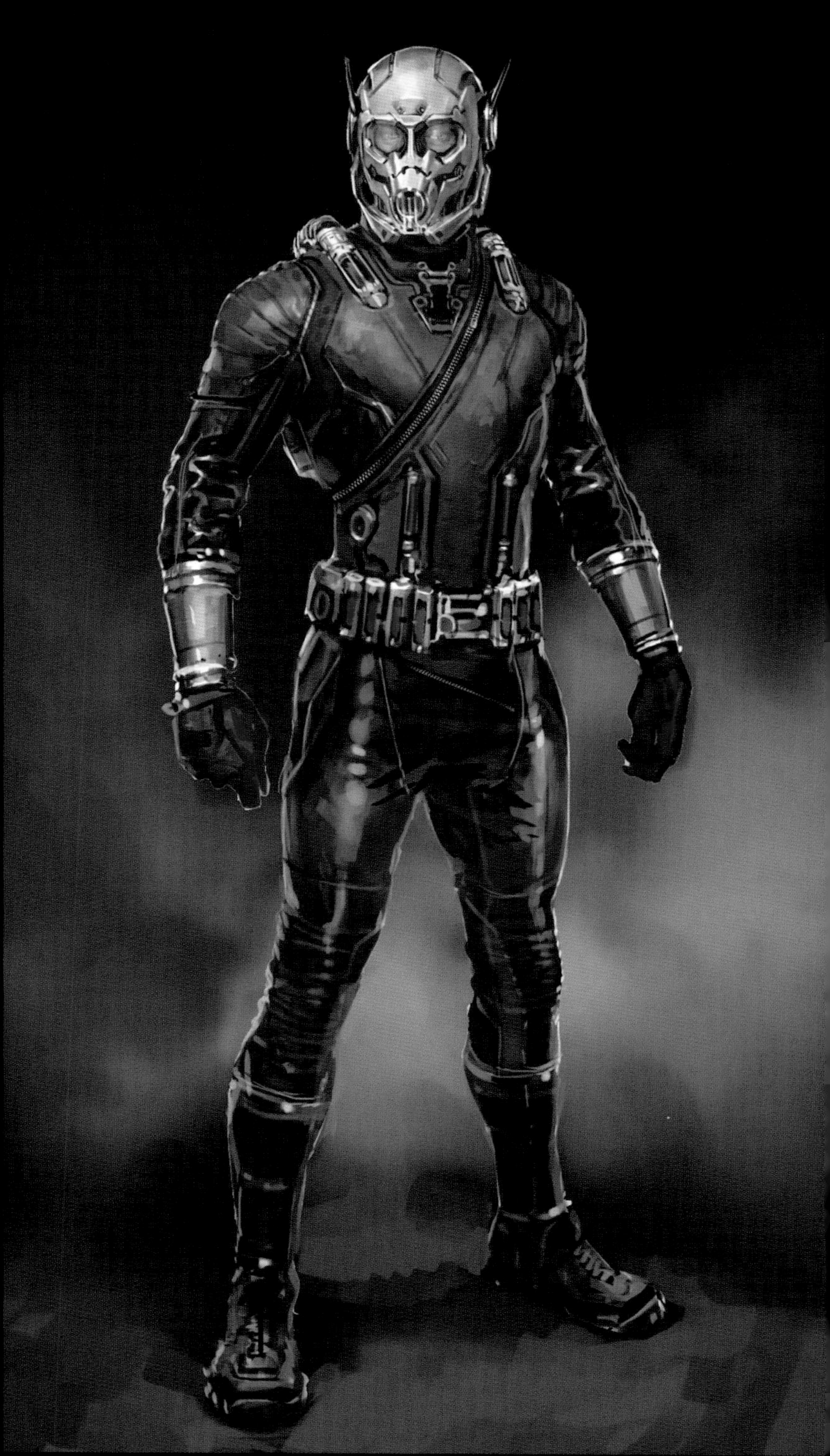

While Ryan Meinerding and the Vis Dev team were working on *Marvel's The Avengers*, they were also busy doing concept art for the early days of *Ant-Man*. Meinerding recalls there being a concerted team effort about the aesthetic of the suit, detailing one influence as, "Calling back to a guy in a super spy, cat burglar-type suit, like a late-sixties or early-seventies spy movie vibe that had the camp of that era of James Bond. We were doing designs along that line for a long time. Charlie [Wen] and I both did takes on Ant-Man. I had done an initial helmet for Ant-Man that was sort of favored. And then Andy [Park] took that and finished it and turned it into what the character is. He nailed the suit and the helmet pretty quickly." When Ant-Man started up again under the directorship of Peyton Reed, Meinerding and his team were working on Hope and Janet Van Dyne. "I did two passes at Janet's suit, and they picked one of them. But ultimately Andy designed the costume. I was essentially helping start the dialogue, doing initial designs on the helmet, and having that be the thing that set some of the direction that Andy ended up finishing wonderfully."

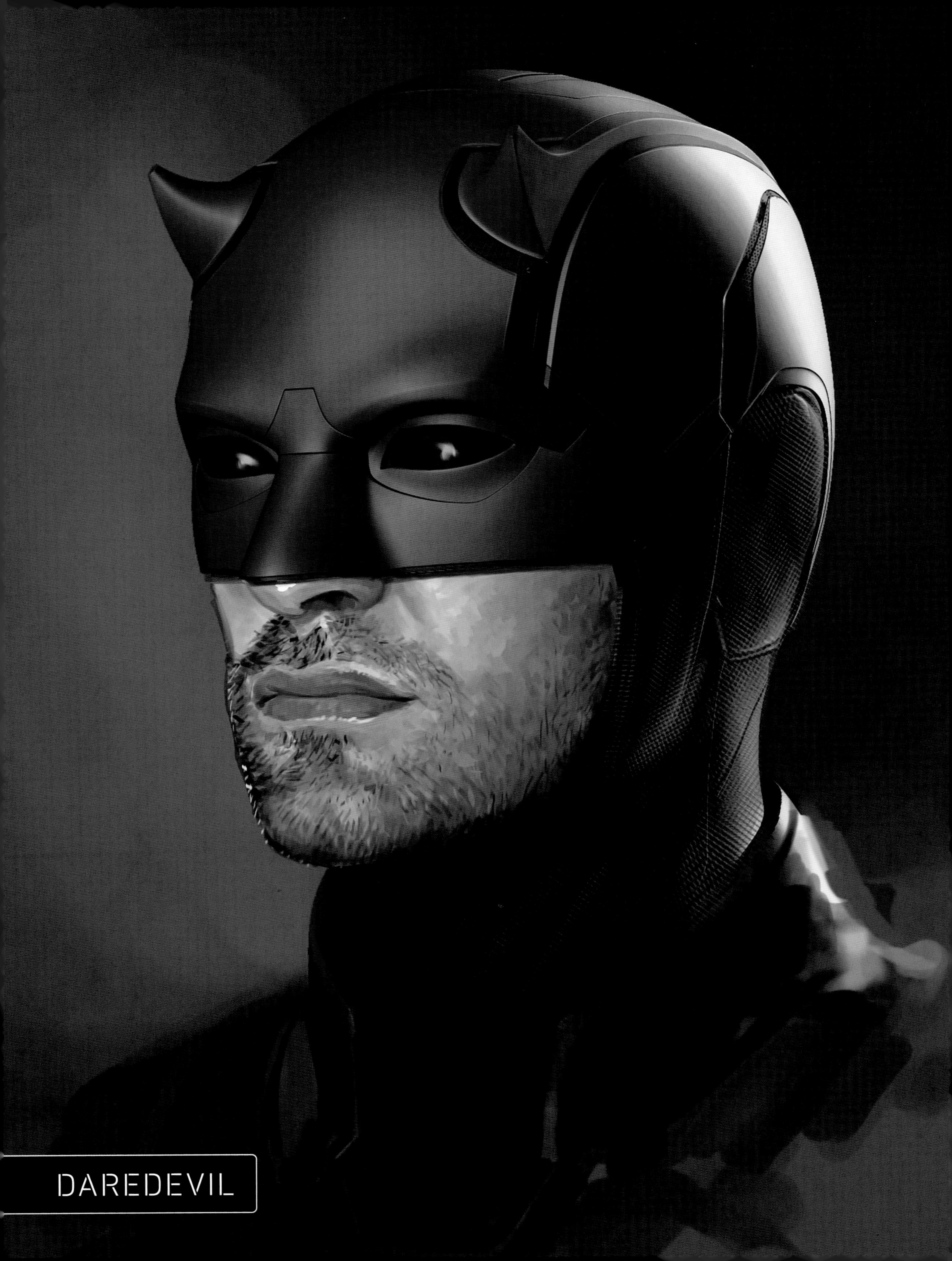

DAREDEVIL

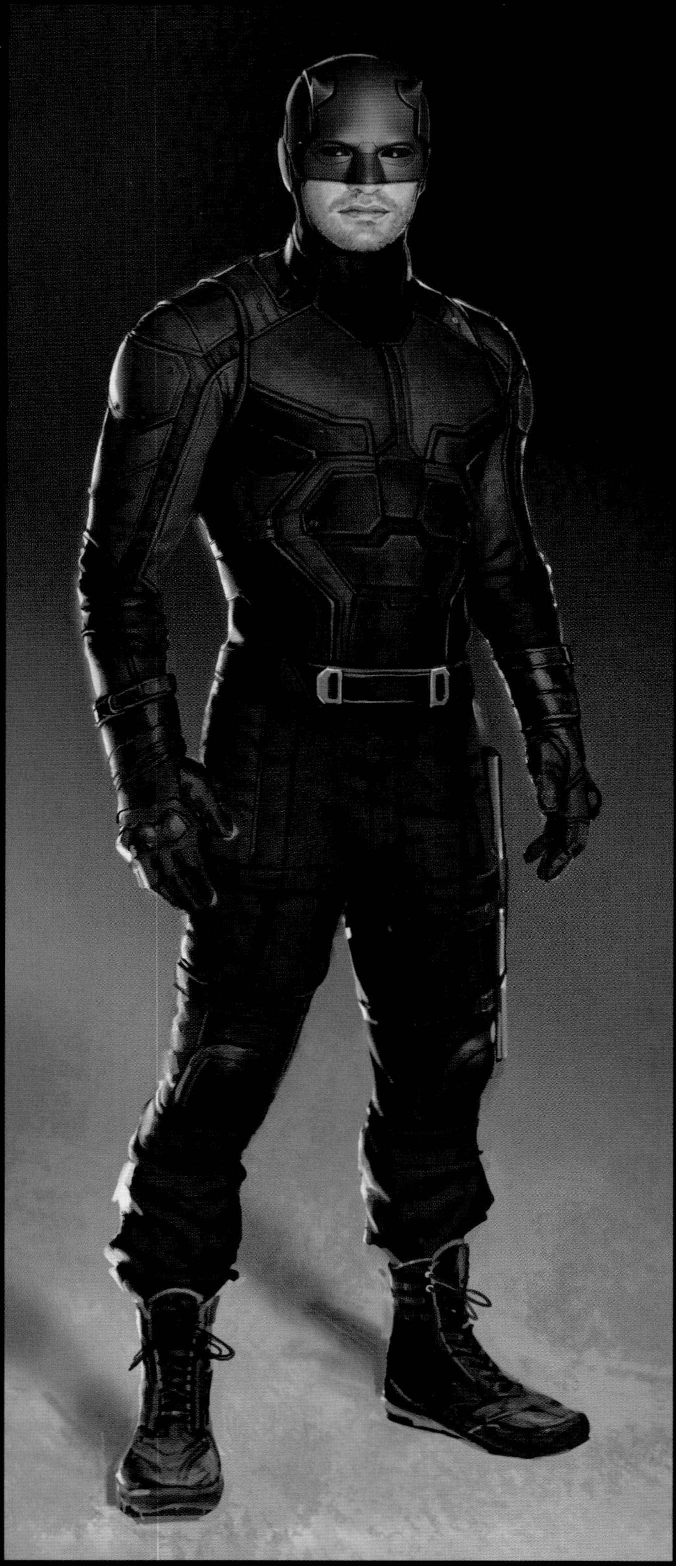

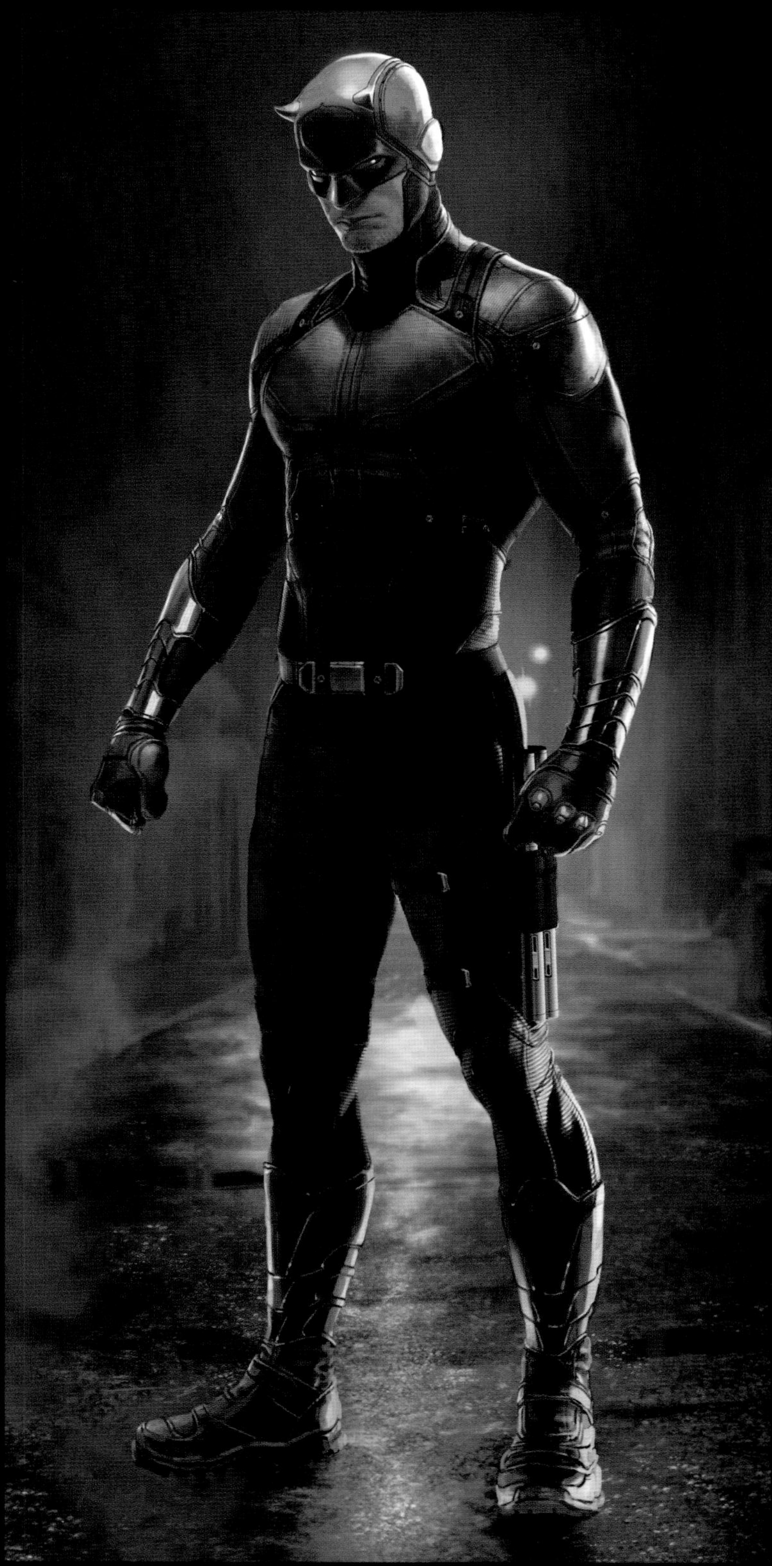

While Ryan Meinerding was working on concept art for Marvel Studios' *Avengers: Age of Ultron* and *Ant-Man*, he was also asked to help out Marvel Entertainment's Netflix show *Daredevil*. "Joe Quesada sent over a document saying what the show wanted to explore and what he was interested in getting out of the Daredevil costume and the billy clubs. They liked the initial pass I did, so I ended up working on that show. These images feature the second season helmet and suit. By the second season, Joe Quesada had made moves to hire somebody like me for his [New York] team. I recommended Joshua James Shaw, and he actually became the person helping out on season two. He worked on the other [Marvel Entertainment] series, too."

OPPOSITE AND ABOVE LEFT Both Daredevil helmets are based on Josh Herman's 3D models.

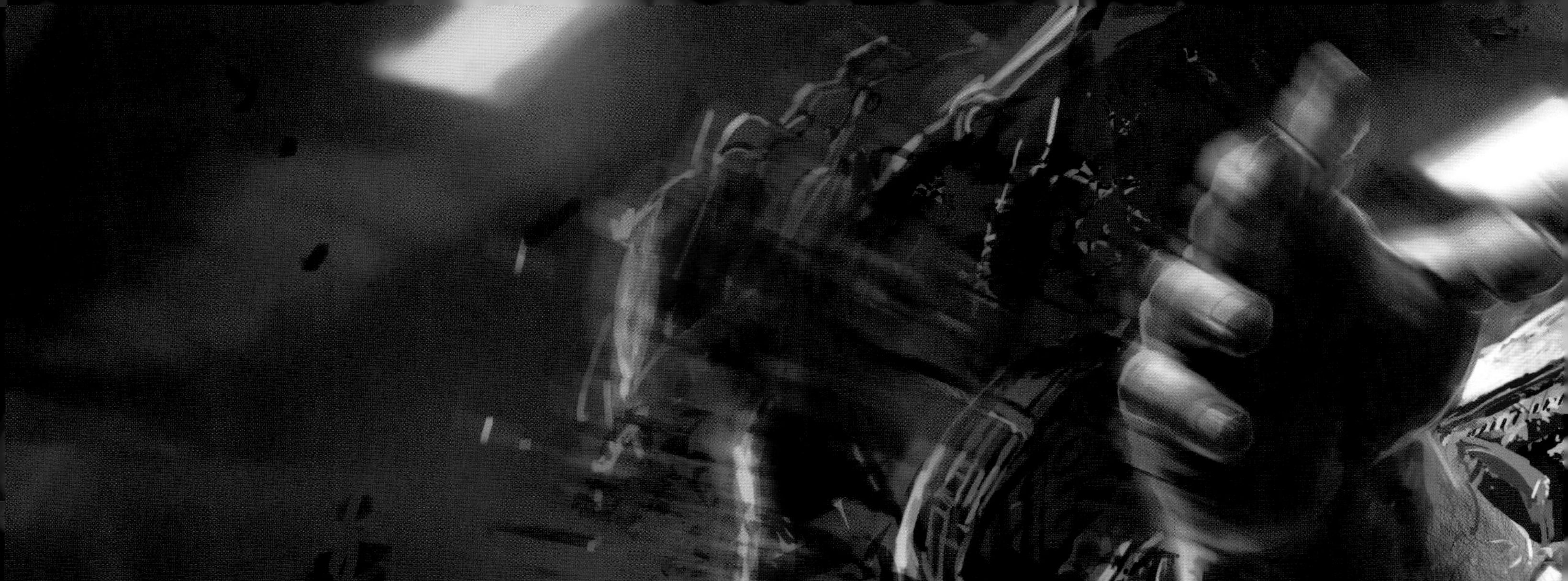

INFINITY WAR AND BEYOND

By the time Marvel Studios was pushing into Phase 3 of their Marvel Cinematic Universe, the Visual Development team had grown to seven full-time artists.

Still the longest serving member of the team, Ryan Meinerding was named the Creative Director of Visual Development at Marvel Studios and worked closely with Kevin Feige, Louis D'Esposito, and the executives for Production and Development who were responsible for guiding the directors already working with, and those just coming into, the MCU on how to visually develop the Super Hero characters in their films.

With a decade of experience developing the house style, Meinerding says his job has evolved into an extremely unique role in the film industry, where he works to achieve the needs of Feige and executive producers for the individual films he works on. He looks at this evolving role as being both a visual storyteller and a problem-solver.

In fact, he developed a creative credo that guides the entire department: "To create concept art in the highest possible quality, but in so doing create a spectrum of design options that allows filmmakers to have the needed conversations to push the project forward."

In essence, it's a formal distillation of the function of the department that, to this day, is still often a novel idea to outside screenwriters, directors, and heads of departments. "We're engineering and proposing options that other people put together into a story," he explains. "It's not saying we do hifalutin art. It's not taking credit for things. It's literally saying we provide options that people get to talk about and then find the right solutions forward. Hopefully, they think it's a cool piece of art and it inspires them."

Personally, Meinerding says he continues to be challenged by finding design solutions for a wide array of creative people. He does that by creating visuals that ideally bridge the gap from one person's brain onto a canvas that then allows for discussion and kinetic ideas.

"I look at it as my brain wants to figure this out, and I'm going to create the design options that solve the problem in five or six different ways, then show those to someone and see how they regard it," he says of his process. "The reality of creating those visuals means that I have to think through things: I have to have ideas, they have to coalesce, and they have to come together in a frame or a costume designer's character design image. The reality is that those ideas, more than the art, are what I love about working here."

"I love the art, too. Don't get me wrong," he emphasizes. "But if I can tell you the reason *why* I did this for Cap, or I did that for Cap, there's a joy that comes out of that for me because I'm taking an idea and making it manifest. It's becoming more real than it was before I drew the picture."

Meinerding does admit that his job carries with it a tremendous amount of pressure and the common lament of all creatives: the wish for more time to create the perfect image. "I am a person that can get overloaded and not be willing to admit that he's been overloaded with stuff," he says. "And what that does to me as an artist is a good thing, as it forces me to prioritize. It forces me to choose. It forces me to say 'this is the thing that's most important to me.'"

"It's also led me down a path of embracing more technology," he continues. "It's led me down a path of thinking more practically about not only how I spend my time, but if I spend time on X, how can I use X down the line? And that is a more production-oriented mentality for still trying to create high-end concept art. It makes me try to be more judicious with how I use my time."

An example of this was when Meinerding was working on designs for Thanos for *Avengers: Infinity War* and *Avengers: Endgame*, as well as character concept designs for *Black Panther*. "I was working on three movies at once," he remembers. "Something had to give, and sadly that was *Black Panther*. But I got to design the suit for Cap, the Iron Spider suit for Spidey, Thanos, Thor, and Stormbreaker and Smart Hulk."

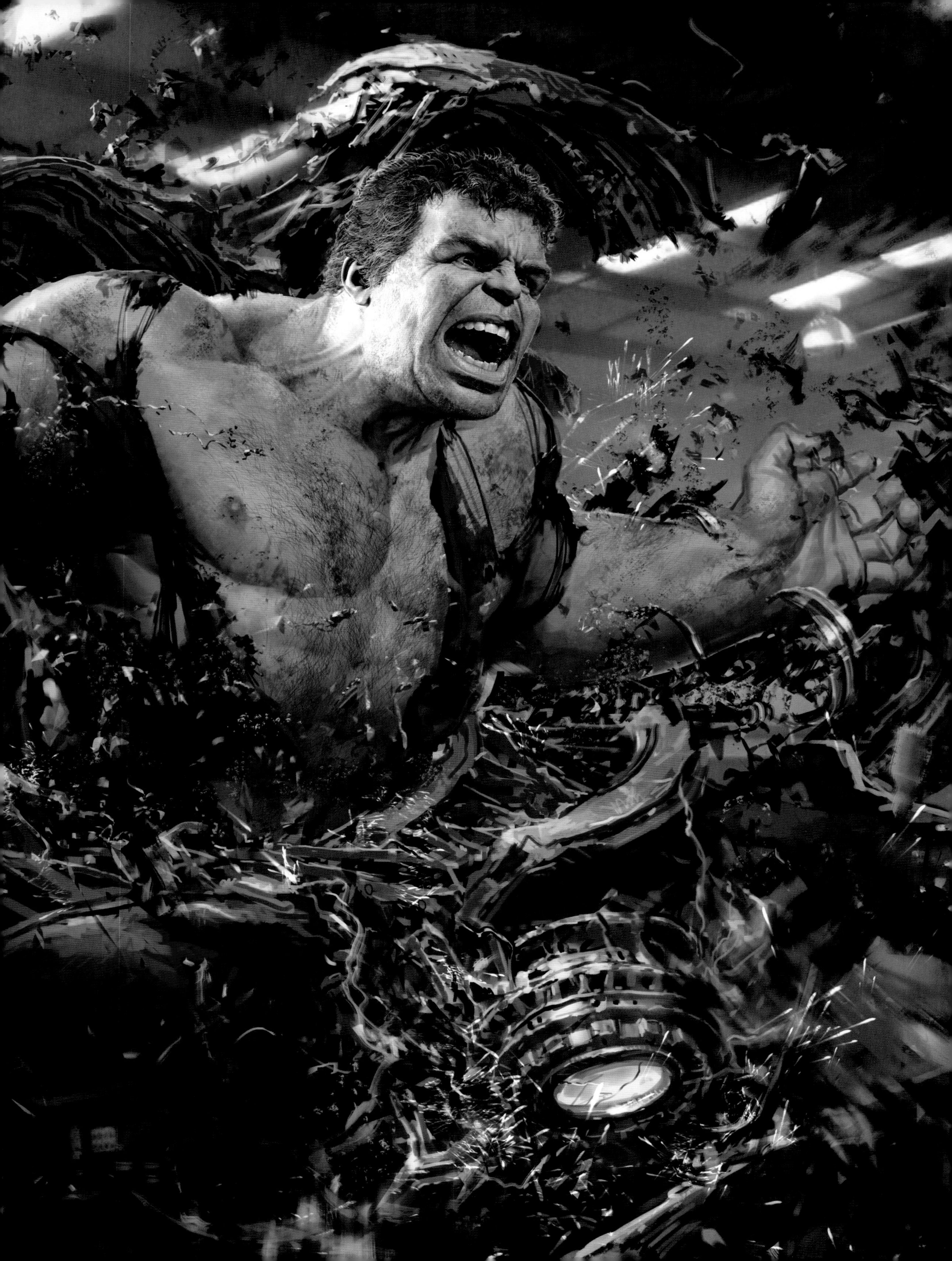

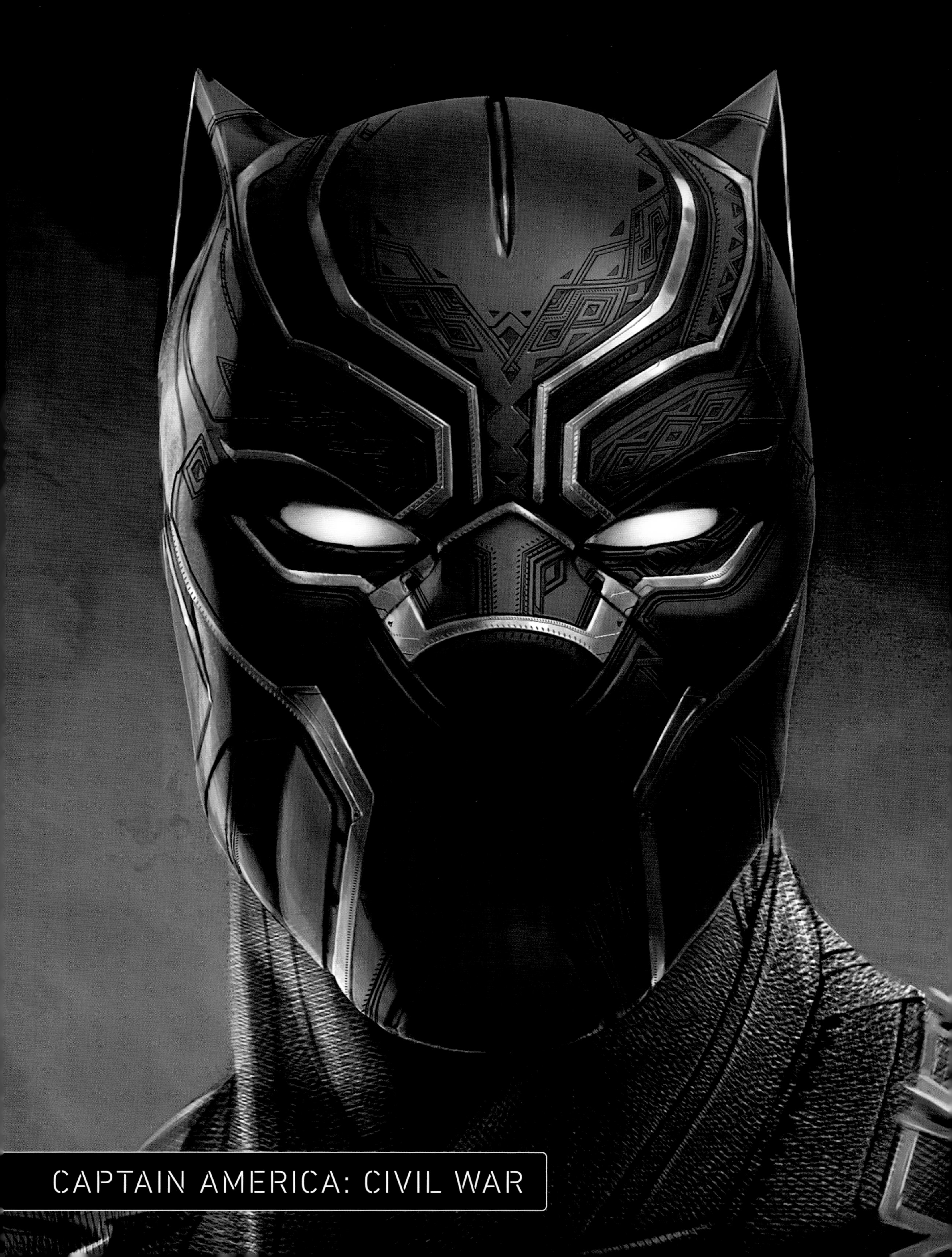

CAPTAIN AMERICA: CIVIL WAR

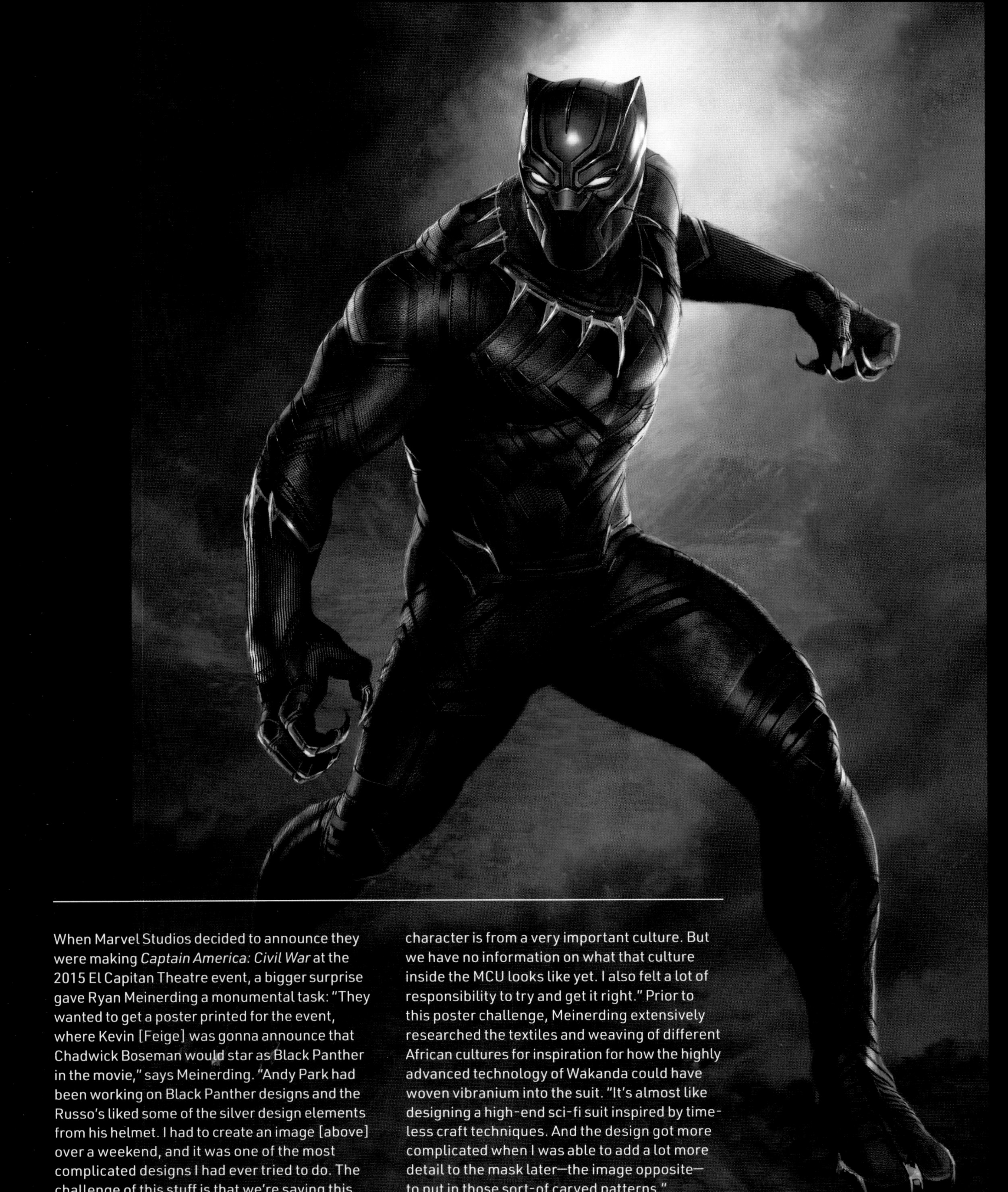

When Marvel Studios decided to announce they were making *Captain America: Civil War* at the 2015 El Capitan Theatre event, a bigger surprise gave Ryan Meinerding a monumental task: "They wanted to get a poster printed for the event, where Kevin [Feige] was gonna announce that Chadwick Boseman would star as Black Panther in the movie," says Meinerding. "Andy Park had been working on Black Panther designs and the Russo's liked some of the silver design elements from his helmet. I had to create an image [above] over a weekend, and it was one of the most complicated designs I had ever tried to do. The challenge of this stuff is that we're saying this character is from a very important culture. But we have no information on what that culture inside the MCU looks like yet. I also felt a lot of responsibility to try and get it right." Prior to this poster challenge, Meinerding extensively researched the textiles and weaving of different African cultures for inspiration for how the highly advanced technology of Wakanda could have woven vibranium into the suit. "It's almost like designing a high-end sci-fi suit inspired by timeless craft techniques. And the design got more complicated when I was able to add a lot more detail to the mask later—the image opposite—to put in those sort-of carved patterns."

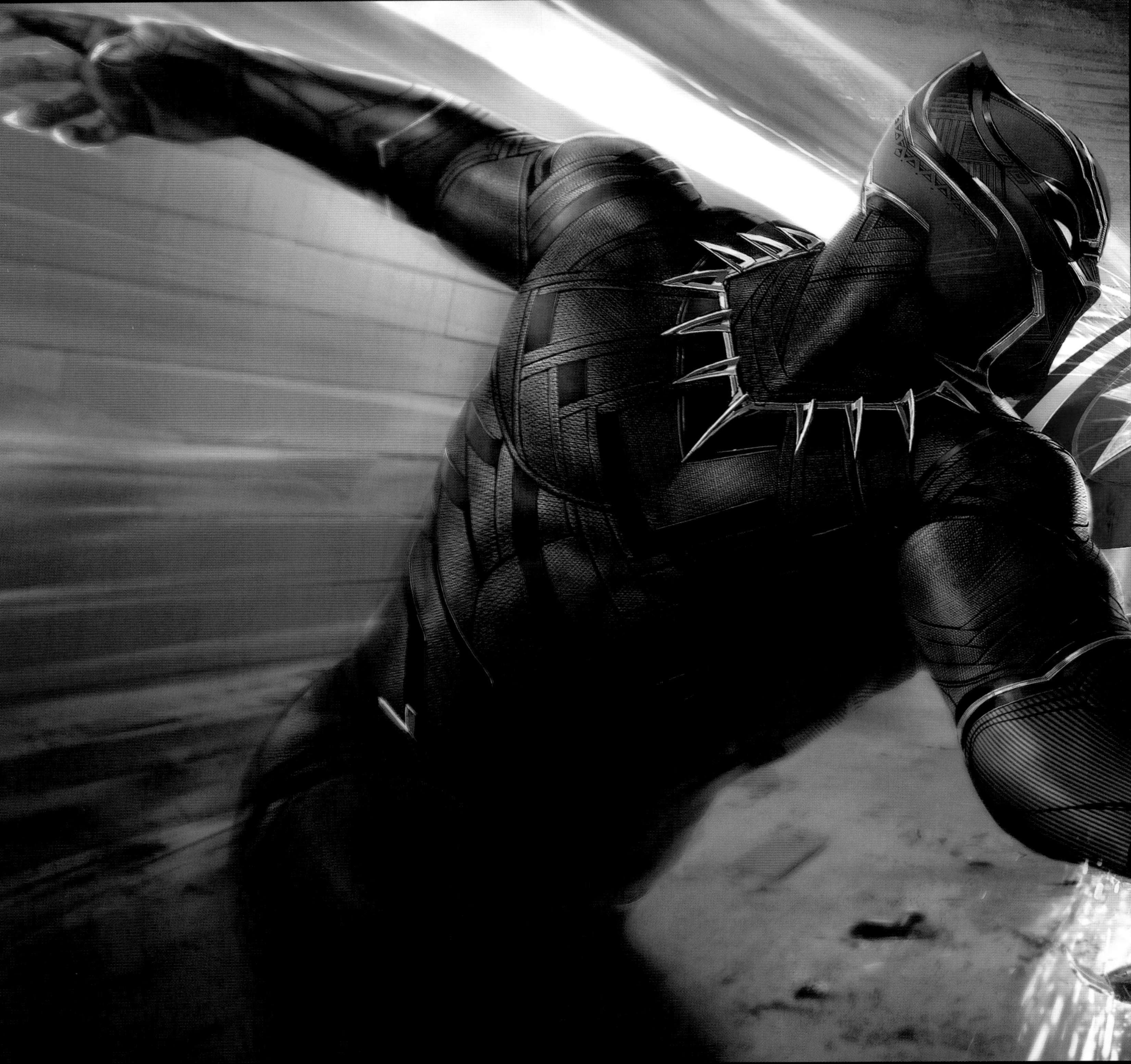

"This is referencing an awesome Mike Zeck cover where Wolverine is slashing at Cap's shield," reveals Meinerding. "To get to create this moment between Panther and Cap as a key film frame and feature two suit designs I'm really proud of—plus the shield, which I also designed—was super exciting."

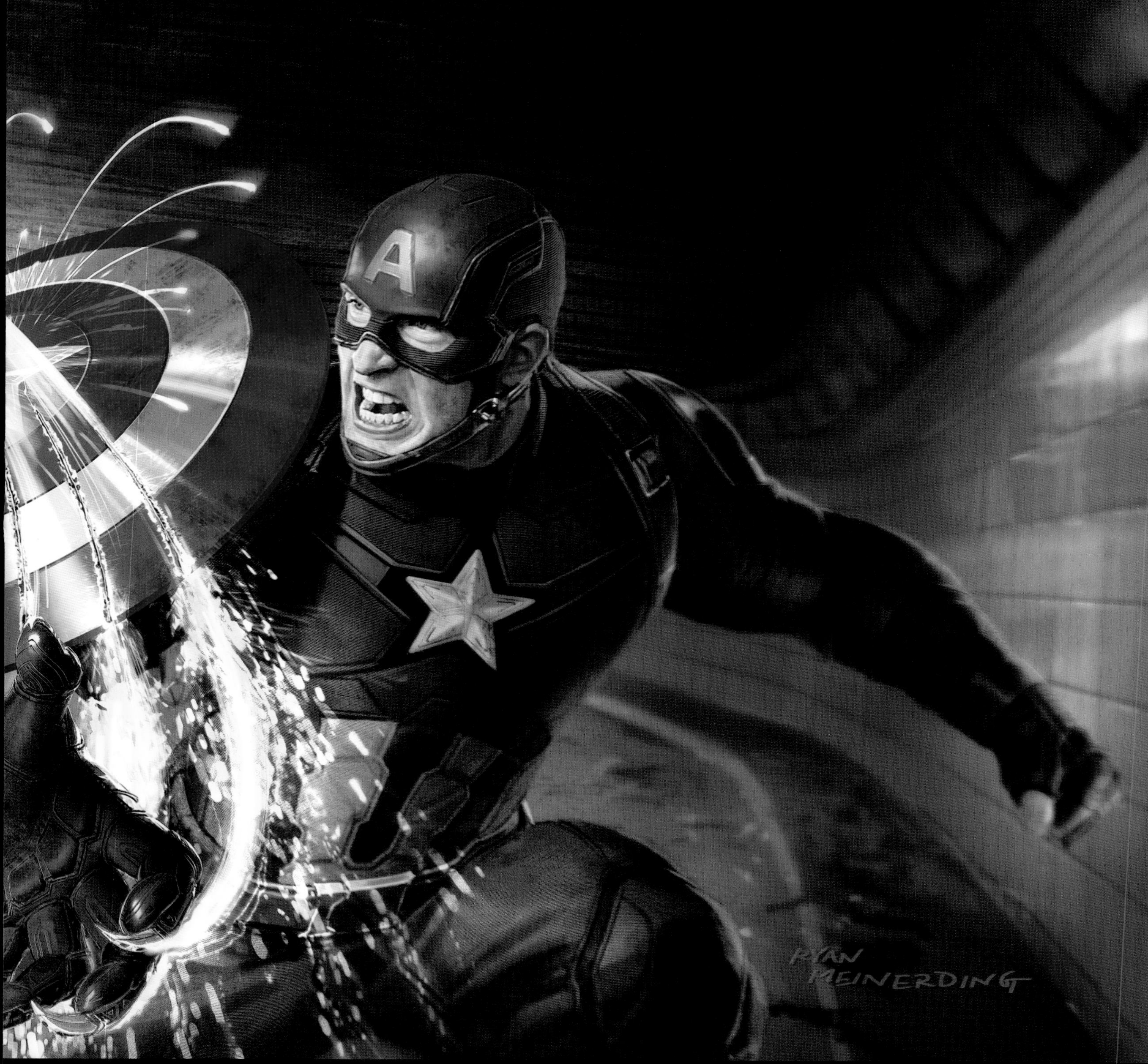
RYAN
MEINERDING

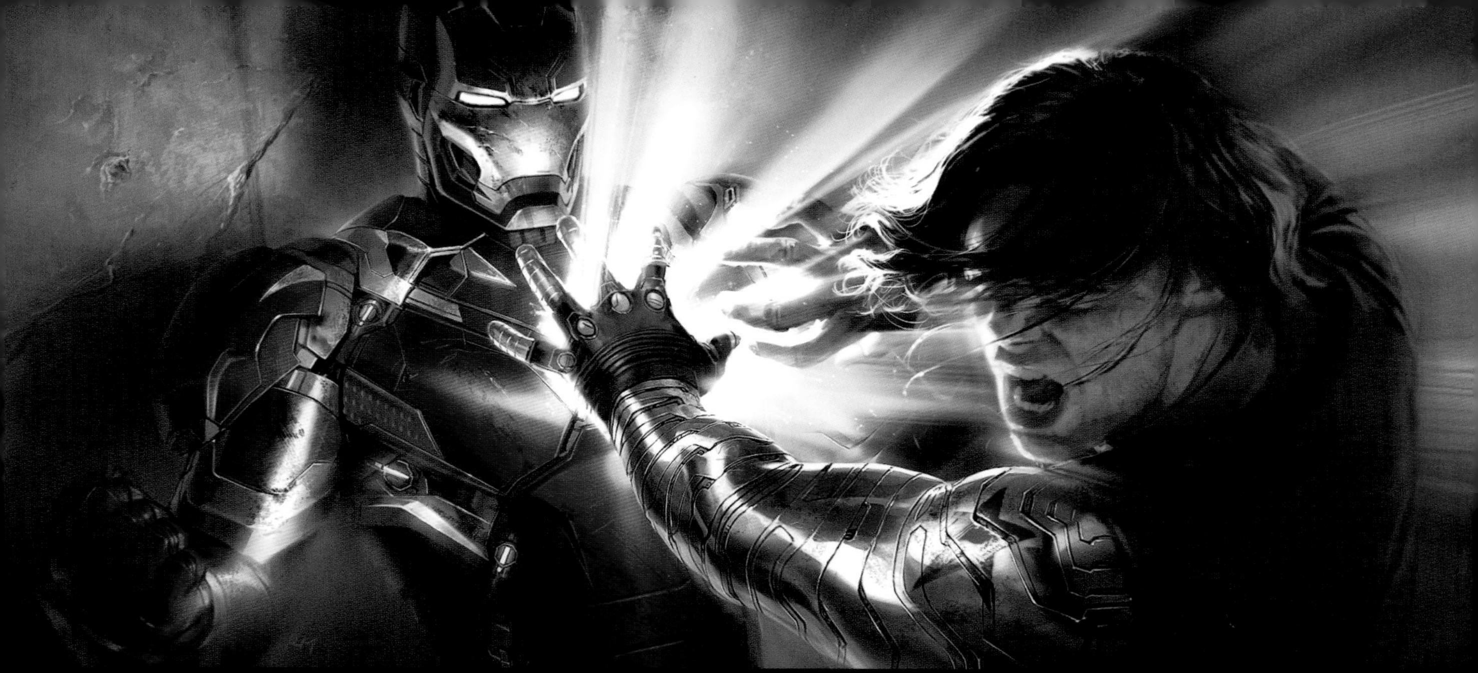

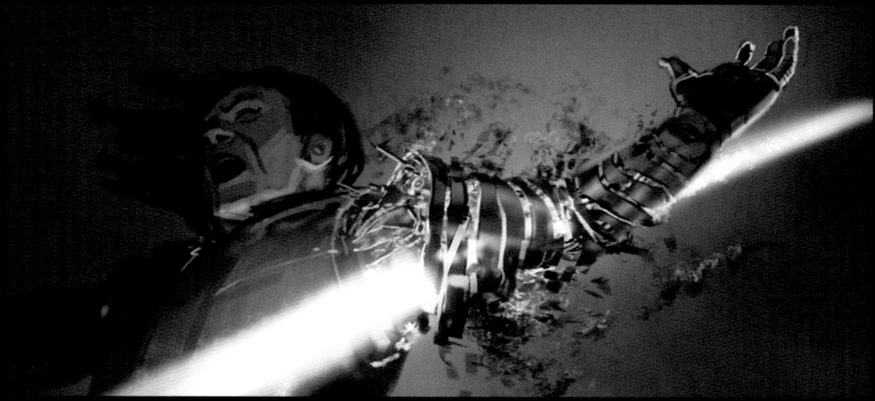

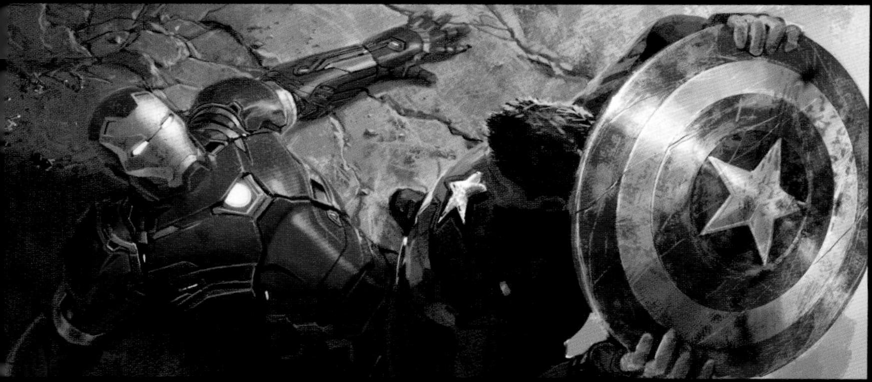

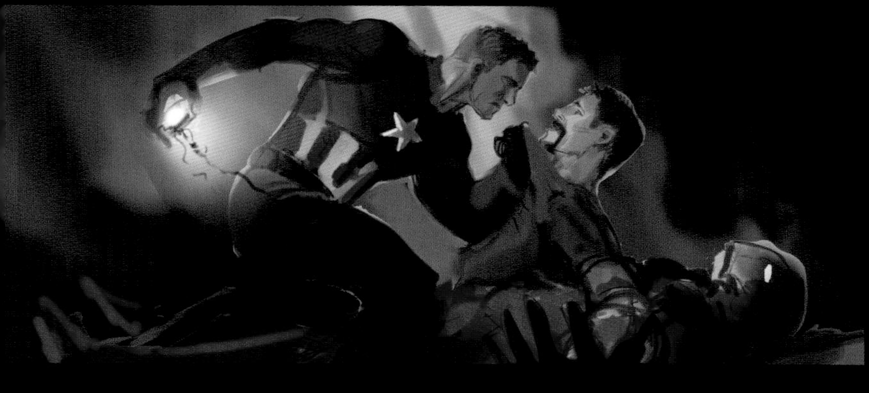

"If I care about the characters, I care about staying with the characters through whatever design changes they need," emphasizes Meinerding. "Even if that means a bunch of different jackets with pouches for Bucky." Meinerding crafted Bucky Barnes's look for the first *Captain America* movie, and then multiple designs for his mysterious role in *The Winter Soldier*. Therefore, the artist asserts, "It was important to me that I work on him for *Civil War*. He's a character I care about a lot. I think of Steve and Bucky as a team. If I'm gonna work on one, it's hard not to work on the other."

Caring deeply for these characters meant that coming up with key frames of their fights with Iron Man and the other Avengers was far from easy. "I'm not gonna lie. I had a hard time doing it," admits the artist. "How do you frame it so they're both still heroic? How do you frame it so that they *both* feel like their point of view is justified when I relate to both characters? It's hard. Because you've still got to put one character kind of 'above' the other, even if you're not trying to state who is 'winning.' I struggled to do these kind of *Civil War* key frames much more than I expected to."

OPPOSITE BOTTOM The left-hand third of this triptych was illustrated by Andy Park, with Meinerding crafting the rest.

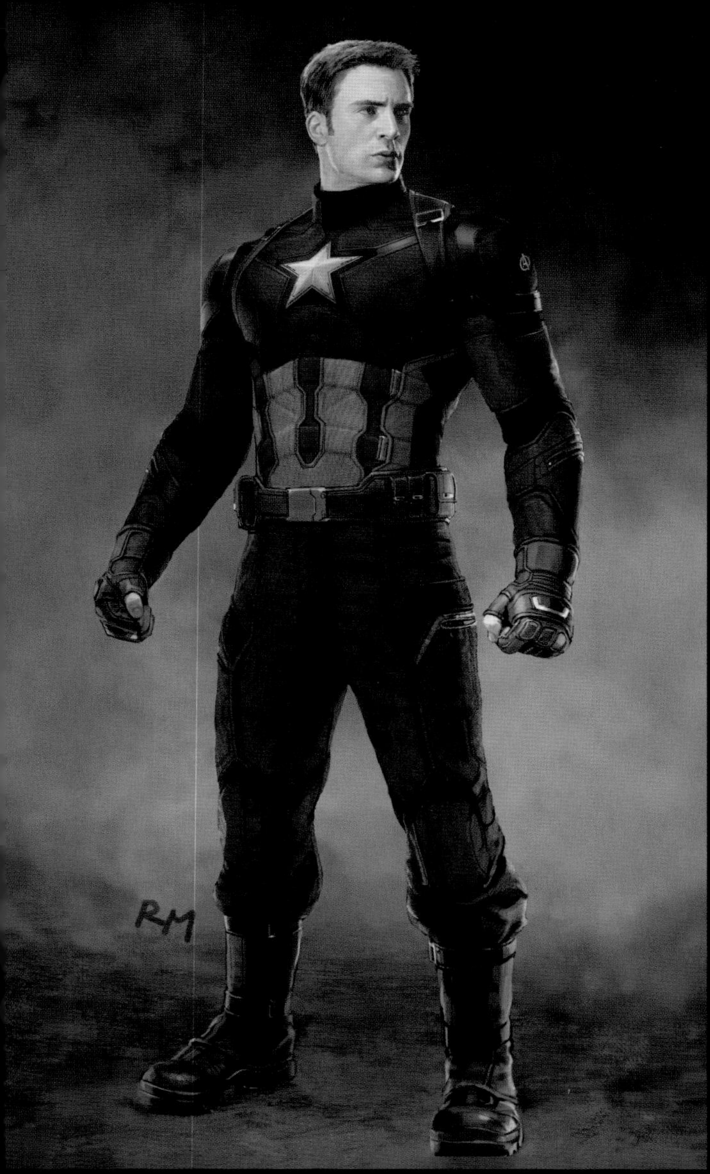
RM

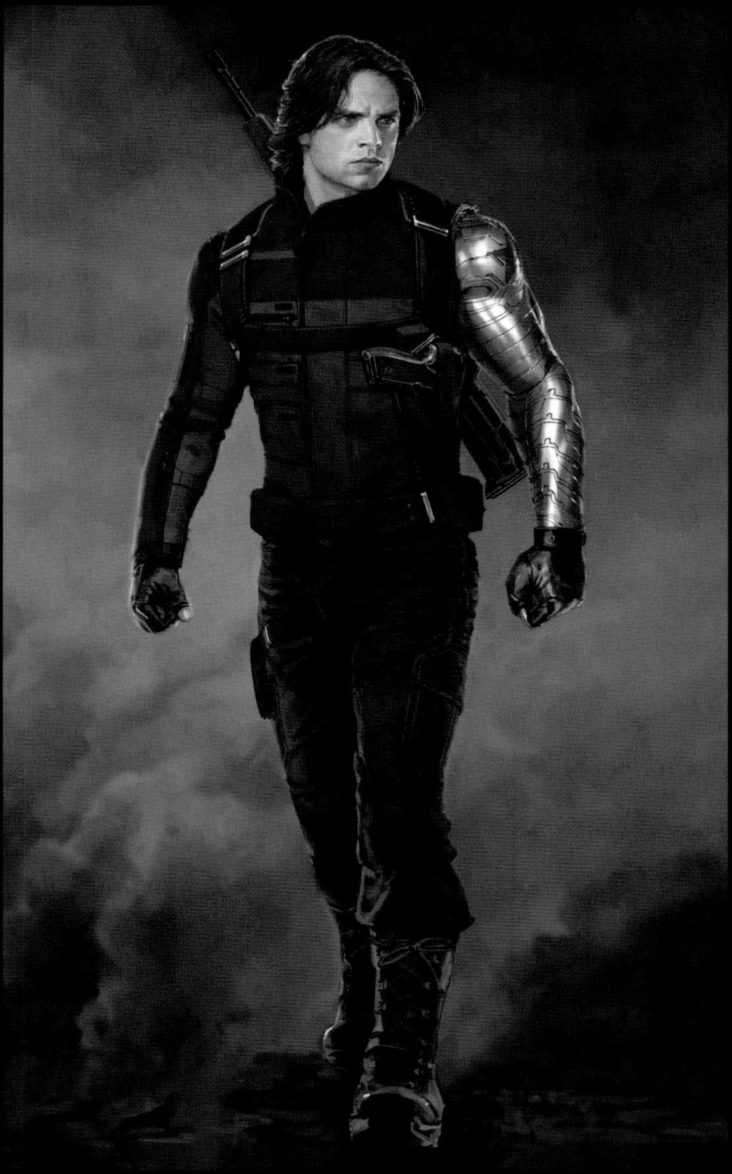

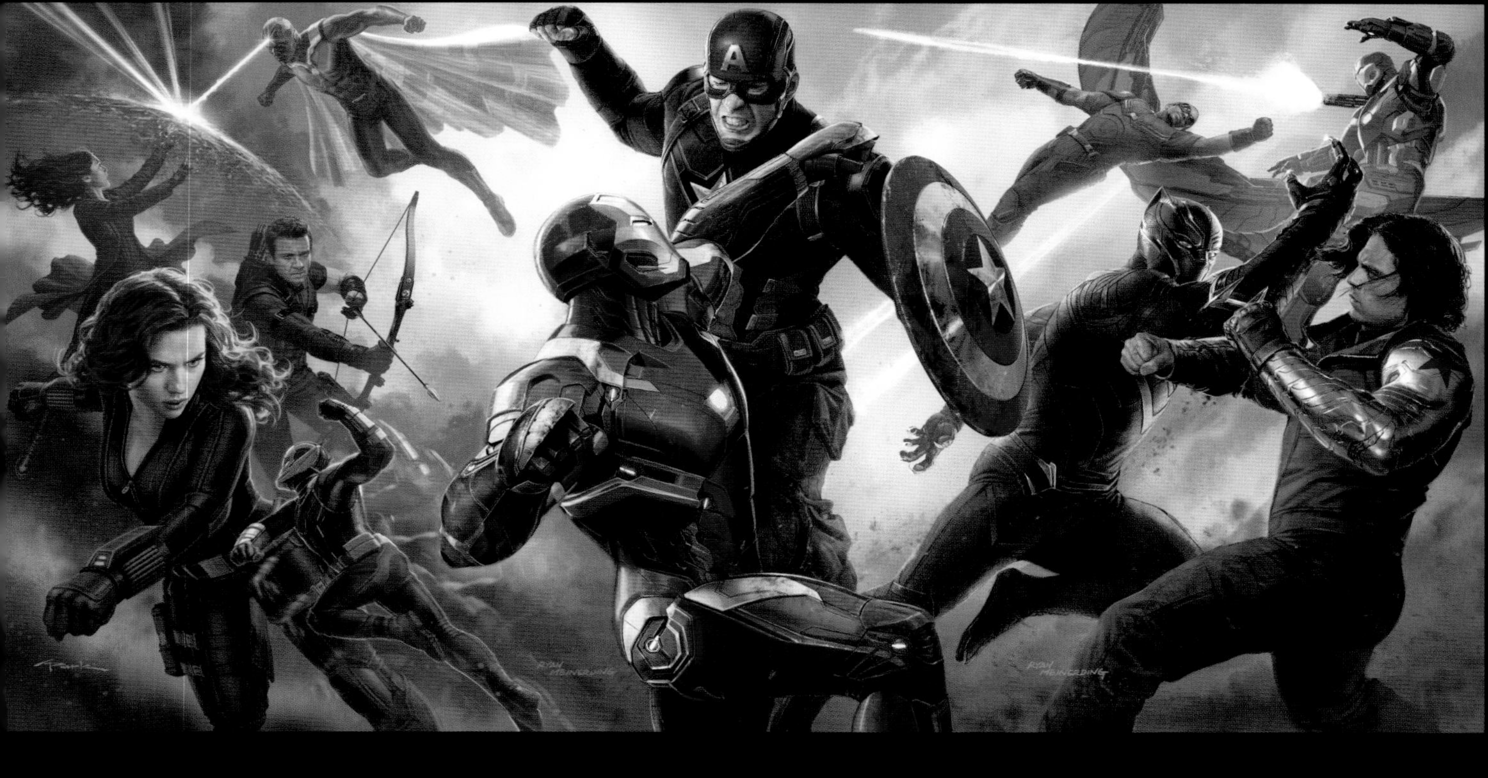

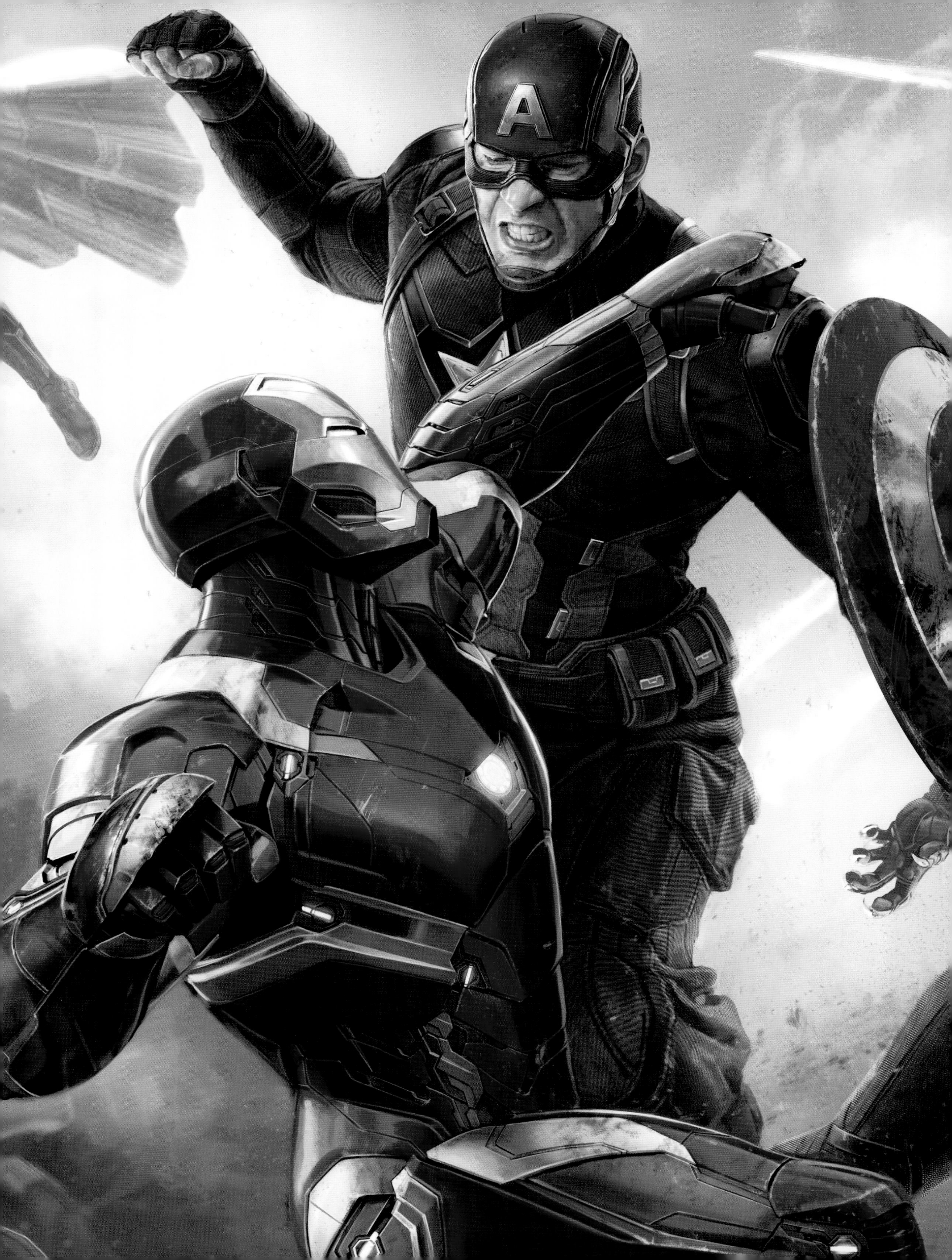

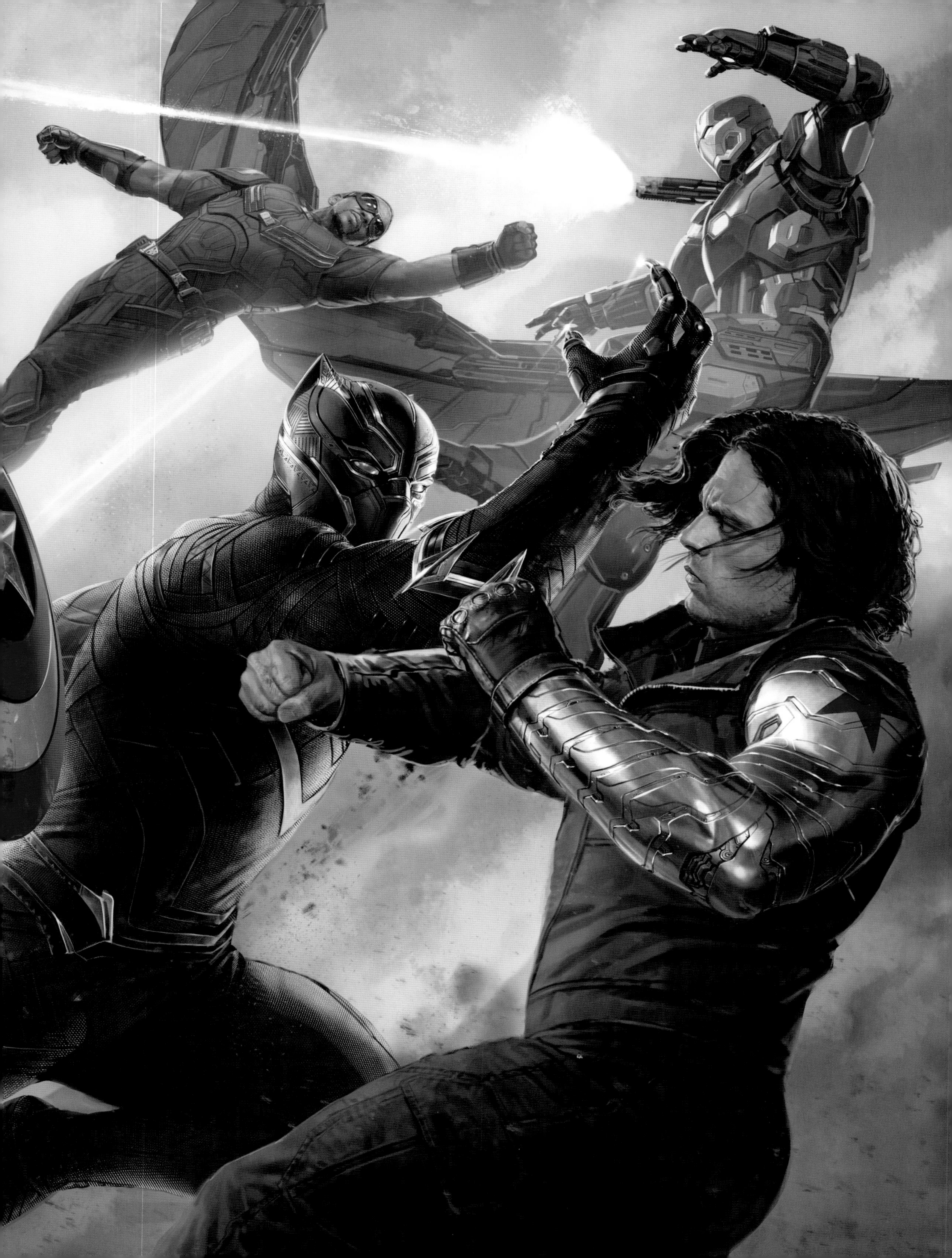

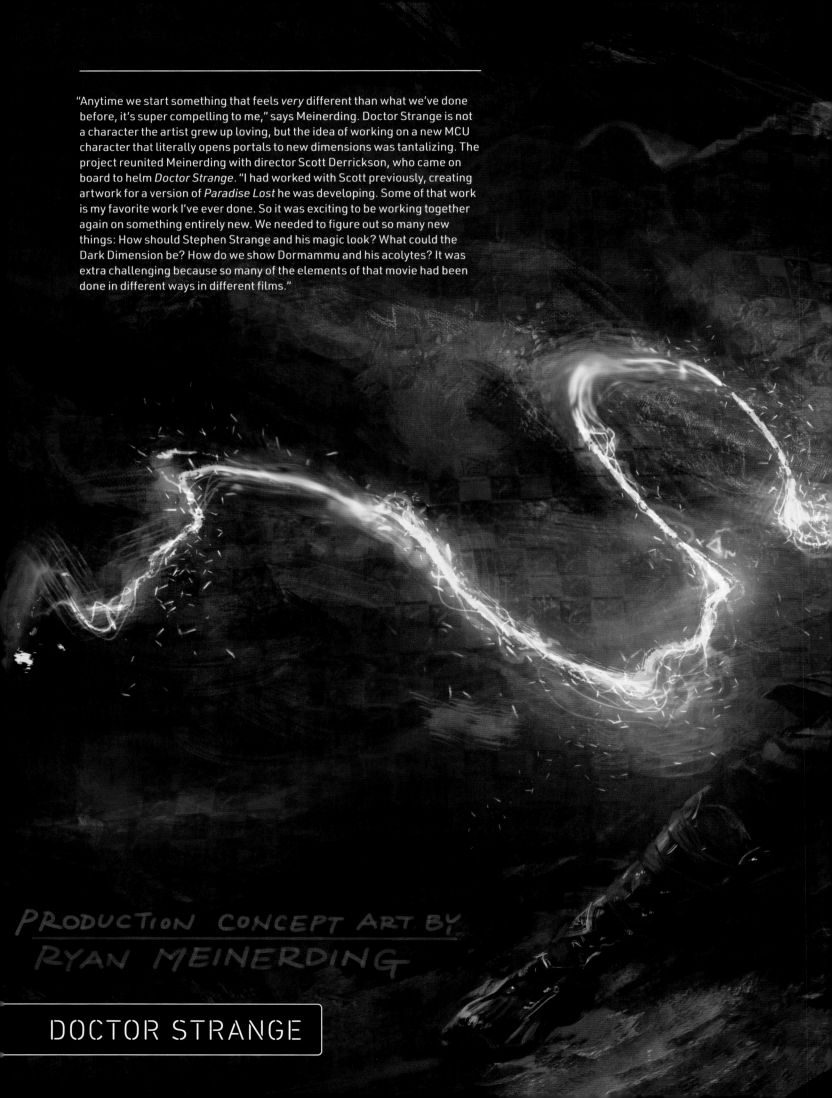

"Anytime we start something that feels *very* different than what we've done before, it's super compelling to me," says Meinerding. Doctor Strange is not a character the artist grew up loving, but the idea of working on a new MCU character that literally opens portals to new dimensions was tantalizing. The project reunited Meinerding with director Scott Derrickson, who came on board to helm *Doctor Strange*. "I had worked with Scott previously, creating artwork for a version of *Paradise Lost* he was developing. Some of that work is my favorite work I've ever done. So it was exciting to be working together again on something entirely new. We needed to figure out so many new things: How should Stephen Strange and his magic look? What could the Dark Dimension be? How do we show Dormammu and his acolytes? It was extra challenging because so many of the elements of that movie had been done in different ways in different films."

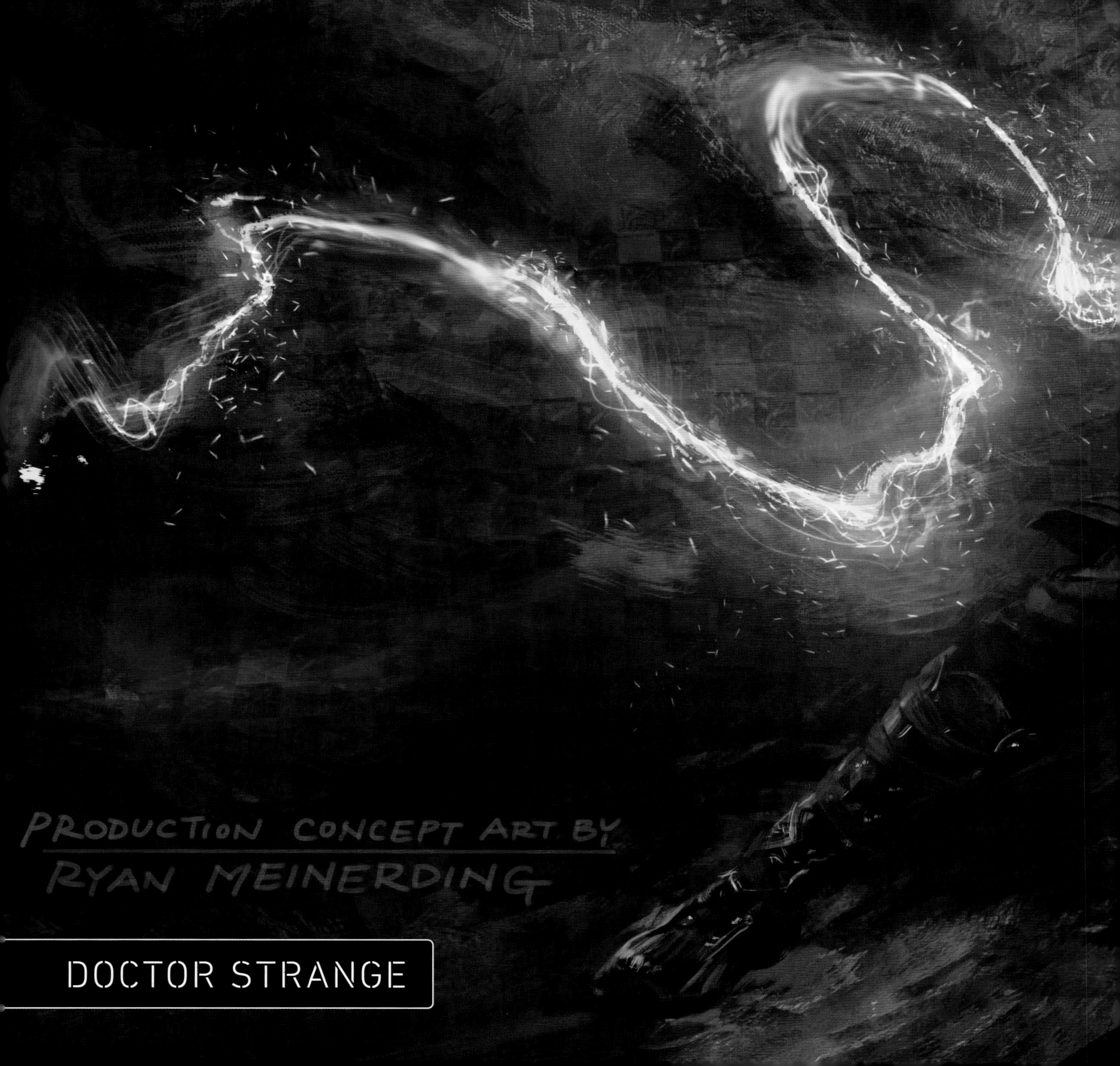

PRODUCTION CONCEPT ART BY RYAN MEINERDING

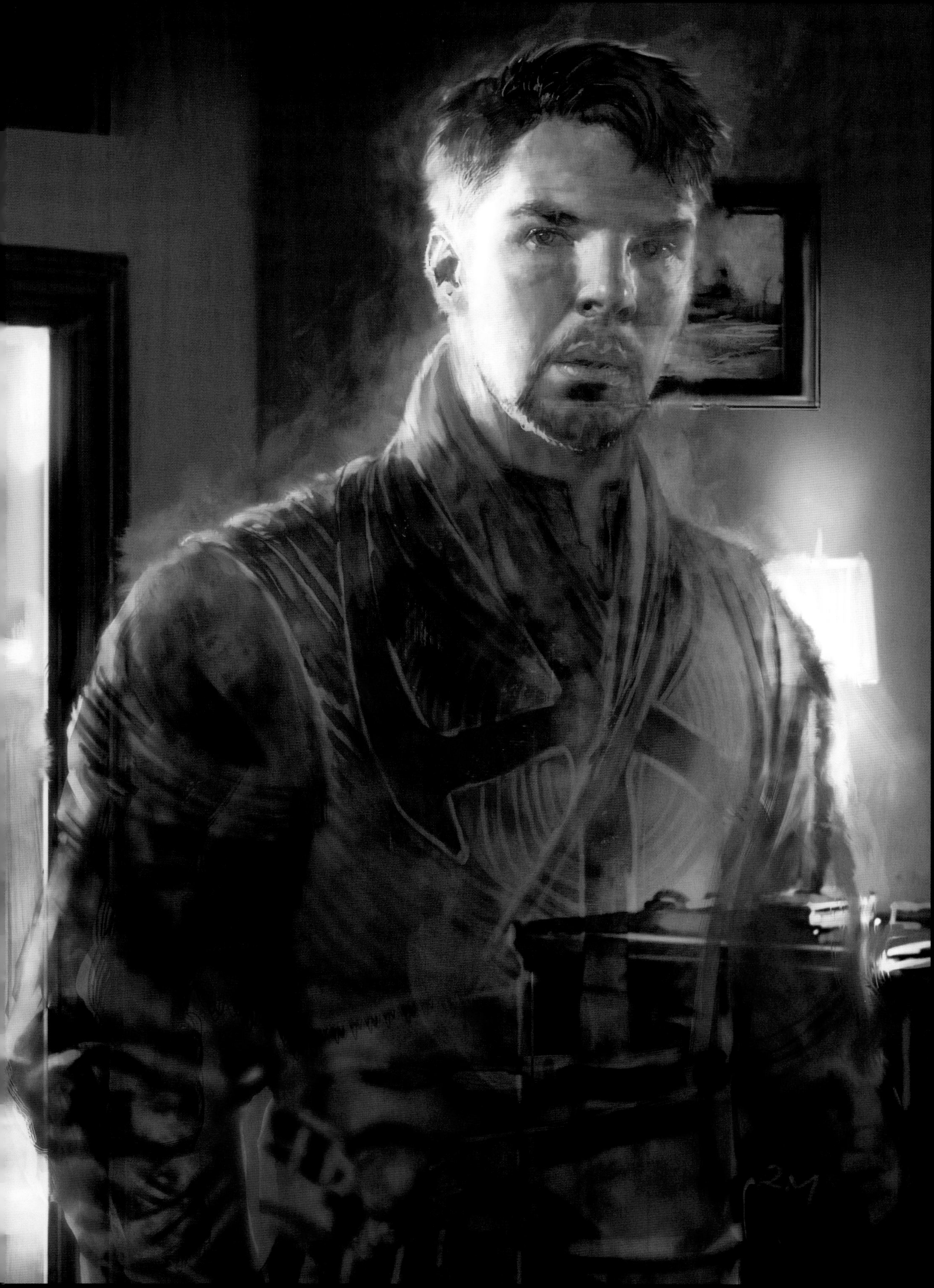

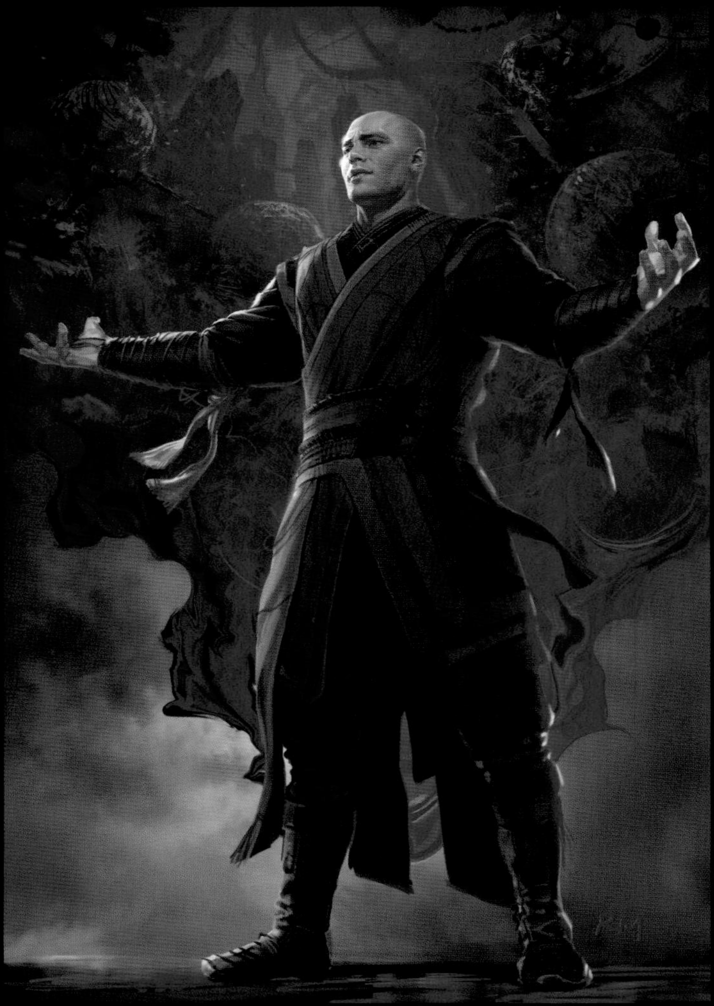

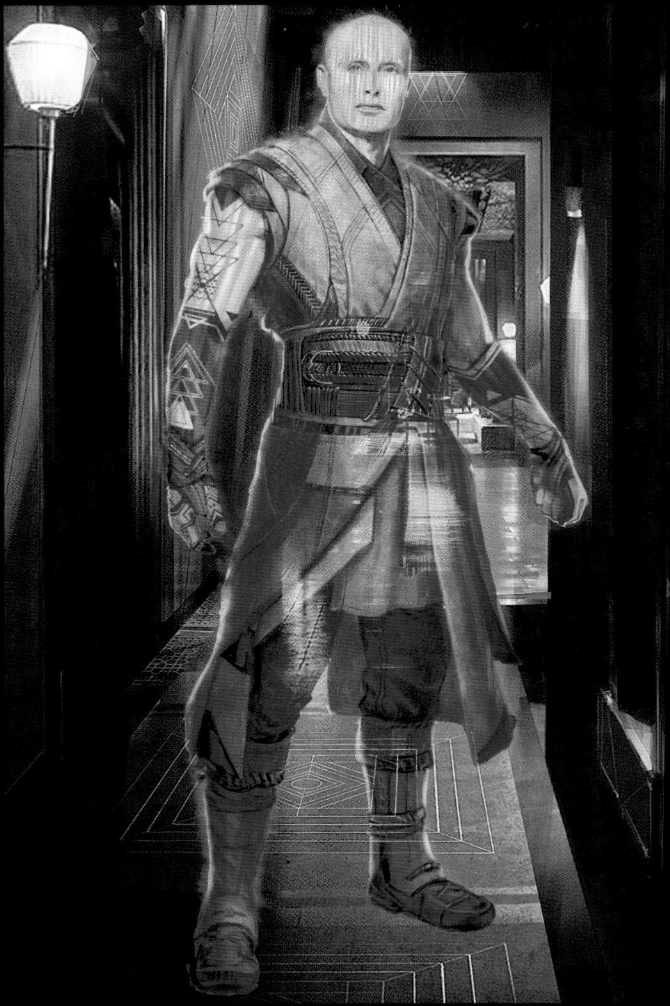

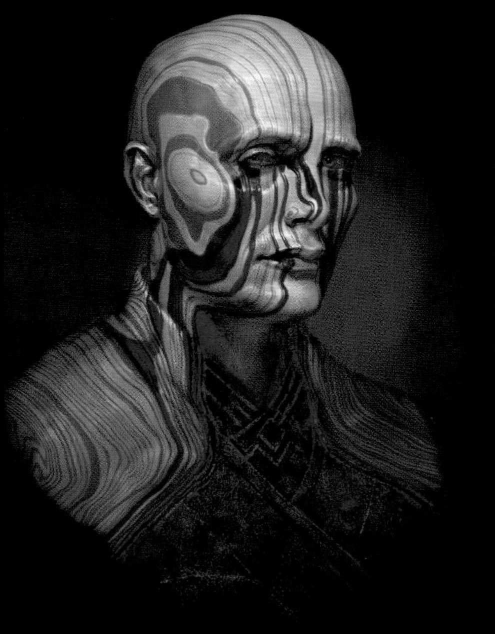

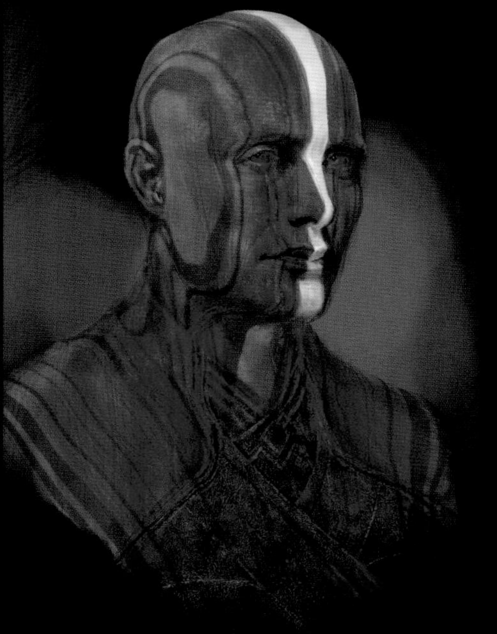

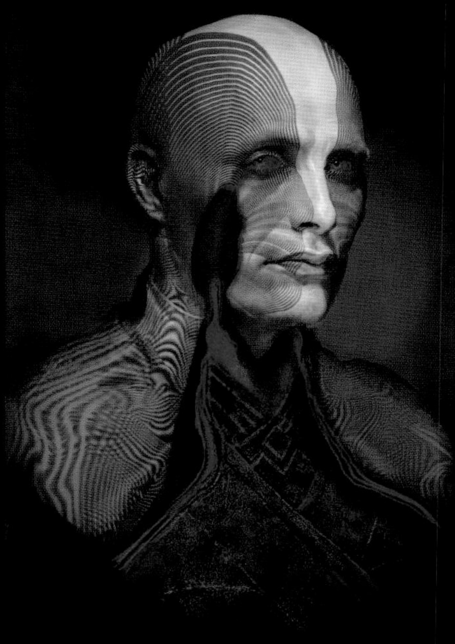

Doctor Strange production designer Charles Wood and his art department came up with the blacklight palette for the Dark Dimension. "A lot of the stuff we ended up doing [in terms of] how Kaecilius or the zealots were affected by the Dark Dimension ended up trying to take some of that [palette] on."

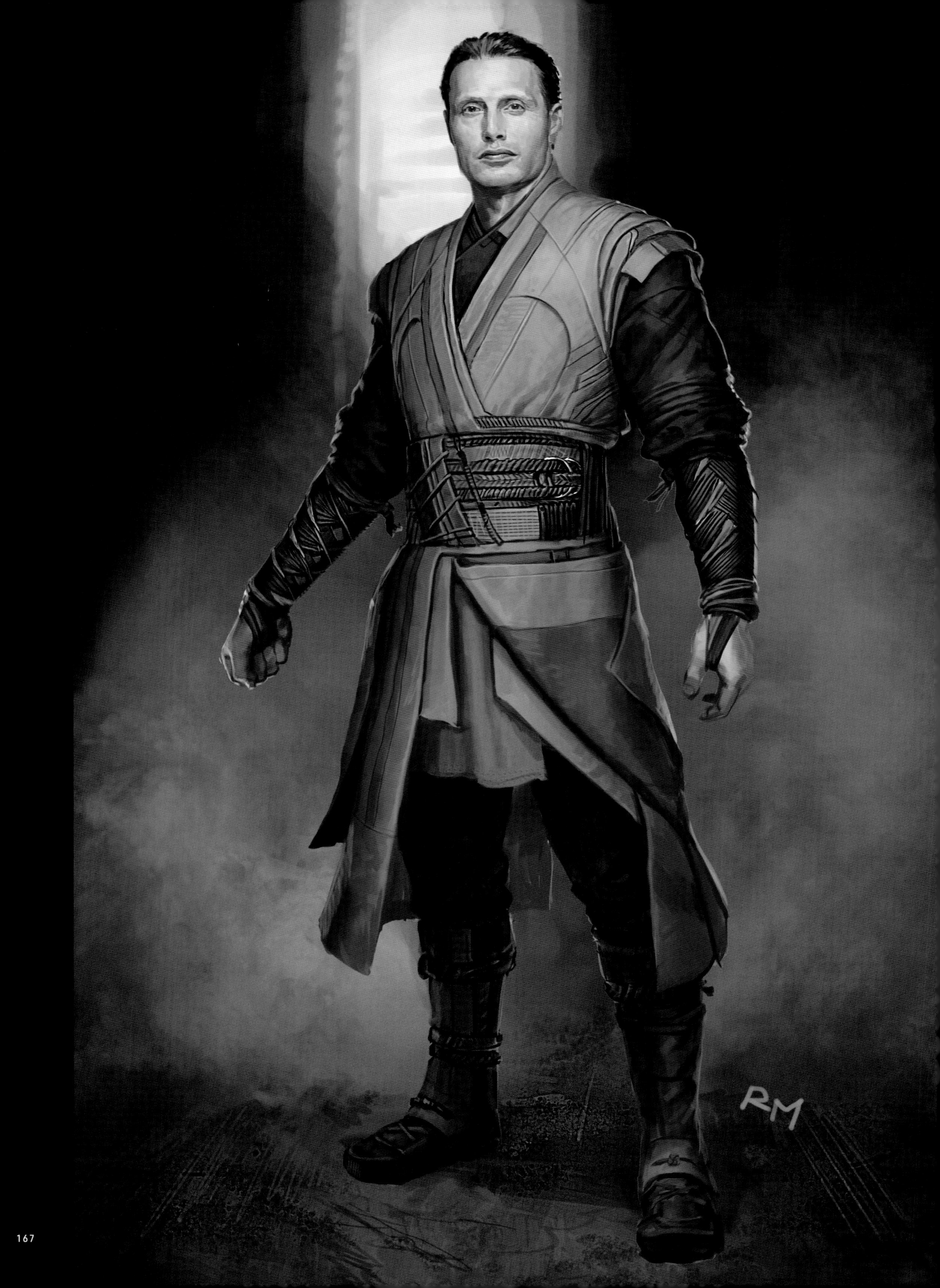
RM

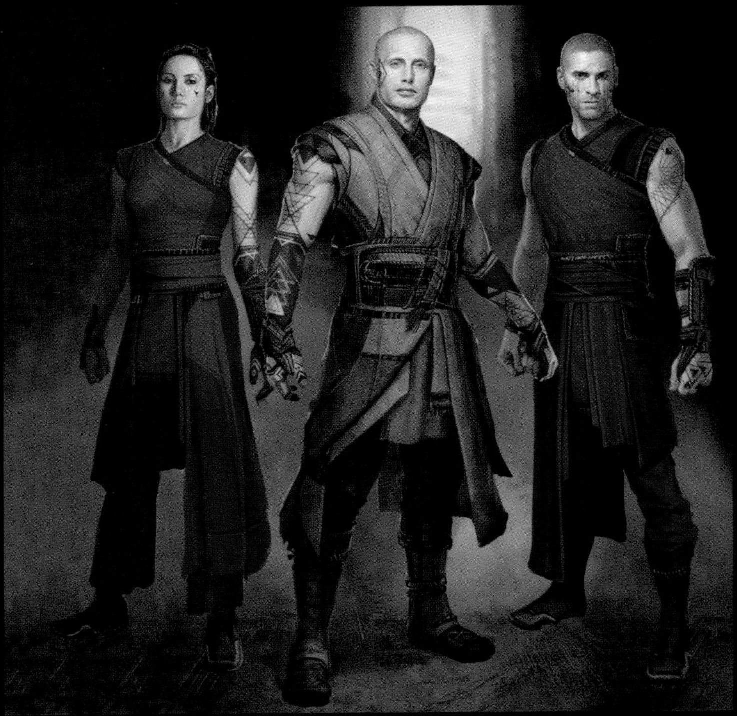

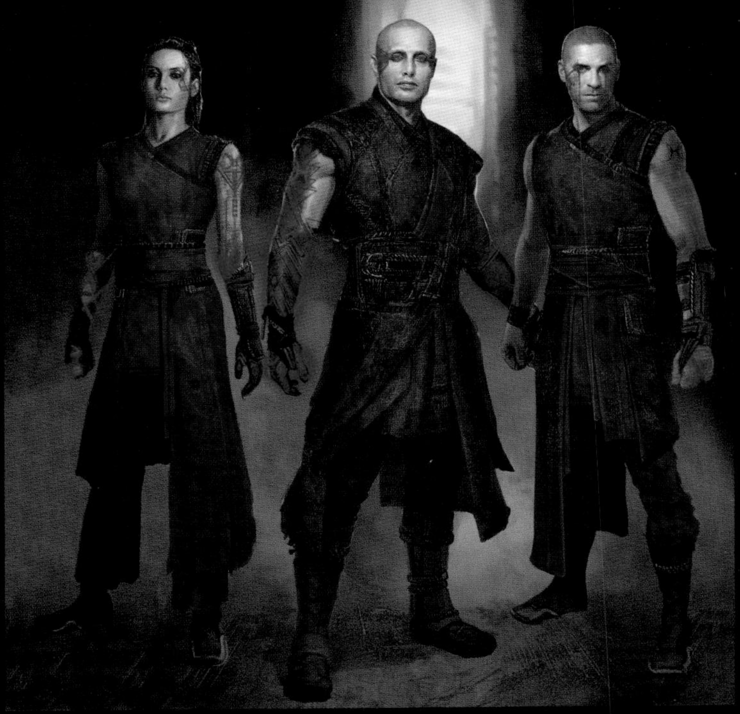

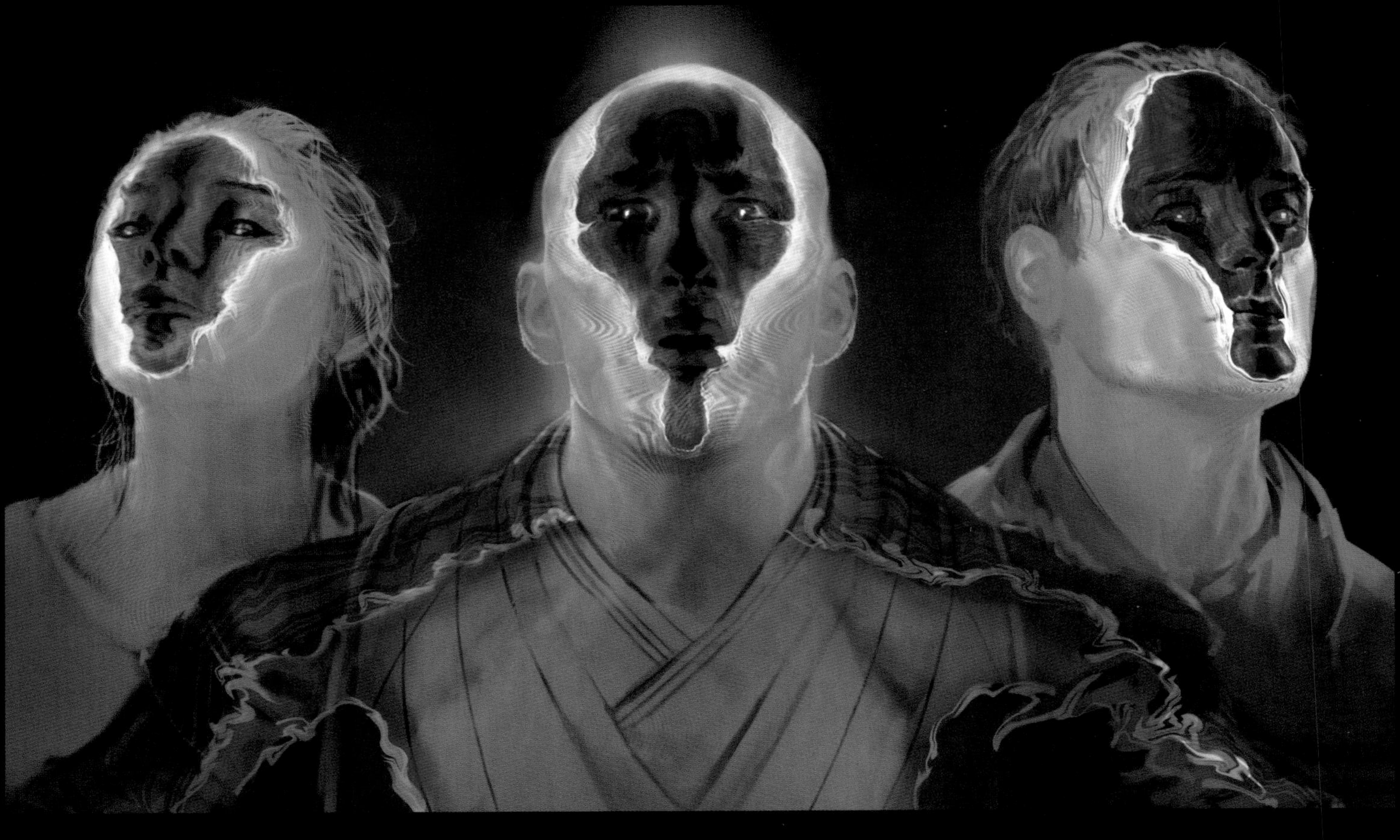

"Initially, what a sorcerer should look like in the MCU was not really fully formed in everybody's mind," shares Meinerding. "Stephen [Broussard] and Kevin [Feige] pitched some different multicolored takes on a Jedi-type costume." Creative conversations about the zealots were detailed and extensive. Meinerding adds, "We were trying to sell not only how the costumes and characters looked, but by what process did they become affected by the Dark Dimension? Is it something internal? Do they cry tears of ecstasy that burn their skin and affect them in strange ways, or is it through some ritual? We quickly realized, as all of those things overlapped, that we needed to figure out everything all at once."

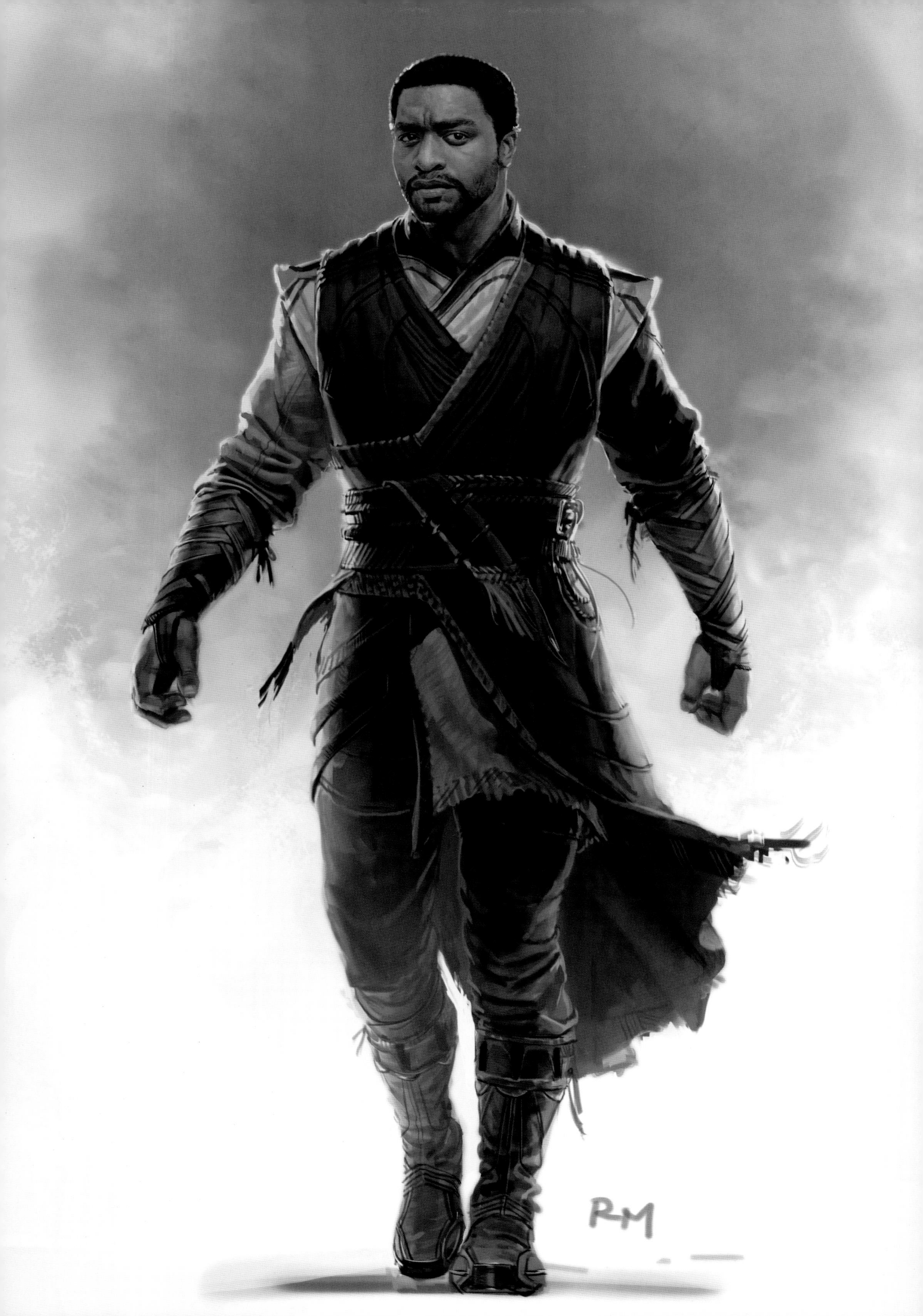
RM

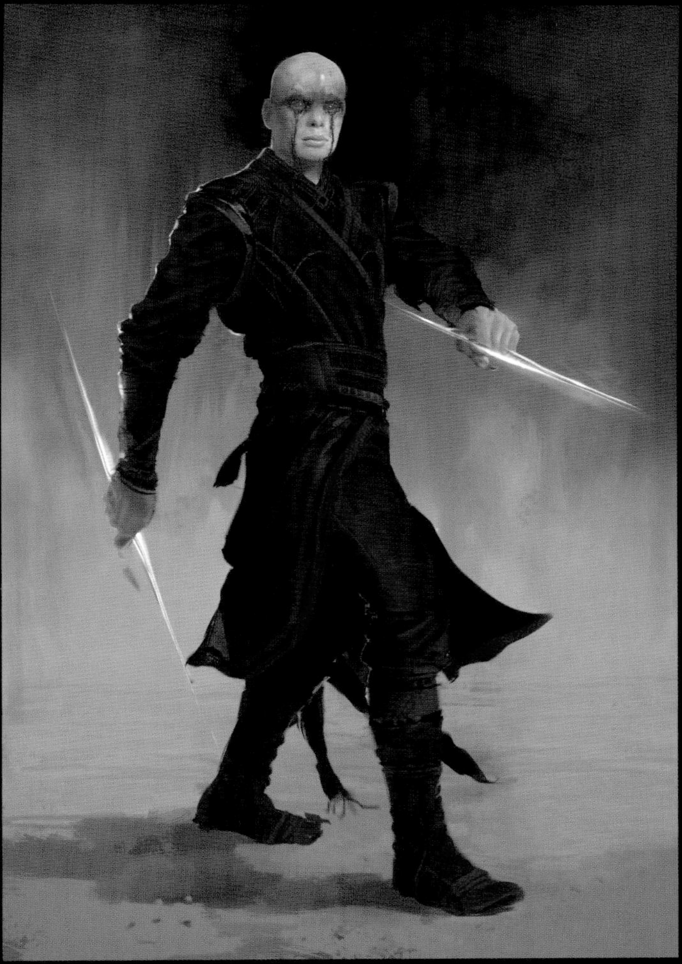

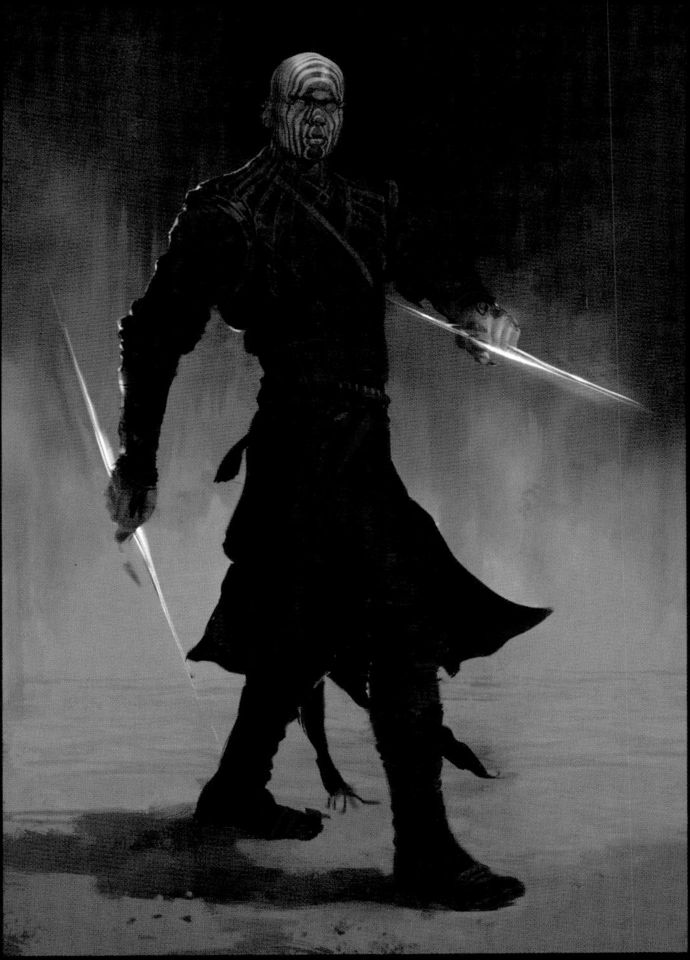

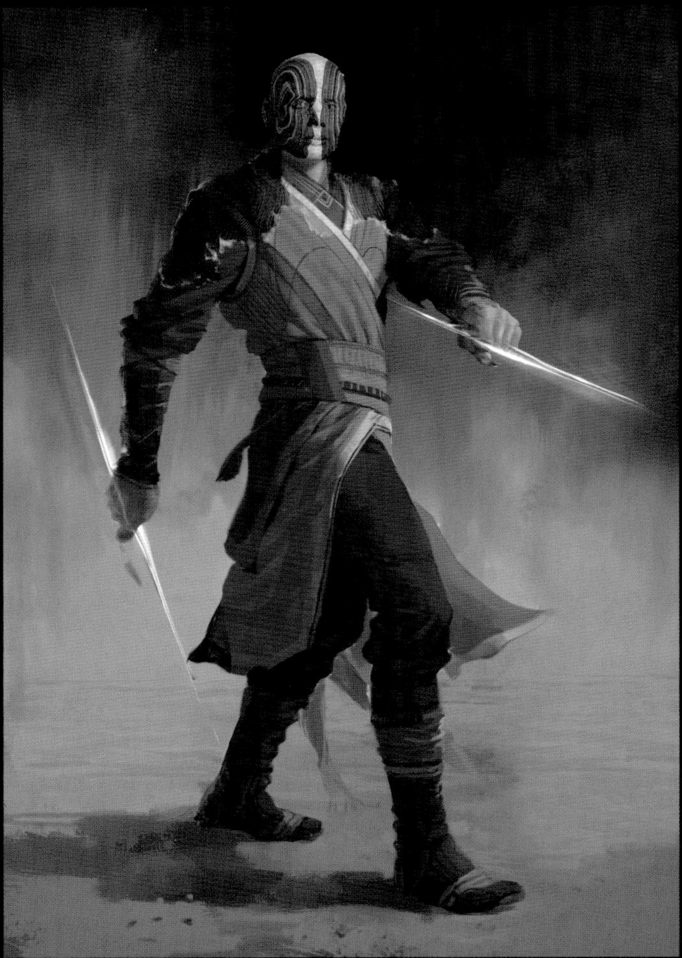

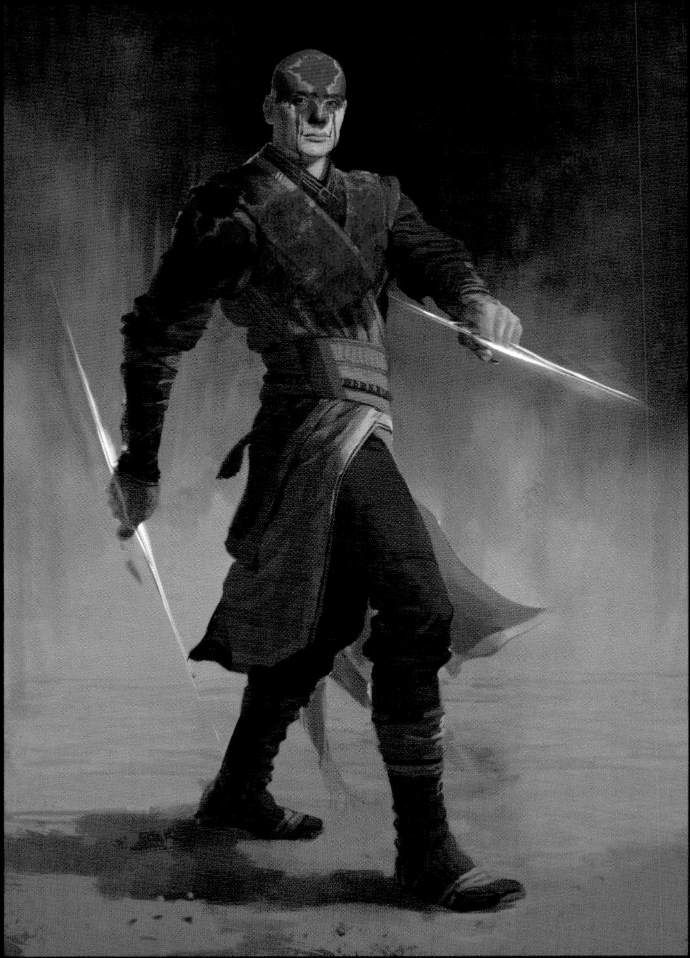

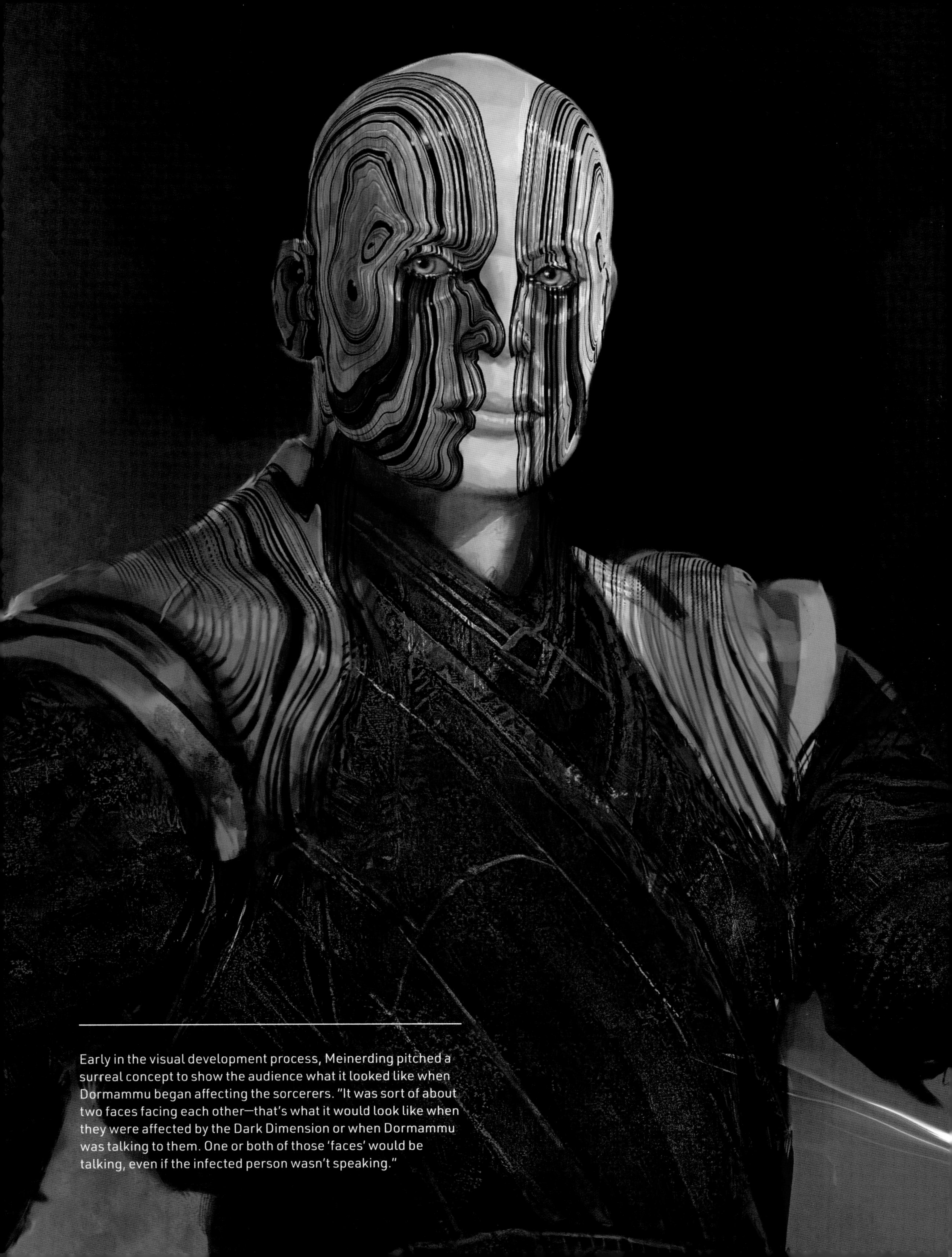

Early in the visual development process, Meinerding pitched a surreal concept to show the audience what it looked like when Dormammu began affecting the sorcerers. "It was sort of about two faces facing each other—that's what it would look like when they were affected by the Dark Dimension or when Dormammu was talking to them. One or both of those 'faces' would be talking, even if the infected person wasn't speaking."

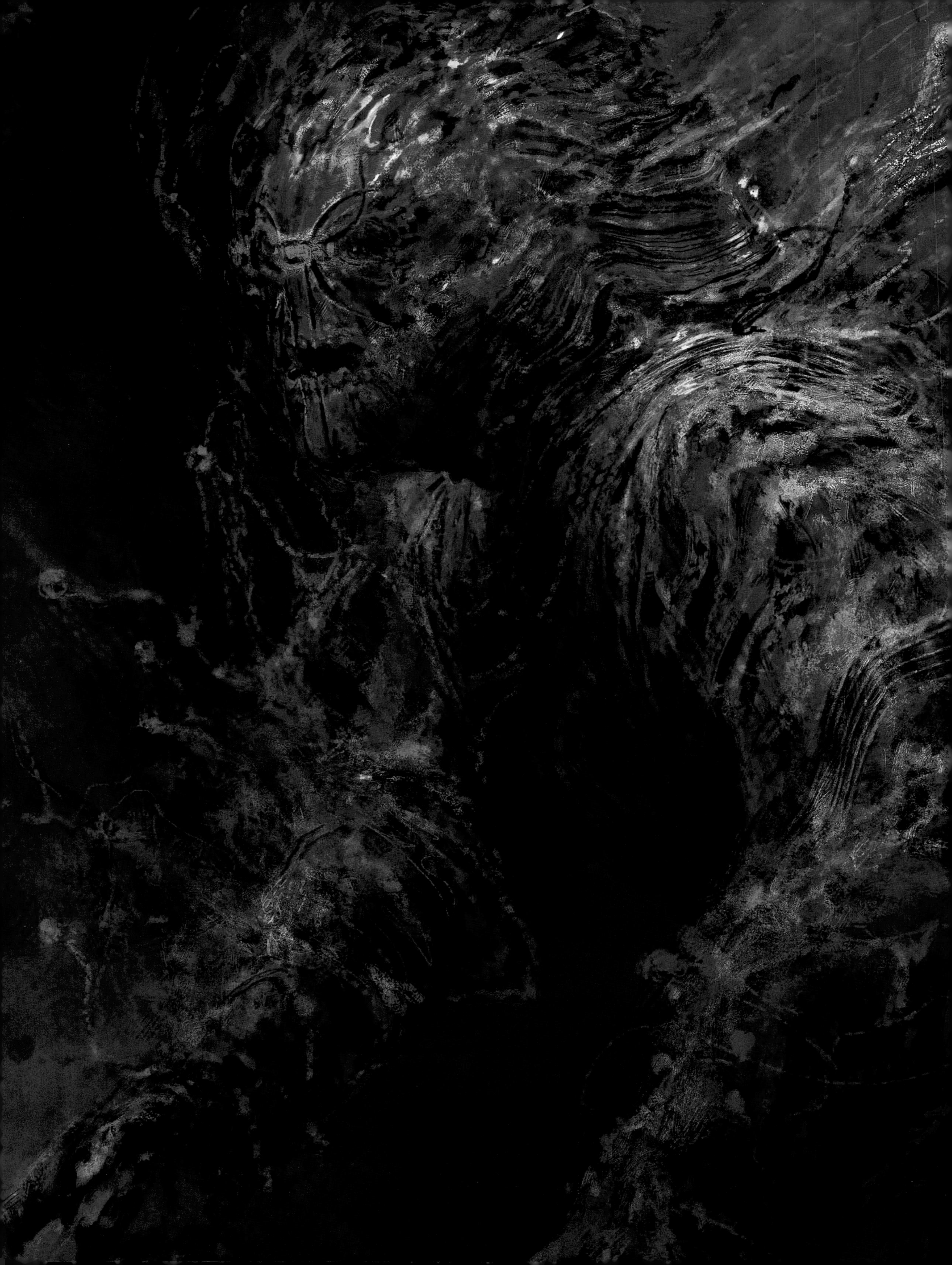

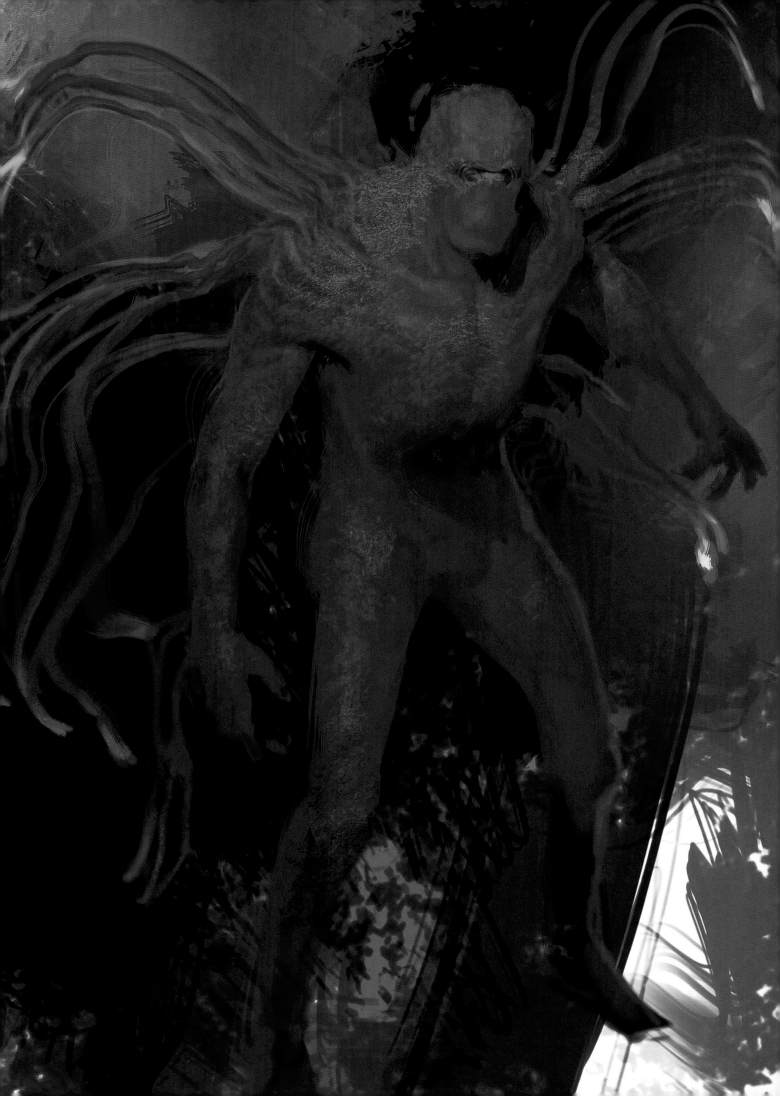

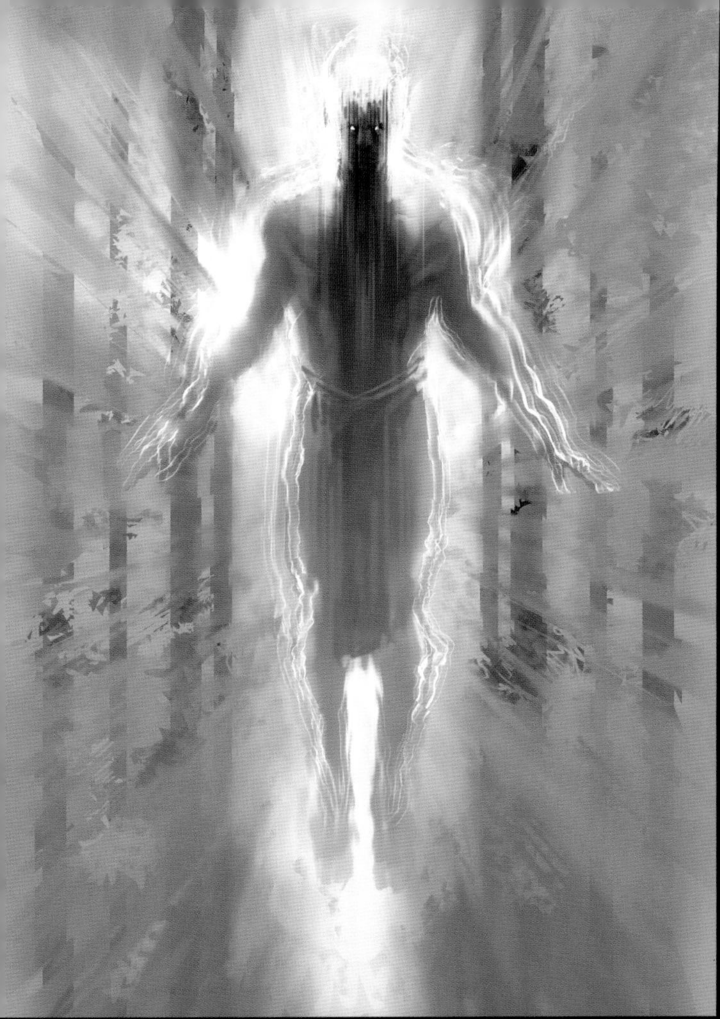

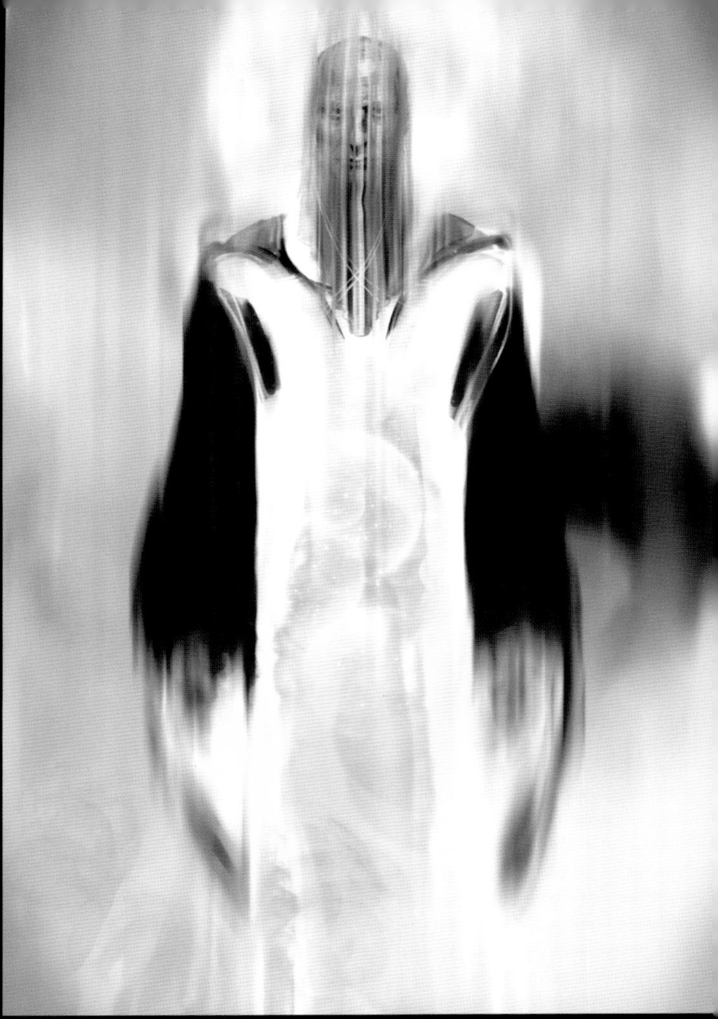

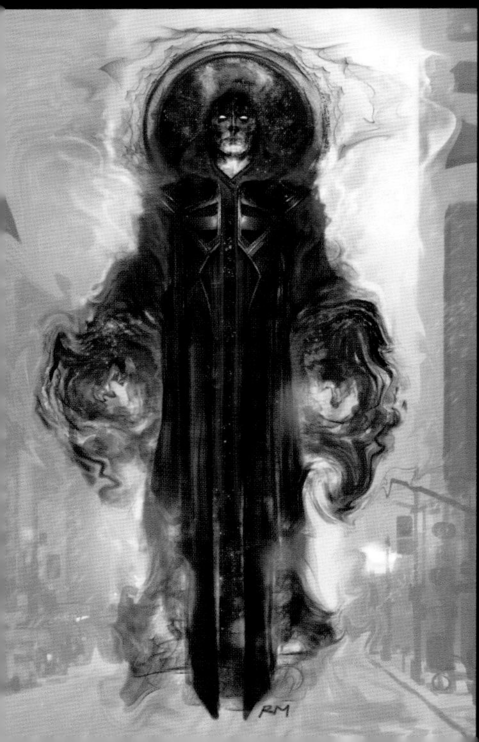
RM

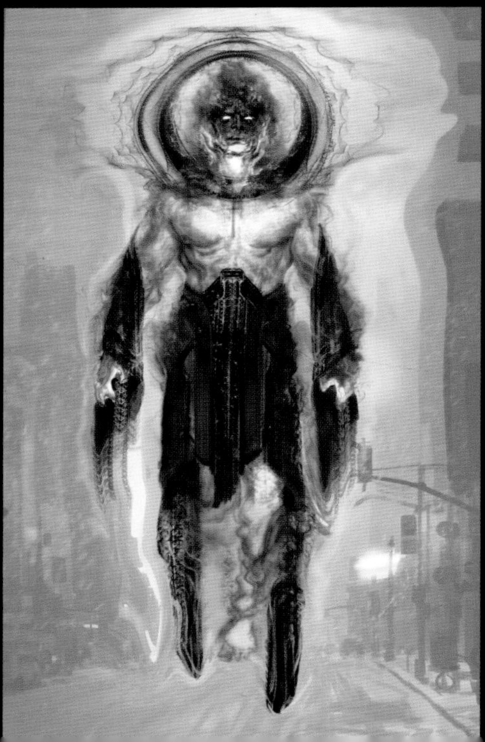

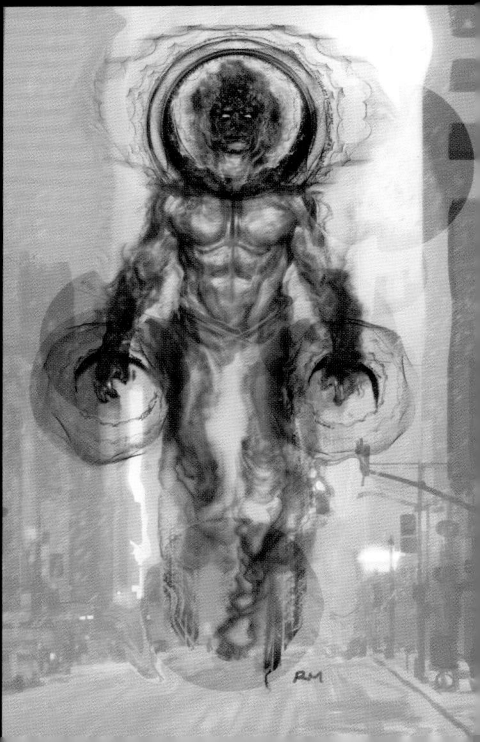
RM

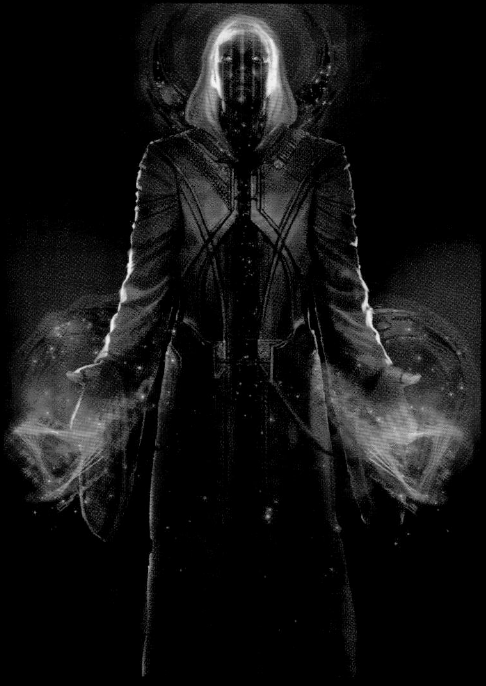

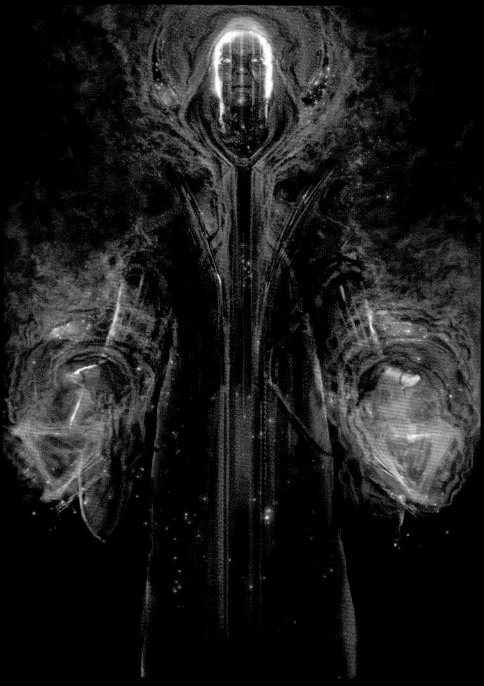

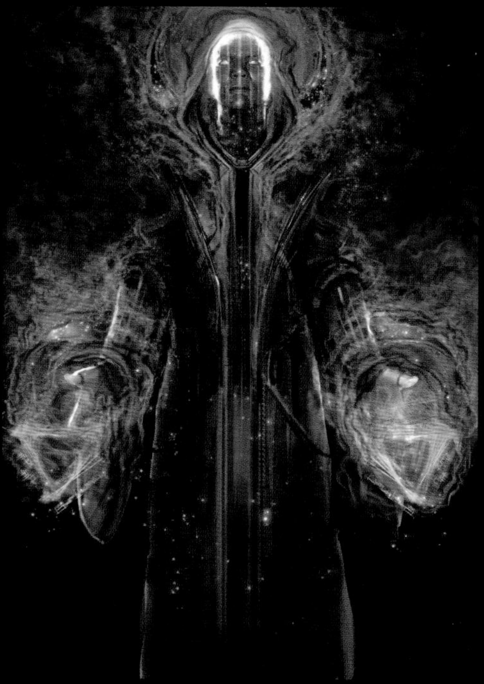

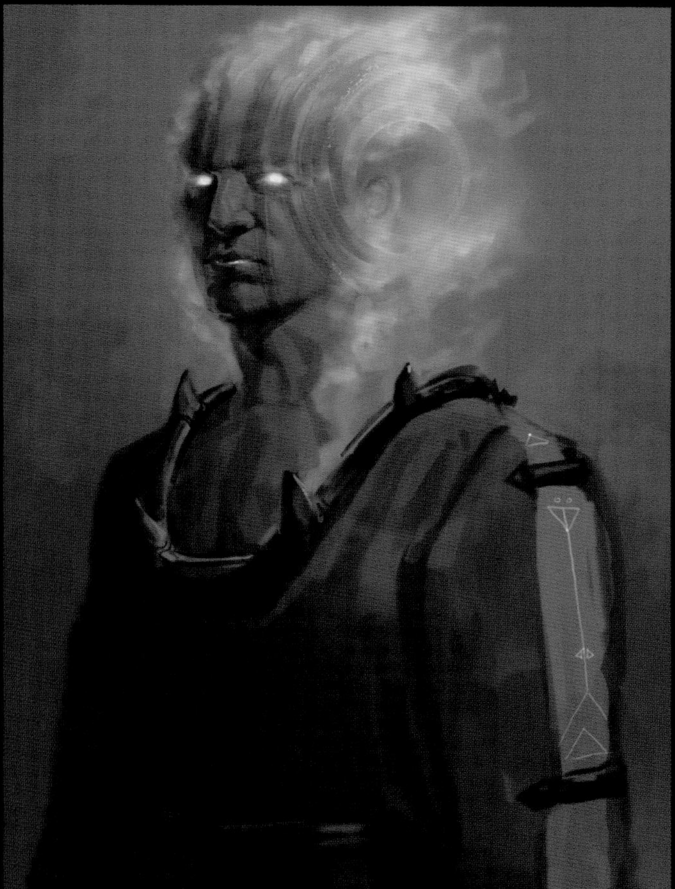

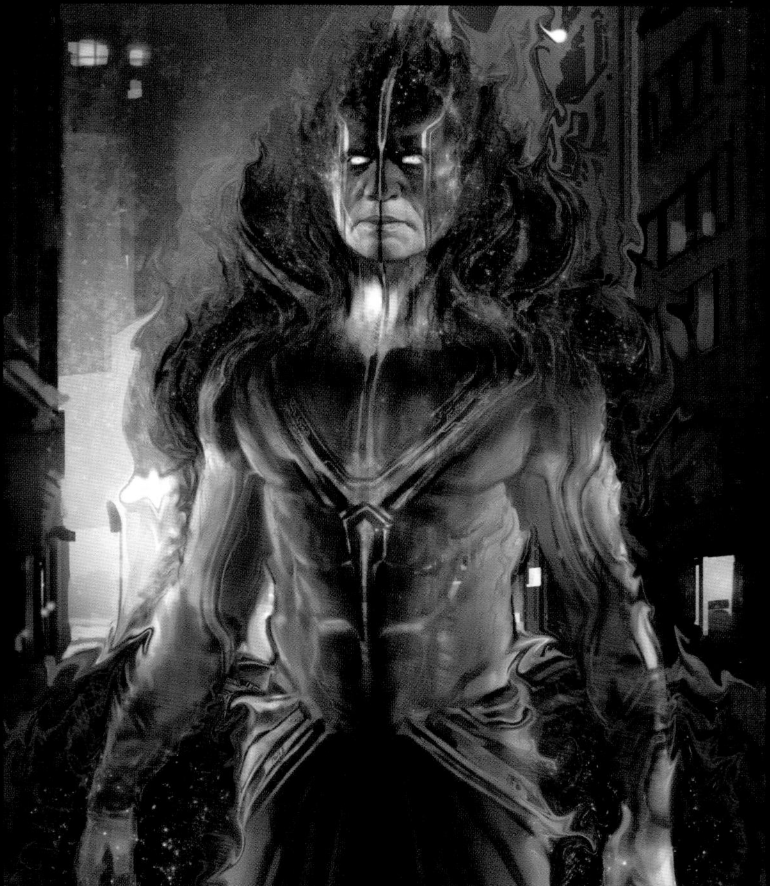

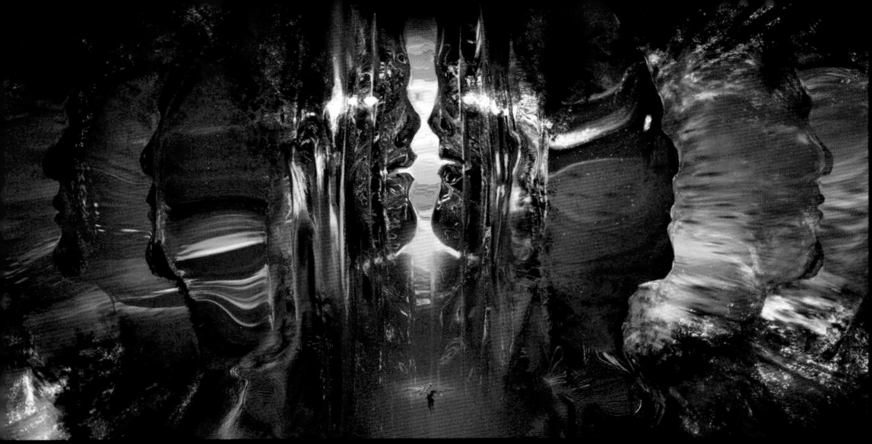

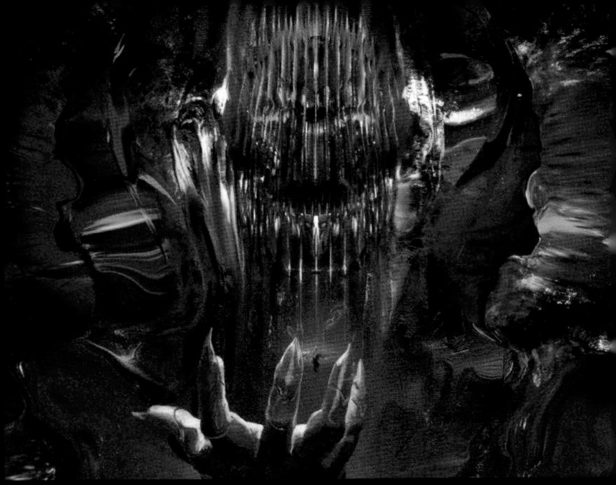

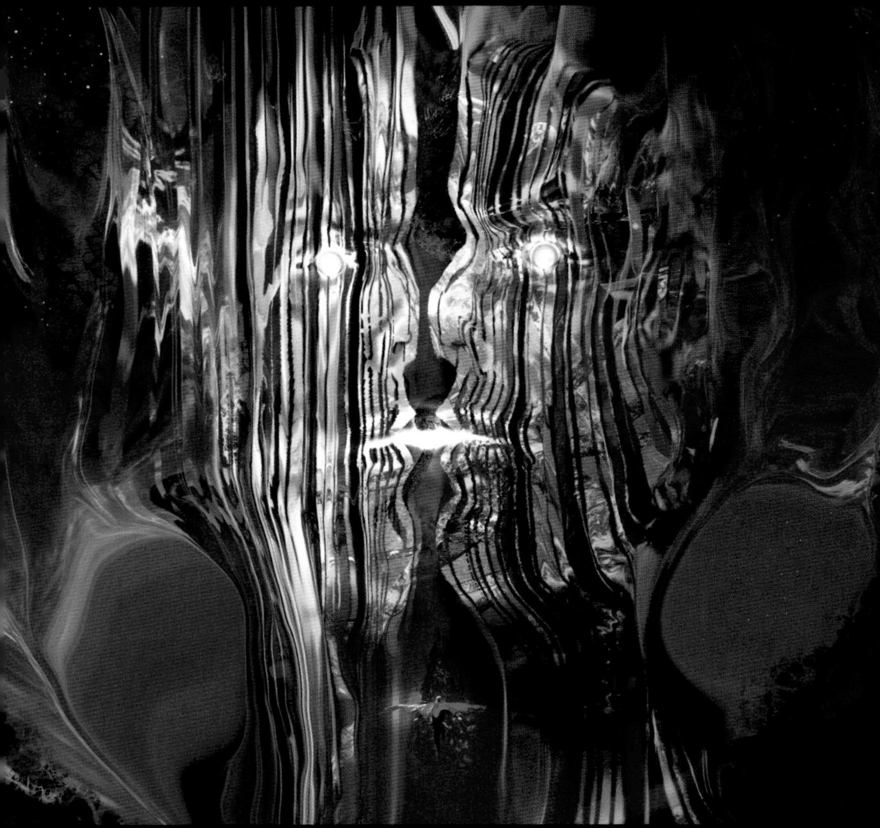

Doctor Strange director/cowriter Scott Derrickson pitched Dormammu as an "eleven-dimensional being." This sent Ryan Meinerding down an extremely experimental path that led to the creation of these images. "I visualized that it could look as though Dormammu is spread *between* dimensions, or you had to look into multiple dimensions to even attempt to comprehend what they looked like," details Meinerding. "Kind of like at the end of *Indiana Jones and the Kingdom of the Crystal Skull*—the alien character exists in other dimensions, so we only ever see slices of them." Developing his idea of the two faces looking inward at each other, the artist expands, "Take the image above left, for example: As you go outward, there are silhouettes that look like facial distortions. If you encountered Dormammu, the idea was that one of those faces talked while the others didn't. Or one said something and then the other echoed it. But, at every turn, you would only ever see a fragmented version of Dormammu, because it's the only thing our brains could process."

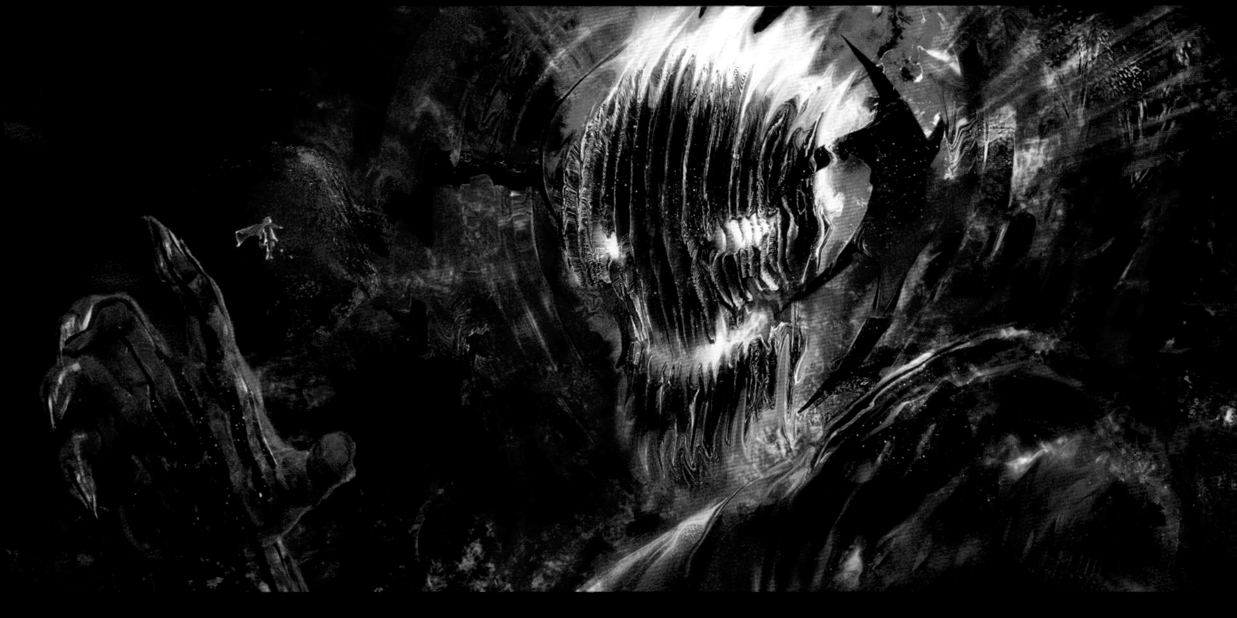

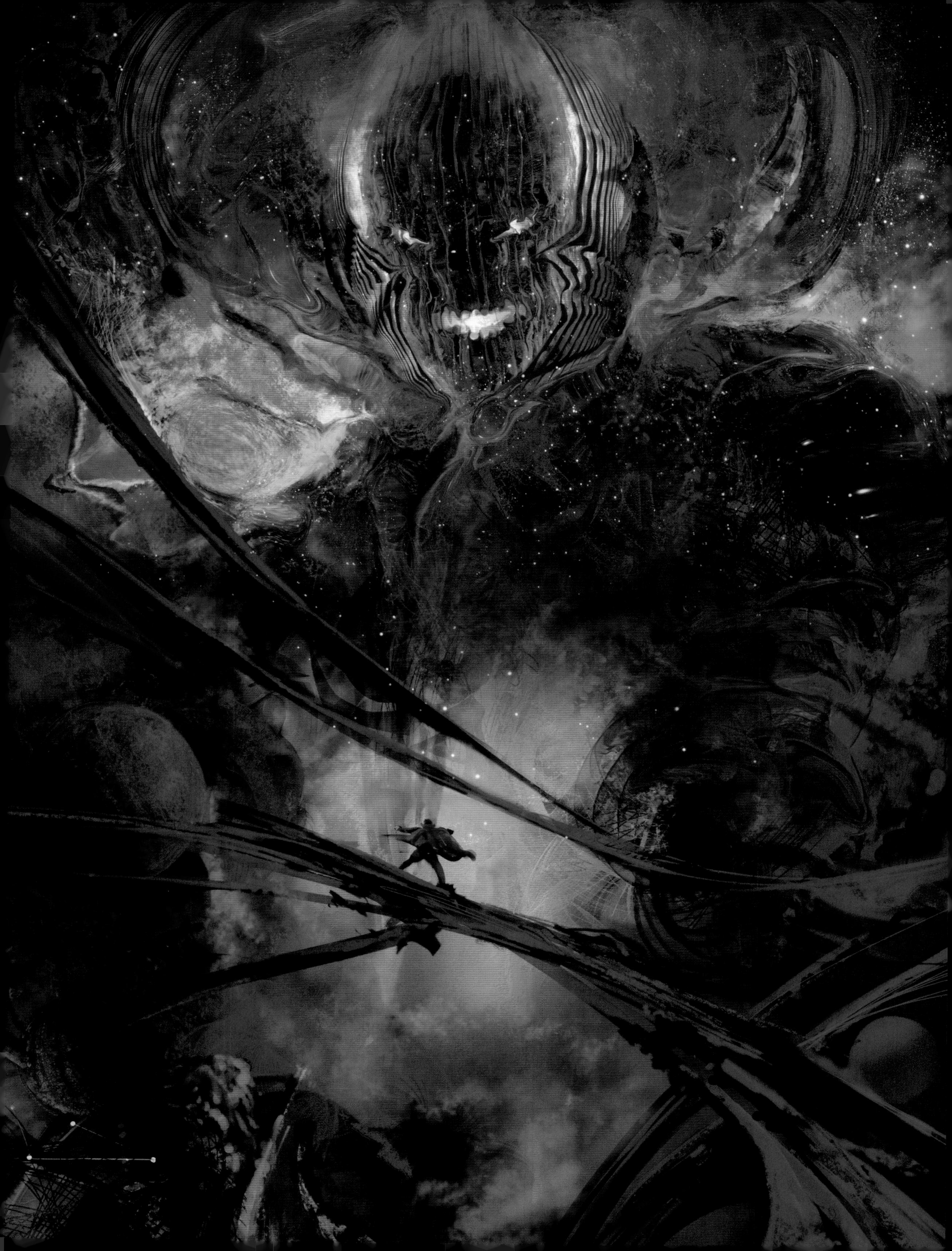

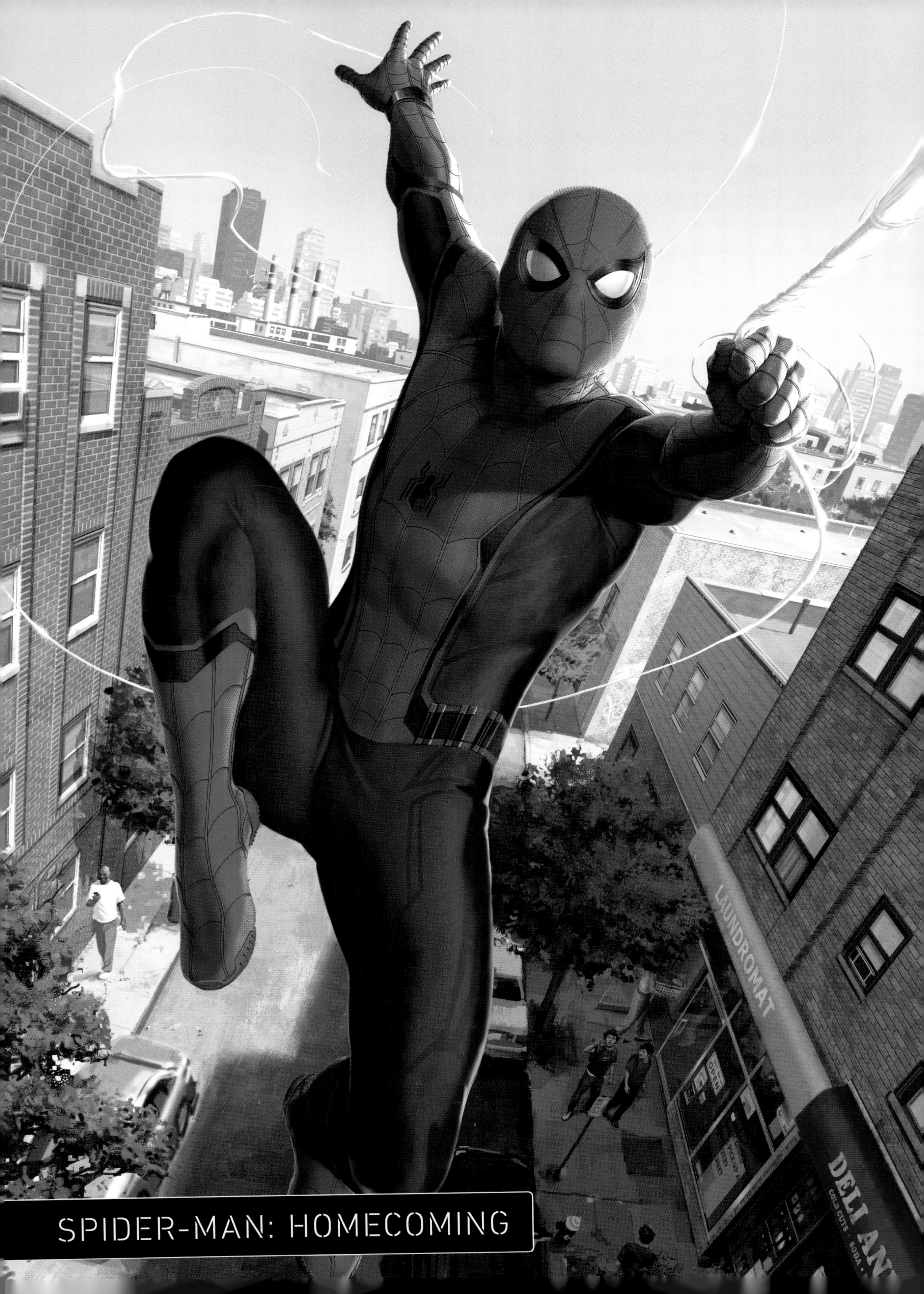
LAUNDROMAT

SPIDER-MAN: HOMECOMING

The development of *Captain America: Civil War* was another massive undertaking, as it was for all intents and purposes another Avengers film, with the added bonus of introducing one of Marvel's most beloved characters: Spider-Man. For Meinerding, it was the unexpected opportunity of a lifetime to develop and design the character for his inclusion into the Marvel Cinematic Universe's ongoing narrative.

Because Spider-Man is a character licensed to Sony Pictures, it was almost impossible to imagine him ever being folded into the MCU. But producer Amy Pascal and Kevin Feige were able to work out the framework of a shared collaboration. However, Meinerding had no idea. In fact, the idea of introducing Spider-Man into the MCU was such a fantasy that he says when he was in England working on *Captain America: The First Avenger*, he connected once more with production designer Michael Riva, who was working on *Spider-Man 4* for director Sam Raimi. Riva floated Meinerding coming to work for him, and he actually considered it for moment, assuming it would be his one and only chance to design a cinematic Spider-Man.

Later, while working on *Captain America 3*, Feige popped into Meinerding's office and asked him to work on designs for Spider-Man. Elated, Meinerding threw himself into conceptual ideas covering every kind of iteration of the character. "I like when they're overtly cool. I like when he's a hero. I like when he's a little campy. And all the versions in between," he explains. "I was trying to find reference points and fun things to draw from in all of those areas."

In particular, he focused on how to make Spider-Man's eyes in the mask work to be emotive but not cartoonish. He pitched the concept of camera lens blades, which was quickly adopted as a feature of this version of the character. Much more challenging was nailing the concept for the costume. Because there were several different personalities to please, including Feige, Pascal, the Russos, and producer Nate Moore, Meinerding says he did more than 150 costume designs before they finally selected the one featured in *Civil War*.

But even in postproduction, Meinerding's pitch was to lean into a design that reflected Stark tech components—especially the tech-y spider within the suit and the movable lenses in the mask—which was eventually adopted.

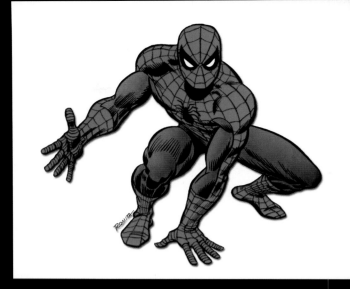

TOP Meinerding says, "I'm hugely inspired by John Romita Sr. and his licensing art for Spider-Man."

MIDDLE One of many homemade Spider-Man masks that Ryan made when he was a teenager

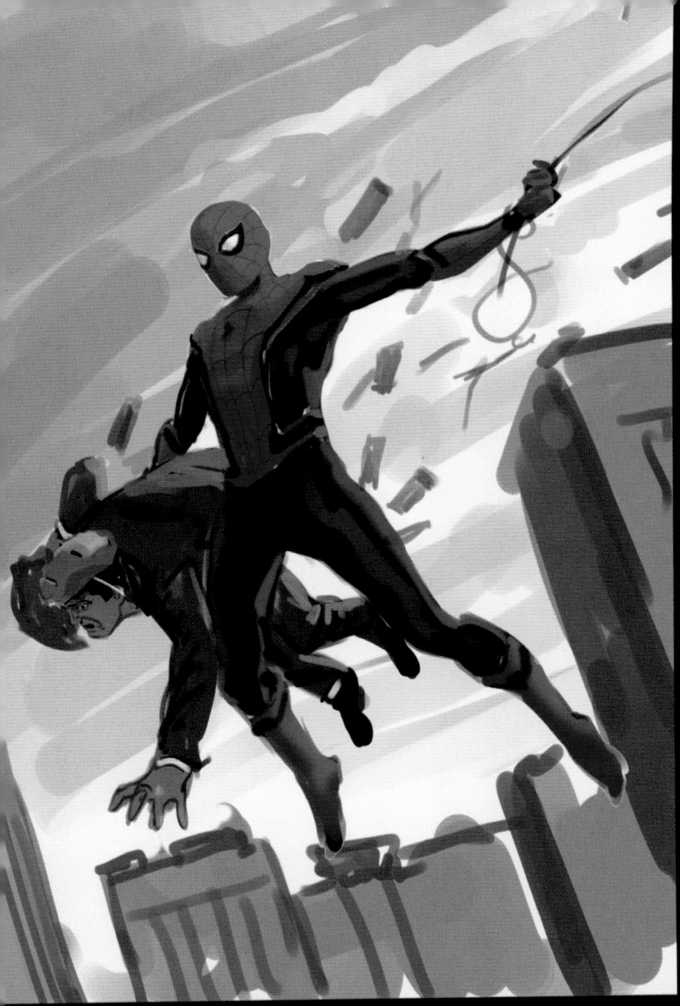
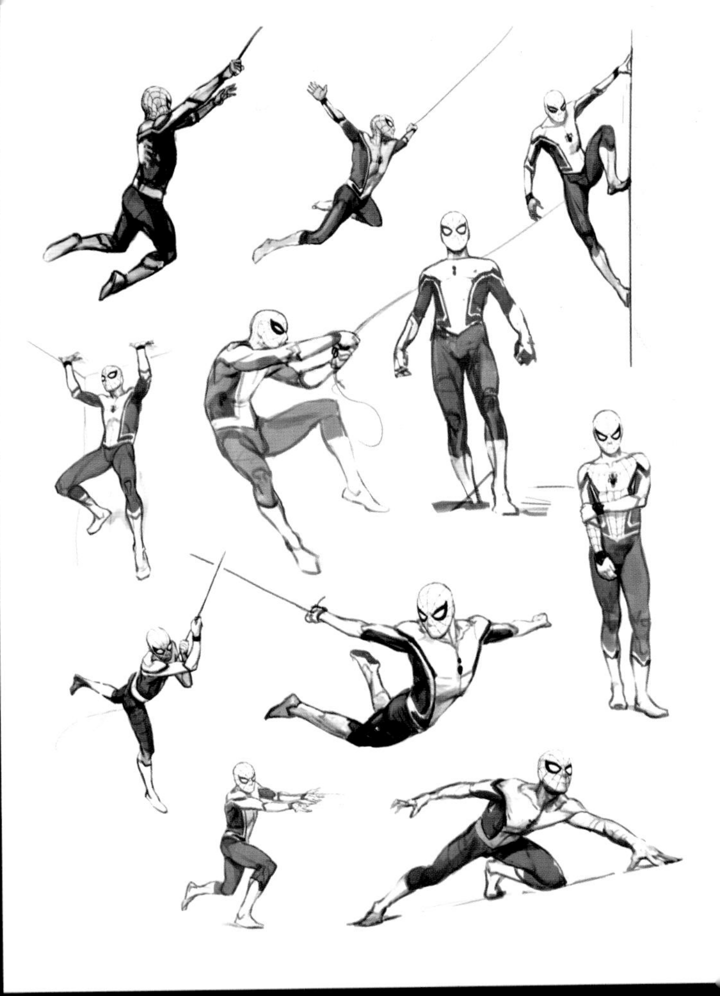
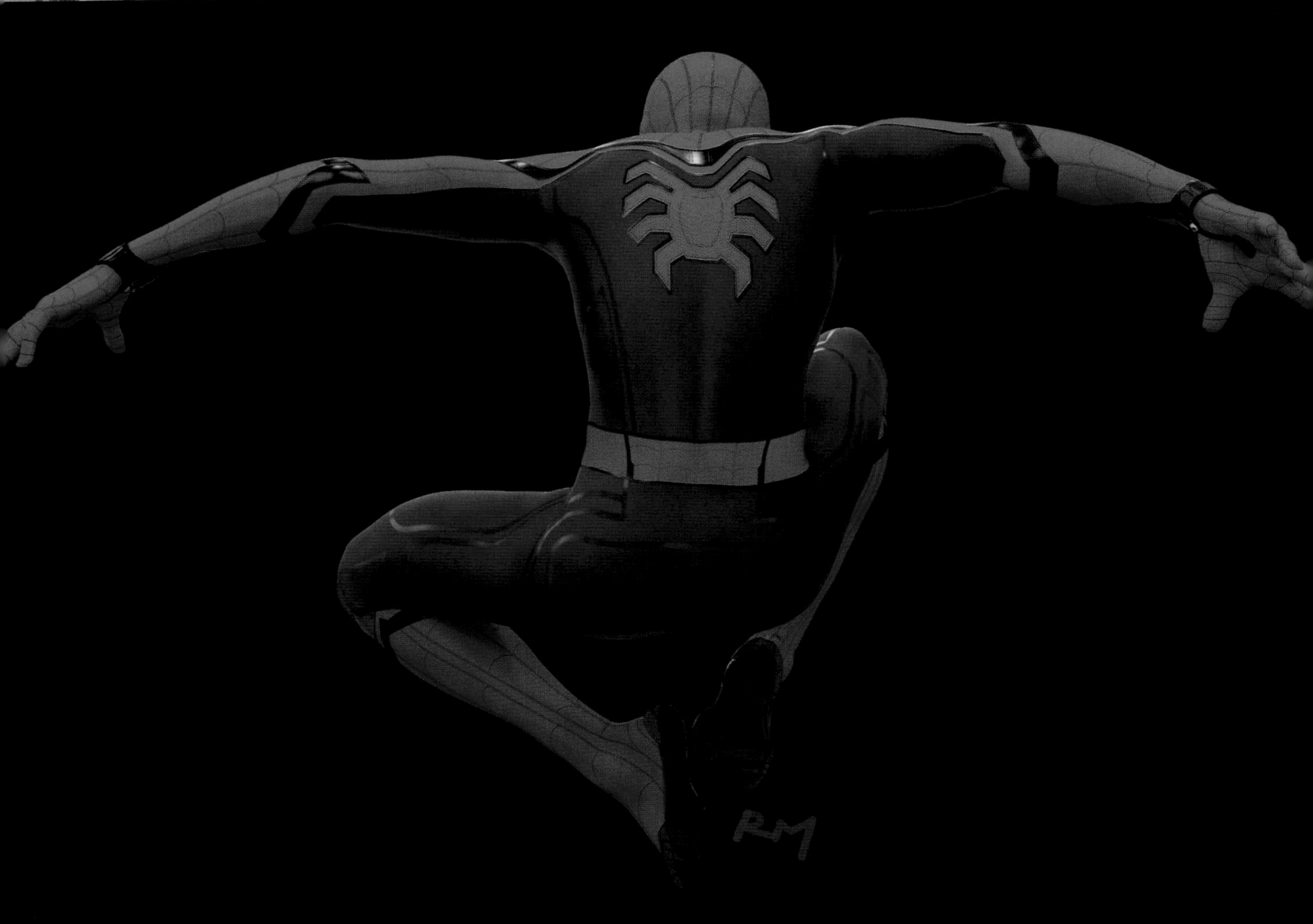
RM

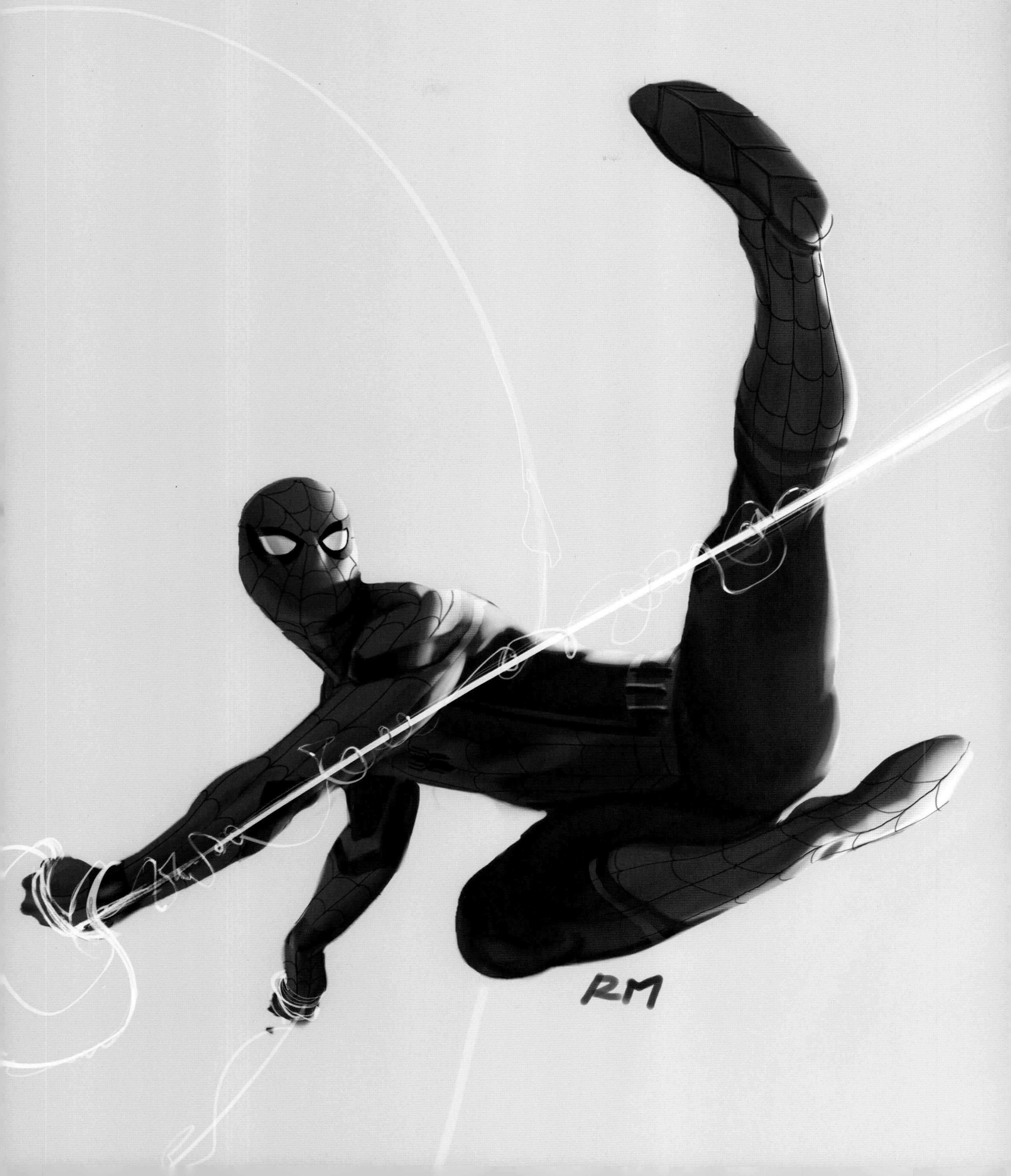
RM

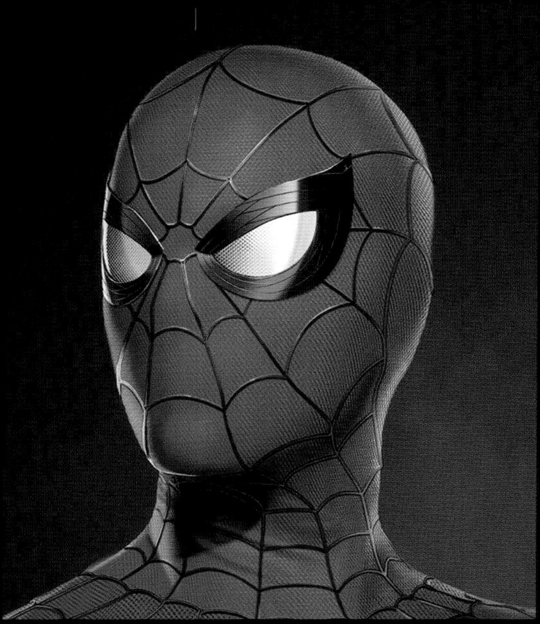
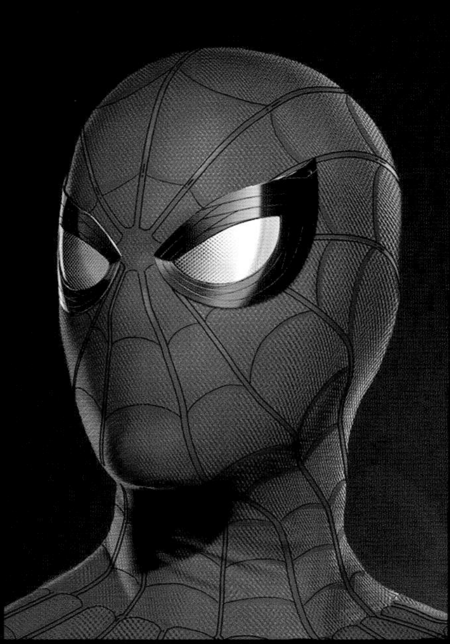
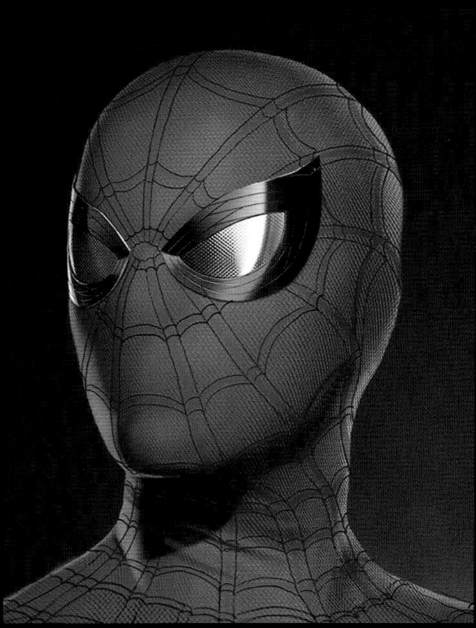
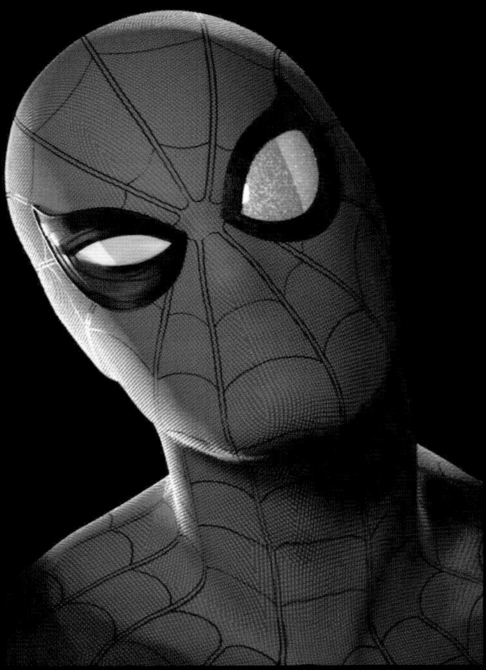
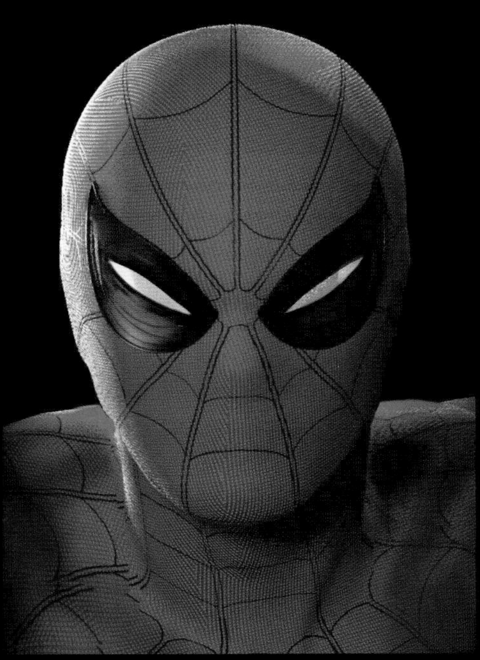
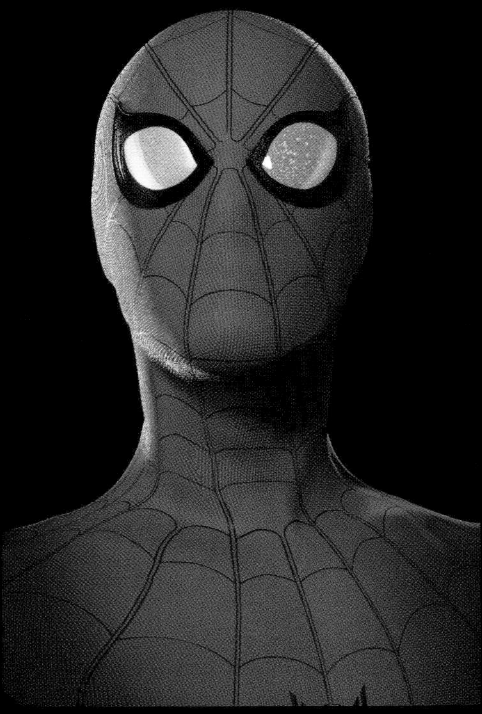
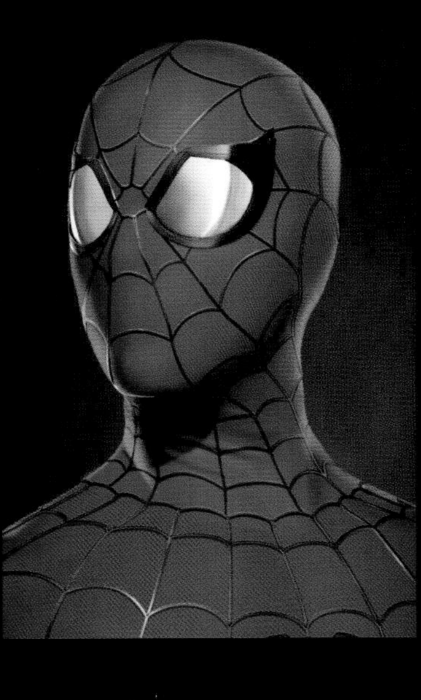
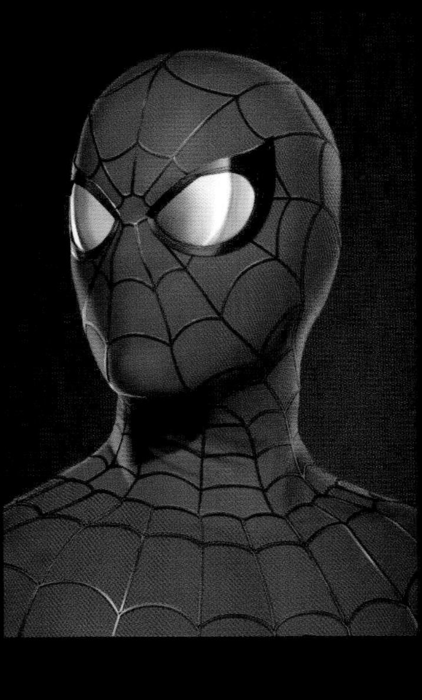
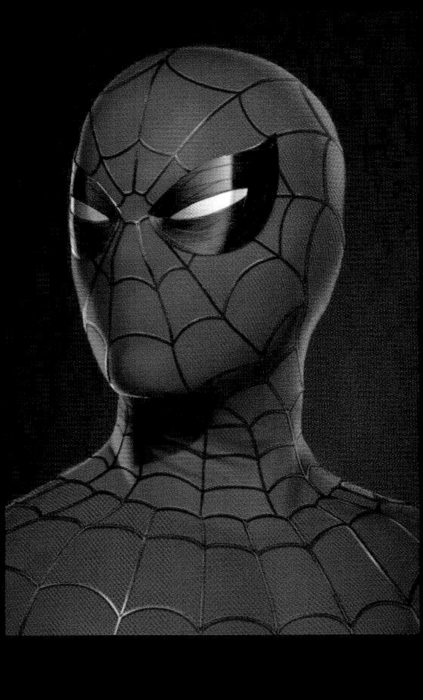
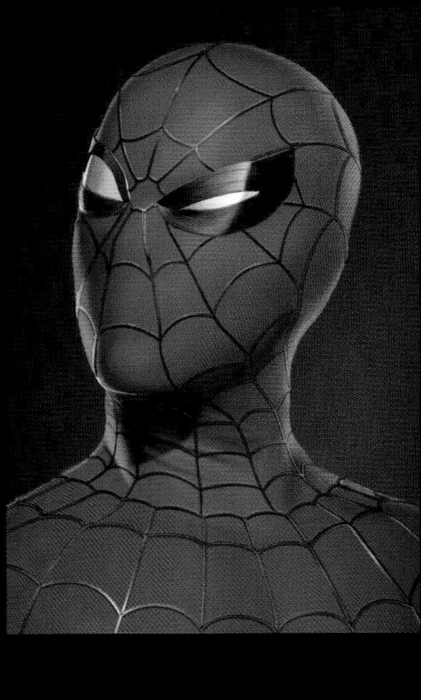

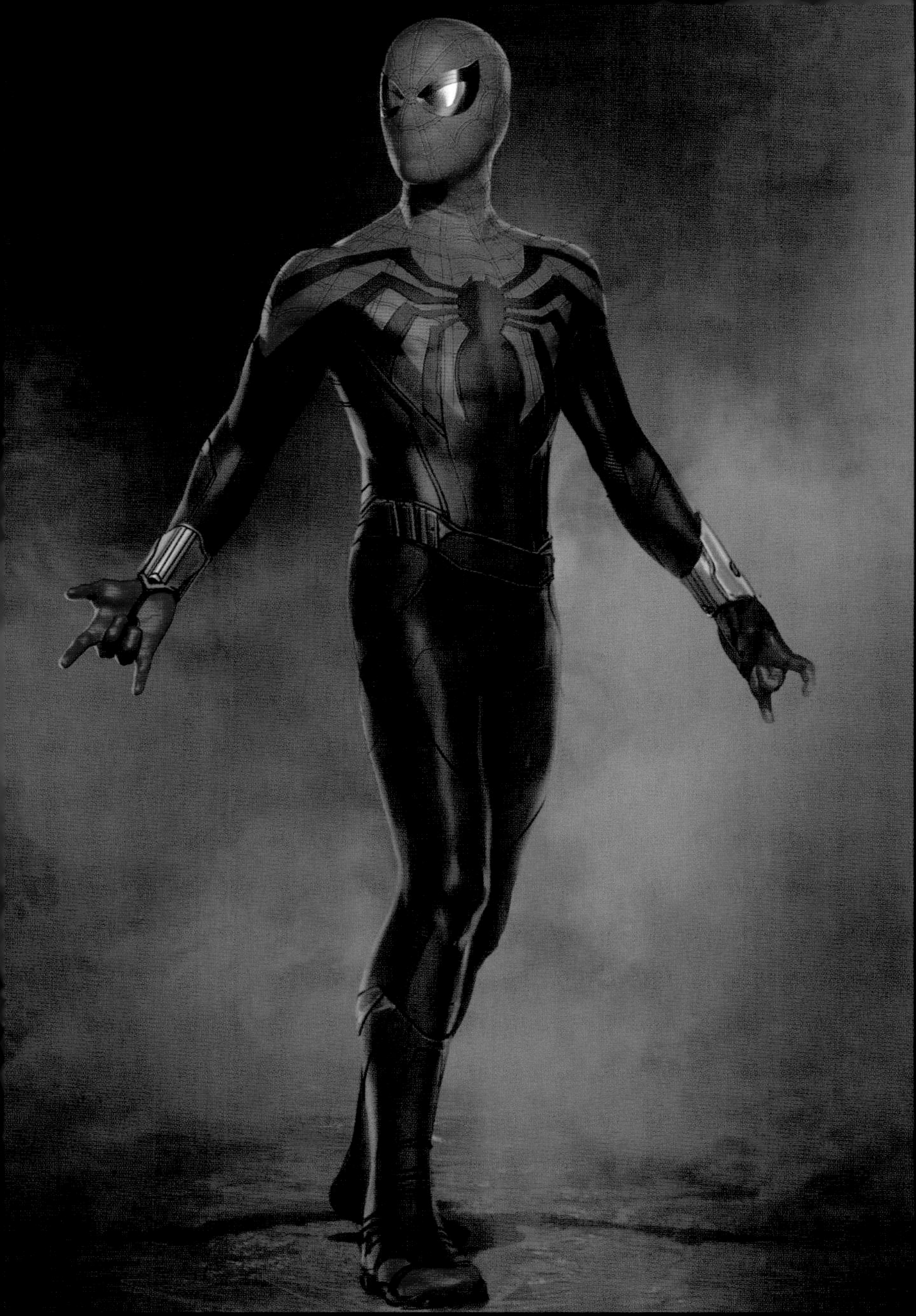
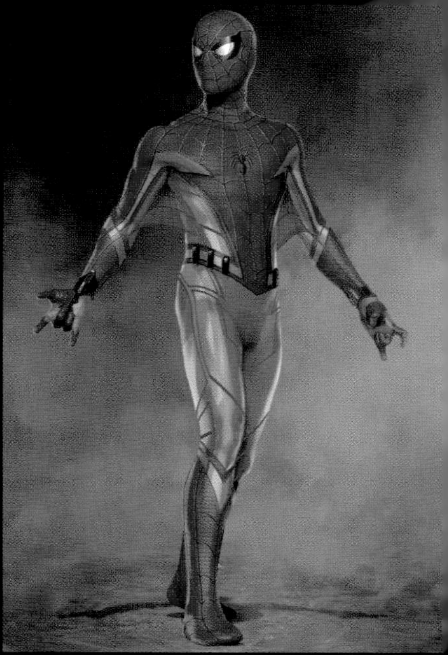
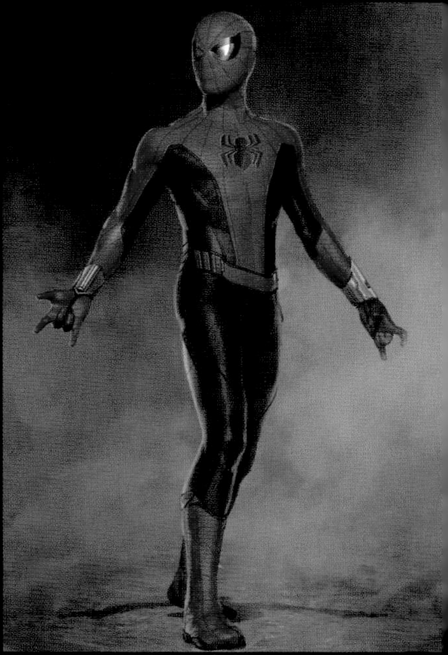
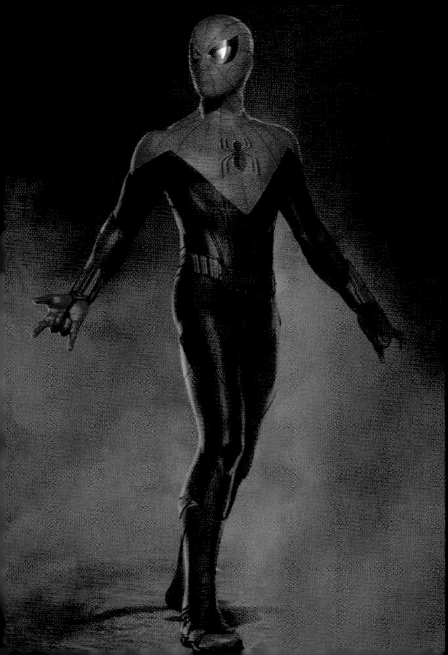
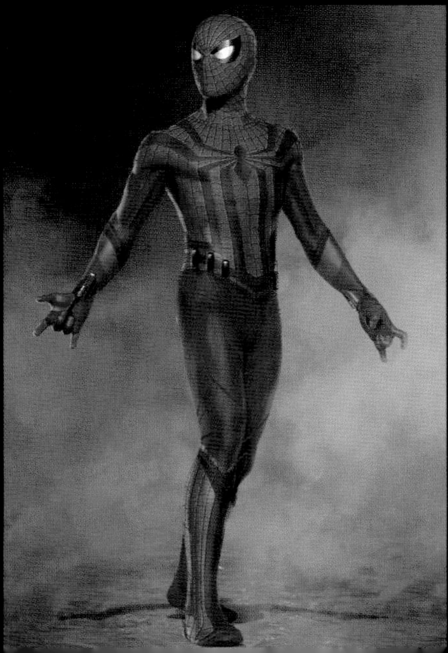
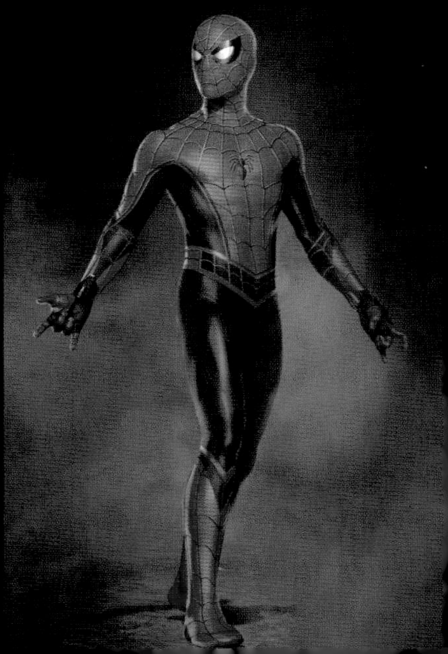

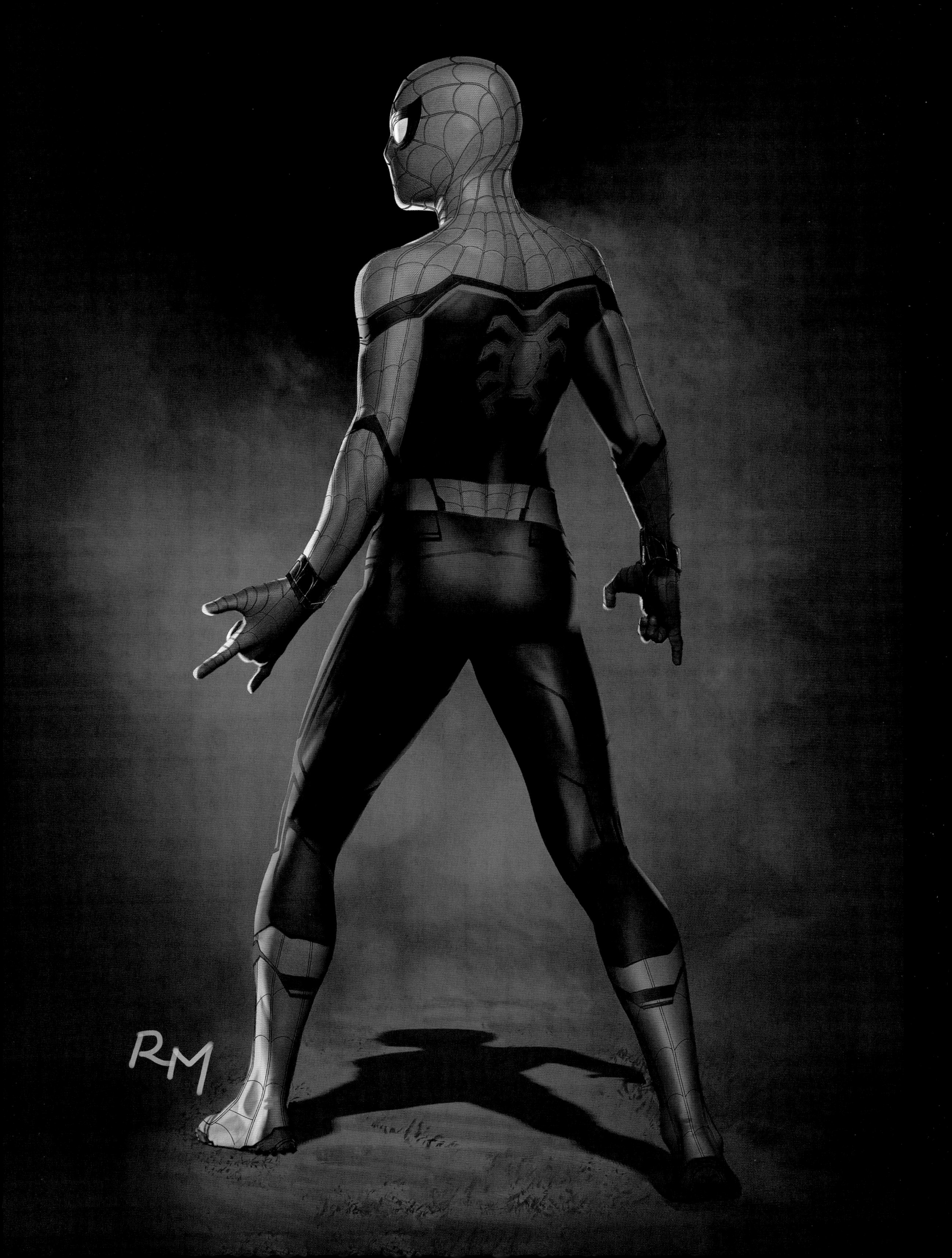

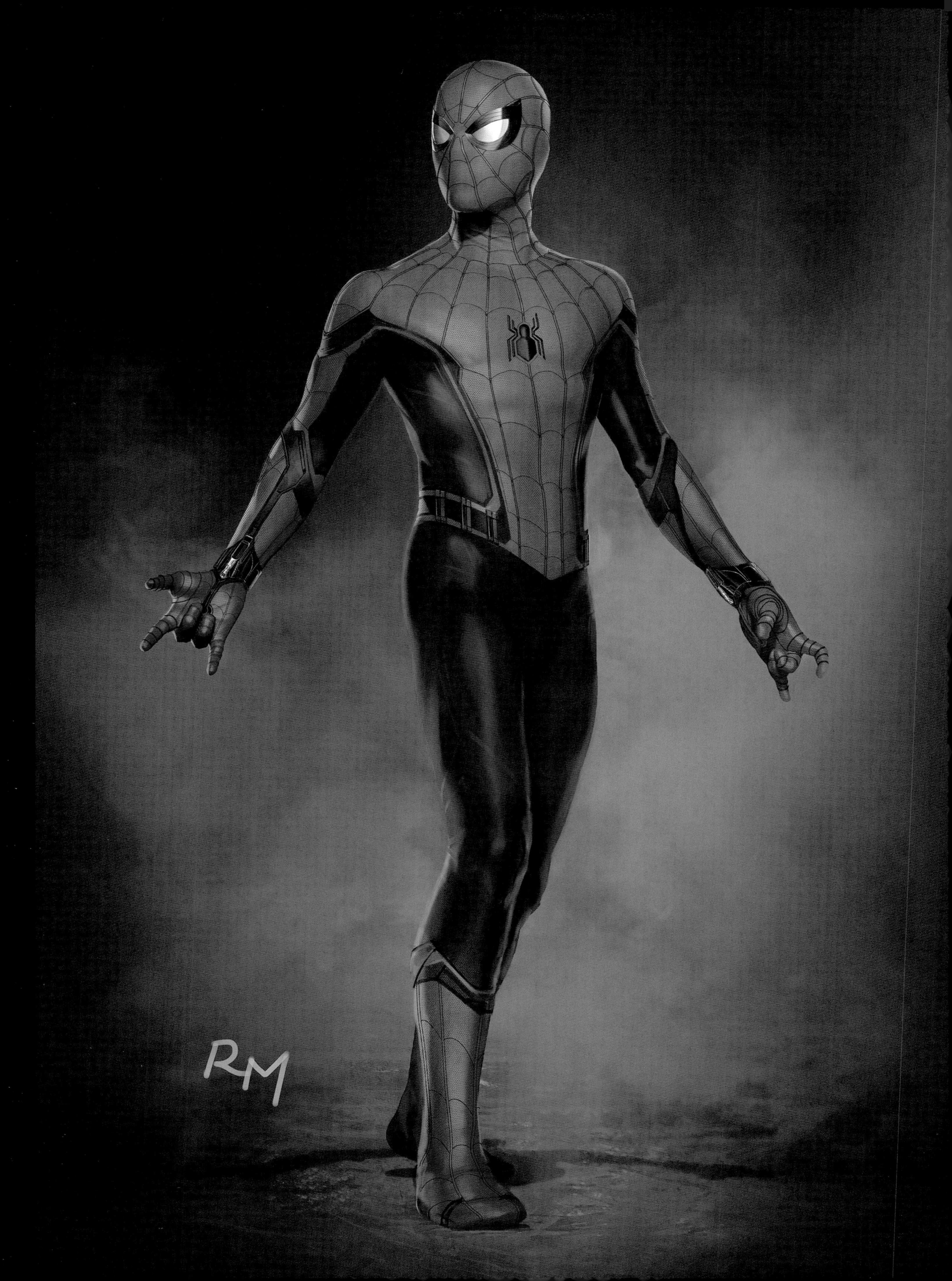
RM

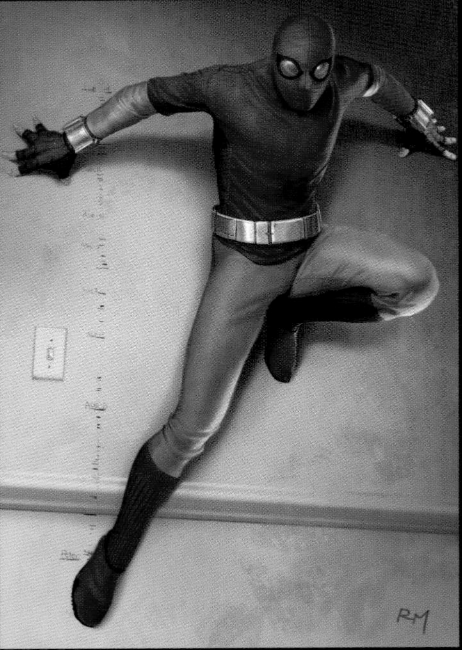
RM

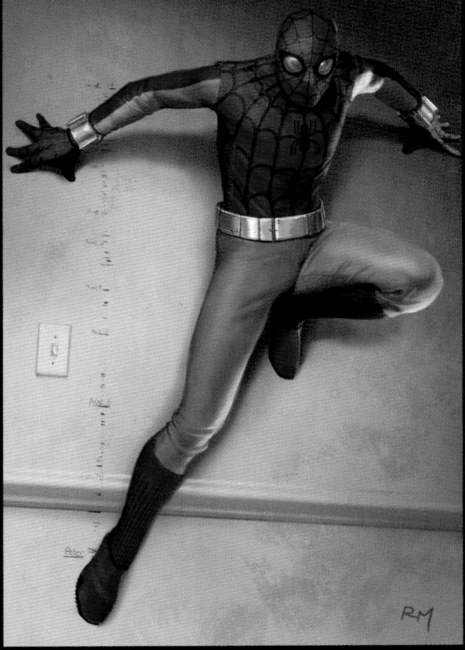
RM

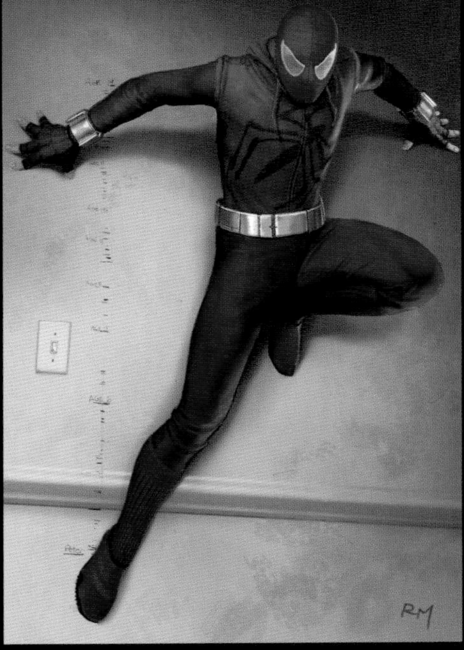
RM

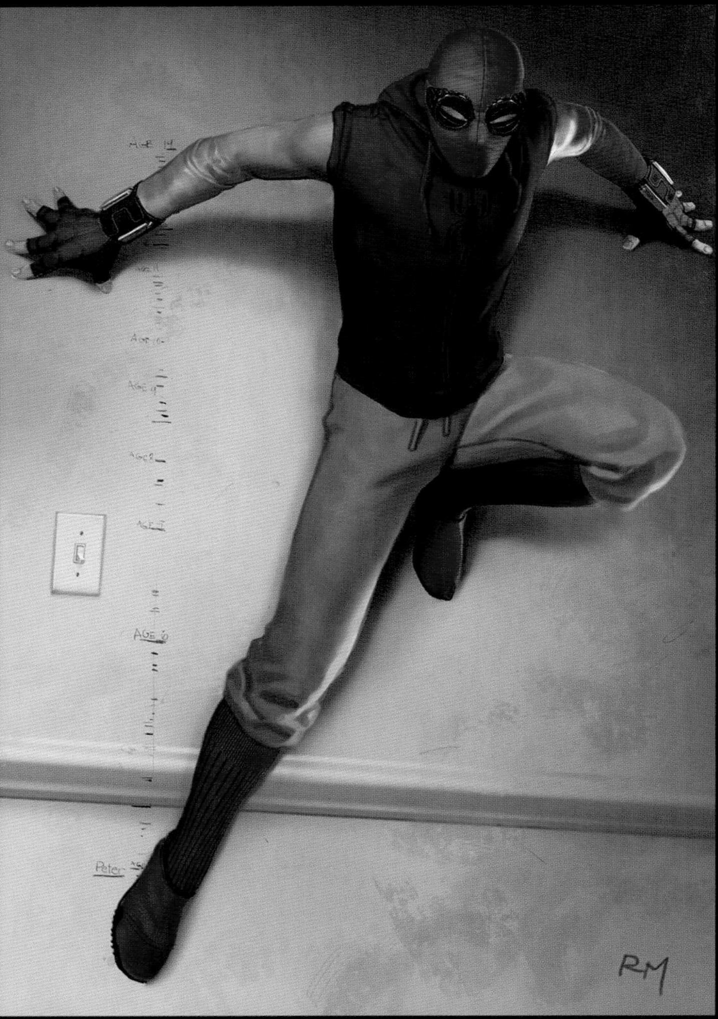
RM

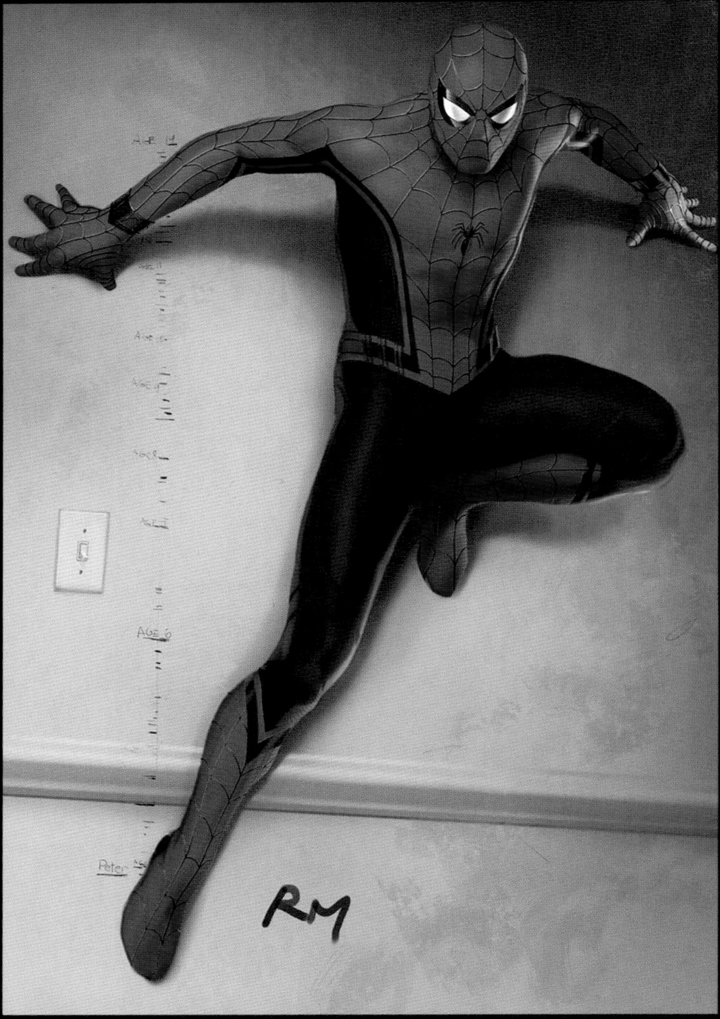
RM

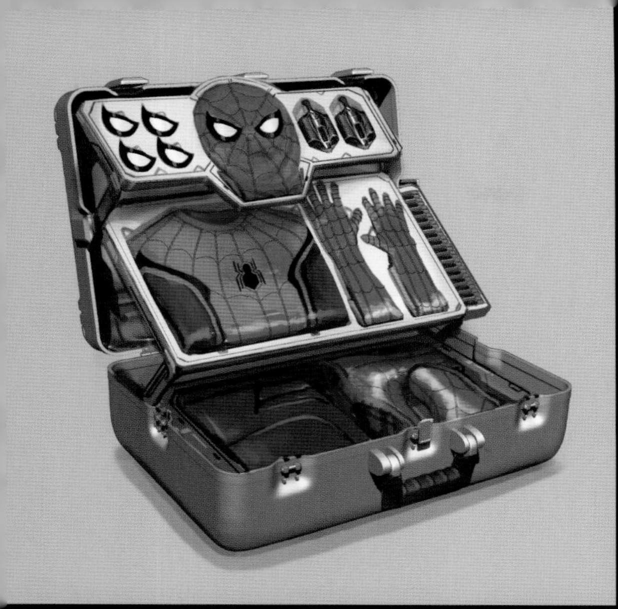

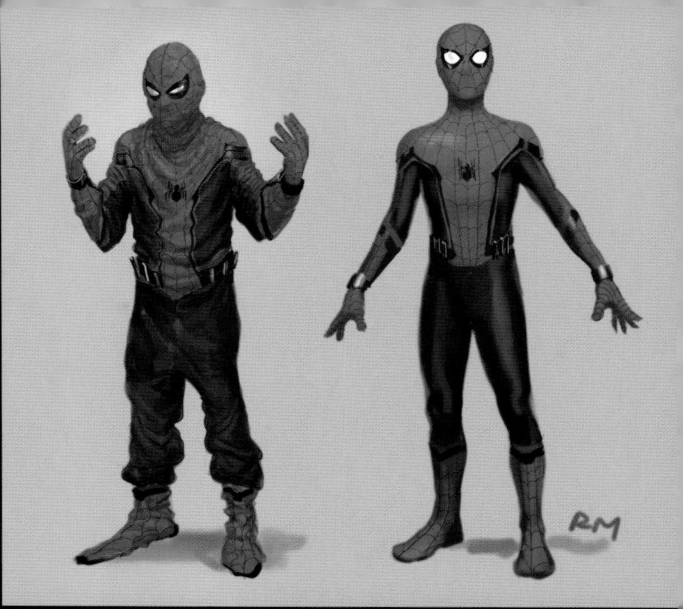
RM

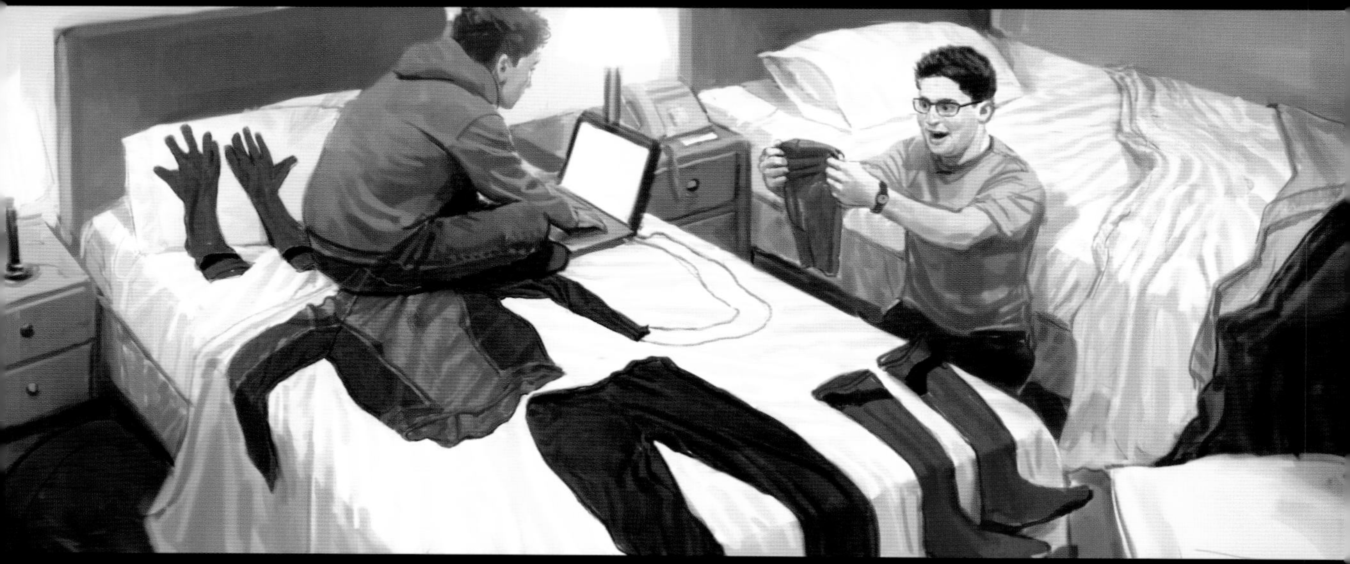

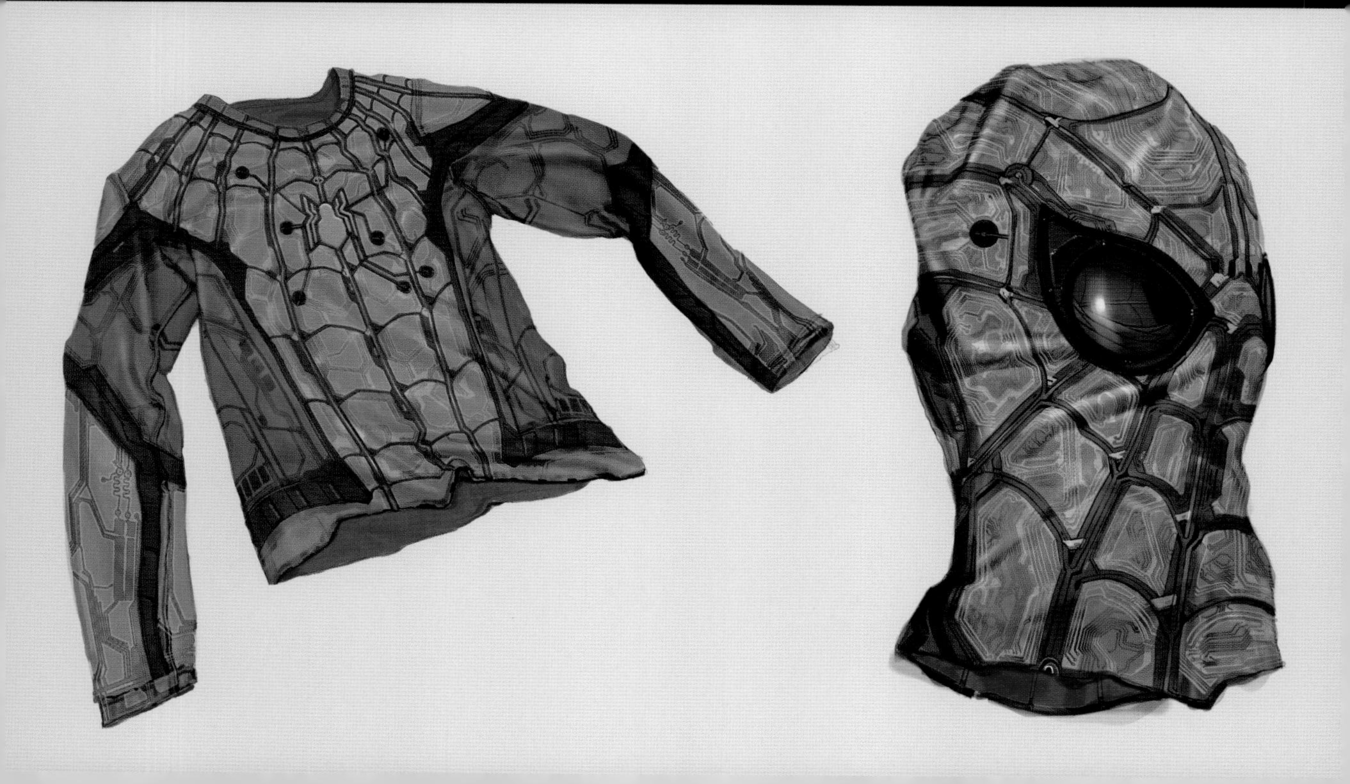

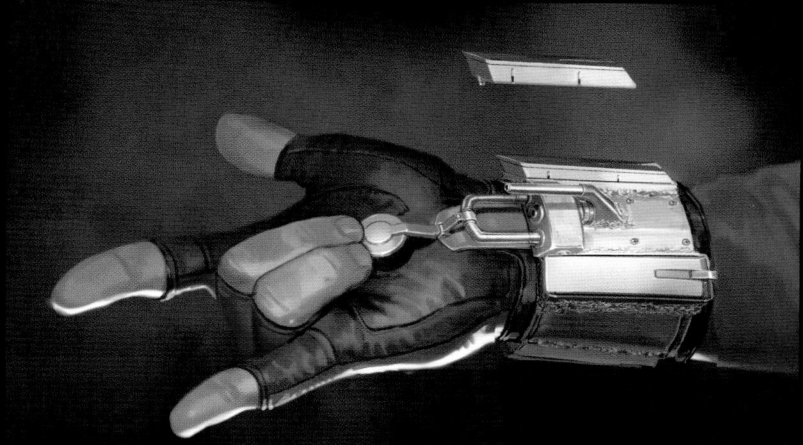

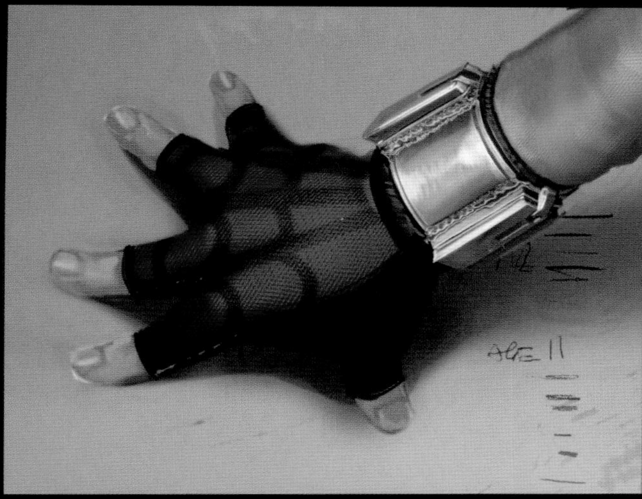

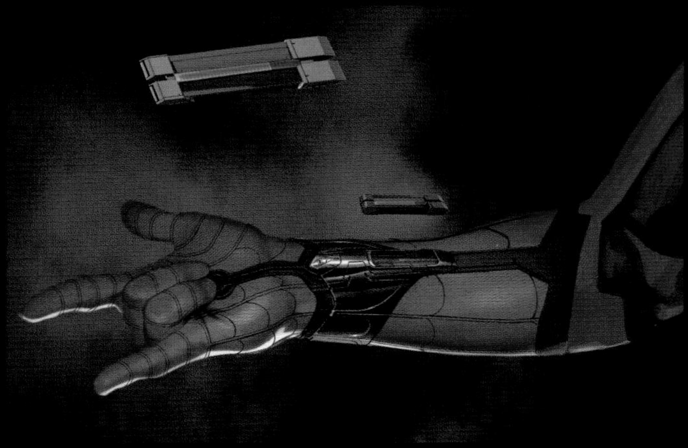

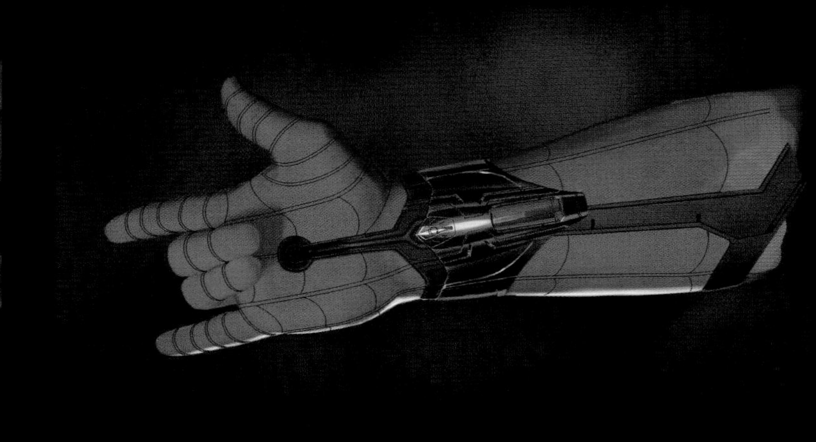

Ryan Meinerding loves a lot of the elements that come directly from the Spider-Man comics. "The idea of web shooters or web cartridges is part of making it hard for Peter to do certain things—he's got to refill something," he says. "I also loved the late 1970s TV show *The Amazing Spider-Man*, where he had those huge silver bracelets. It means it's about gadgets. It's a relatable moment. We took that into a space where it becomes Tony Stark technology to make it even more understandable and grounded."

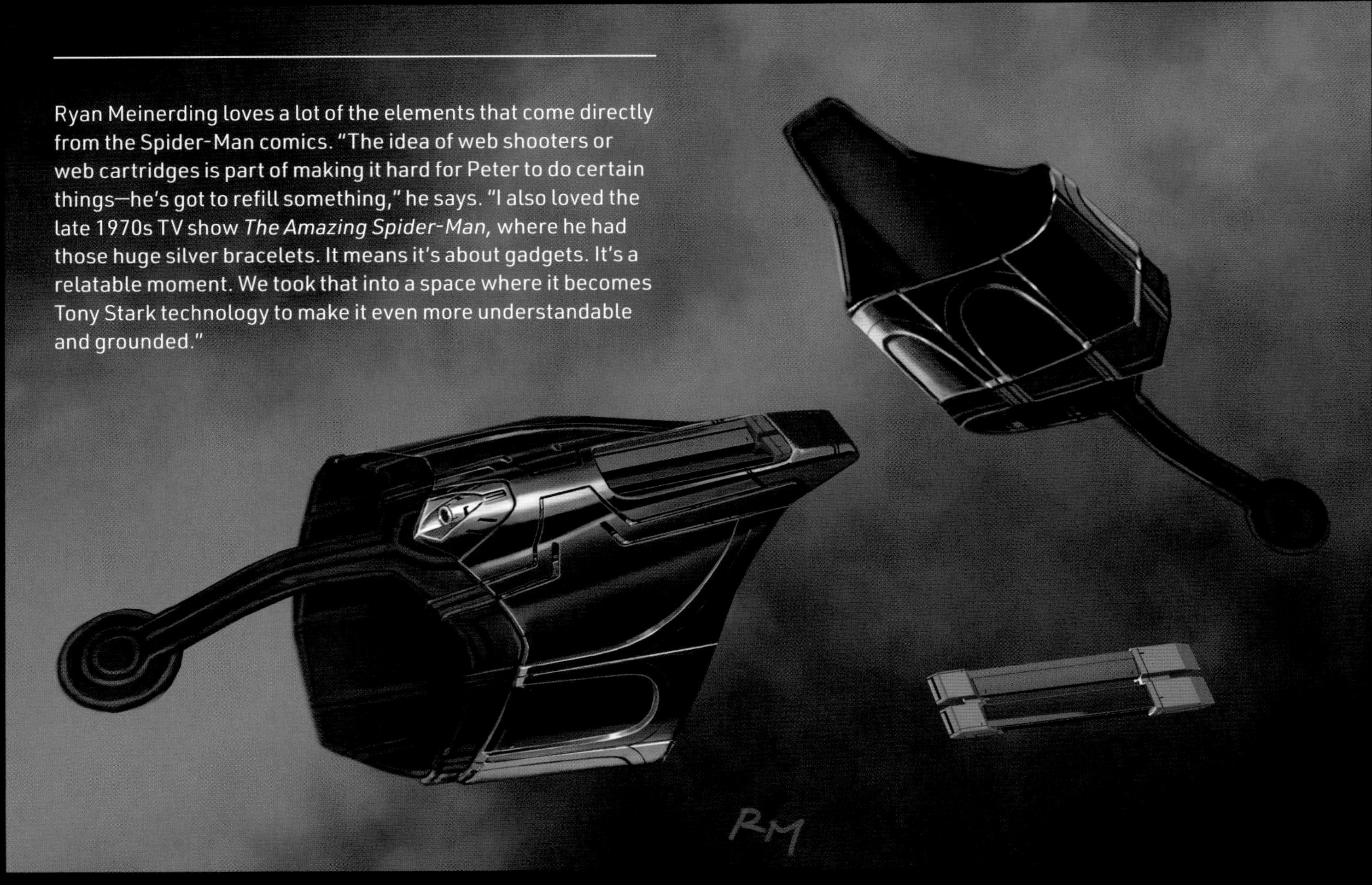
RM

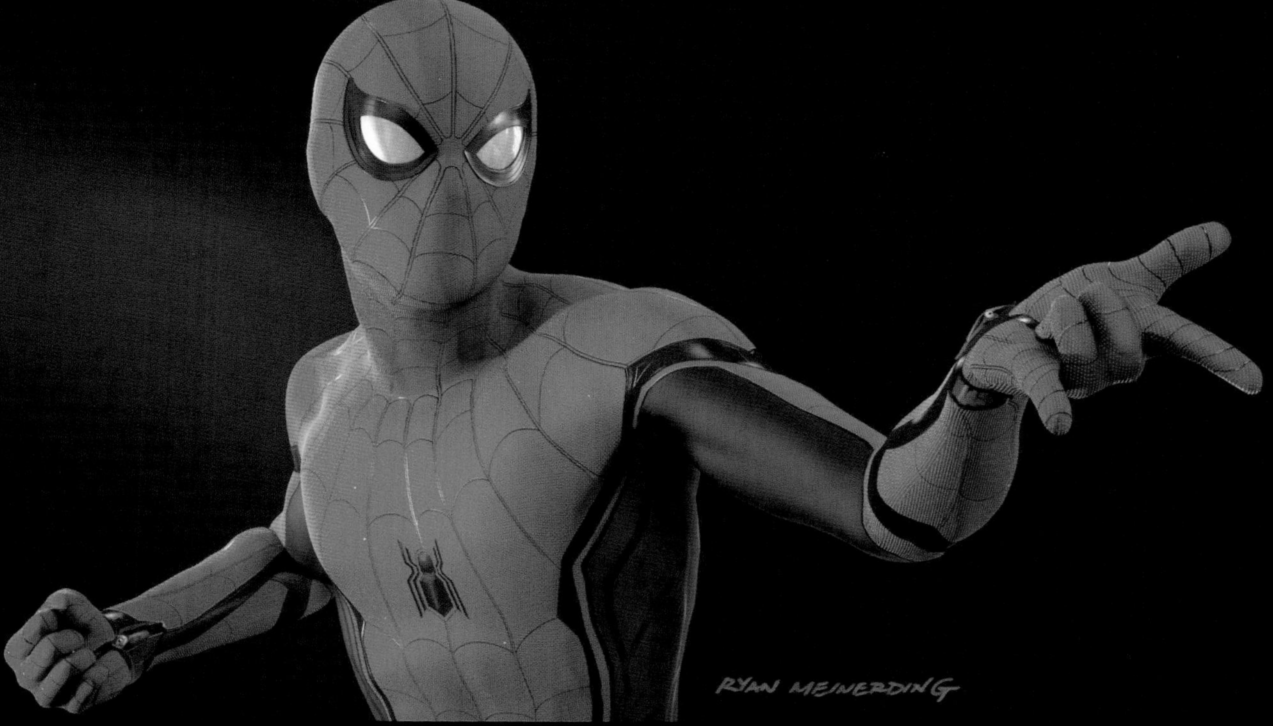
RYAN MEINERDING

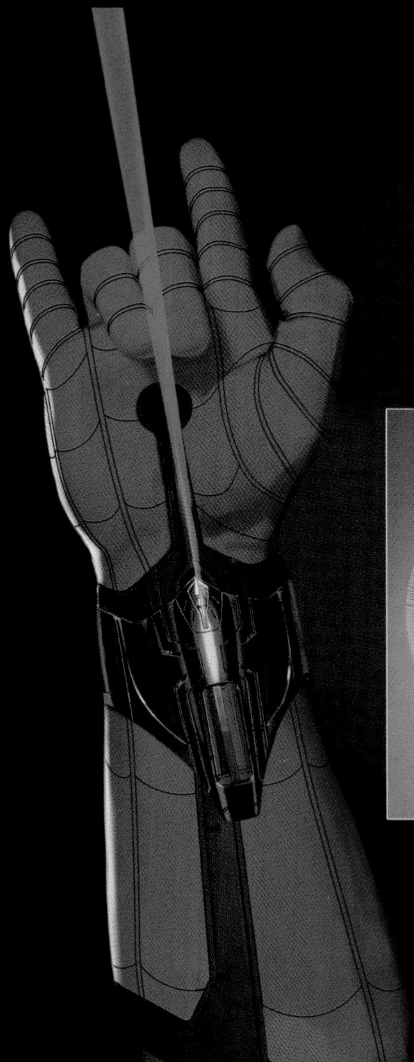

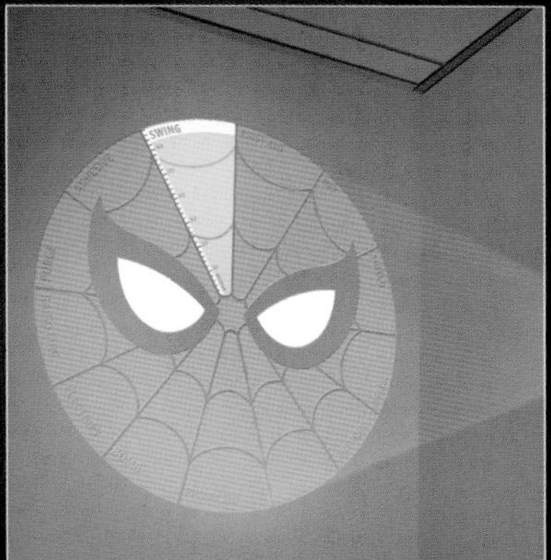
SWING

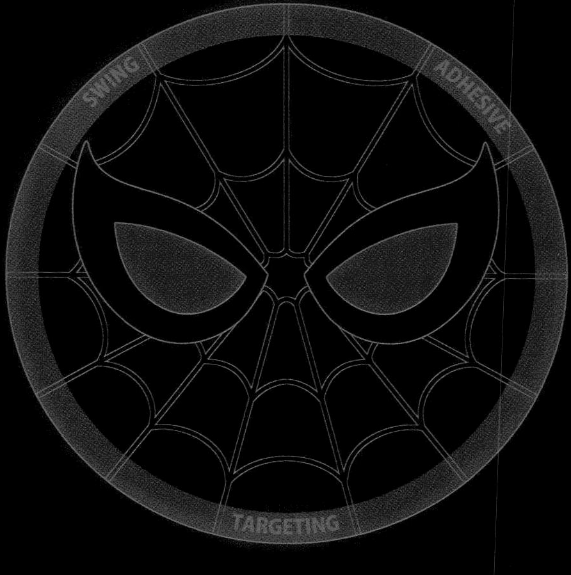
SWING
ADHESIVE
TARGETING

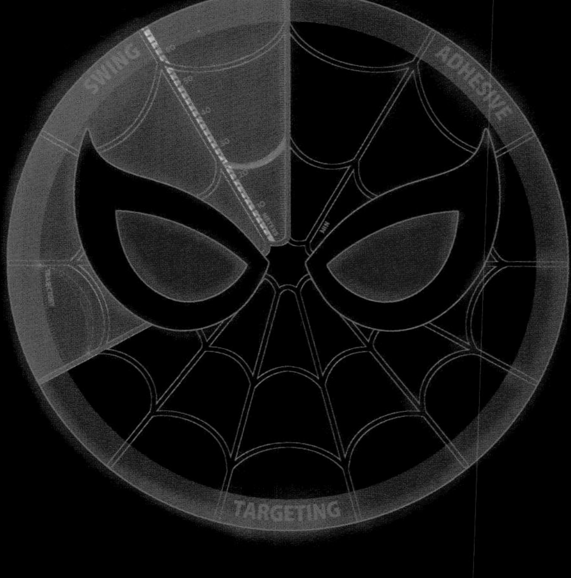
SWING
ADHESIVE
TARGETING

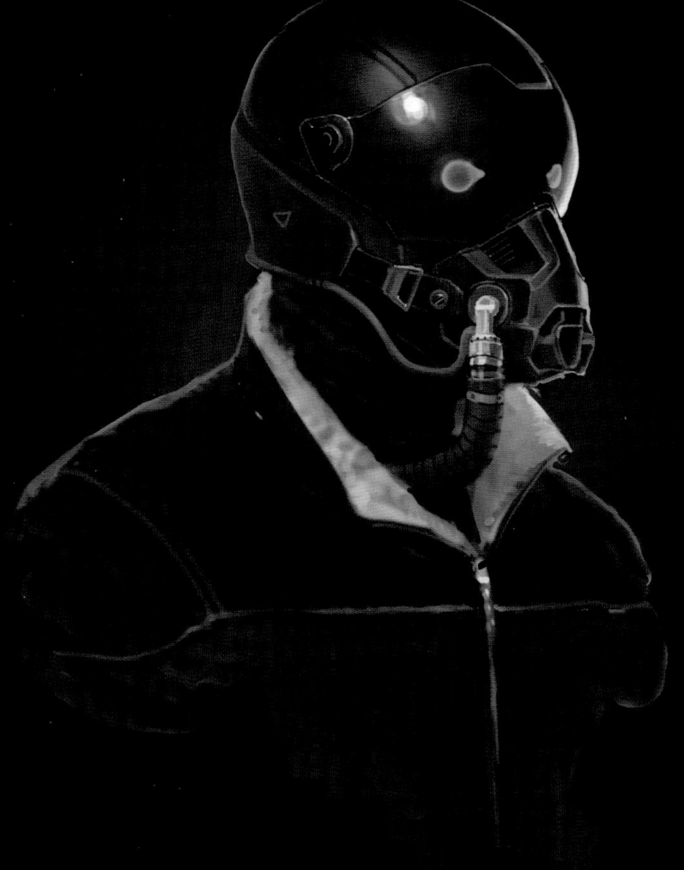
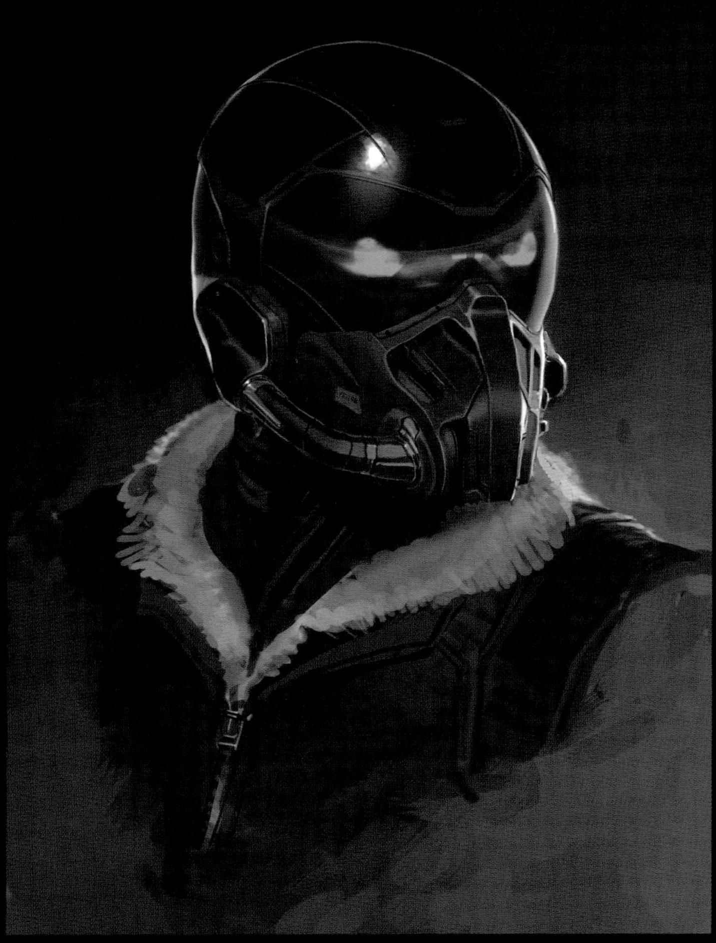
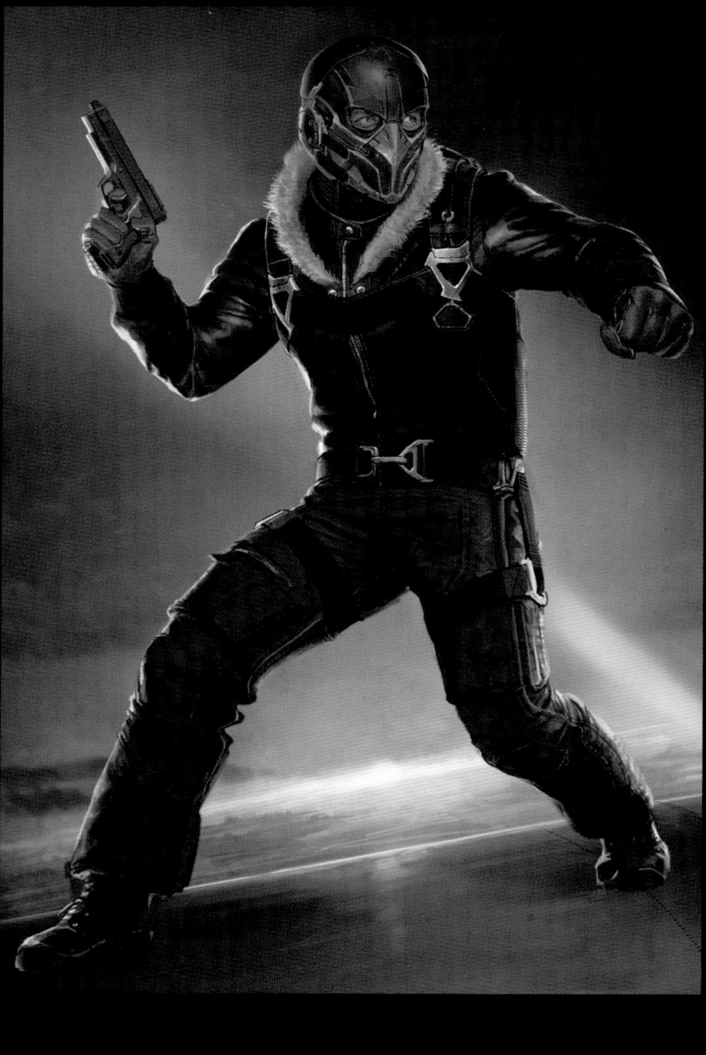
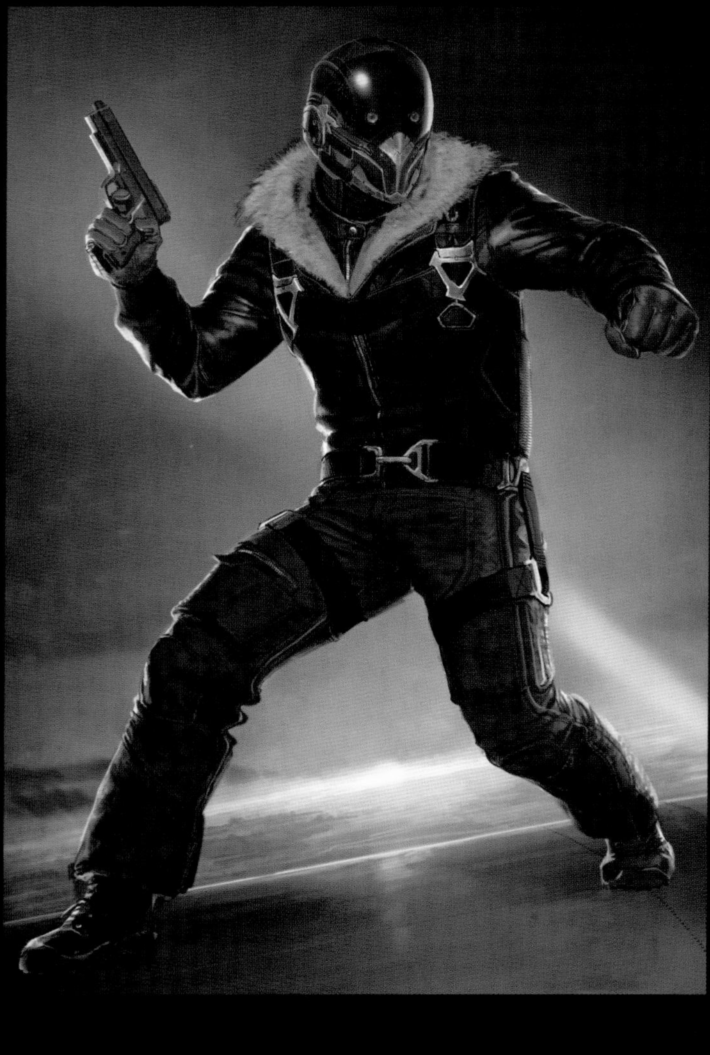

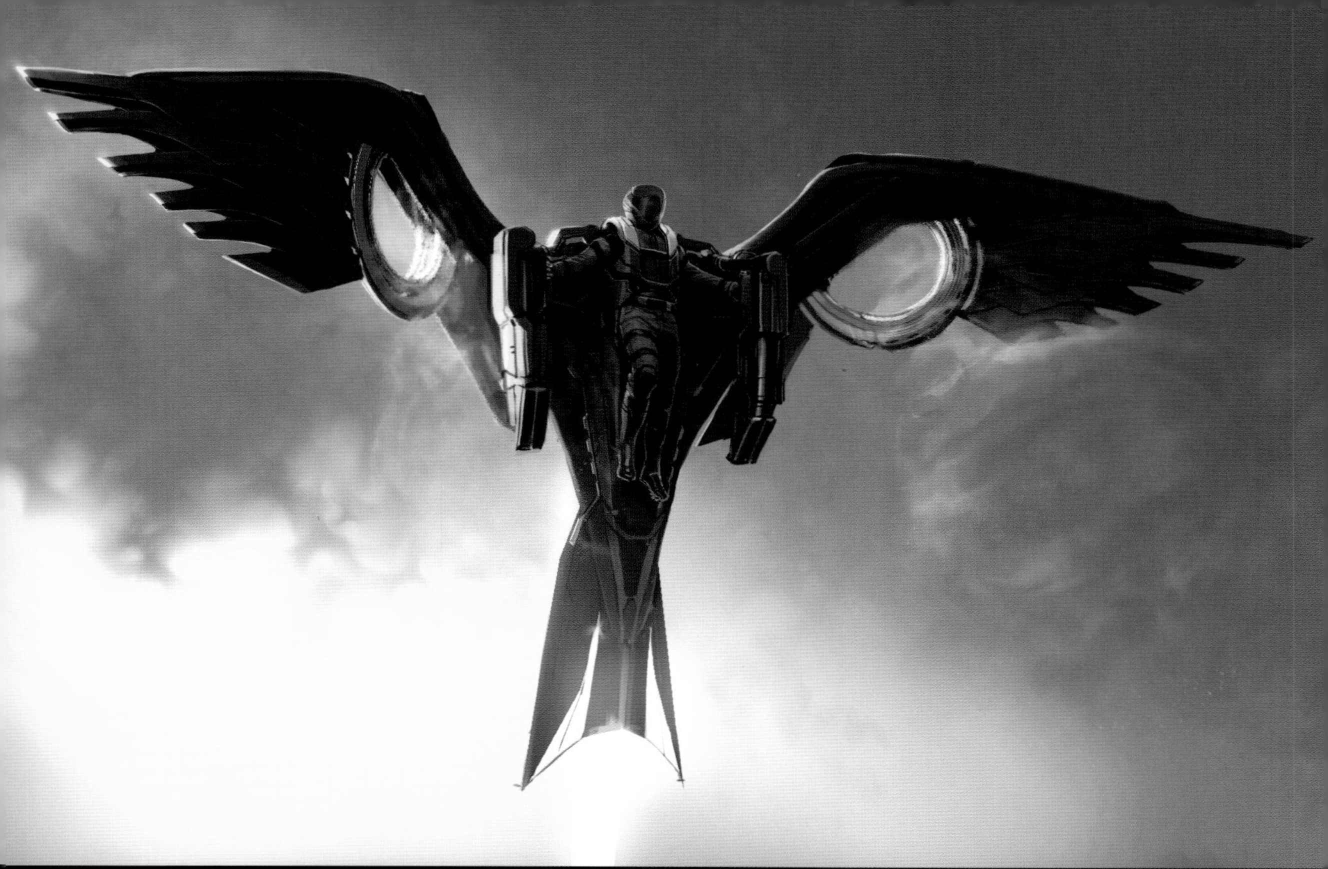

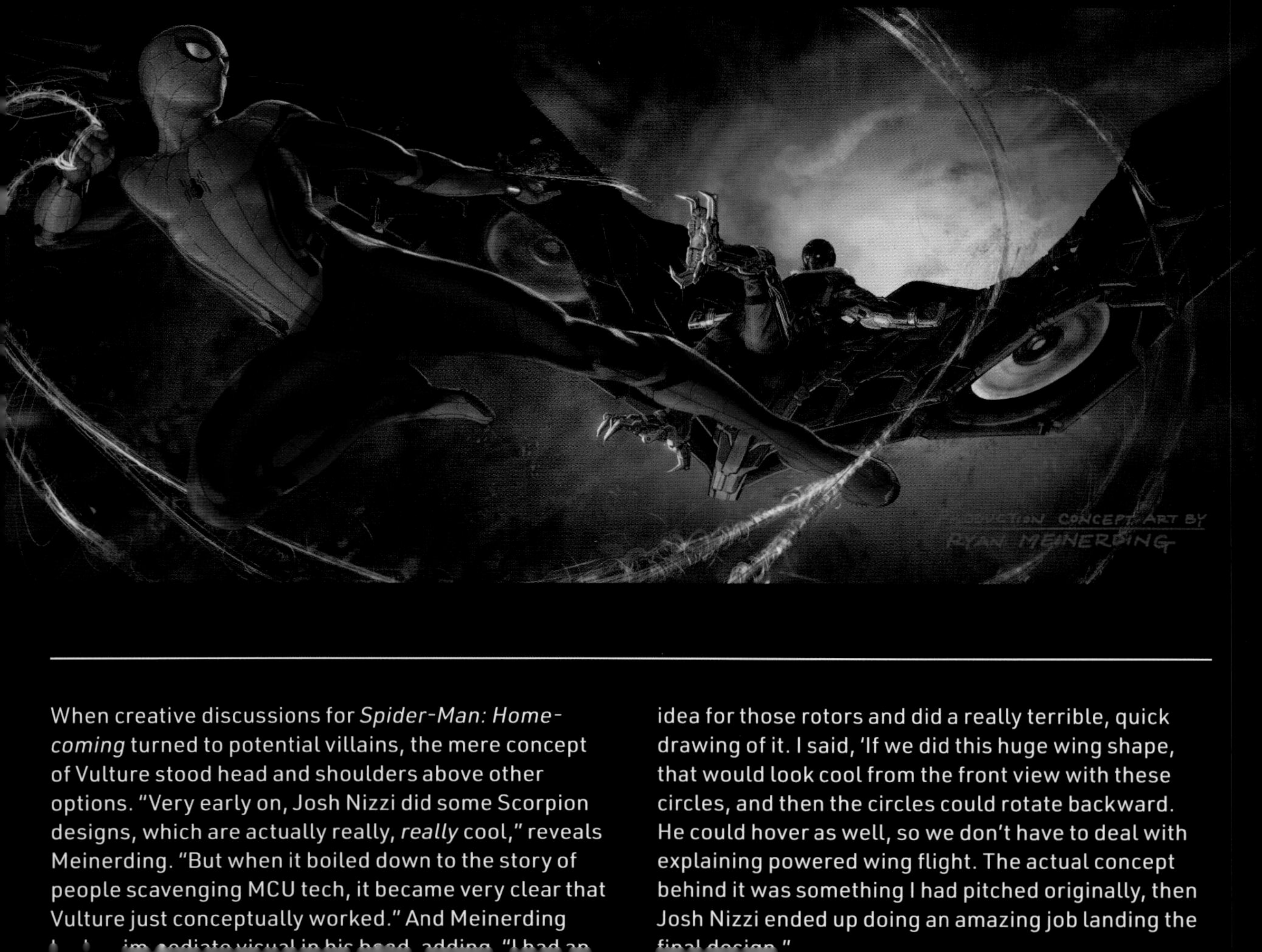
CONCEPT ART BY
RYAN MEINERDING

When creative discussions for *Spider-Man: Home-coming* turned to potential villains, the mere concept of Vulture stood head and shoulders above other options. "Very early on, Josh Nizzi did some Scorpion designs, which are actually really, *really* cool," reveals Meinerding. "But when it boiled down to the story of people scavenging MCU tech, it became very clear that Vulture just conceptually worked." And Meinerding had an immediate visual in his head, adding, "I had an idea for those rotors and did a really terrible, quick drawing of it. I said, 'If we did this huge wing shape, that would look cool from the front view with these circles, and then the circles could rotate backward. He could hover as well, so we don't have to deal with explaining powered wing flight. The actual concept behind it was something I had pitched originally, then Josh Nizzi ended up doing an amazing job landing the final design."

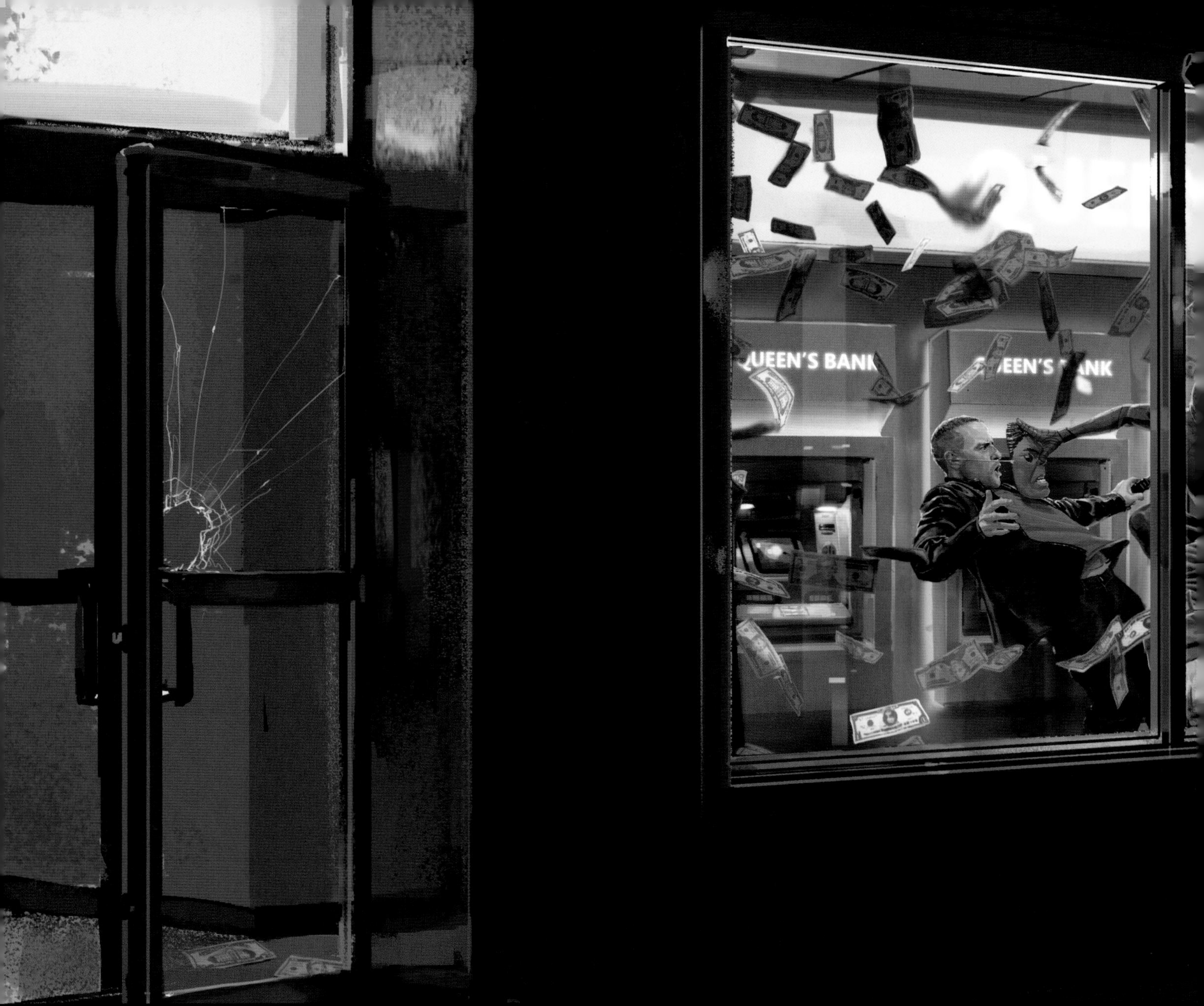
QUEEN'S BANK

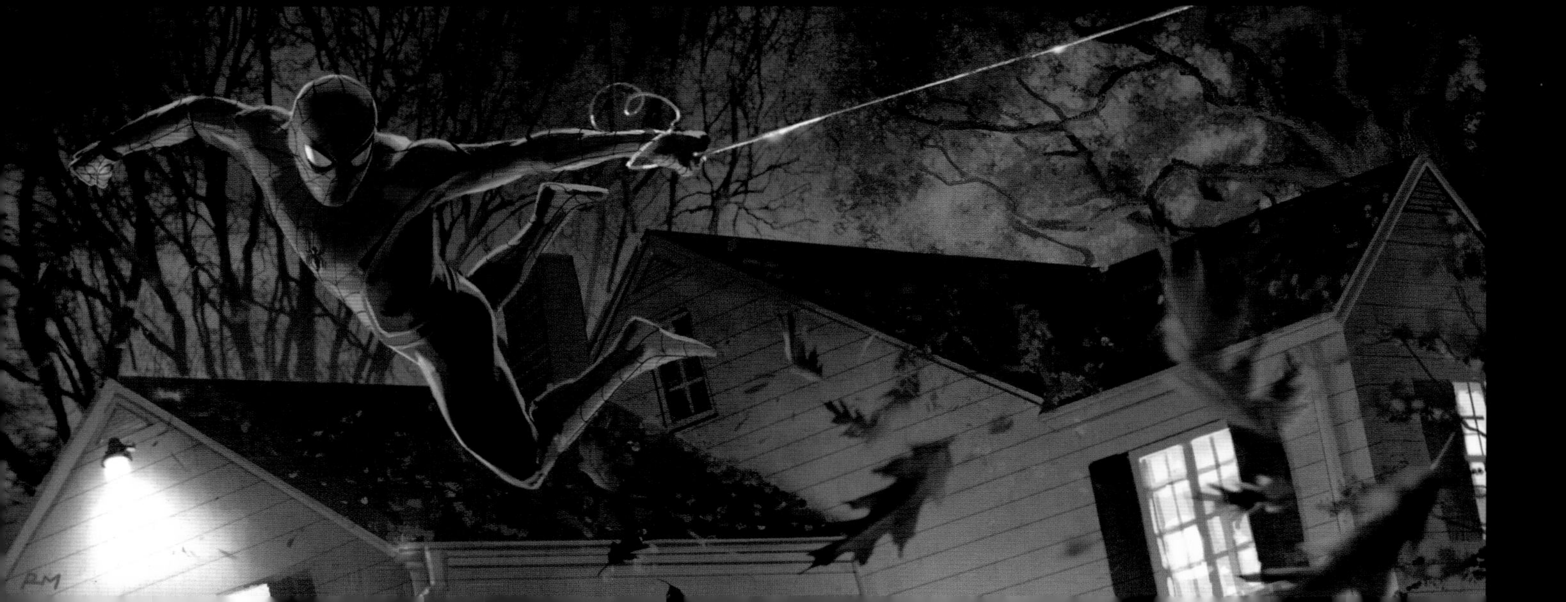

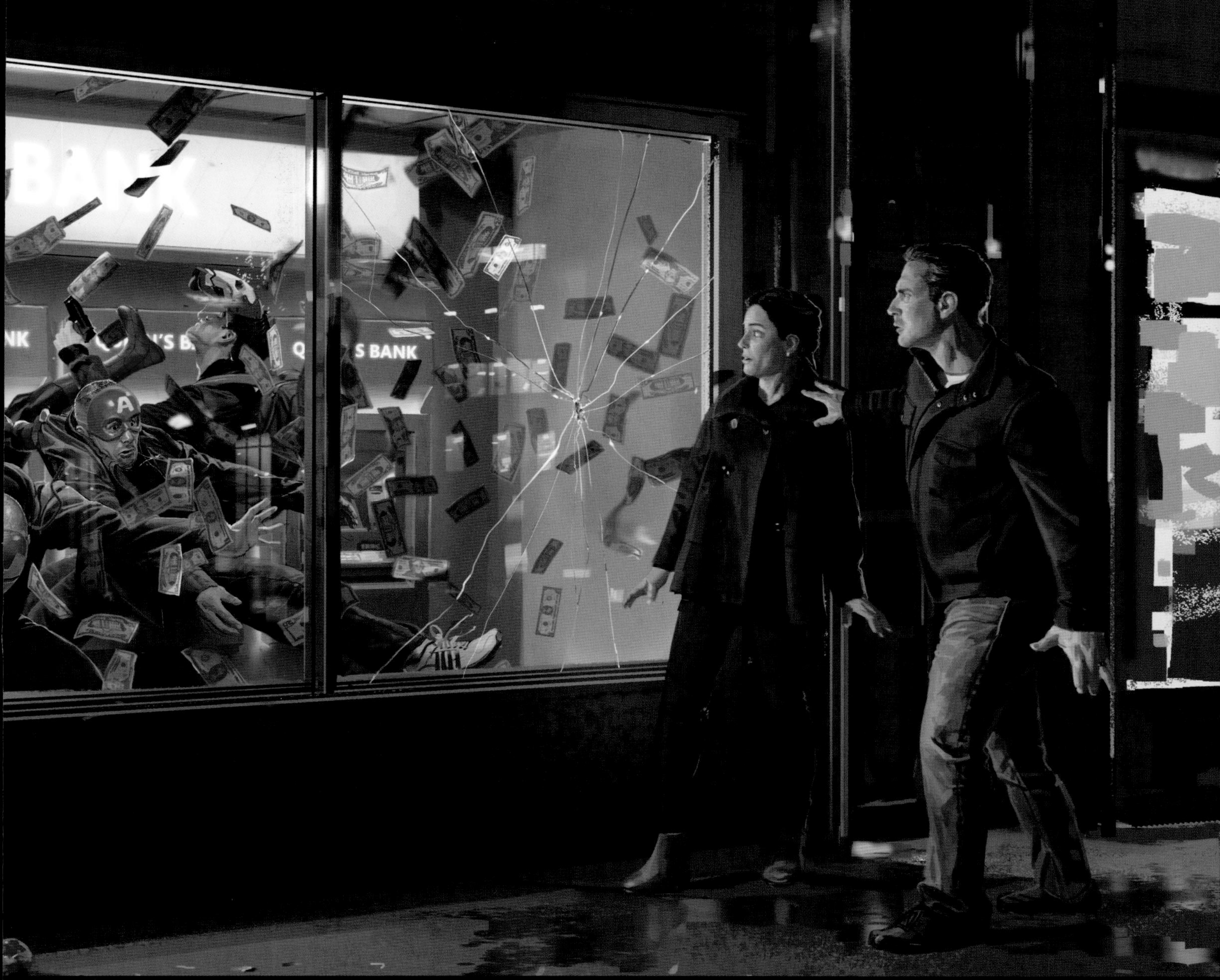
BANK

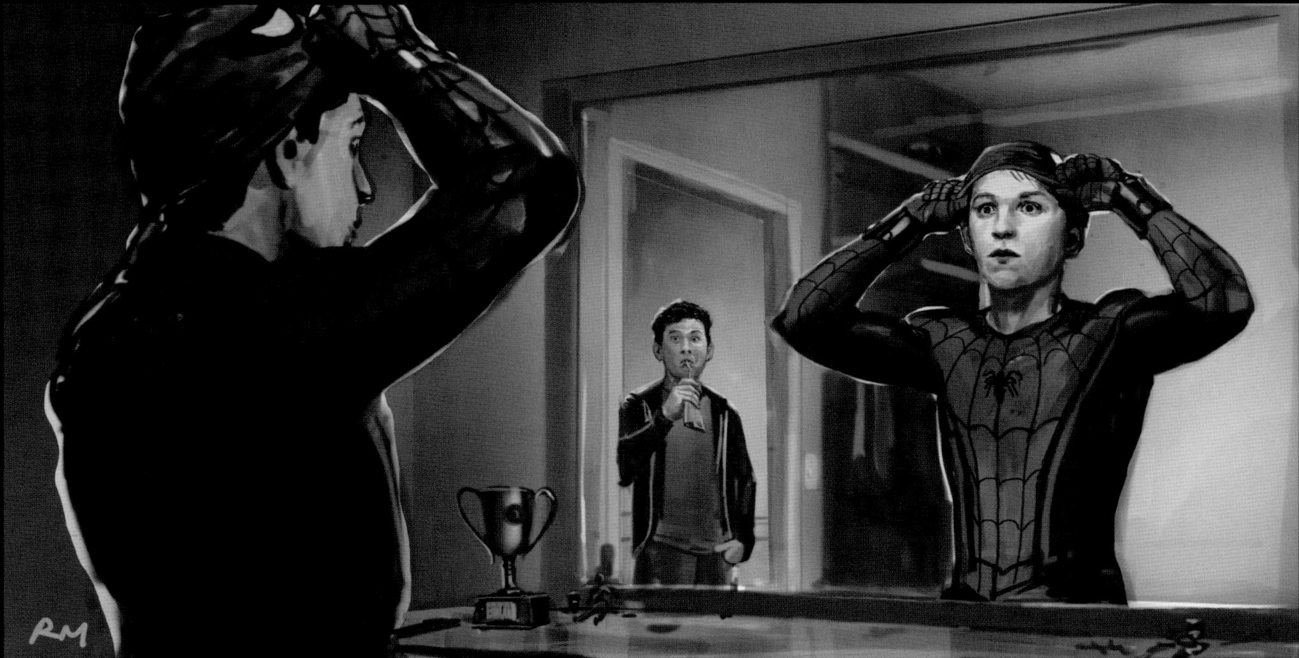
RM

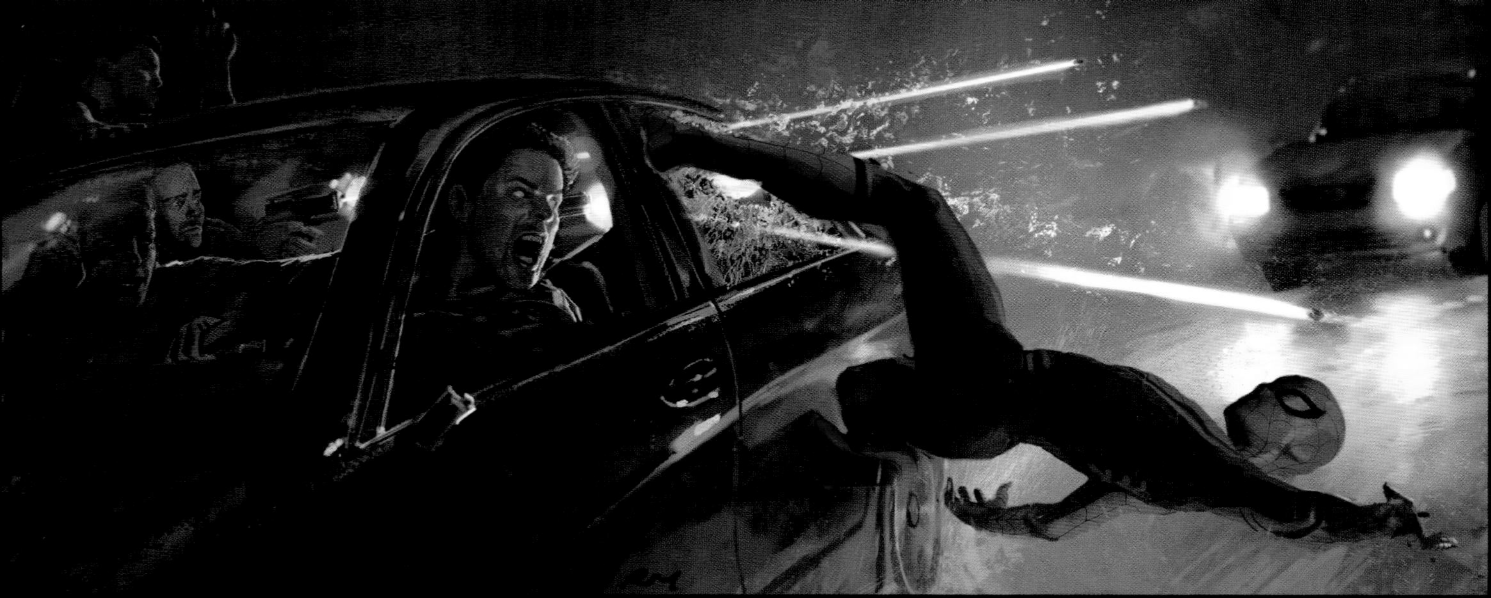

ABOVE "I was really looking forward to doing this key frame," shares Meinerding. "Initially, it was going to be Shocker in the car. Shocker was going to be punching out that window. When they turned it into a car chase and Shocker was in the other vehicle, I changed it to the bullets."

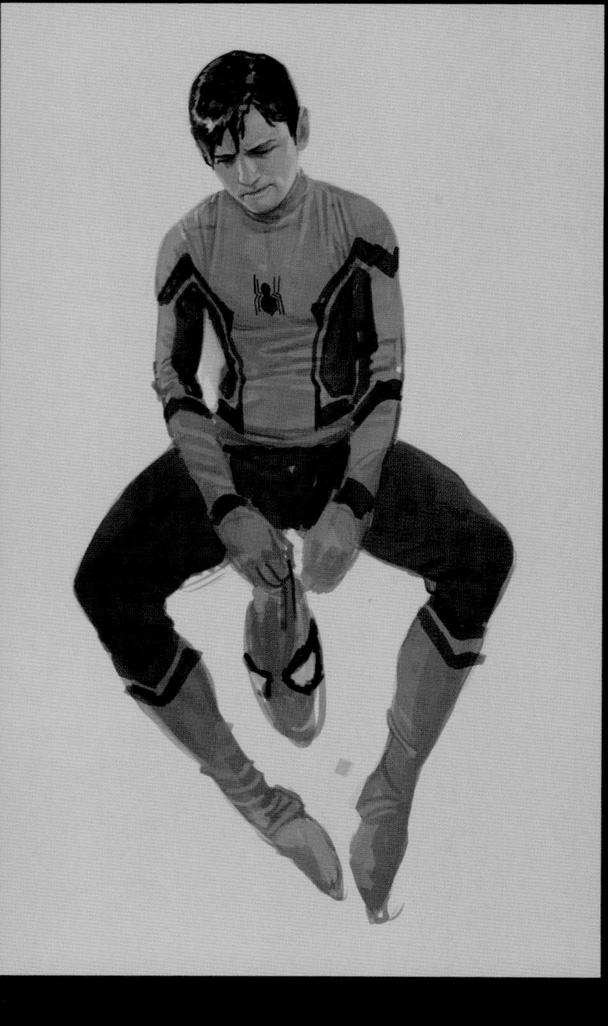

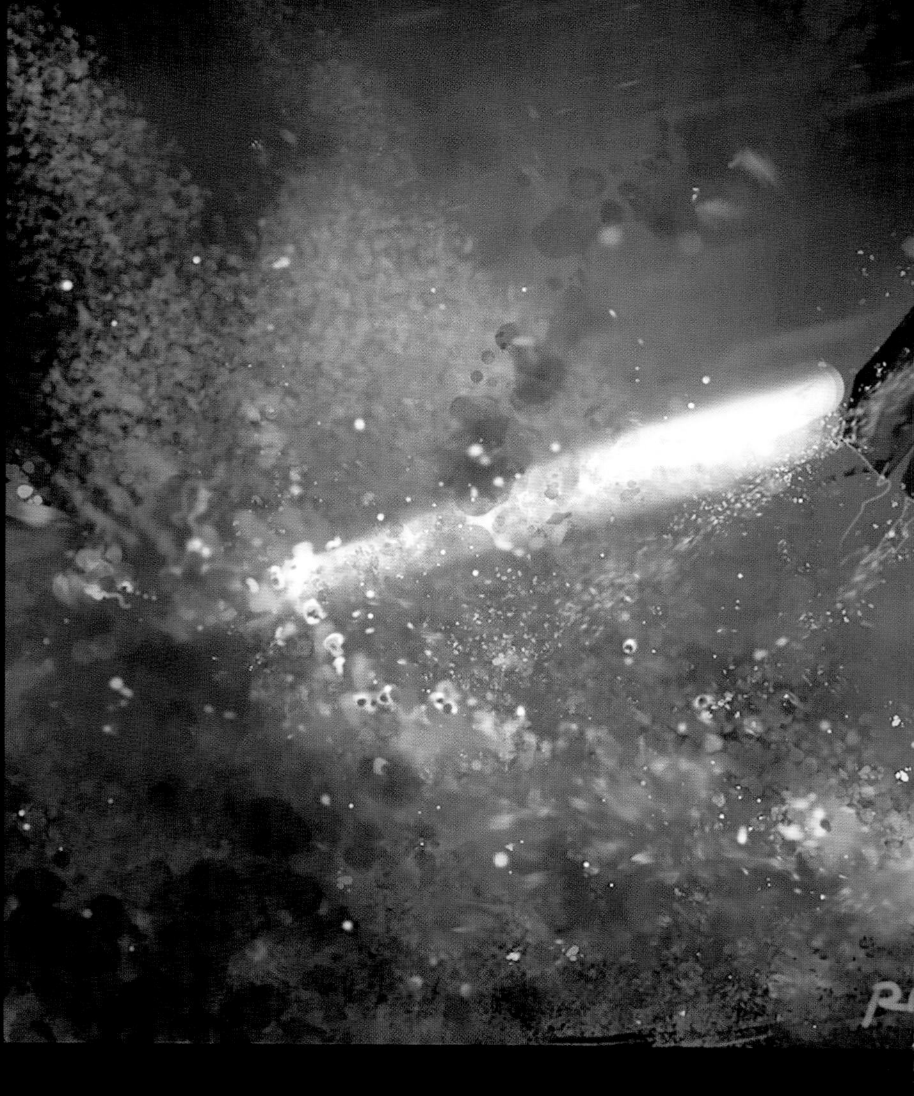

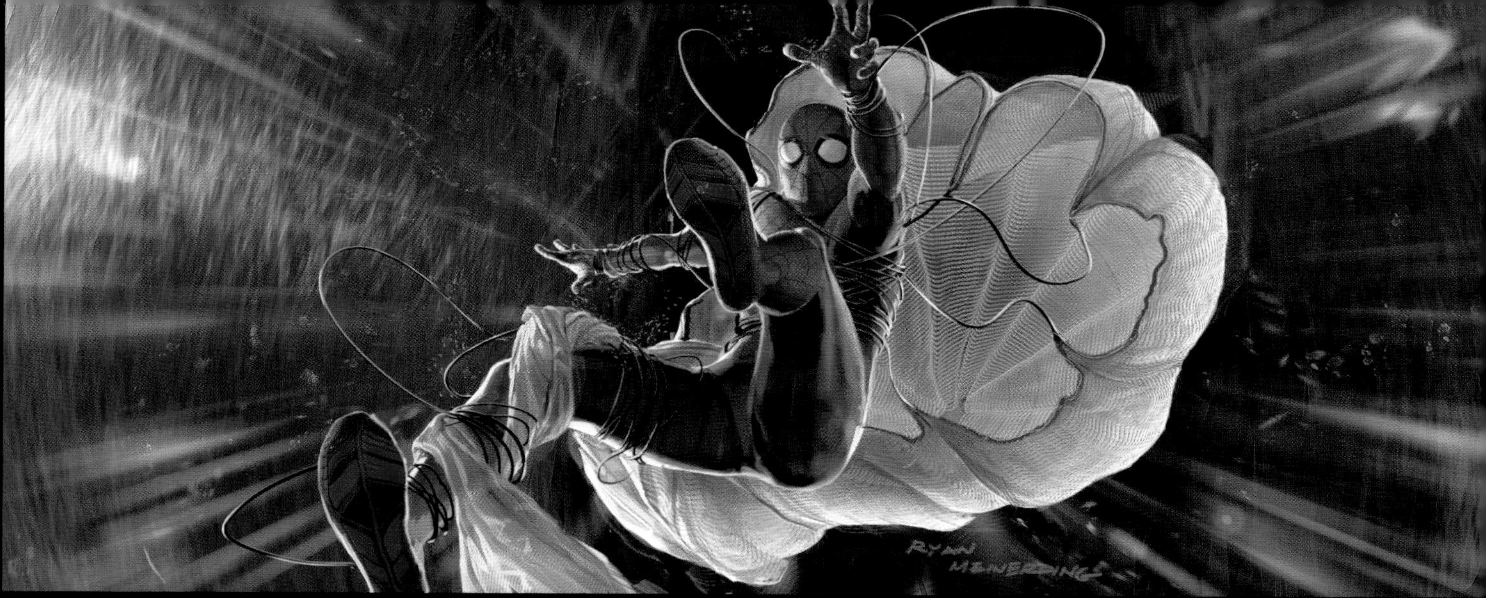
RYAN
MEINERDING

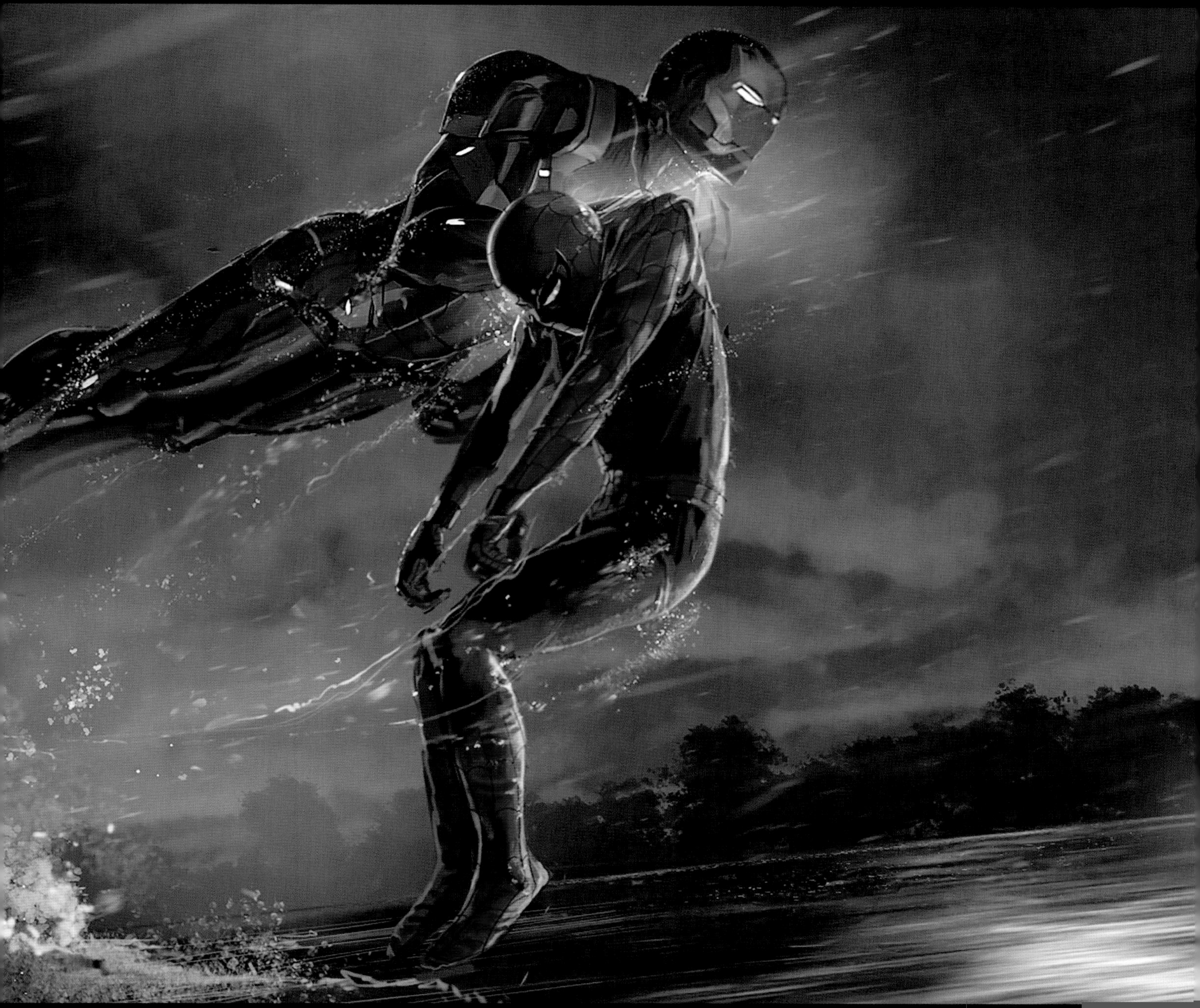

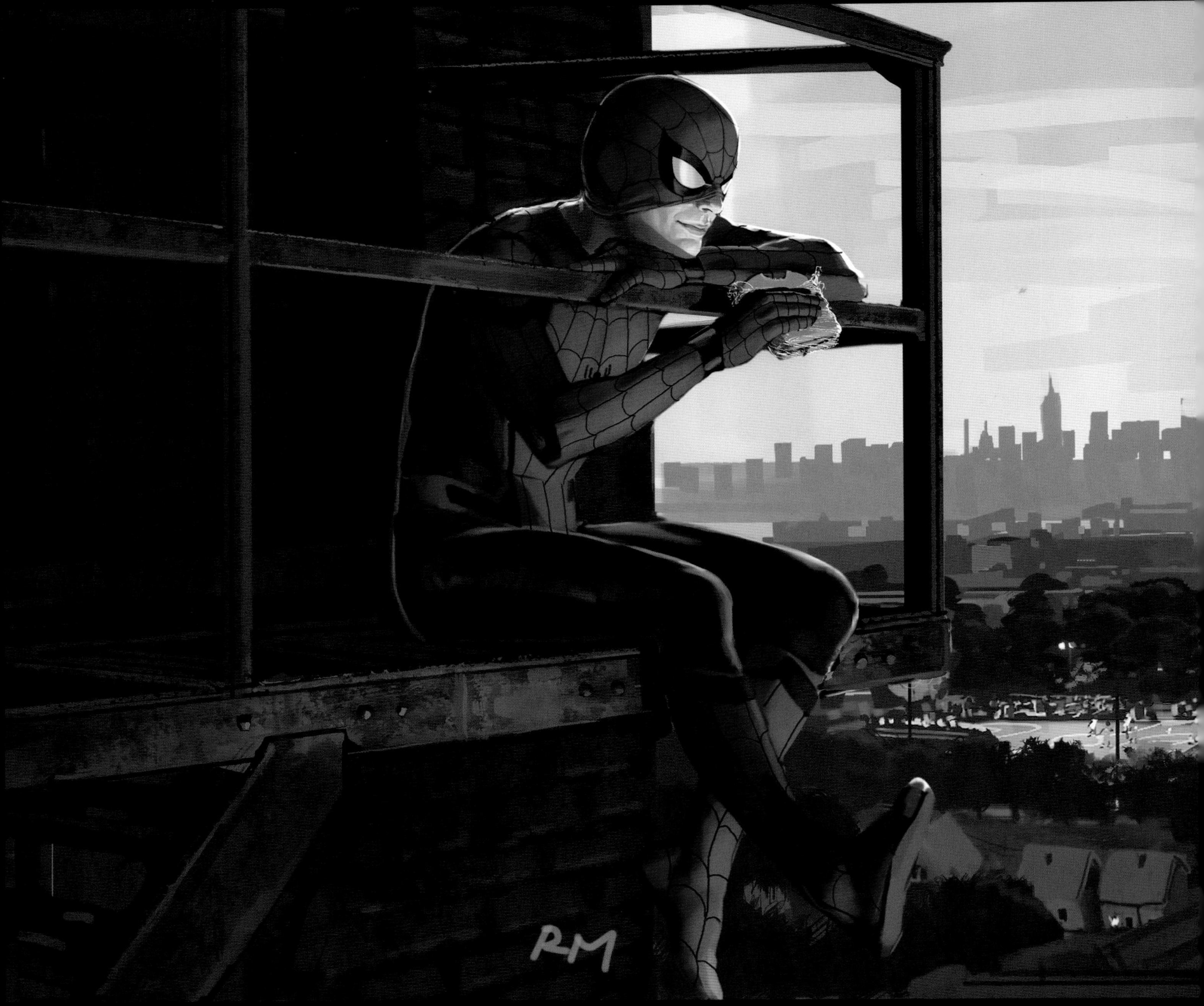
RM

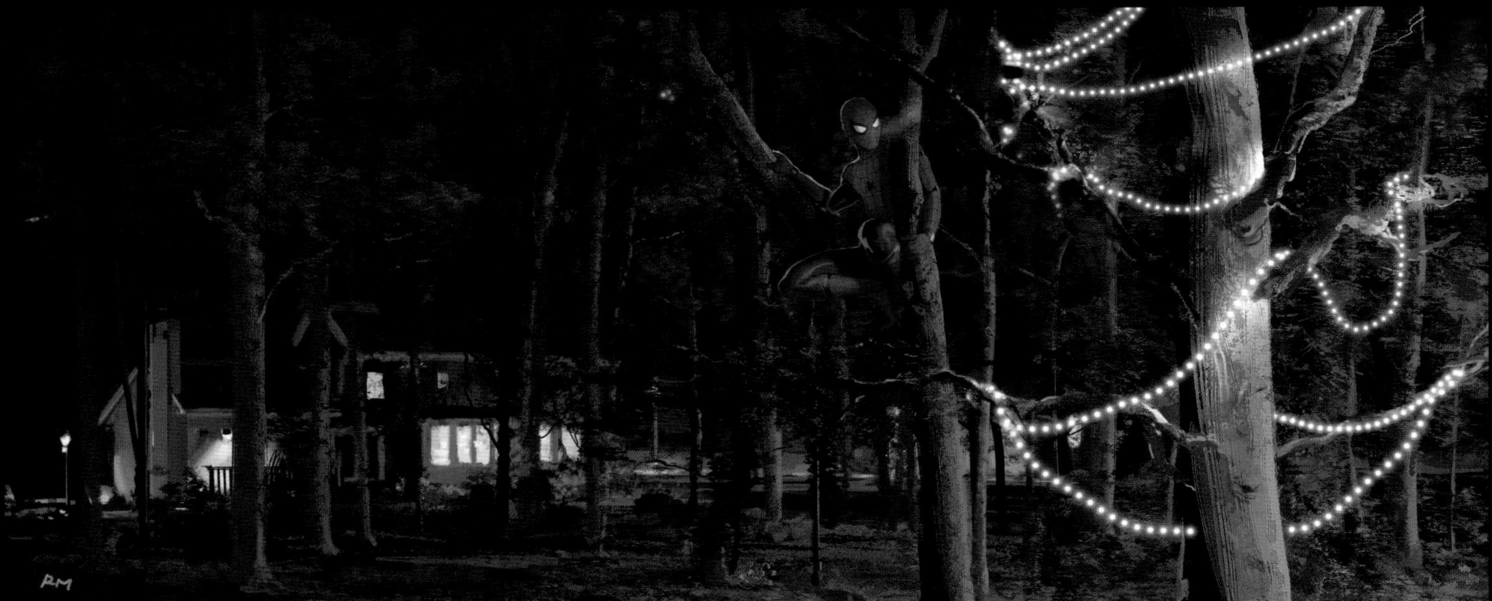
RM

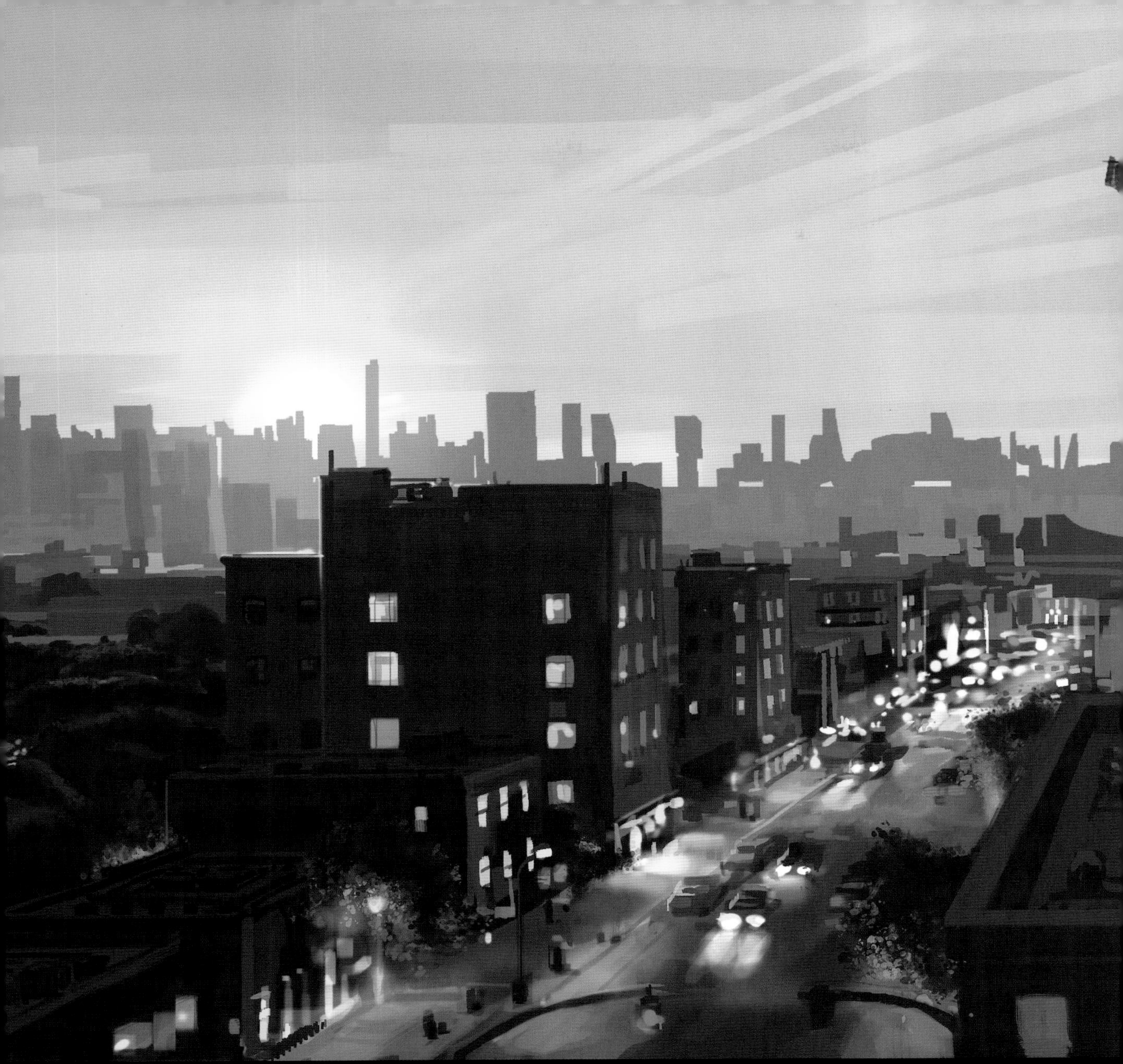

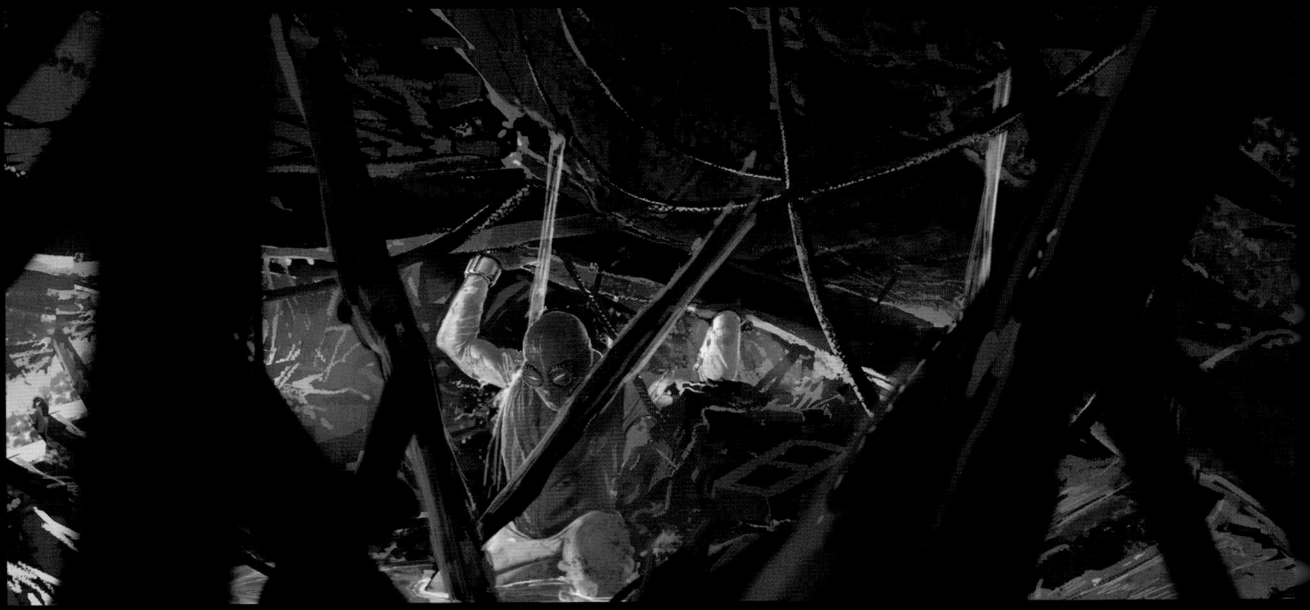

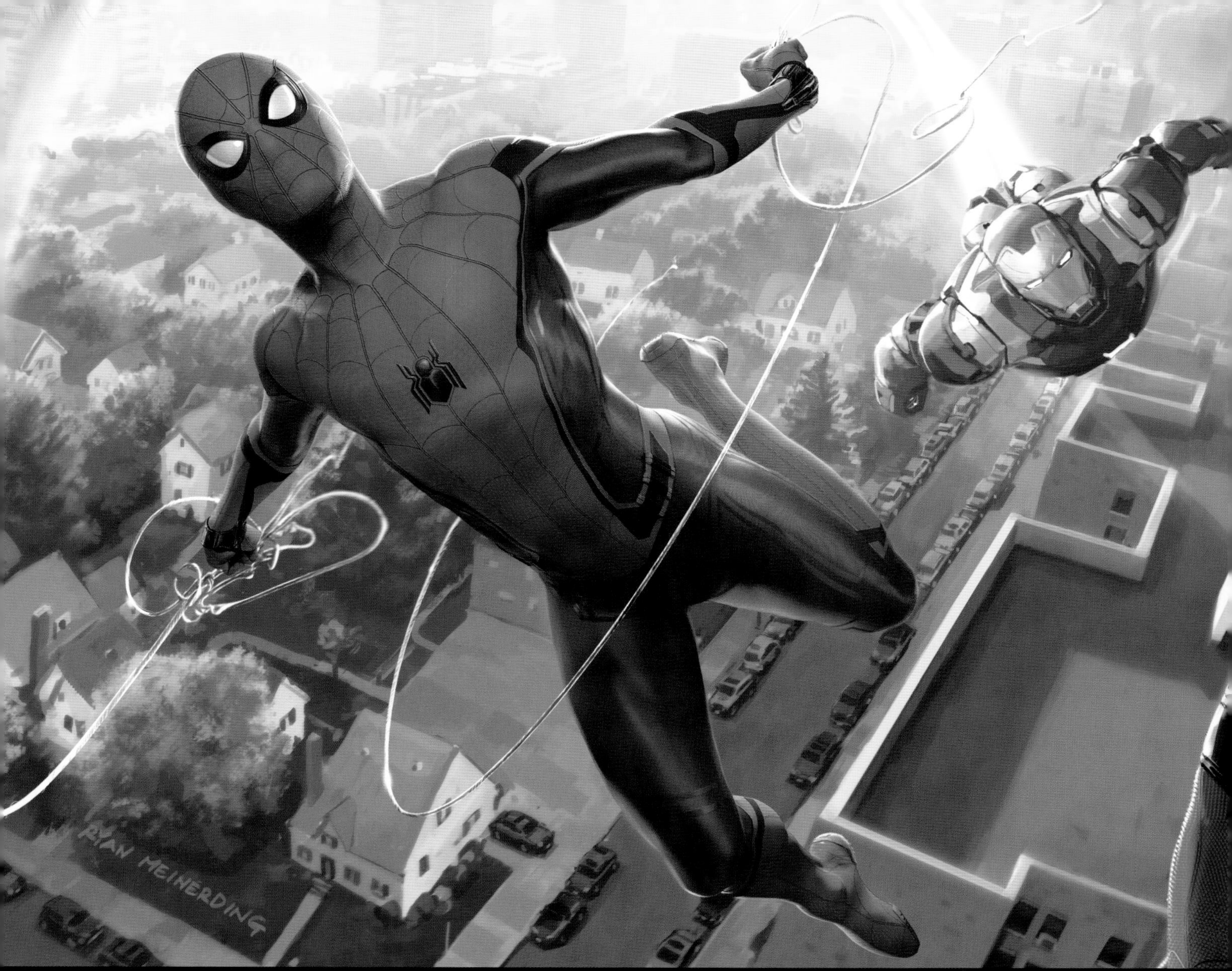
RYAN MEINERDING

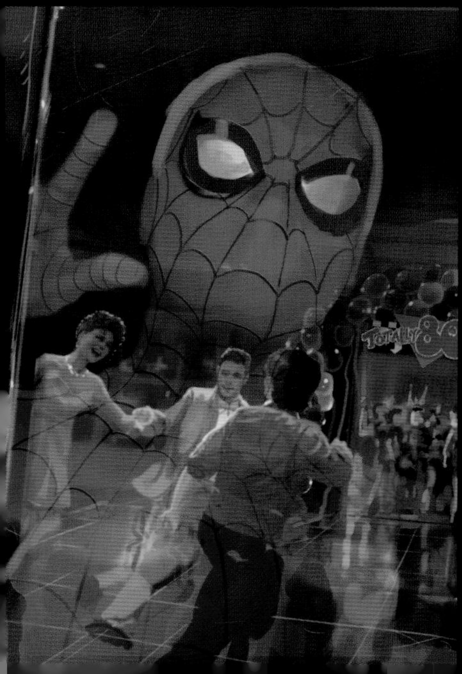

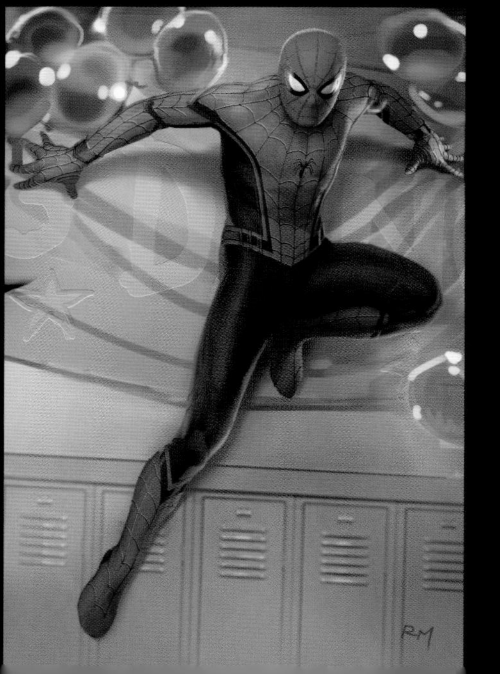
RM

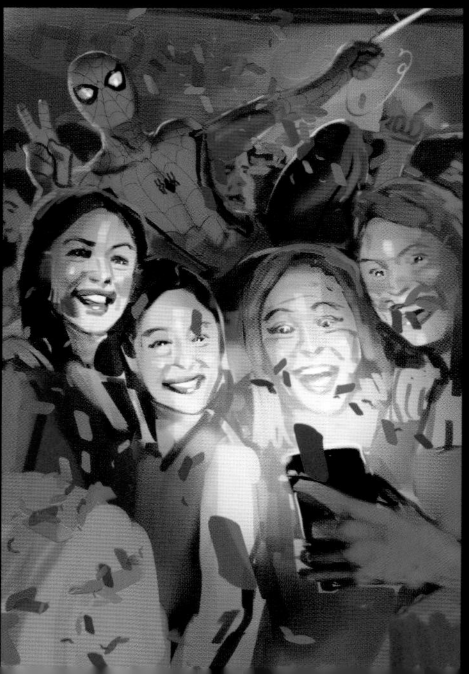

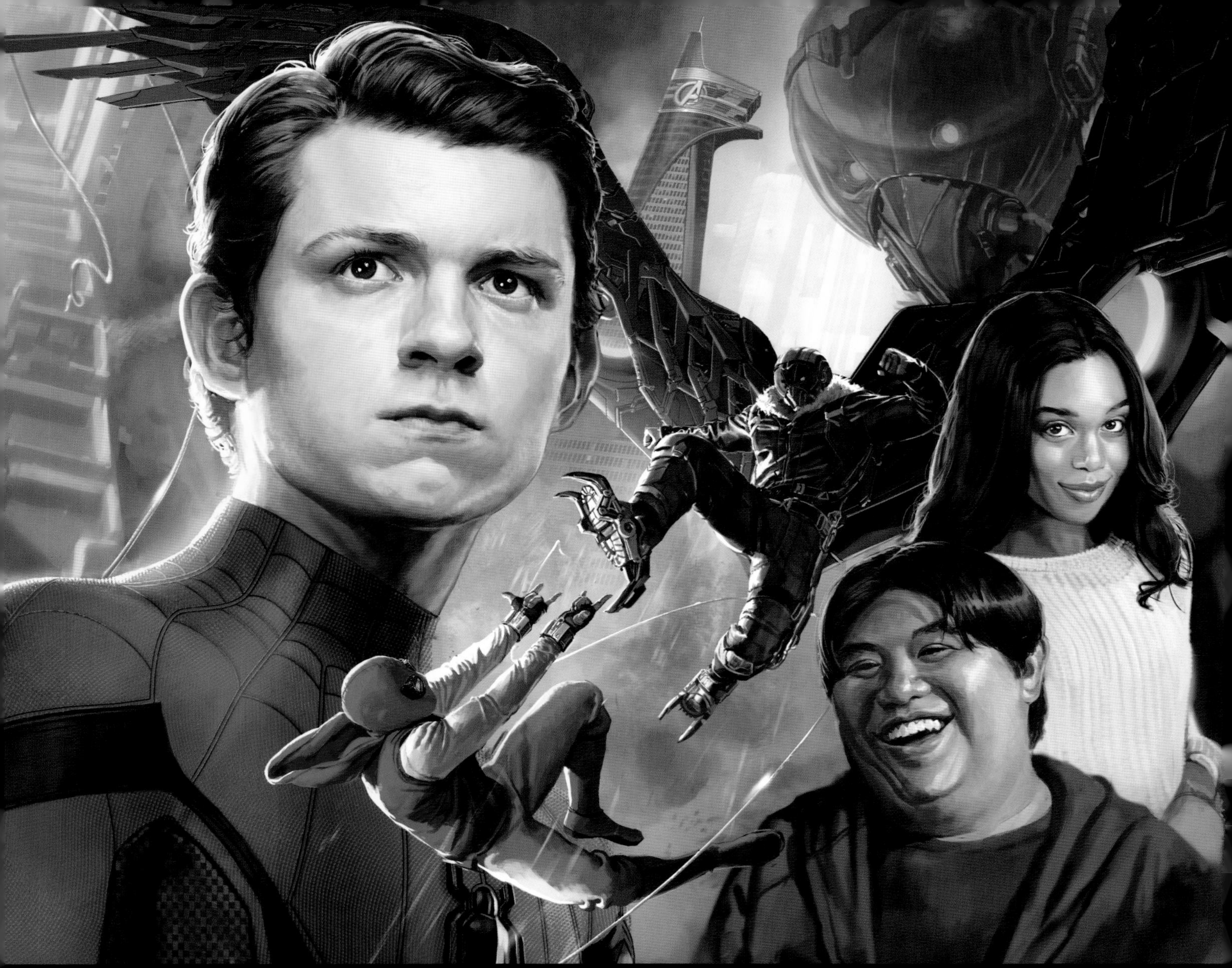

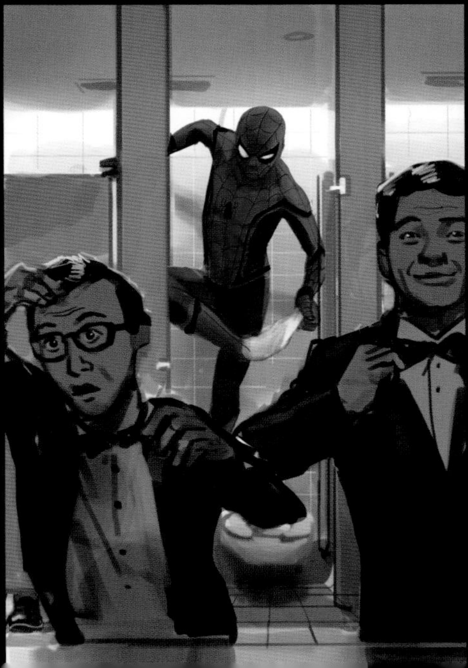

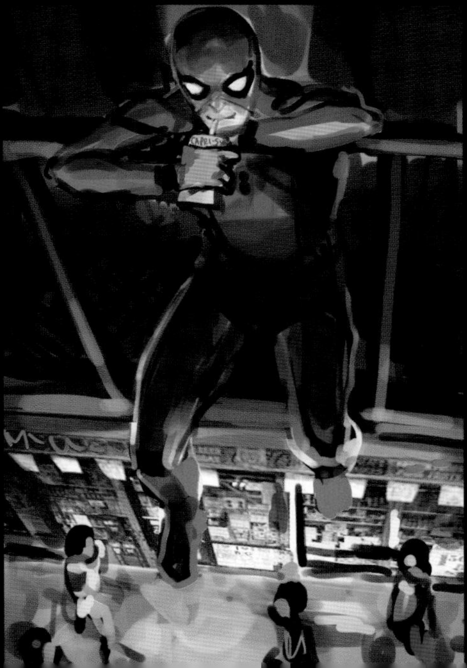

BOTTOM ROW When *Spider-Man: Homecoming* executive producer Jeremy Latcham came to Ryan Meinerding to ask him to come up with some ideas for promo posters, the artist admits, "I kinda got into it a little *too* much. The one on the far left, opposite—I don't know why I thought they would ever pick that because it's literally not like a one-sheet poster. But it took a fair amount of time to make that one work. And I loved coming up with these, even just as possible ideas."

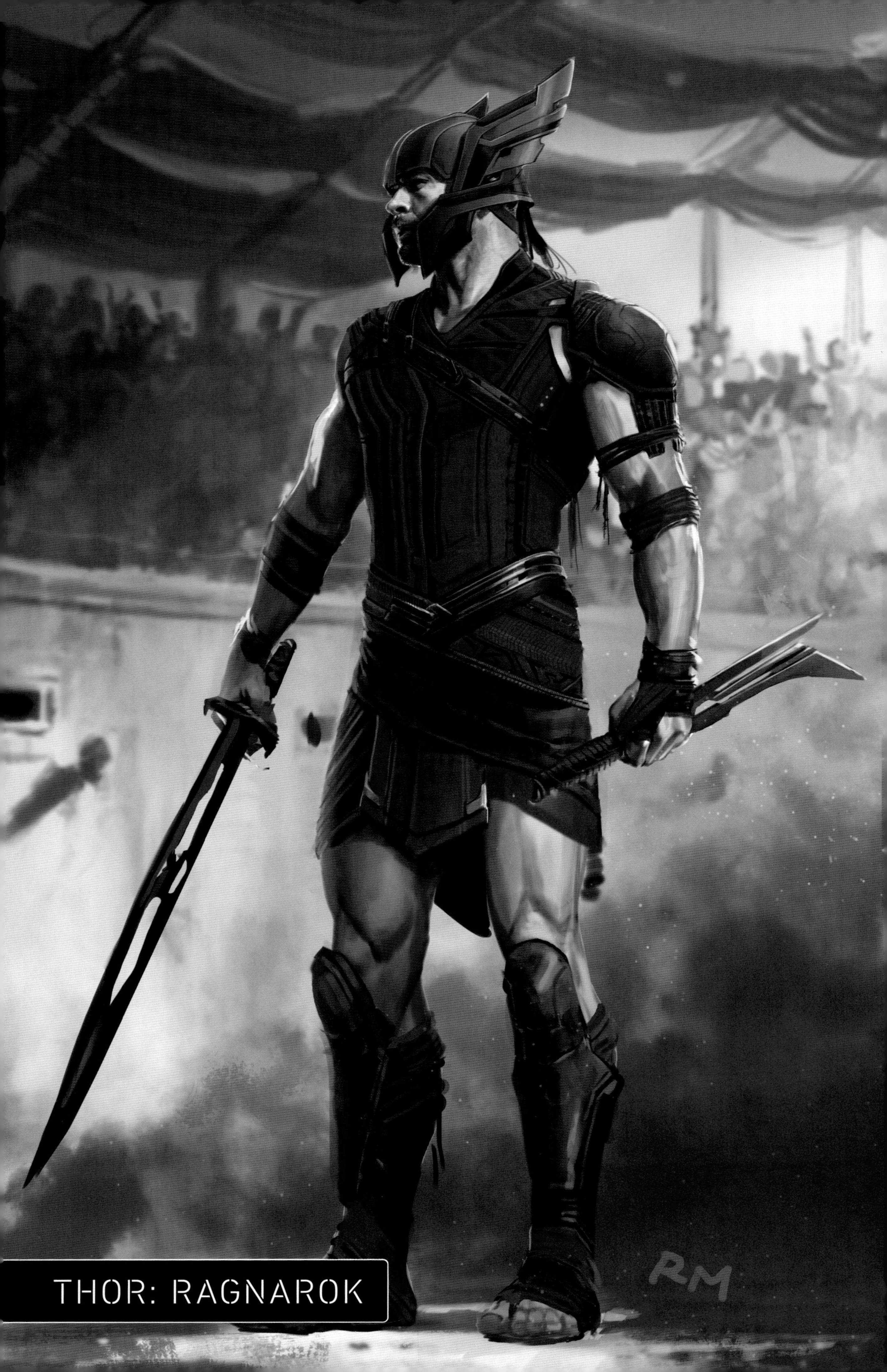
RM

THOR: RAGNAROK

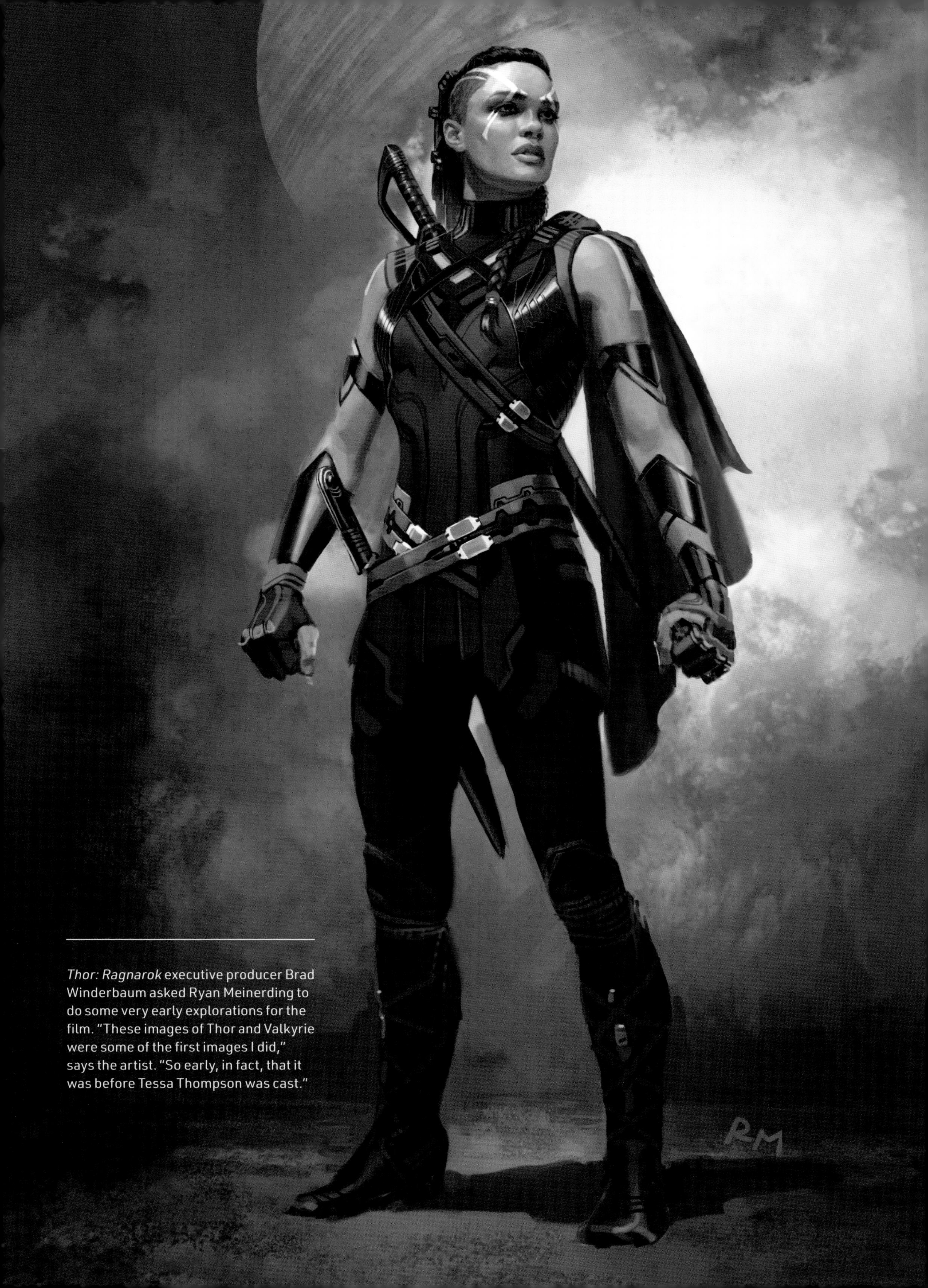
RM

Thor: Ragnarok executive producer Brad Winderbaum asked Ryan Meinerding to do some very early explorations for the film. "These images of Thor and Valkyrie were some of the first images I did," says the artist. "So early, in fact, that it was before Tessa Thompson was cast."

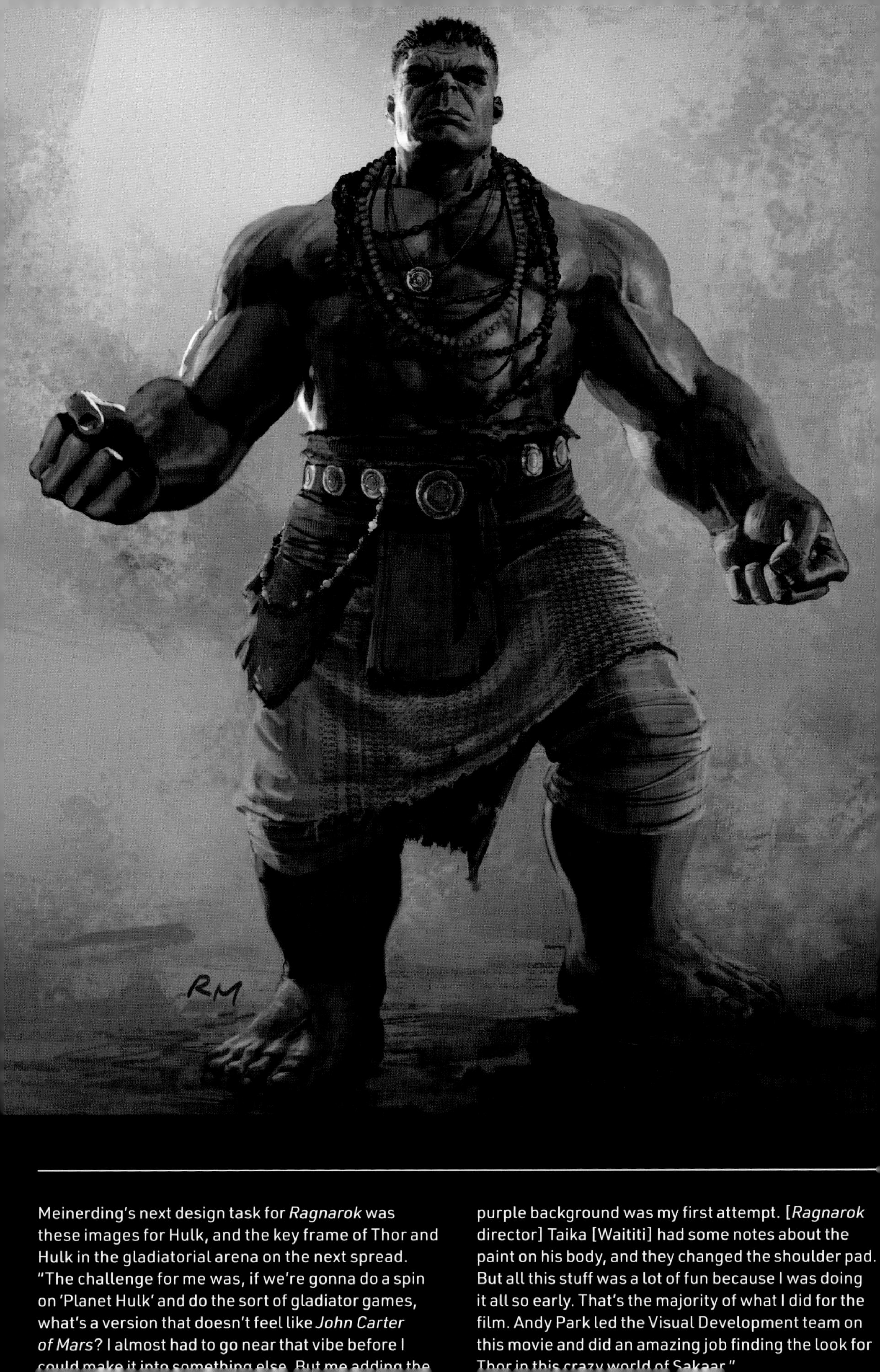
RM

Meinerding's next design task for *Ragnarok* was these images for Hulk, and the key frame of Thor and Hulk in the gladiatorial arena on the next spread. "The challenge for me was, if we're gonna do a spin on 'Planet Hulk' and do the sort of gladiator games, what's a version that doesn't feel like *John Carter of Mars*? I almost had to go near that vibe before I could make it into something else. But me adding the purple background was my first attempt. [*Ragnarok* director] Taika [Waititi] had some notes about the paint on his body, and they changed the shoulder pad. But all this stuff was a lot of fun because I was doing it all so early. That's the majority of what I did for the film. Andy Park led the Visual Development team on this movie and did an amazing job finding the look for Thor in this crazy world of Sakaar."

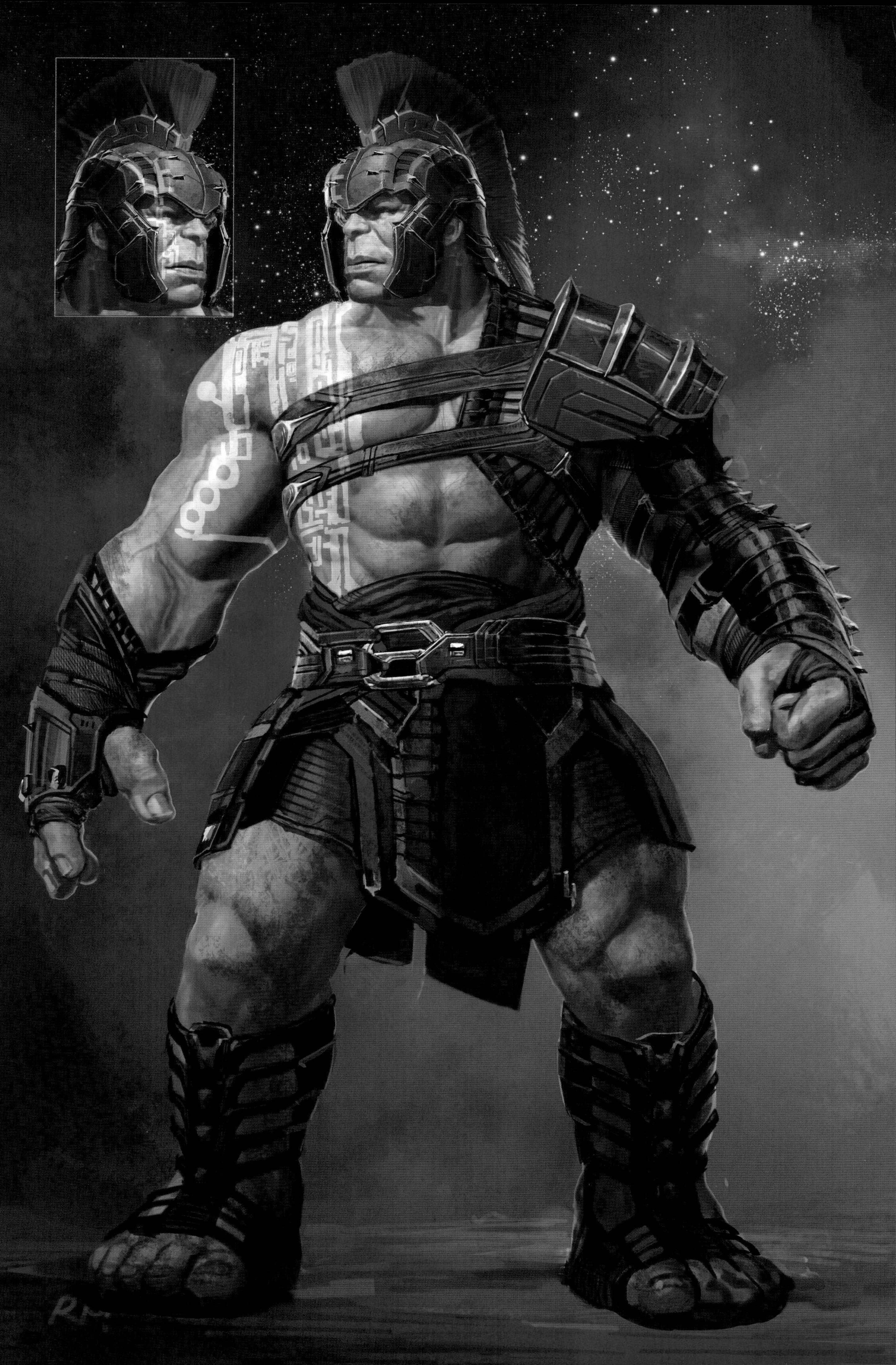

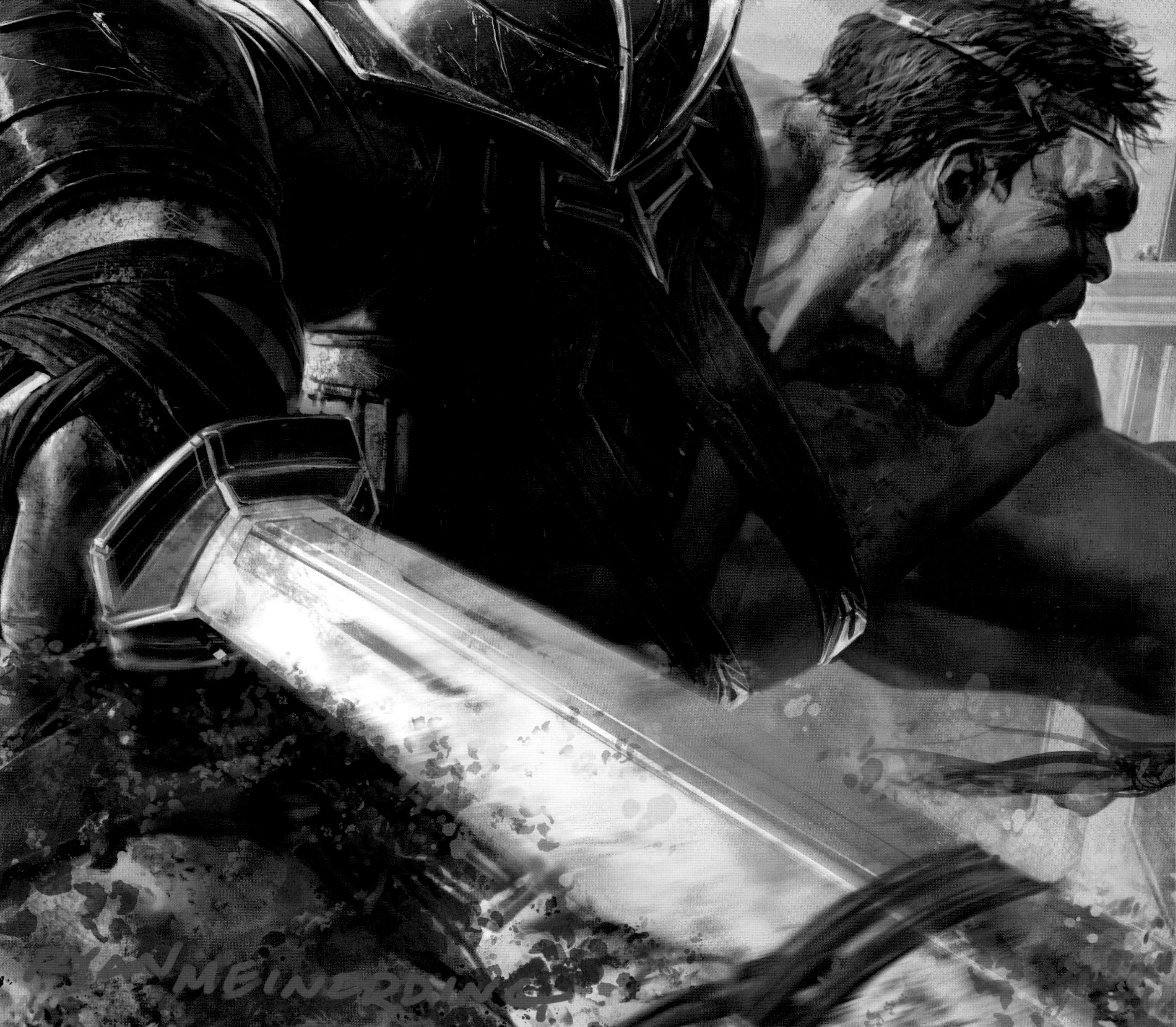
MEINERDING

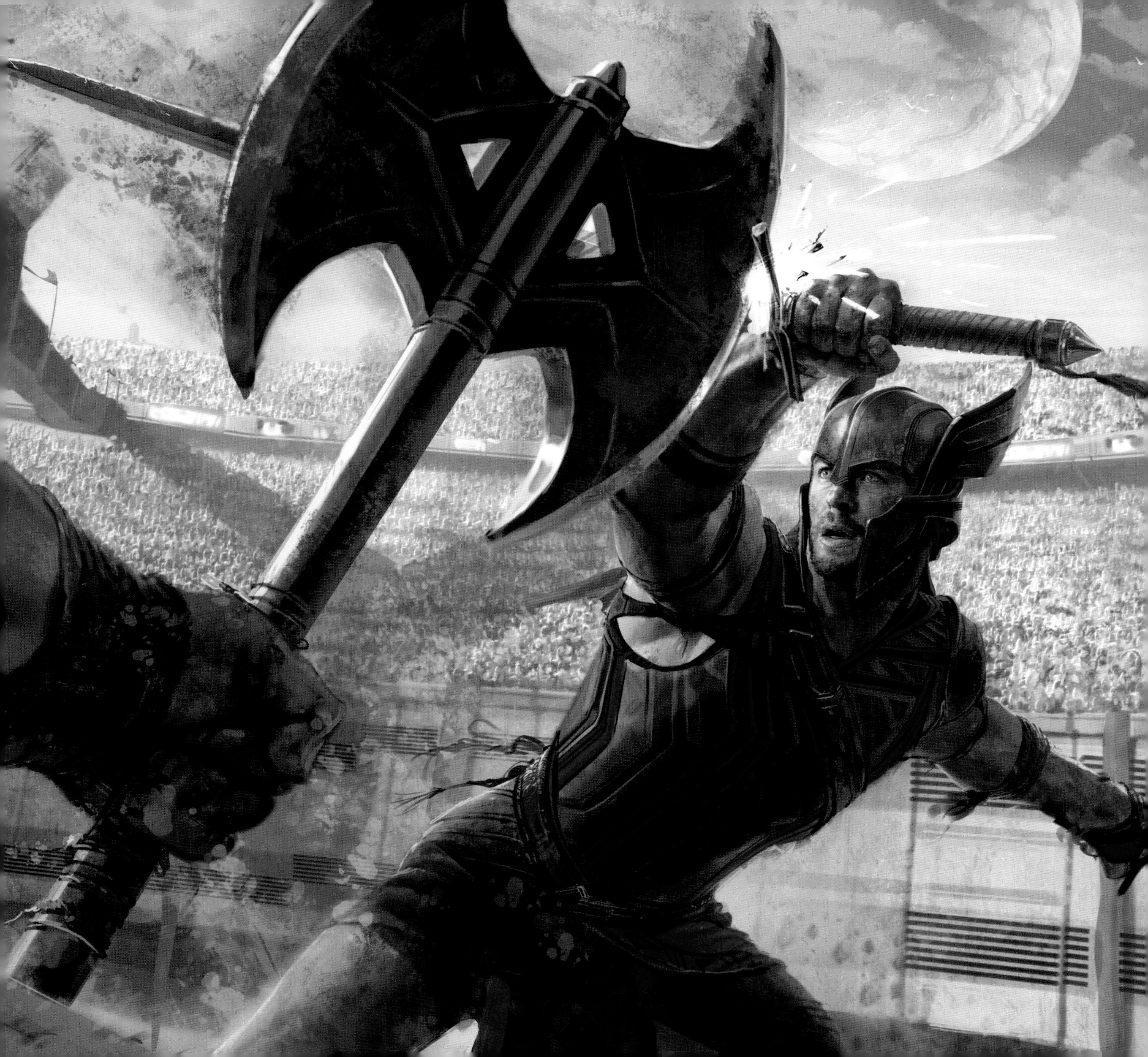

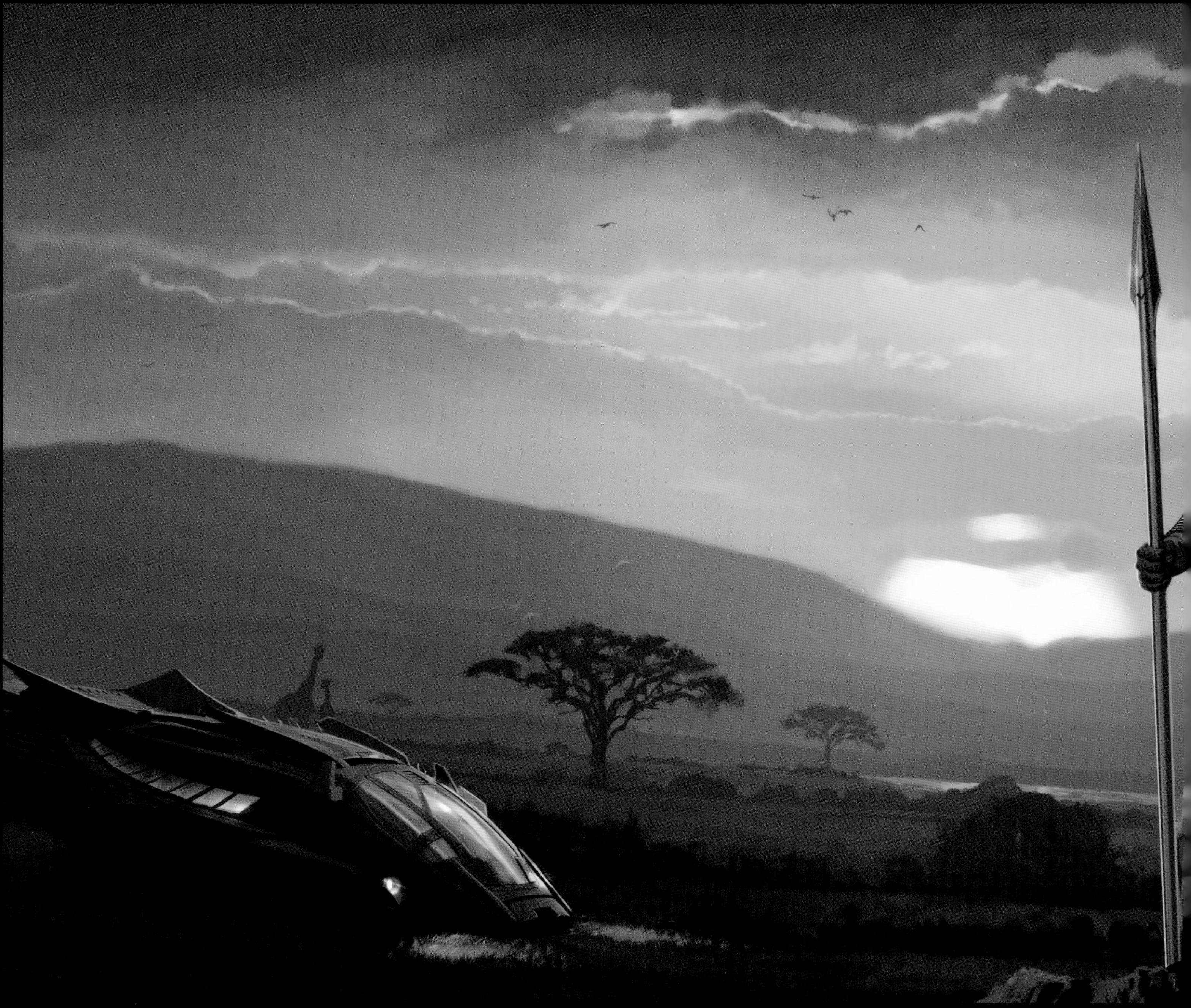

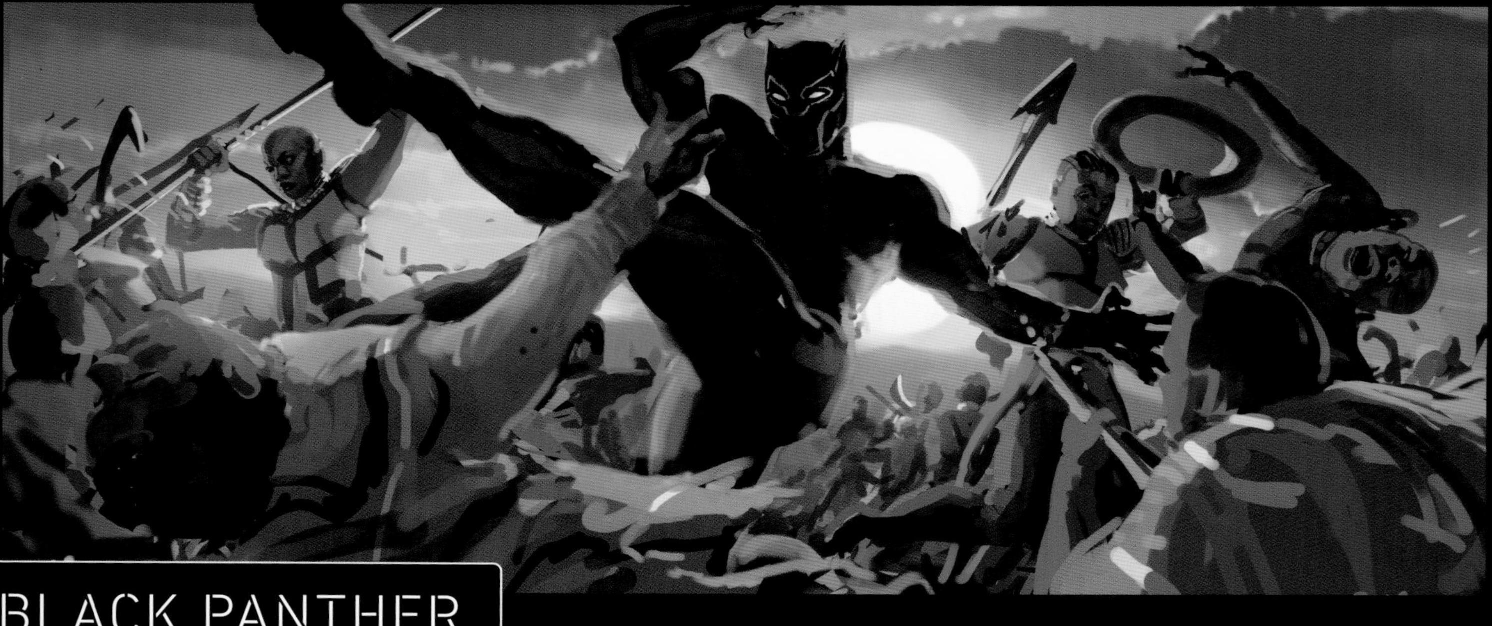

BLACK PANTHER

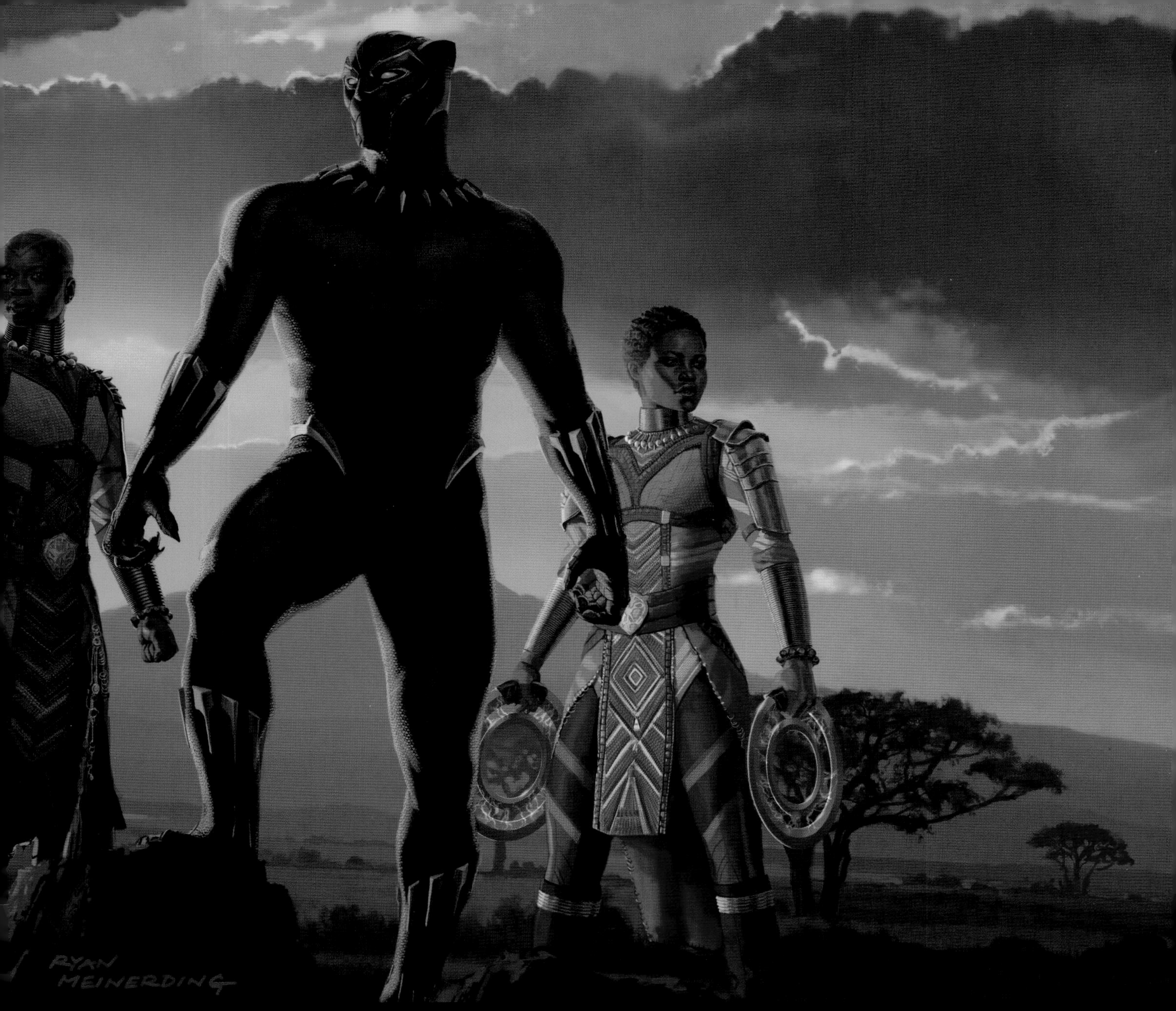
RYAN
MEINERDING

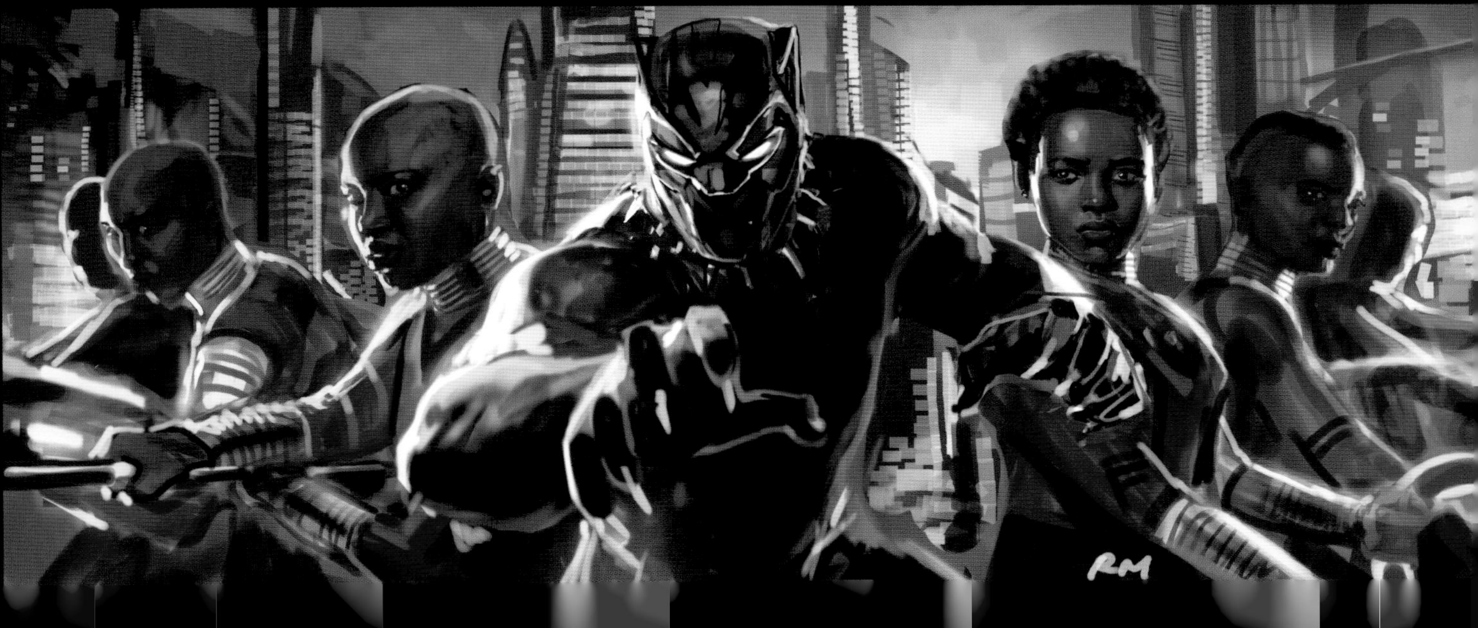
RM

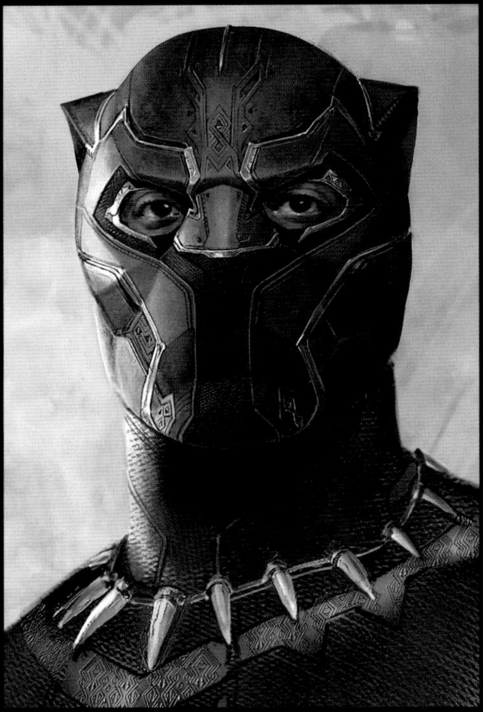

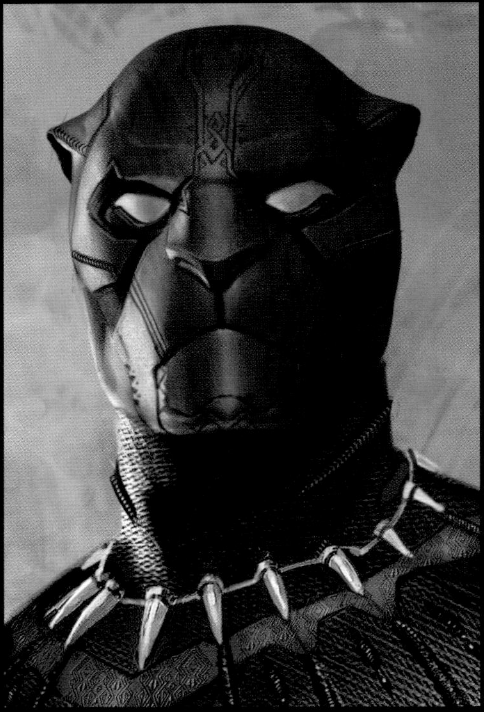

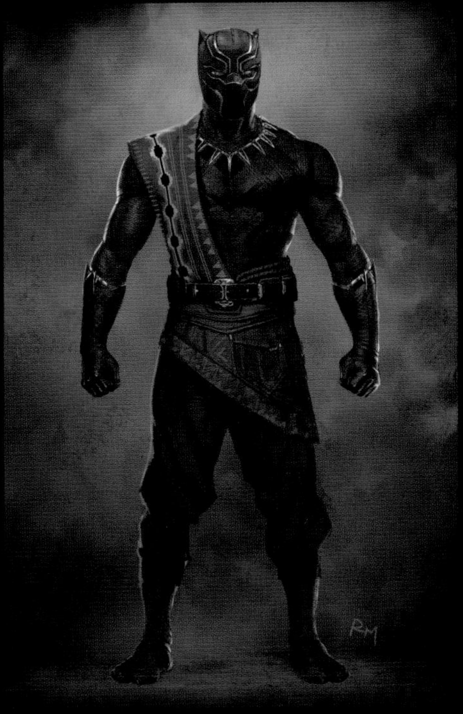

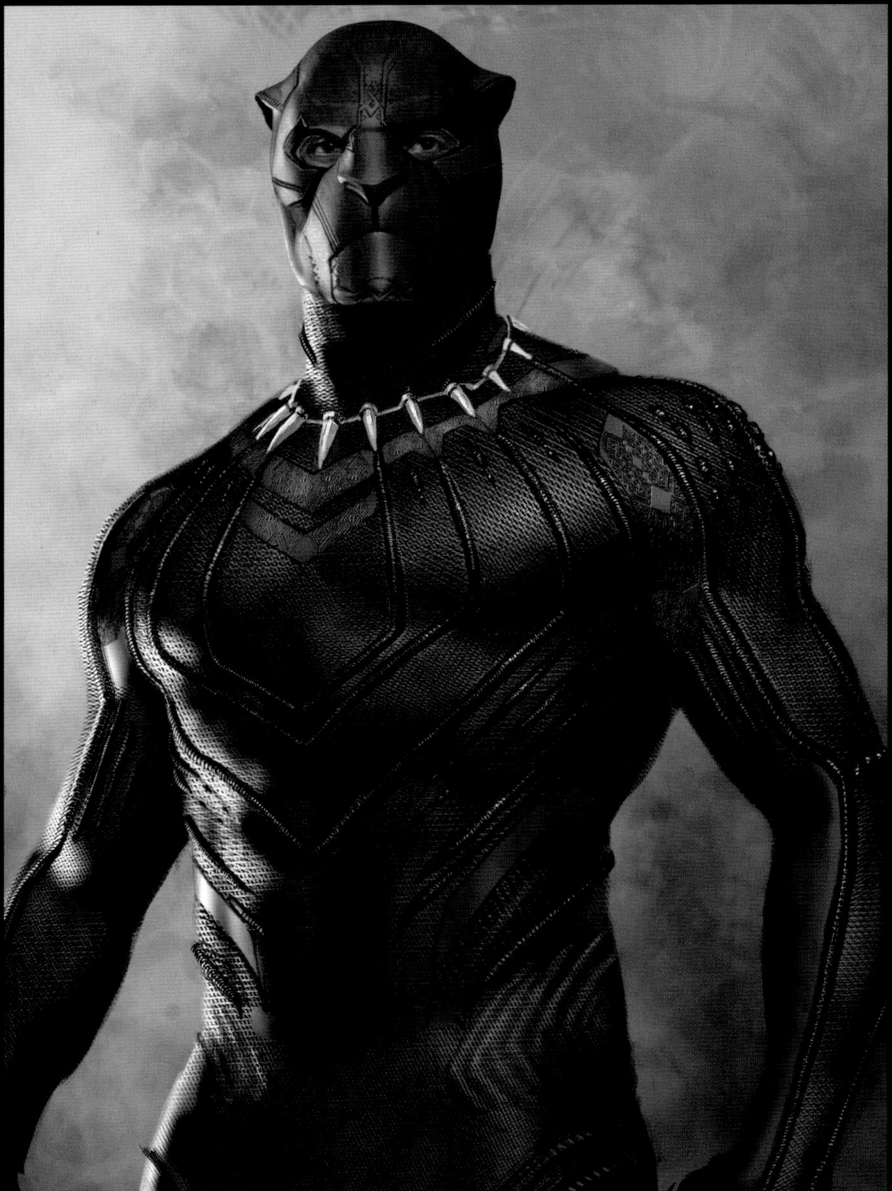

Although Ryan Meinerding originated the design for Black Panther in *Captain America: Civil War*, for the visual development of *Black Panther* he took more of a managing role. "The reason why I was not as involved was because of how big *Infinity War* and *Endgame* were," he explains. "Essentially, if I led design on *Black Panther*, it would've meant I was working on *three* gigantic movies at once." However, he did contribute design and key frames, including for T'Challa/Panther and T'Chaka (above right) with a sash and skirt, based on Rodney Fuentebella's T'Chaka design. "Overall, collaboration needs to happen when it's about designing an entire *world*—Wakanda—as opposed to just designing a cool Super Hero. A lot of that collaboration is made possible by Kevin [Feige] and [director] Ryan [Coogler] finding the common themes between what every other department is doing. I had lots of conversations with Ryan and really enjoyed working with him." Other artists that contributed to figuring out the look of Wakanda and Black Panther himself were Adi Granov, Wes Burt, Andy Park, and Anthony Francisco. Meinerding adds, "Ryan [Coogler] really started to gravitate toward Adi's designs in a strong way for Panther and Anthony's designs for the Dora Milaje."

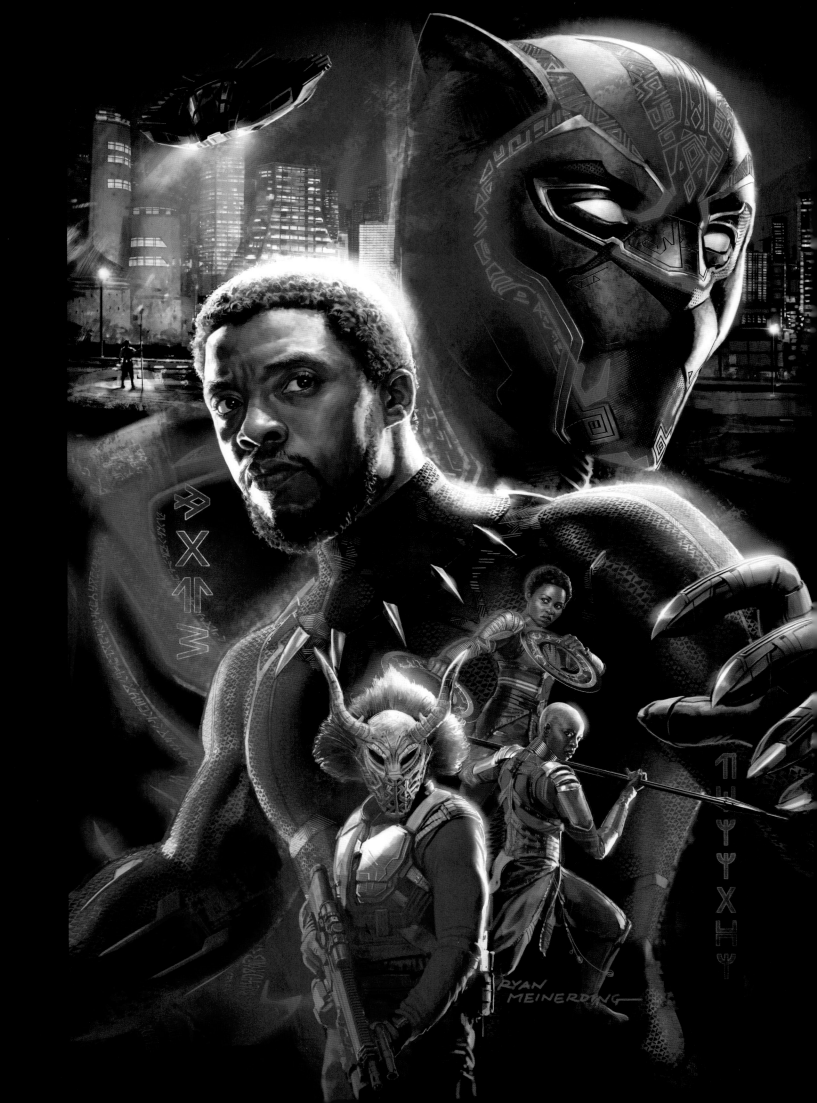

RYAN
MEINERDING

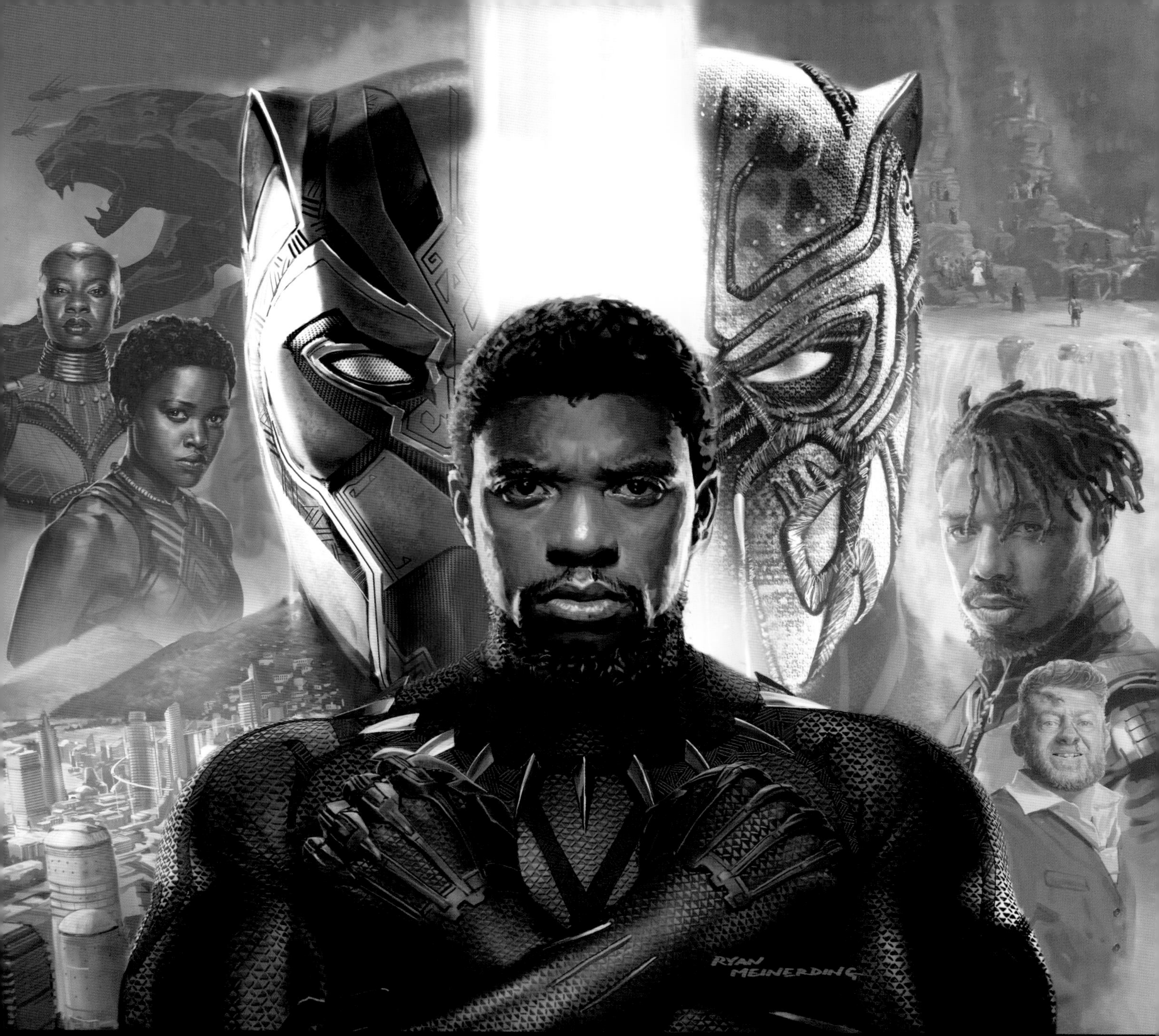
RYAN
MEINERDING

Much of the completed artwork that Meinerding did for *Black Panther* was done toward the end of the project, for the film's marketing. (This includes the 2017 D23 Expo poster shown at the top of pages 206–207.) The main image here expands upon his initial idea for Killmonger's suit. Meinerding details, "I was pitching turning the stitching of his suit into something that looks like the keloid scarring that Killmonger was doing to himself. As he had the scarification over his body, this was the version of his suit had a visual manifestation of that, but in the actual fabric."

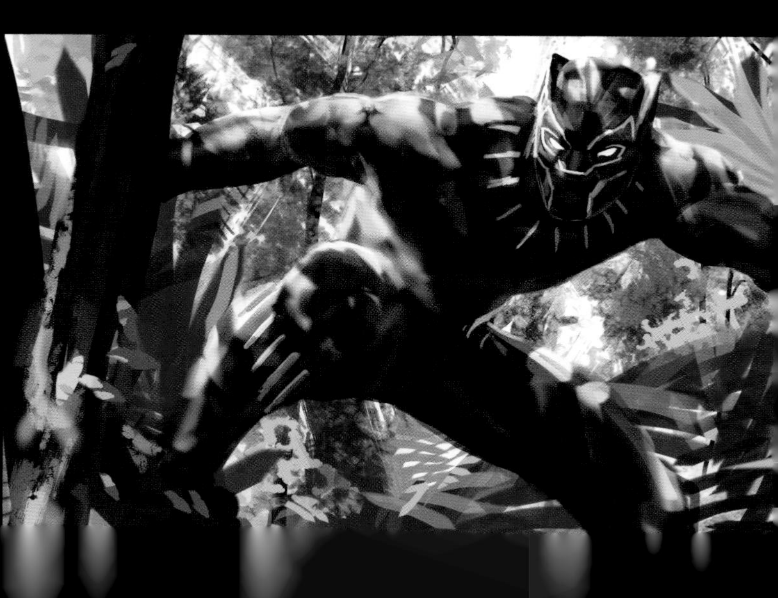

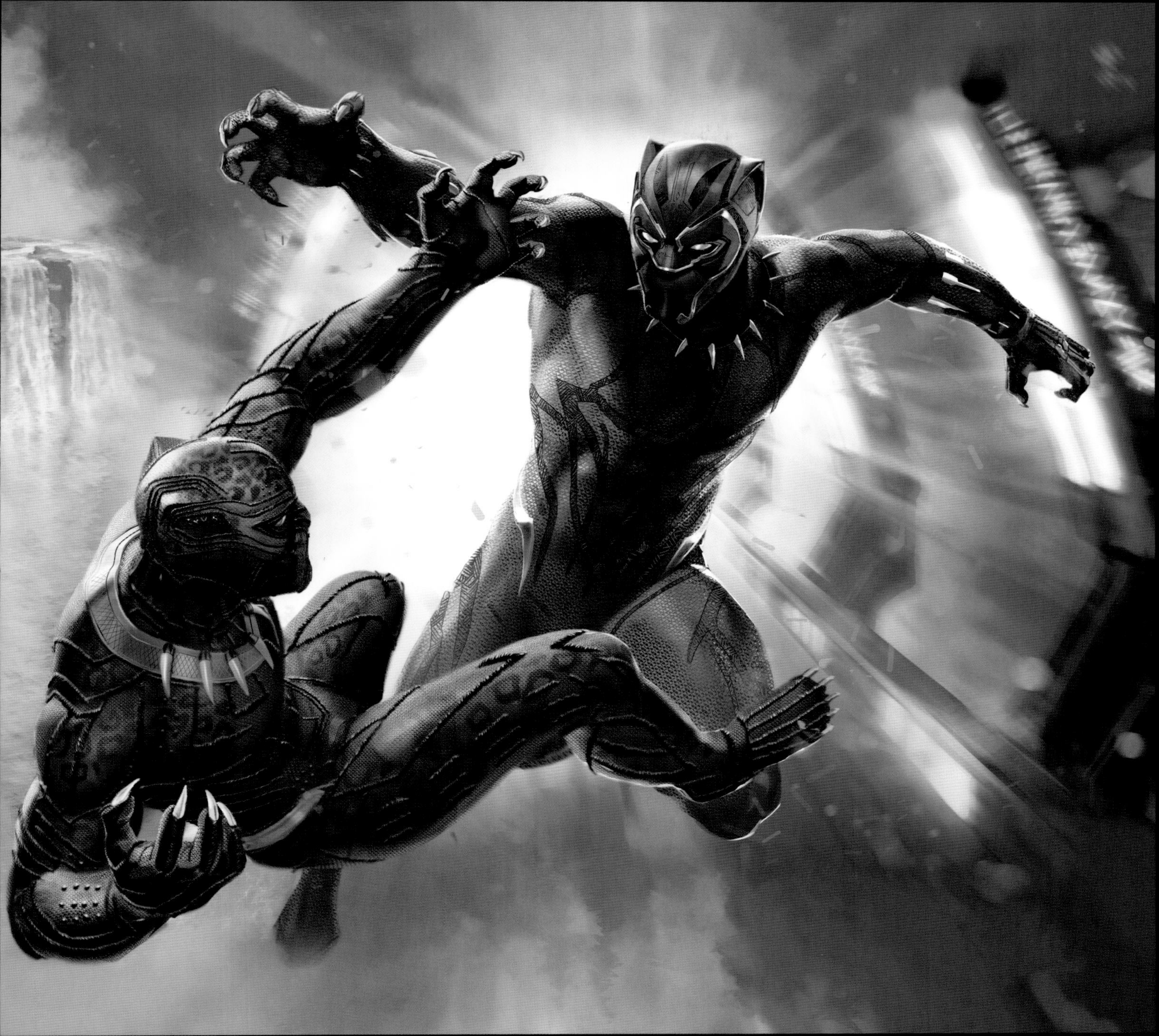

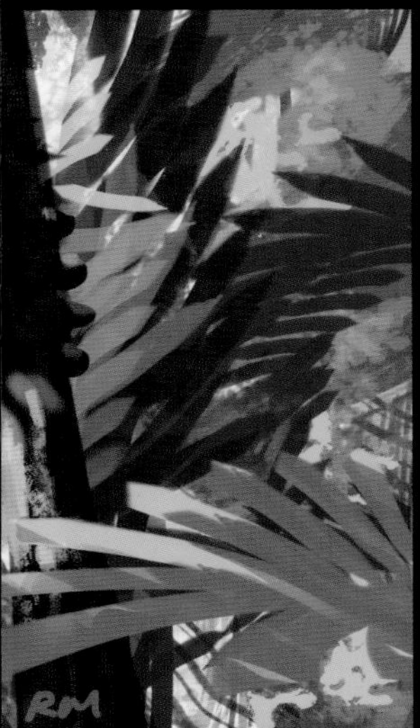
RM

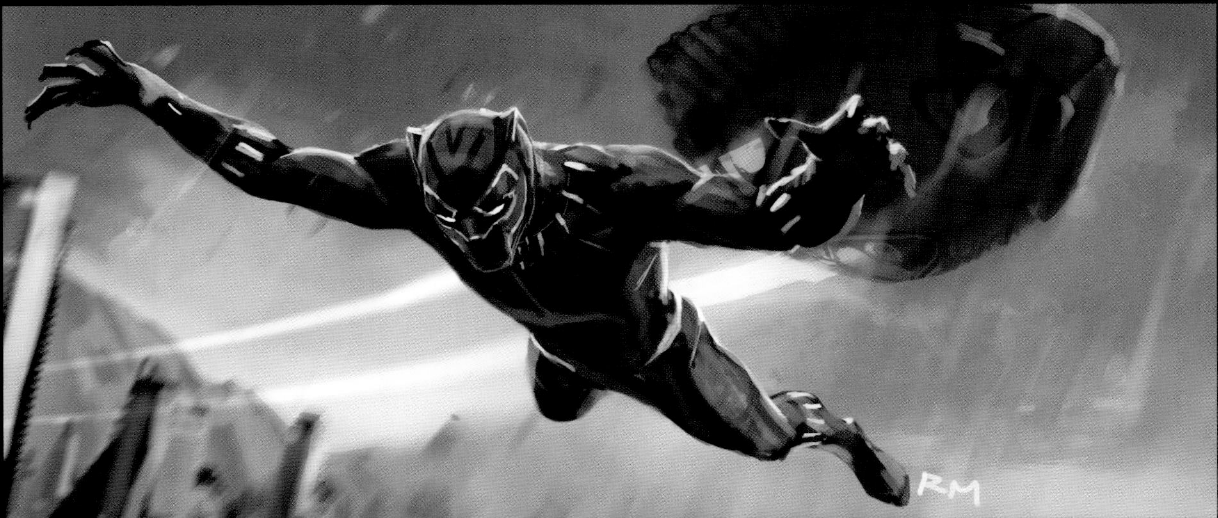
RM

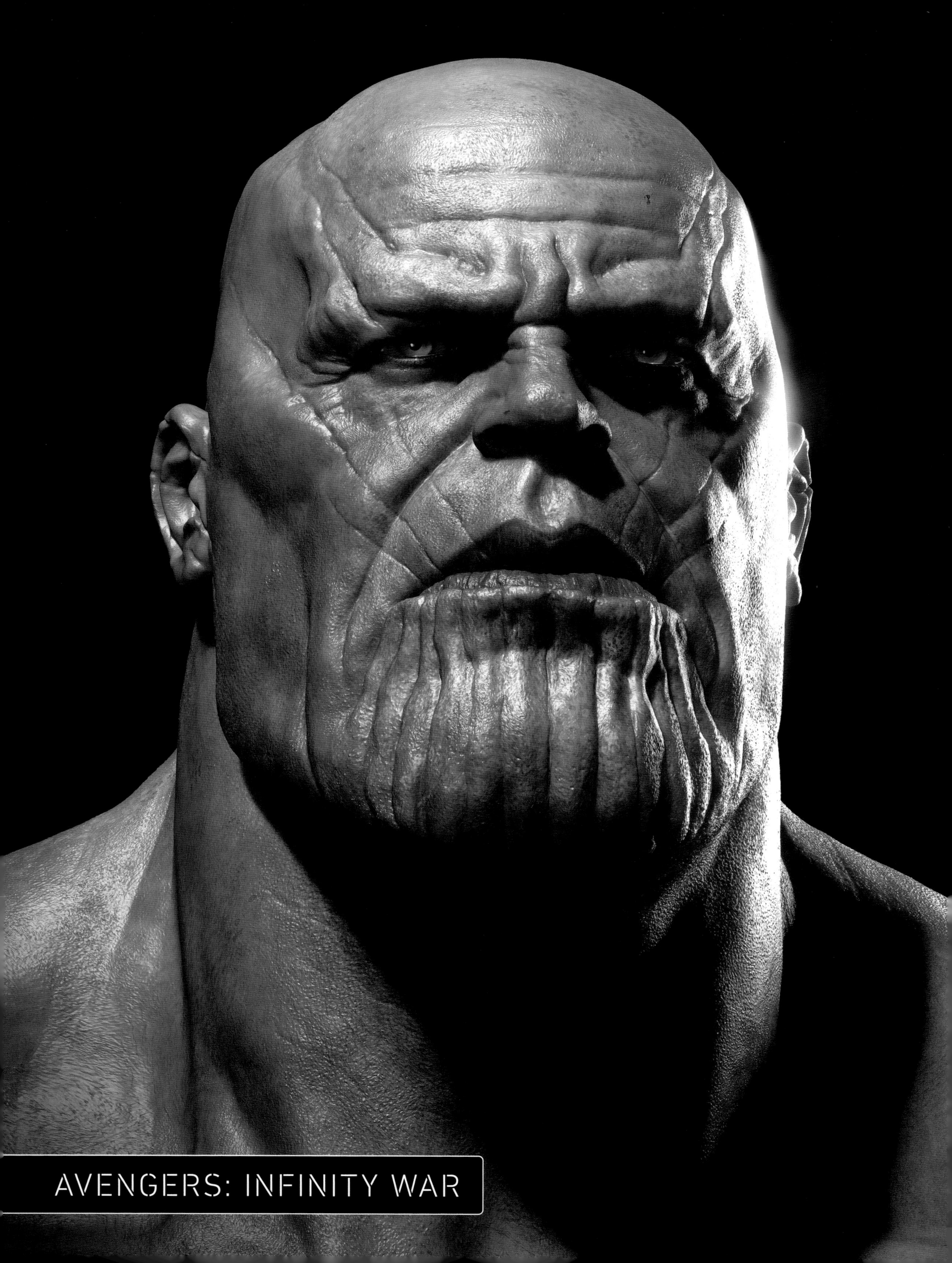

AVENGERS: INFINITY WAR

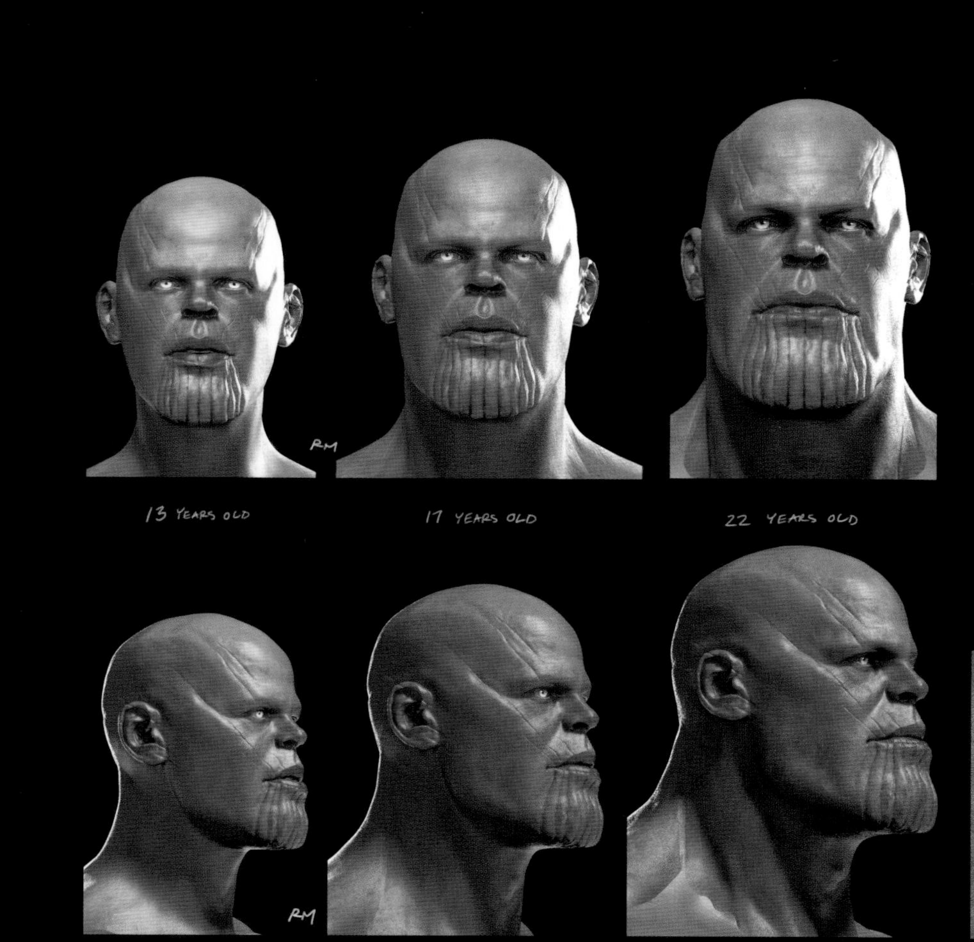
RM
13 YEARS OLD
17 YEARS OLD
22 YEARS OLD
RM

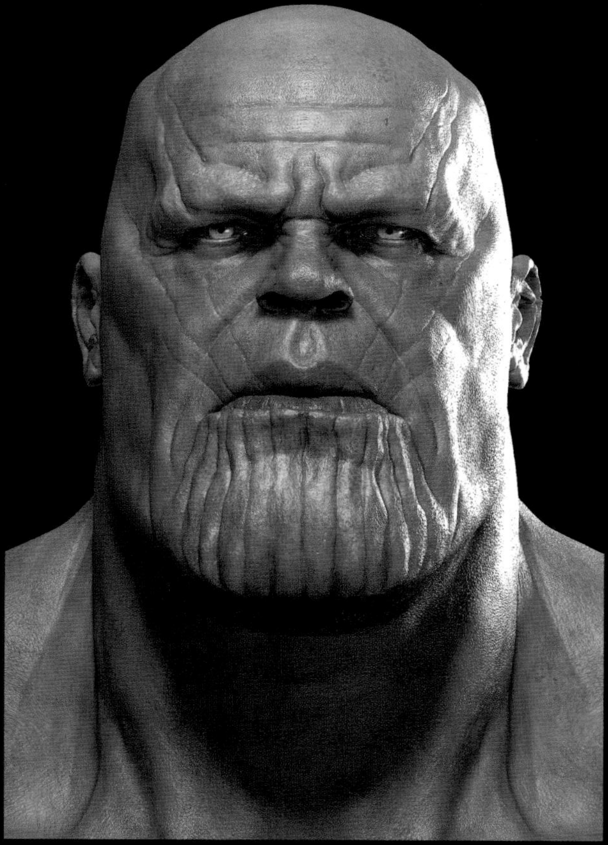

Landing the design of the entirely digital character of Thanos—featuring Josh Brolin's motion-captured performance—was Meinerding's biggest challenge to date. "With my concept art, I started doing paintings of basically a purple Josh Brolin and then turning him into Thanos slightly more each time," he says. "My point of view was that the Thanos from *Guardians of the Galaxy* was successful in a lot of ways, but his face was a little too cartoony. His mouth was just massive. So I wanted to bring a greater sense of realism. My design kind of has the same termination points, but I just made the lips overlap in a way that ended up feeling more like a real mouth. And it's fooling you into thinking that he's sneering at you a little bit." But in order to *fully* sell Thanos as a real, living, breathing entity, Meinerding came to realize he needed to do something different. He learned some new rendering software programs, went through numerous iterations, then built Thanos in 3D to push the photorealism more than he previously had with any other character design. "That model went straight to Digital Domain," he continues. "Within a month, they were able to do an animation test using that as a starting point." Kevin Feige showed that VFX test, based on Meinerding's provable concept design, to Bob Iger (CEO of the Walt Disney Company), who personally expressed how thrilled he was with the work. "Getting the design to that place remains one of the things I'm most proud of, too."

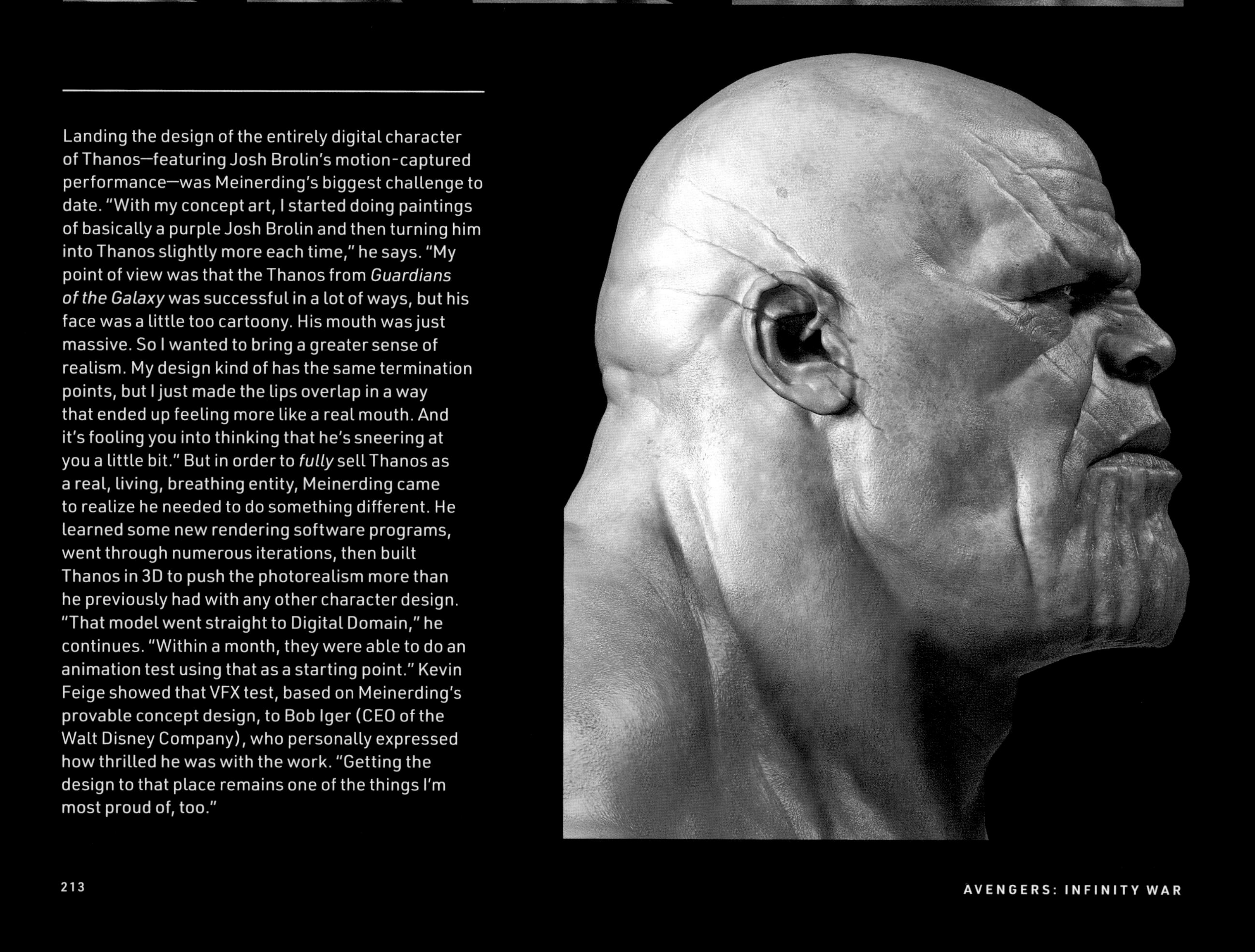

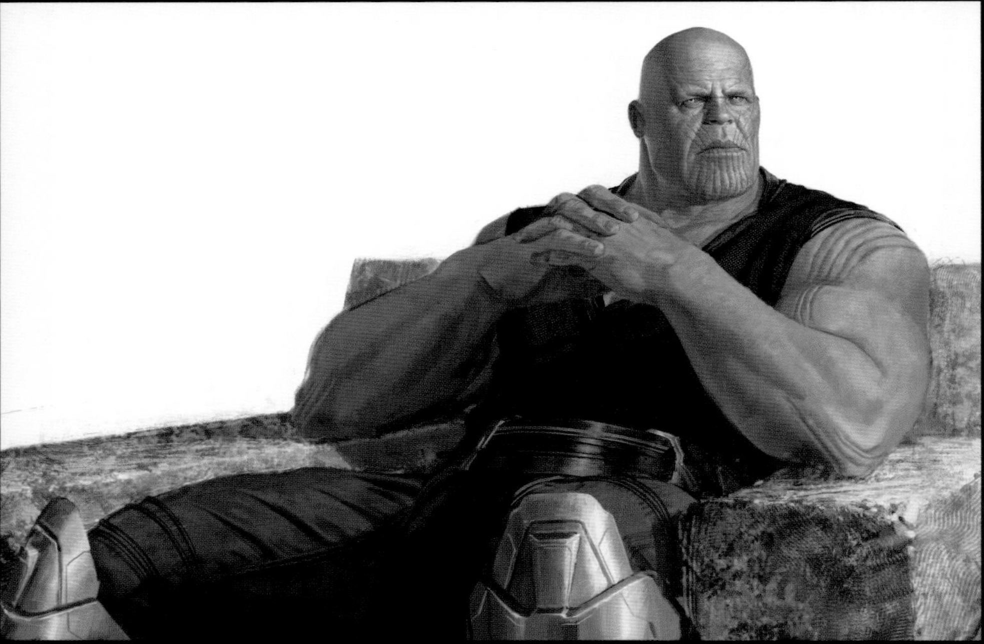

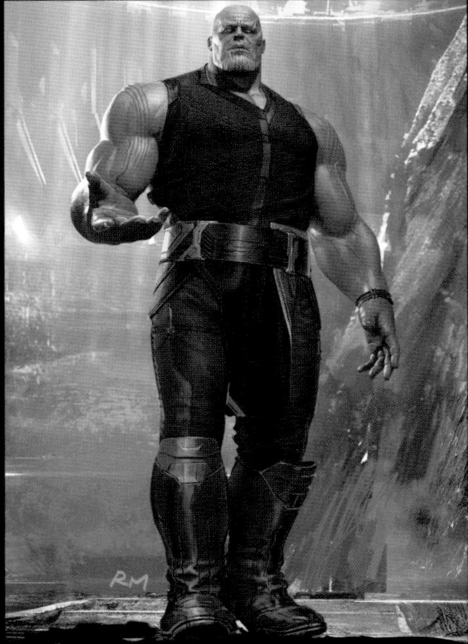
RM

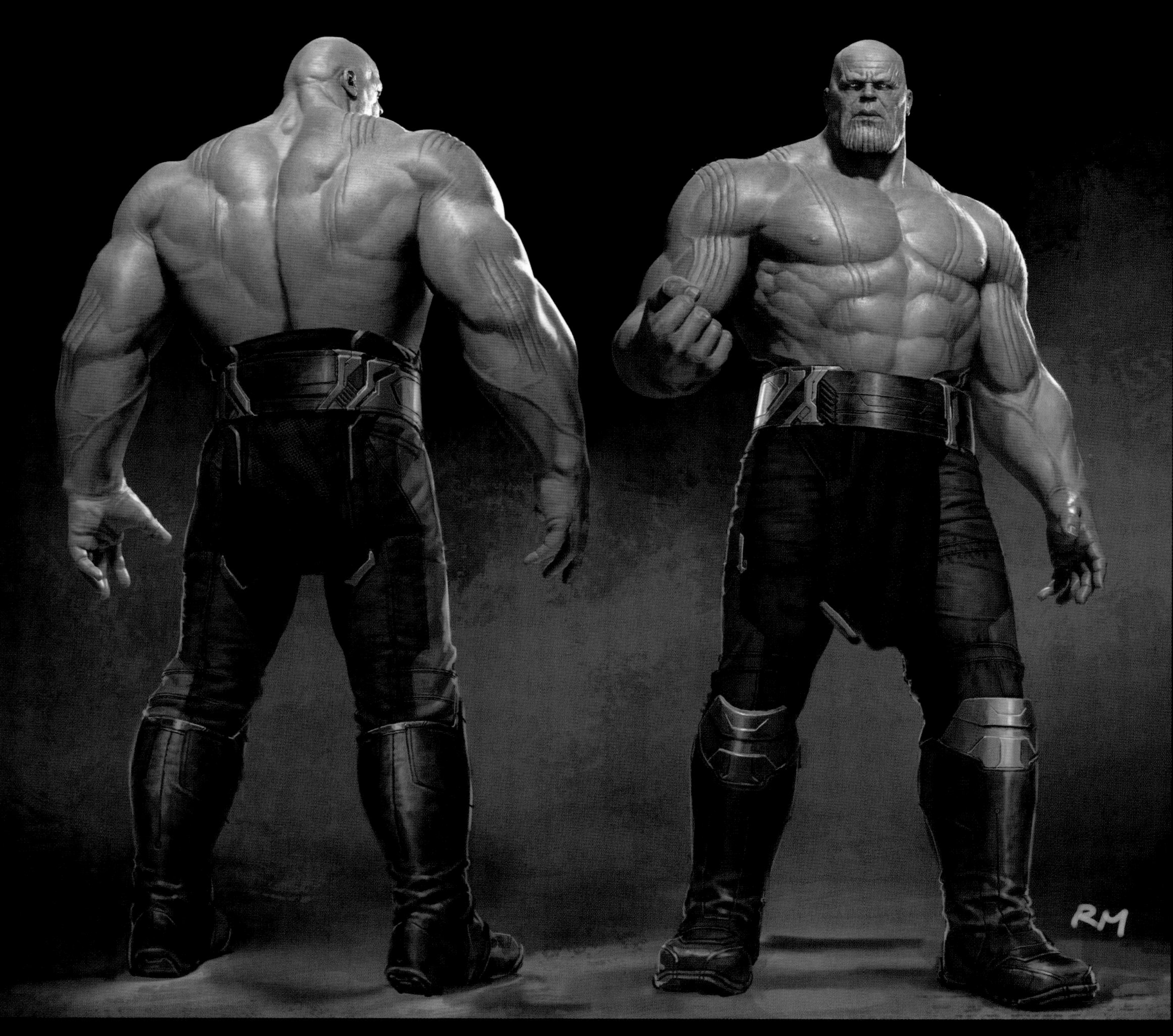
RM

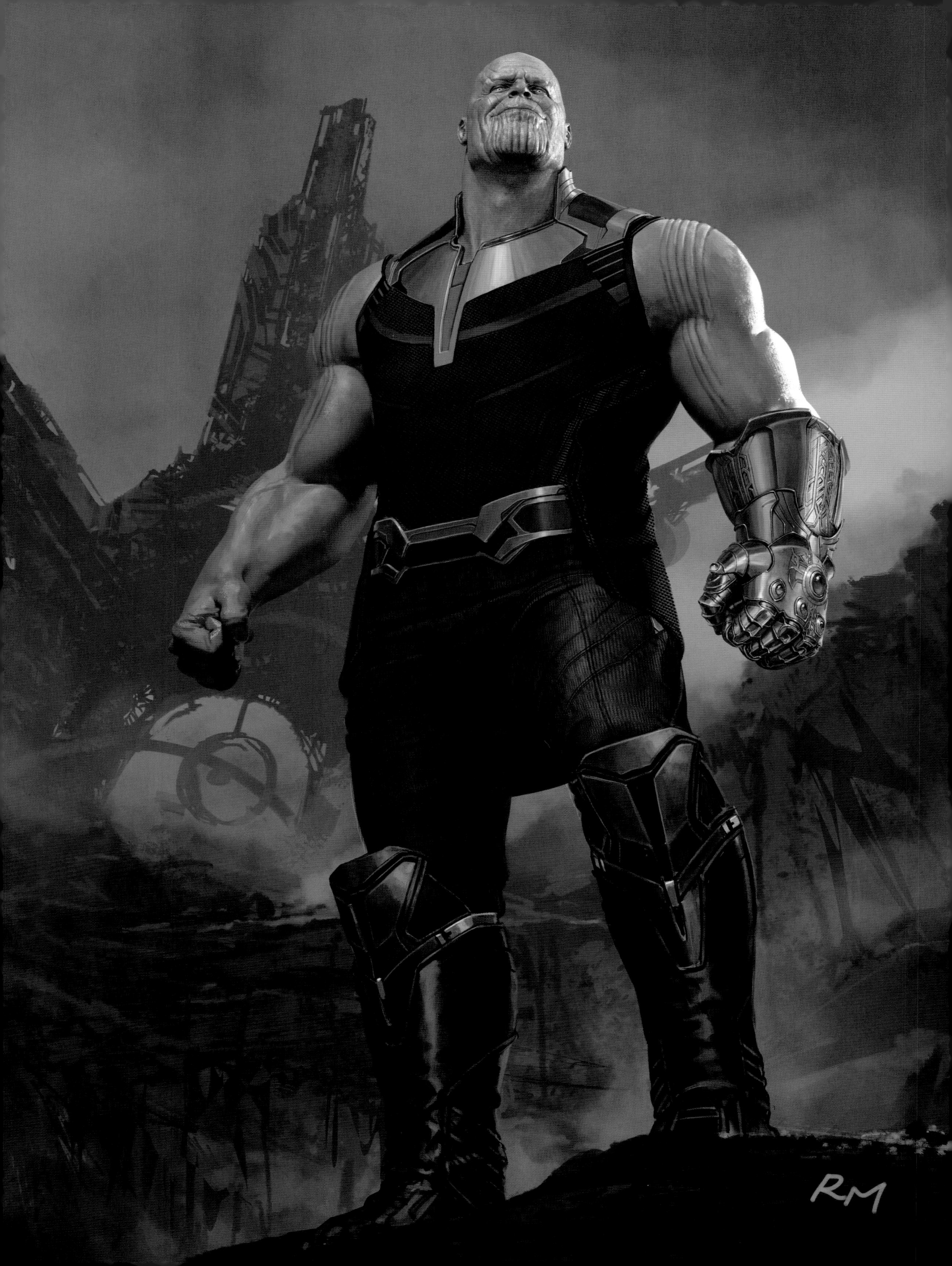
RM

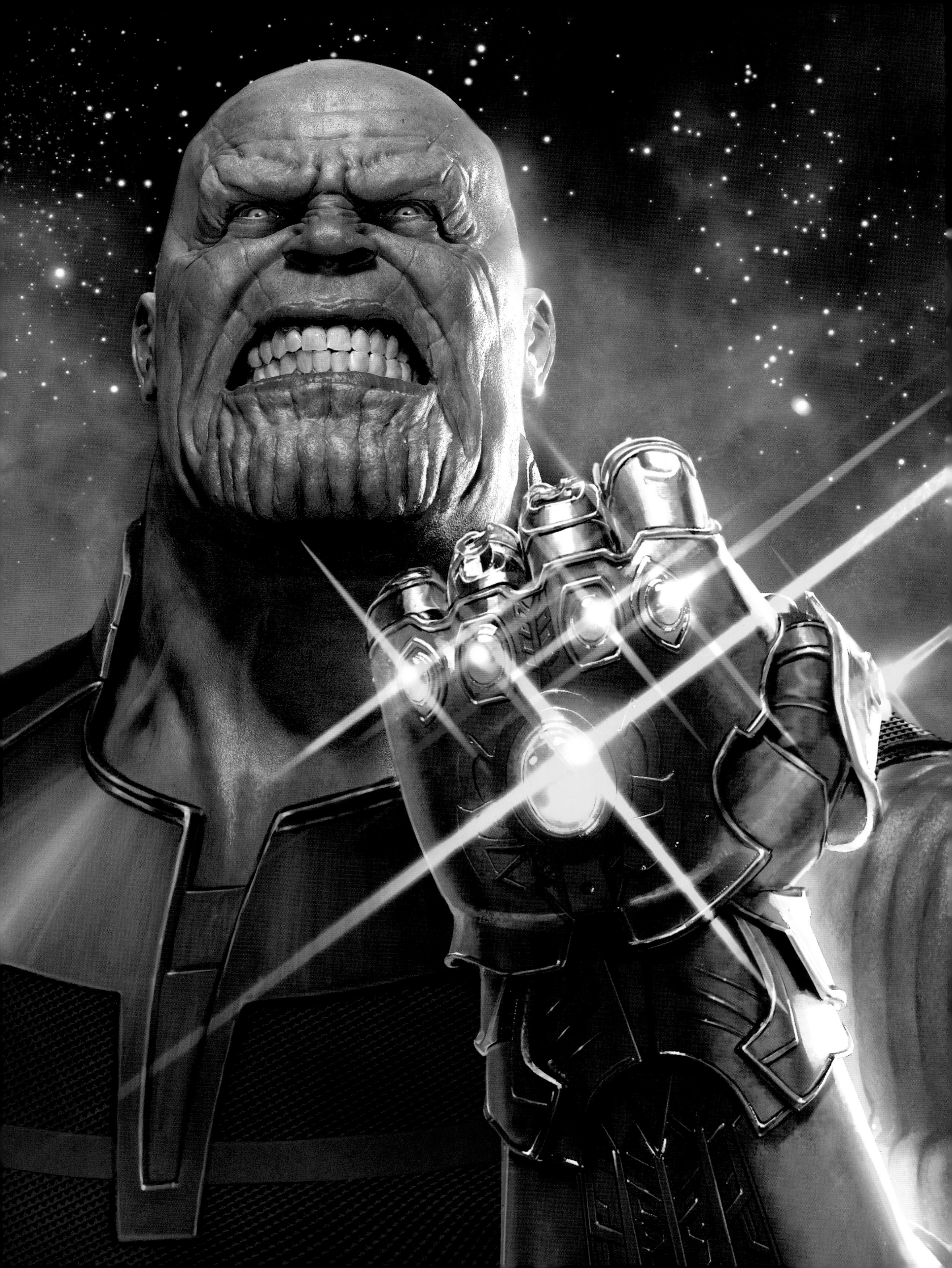

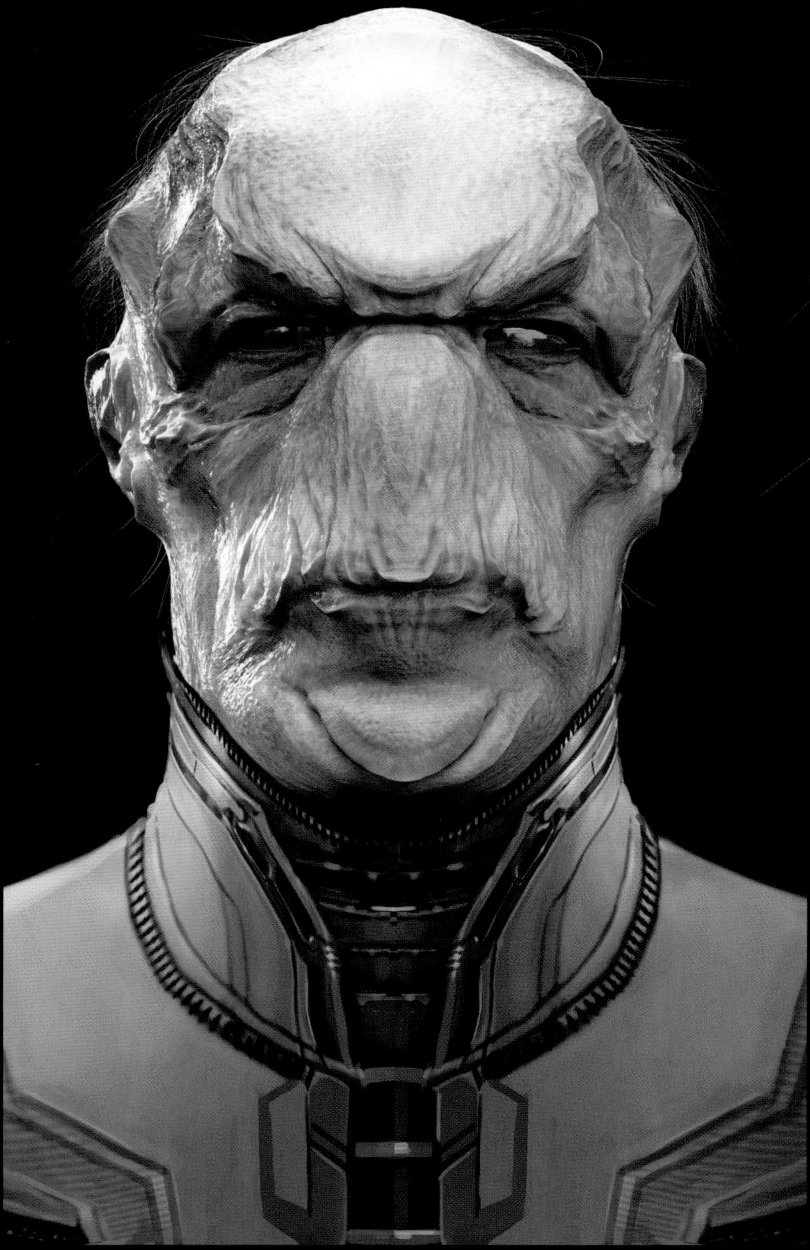

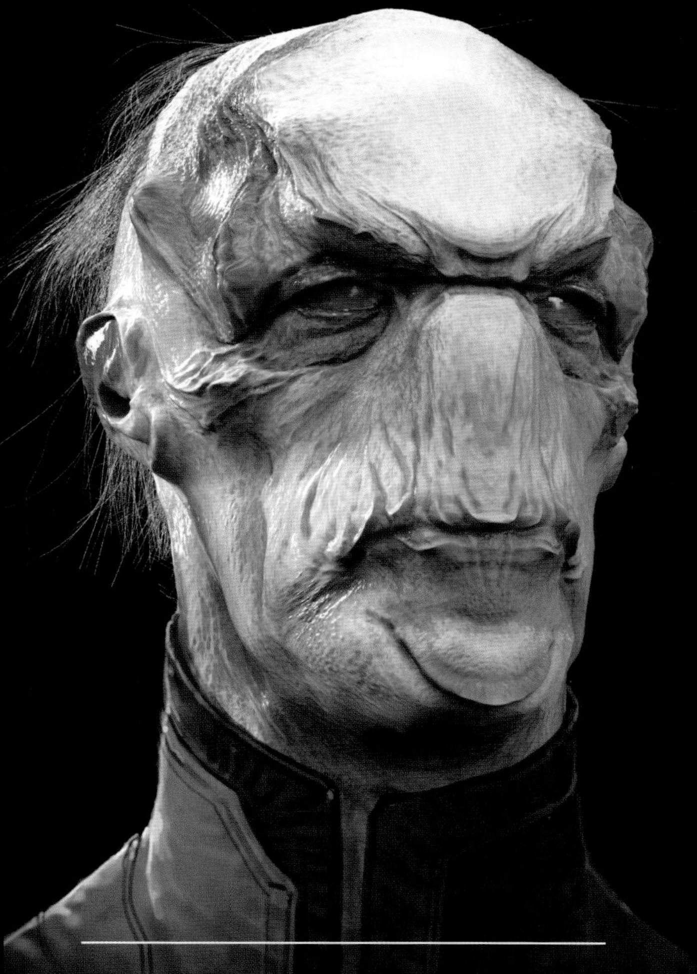

"There was a real push to make the Black Order feel legitimate and real, too, and not like generic henchman," says Meinerding. After going through the 3D design process, the artist already had a workflow developed to render them in relatively high resolution. He sculpted Ebony Maw's and Cull Obsidian's heads in the same way as Thanos.

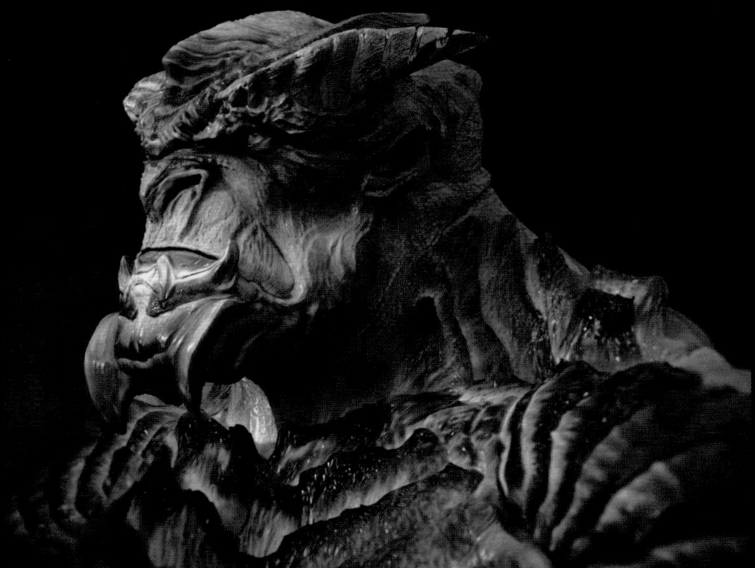

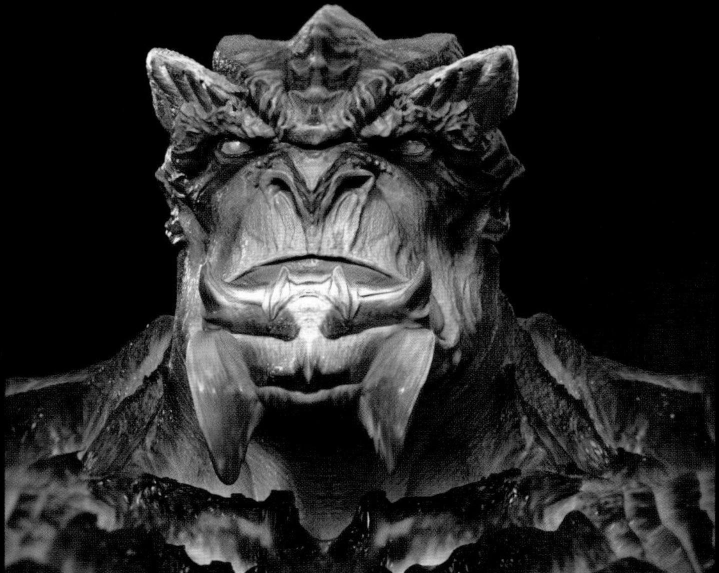

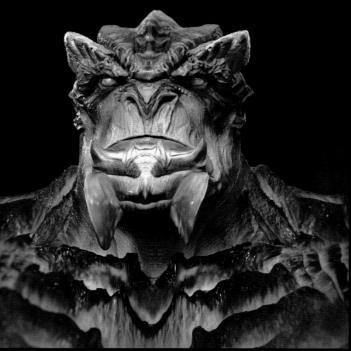

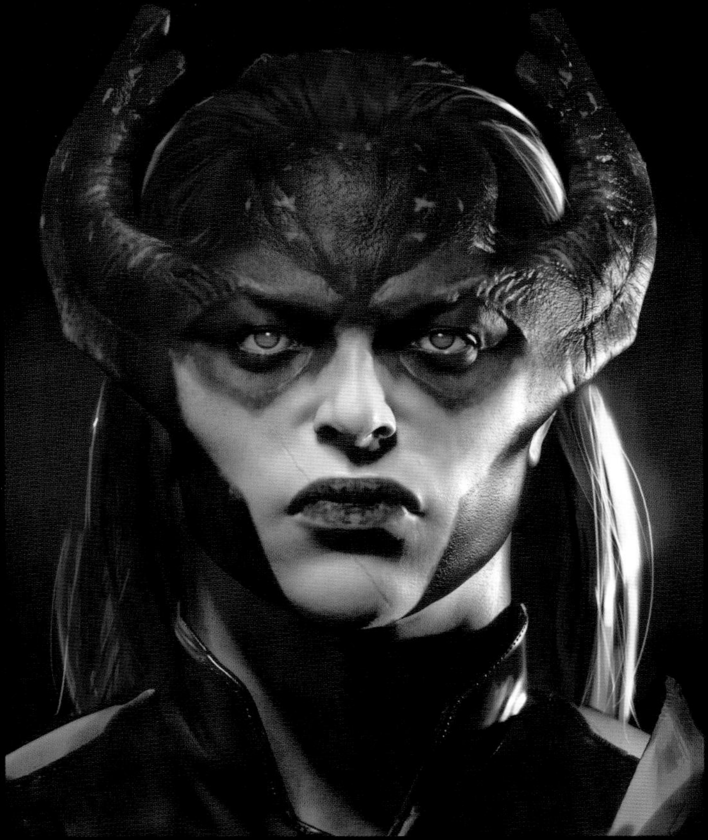

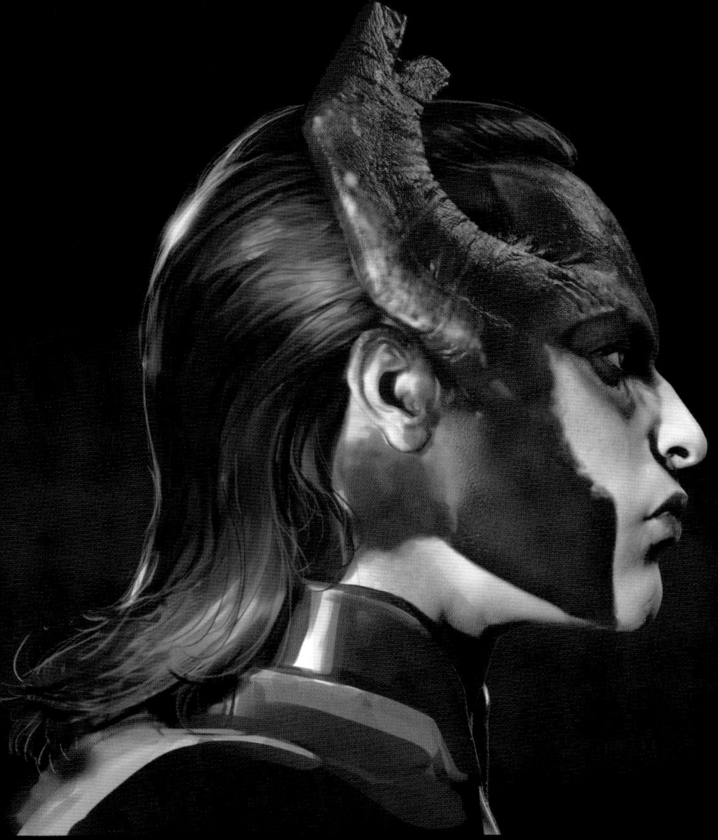

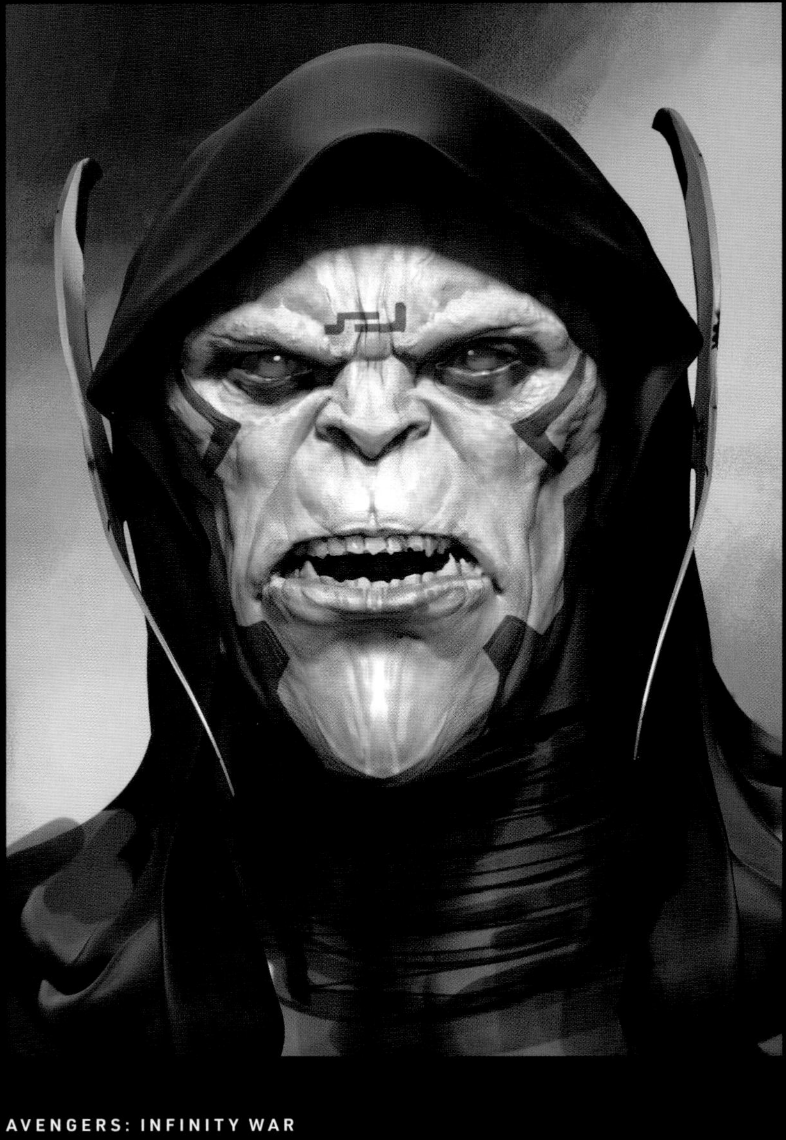

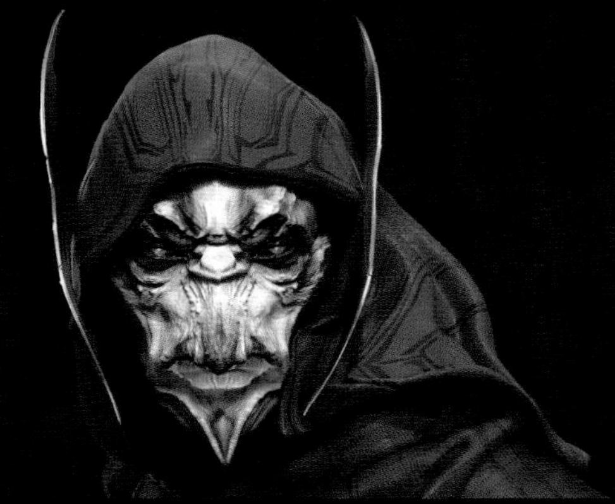

Meinerding helped model Proxima Midnight along with Adam Ross, based on Jerad Marantz's design, with some elements mixed in from Wes Burt's takes. For Corvus Glaive, the artist admits, "I did some *really* out there takes for him. But working on digital characters that are as visually important as these is a lot of fun because you're building them from the ground up." When it comes to the costuming, the vis-dev approach depends on the digital character. Meinerding designed Thanos's costume. For the Black Order clothing, their outfits were 50 percent figured out by Meinerding and his team before the visual effects house added the details to make them work.

TOP These Proxima Midnight studies were a result of Meinerding collaborating with Adam Ross and Wes Burt.

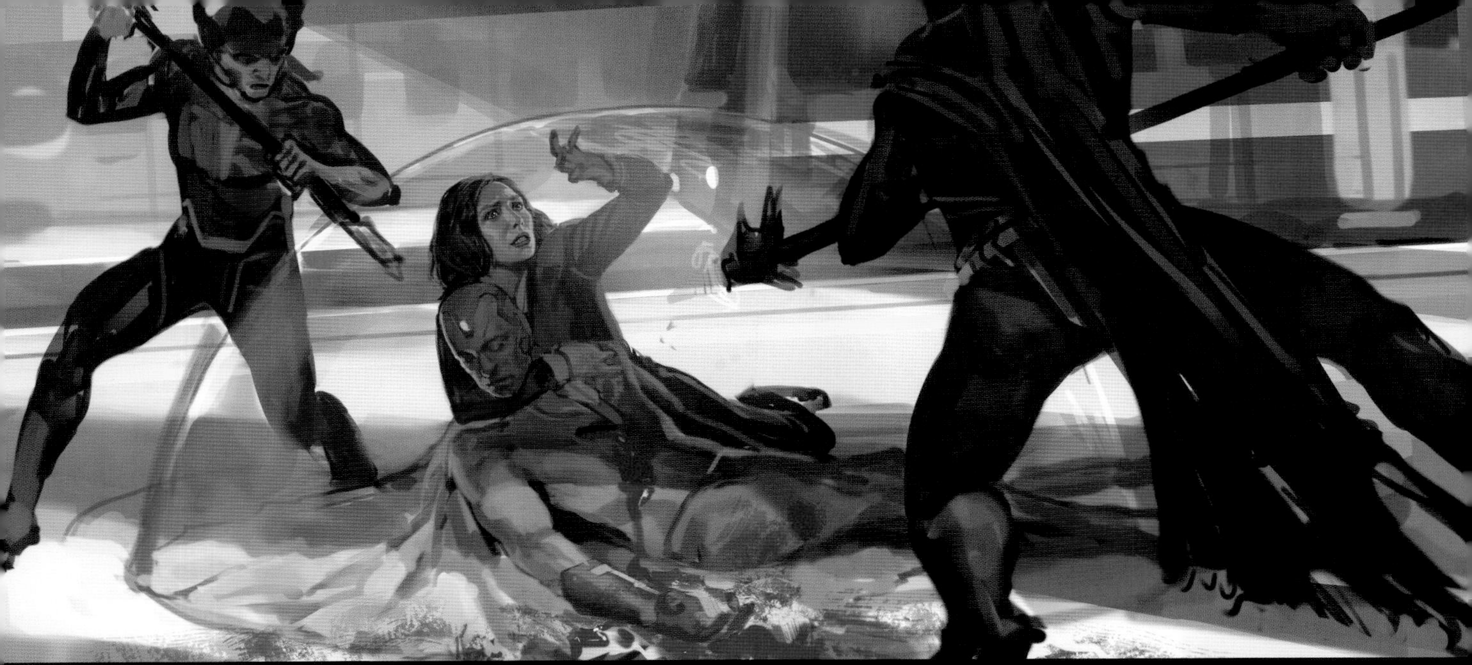

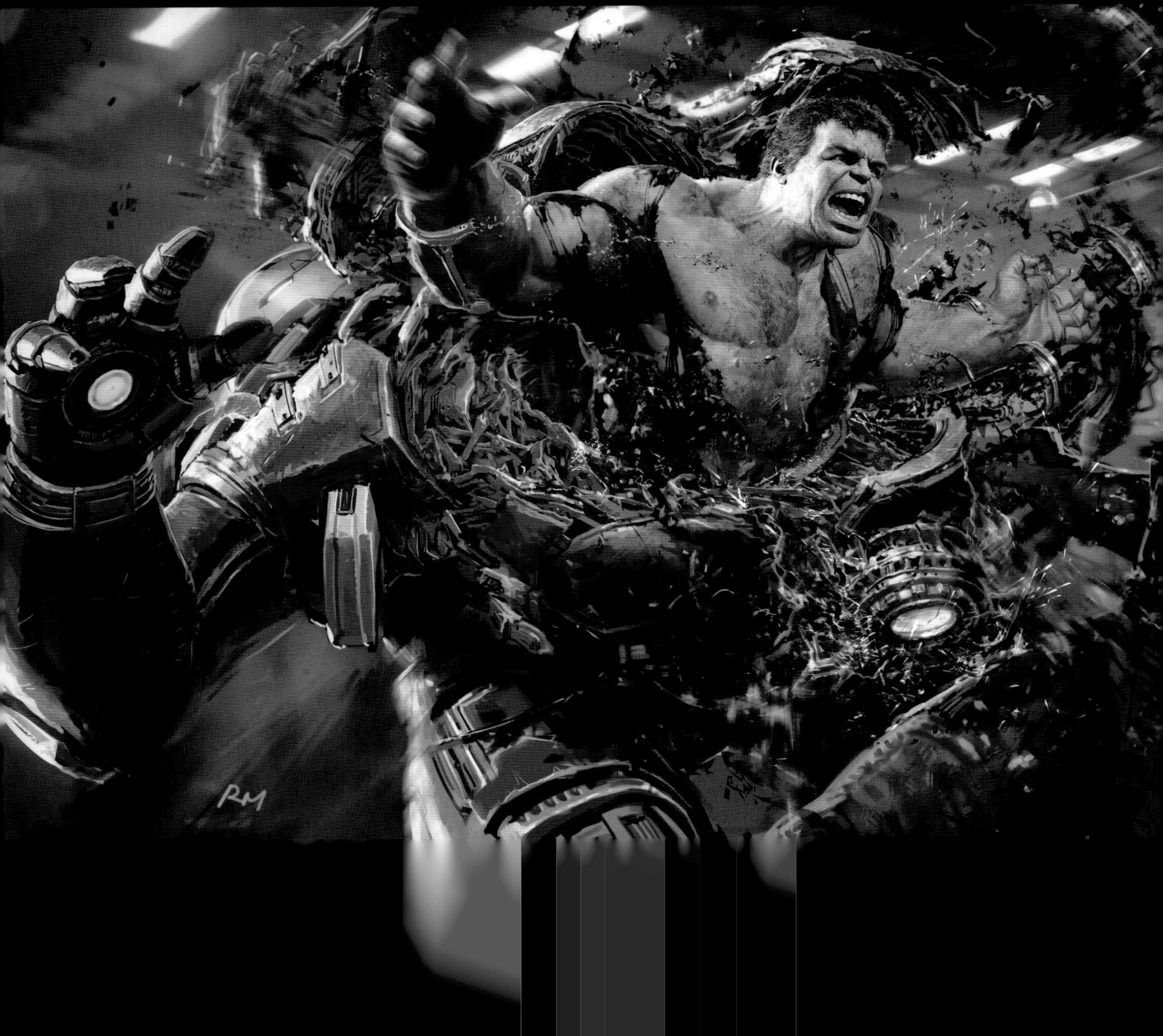
RM

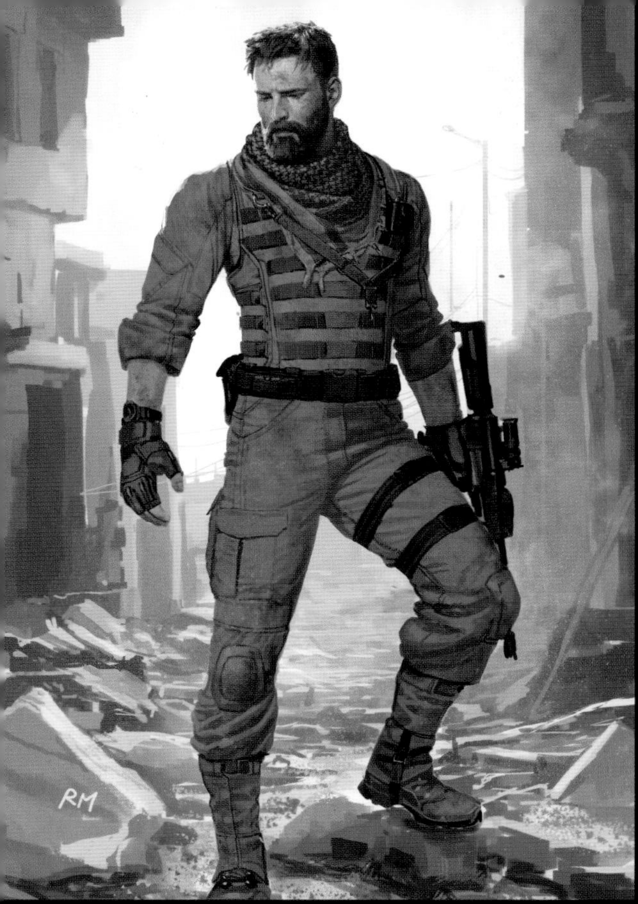
RM
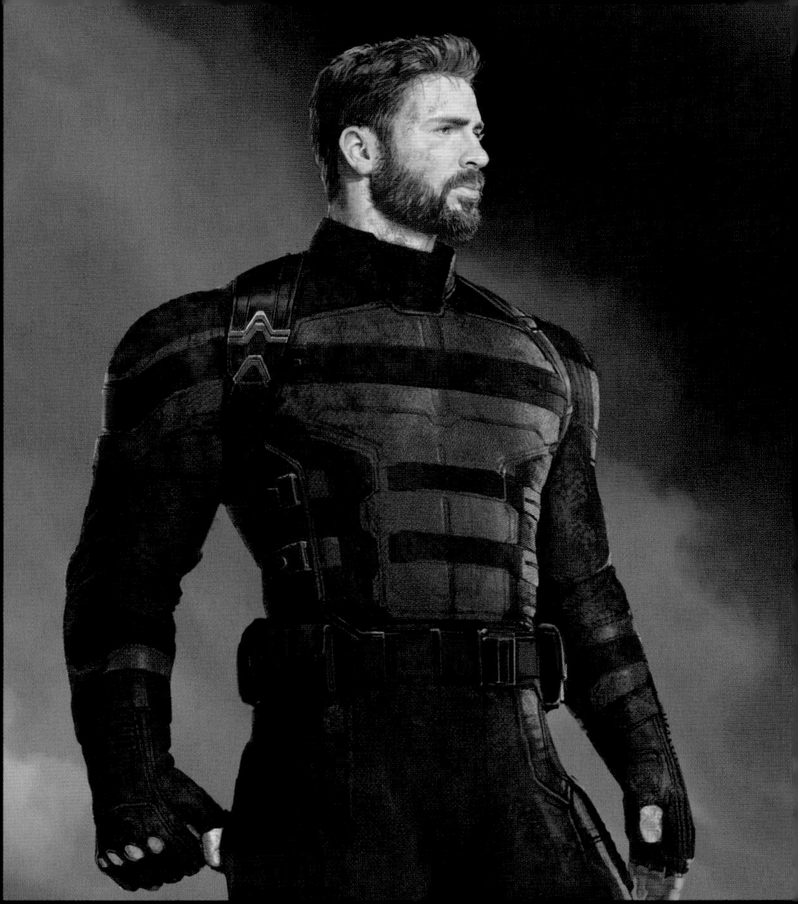
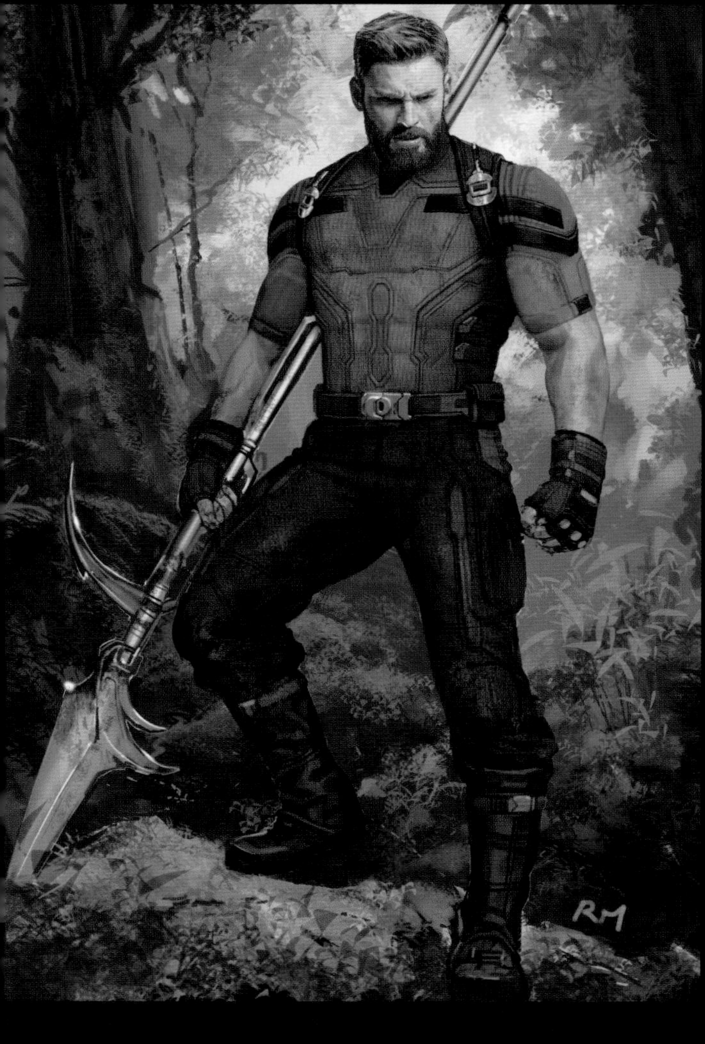
RM
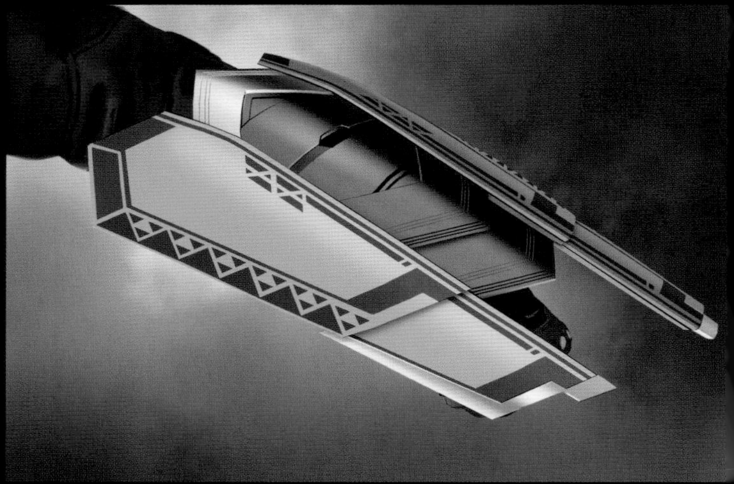
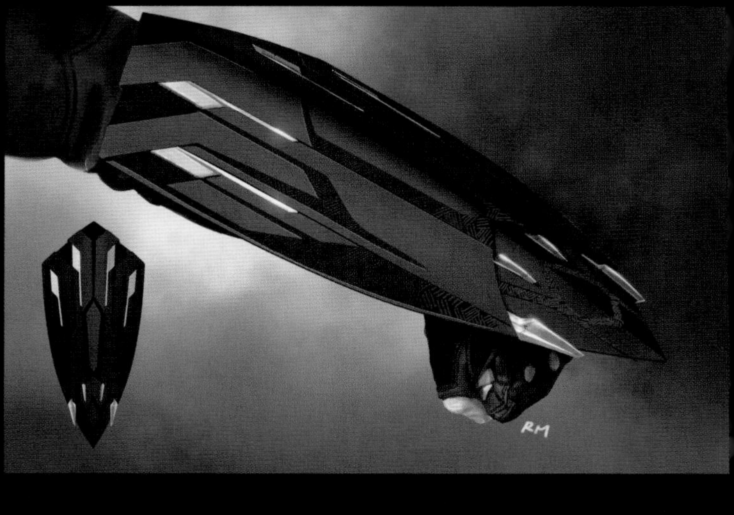
RM

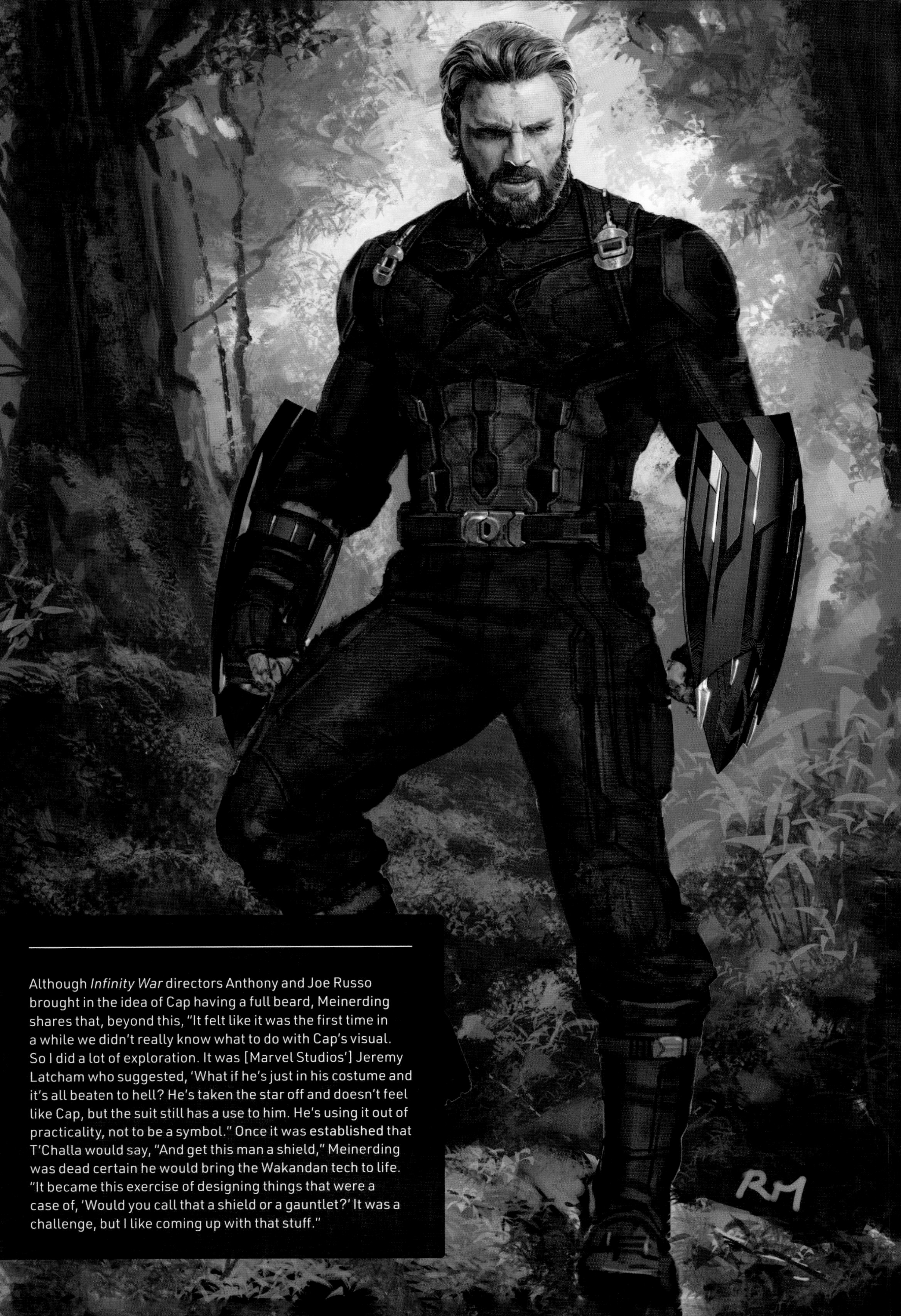
RM

Although *Infinity War* directors Anthony and Joe Russo brought in the idea of Cap having a full beard, Meinerding shares that, beyond this, "It felt like it was the first time in a while we didn't really know what to do with Cap's visual. So I did a lot of exploration. It was [Marvel Studios'] Jeremy Latcham who suggested, 'What if he's just in his costume and it's all beaten to hell? He's taken the star off and doesn't feel like Cap, but the suit still has a use to him. He's using it out of practicality, not to be a symbol." Once it was established that T'Challa would say, "And get this man a shield," Meinerding was dead certain he would bring the Wakandan tech to life. "It became this exercise of designing things that were a case of, 'Would you call that a shield or a gauntlet?' It was a challenge, but I like coming up with that stuff."

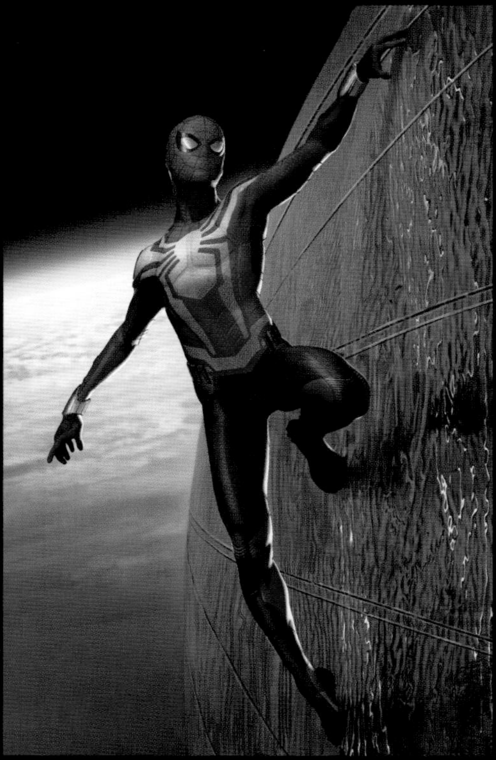

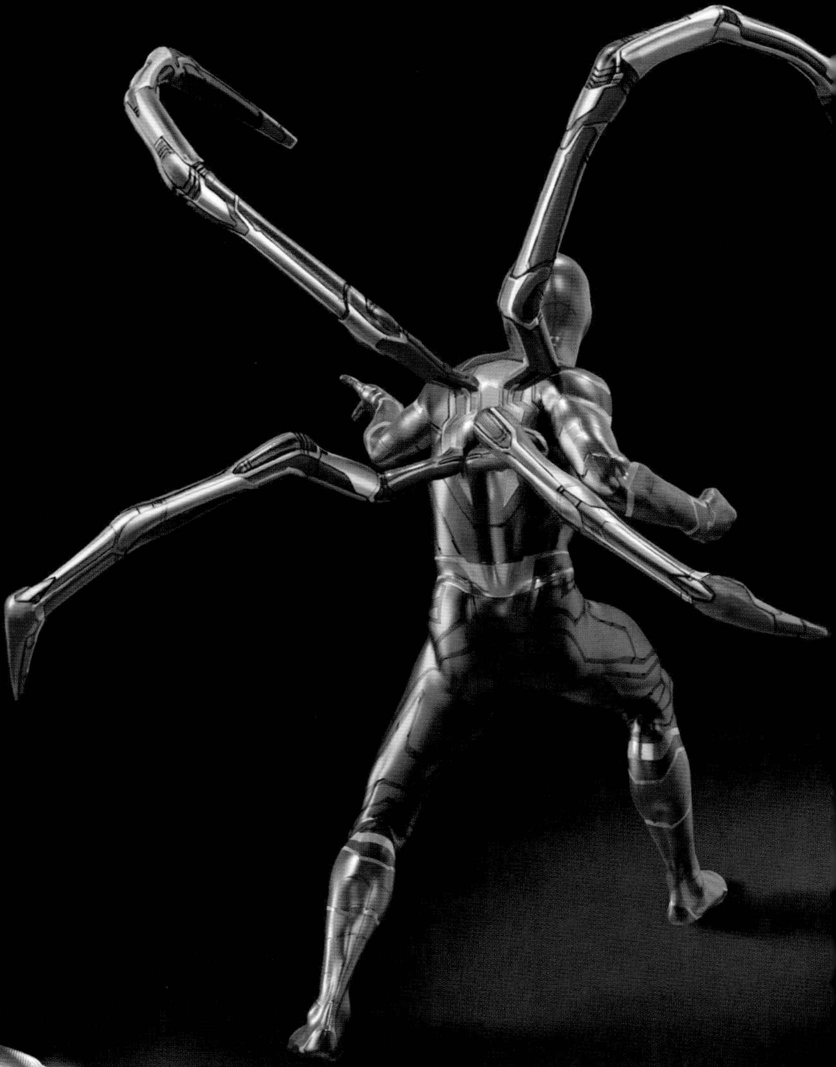

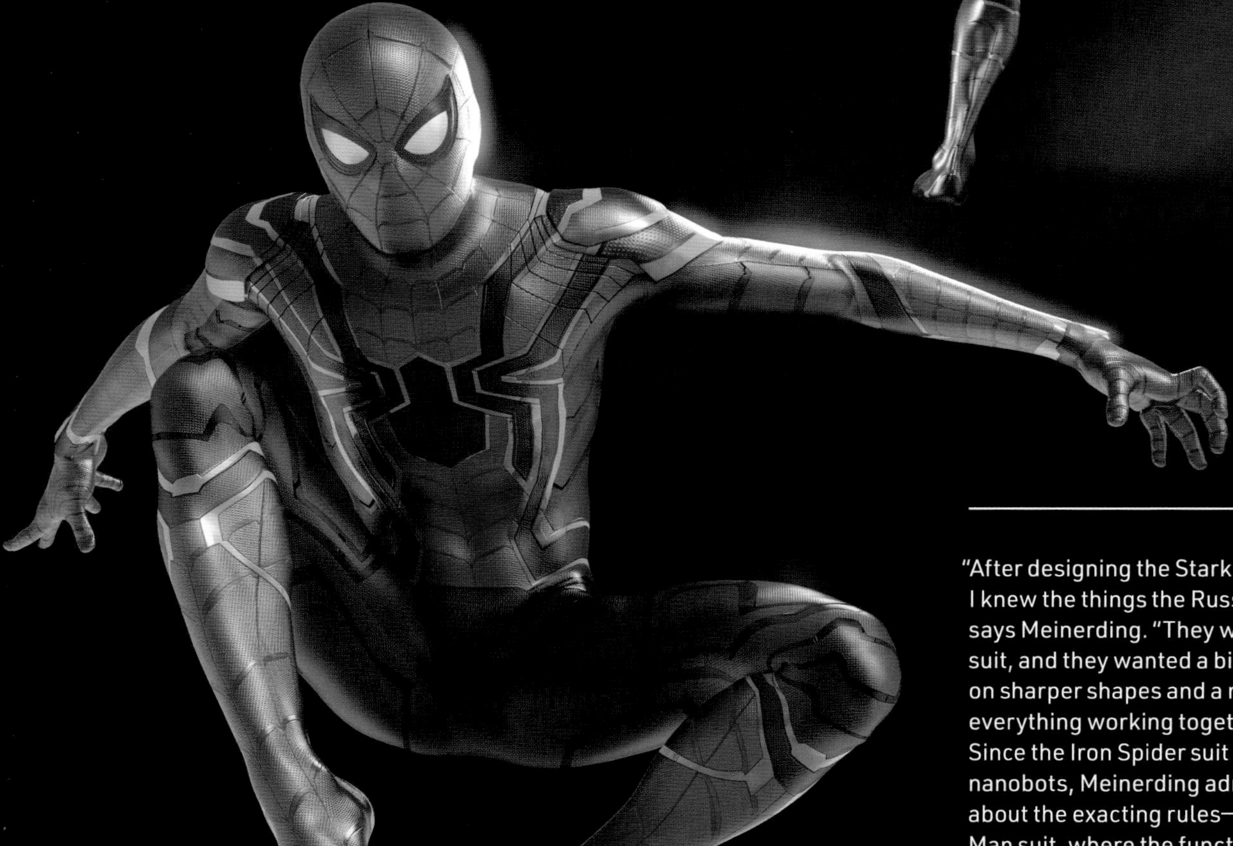

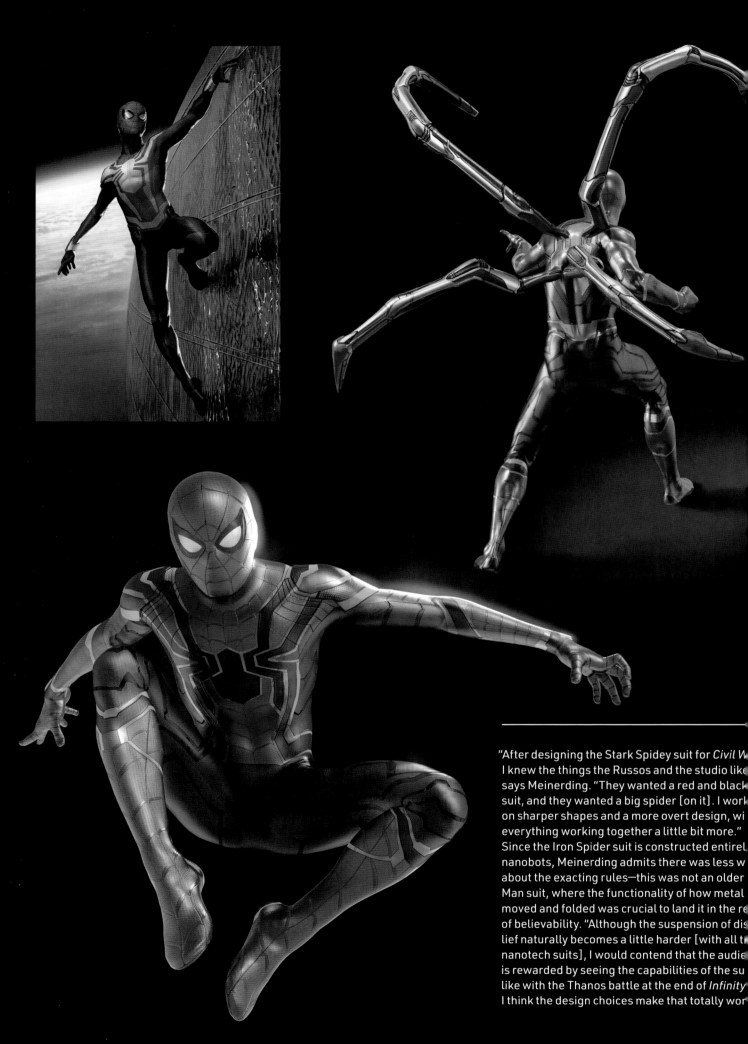

"After designing the Stark Spidey suit for *Civil W*
I knew the things the Russos and the studio like
says Meinerding. "They wanted a red and black
suit, and they wanted a big spider [on it]. I work
on sharper shapes and a more overt design, wi
everything working together a little bit more."
Since the Iron Spider suit is constructed entirel
nanobots, Meinerding admits there was less w
about the exacting rules—this was not an older
Man suit, where the functionality of how metal
moved and folded was crucial to land it in the re
of believability. "Although the suspension of dis
lief naturally becomes a little harder [with all t
nanotech suits], I would contend that the audie
is rewarded by seeing the capabilities of the su
like with the Thanos battle at the end of *Infinity*
I think the design choices make that totally wor

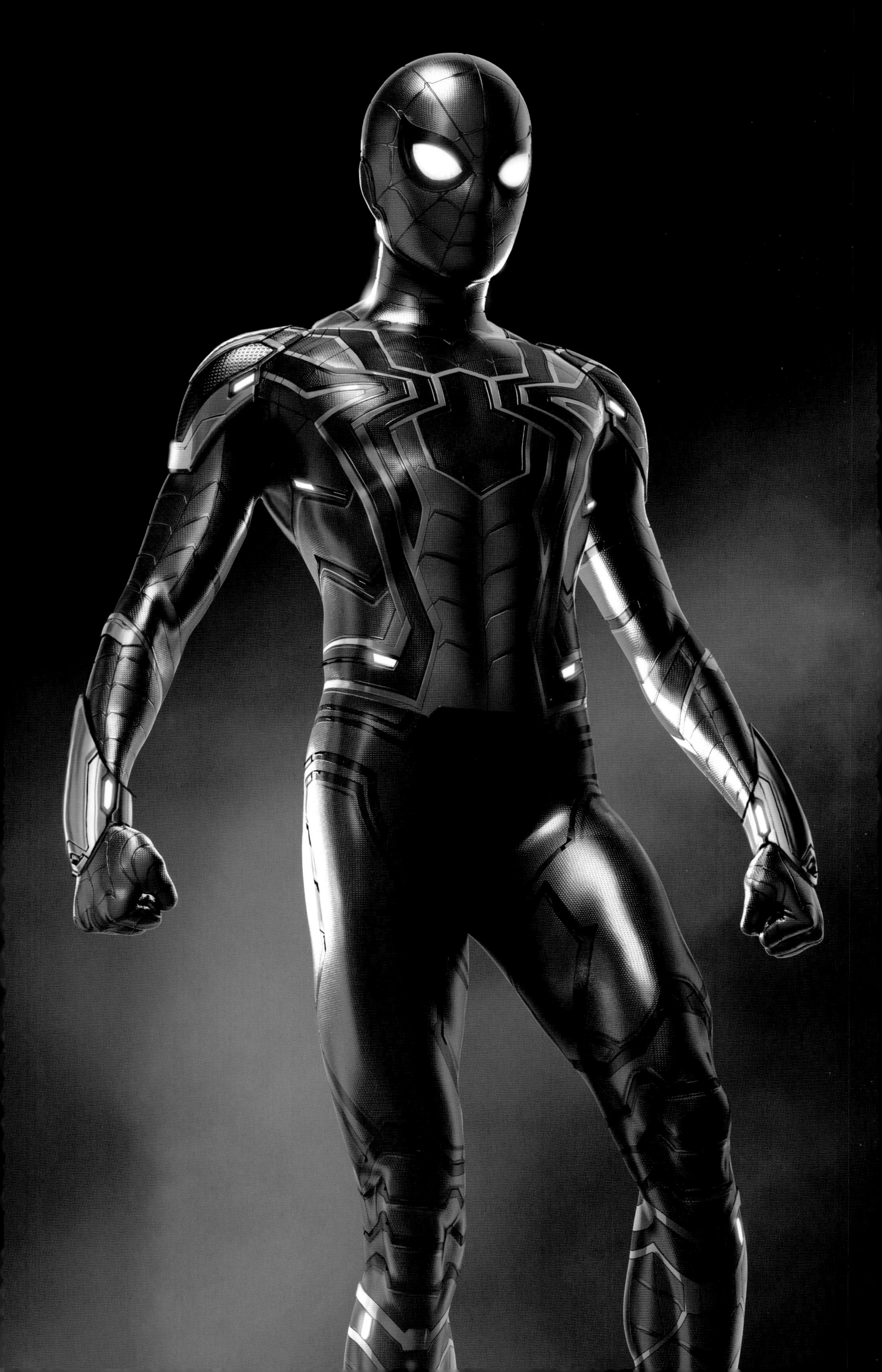

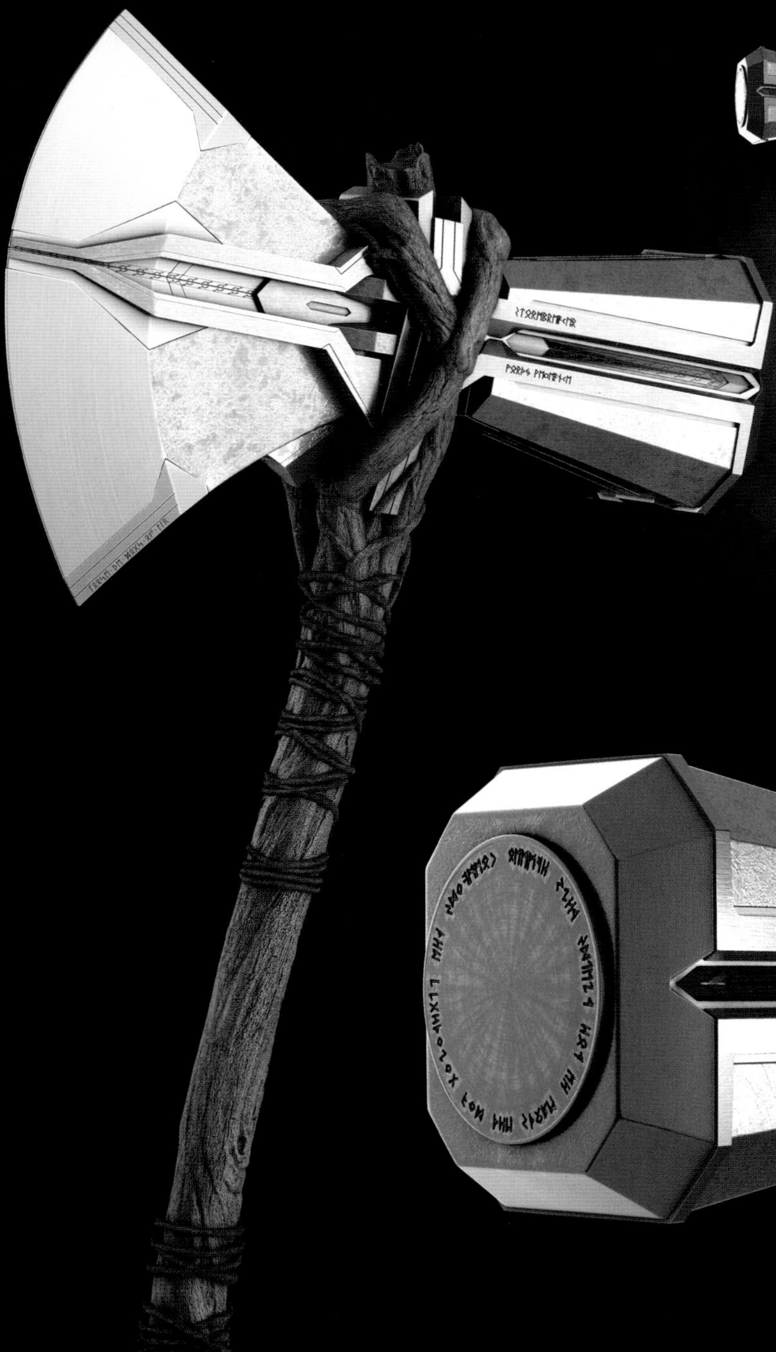

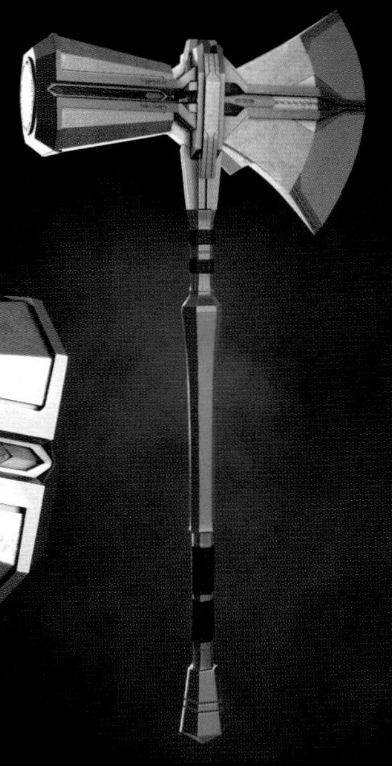

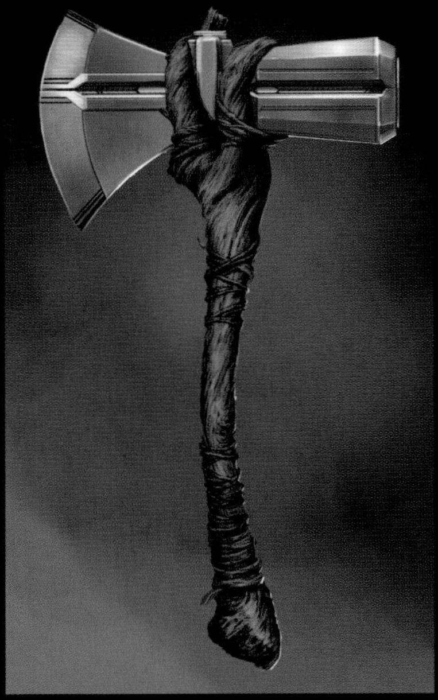

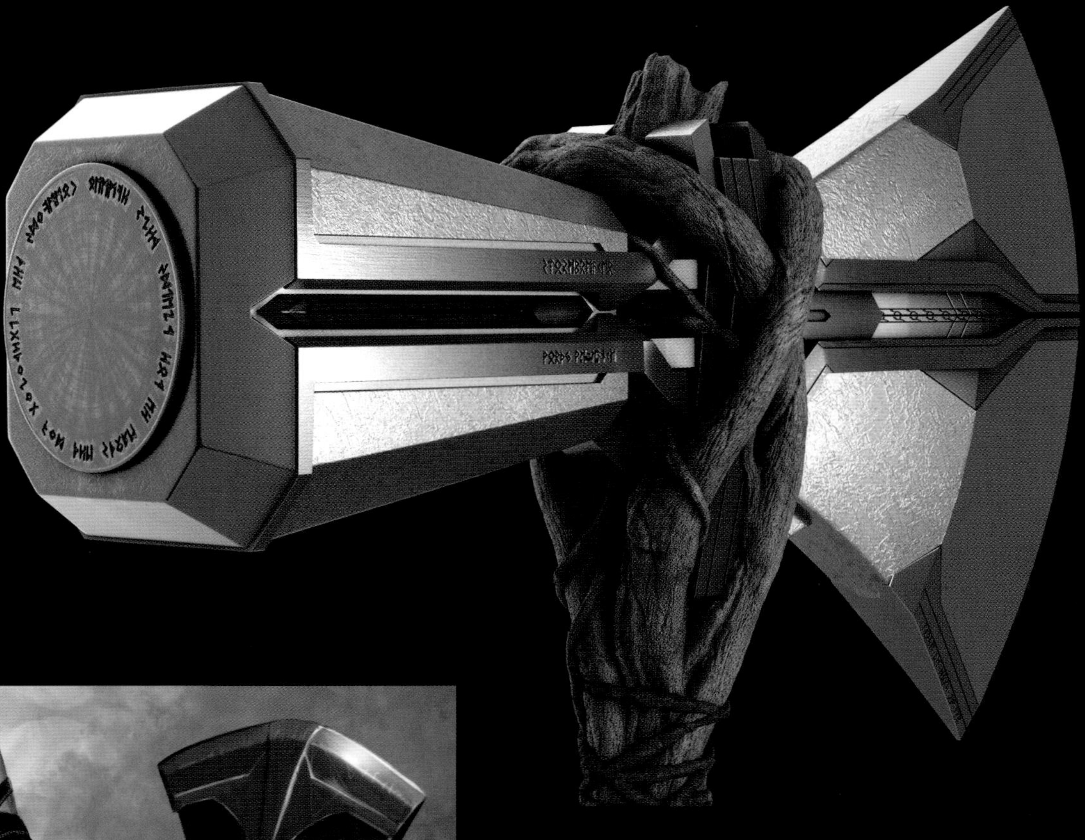

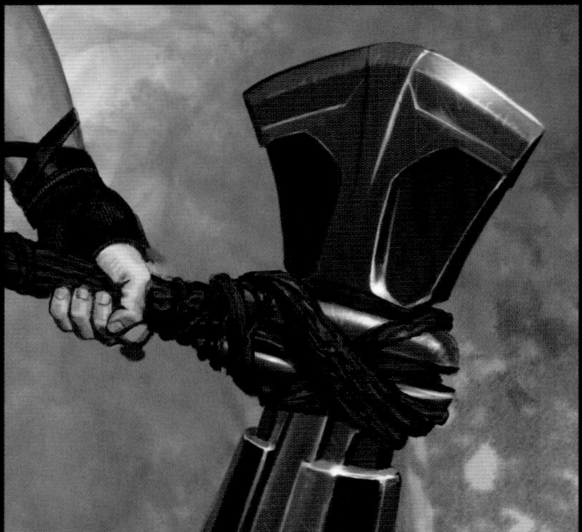

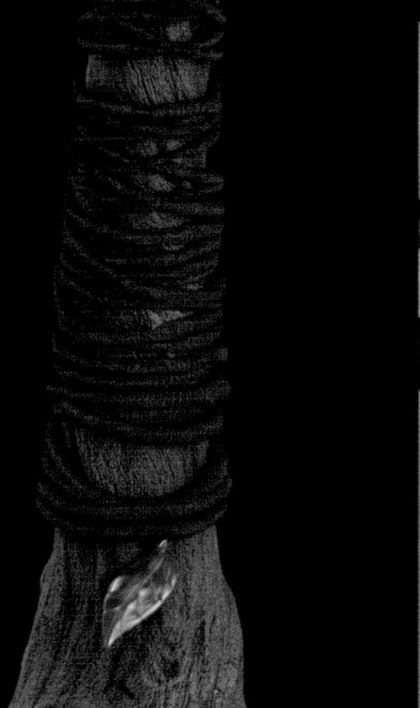

"If I was gonna work on Thor, I *had* to work on the weapon," says Meinerding about how passionate he was to get the opportunity to design Thor with Stormbreaker. "Even if it's sort of the most simplified version of him, I really enjoyed working on this version of Thor."

THIS PAGE Additional 3D modeling for Stormbreaker was done by Adam Ross.

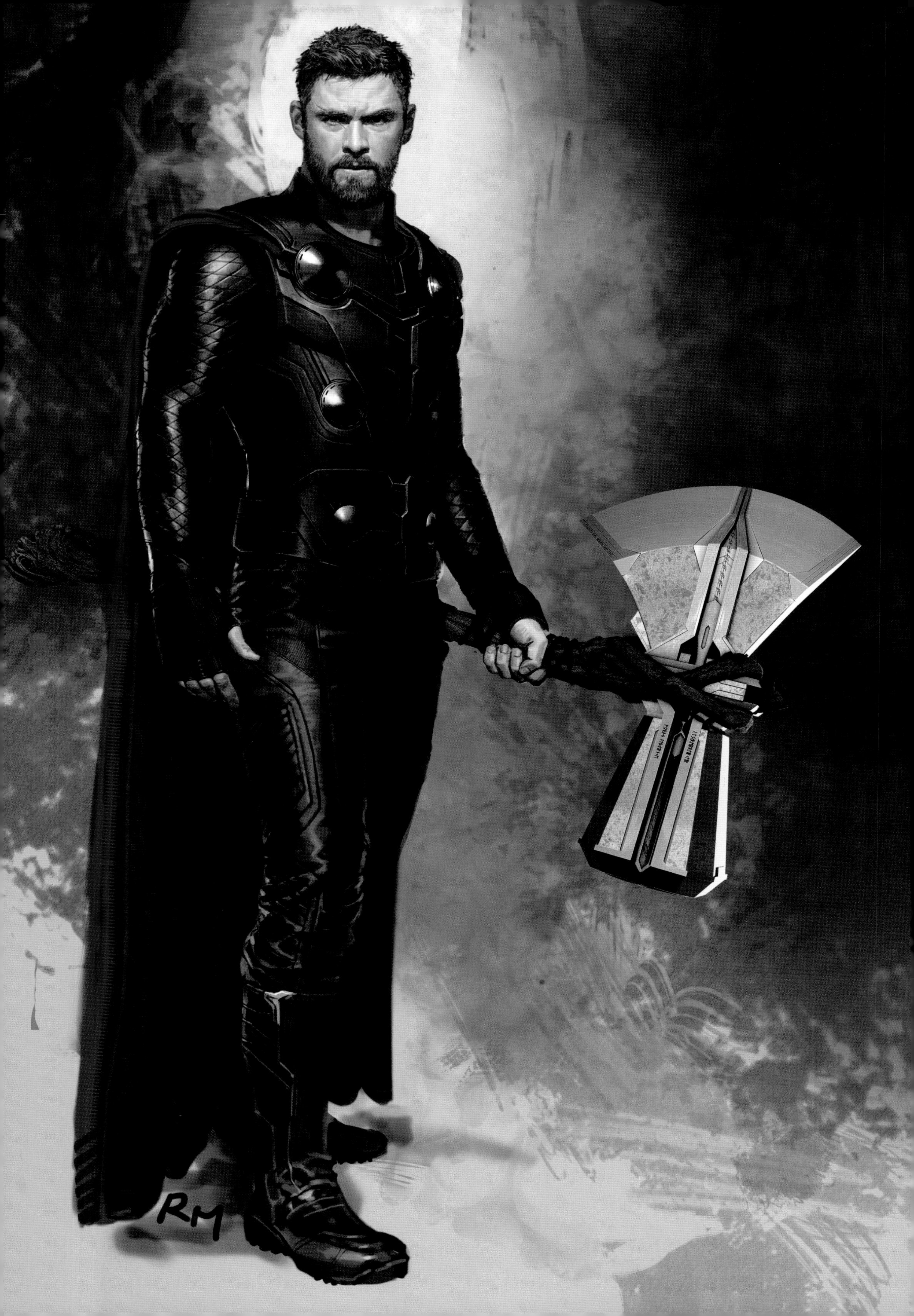
RM

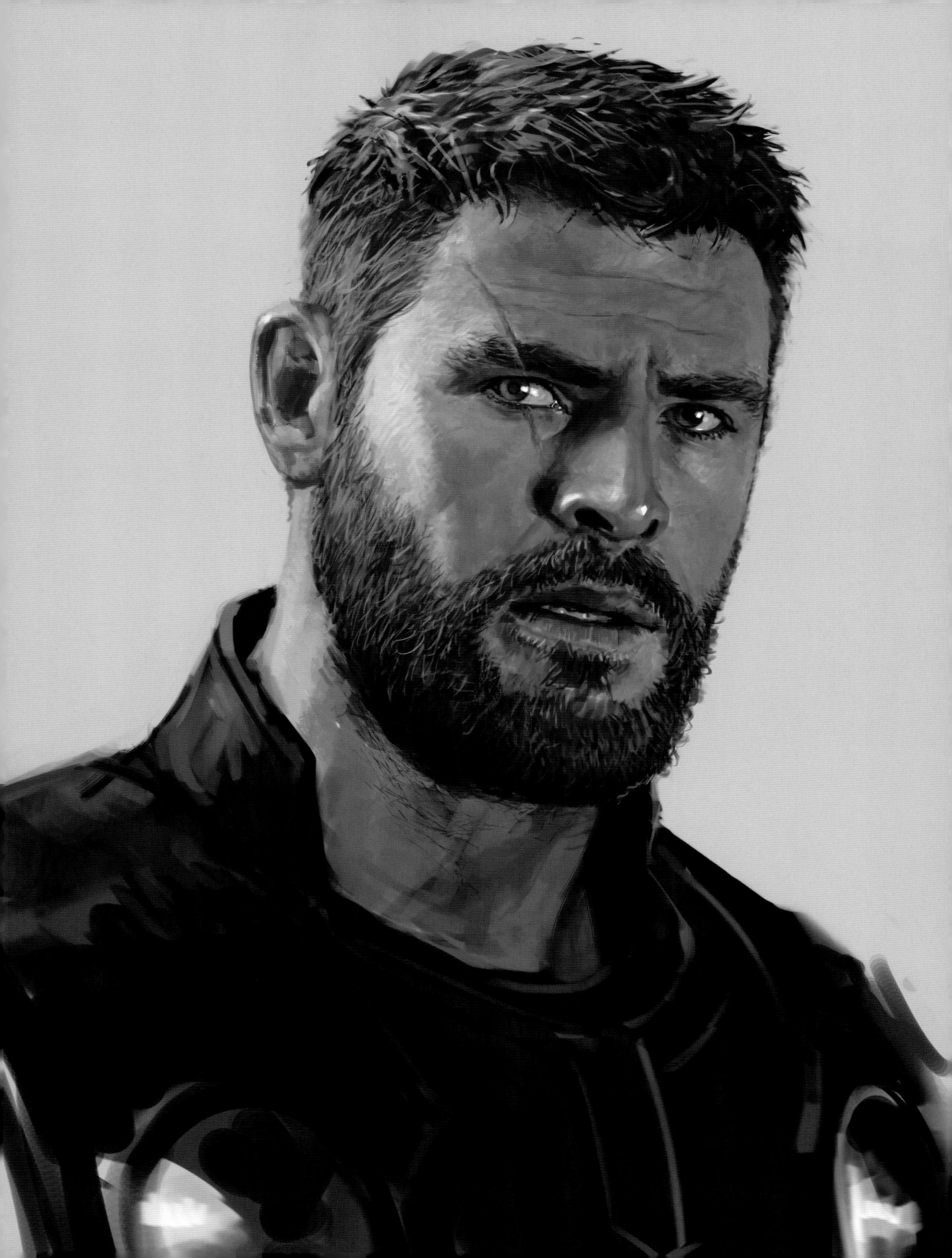

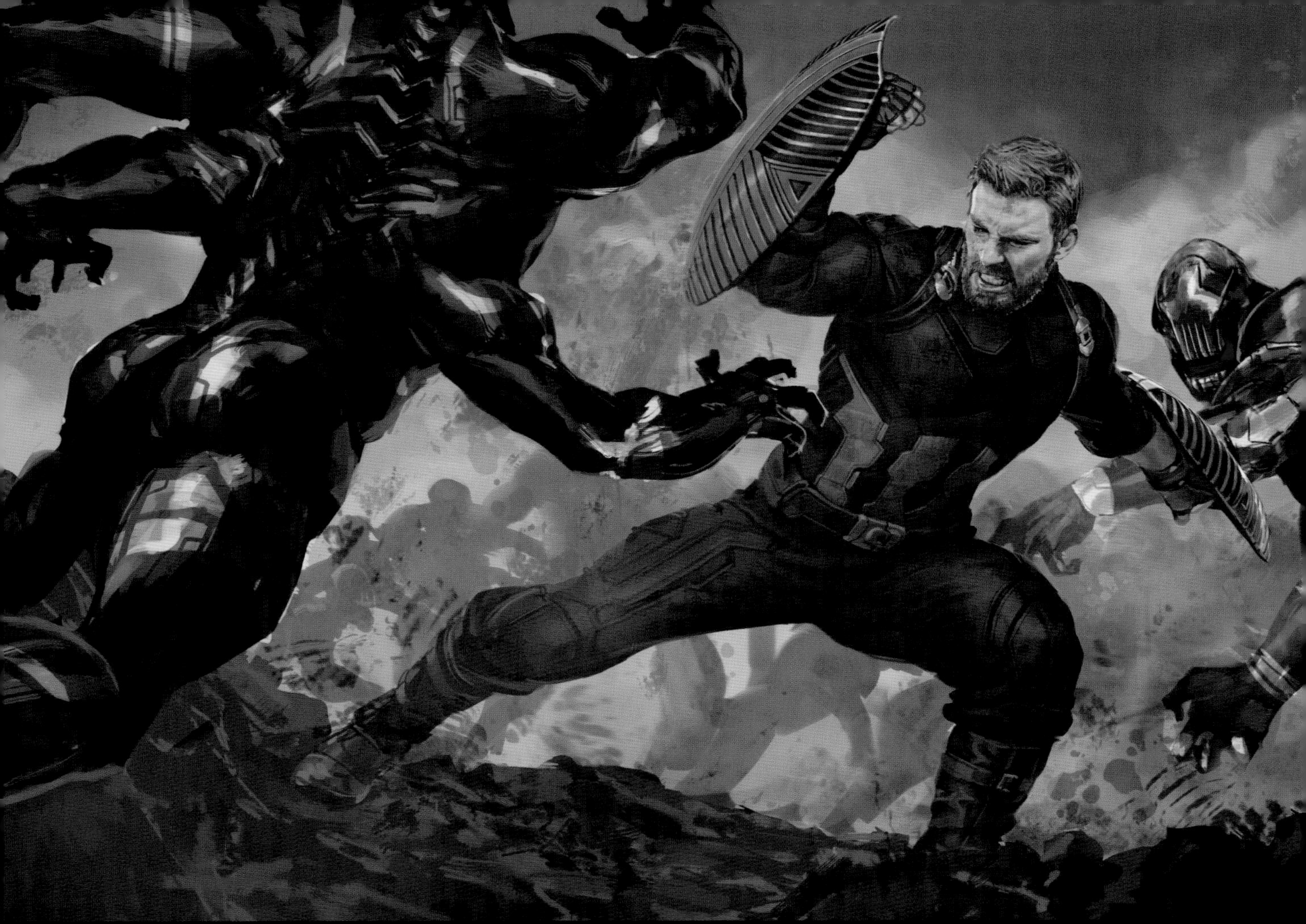

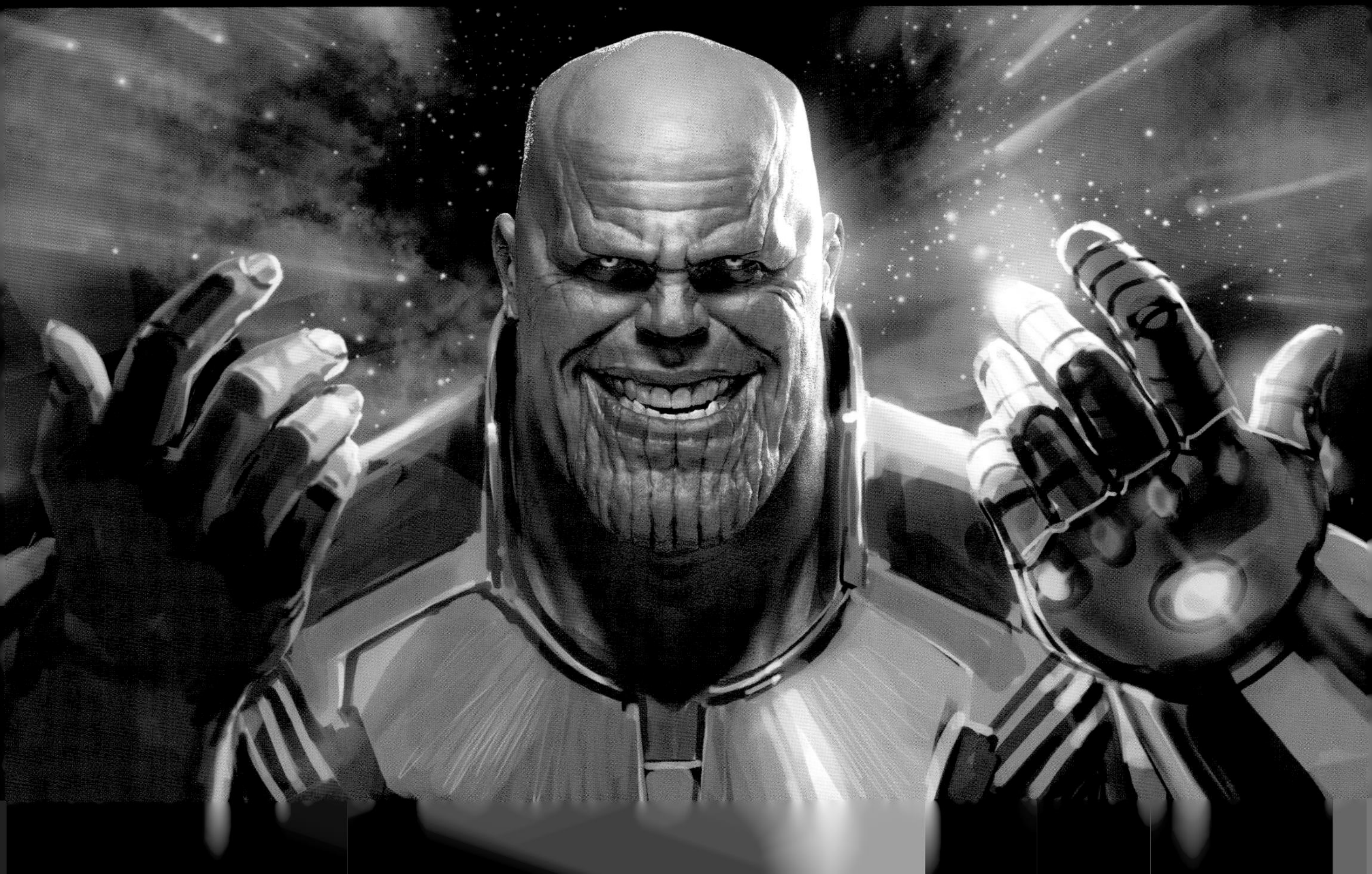

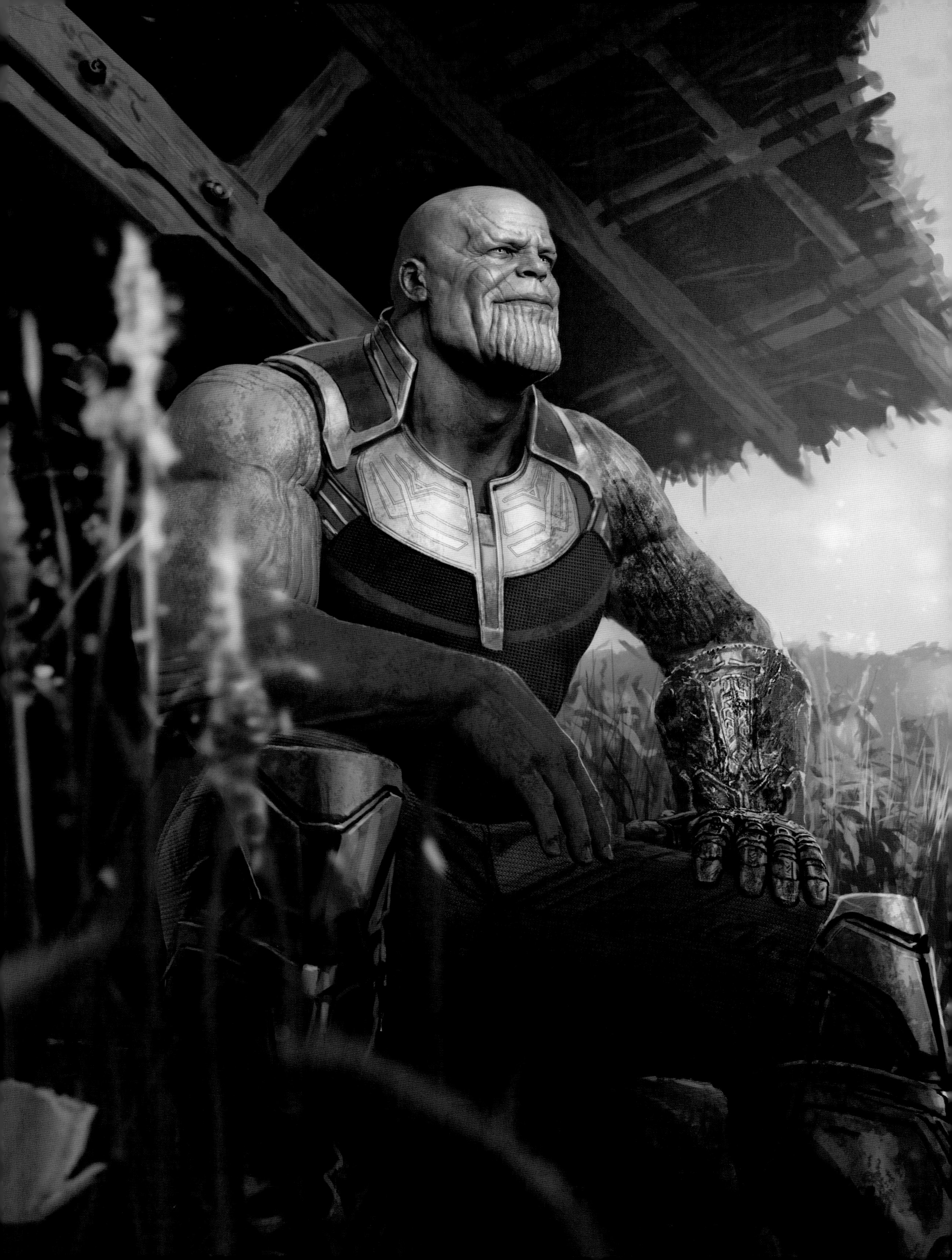

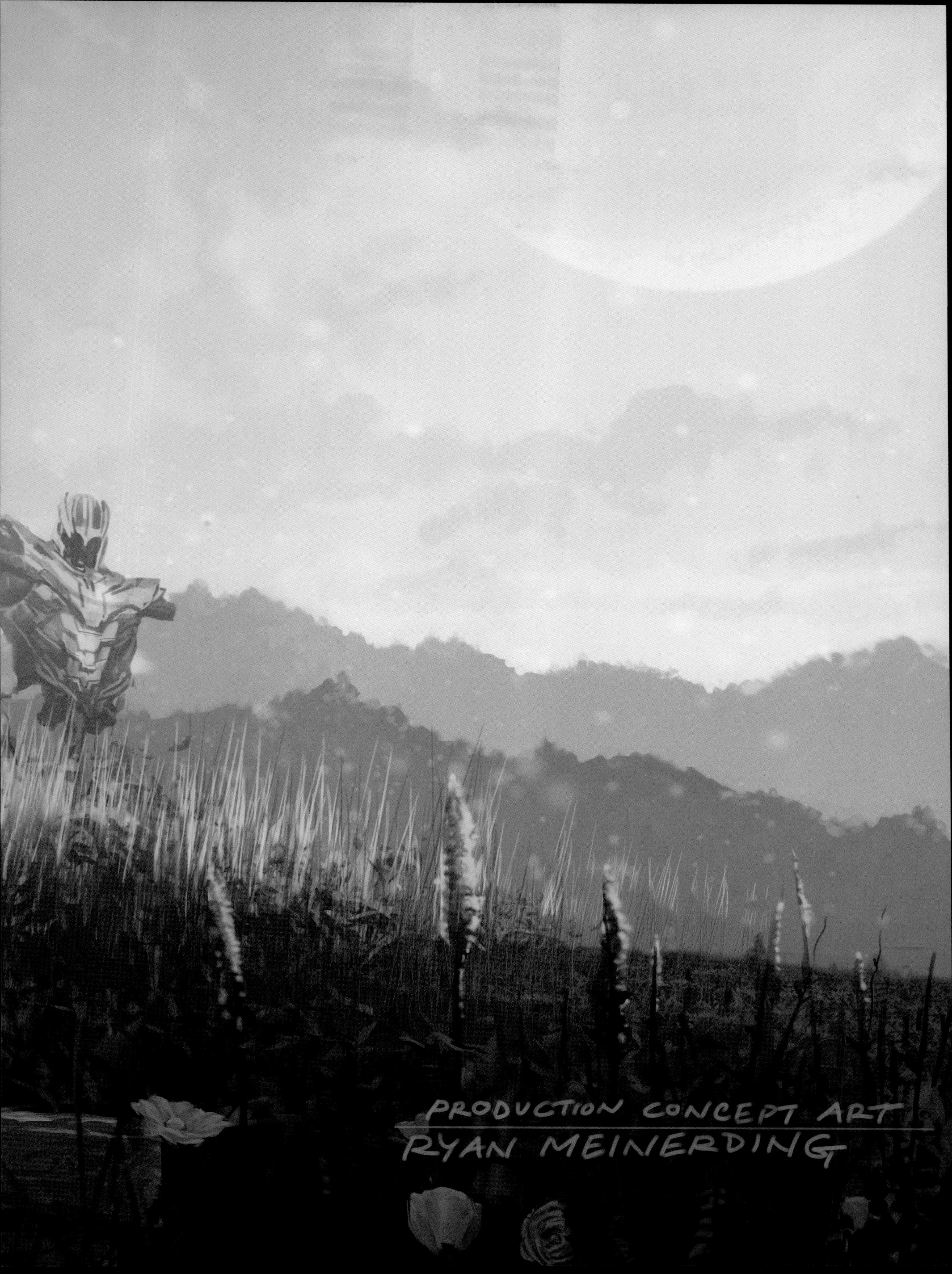
PRODUCTION CONCEPT ART
RYAN MEINERDING

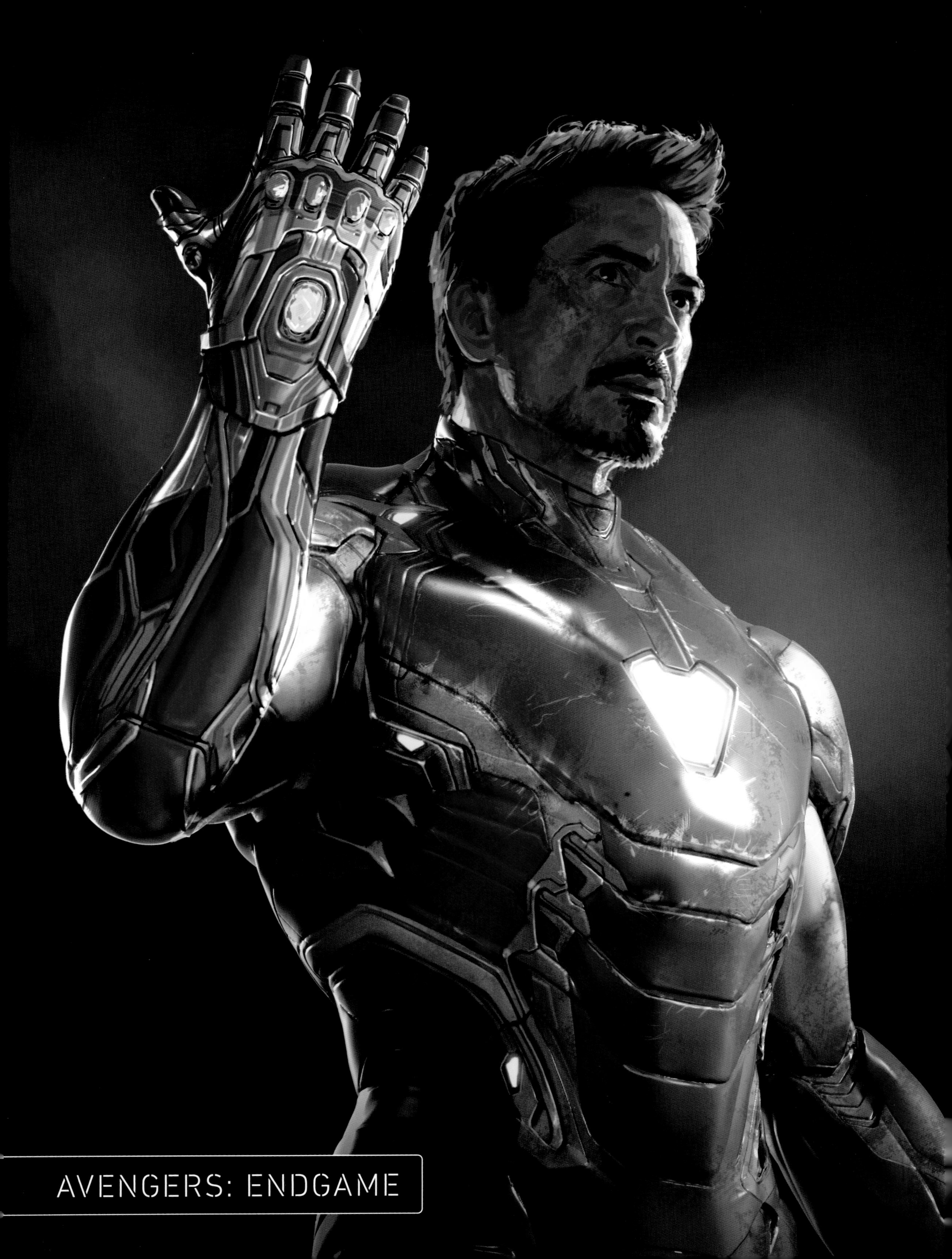

AVENGERS: ENDGAME

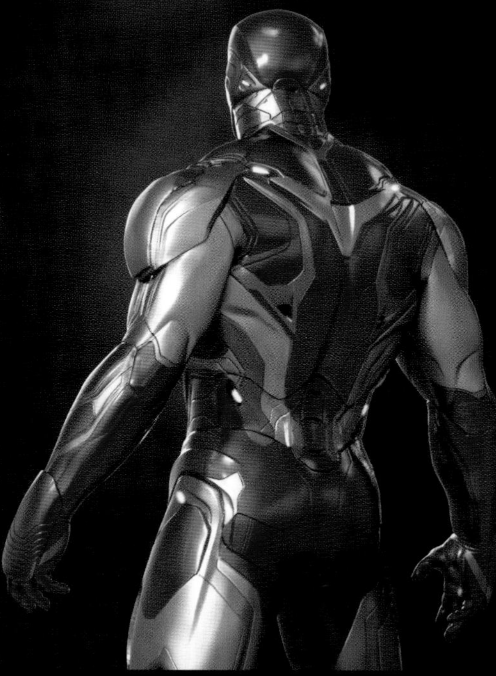

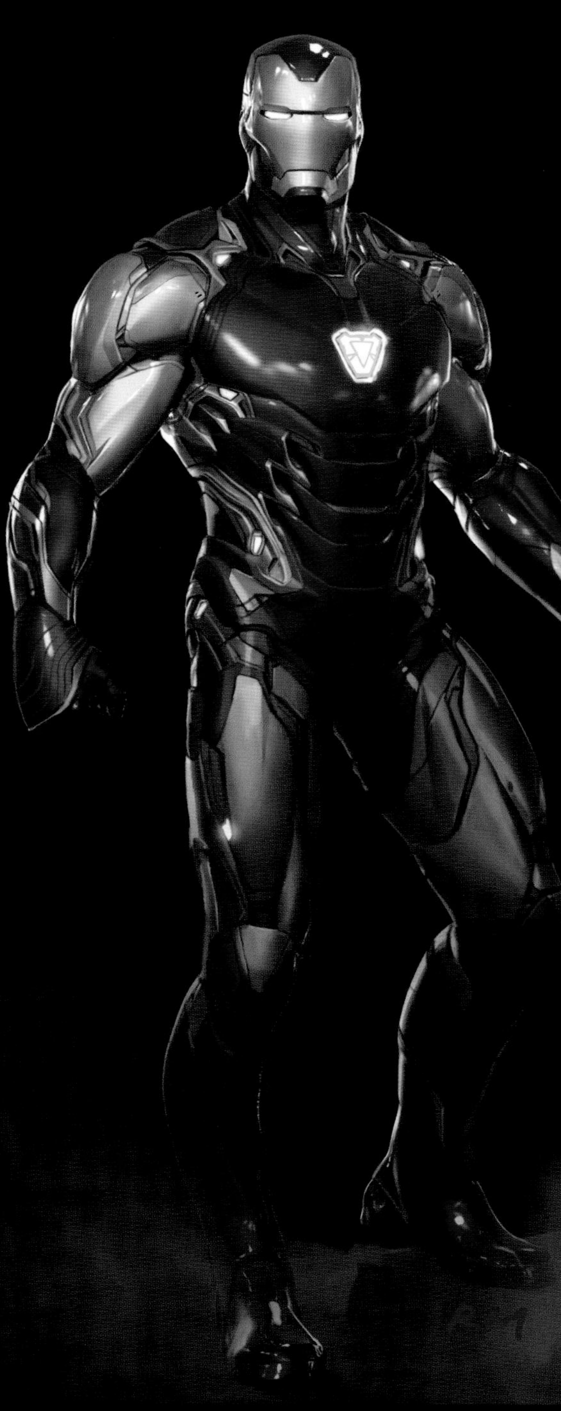

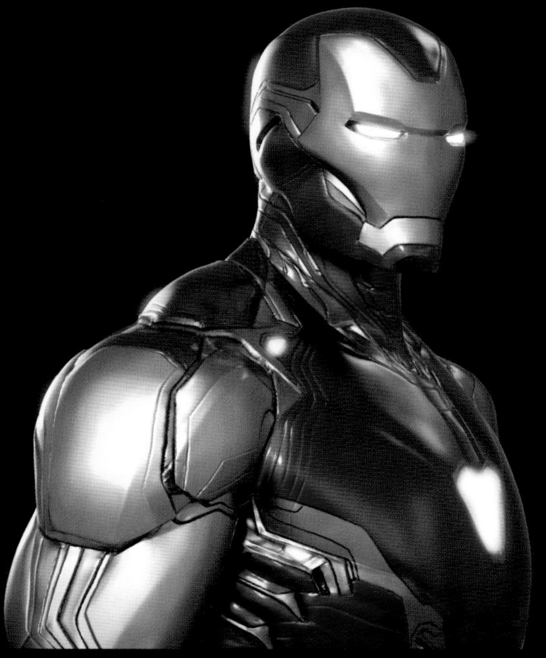

The Mark LXXXV was the final Iron Man armor Tony Stark created. Meinerding admits, "Just the idea that I got to design Tony's first suit—the Mark I in the cave—as well as his last suit, was amazing, and emotional." Because Phil Saunders designed the Mark L nanotech suit for *Infinity War*, Meinerding got in touch with him to collaborate on the Mark LXXXV. "Phil had some ideas from the Mark L era that he was excited about exploring more, rather than trying to do something that was a radical reinvention of the nanotech look." For the first presentation of designs, they reskinned the Mark L, changed a few things, but kept the same visual language. "Then I did another version that was more like a classic muscle breakup—close to the one on the top right with the gold shoulders and thighs. I love the Mark L, but its form language is clearly supposed to read as like a liquid metal." The Russos and Kevin [Feige] liked Meinerding's idea of making the Mark LXXXV have the look and feel of muscle, like a classic Iron Man suit from the comics, but still read as advanced technology. "It was a labor of love, but I'm really excited with how it turned out. It's probably my favorite Iron Man design I've done. I love the Mark I because its cobbled together and feels rough and practical. And it's the first thing I ever really got to work on for film. But the Mark LXXXV feels like I was able to take everything that I'd learned since I'd been here working on all these movies, working with Phil, working with all the different artists, and put it into that suit. I'm still excited by it."

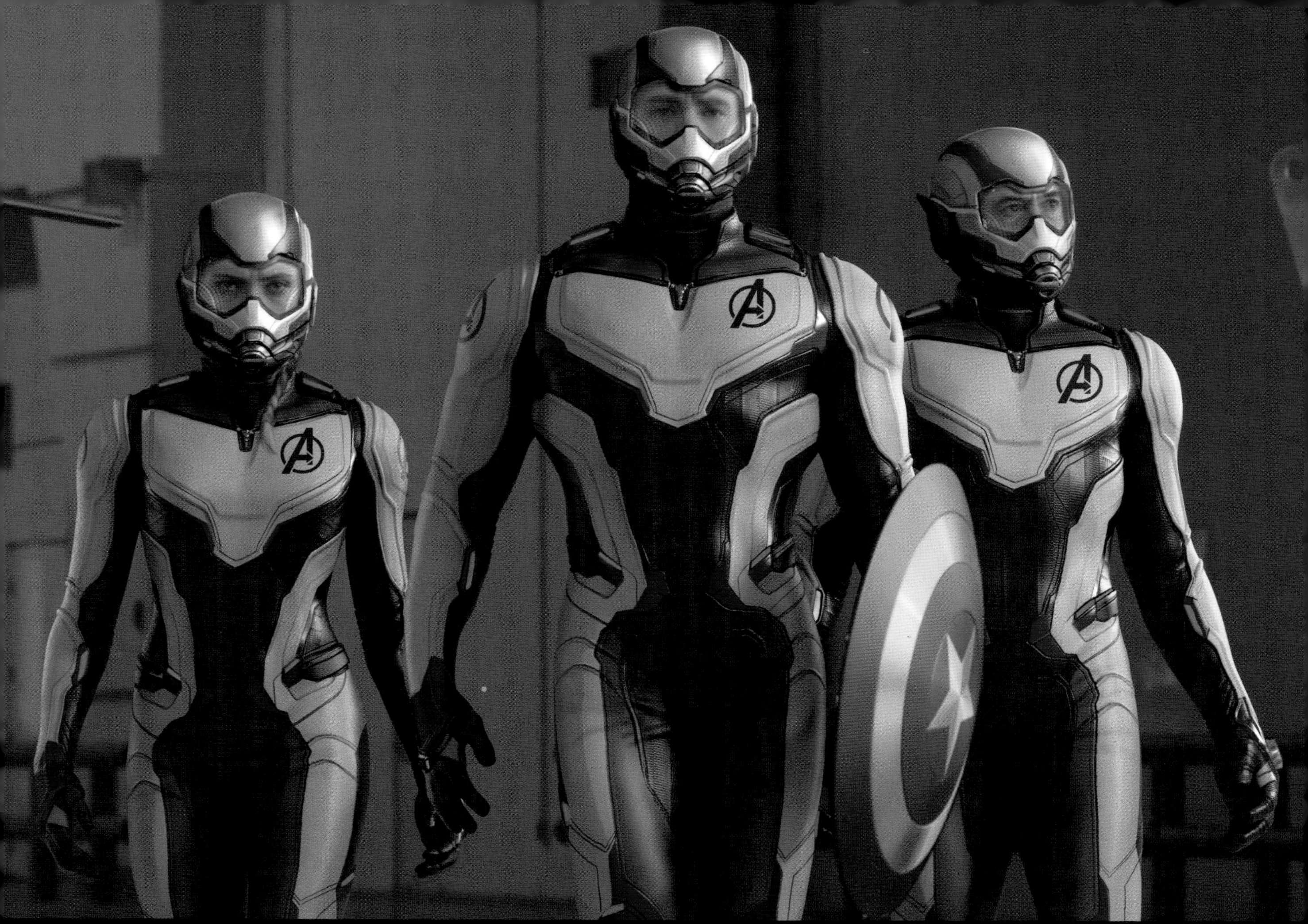

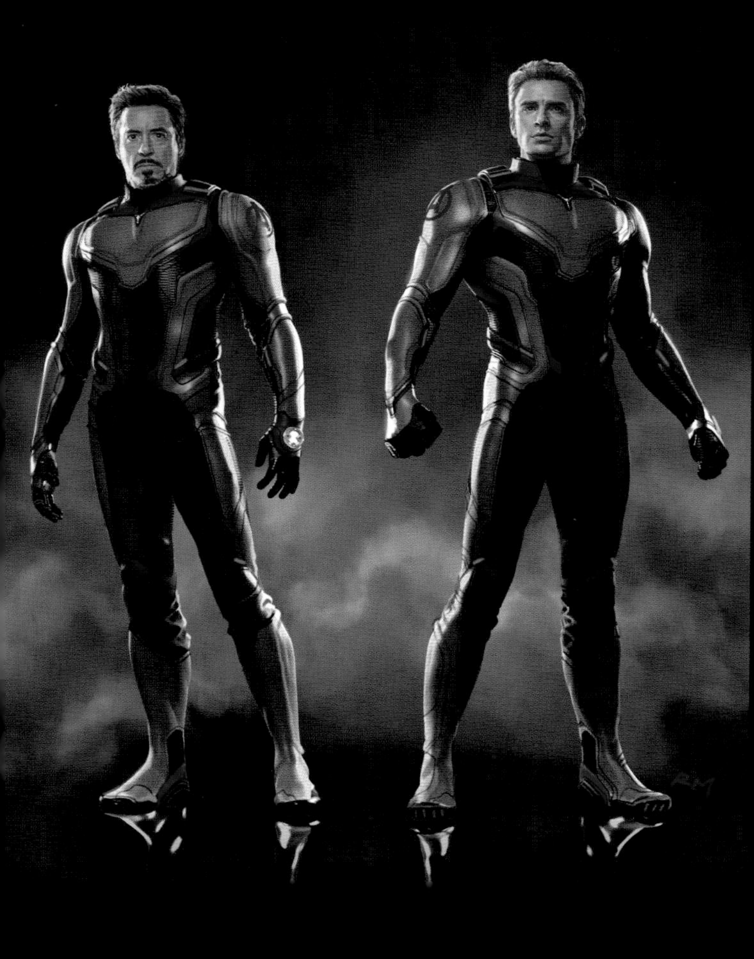

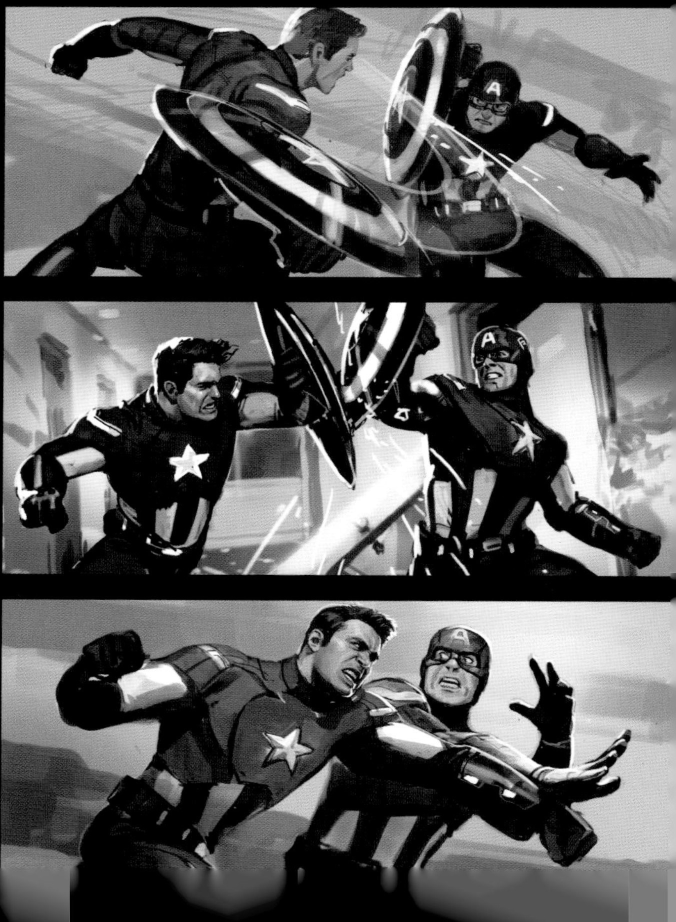

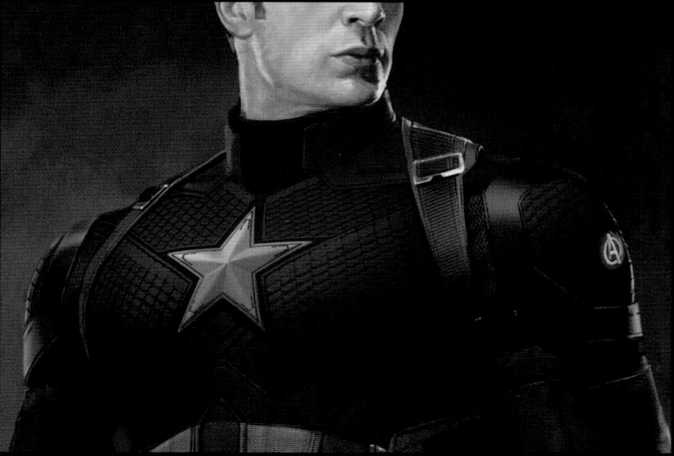

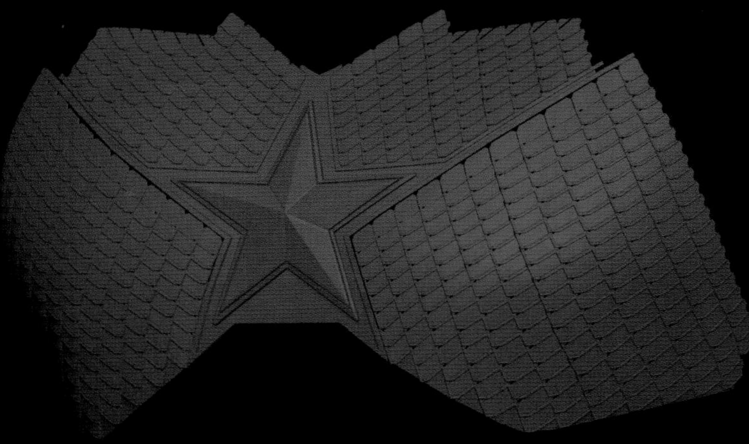

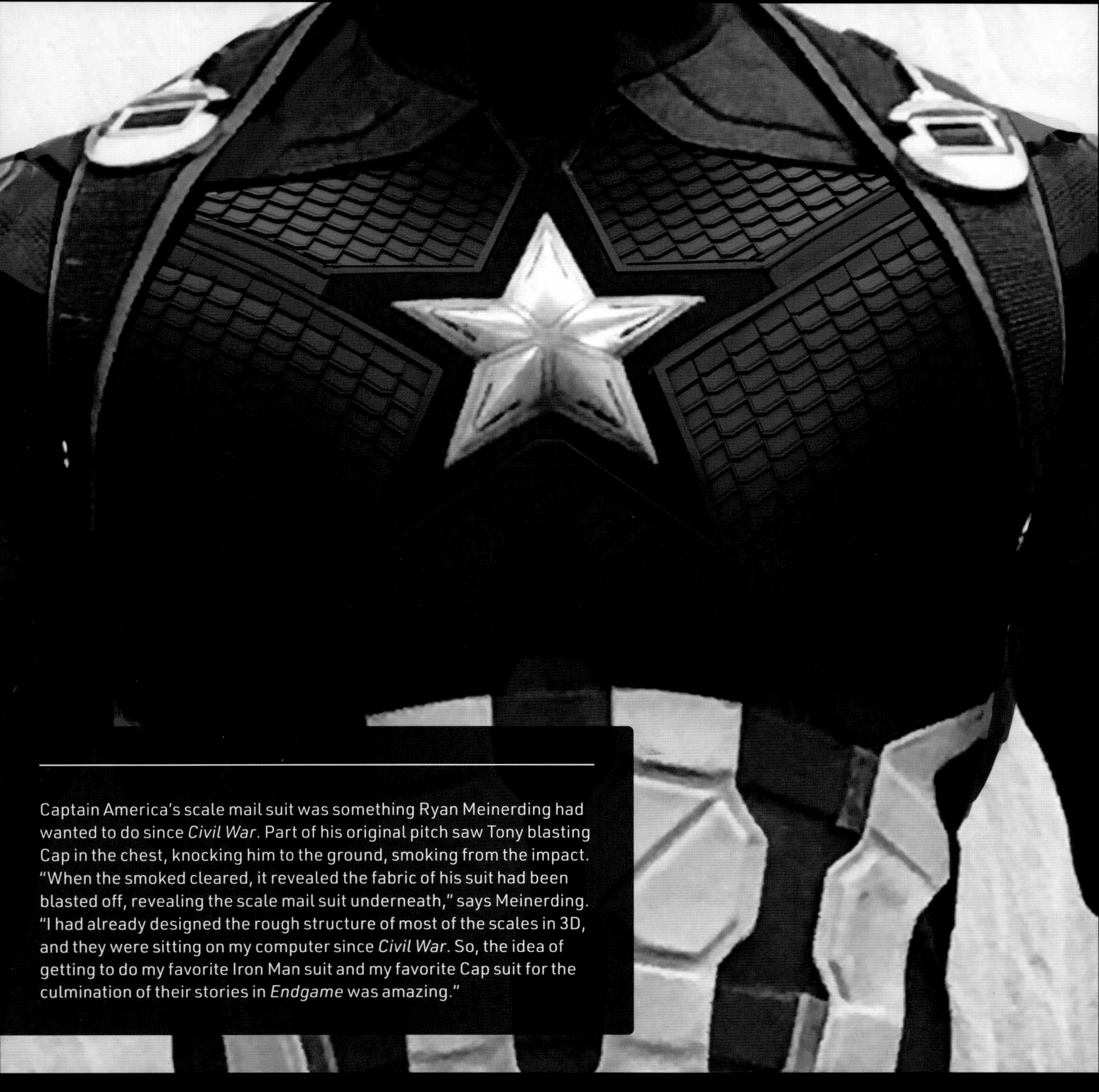

Captain America's scale mail suit was something Ryan Meinerding had wanted to do since *Civil War*. Part of his original pitch saw Tony blasting Cap in the chest, knocking him to the ground, smoking from the impact. "When the smoked cleared, it revealed the fabric of his suit had been blasted off, revealing the scale mail suit underneath," says Meinerding. "I had already designed the rough structure of most of the scales in 3D, and they were sitting on my computer since *Civil War*. So, the idea of getting to do my favorite Iron Man suit and my favorite Cap suit for the culmination of their stories in *Endgame* was amazing."

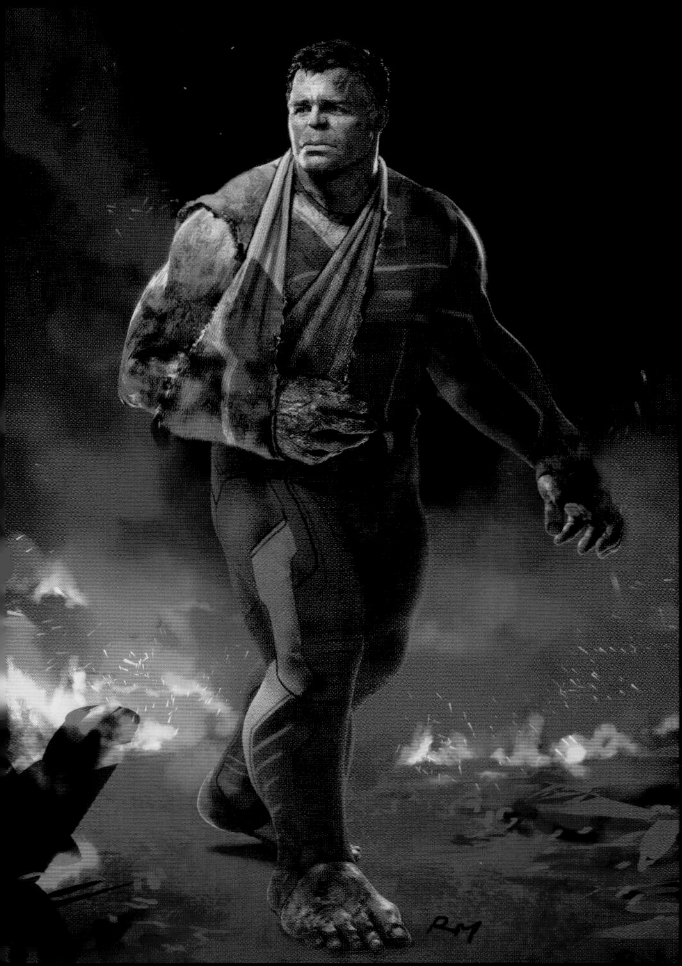
RM
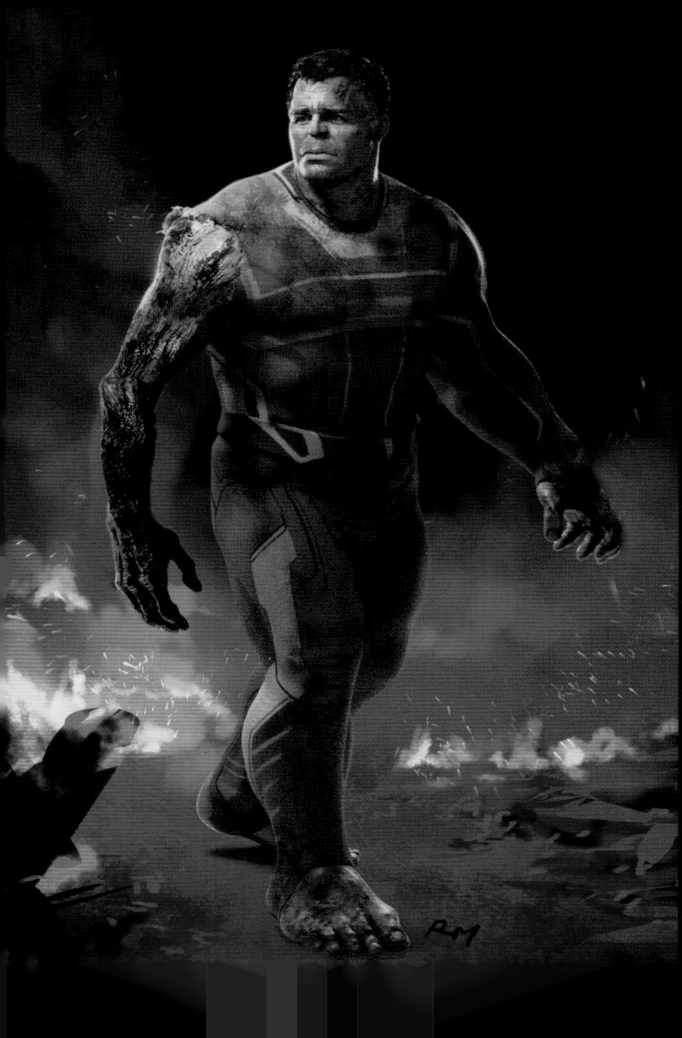
RM
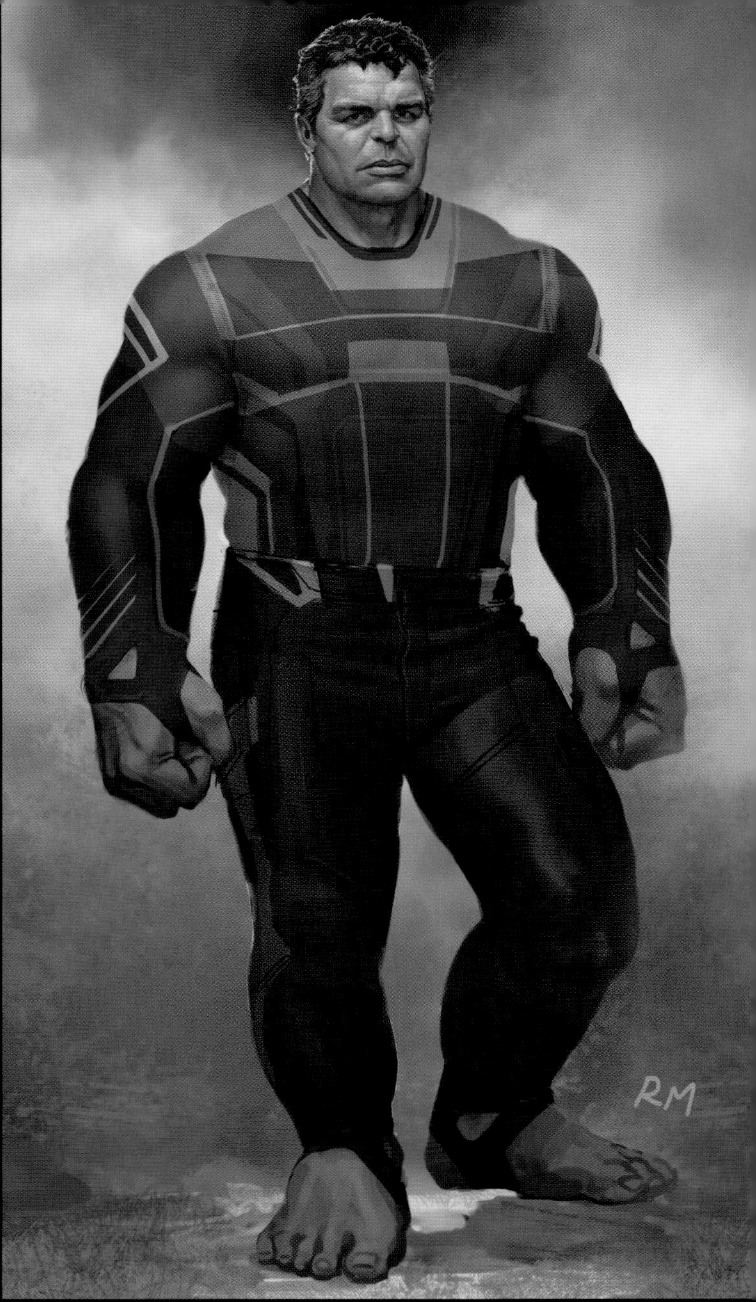
RM
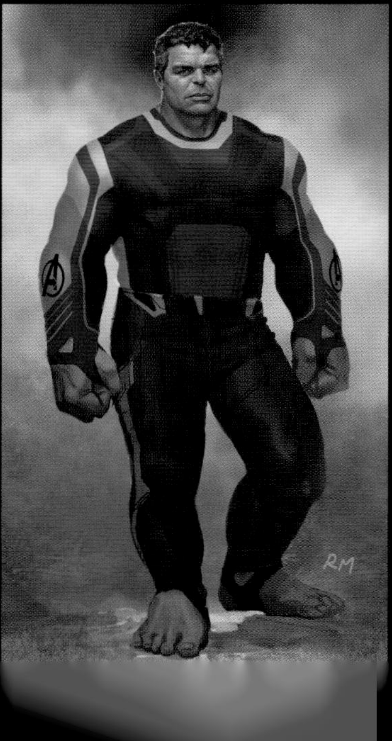
RM
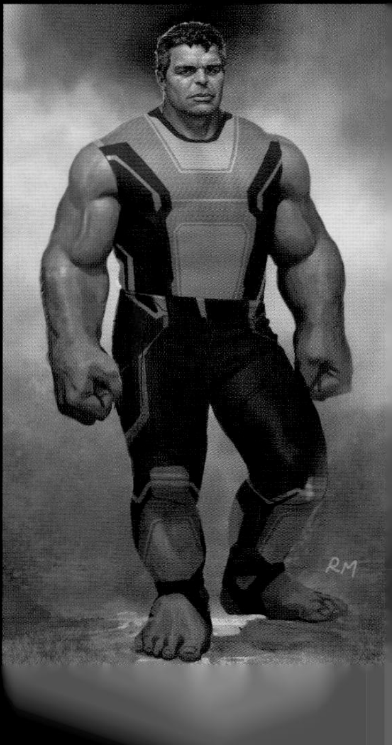
RM

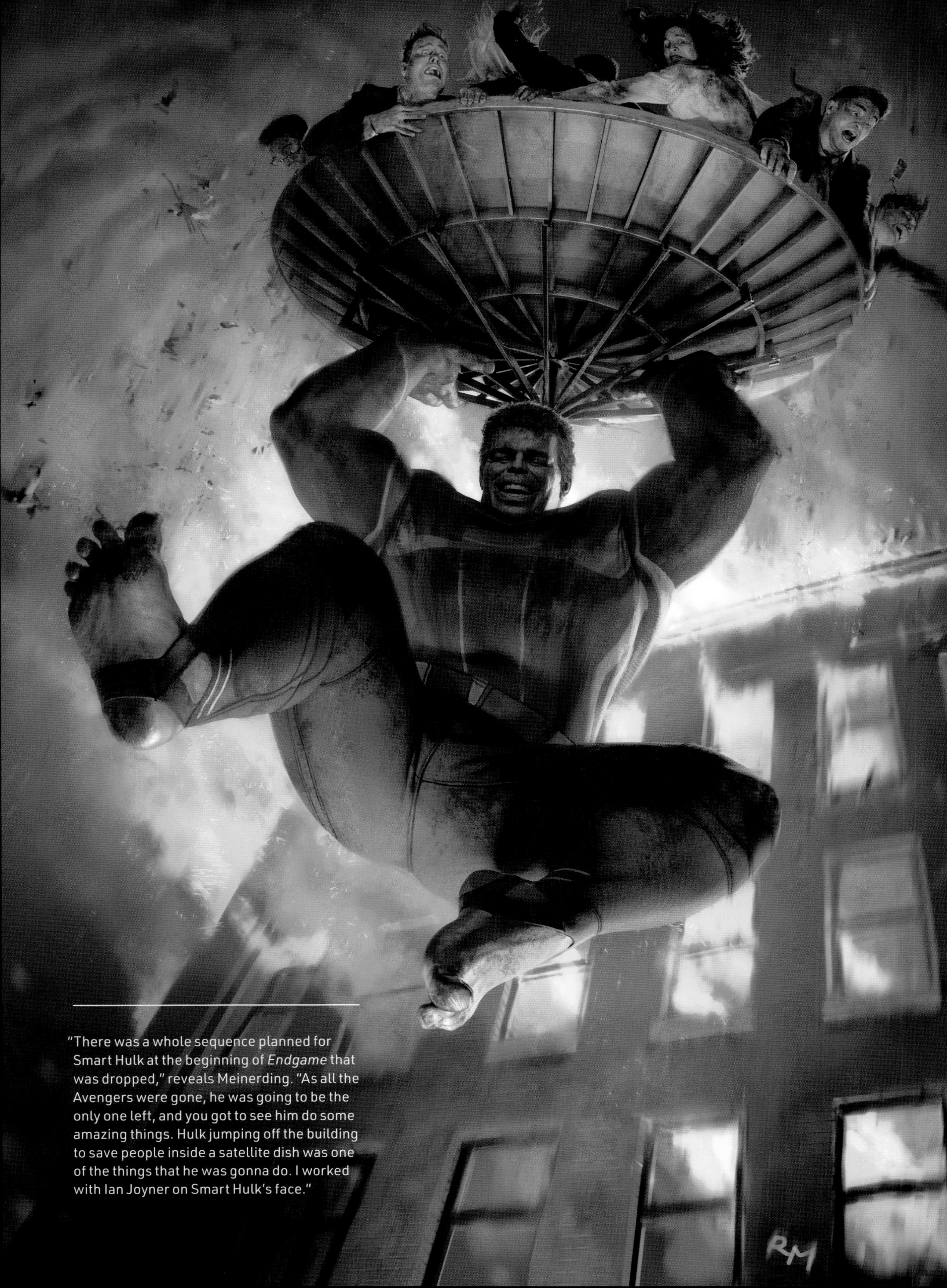
RM

"There was a whole sequence planned for Smart Hulk at the beginning of *Endgame* that was dropped," reveals Meinerding. "As all the Avengers were gone, he was going to be the only one left, and you got to see him do some amazing things. Hulk jumping off the building to save people inside a satellite dish was one of the things that he was gonna do. I worked with Ian Joyner on Smart Hulk's face."

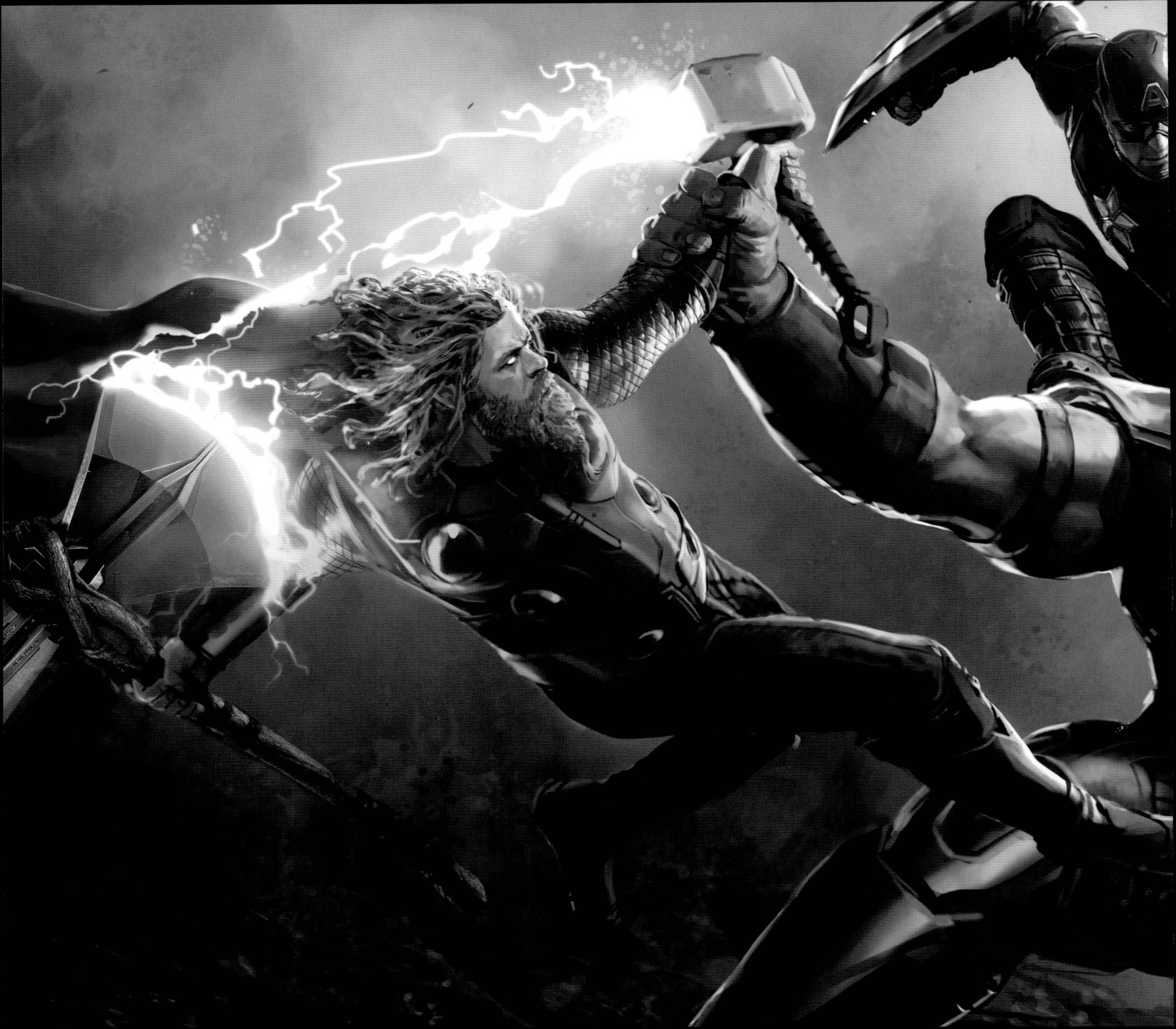

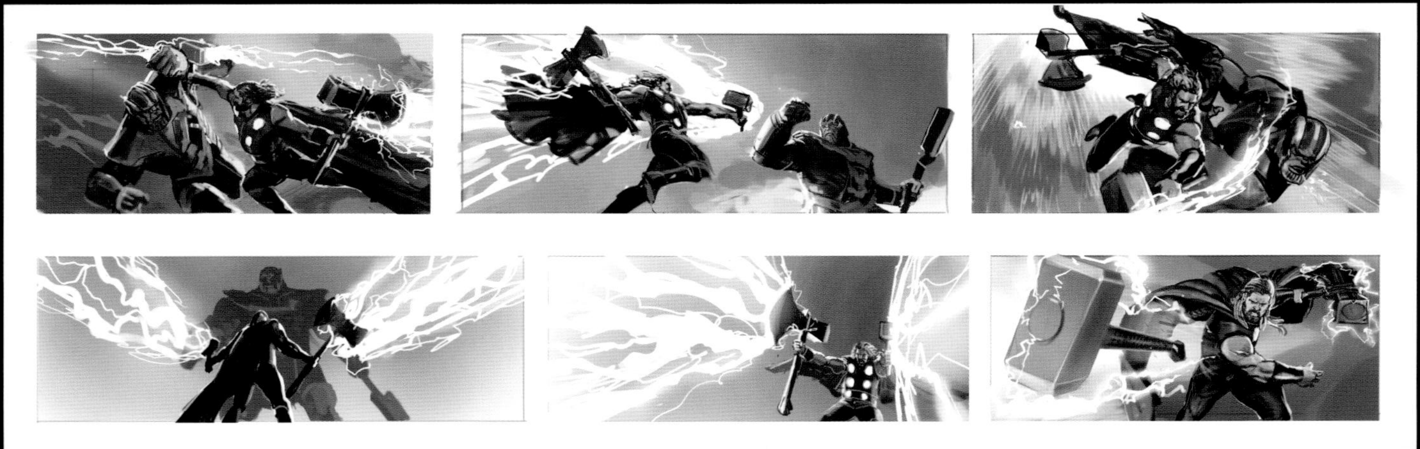

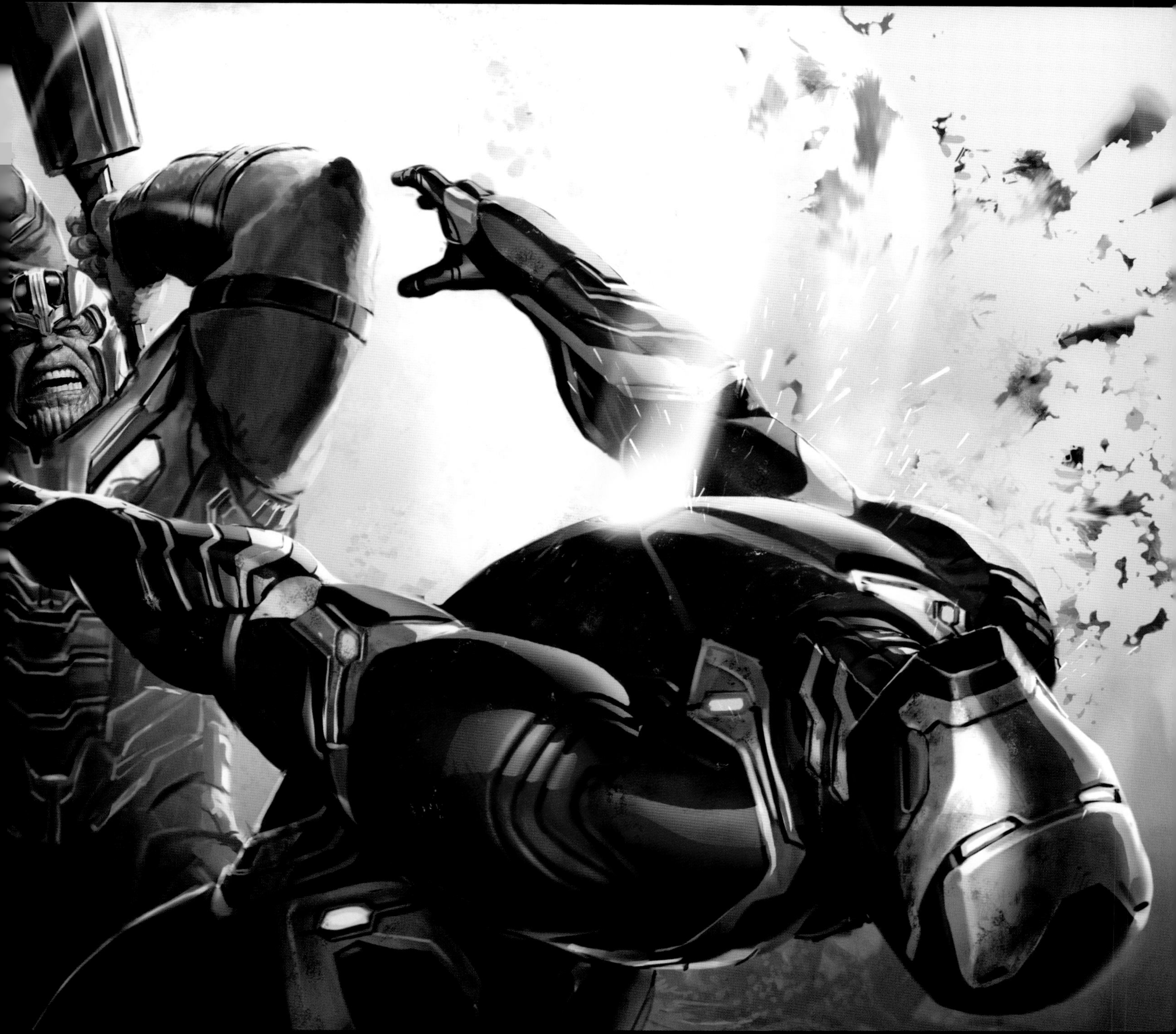

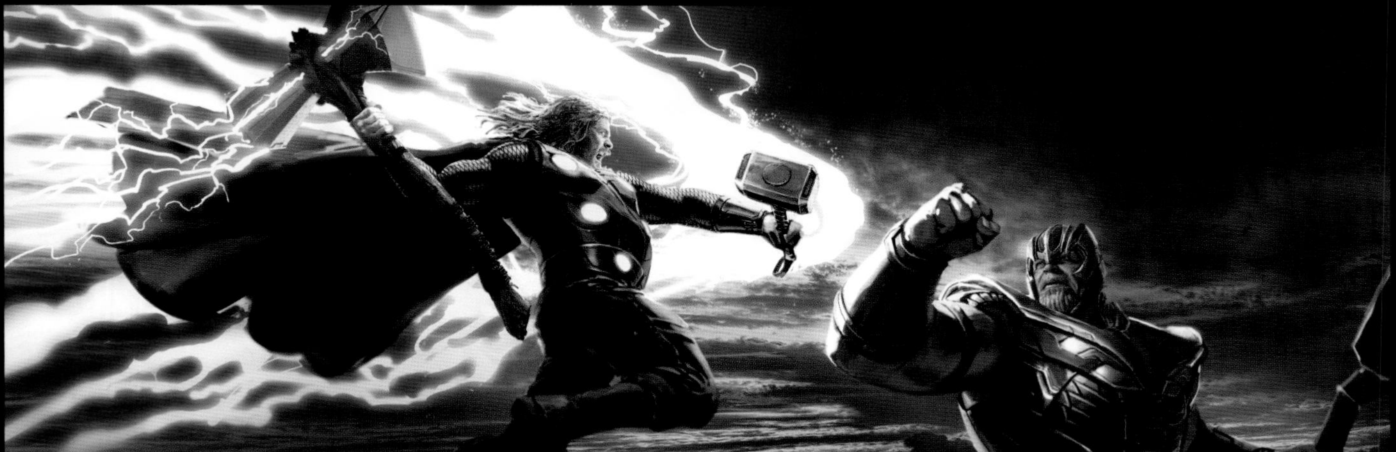
RYAN MEINERDING

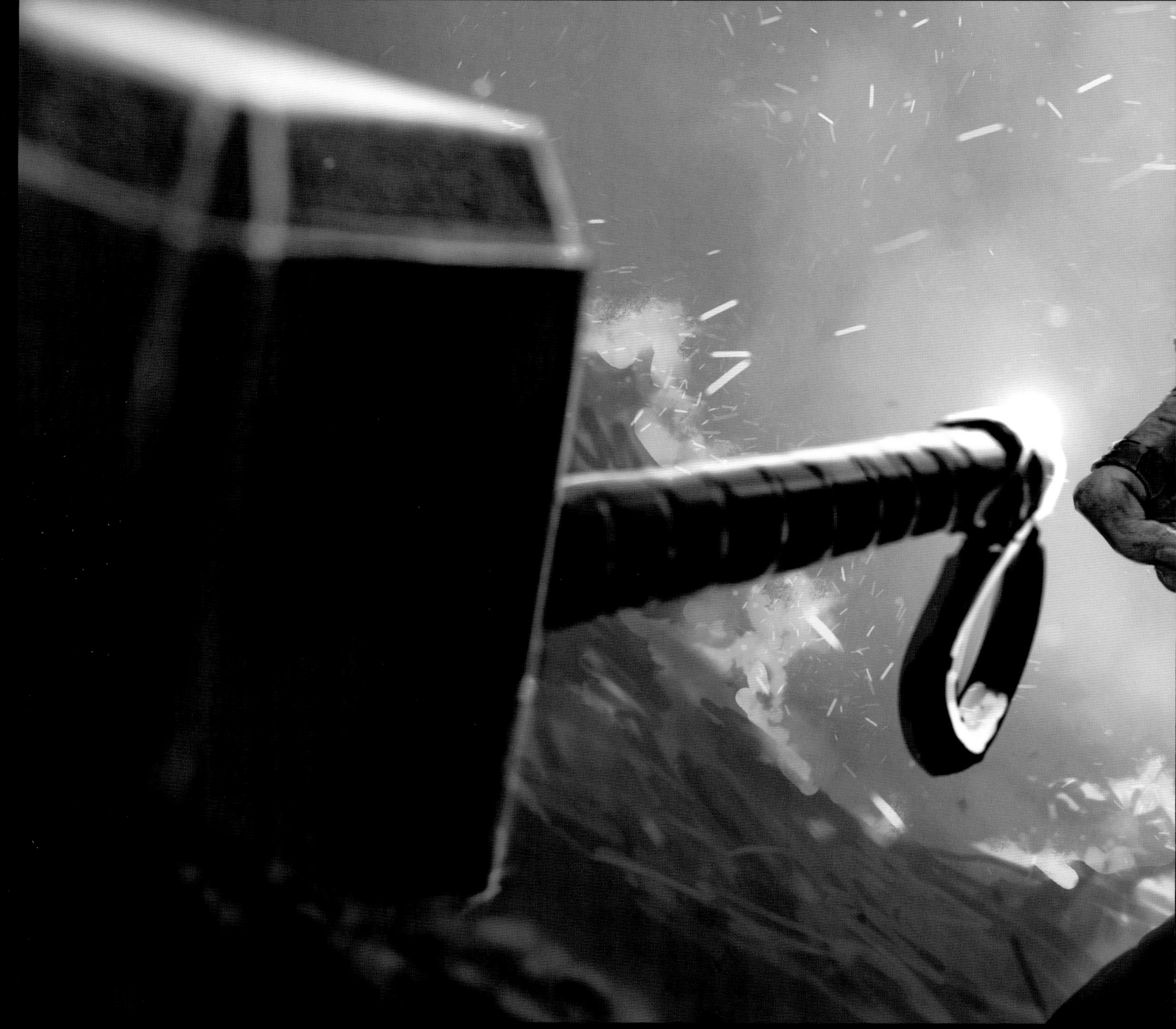

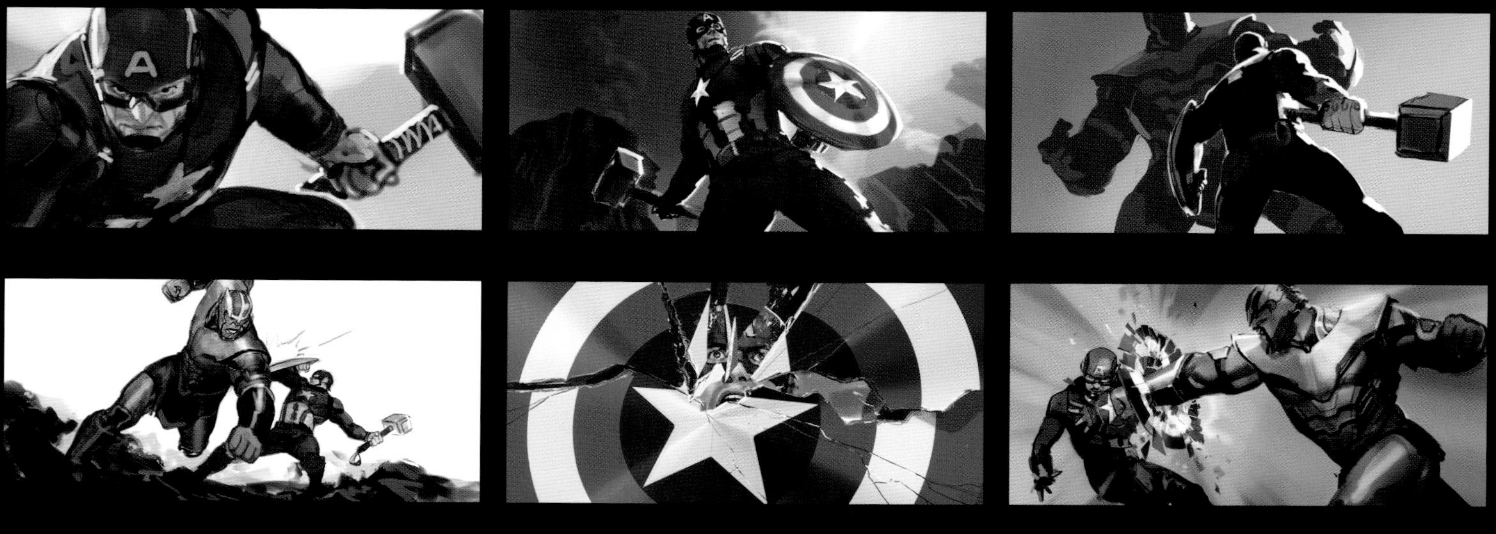

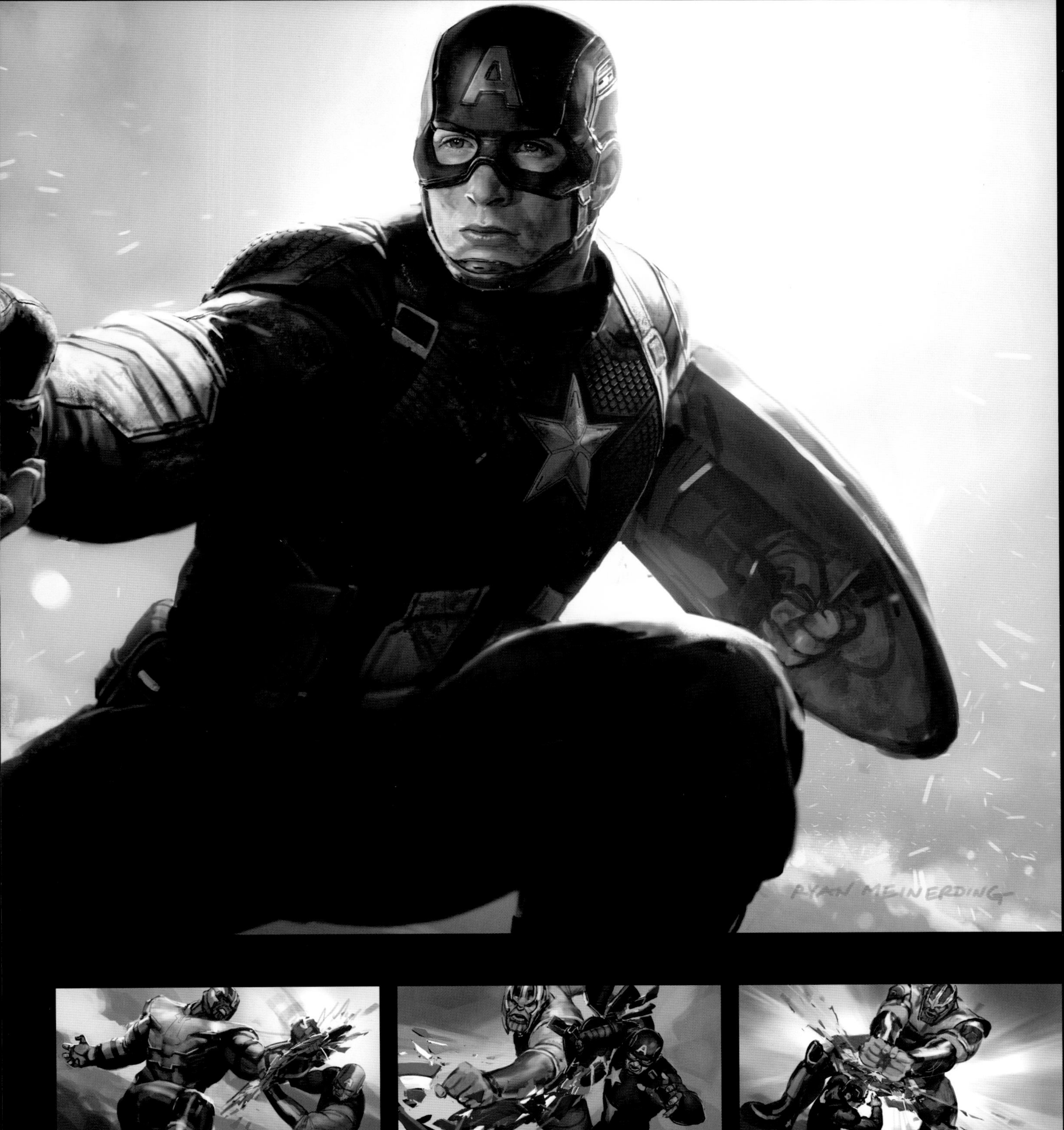
RYAN MEINERDING

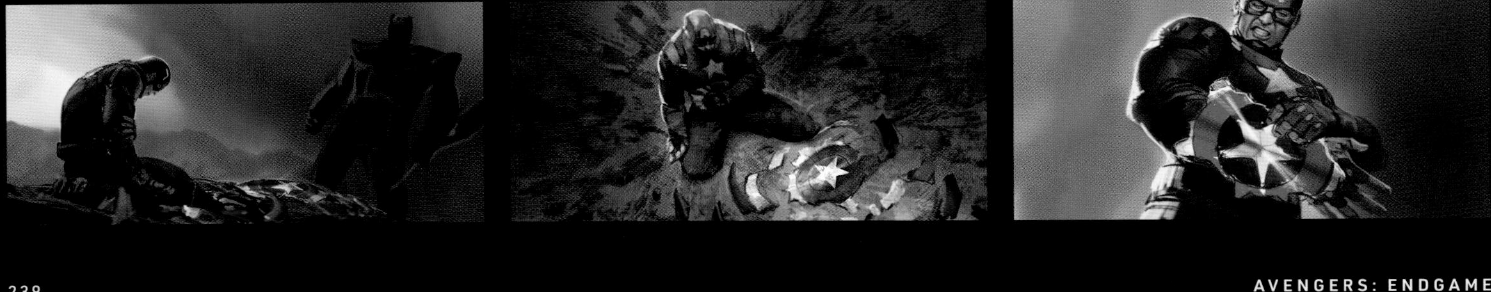

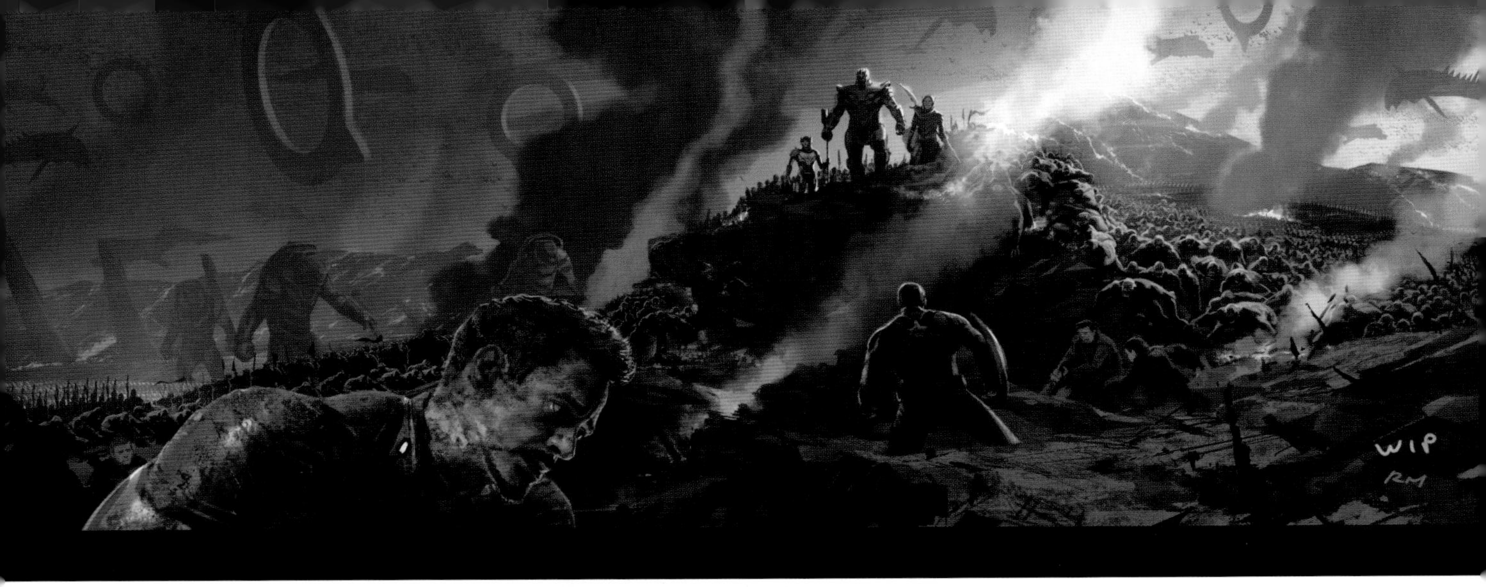
WIP
RM

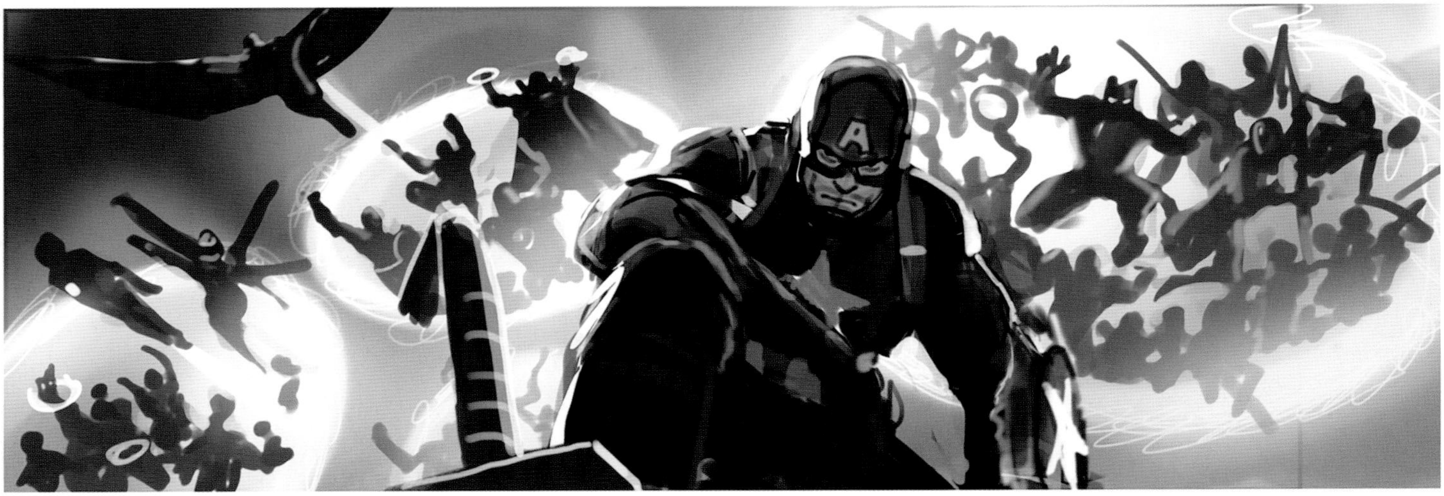

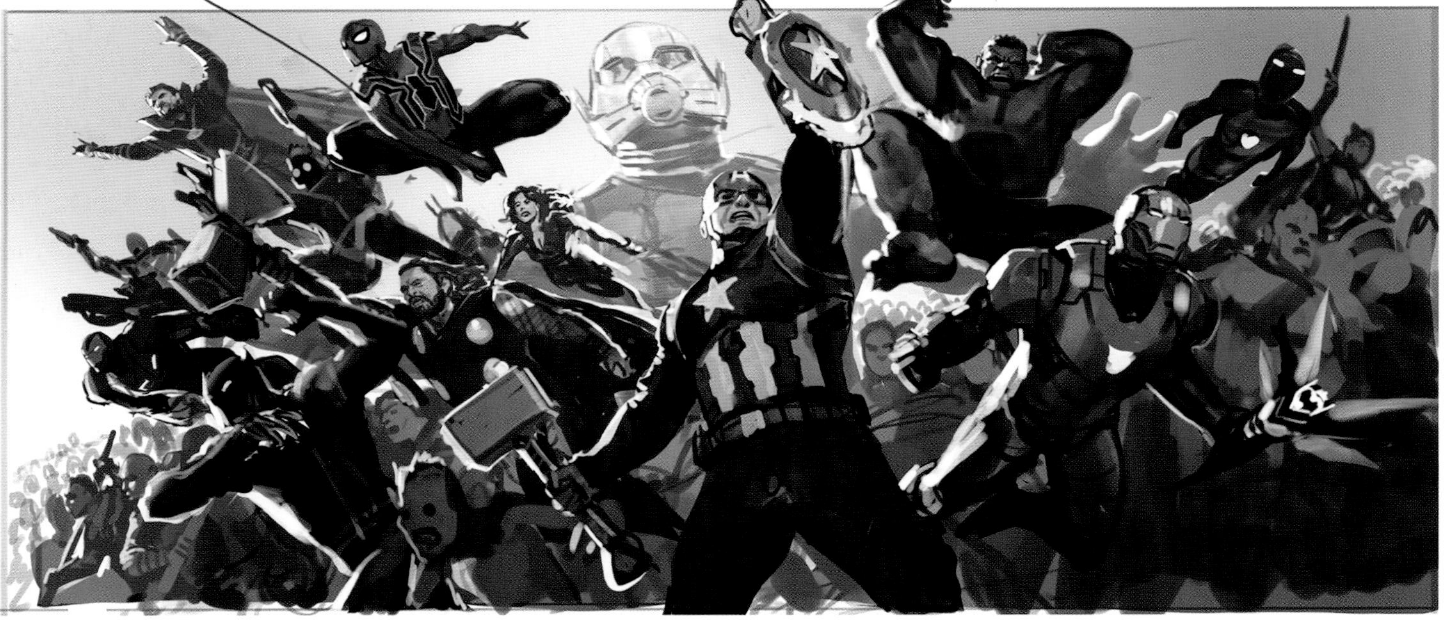

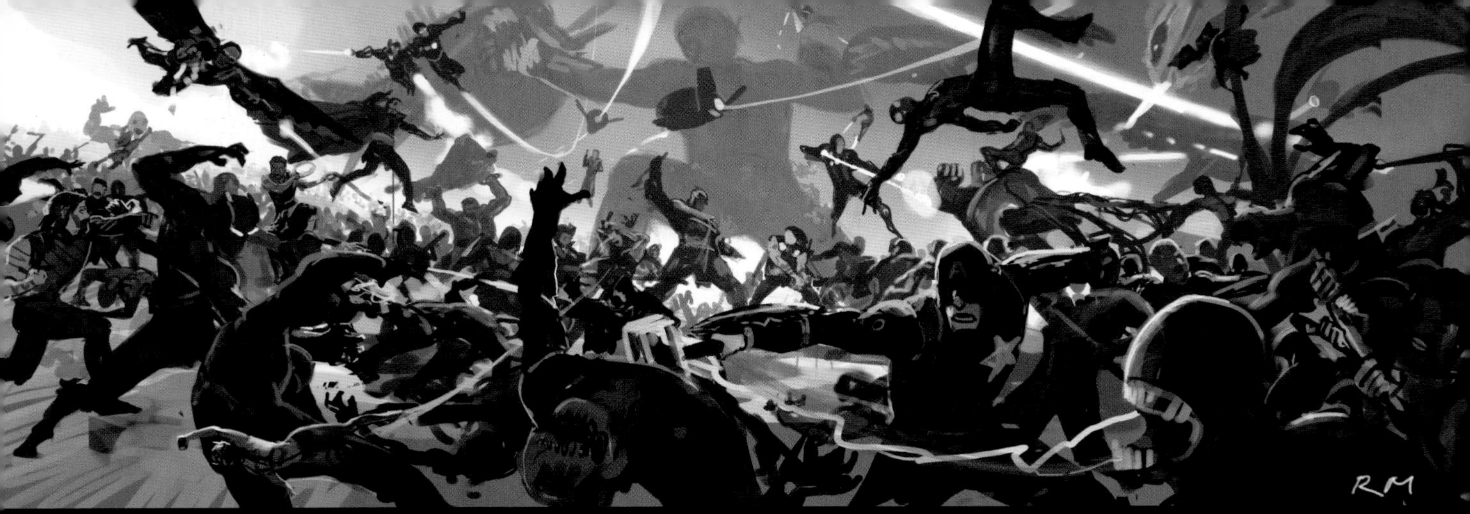
RM

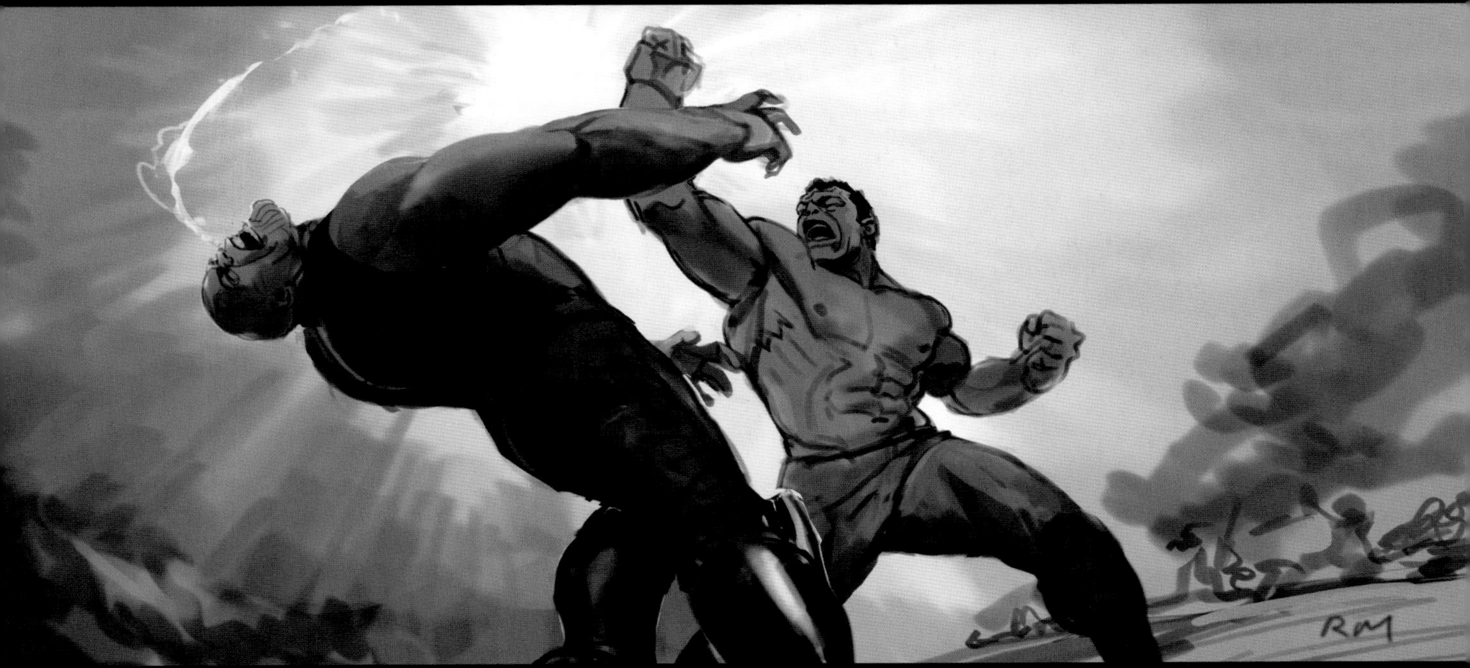
RM

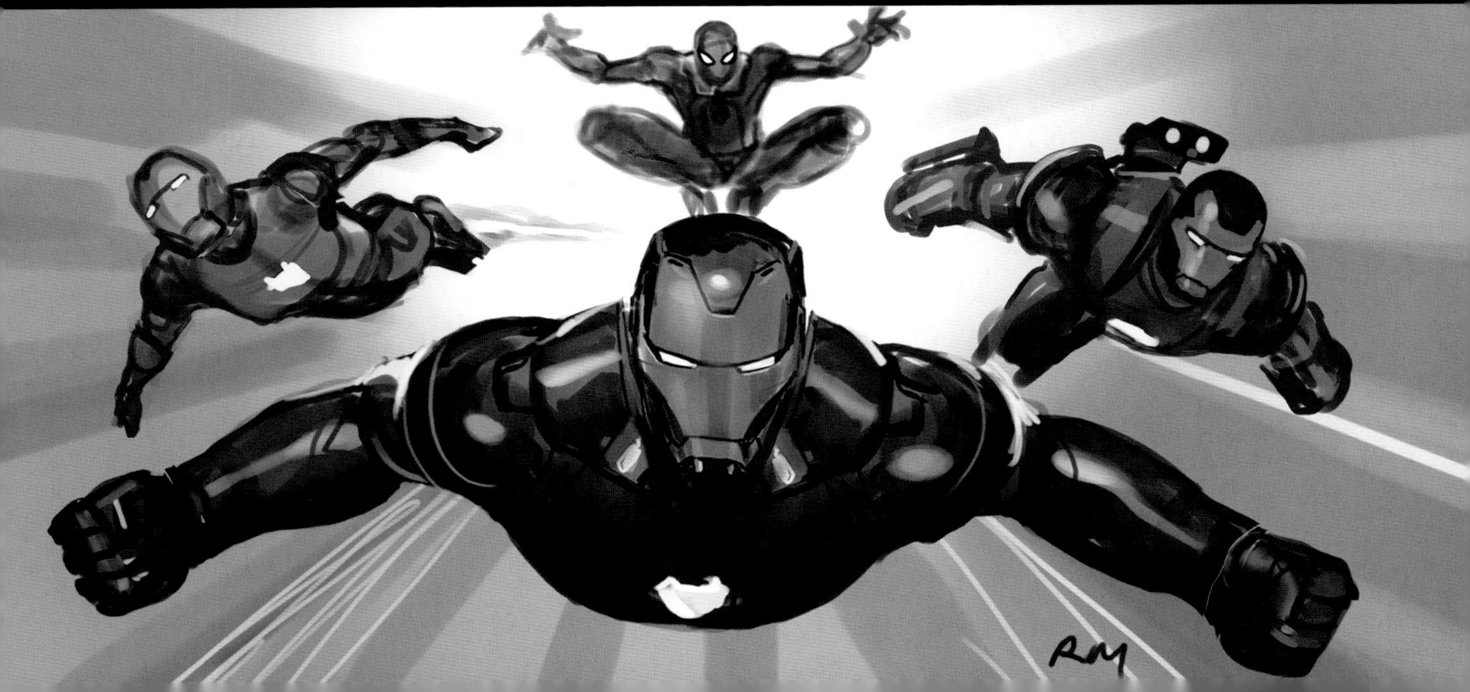
RM

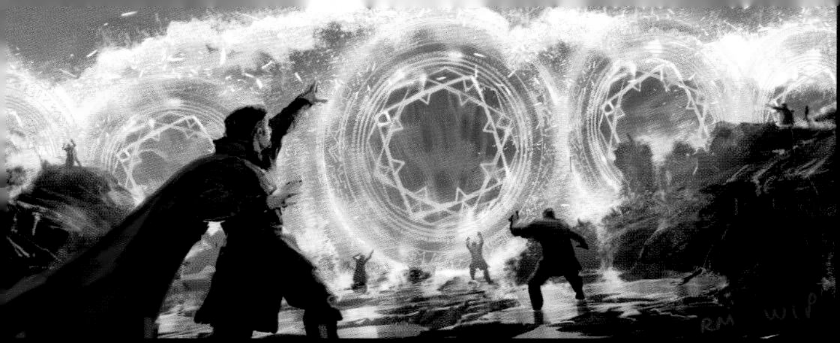

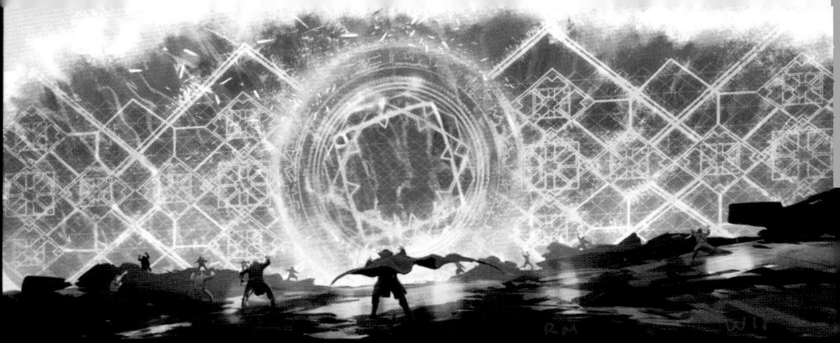

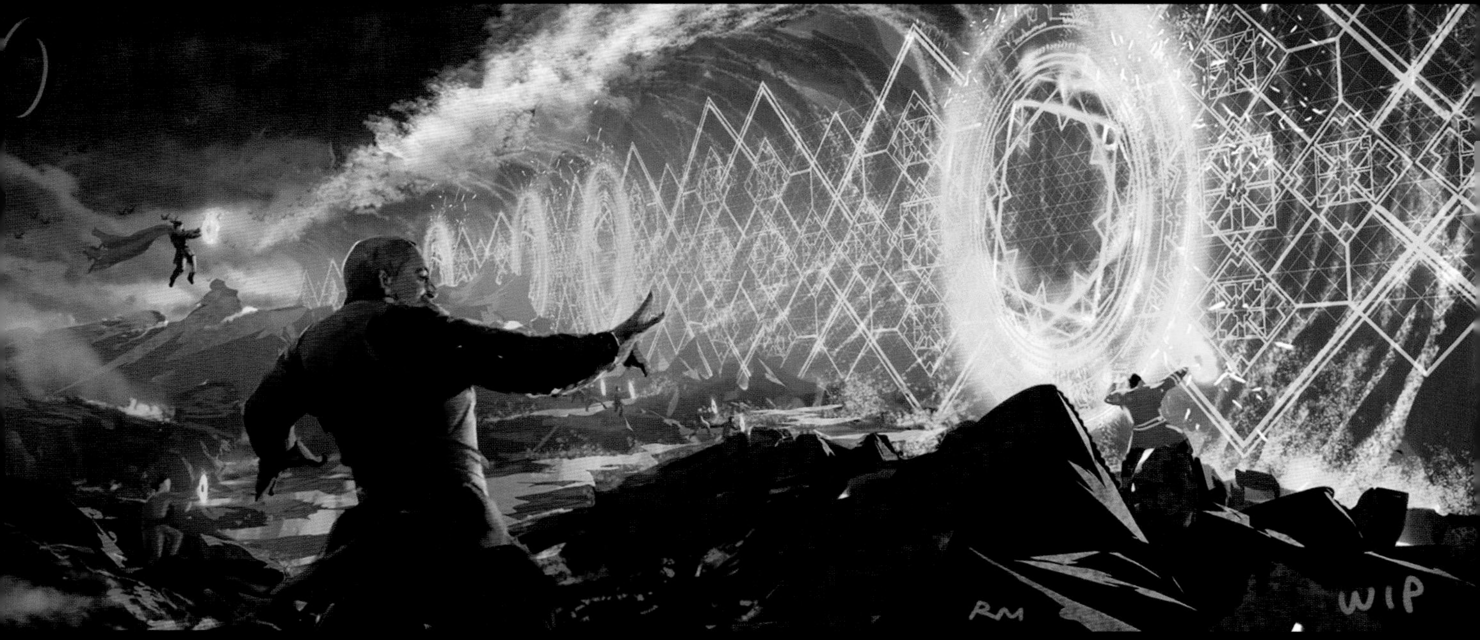
RM
WIP

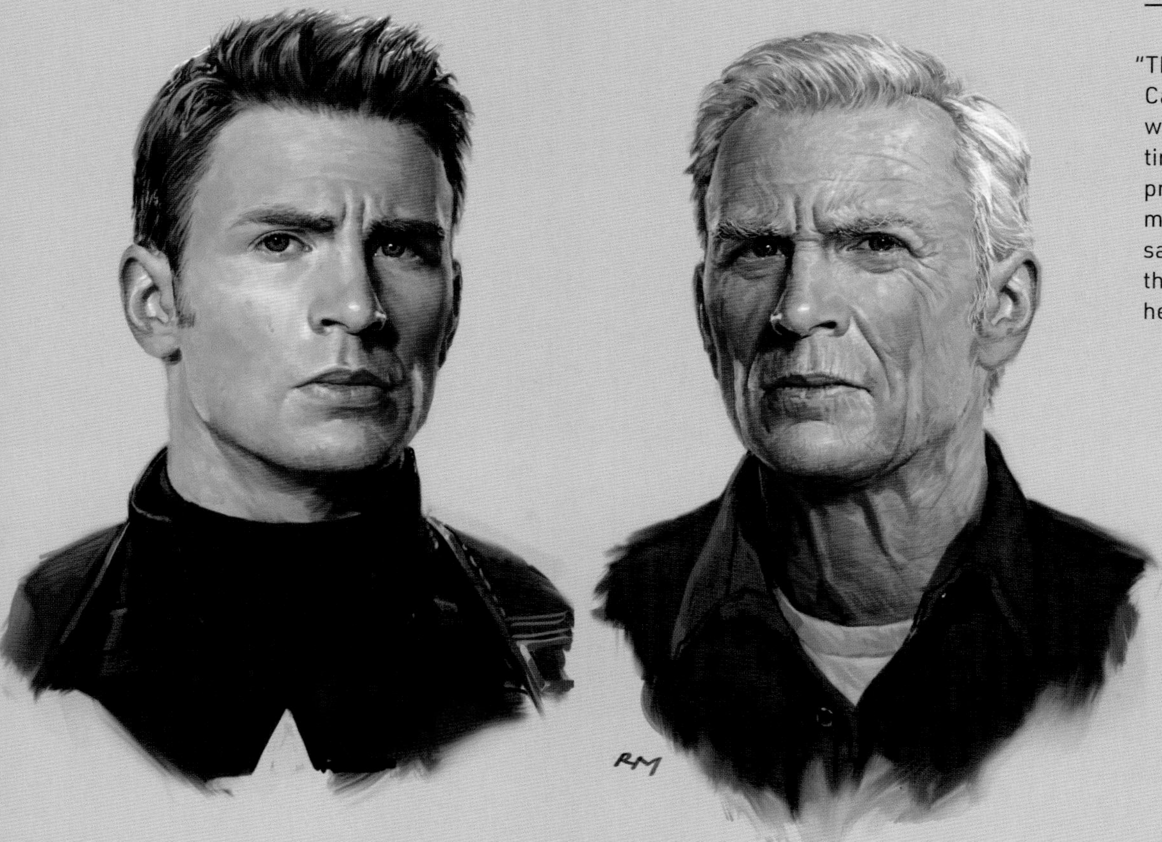
RM

"These paintings of Cap and Old Man Cap were created ahead of time, way before the prosthetics had to be made for Chris Evans," says Meinerding. "So that was me trying to help with that."

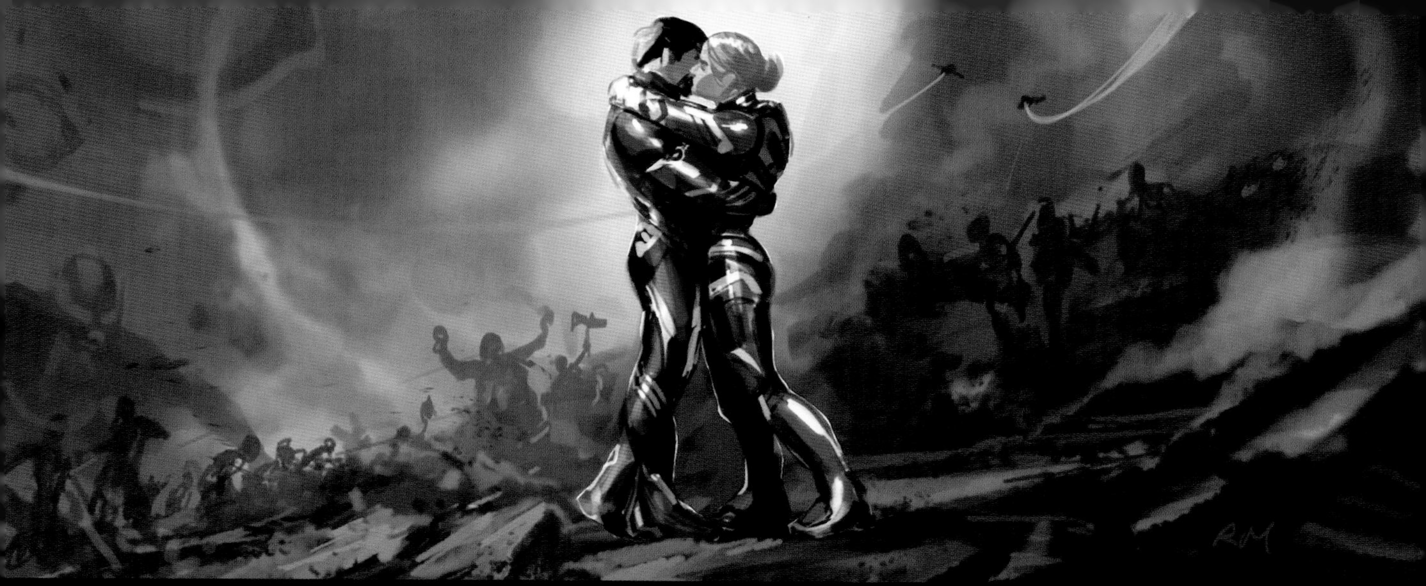
RM

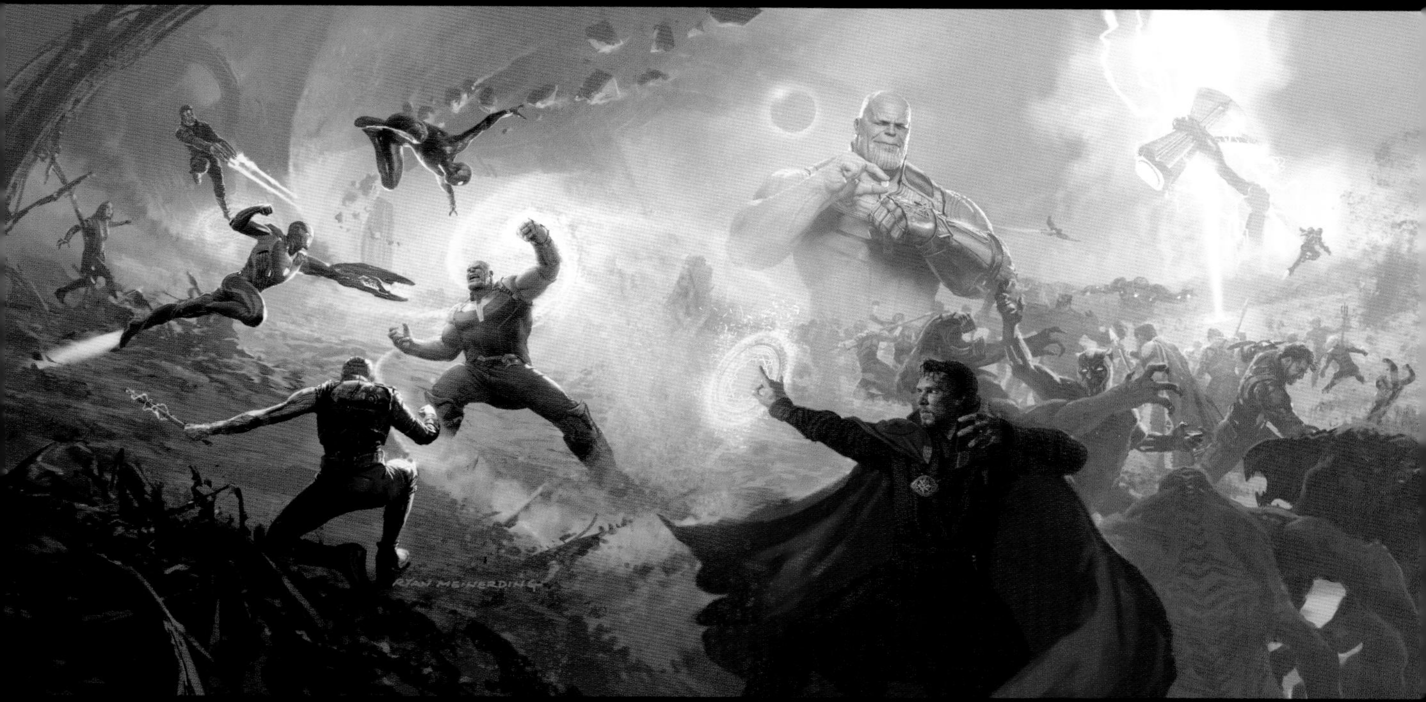
RYAN MEINERDING

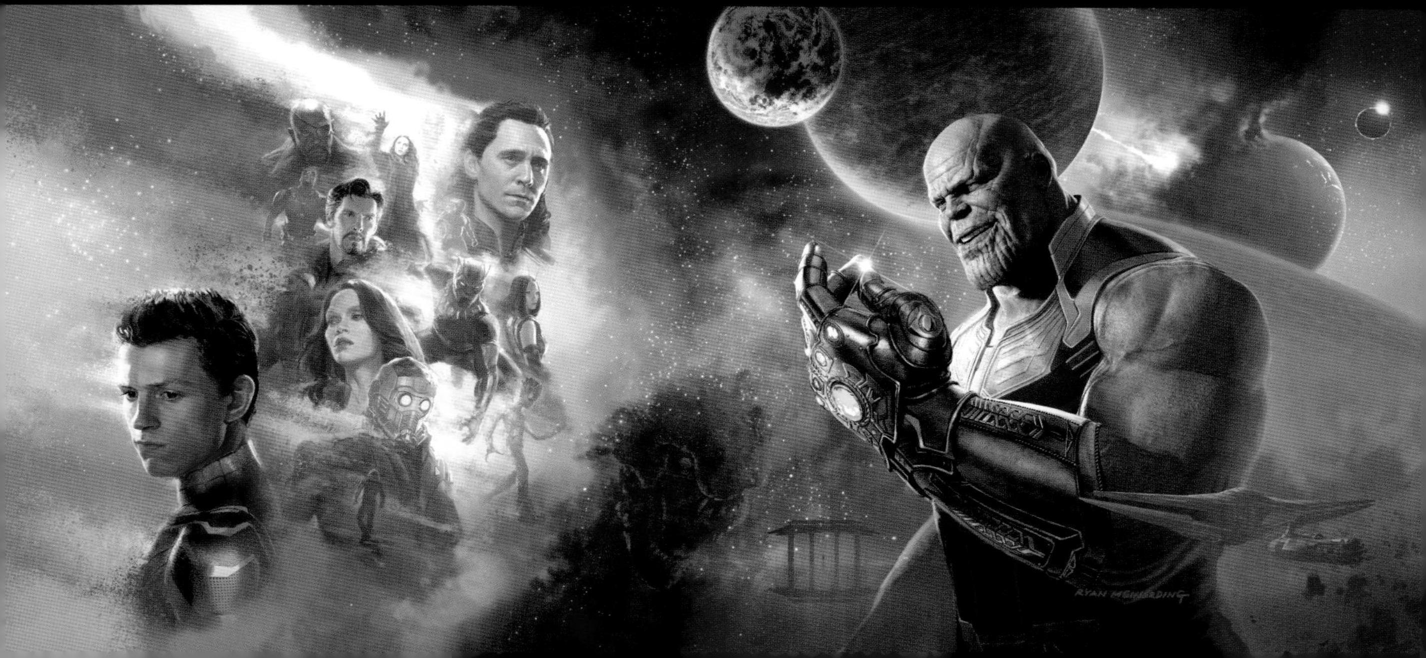
RYAN MEINERDING

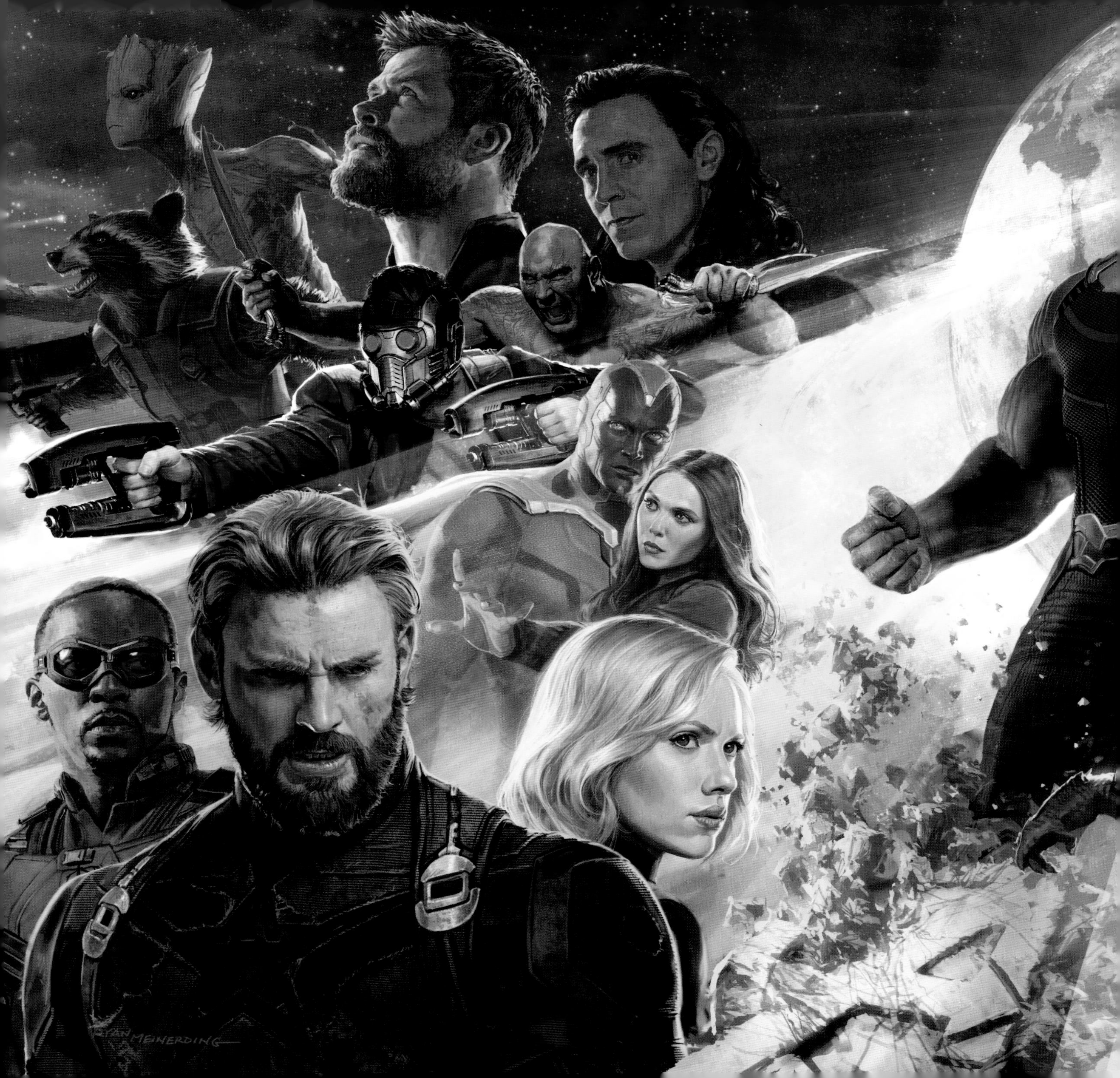
MEINERDING

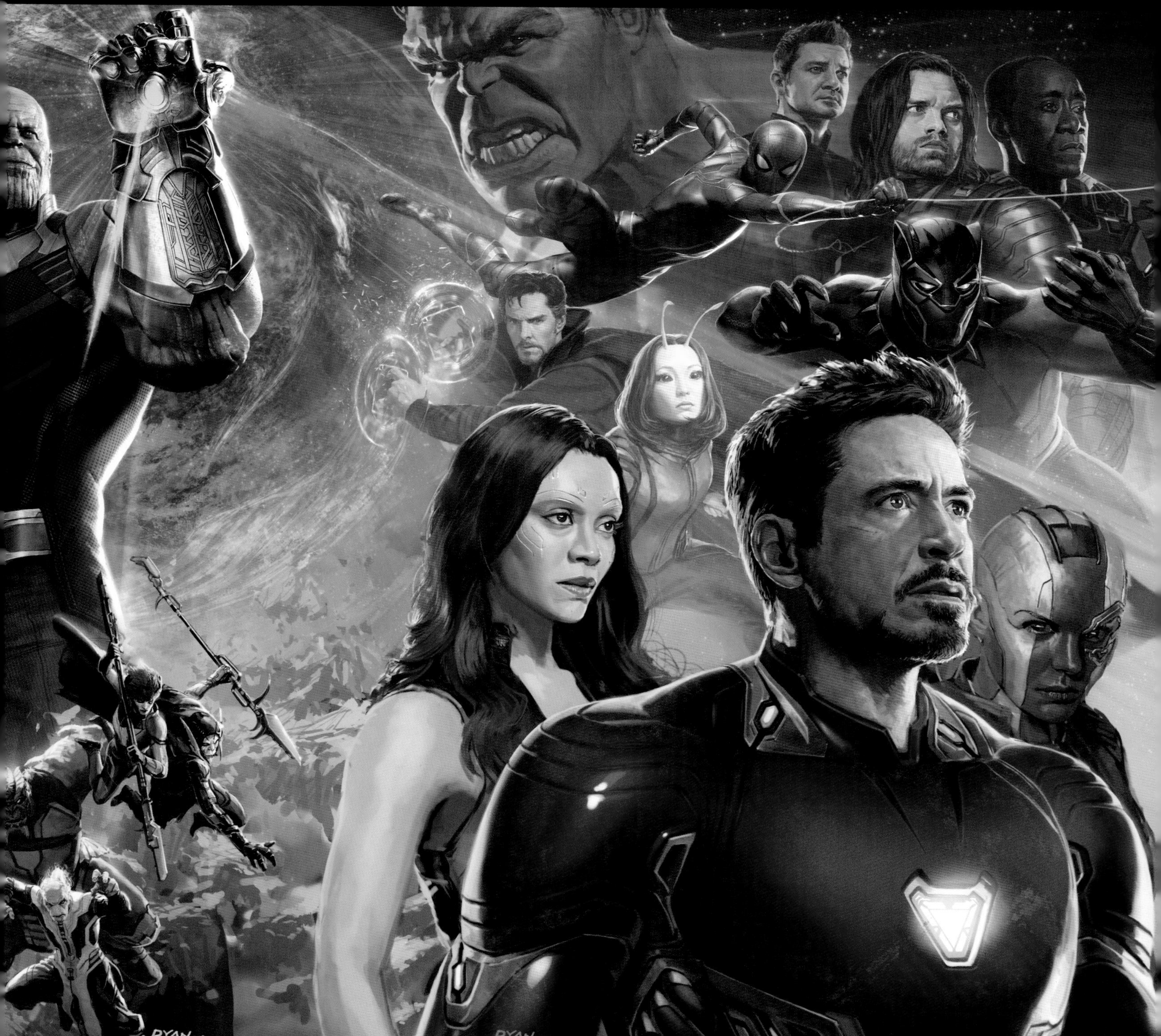
RYAN MEINERDING
RYAN MEINERDING

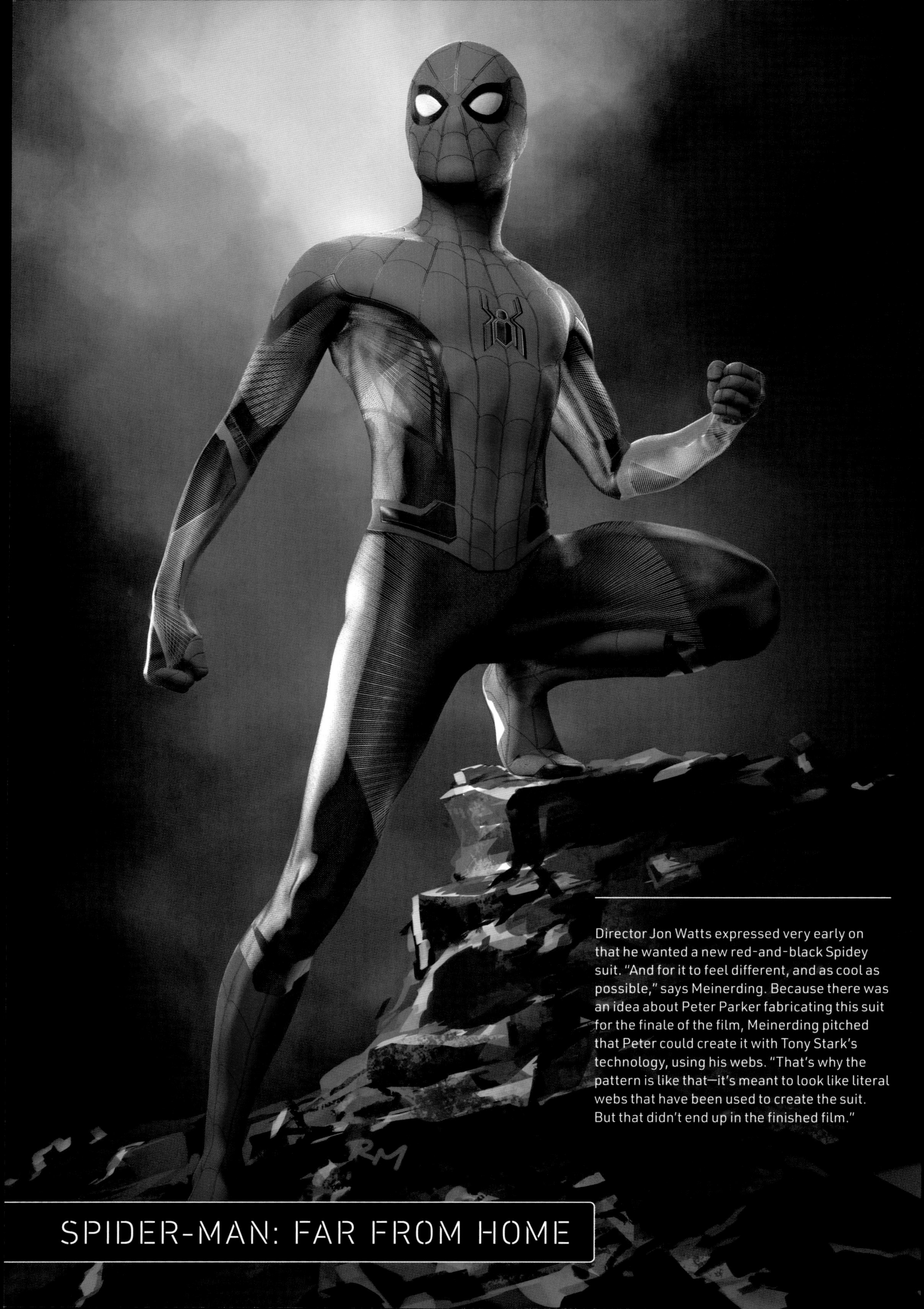

Director Jon Watts expressed very early on that he wanted a new red-and-black Spidey suit. "And for it to feel different, and as cool as possible," says Meinerding. Because there was an idea about Peter Parker fabricating this suit for the finale of the film, Meinerding pitched that Peter could create it with Tony Stark's technology, using his webs. "That's why the pattern is like that—it's meant to look like literal webs that have been used to create the suit. But that didn't end up in the finished film."

SPIDER-MAN: FAR FROM HOME

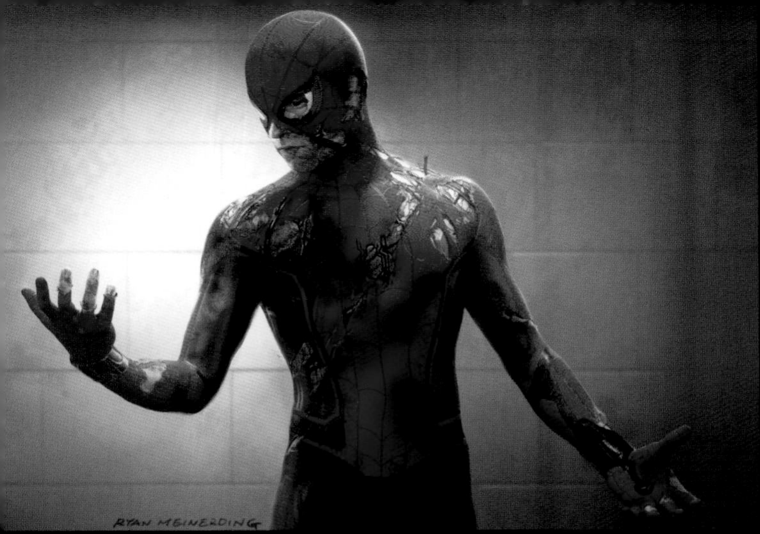
RYAN MEINERDING

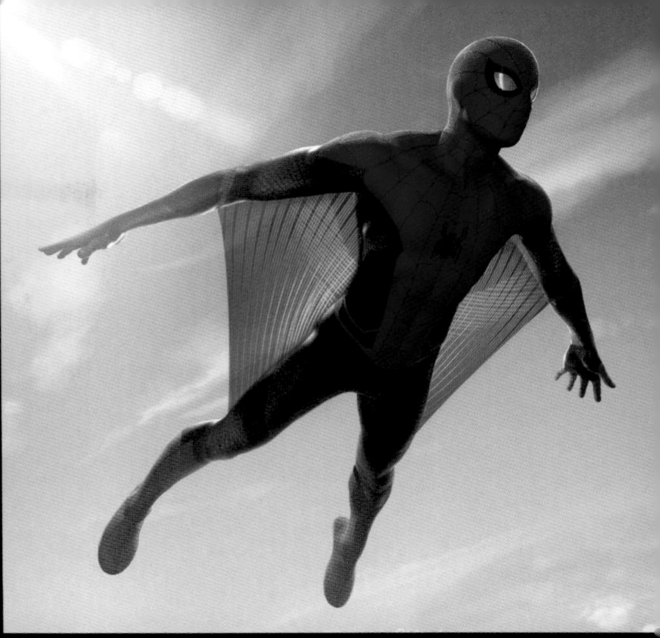

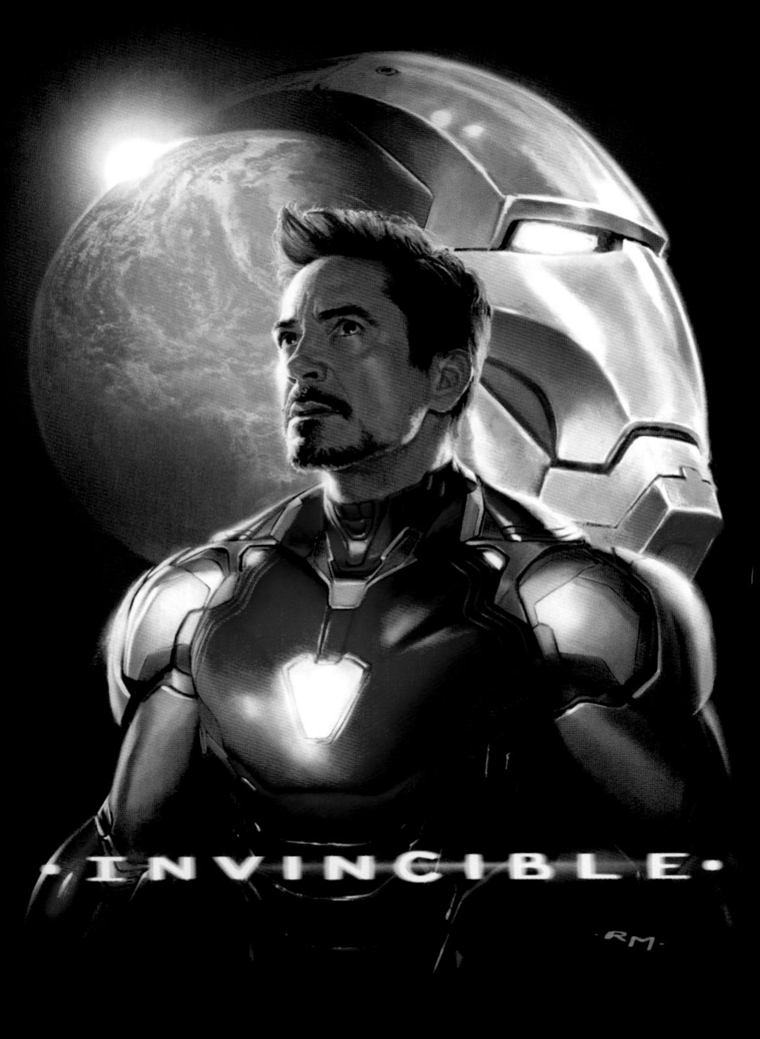
INVINCIBLE
RM

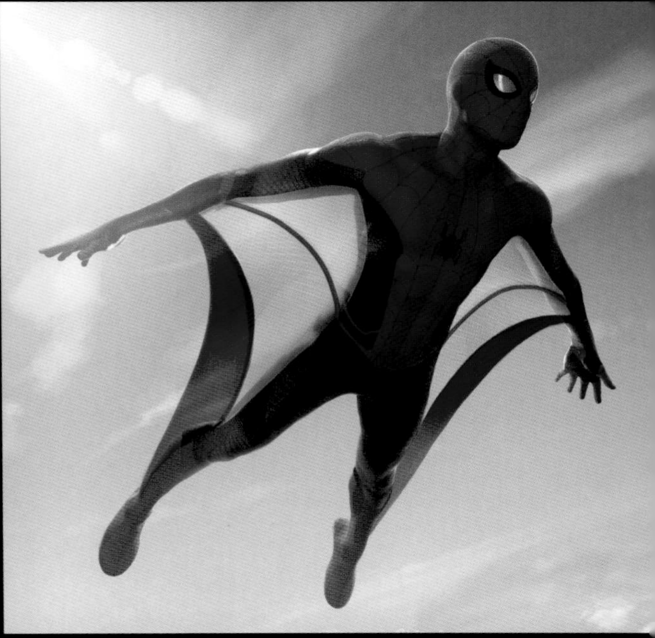

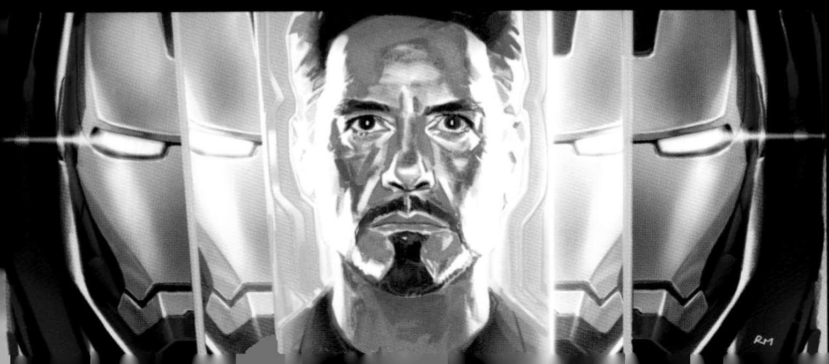
RM

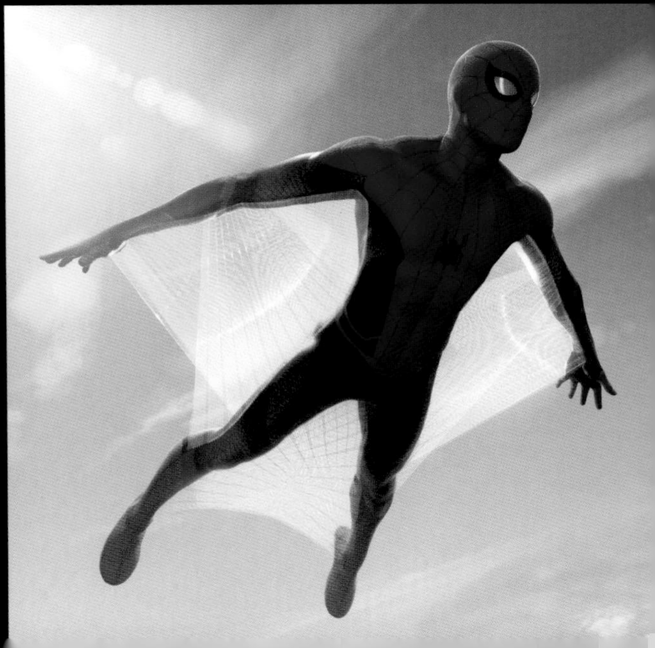

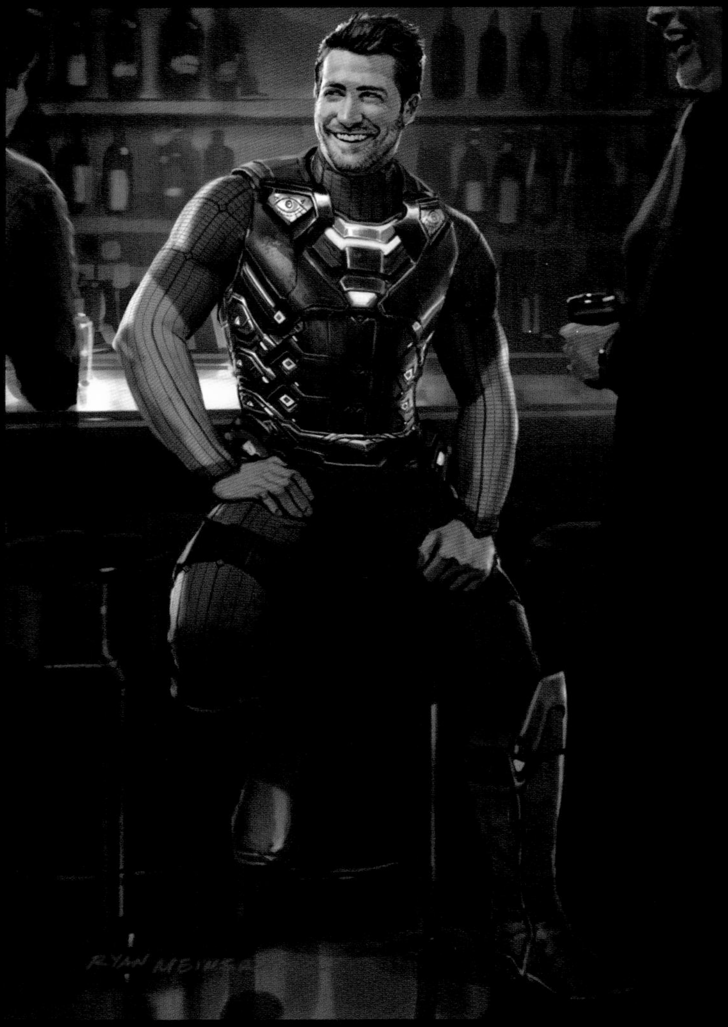

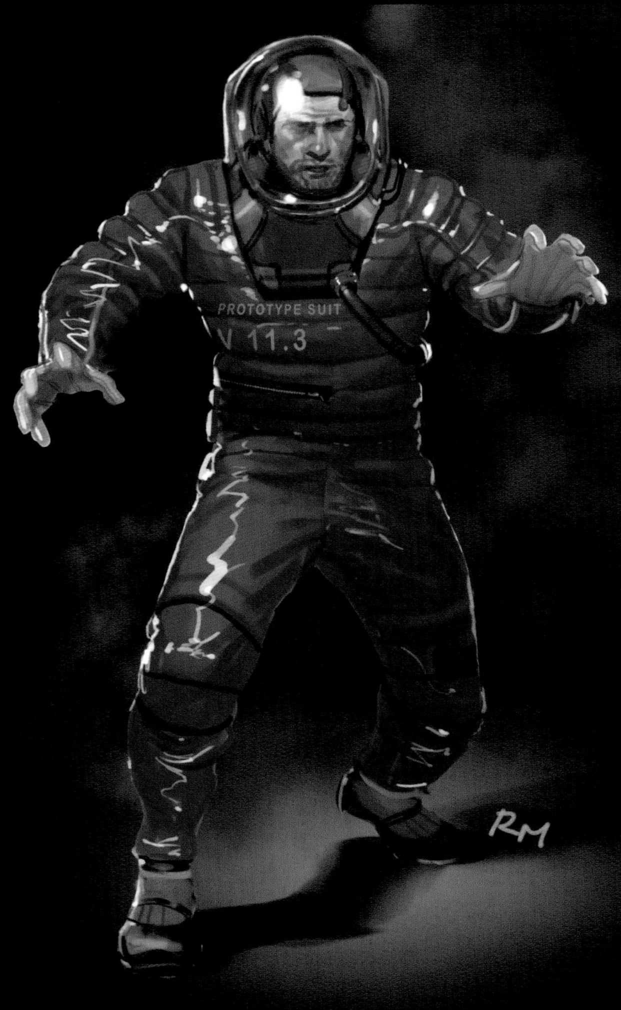
PROTOTYPE SUIT
V 11.3
RM

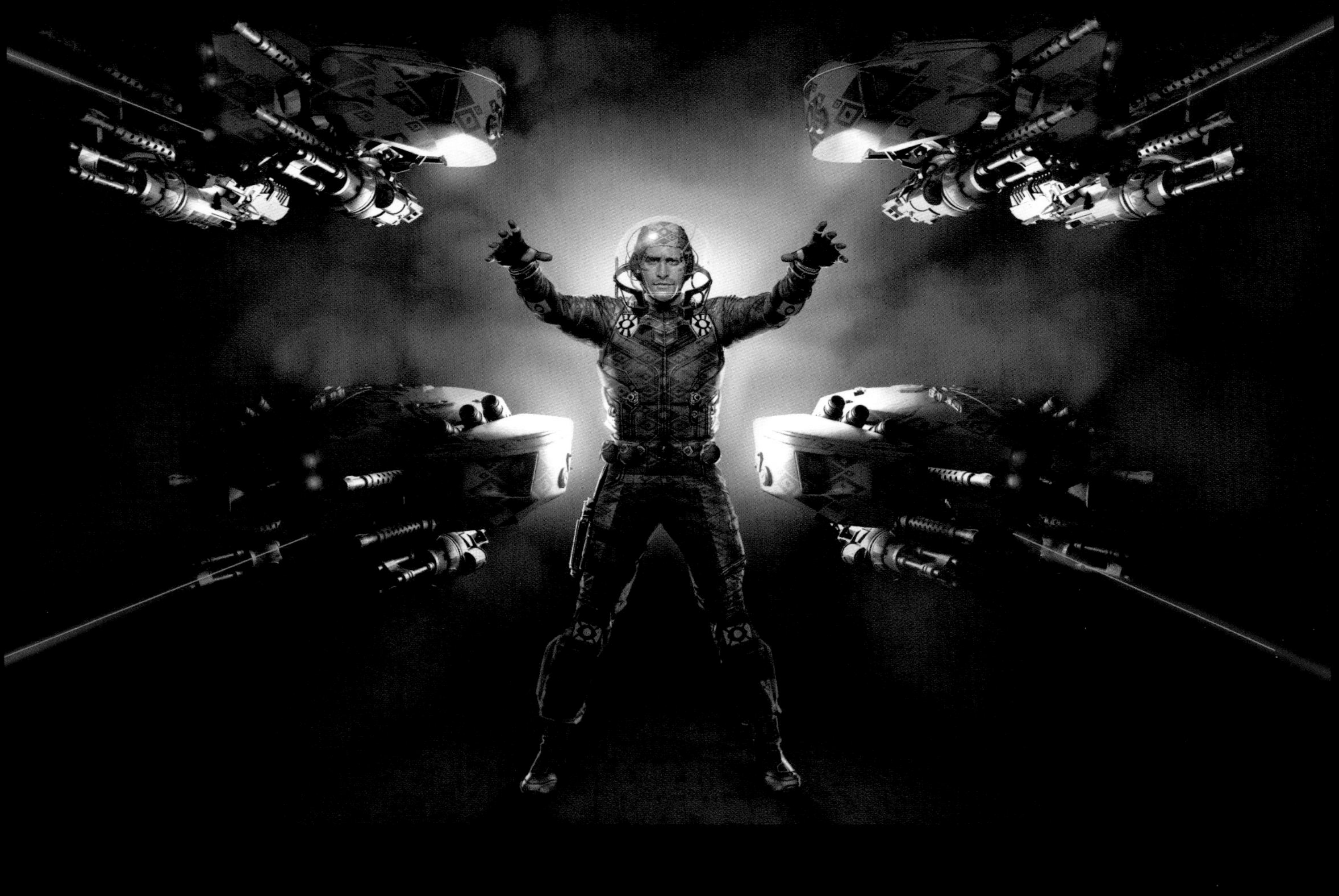

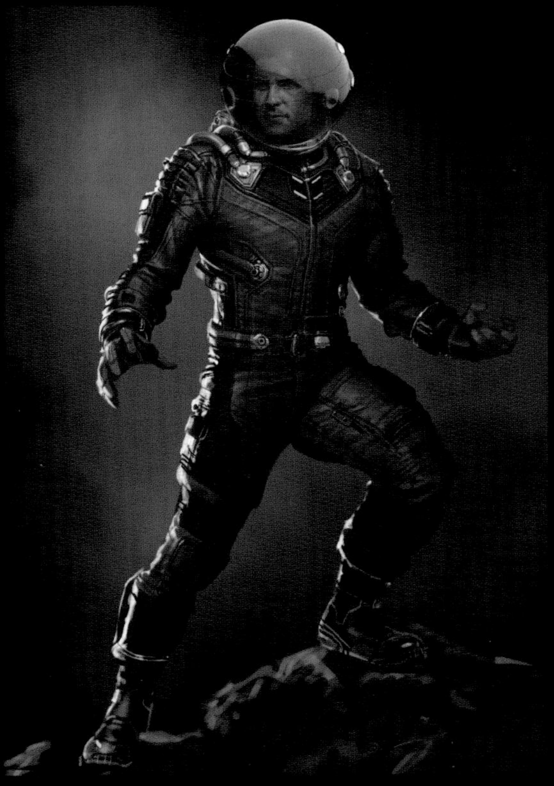

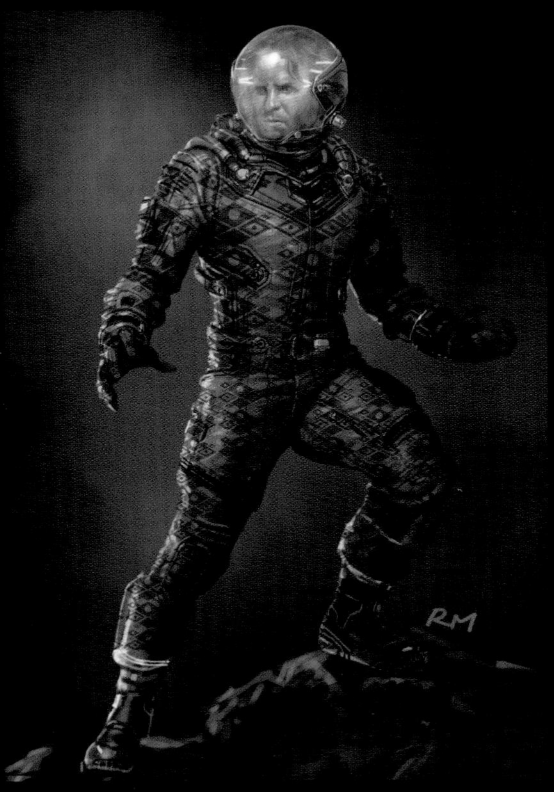
RM

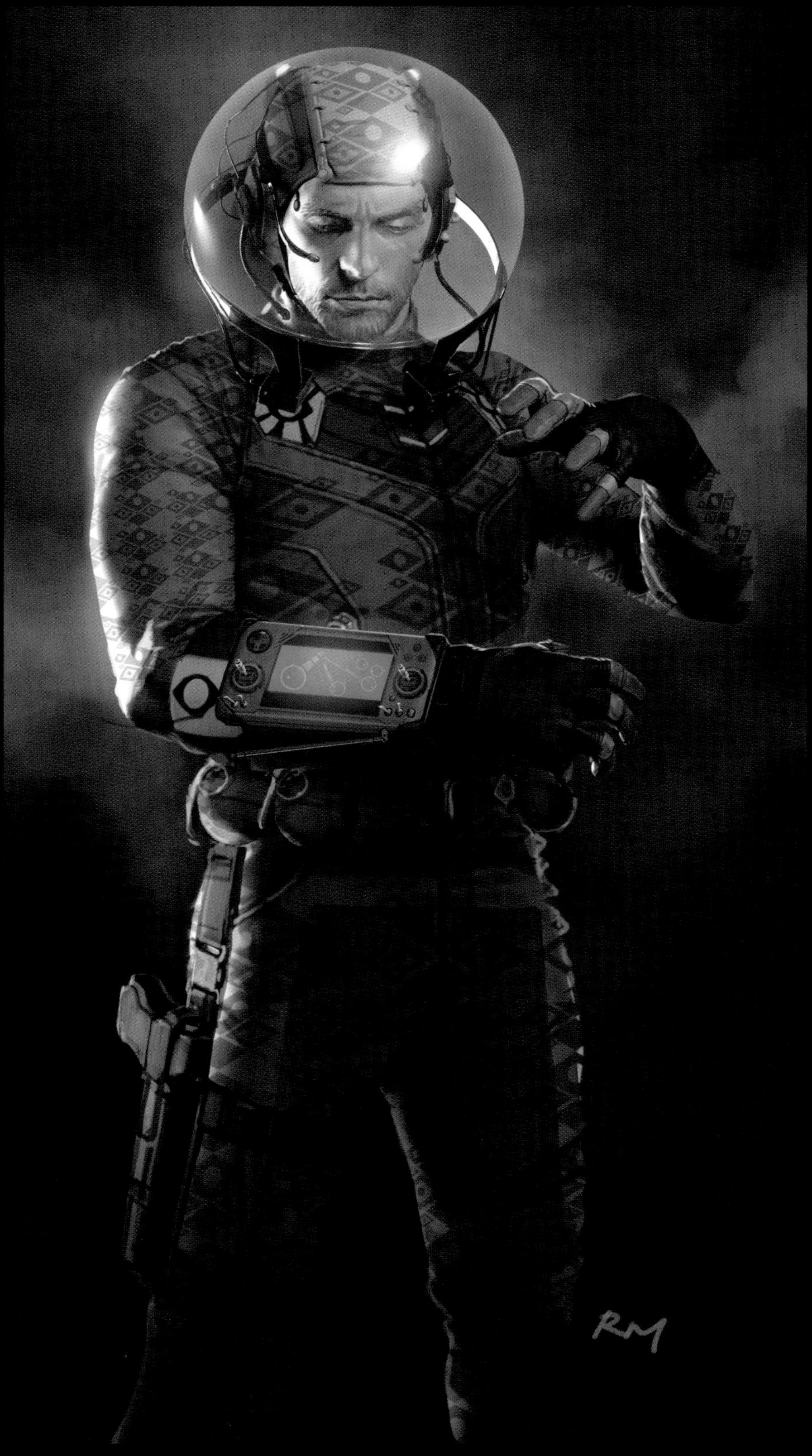
RM

Most of the visual development conversations that happened early for *Spider-Man: Far From Home* were about Mysterio. "Because, although we were excited about using him, we were also *terrified*," shares Meinerding. "We didn't know how to do him in a way that wasn't gonna look ridiculous." After multiple conversations and designs, Meinerding pitched the idea that Mysterio could have a motion-capture suit—engineered with the "eyes" pattern used on real mo-cap suits—to look like it was supposed to be replaced. "Then Mysterio is putting his costumed look together by copying the MCU heroes," says Meinerding. "Sort of like Doctor Strange mixed with Vision mixed with Thor. And, beyond his look, a lot of exploration was done on how to make Mysterio's technology work and make sense so that audiences weren't confused, thinking, *What is it doing?*"

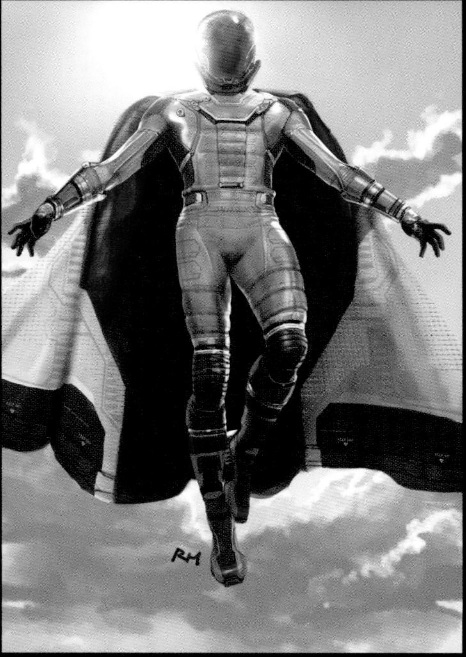
RM

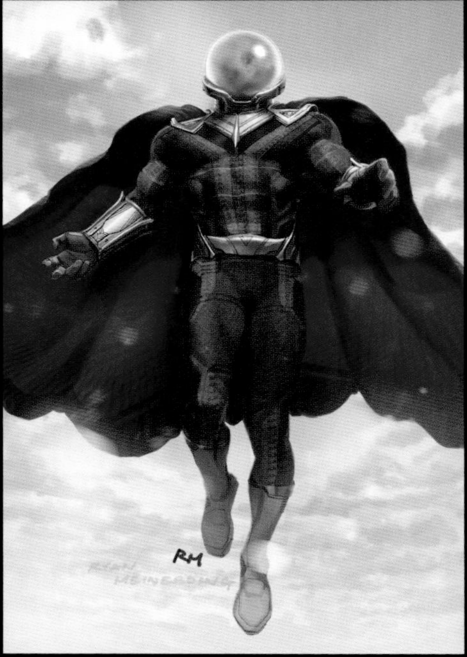
RM

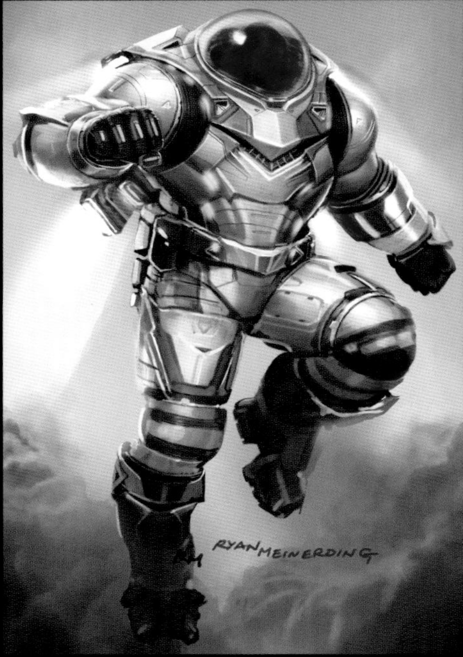
RM
RYAN MEINERDING

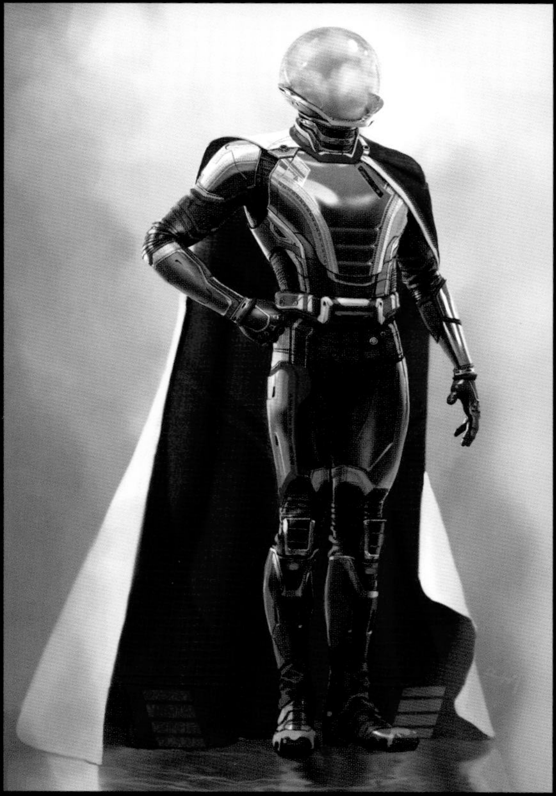

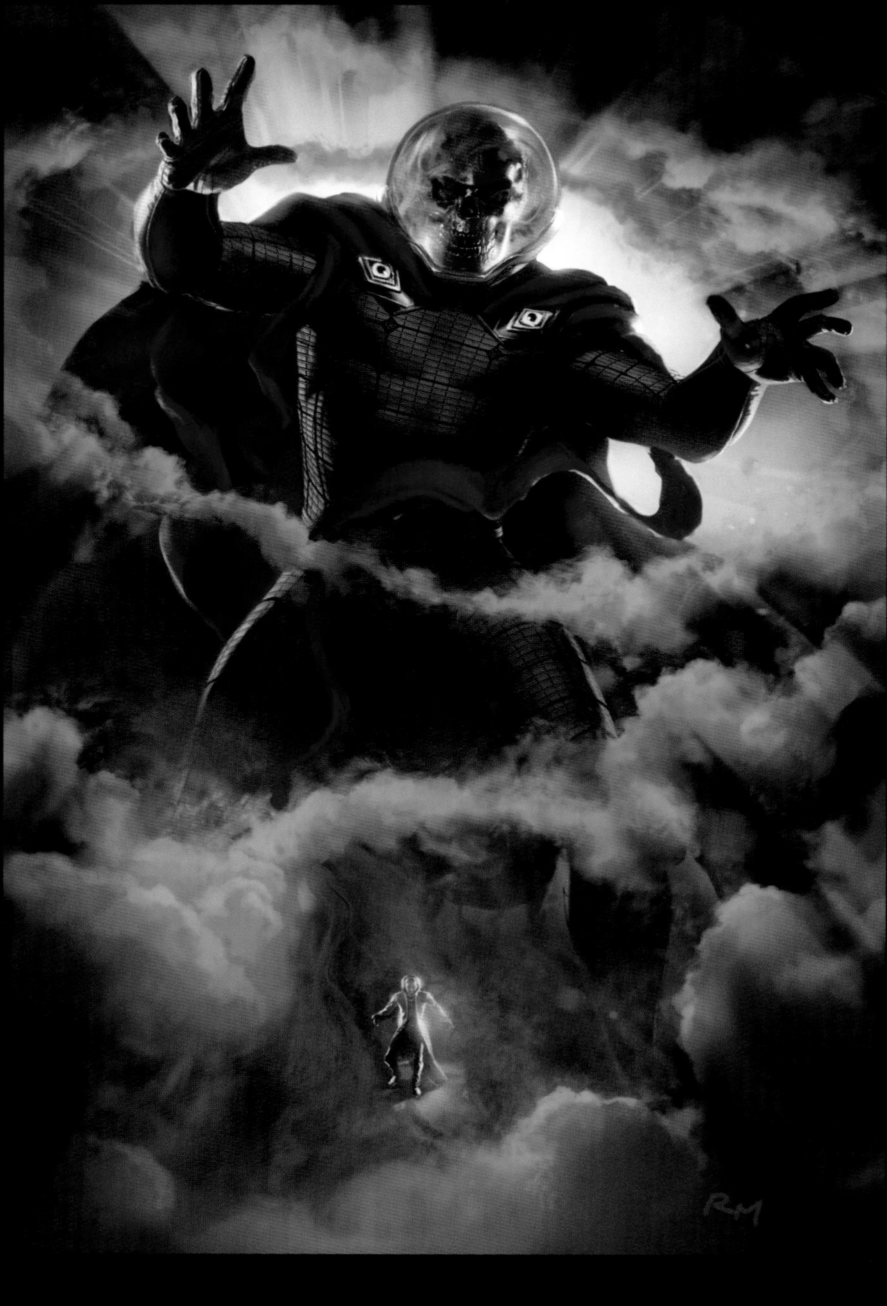
RM

"For some reason, I love Mysterio," enthuses Meinerding. "I think he's one of the cooler villains in Spider-Man's catalogue. It's the hallmark of a lot of [Steve] Ditko's stuff—it just shouldn't work, but there's enough cool stuff about it that it does. I think the touchstones that we were able to find really launched him into that story in a strong way conceptually, visually, and story-wise. I really enjoyed working on that film."

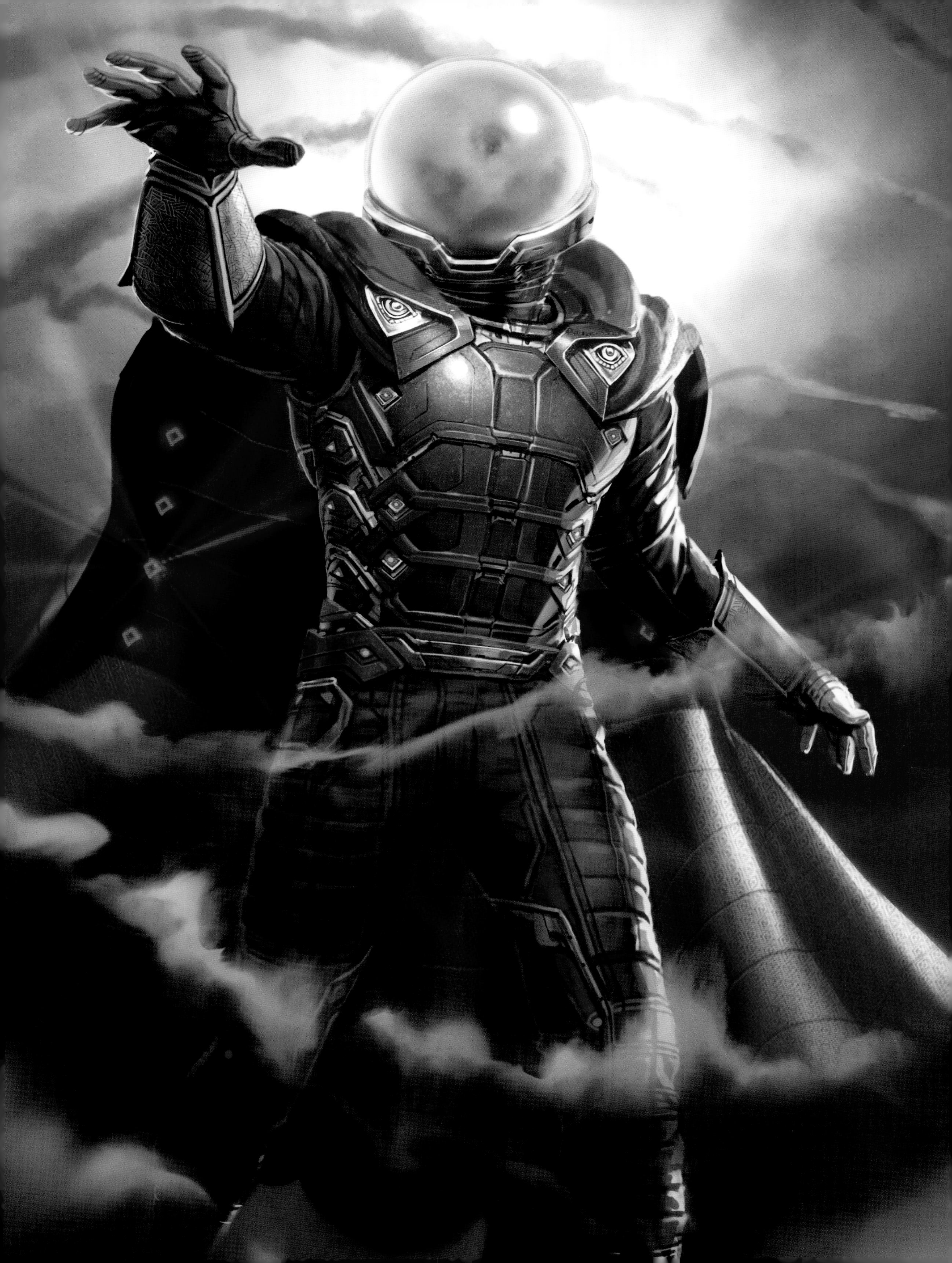

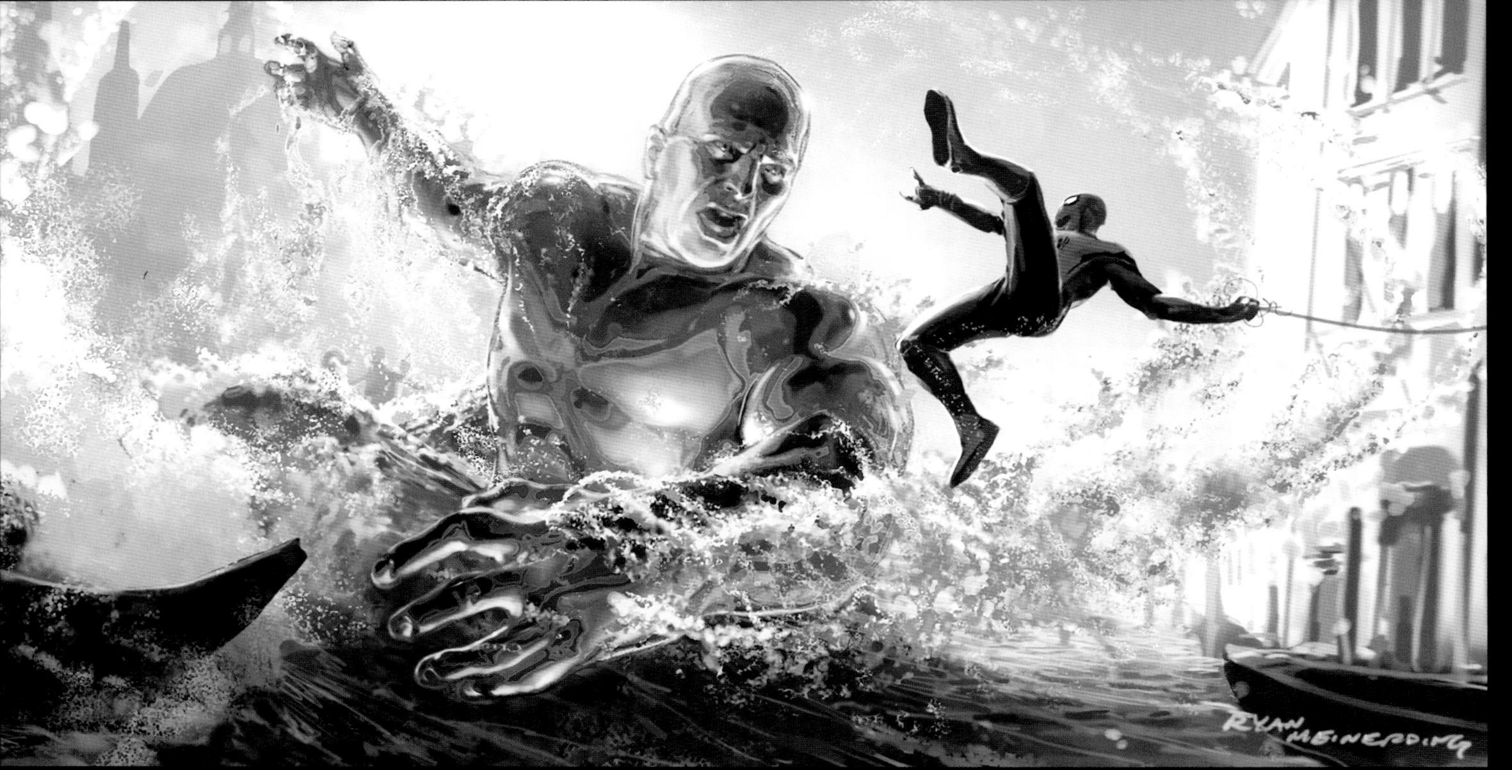
RYAN MEINERDING

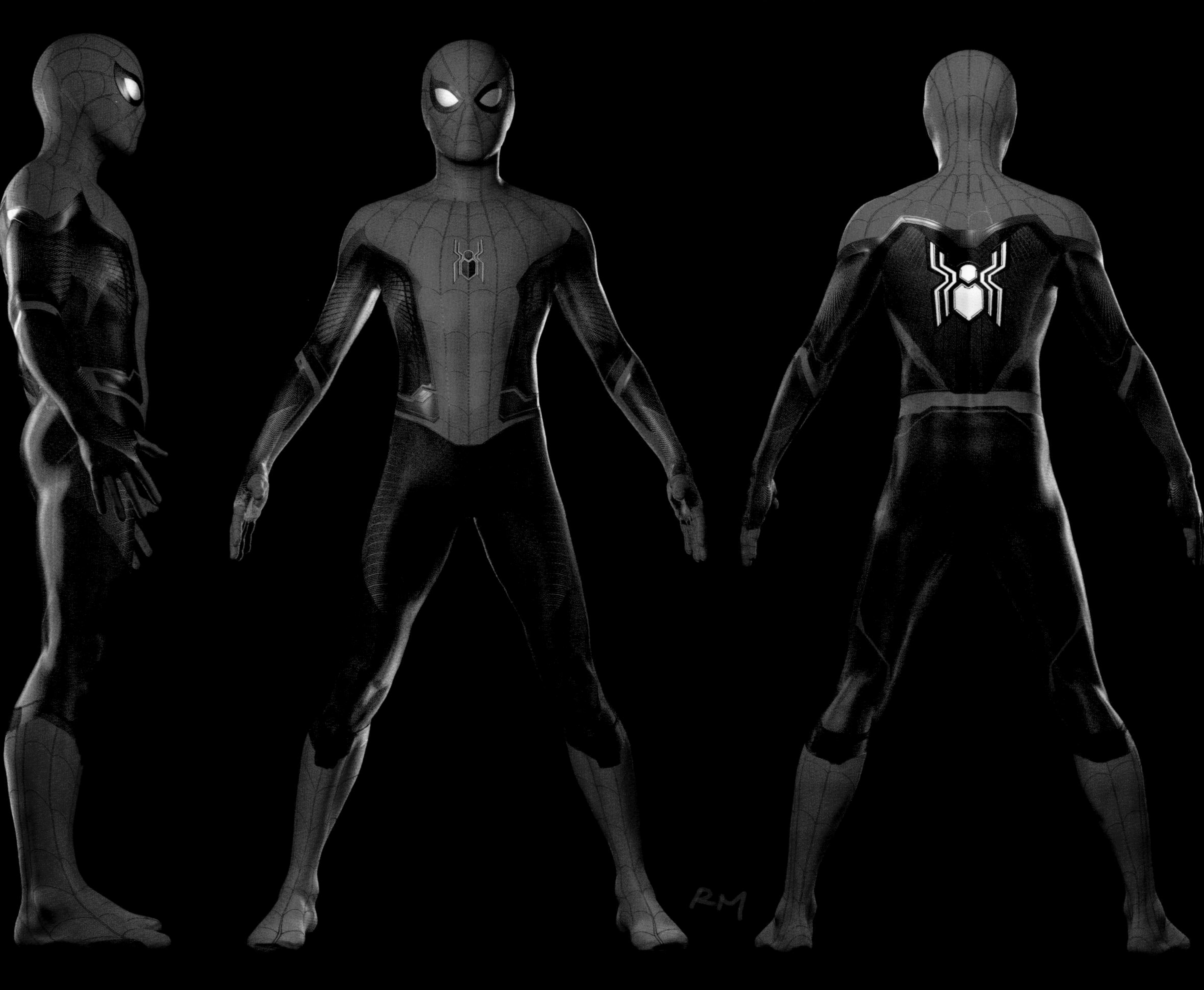
RM

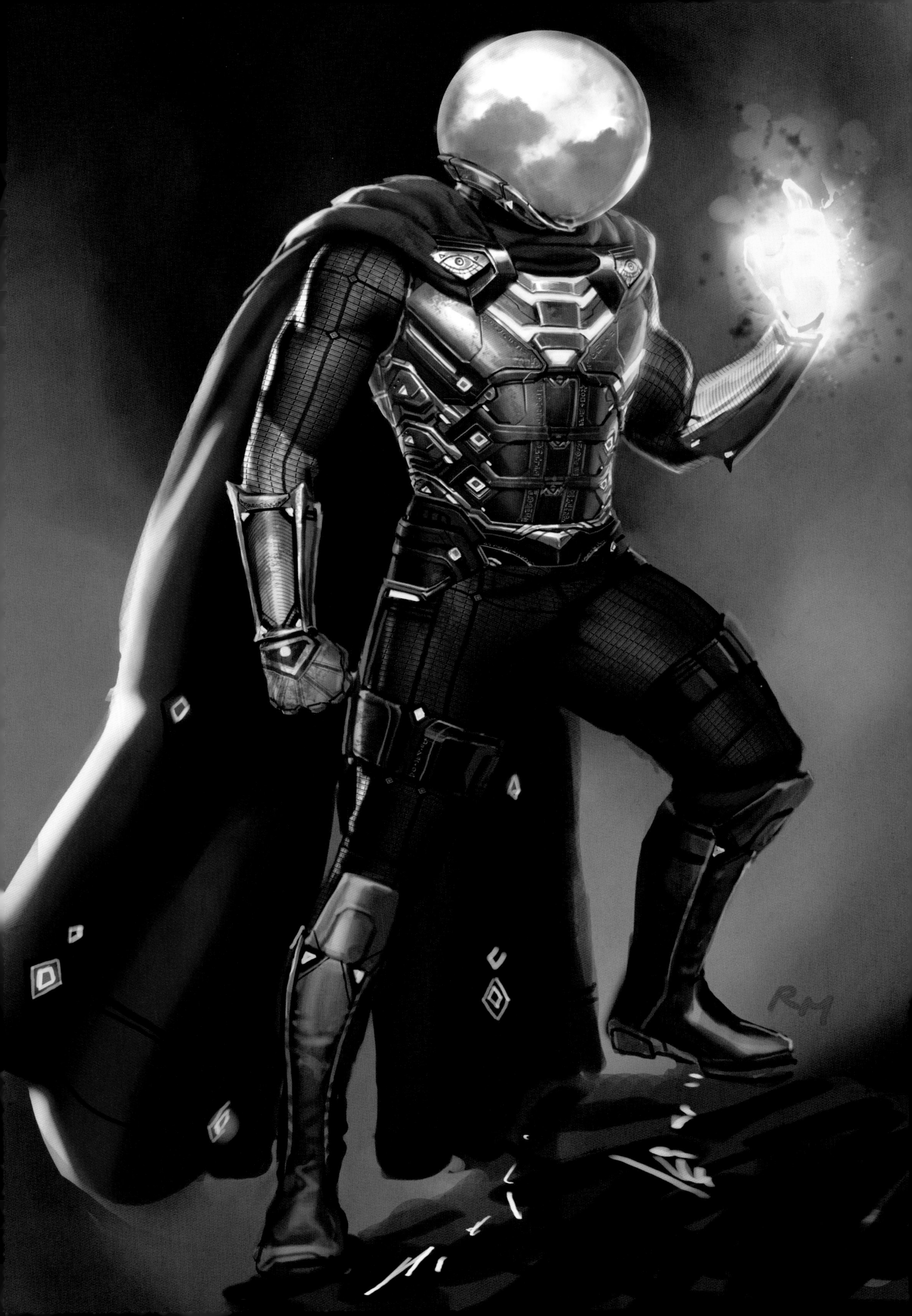
RM

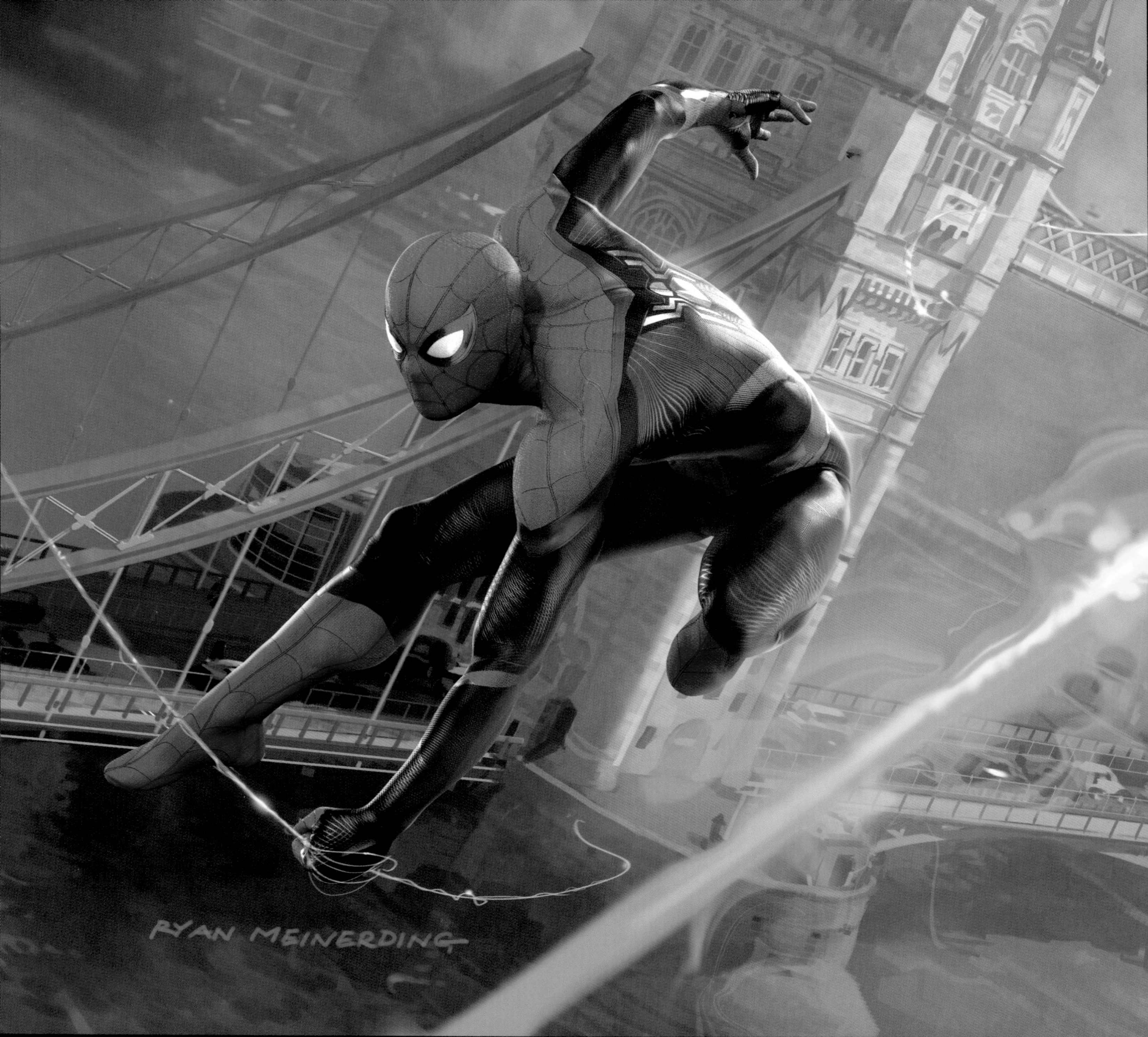
RYAN MEINERDING

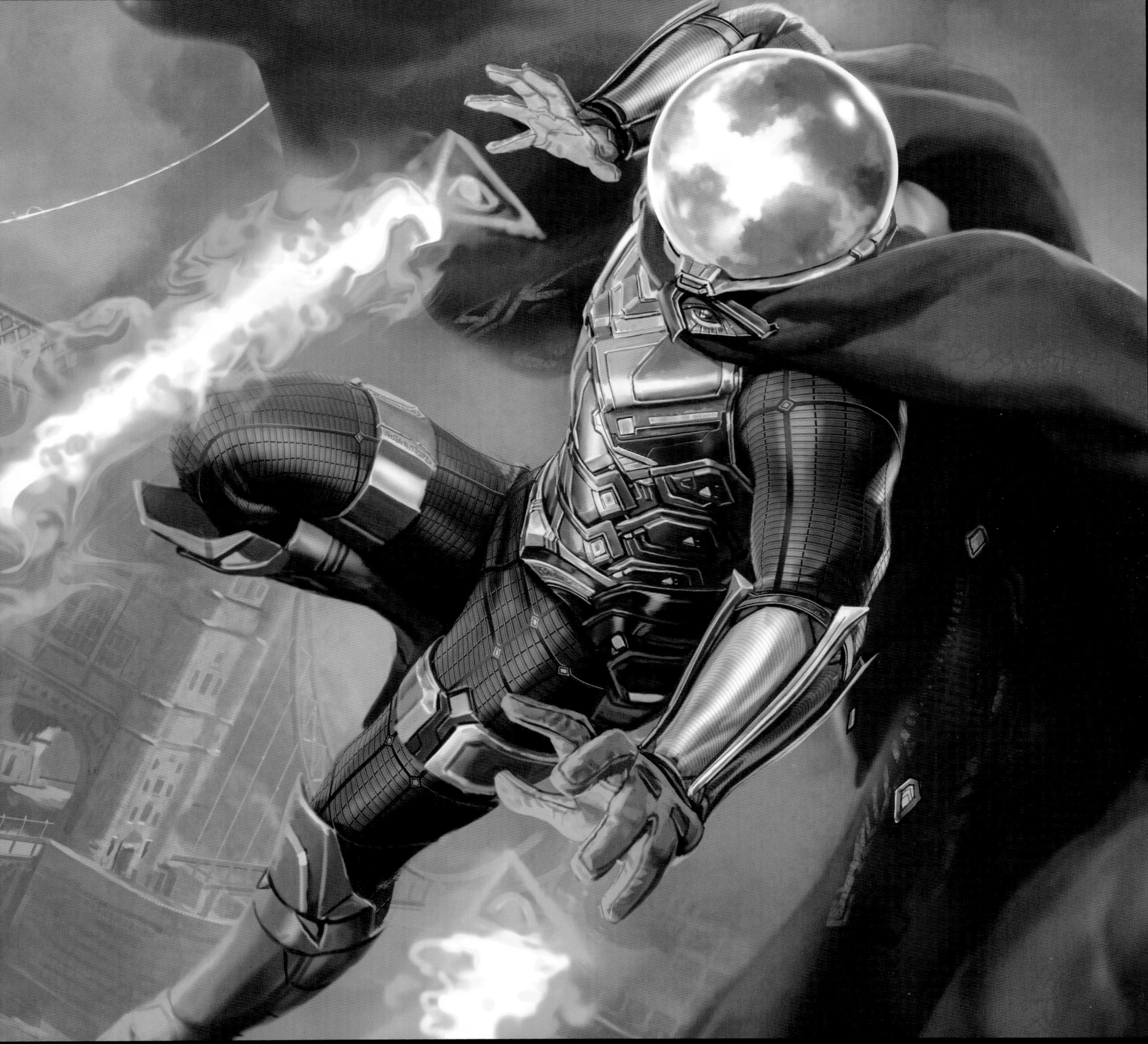

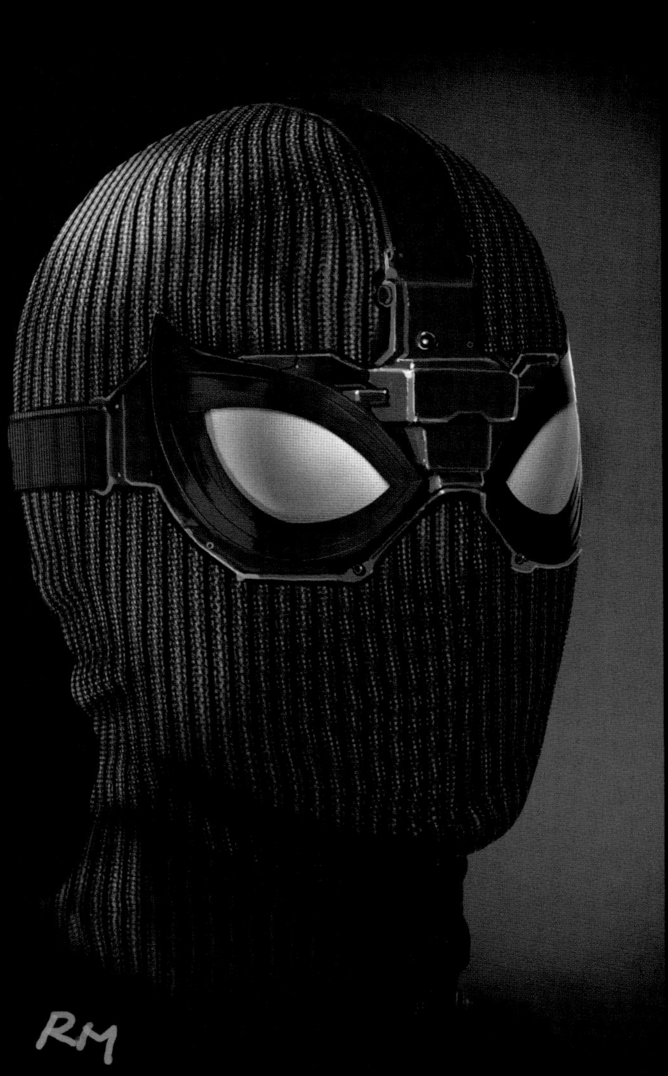
RM

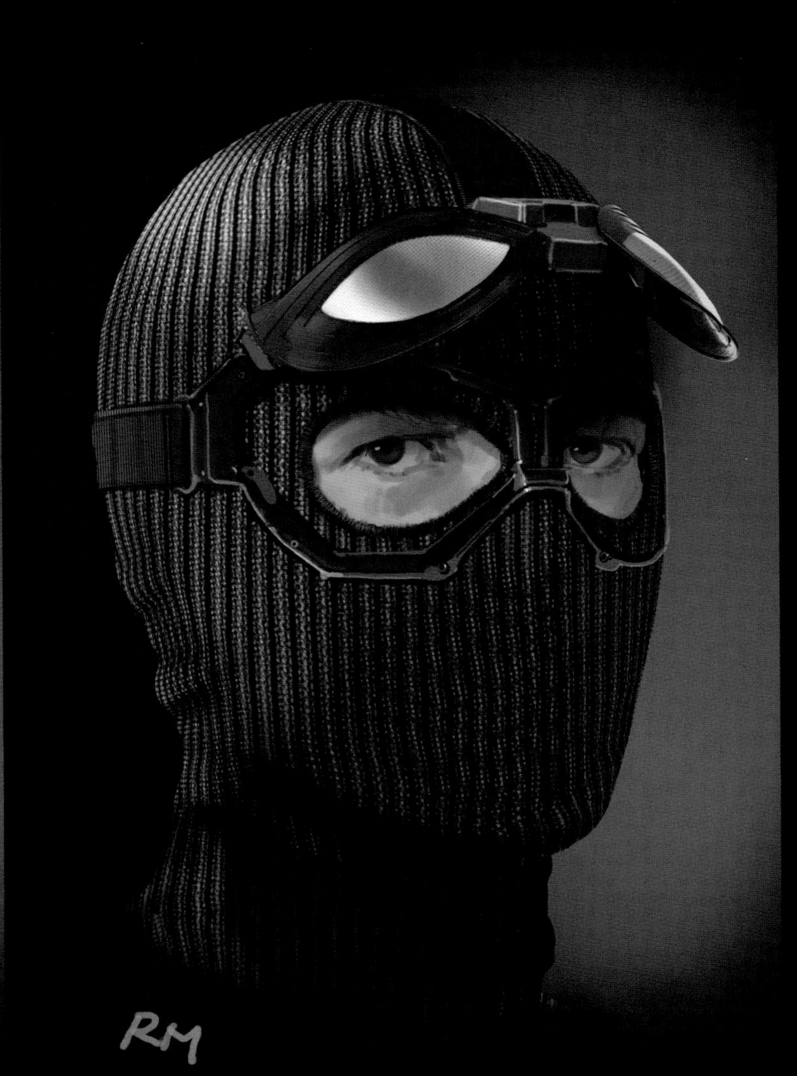
RM

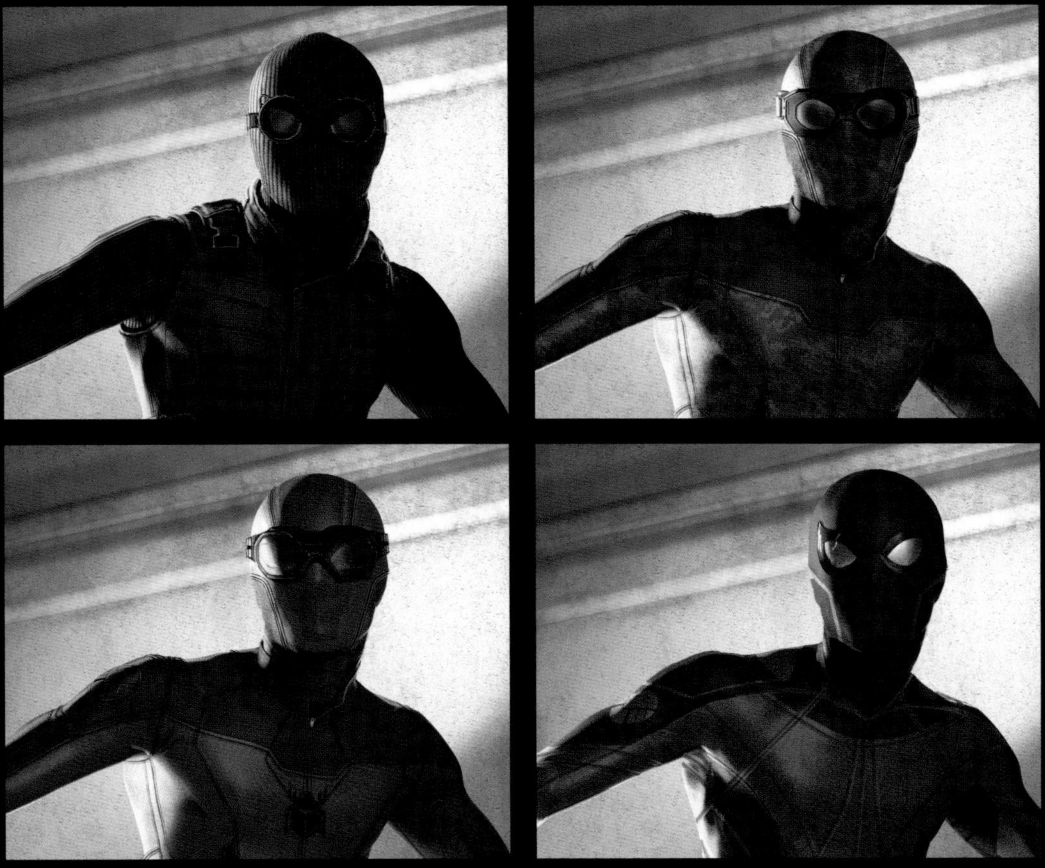

"The black stealth suit was initially supposed to be a left-over S.H.I.E.L.D. outfit," explains Meinerding. "The circle missing on his chest is actually meant to be a S.H.I.E.L.D. insignia that's been pulled off. It was originally going to be a leftover Black Widow outfit. I actually did versions of this with a Black Widow belt buckle, too. The joke was gonna be that he opens up the bag and looks at it and goes, 'Oh, come on, guys.' But as this movie was playing after Black Widow had just died in *Endgame*, we all quickly realized that was never gonna work."

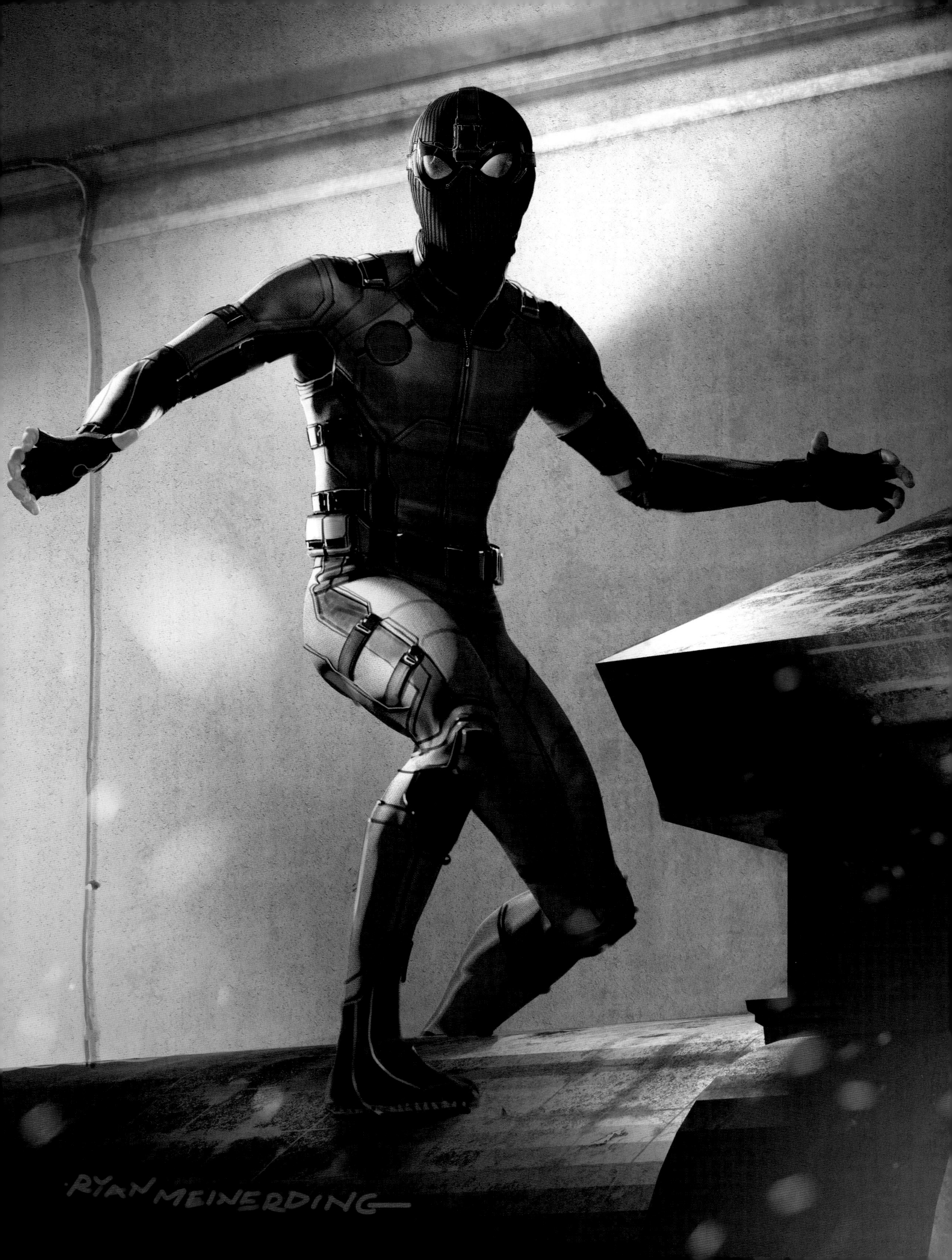
RYAN MEINERDING

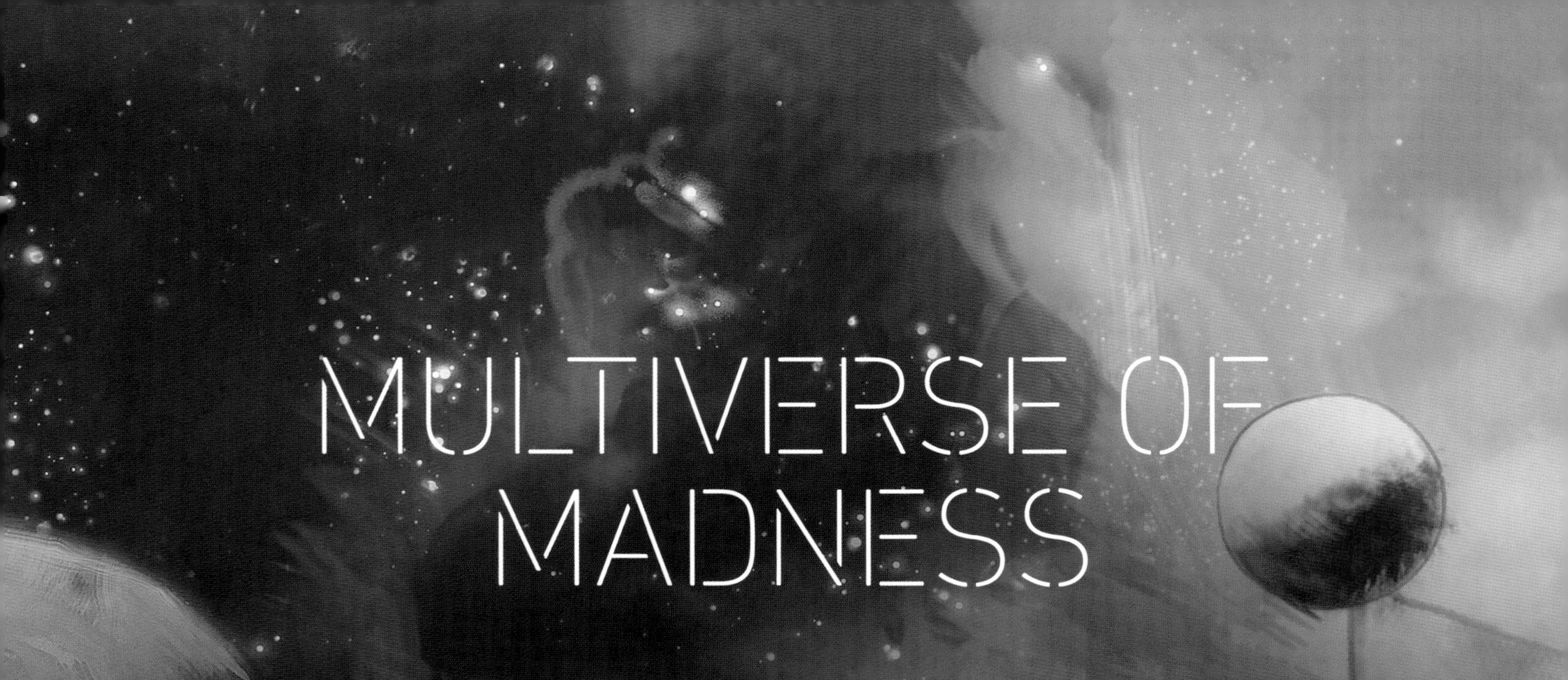

MULTIVERSE OF MADNESS

In 2018, Marvel Studios was gearing up for an expansion unlike anything the studio had embraced before. Bob Iger, the chief executive officer of the Walt Disney Company, asked Kevin Feige, Louis D'Esposito, and Victoria Alonso to develop original streaming series set within the Marvel Cinematic Universe for the upcoming Disney+ subscription service that would launch in November 2019.

Now the Visual Development team would be working not only on theatrical films, but an array of episodic series featuring existing characters like Vision, The Scarlet Witch, the Falcon, and Loki. There would also be brand-new characters from the Marvel Comics library, and for the first-time ever, an original animated series, *What If...?* The scaling up of projects meant Meinerding and his fellow artists had to find a new paradigm of design windows for the streaming shows. For Meinerding, it was an opportunity to design characters for a medium he had longed to experience: animation.

"I had moved out to California to be an animation character designer," he says of his early career aspirations. "I always wanted to do it, but switched gears when I had a lot more opportunities in live action." Knowing he would always regret not throwing his hat into the ring for *What If...?,* Meinerding pitched designing the characters to Feige and series executive producer Brad Winderbaum.

They approved, allowing Meinerding to passionately jump into the series' development. "I did as much work as quickly as I could," he says of their tight turnaround for the series' preproduction. "I tried to help define the style of the characters and the look of the show. Honestly, I was most useful with the characters because I was riffing on a lot of stuff I had already designed."

Having an intimate design knowledge about many of the bedrock MCU characters, Meinerding was able to use a shorthand when tweaking characters for certain episodic concepts. He worked closely with series director Bryan Andrews, who suggested early on that *What If...?* be modeled in the visual style of famed illustrator J.C. Leyendecker.

As it turns out, Leyendecker was one of Meinerding's artistic inspirations, and his style was one he was eager to explore. "I had never purposely tried to draw or paint like Leyendecker, but the challenge of trying to do that and bring it to an animated series was too amazing to pass up," he says. "I had to give it a shot." For the first season of *What If...?,* Meinerding designed close to seventy characters.

For almost twenty years, Ryan Meinerding has been an integral part of the shaping how audiences around the globe see and embrace the characters of the Marvel Cinematic Universe. Rarely one to stop and take stock of his own career evolution (there's always more work to do), Meinerding admits that he has recently slowed down a bit to appreciate the depth and breadth of what Marvel Studios has accomplished over the span of numerous phases of interconnected storytelling via hundreds of individual characters.

"The ride for me has been amazing. When I was leaving art school, had somebody asked me to write down the ideal course for my career, I couldn't have written a script that would be better than what this has turned out to be. There's no other position I could have in the film business that would be as similar. I look back with joy on almost all parts of it. The only things that I lament are things like, I wish I could work a little harder or with more energy," he admits with his typical Midwestern candor.

"I never thought it was gonna be this big," he continues. "I thought we would make it to *Avengers*, and that's incredible. But Kevin has found a way to do things that at every stage feel like they're special. When I look back at that specialness in the stages, I have tried to fully appreciate every moment they've allowed me to participate in. I think of those moments and the great people I've gotten to work with and the artwork that I've done that I'm really proud of. These characters, right now, are finding a new popularity that they've never really achieved in the past. Some of them have, but not all of them."

"And whether I'm remembered at all or as part of the films, I'm still fortunate that I've gotten to make art in a similar way to any of the amazing *Captain America* comic book artists that have drawn him in the past," he says of his place in Marvel's long artistic history. "It's been a lot of hard work, a lot of blood, sweat, and tears, but I'm looking forward to when each and every one of these projects comes out. This feels like the next culmination, and then hopefully a reinvigoration. I'm ready for what's coming after that."

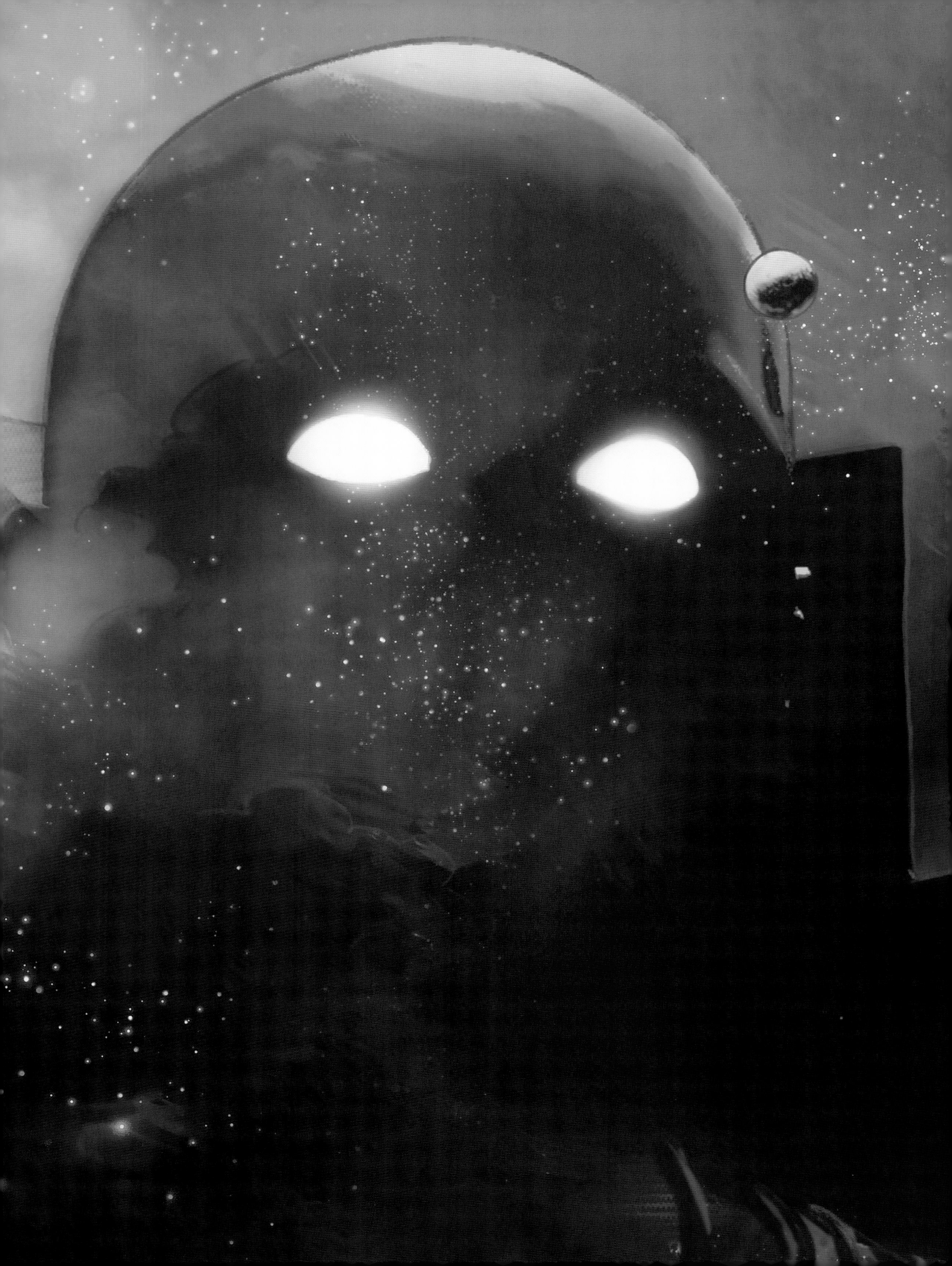

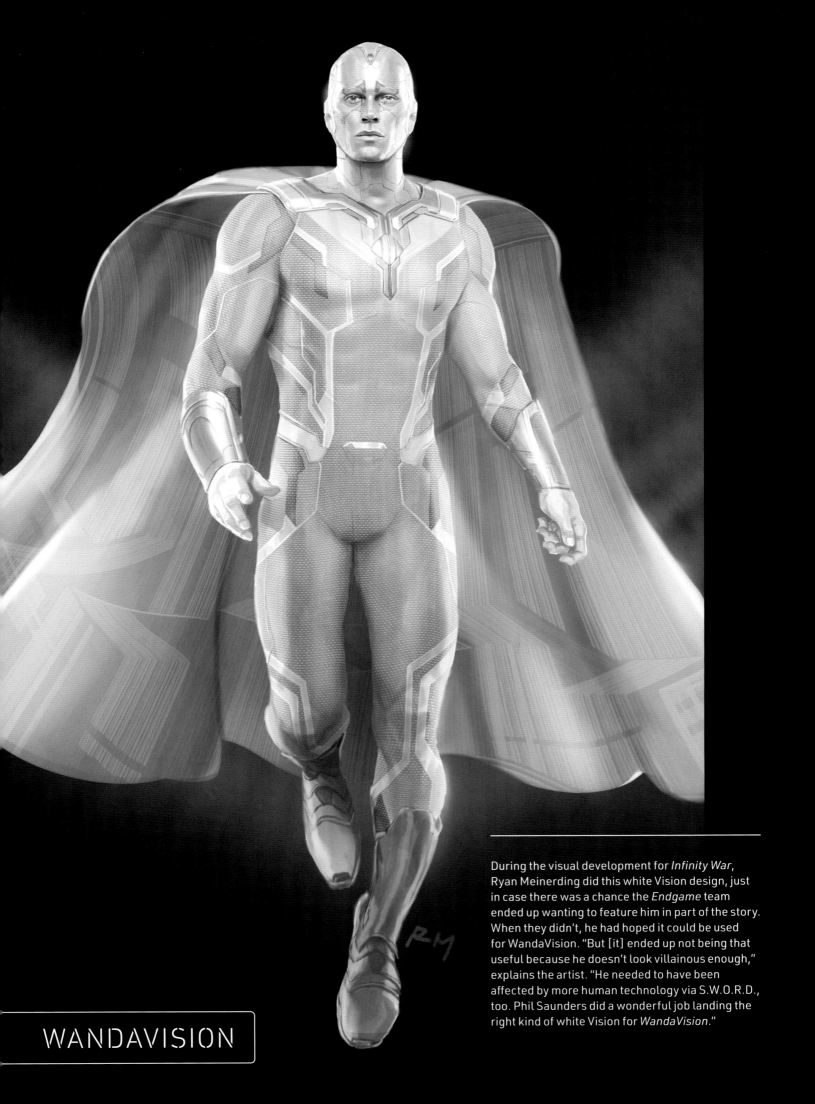

During the visual development for *Infinity War*, Ryan Meinerding did this white Vision design, just in case there was a chance the *Endgame* team ended up wanting to feature him in part of the story. When they didn't, he had hoped it could be used for WandaVision. "But [it] ended up not being that useful because he doesn't look villainous enough," explains the artist. "He needed to have been affected by more human technology via S.W.O.R.D., too. Phil Saunders did a wonderful job landing the right kind of white Vision for *WandaVision*."

WANDAVISION

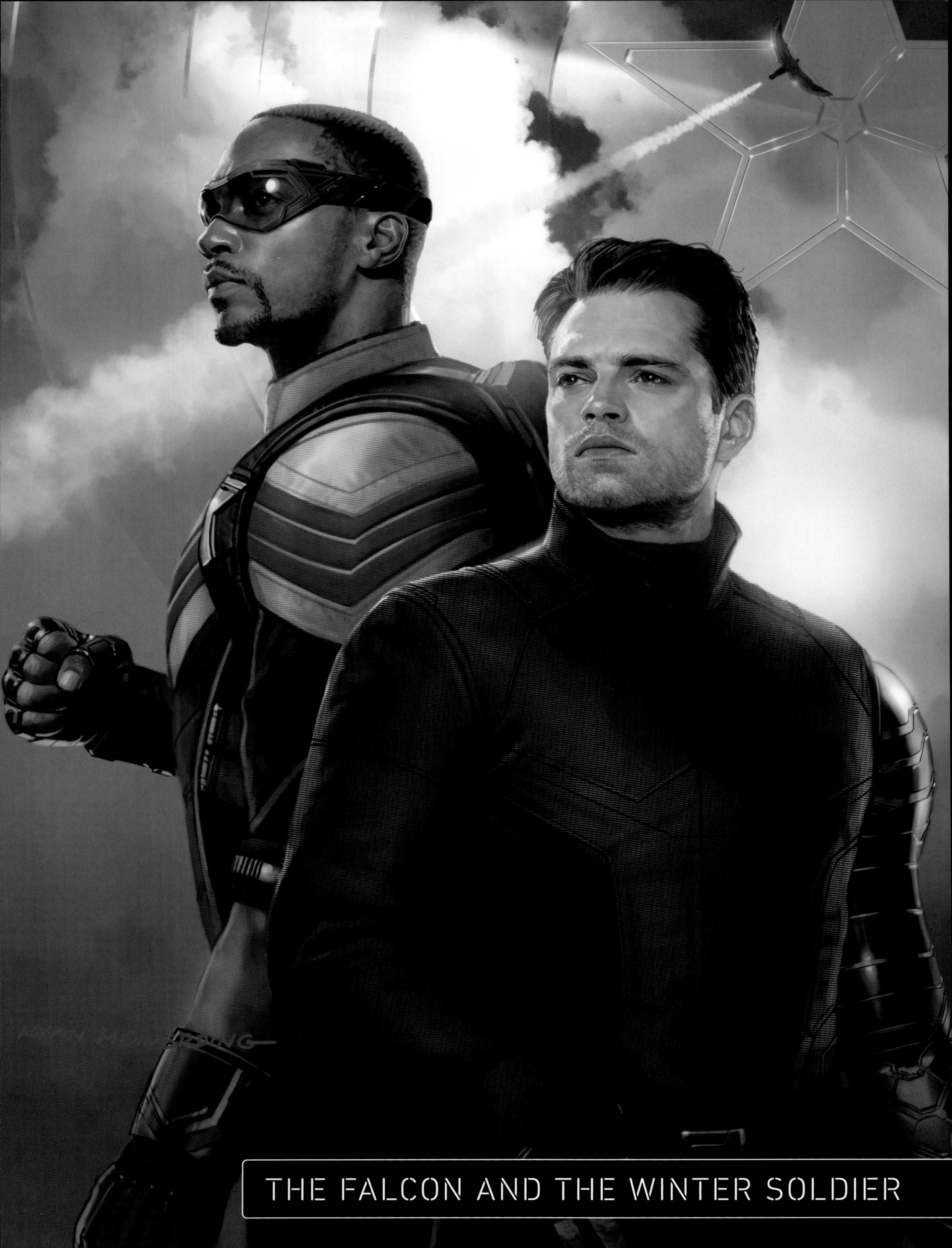

THE FALCON AND THE WINTER SOLDIER

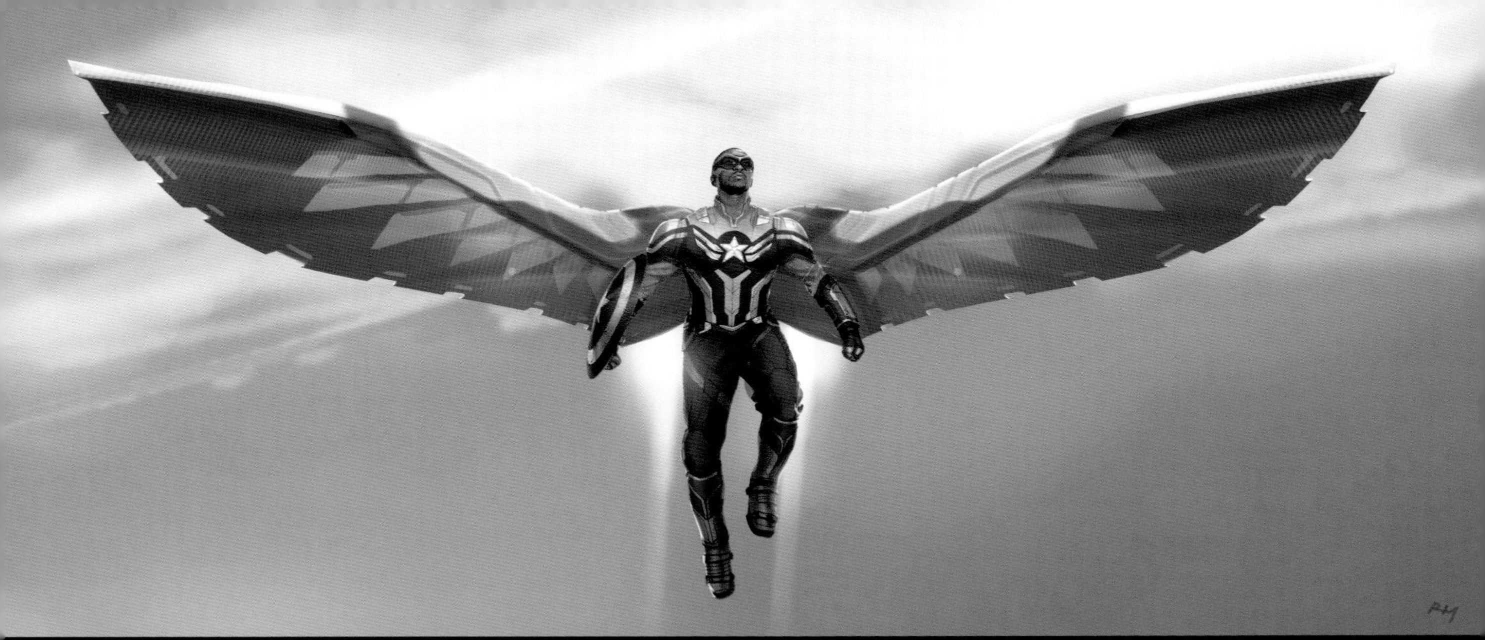
RM

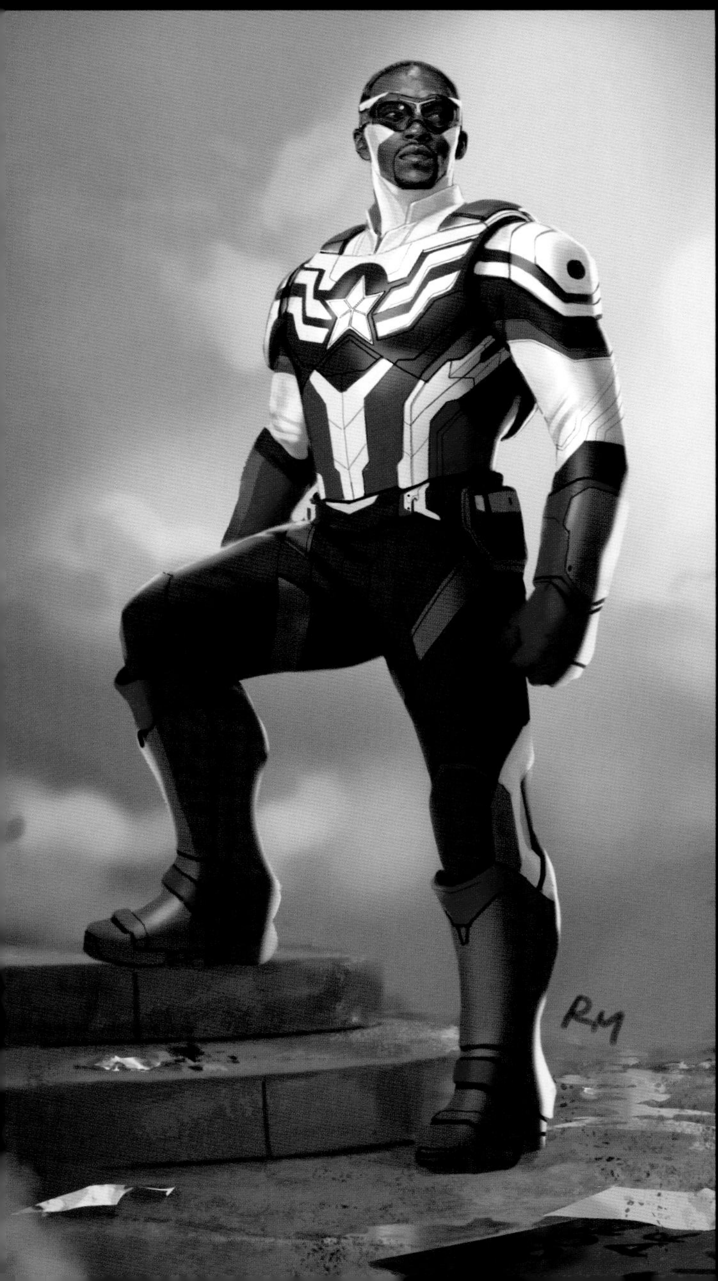
RM

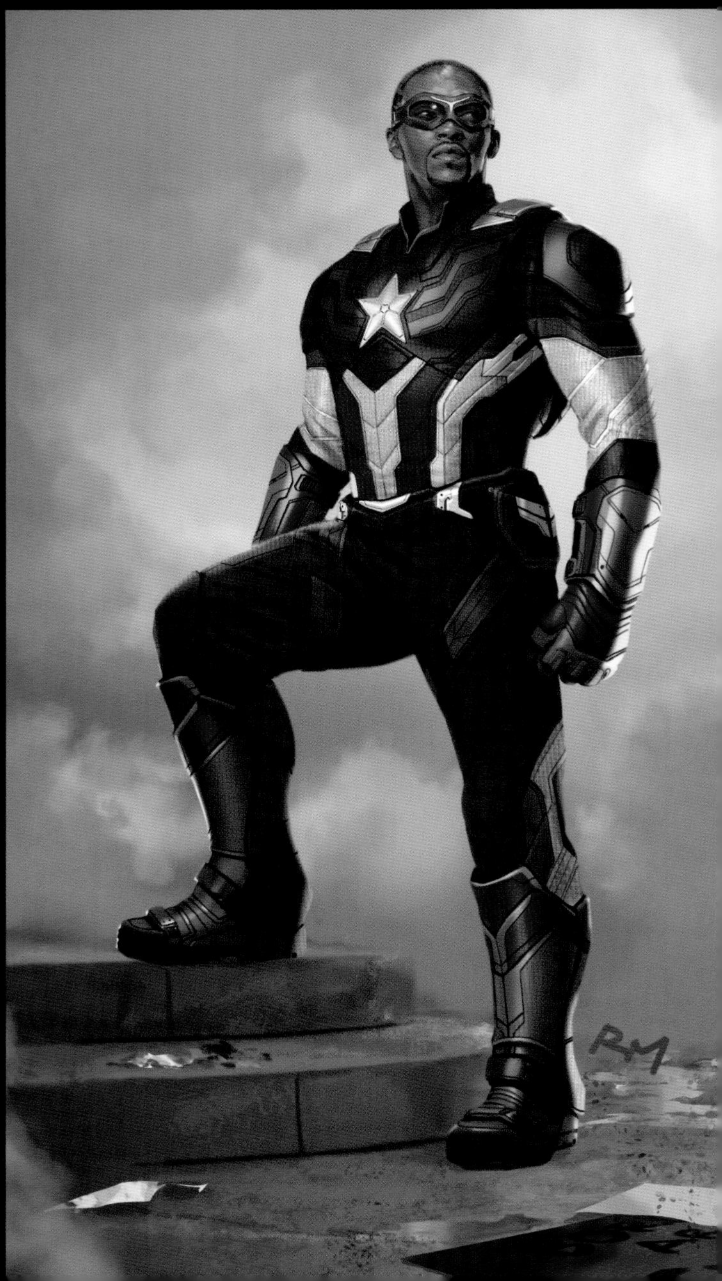
RM

In regard to Sam Wilson transitioning from the Falcon into the next Captain America, the only note Meinerding got from Kevin Feige was that he had to have the cowl and the goggles. "It's from the comics, and it's a unique costume detail for Sam as Captain America," he says. "But I did explorations with only the goggles, too, just to explore how it might look and feel without the cowl. It's a challenging outfit. I was trying to keep a lot of the bulk that he had as Falcon. It was a lot of fun trying to find a new look for Sam."

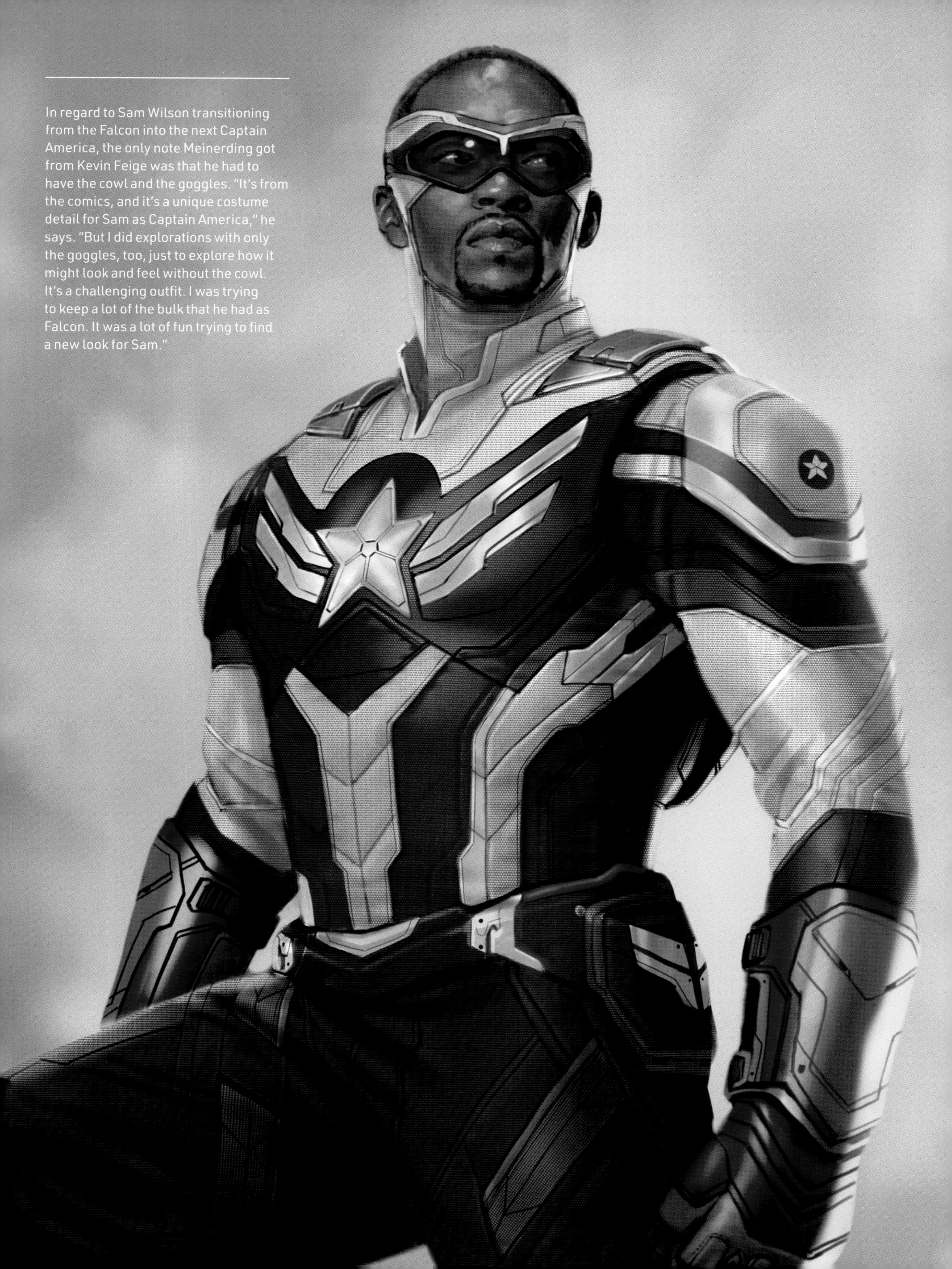

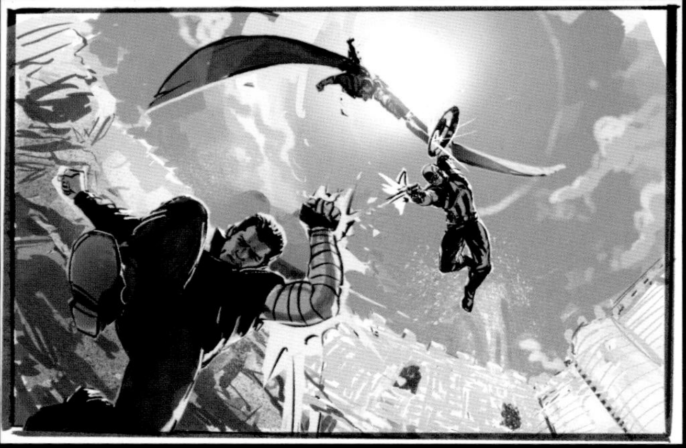

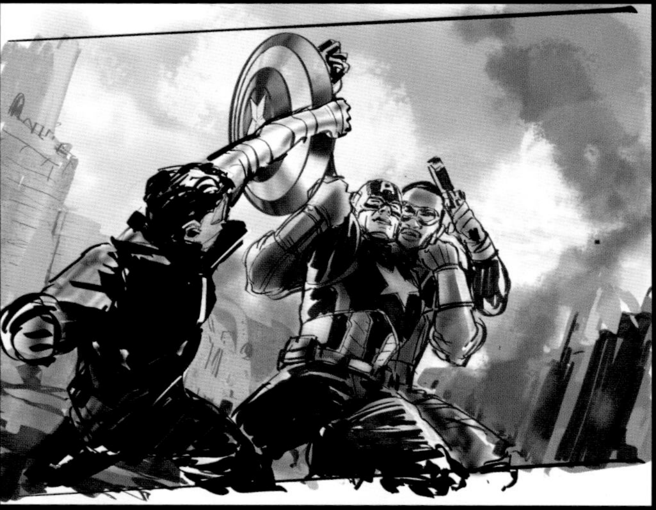

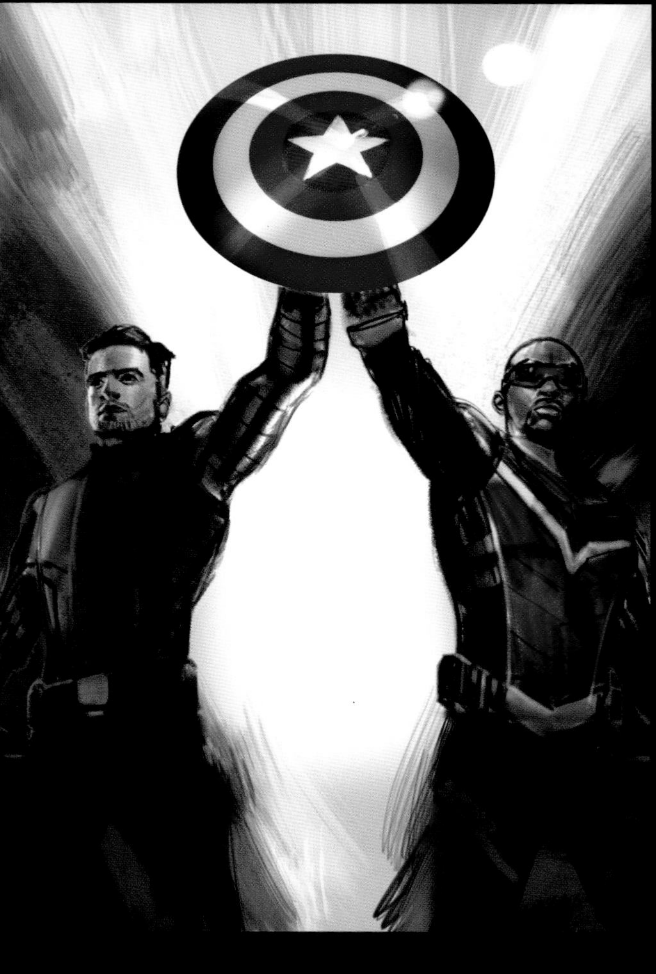

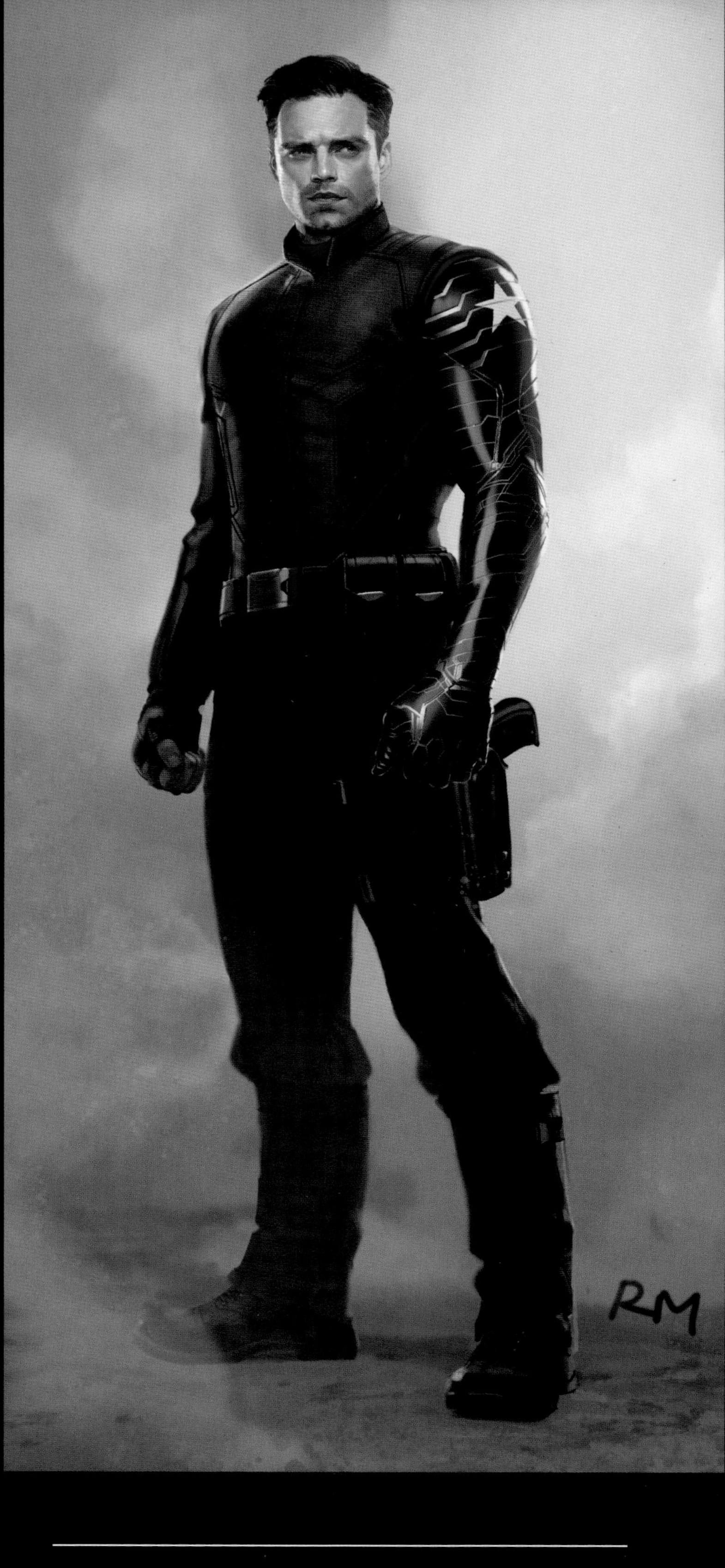
RM

"Working on Bucky is always fun, and having to design John Walker's Cap and U.S.Agent costumes was also really interesting," says Meinerding. "I approached it like Walker's Cap look was kind of the less inspired and unworthy successor to Steve Rogers's Captain America. As I already had the previous Cap designs from the other movies to base it on, I felt like I had a bit of a leg up with that one."

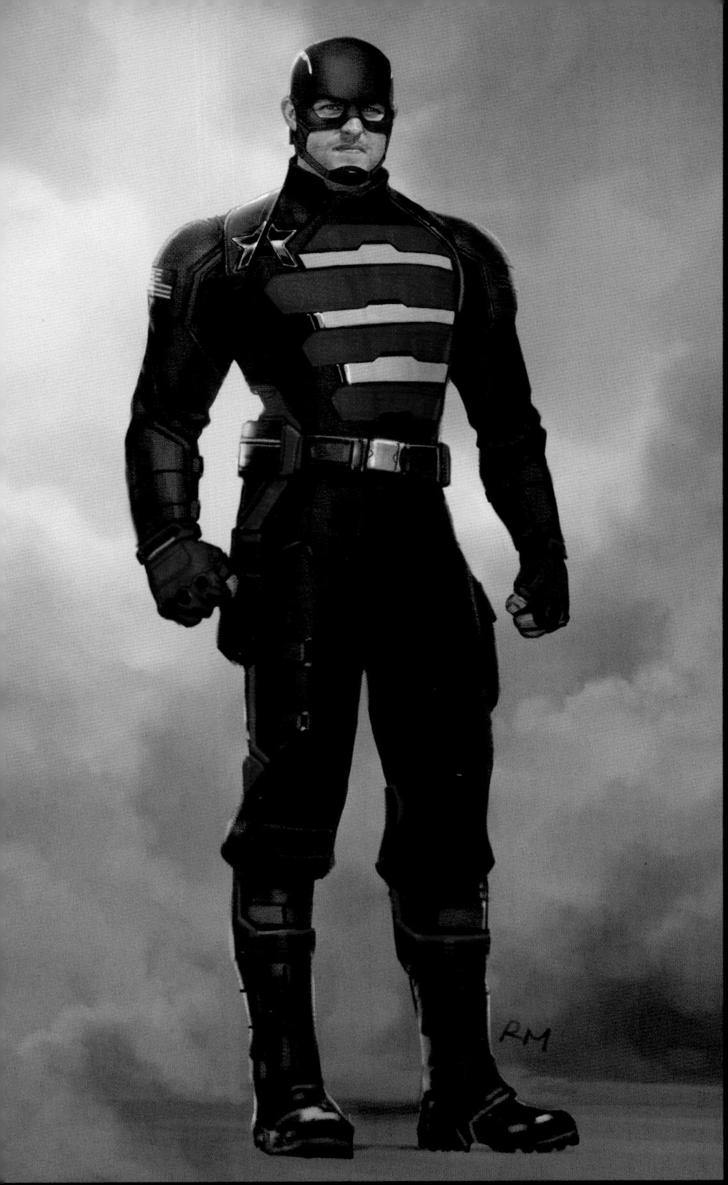
RM

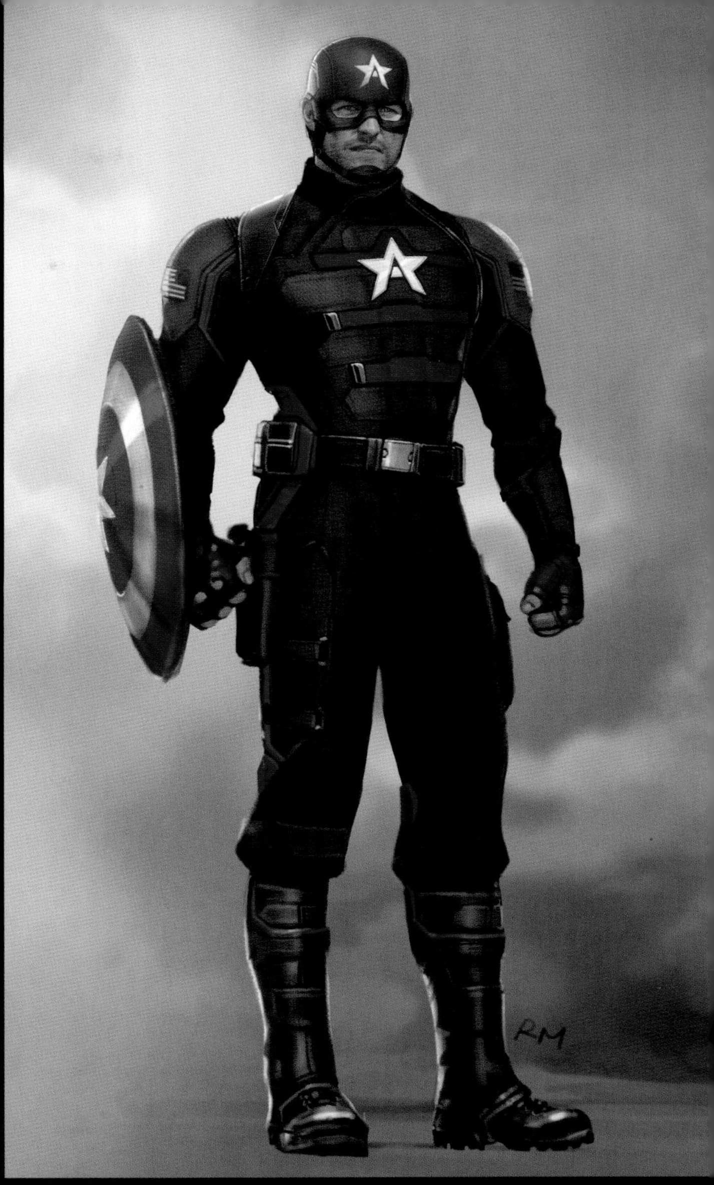
RM

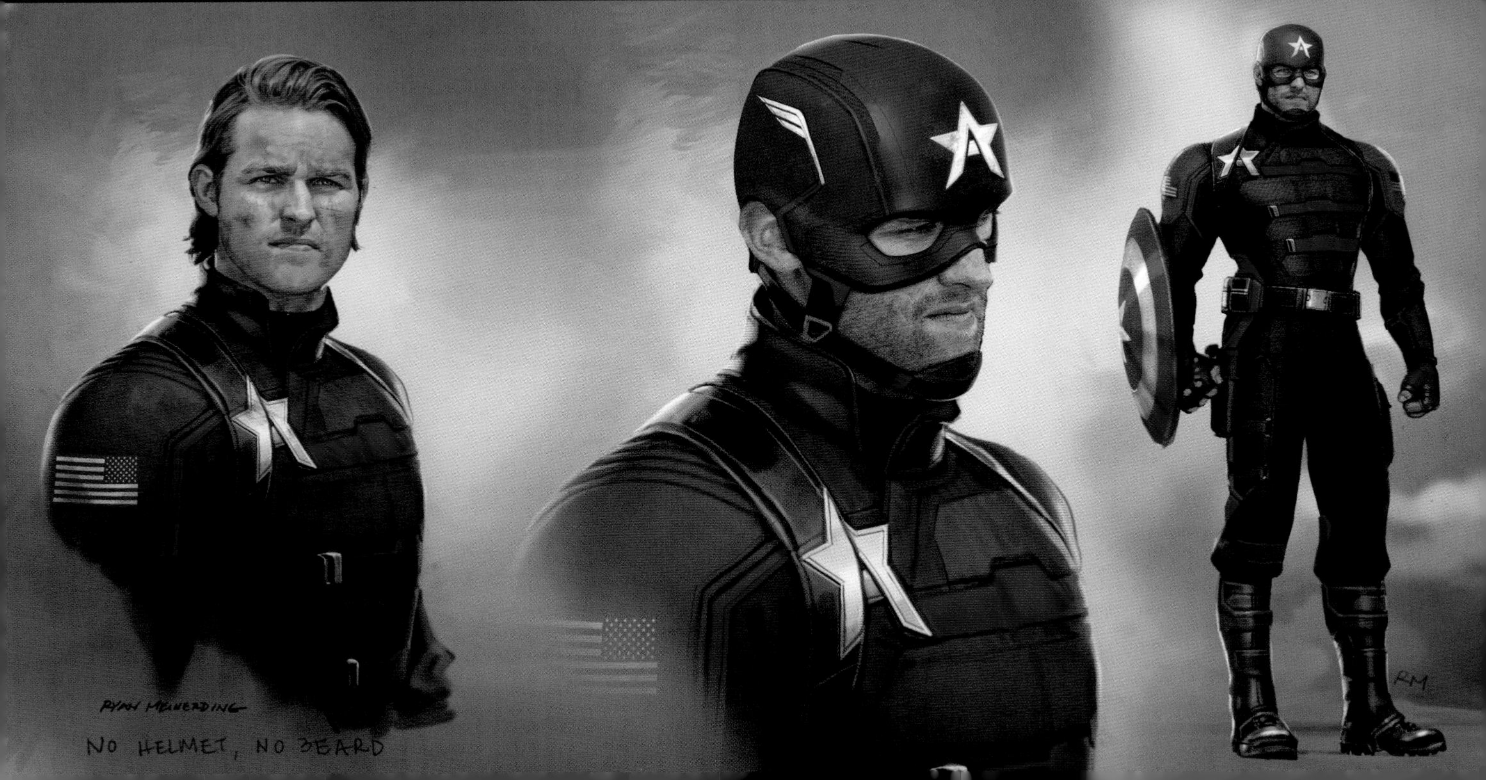
RYAN MEINERDING
NO HELMET, NO BEARD
RM

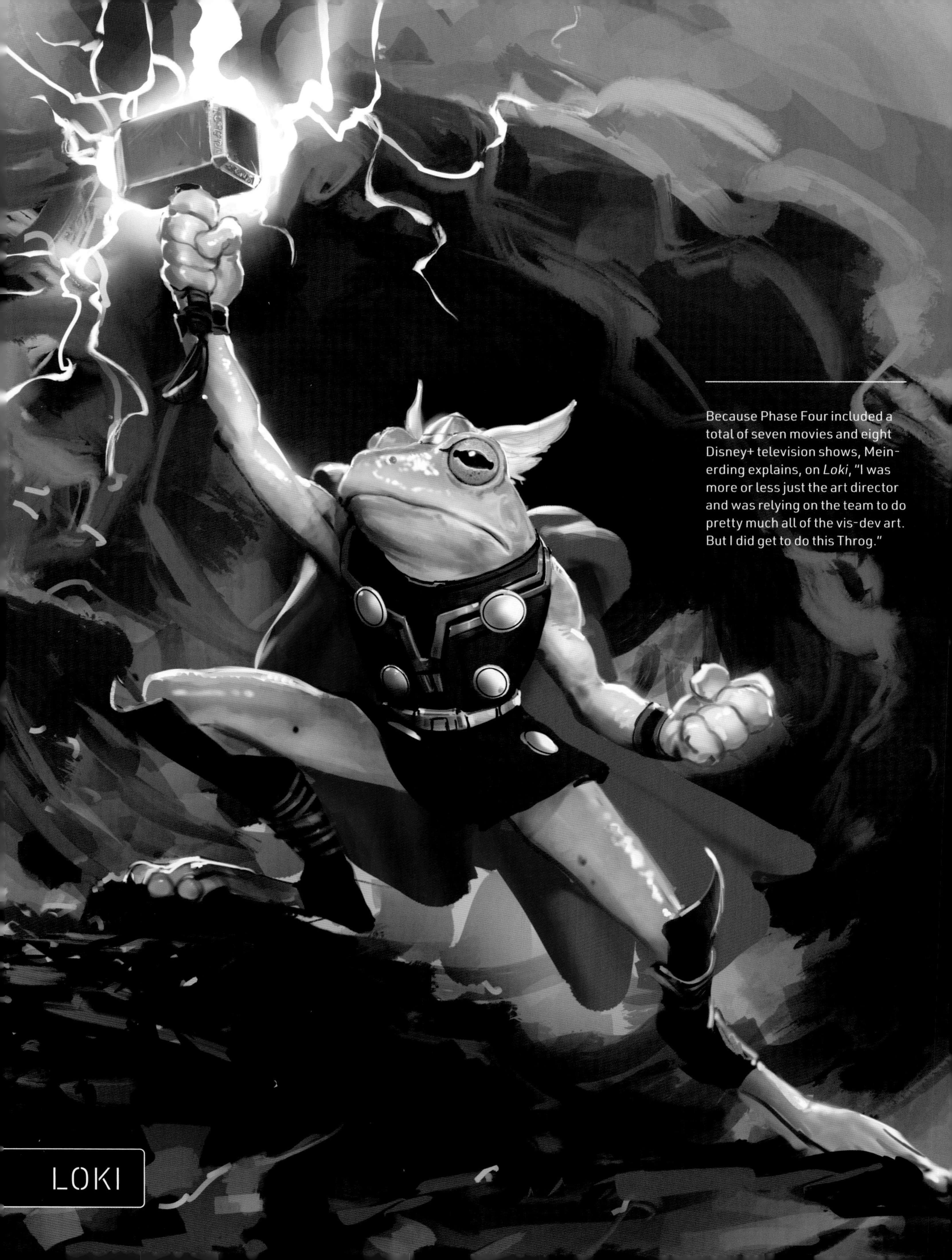

Because Phase Four included a total of seven movies and eight Disney+ television shows, Meinerding explains, on *Loki*, "I was more or less just the art director and was relying on the team to do pretty much all of the vis-dev art. But I did get to do this Throg."

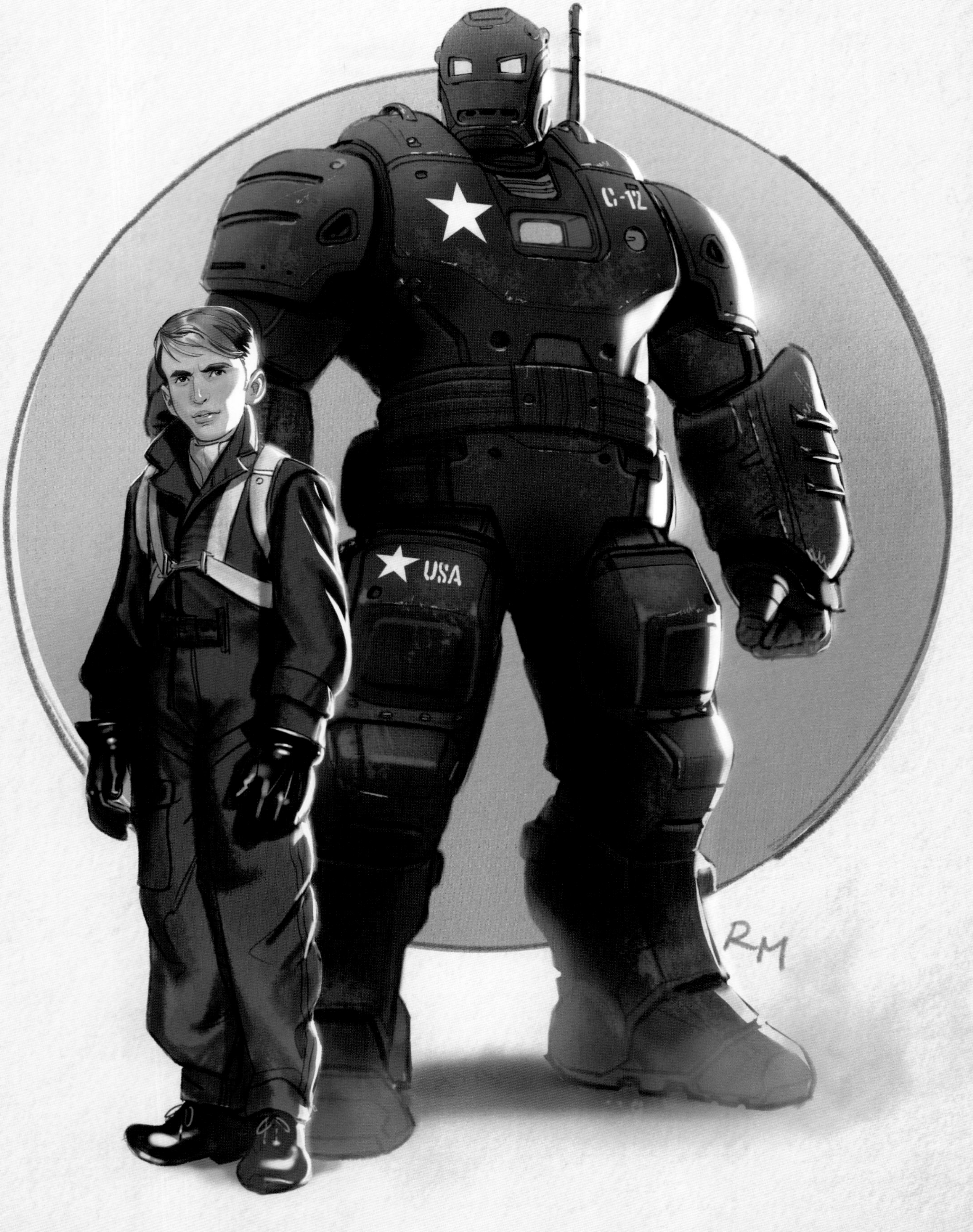
C-12
USA
RM

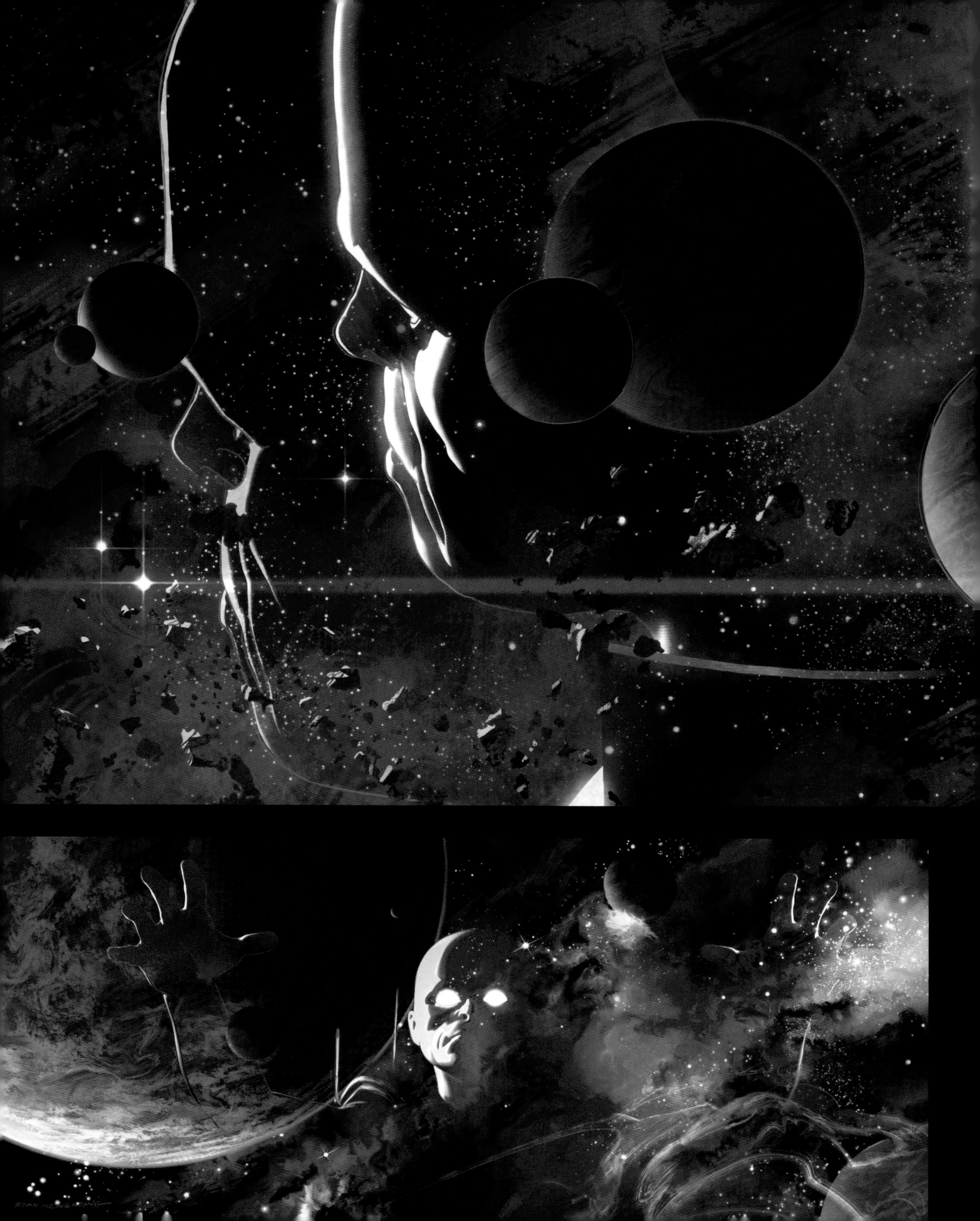

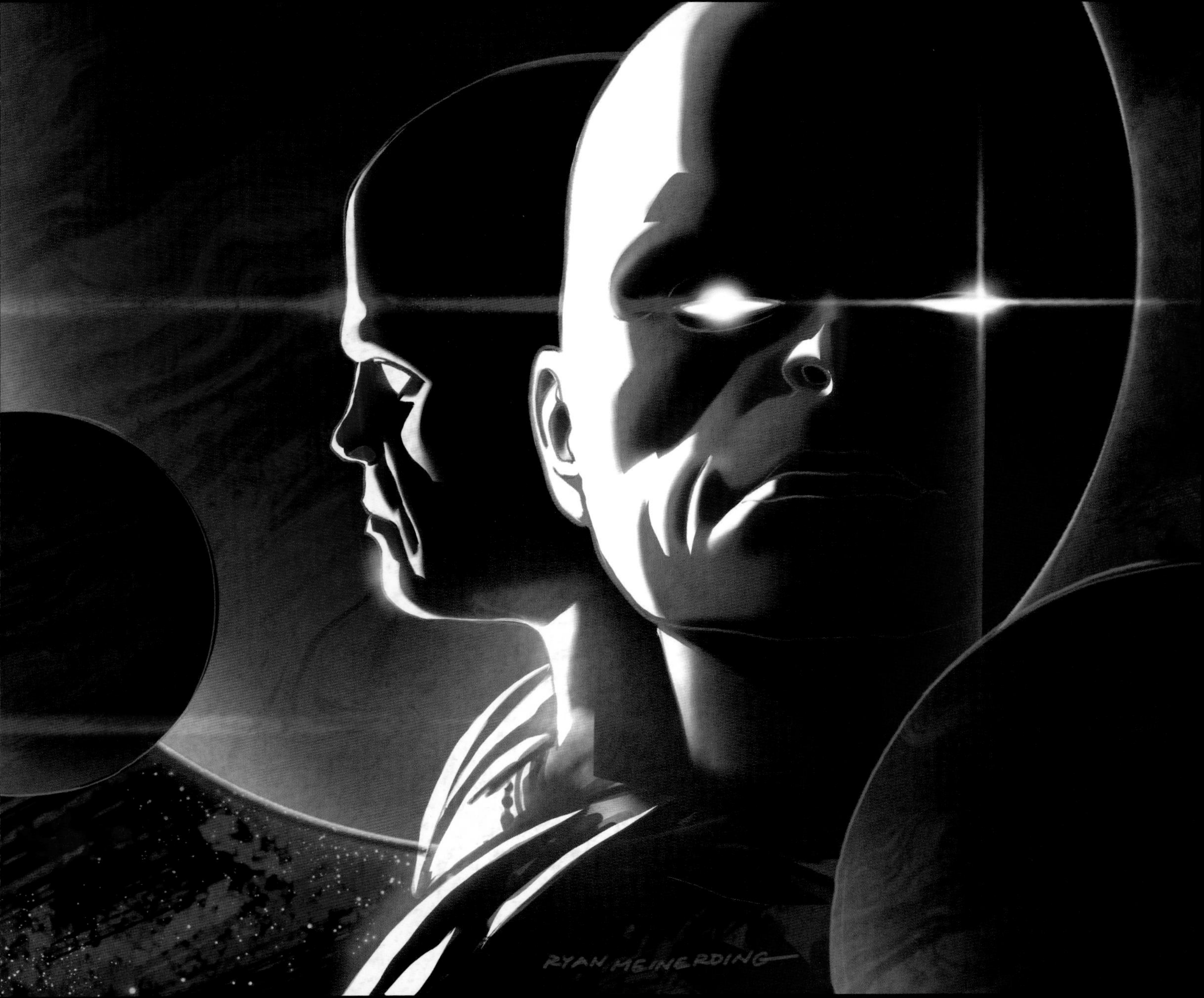
RYAN MEINERDING

The big difference between Ryan Meinerding's character designs for the animated series *What If...?* and his vis-dev art for the live-action projects is how much more quickly ideas can come together because photorealism isn't the goal. "The drawing, the iterations, and the actual design work for that show is not the time-consuming part," shares the artist. Which was necessary as he had around *seventy* characters to design for the first season. "It's all the work with the vendor—transitioning them into 3D and then into the animation pipeline—that takes the most time," he adds.

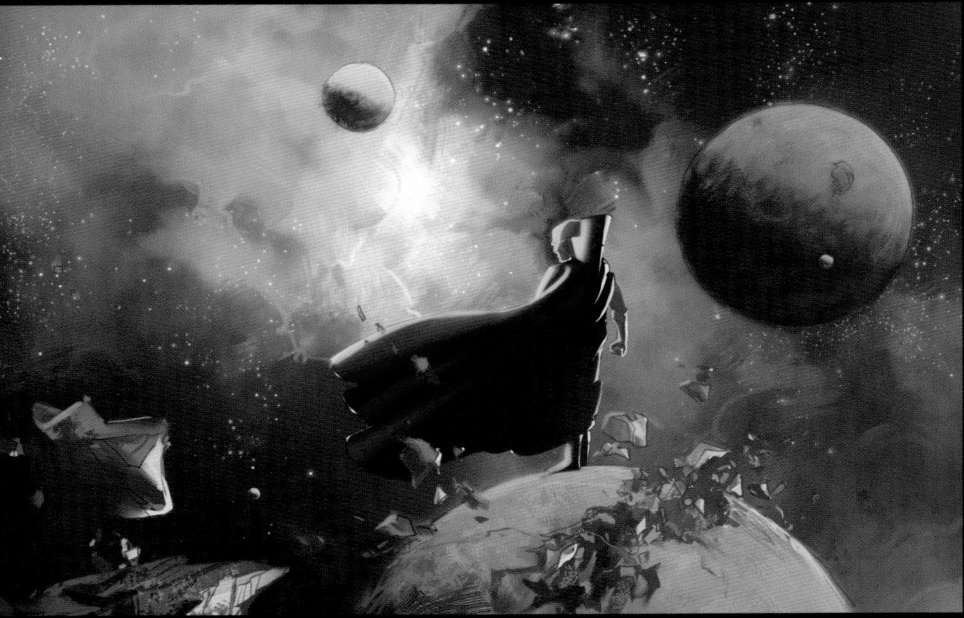

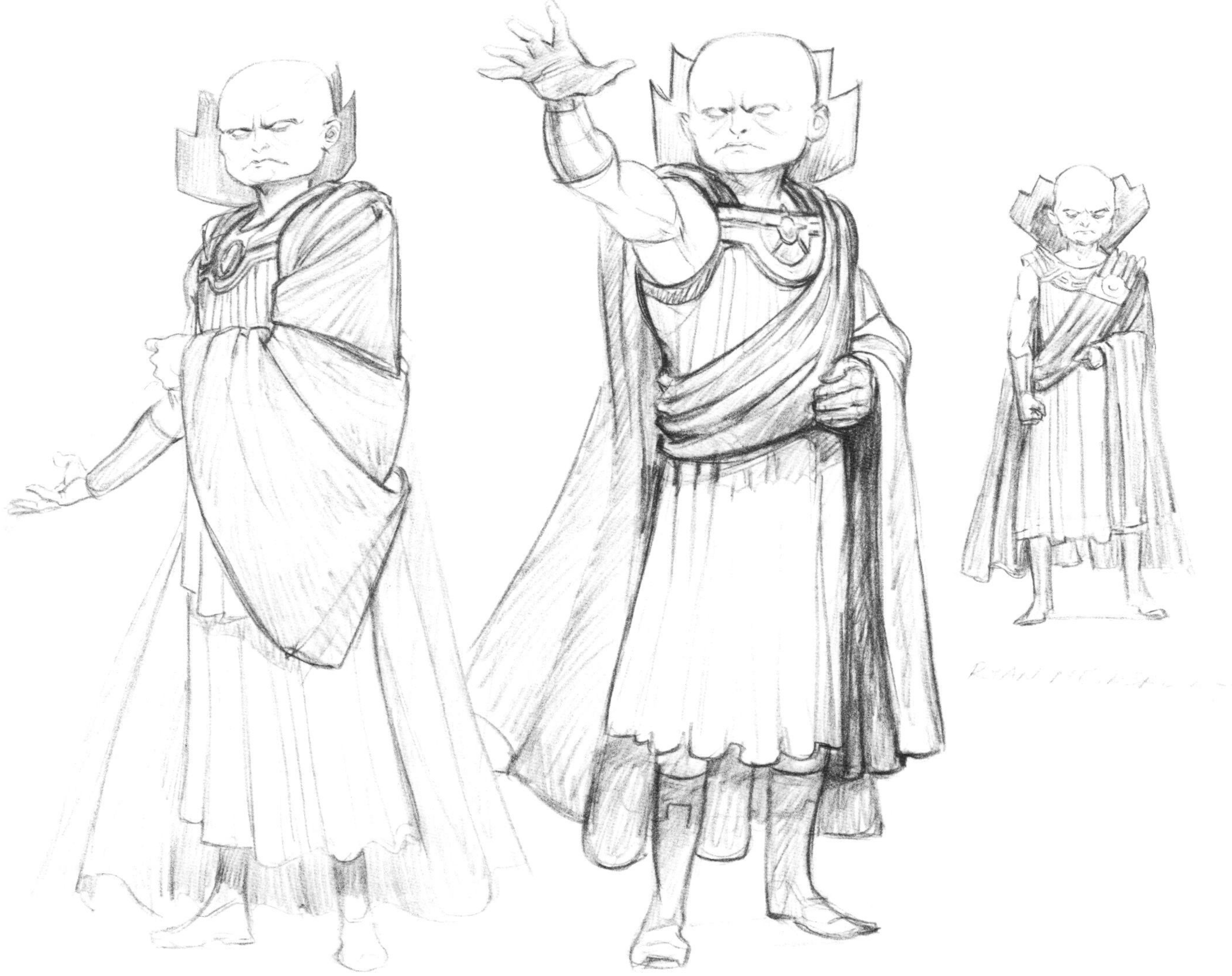

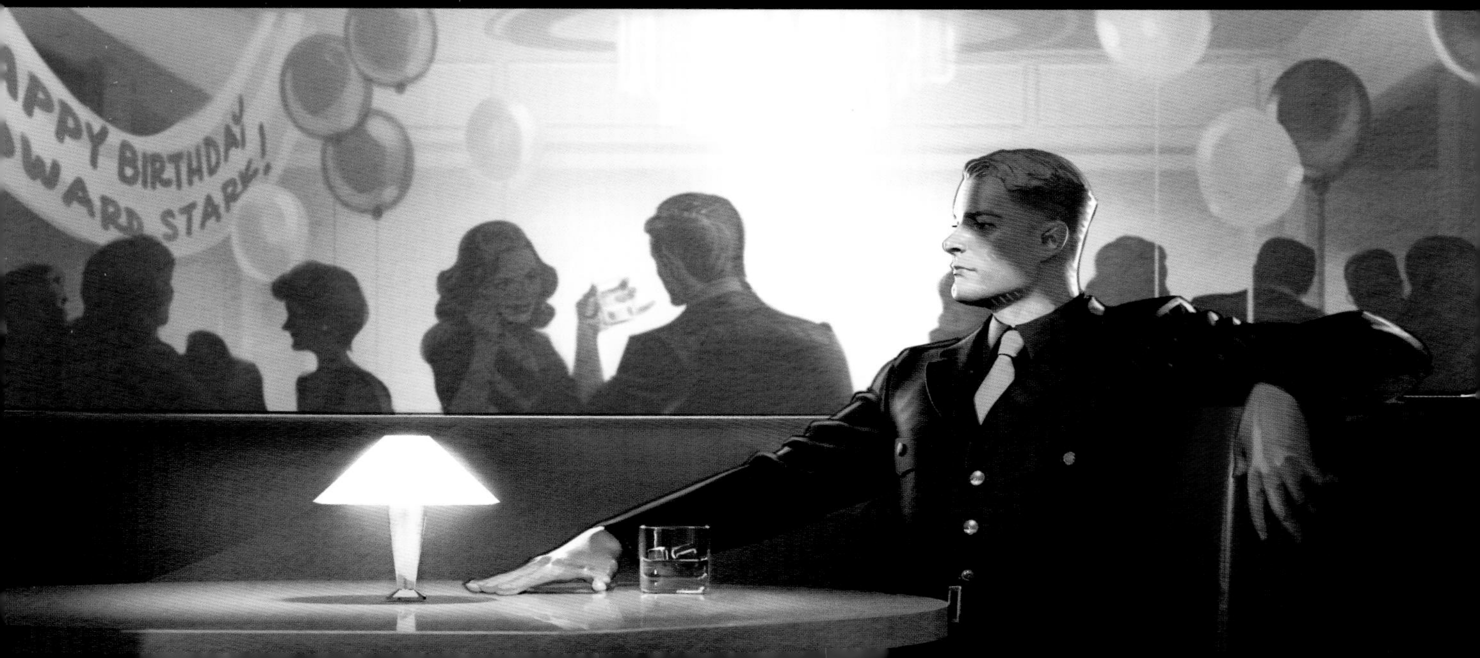

APPY BIRTHDAY
WARD STARK!

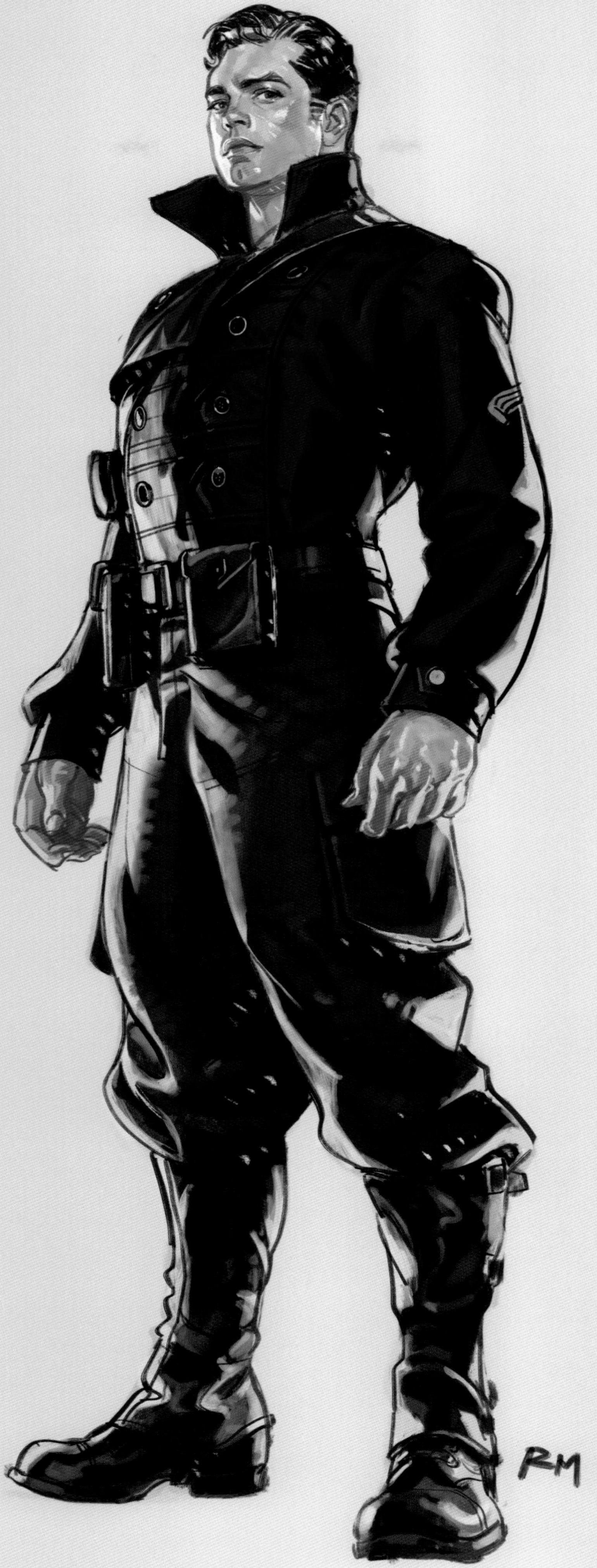
RM

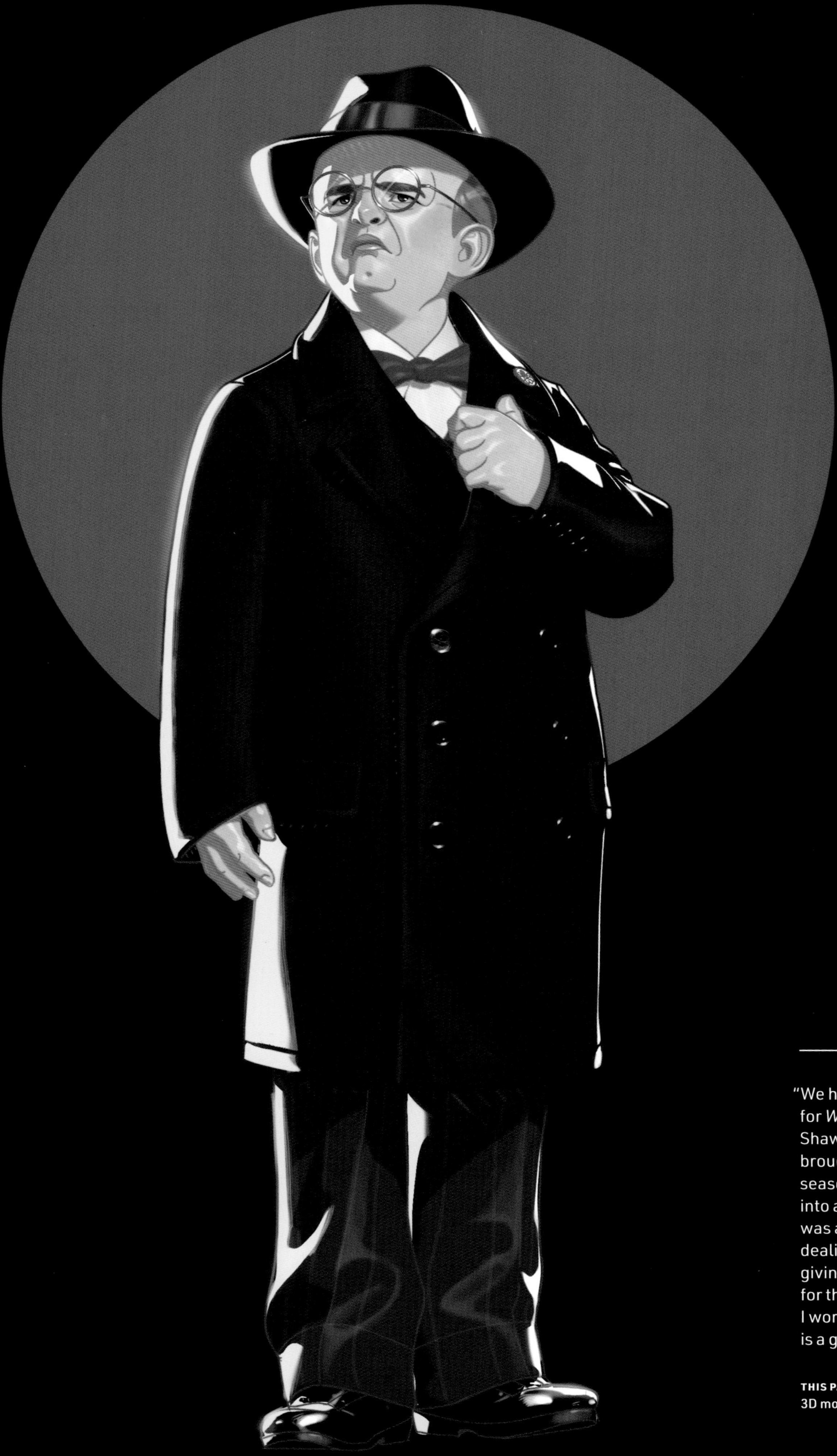

"We had a crew of talented artists for *What If...?* including Joshua Shaw," says Meinerding. "We brought Joshua on in the first season, and he really turned into an amazing art director. He was able to take on the brunt of dealing with the vendors and giving them notes and stuff. Also, for the first and second season I worked with Amelia Vidal, who is a great character designer."

THIS PAGE A collaboration with 3D modeller Adam Ross

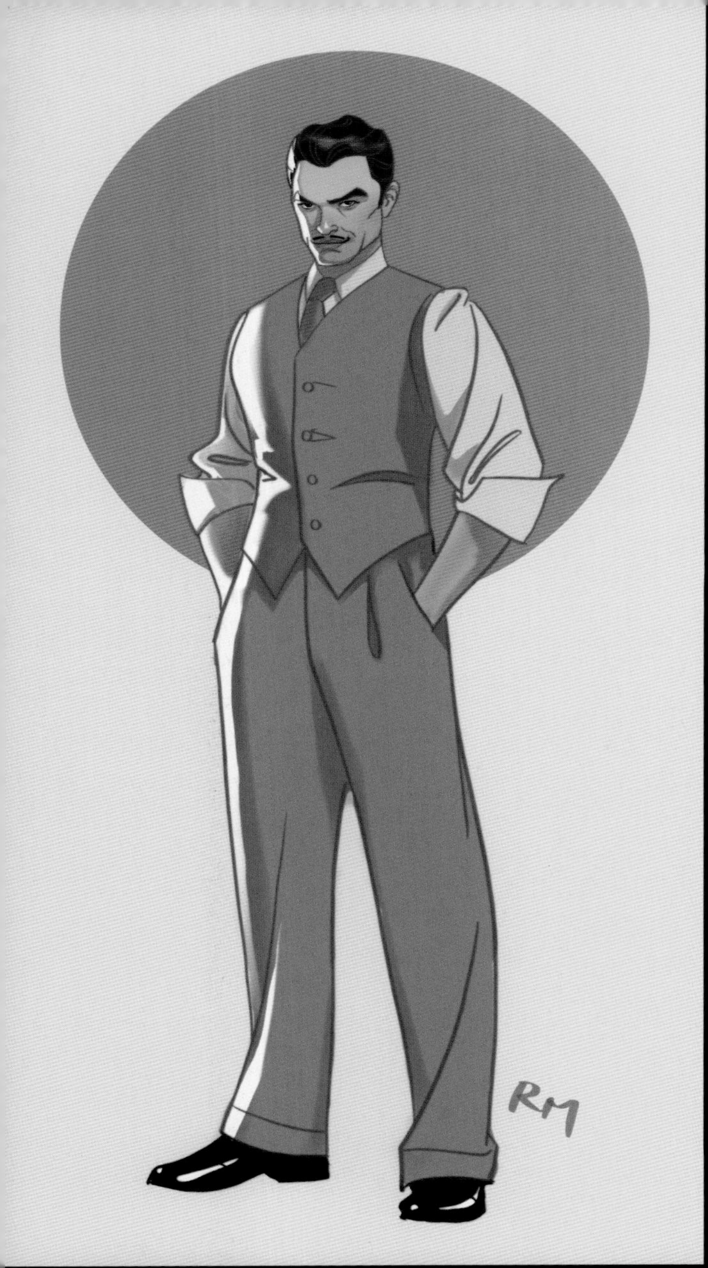
RM

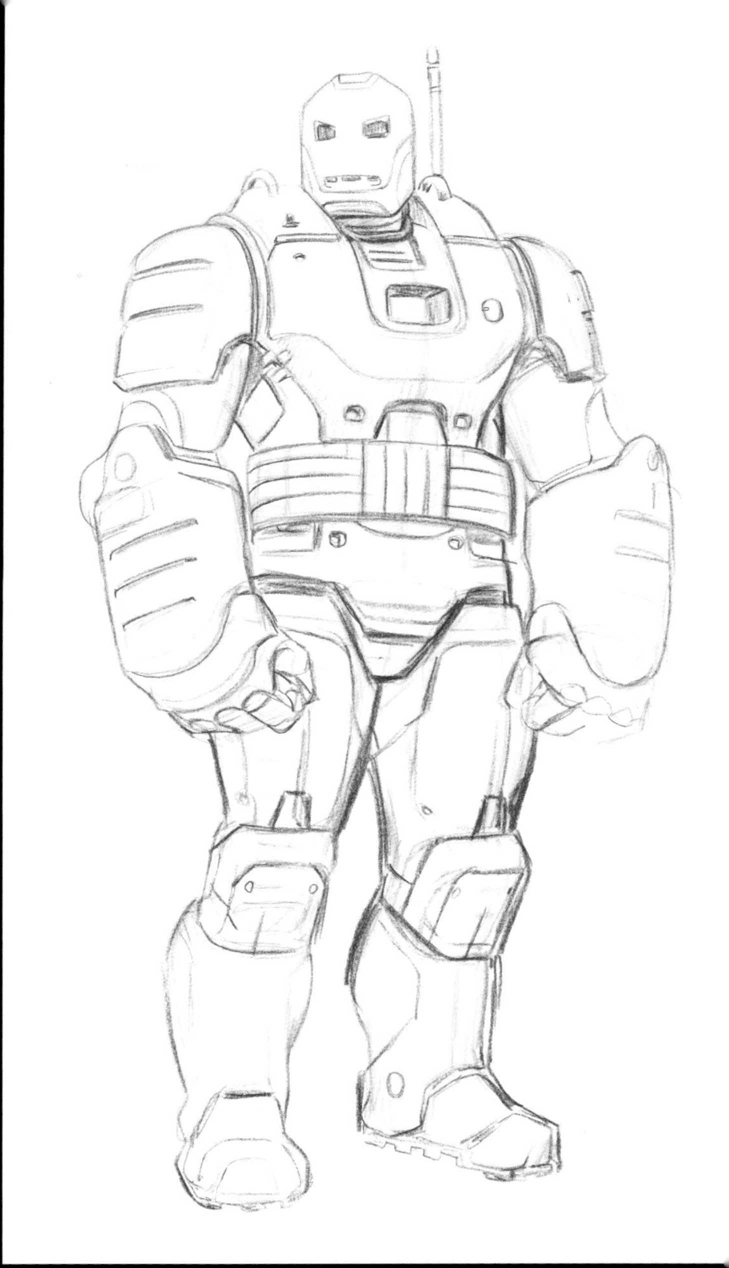

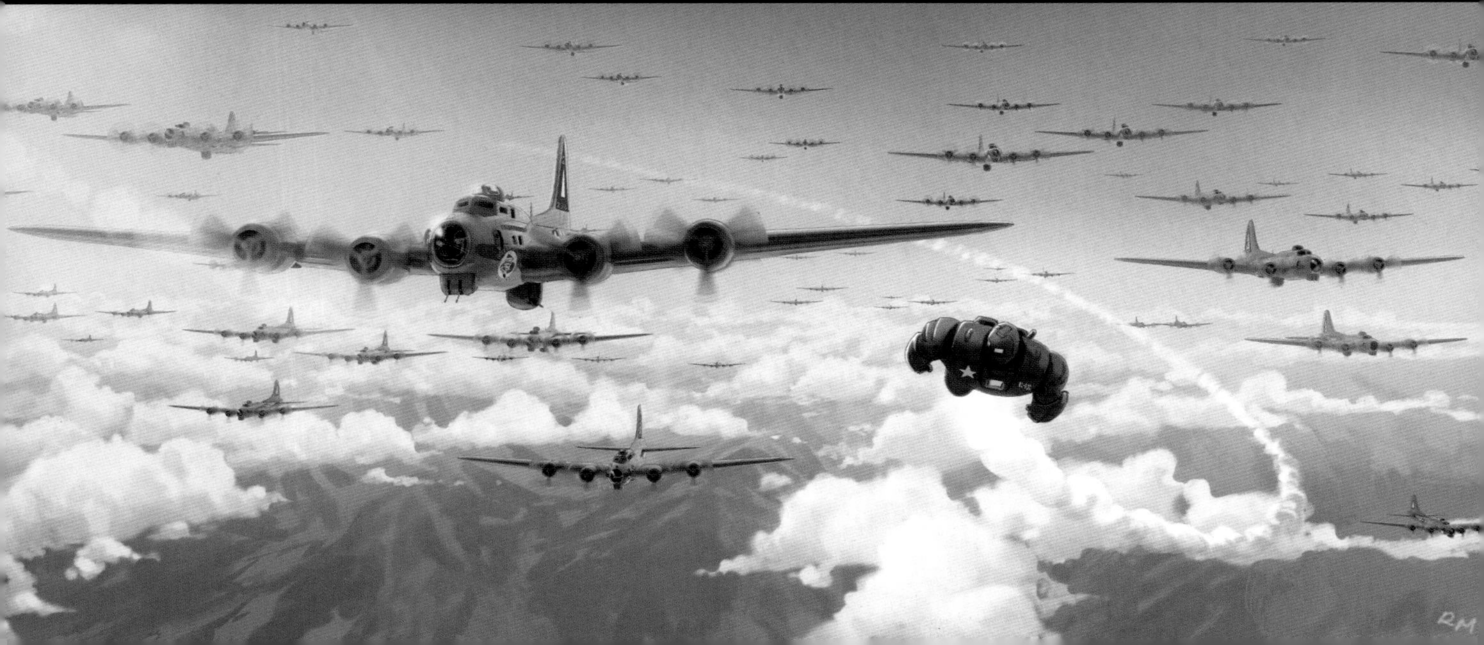
RM

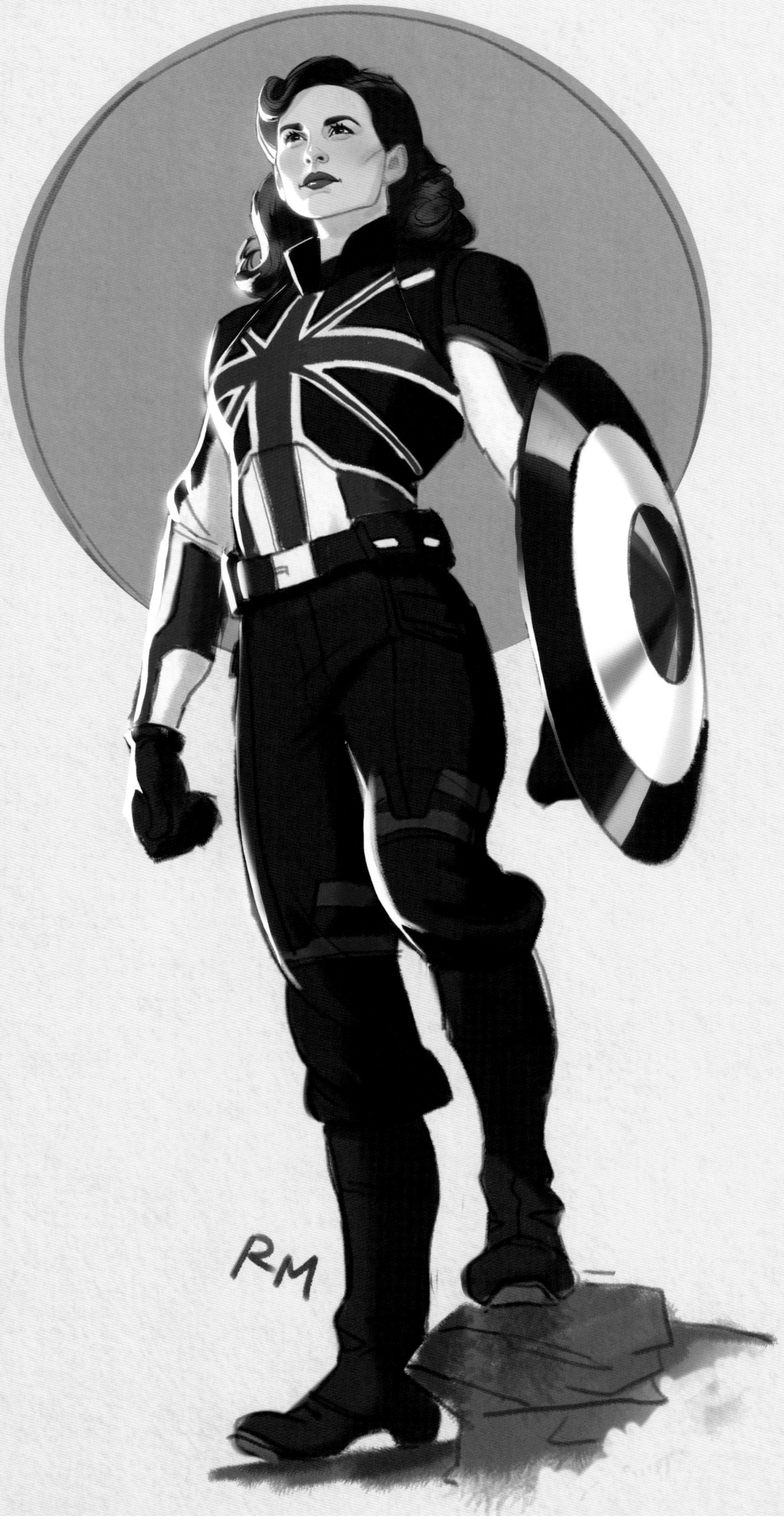
RM

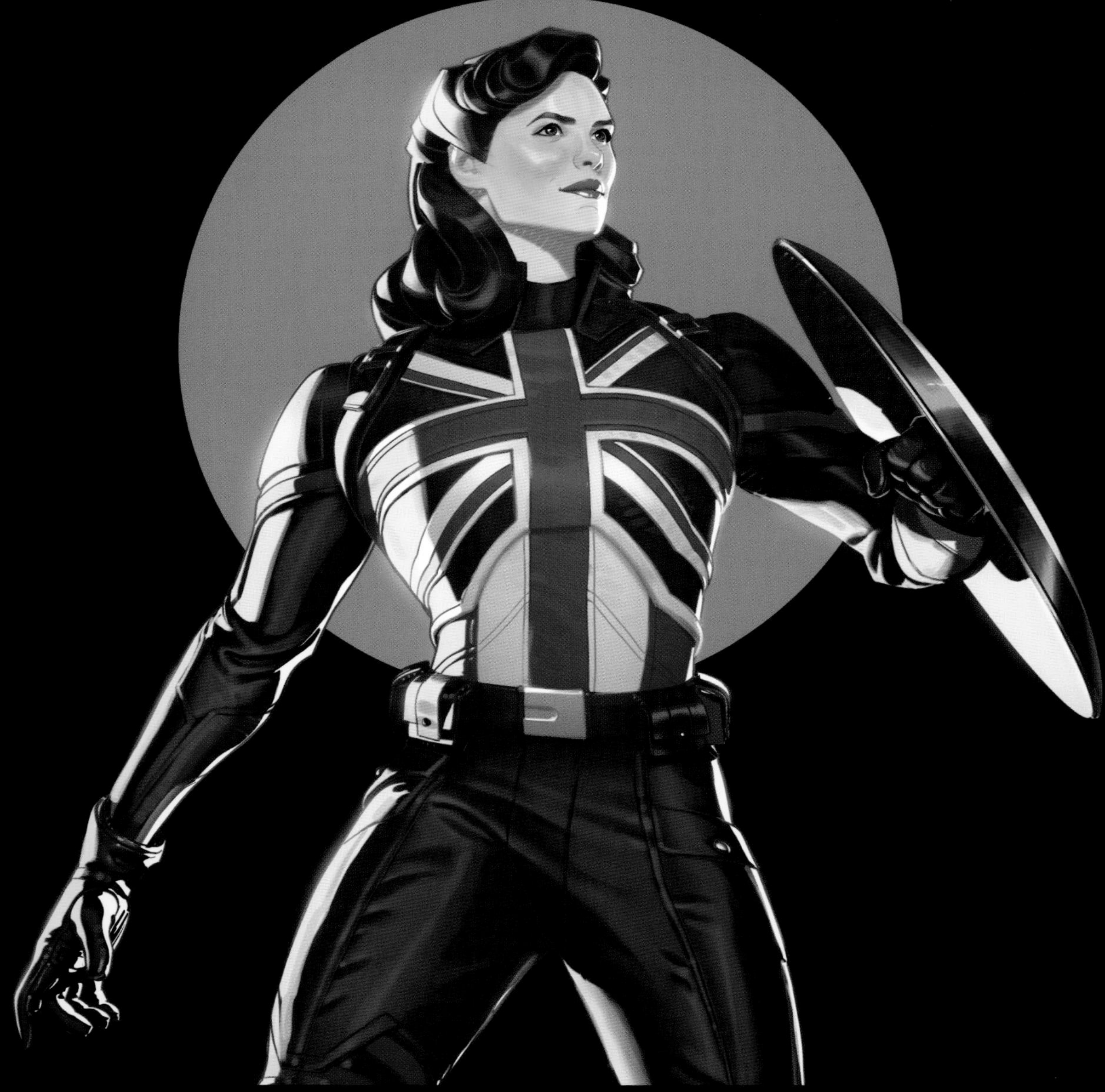

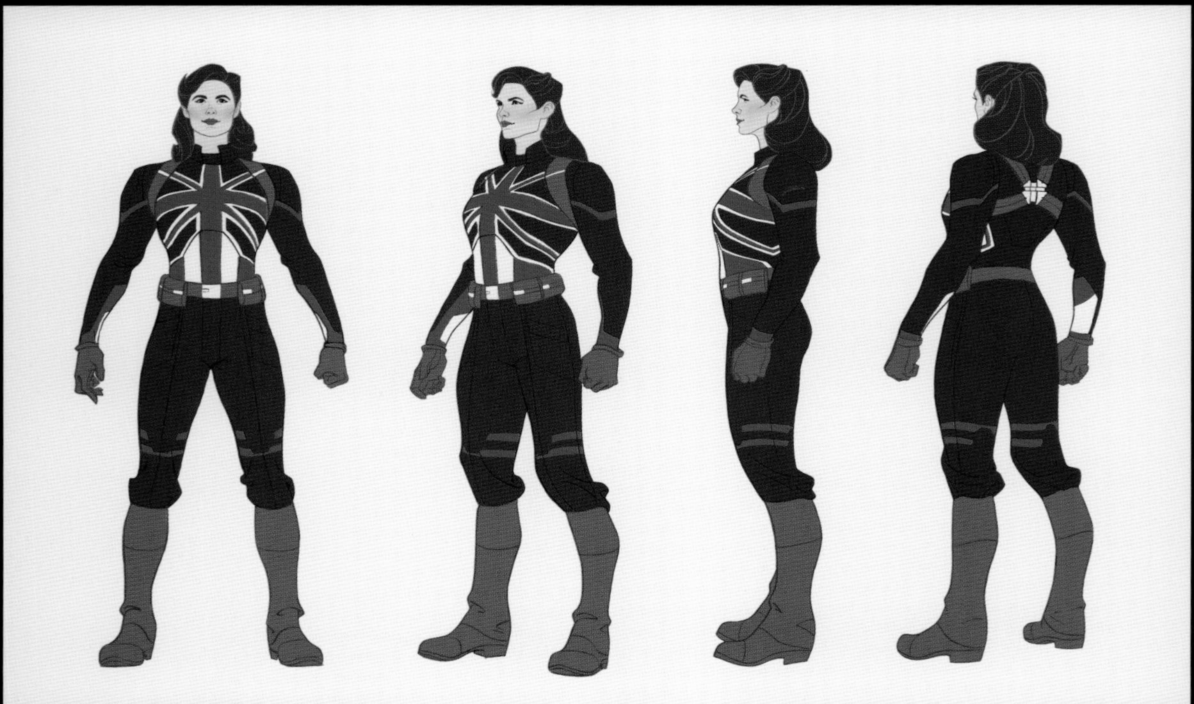

RIGHT A collaboration with 3D modeller Adam Ross

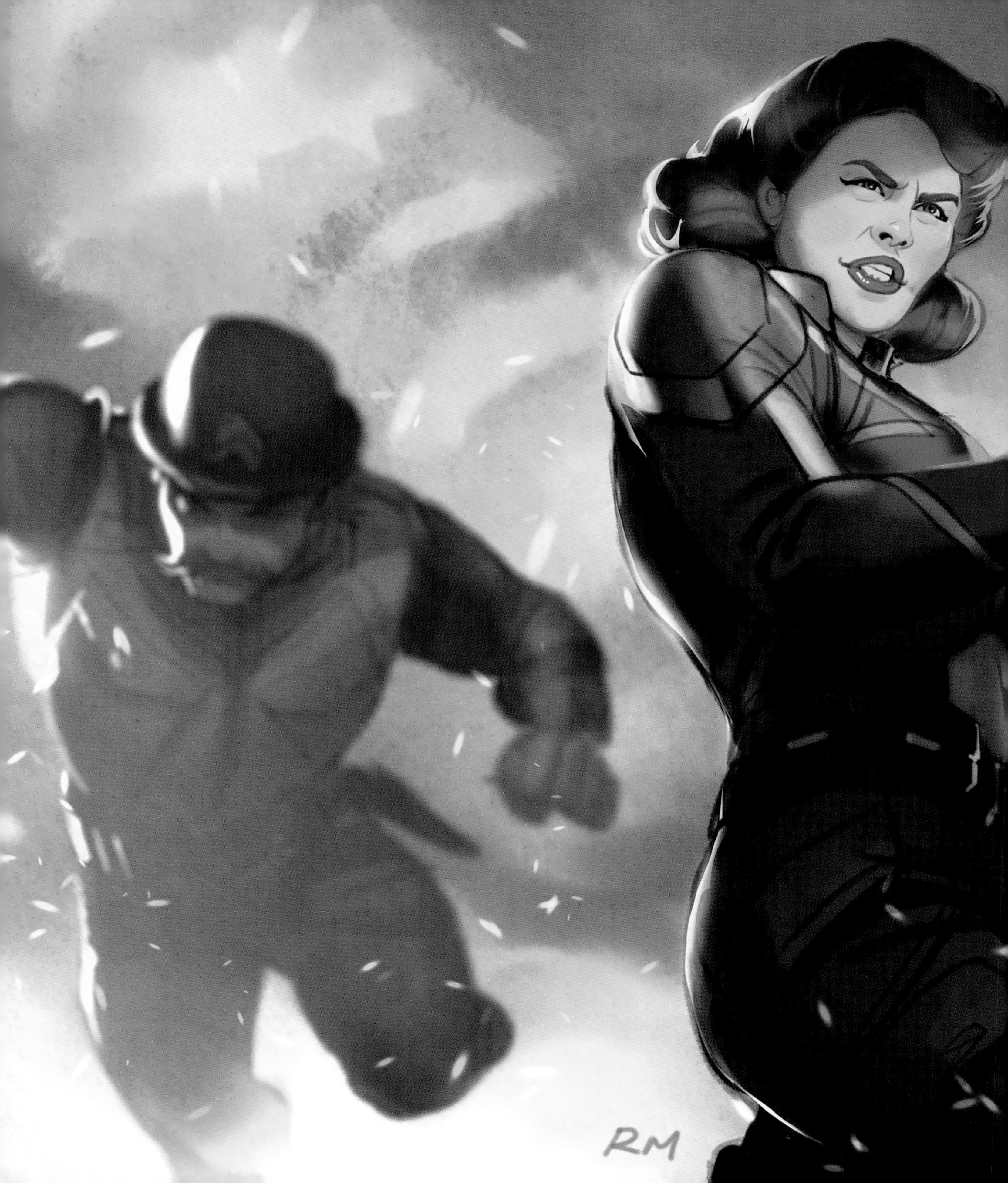
RM

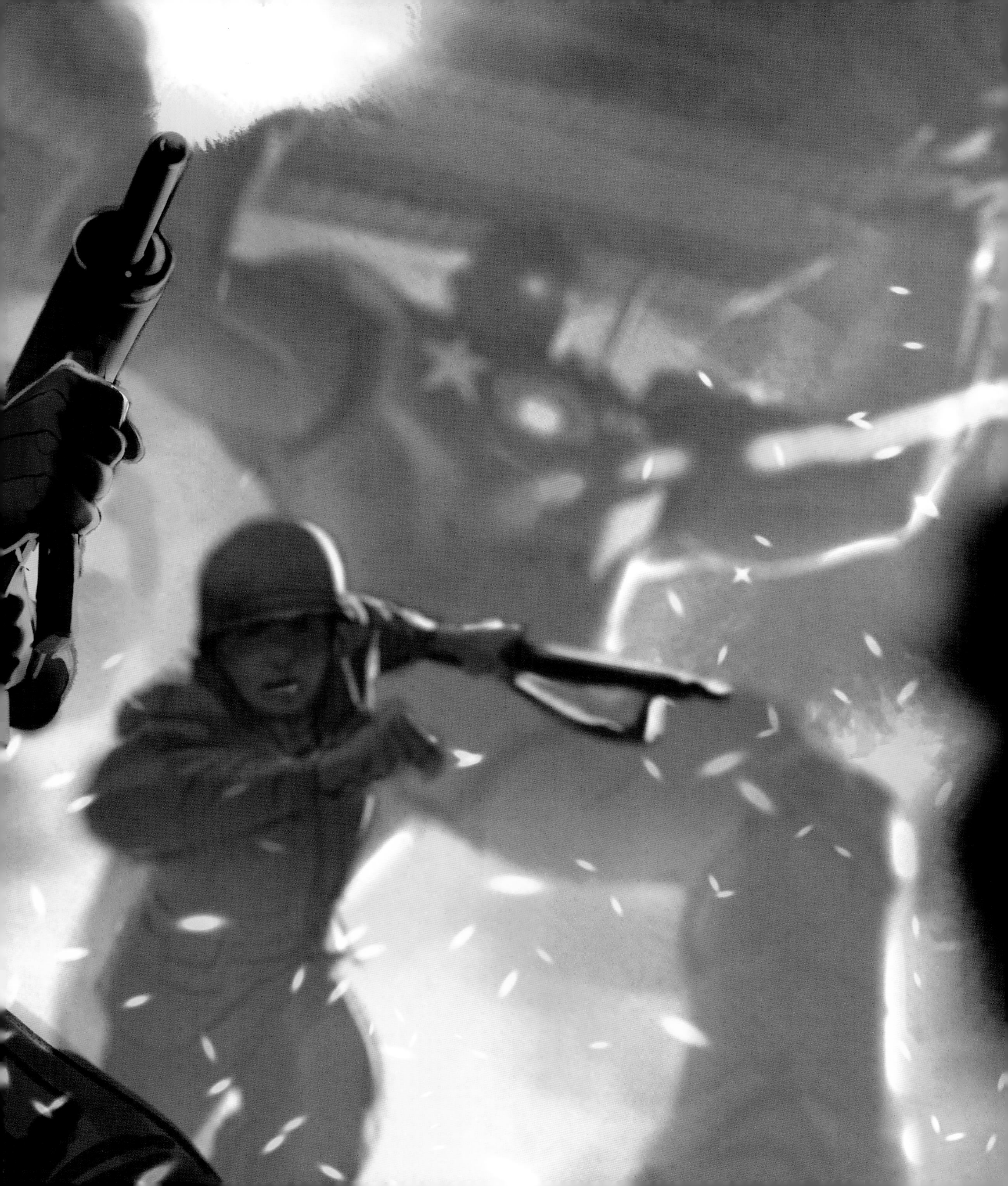

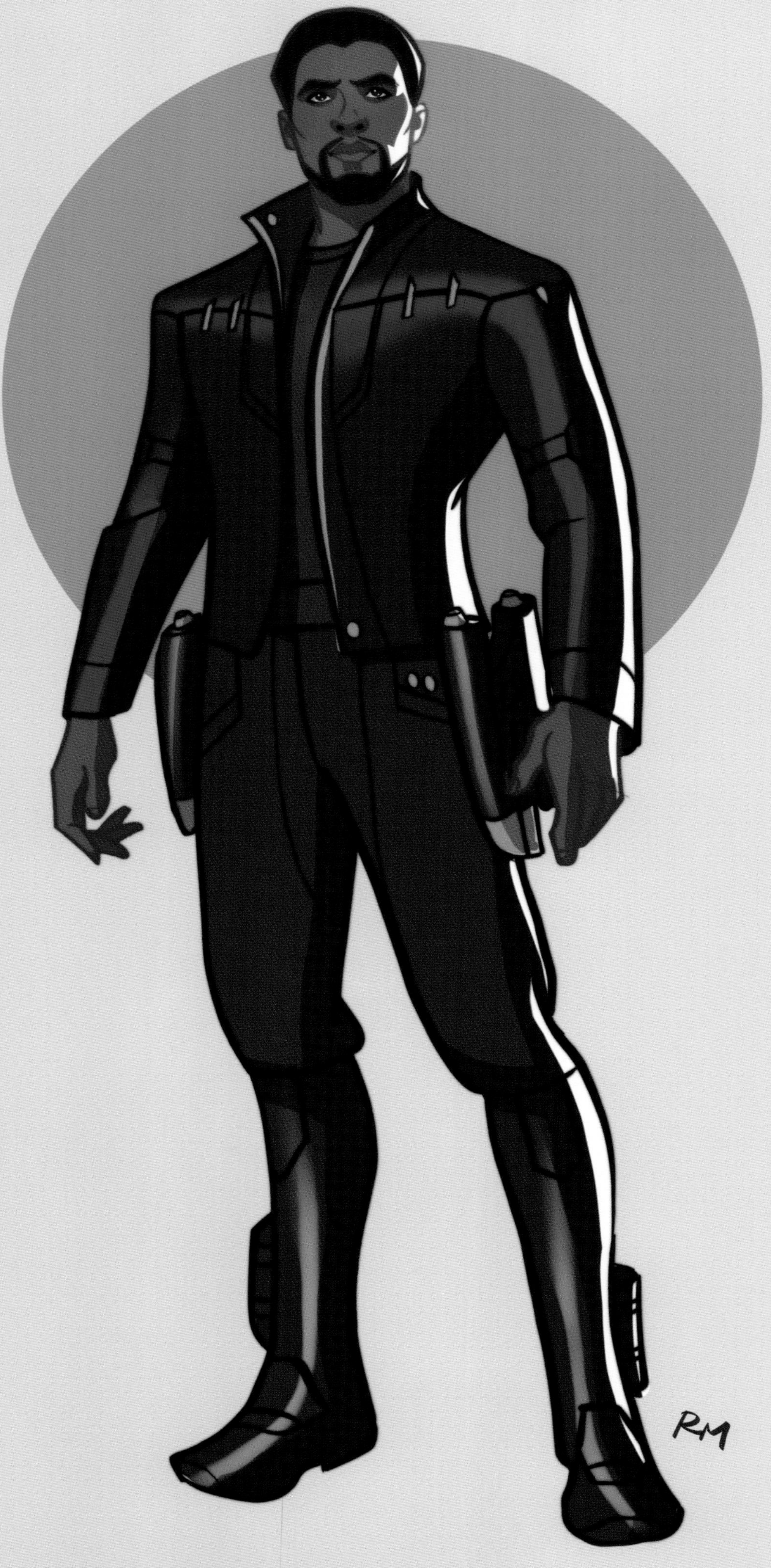
RM

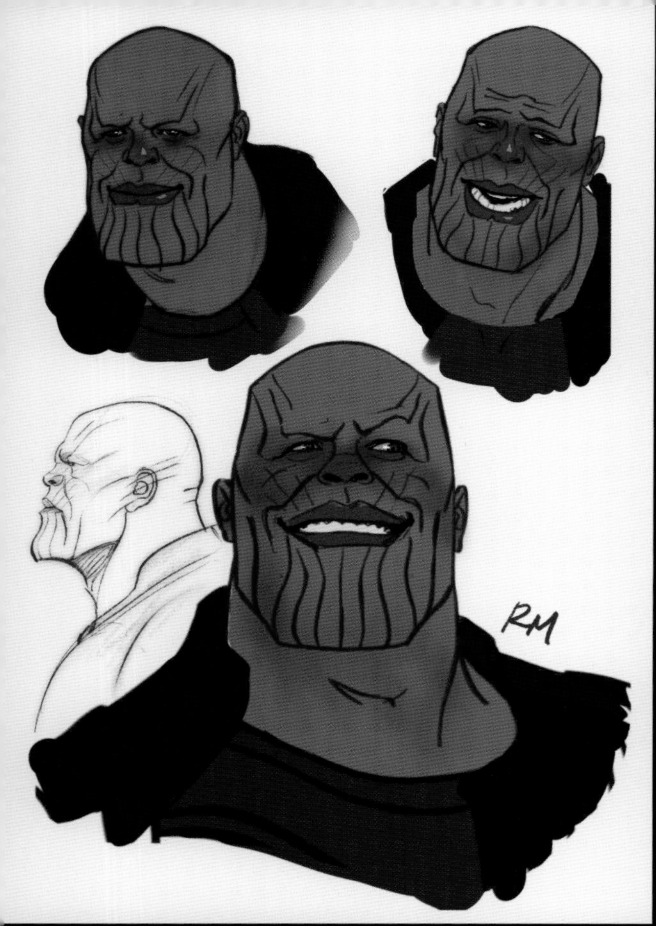
RM
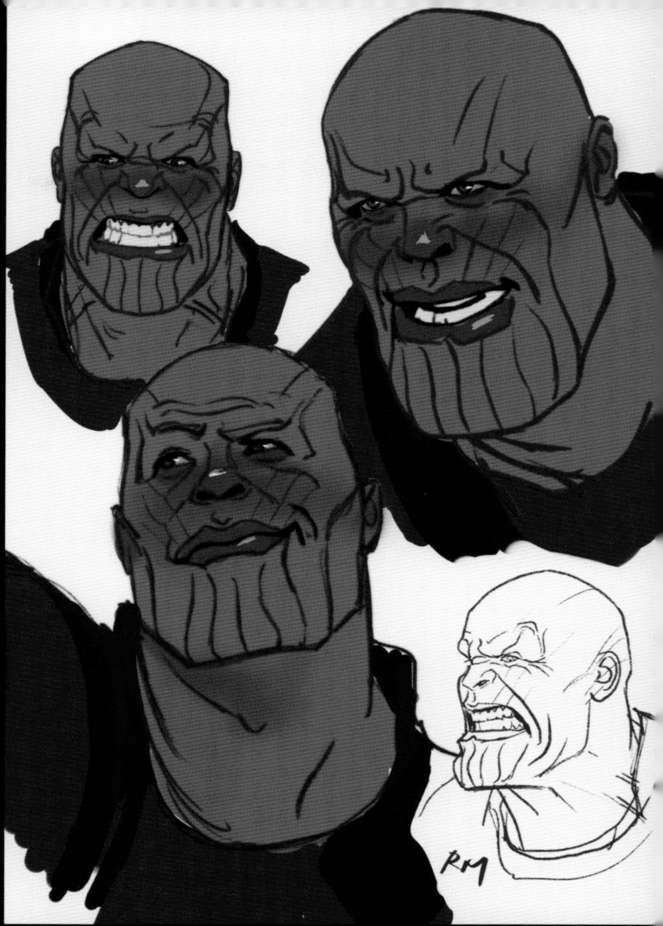
RM
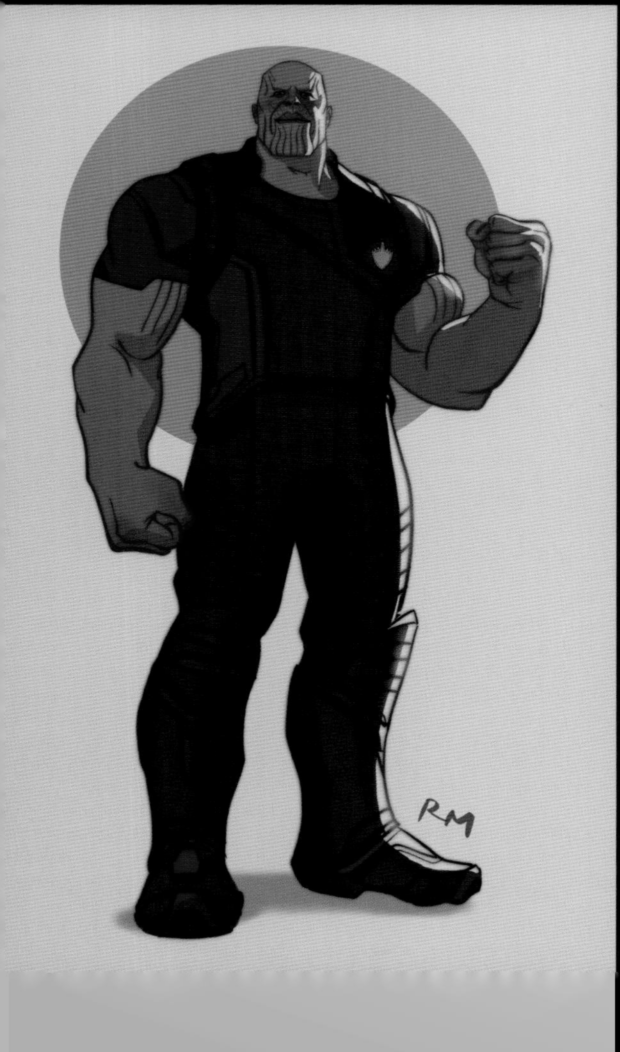
RM
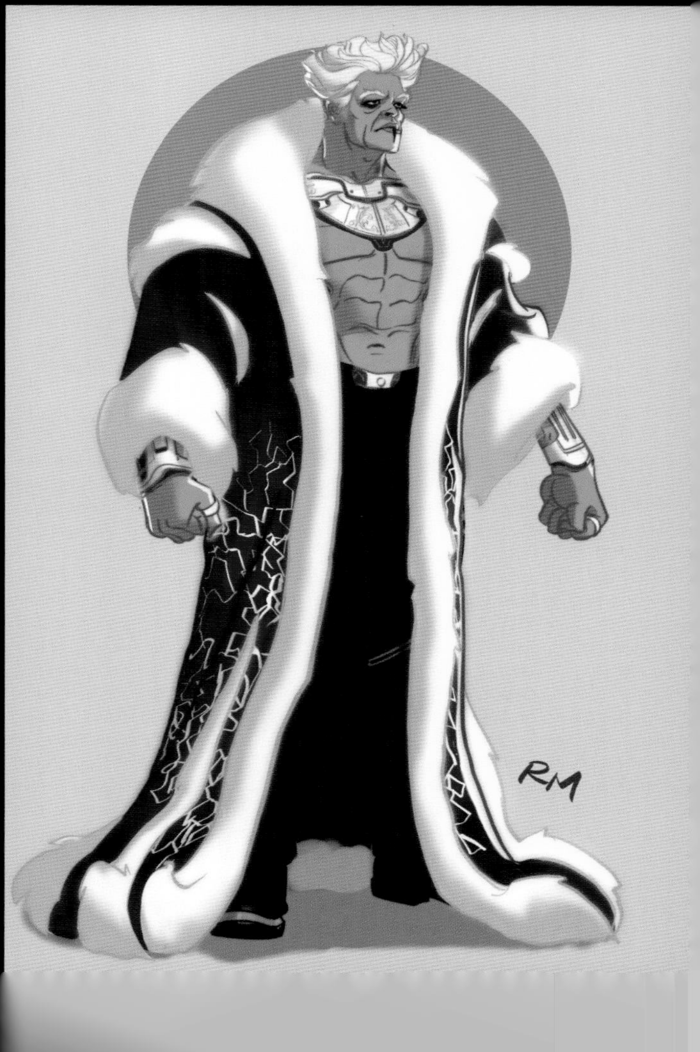
RM

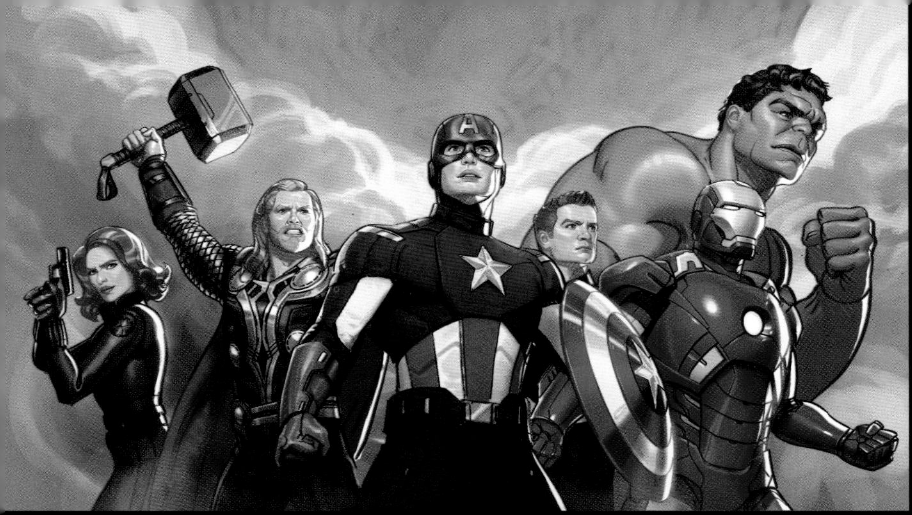

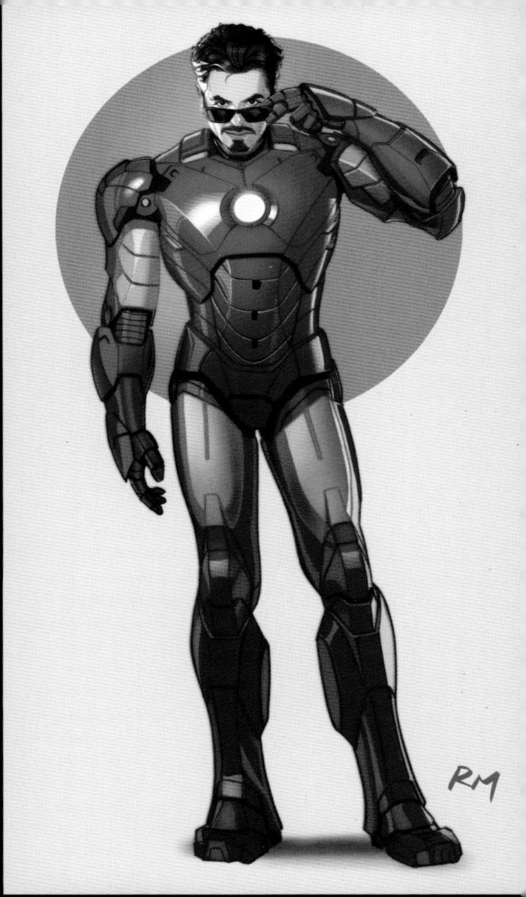
RM

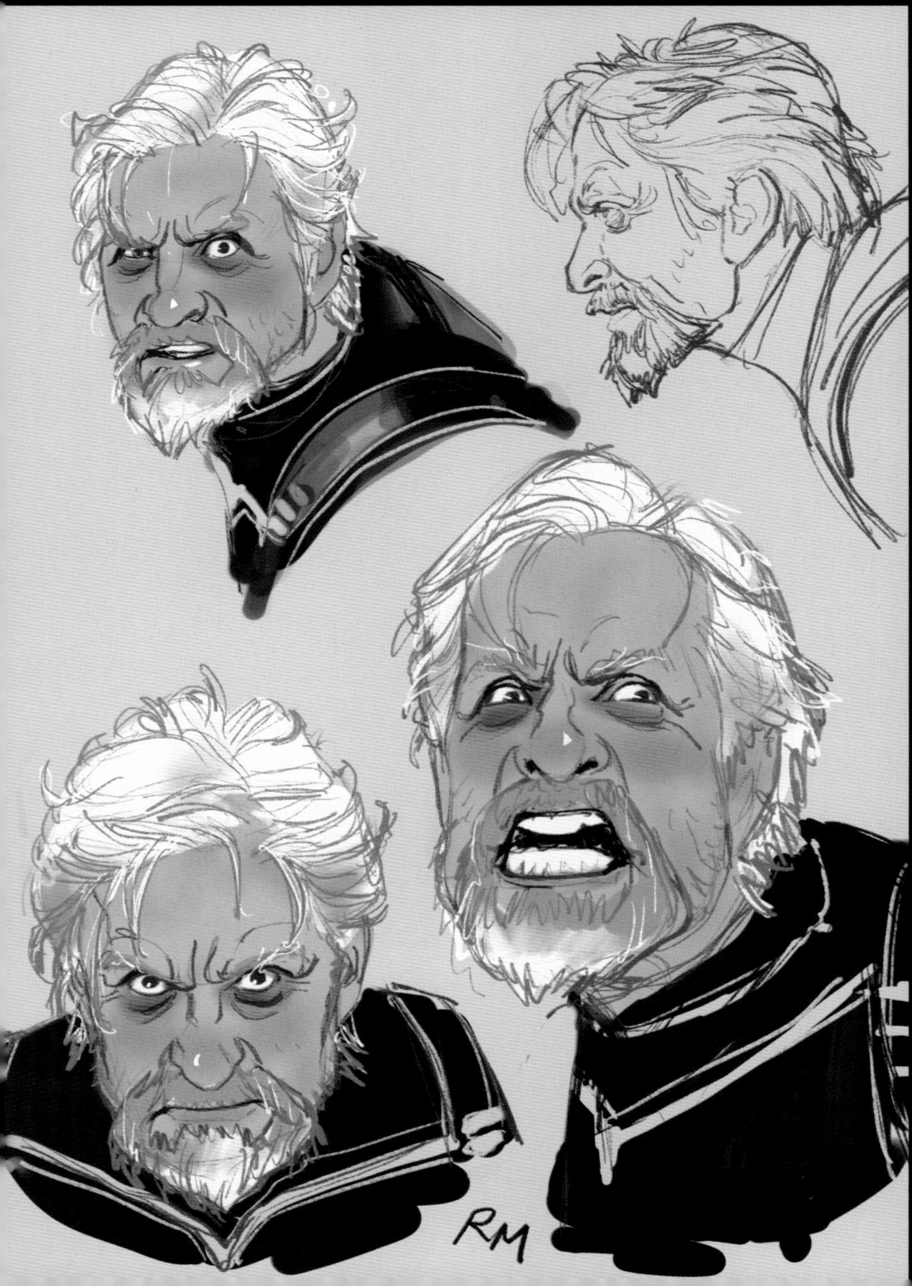
RM

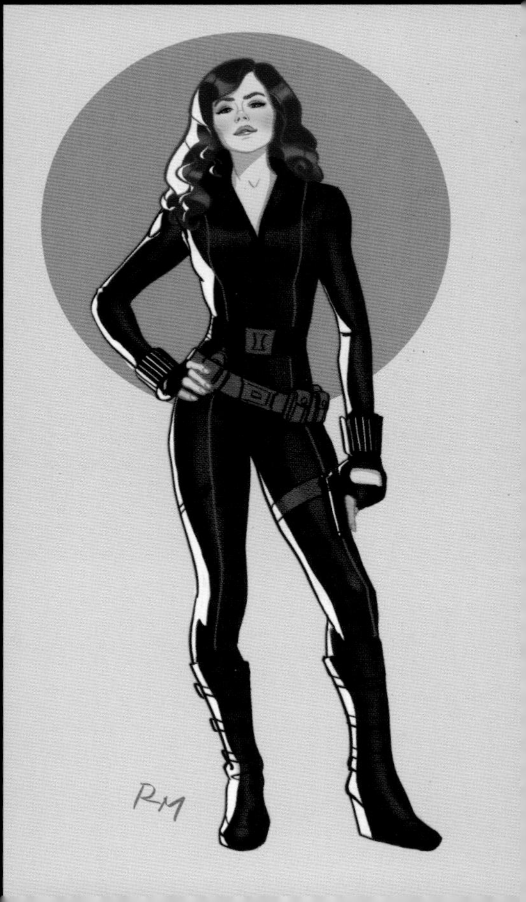
RM

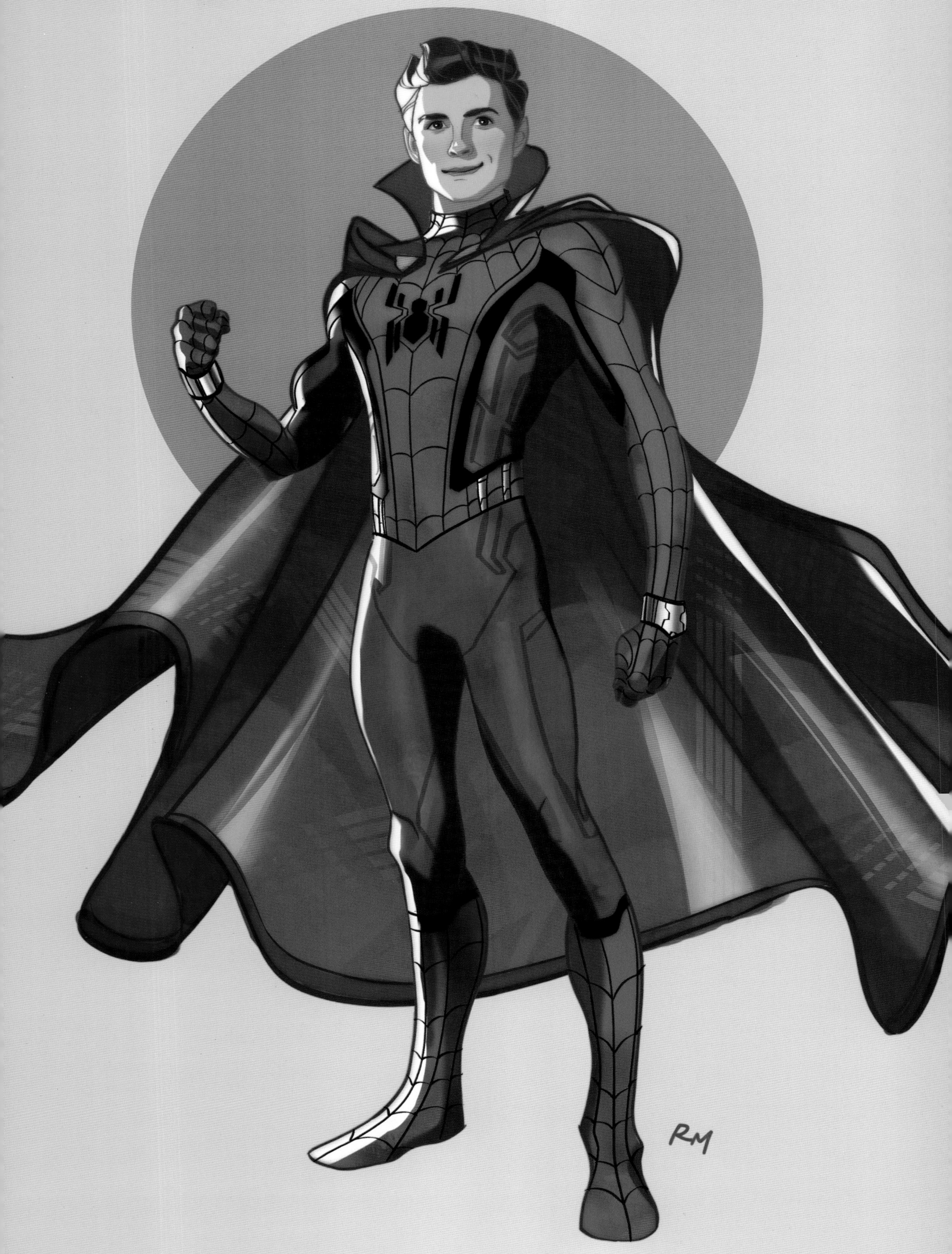
RM

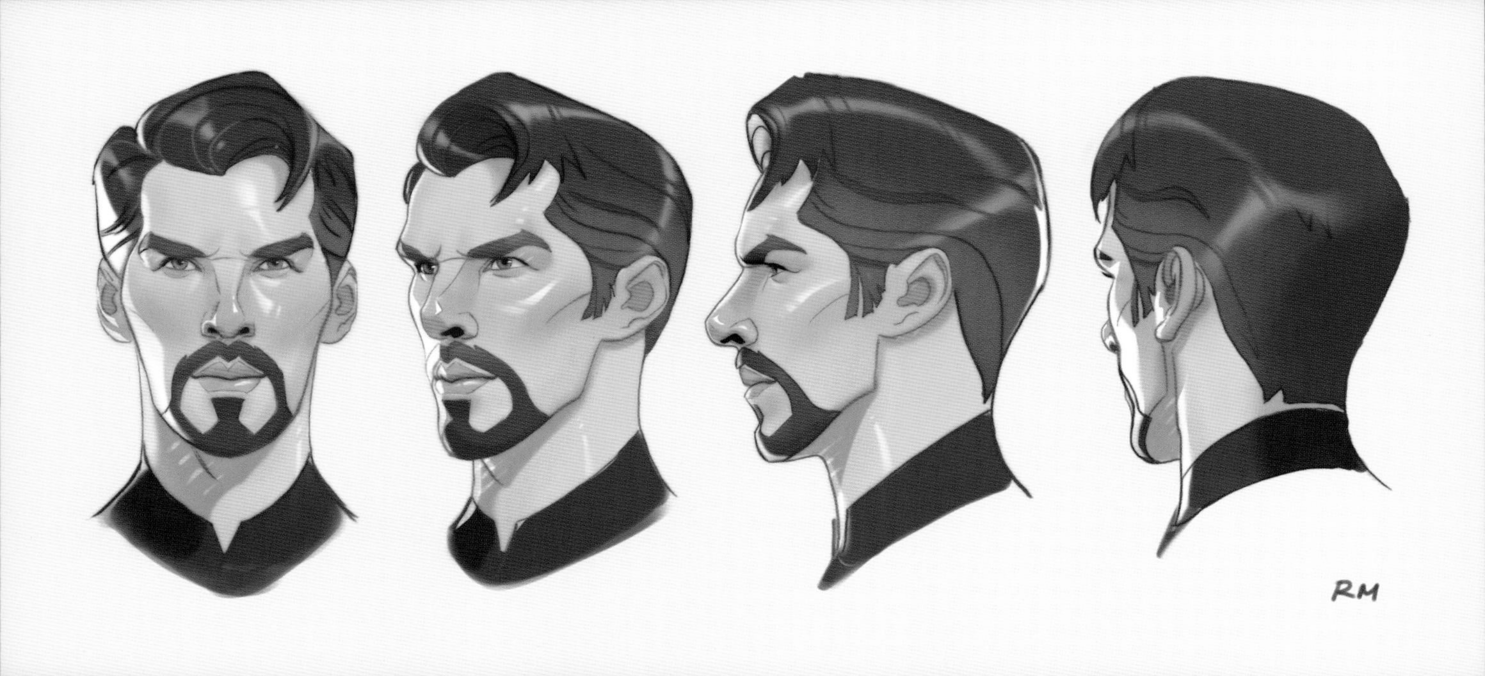
RM

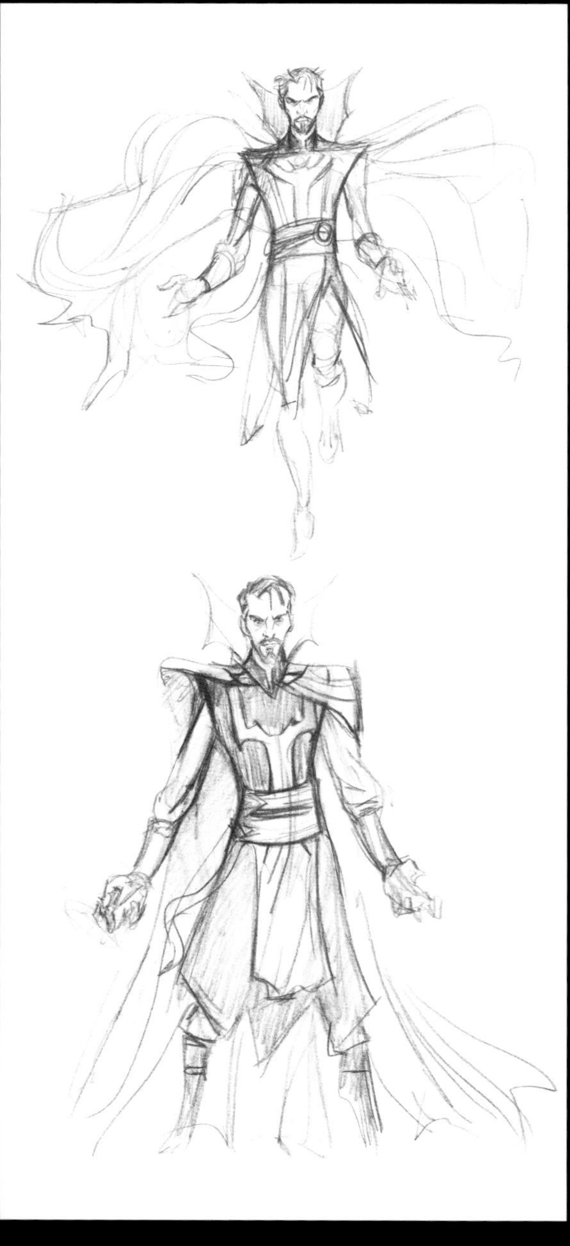

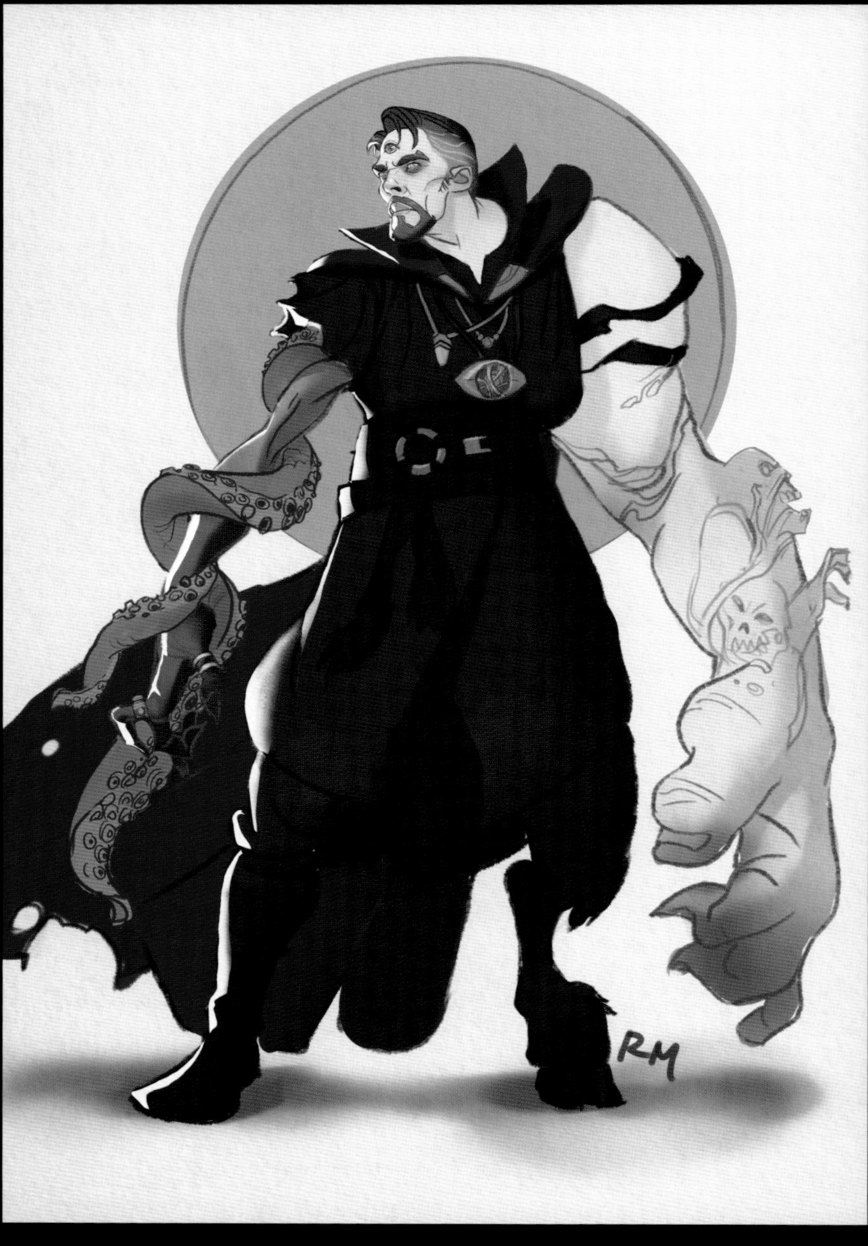
RM

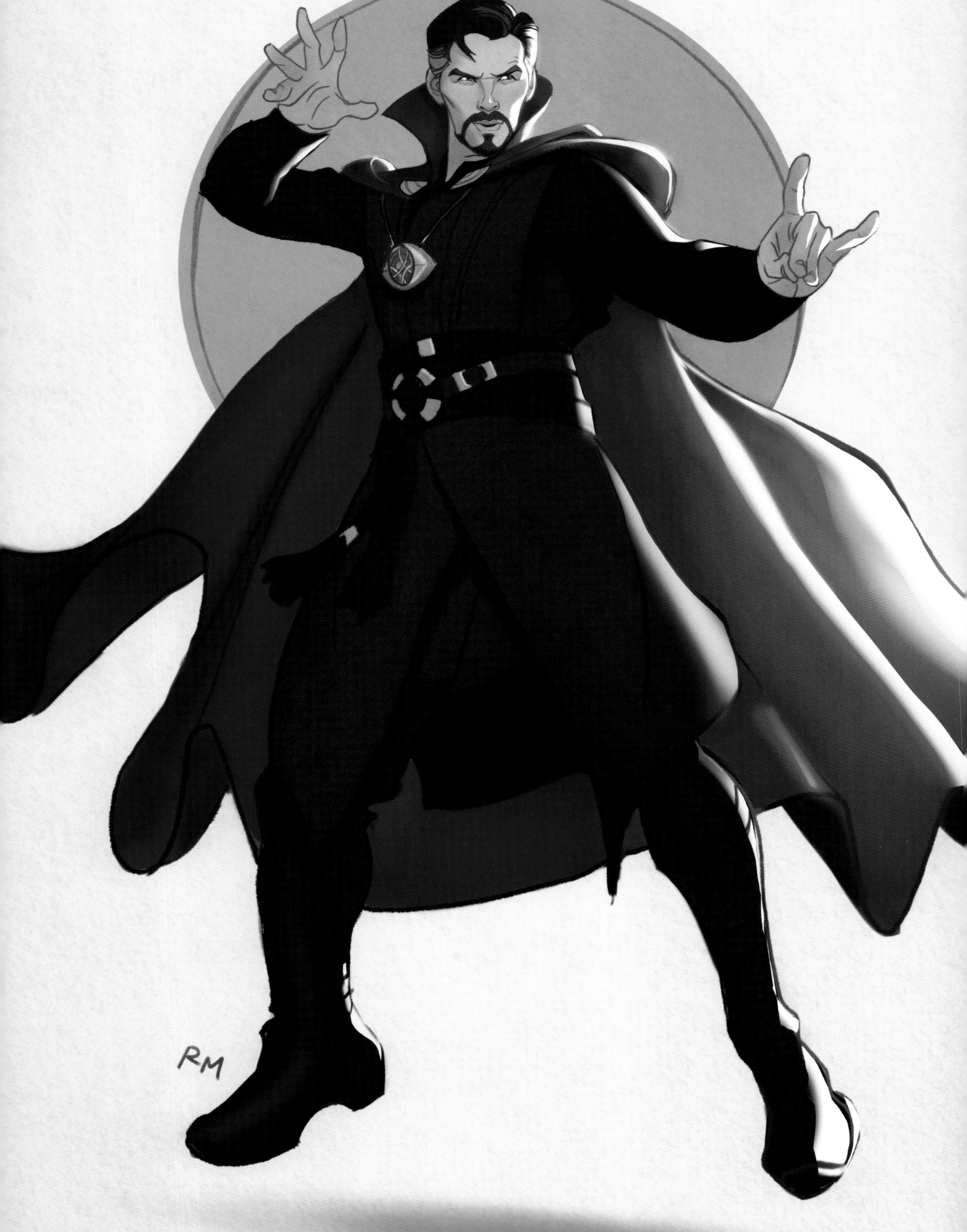
RM

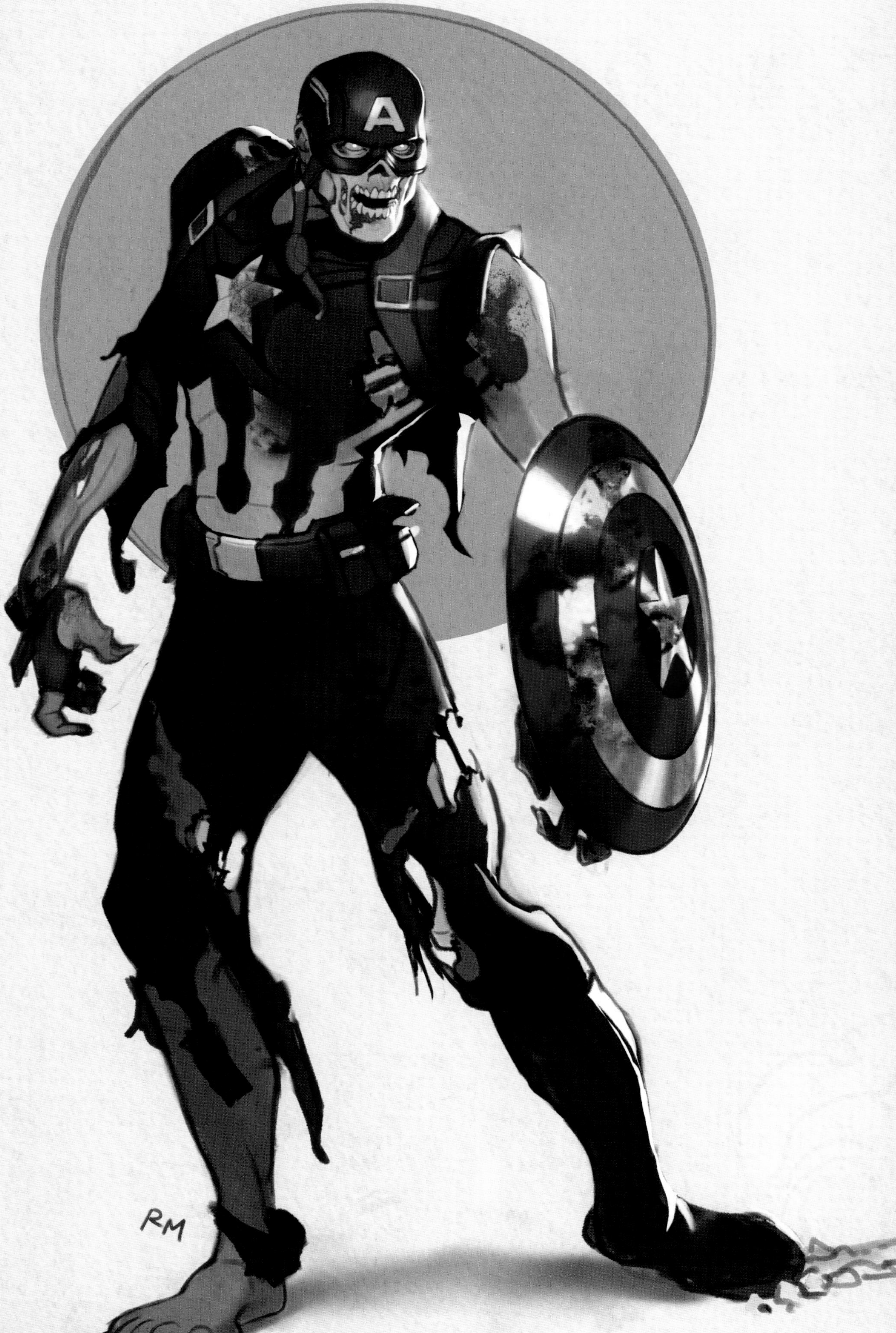
RM

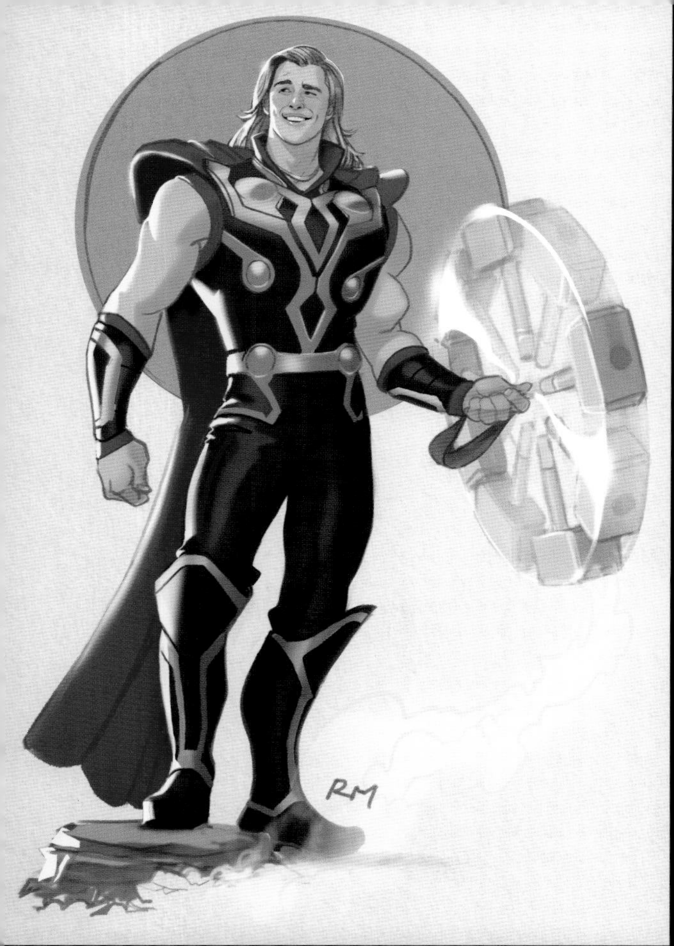
RM

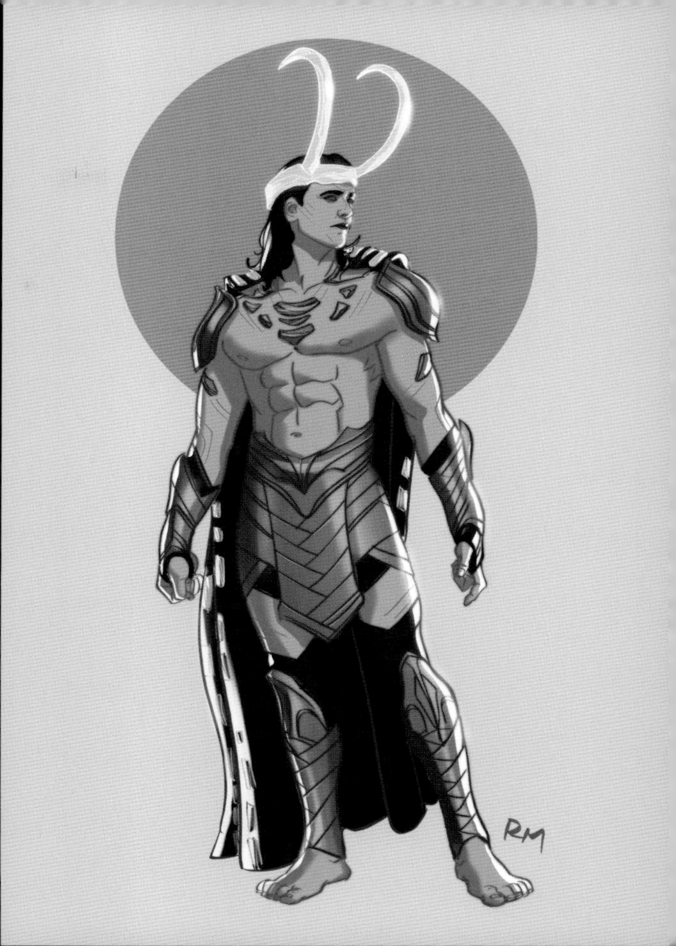
RM

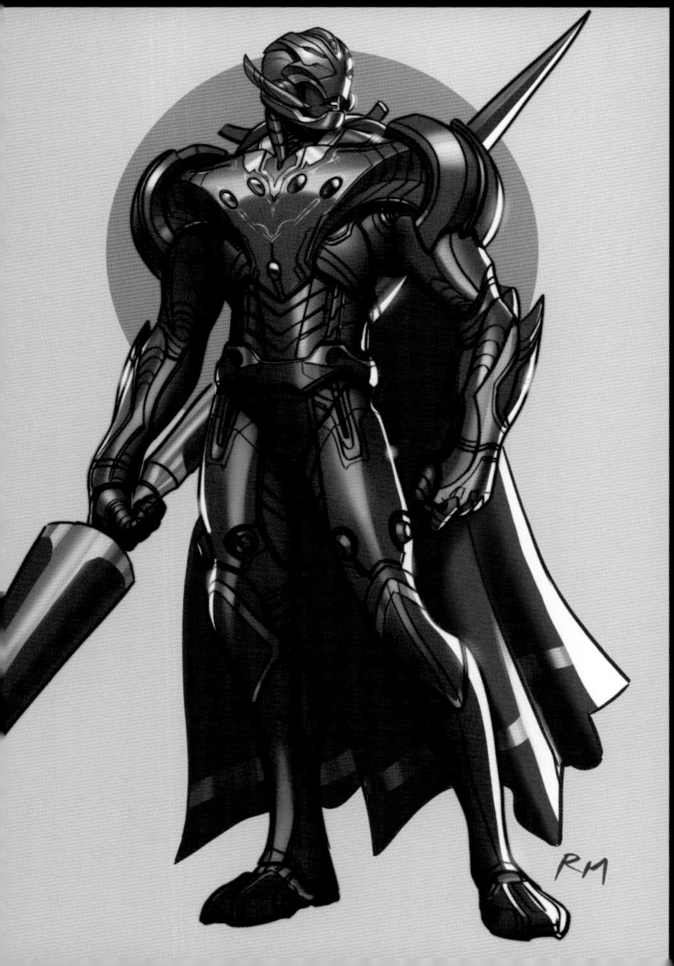
RM

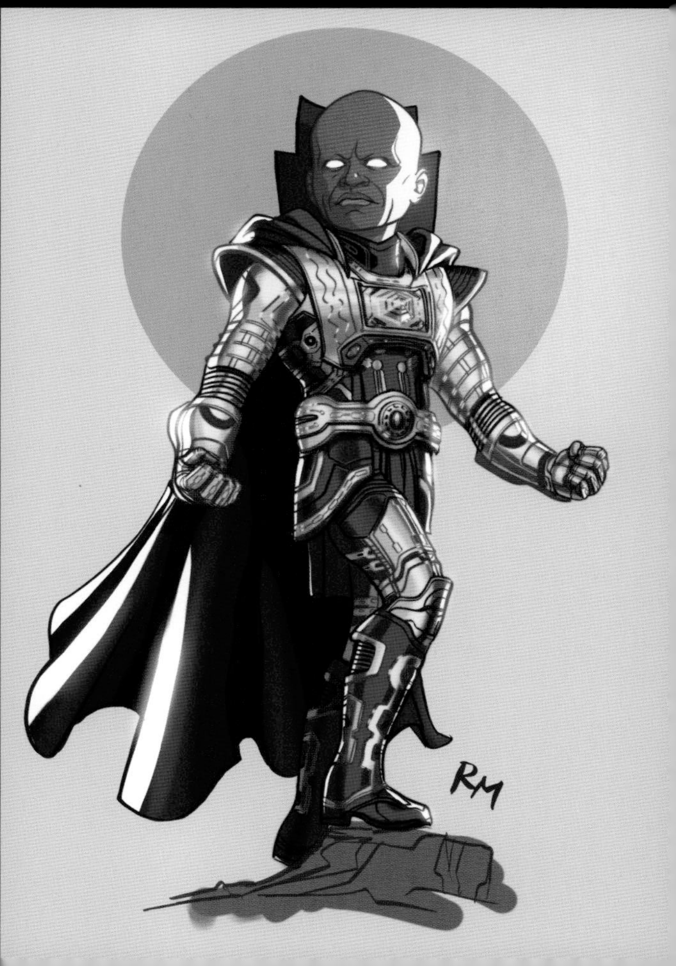
RM

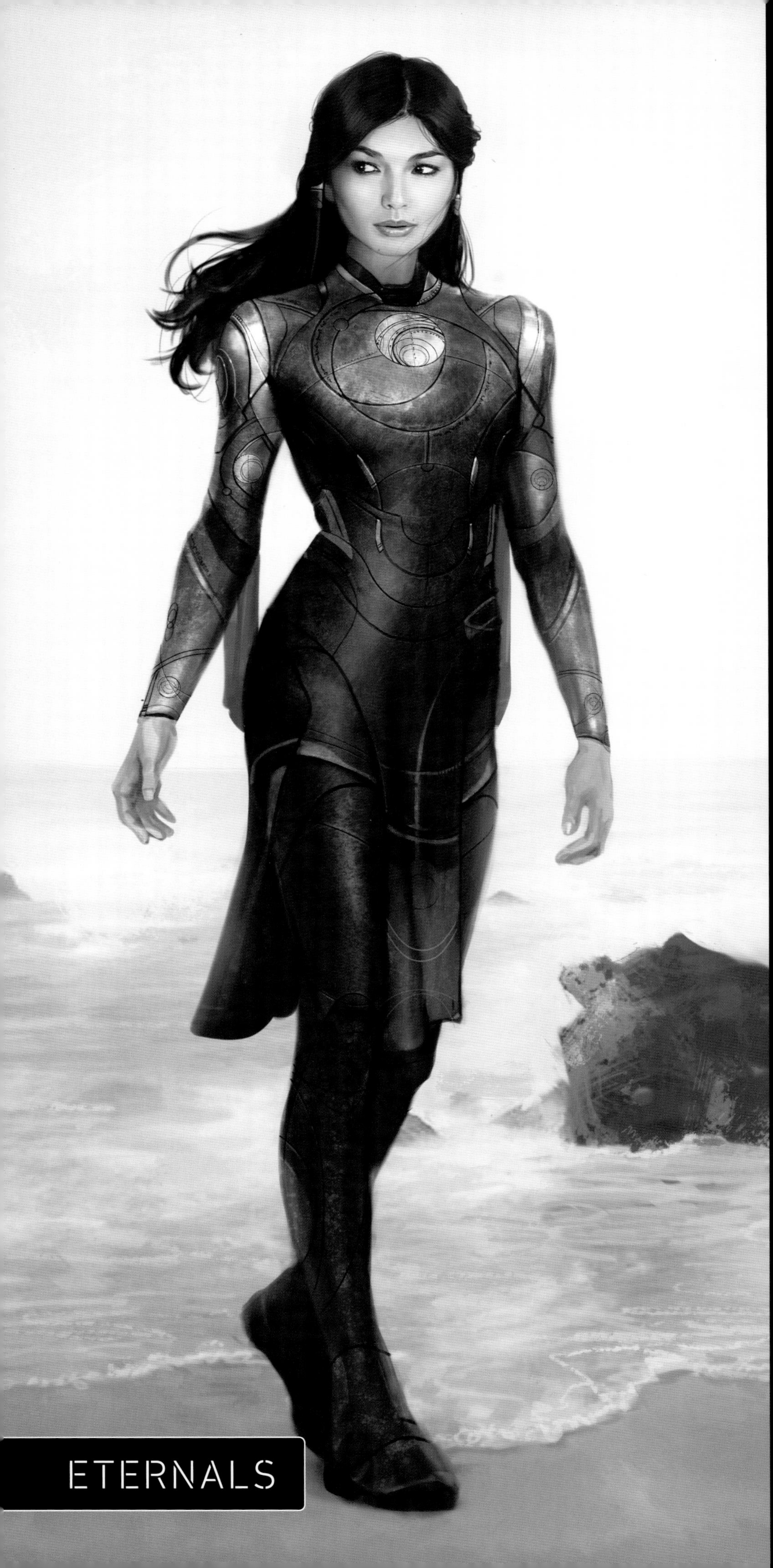

ETERNALS

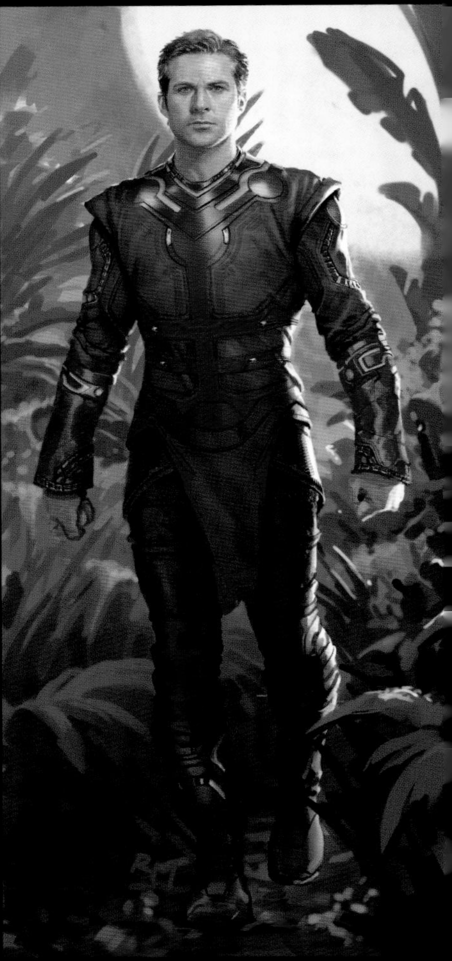

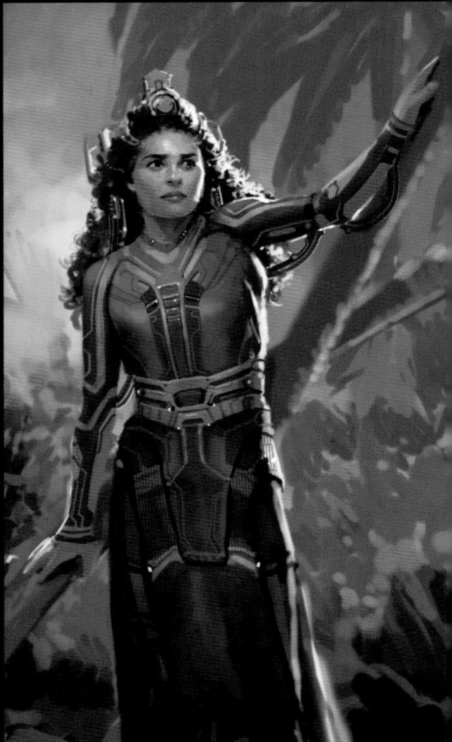

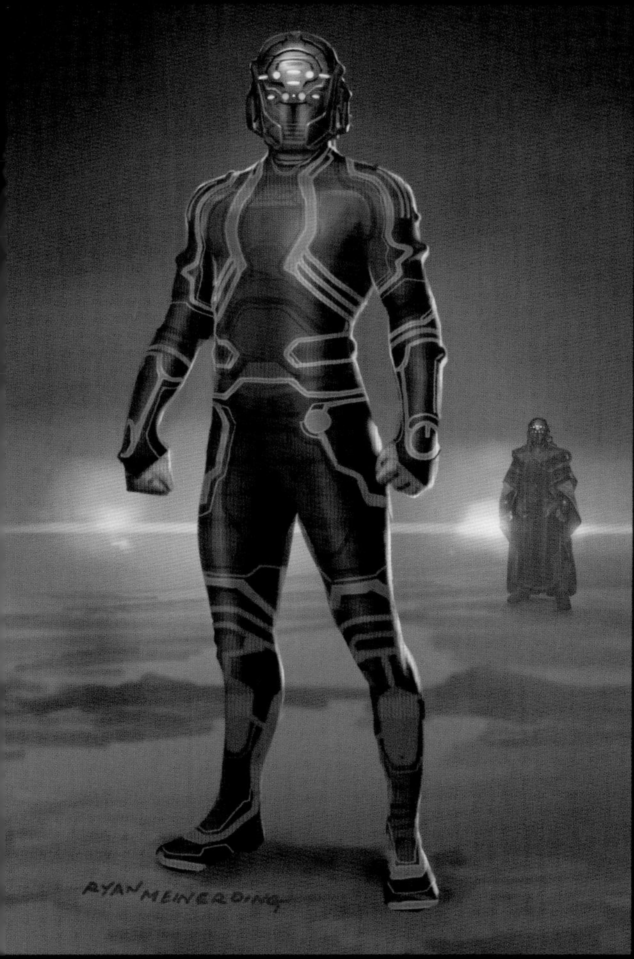
RYAN MEINERDING

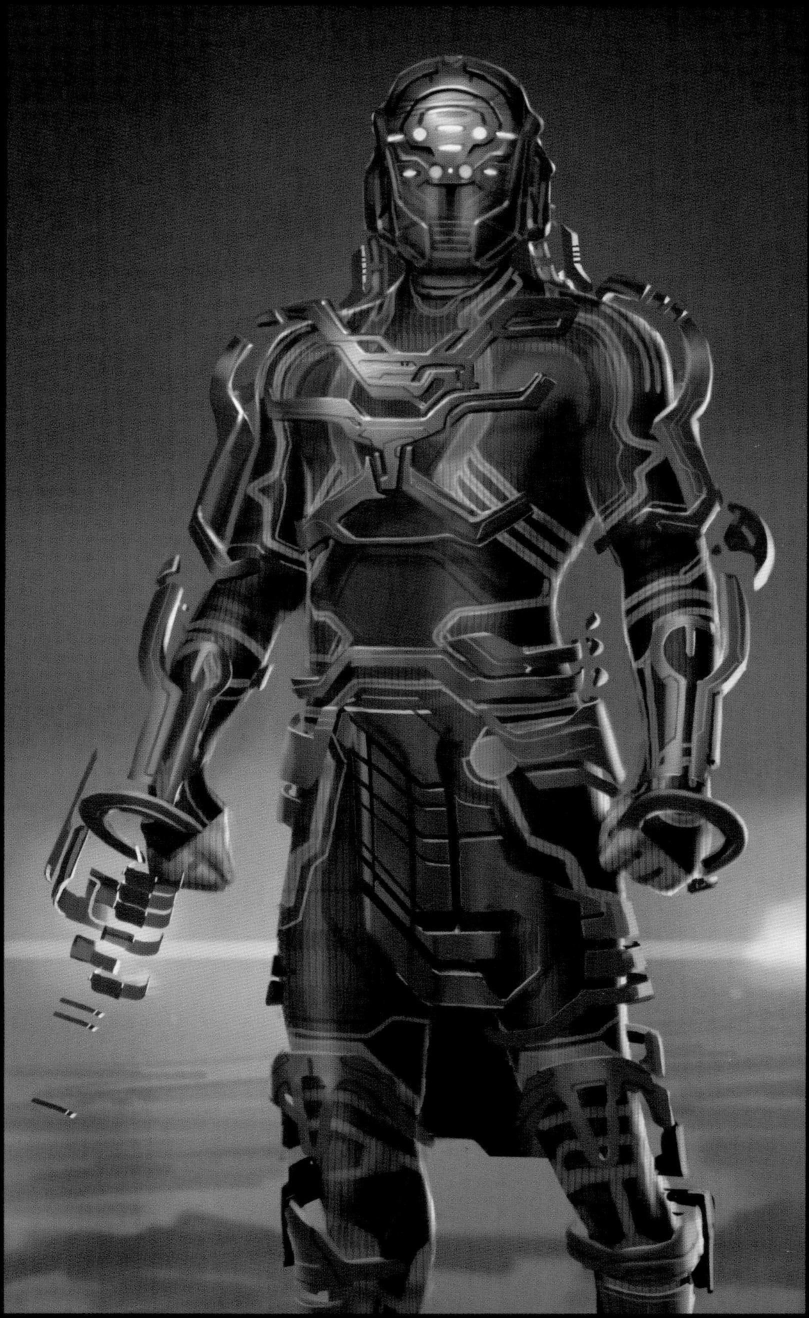

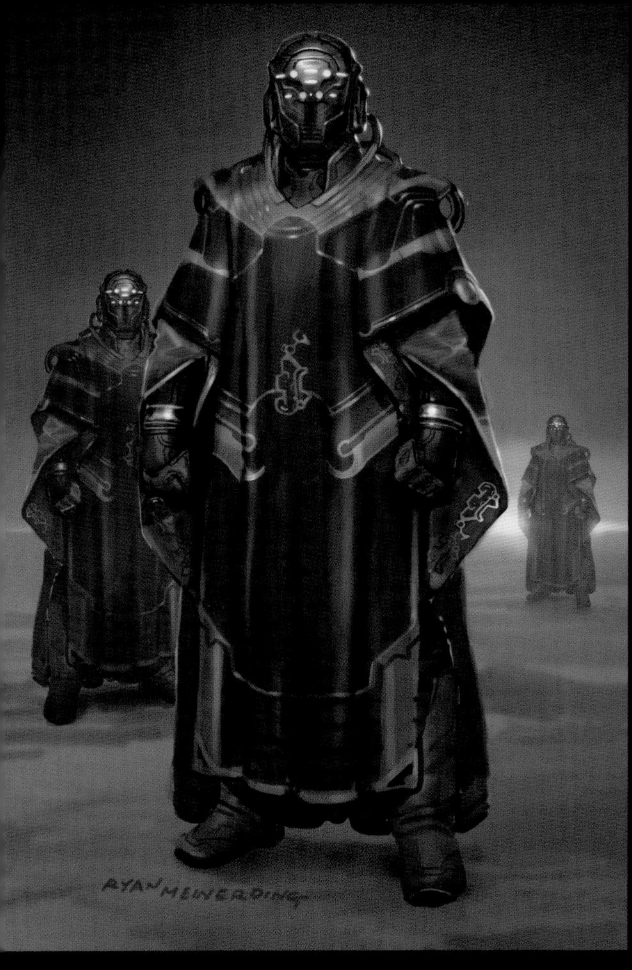
RYAN MEINERDING

For *Eternals*, Kevin Feige wanted to create a film that was much different than what Marvel Studios had typically created to that point. Adding to that challenge: ten main, brand-new characters and an entire world and mythology never before seen in the MCU. "I'd done a very early pass on *Eternals*, which I saw as a chance to do a romantic epic using human history as a base and setting the love story in the most magnificent vistas from different locations and eras." Meinerding cites artists Wes Burt and Keith Christiansen as being crucial to figuring out the designs for the Eternals themselves. "The Sersi image I did [opposite] is based on the design language that Wes Burt was developing for the film," he says. Looking back at the overall *Eternals* creative process, Meinerding adds, "In terms of trying to create something that felt new and different than our other films, I think the team did a fantastic job achieving that. We're always striving to create the artwork that allows the conversations that need to happen to occur."

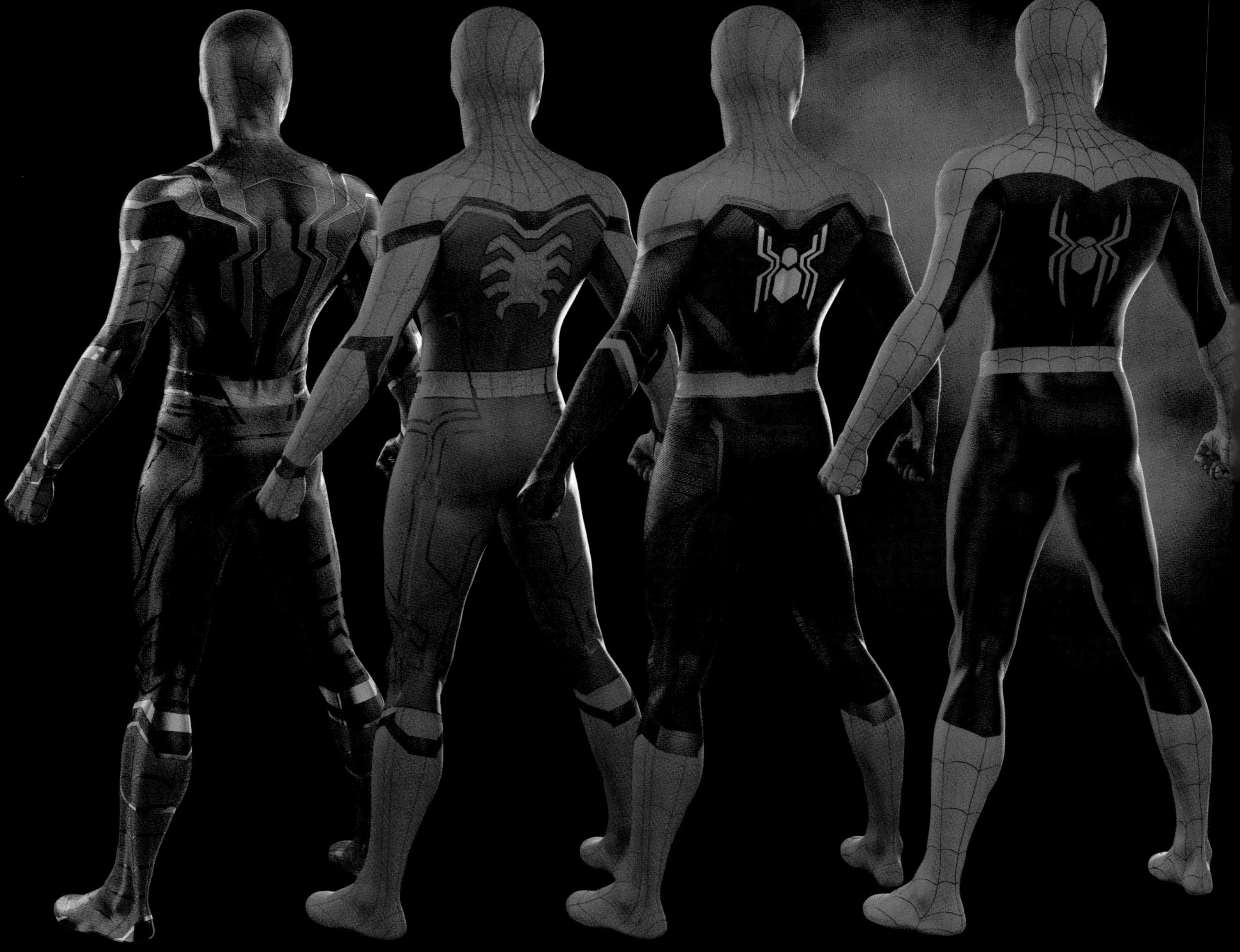

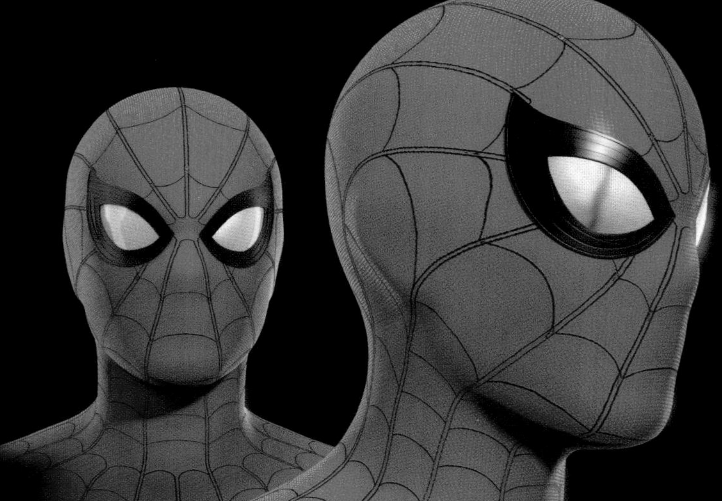

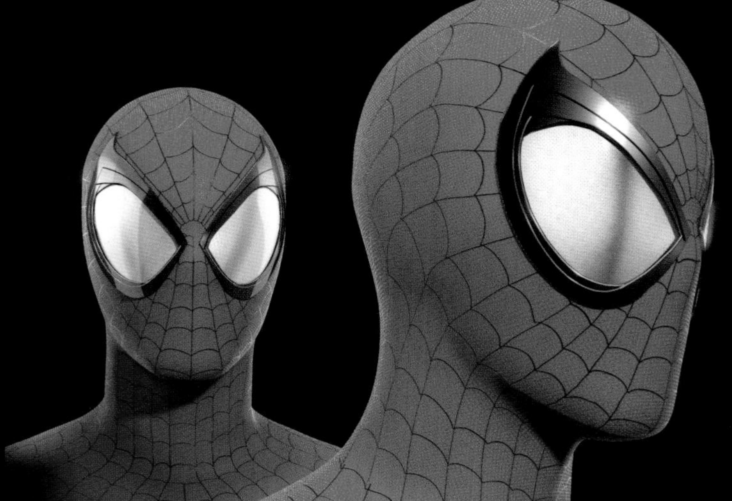

SPIDER-MAN: NO WAY HOME

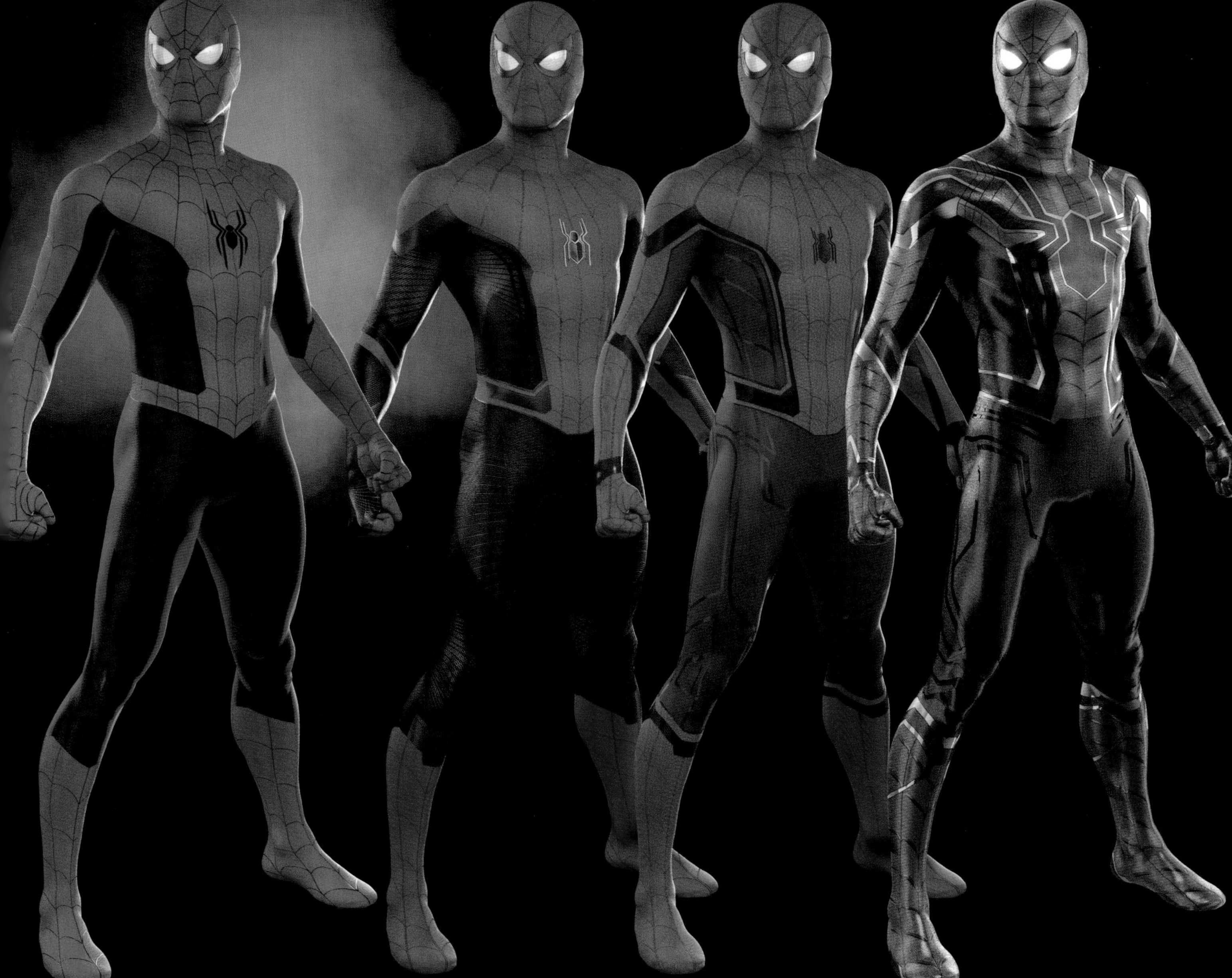

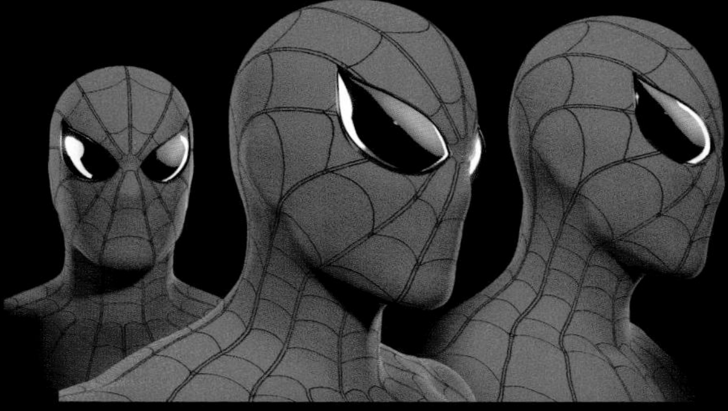

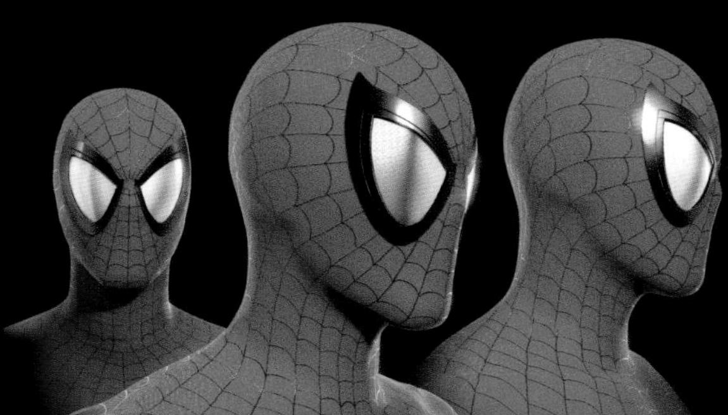

Very early on in the vis-dev process for *Spider-Man: No Way Home*, director Jon Watts talked to Ryan Meinerding about wanting to have a final suit design that could have more of a classic Marvel Comics look. "So a lot of the exploration for me during that time was simply, what does 'classic' mean in the context of what we've already done in the previous films?" says Meinerding. "What could we do that *was* 'classic' but in a way that still felt like we hadn't seen it *on screen* before." A lot of that design exploration saw Meinerding trying to figure out how to do the iconic Spider-Man costume, where most of the leg and outside torso sections look black but then the edging is blue, "Just like they rendered in the comics," he continues. "Because Tobey Maguire's suit is dark like that—and kind of has that same feel—some people were generally a little bit scared to try and go there with Tom's suit." For a different approach to eyes for Tom Holland's costume, Meinerding explored versions inspired by the Spider-Man comic book artwork of Todd McFarlane, Eric Larson, and Ryan Stegman.

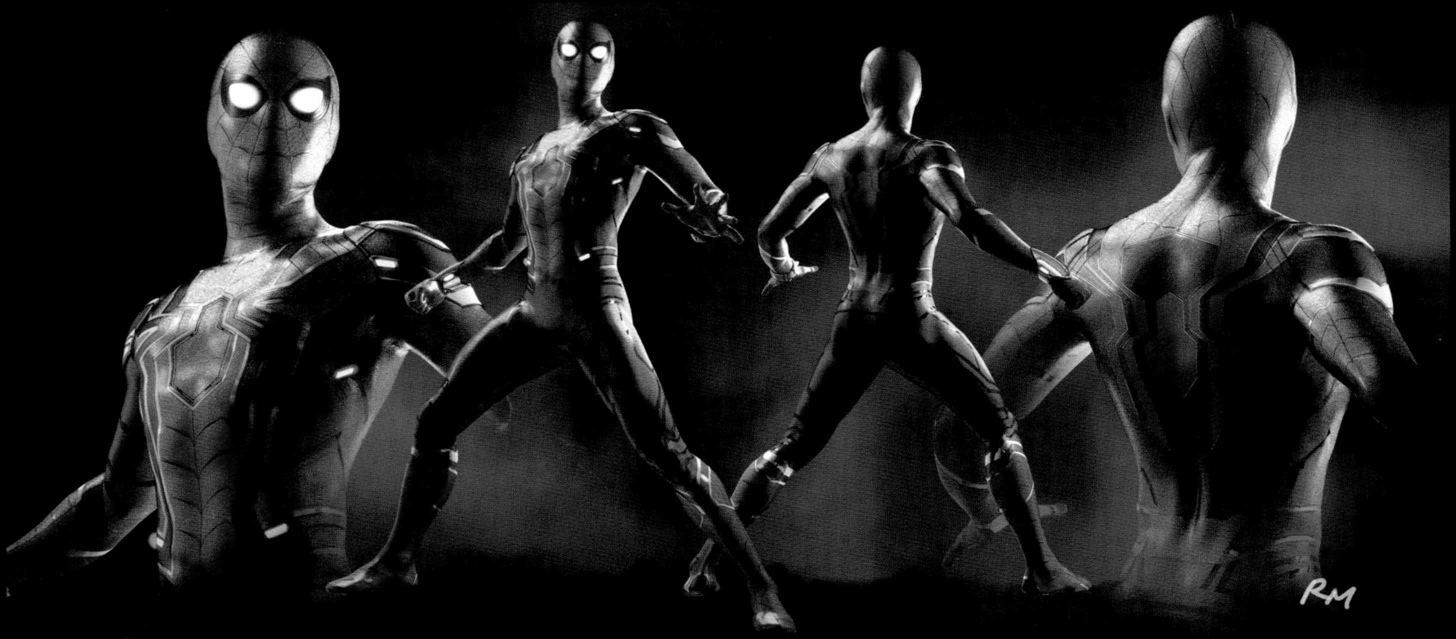
RM

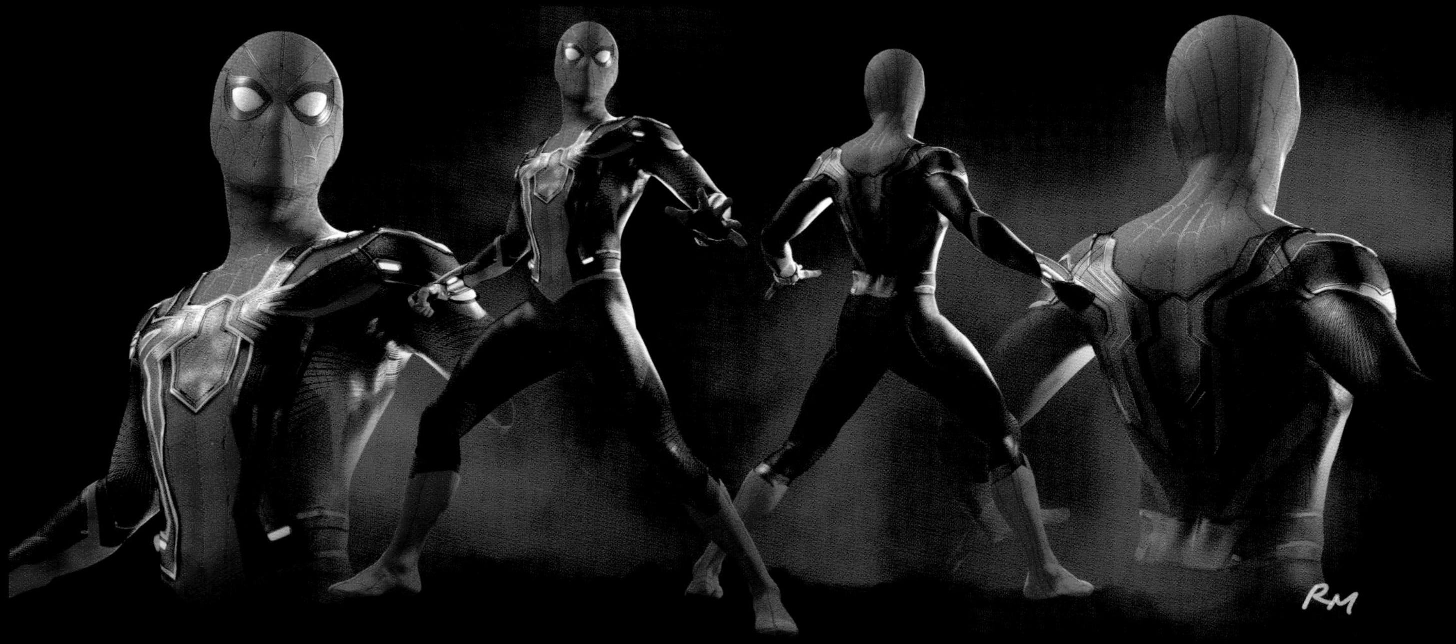
RM

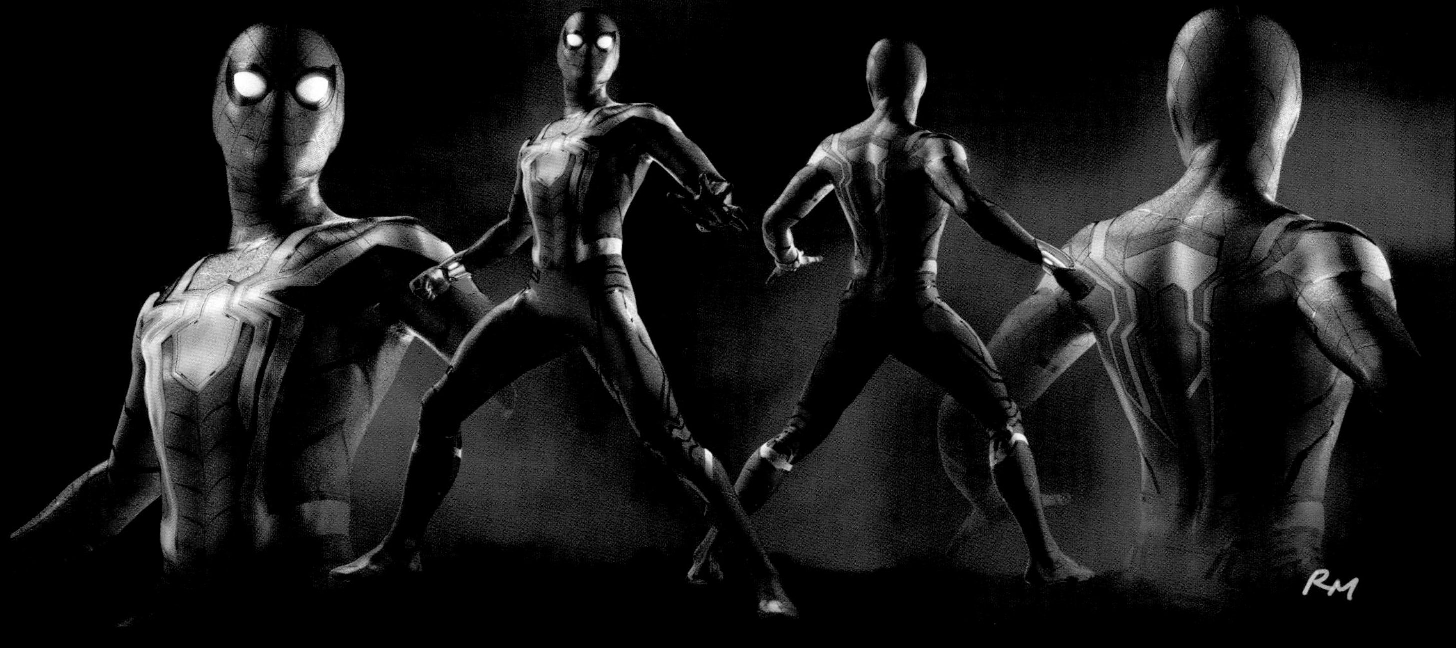
RM

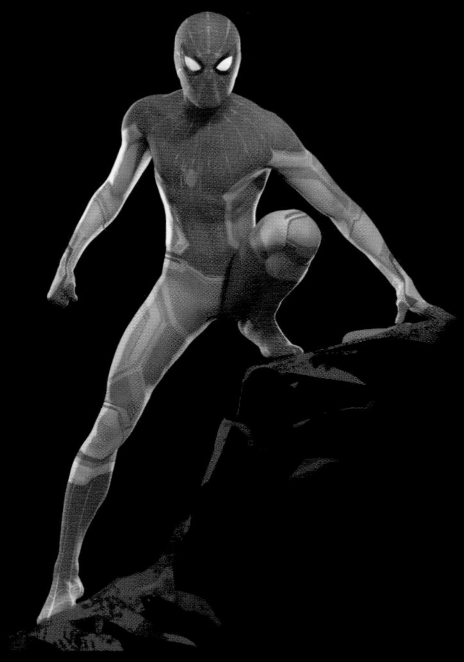
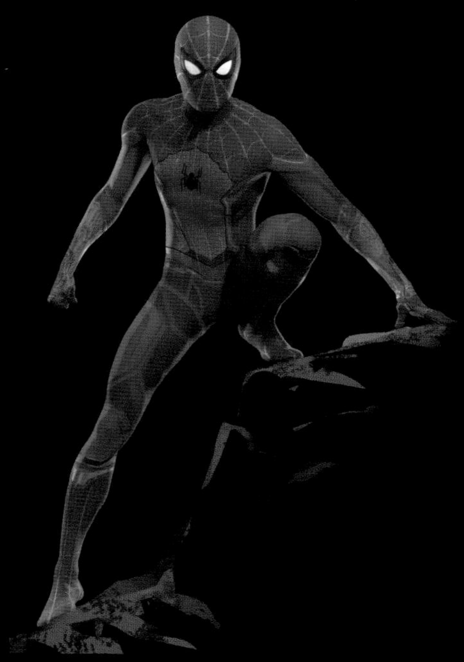
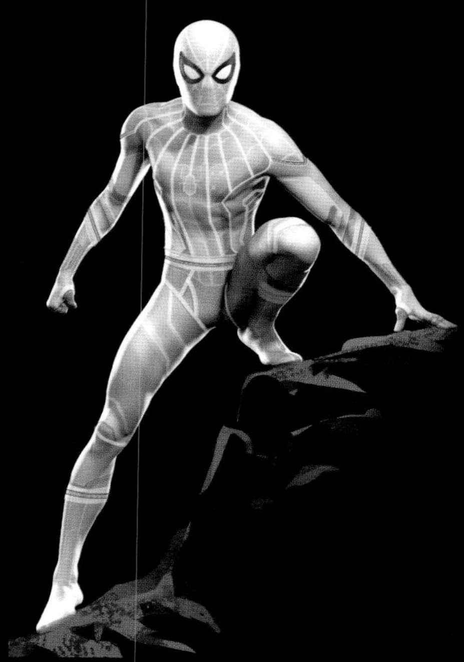
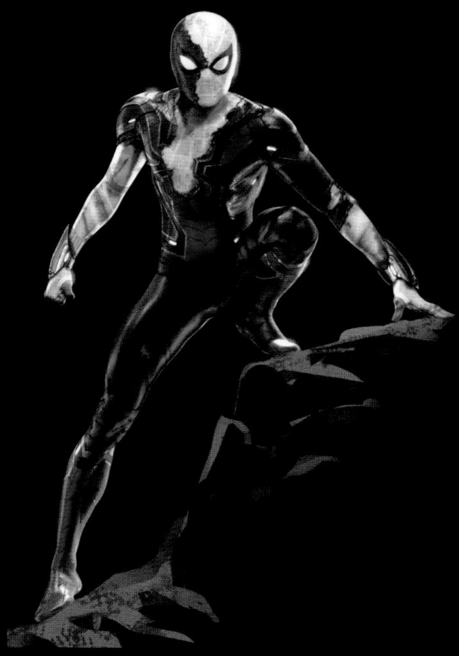
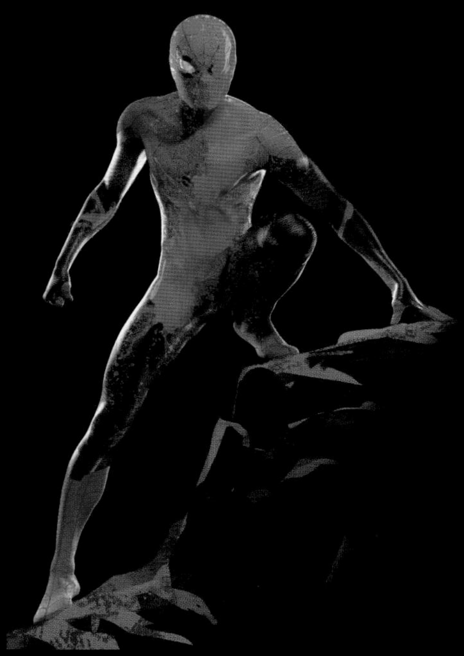
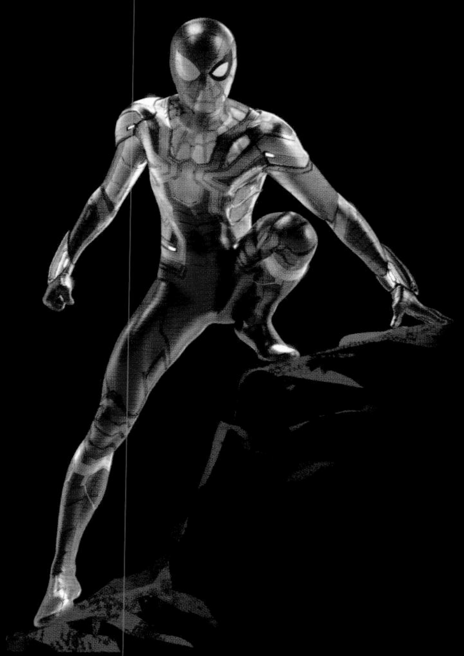

"This was a very interesting time, because my first round of *Spider-Man: No Way Home* suit designs was the last meeting I had at the Marvel Studios offices before we were all gone due to the pandemic," reveals Meinerding. "On the Friday before that meeting, I had said to my whole team, 'You should all go home and think about figuring out working from home if we have to for a period of time.' On the following Monday, we all came in. Then lockdown happened. And that was the last in-person meeting for *two years*."

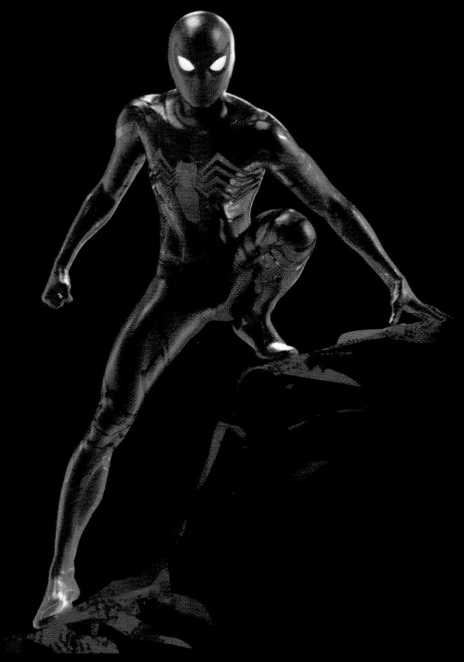
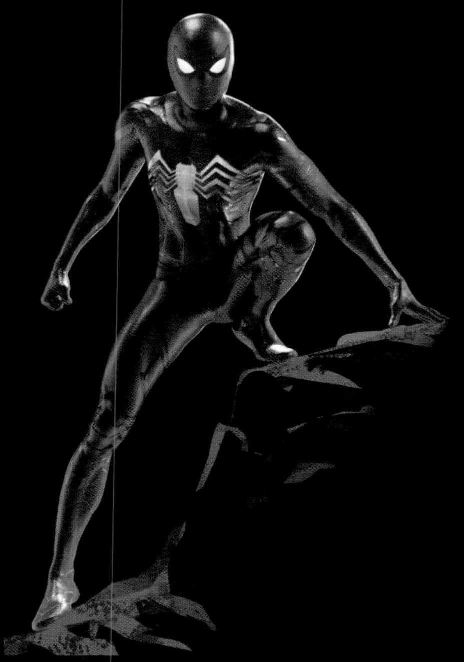

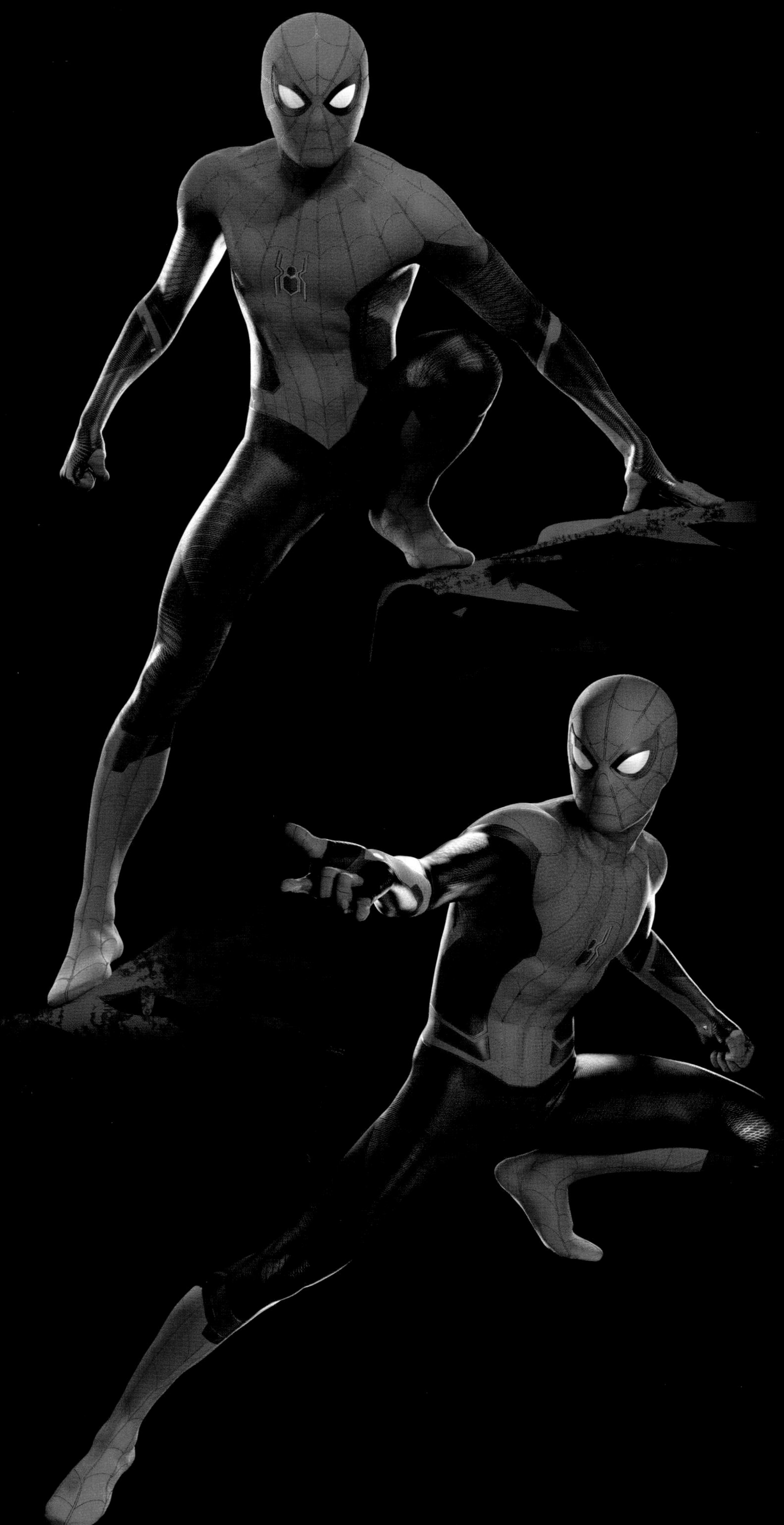

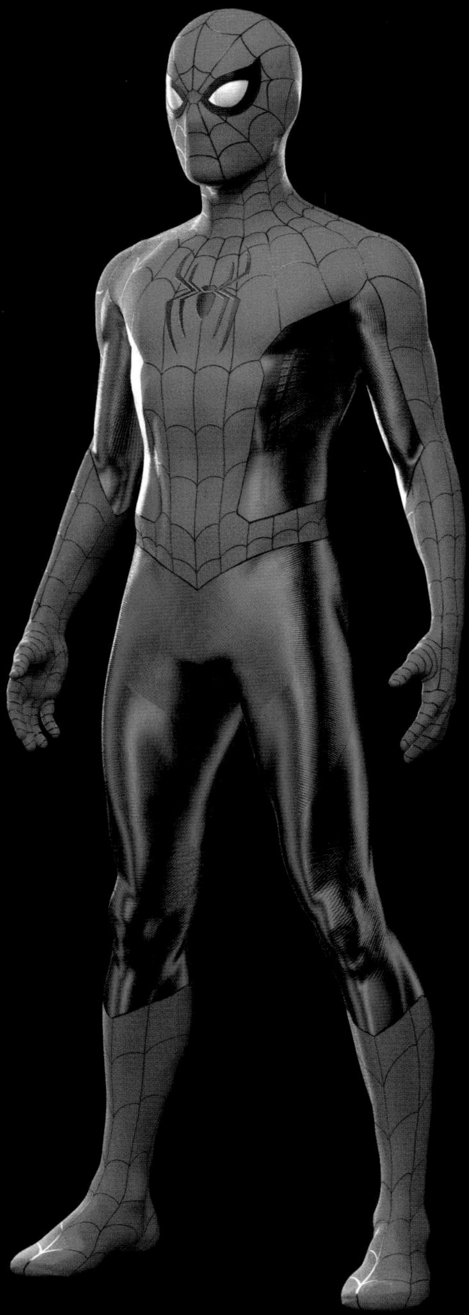

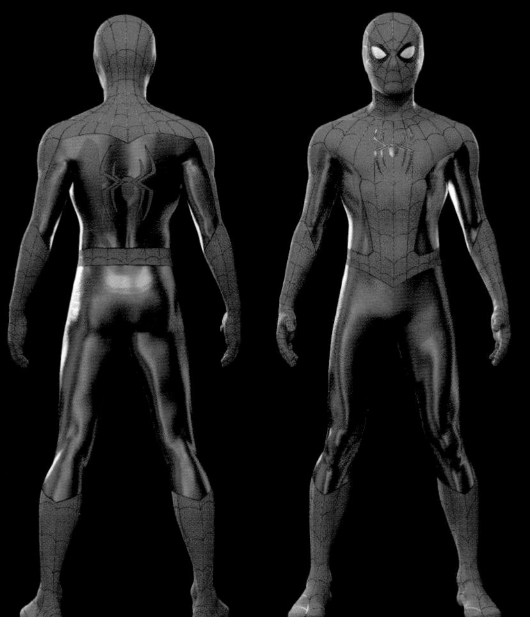

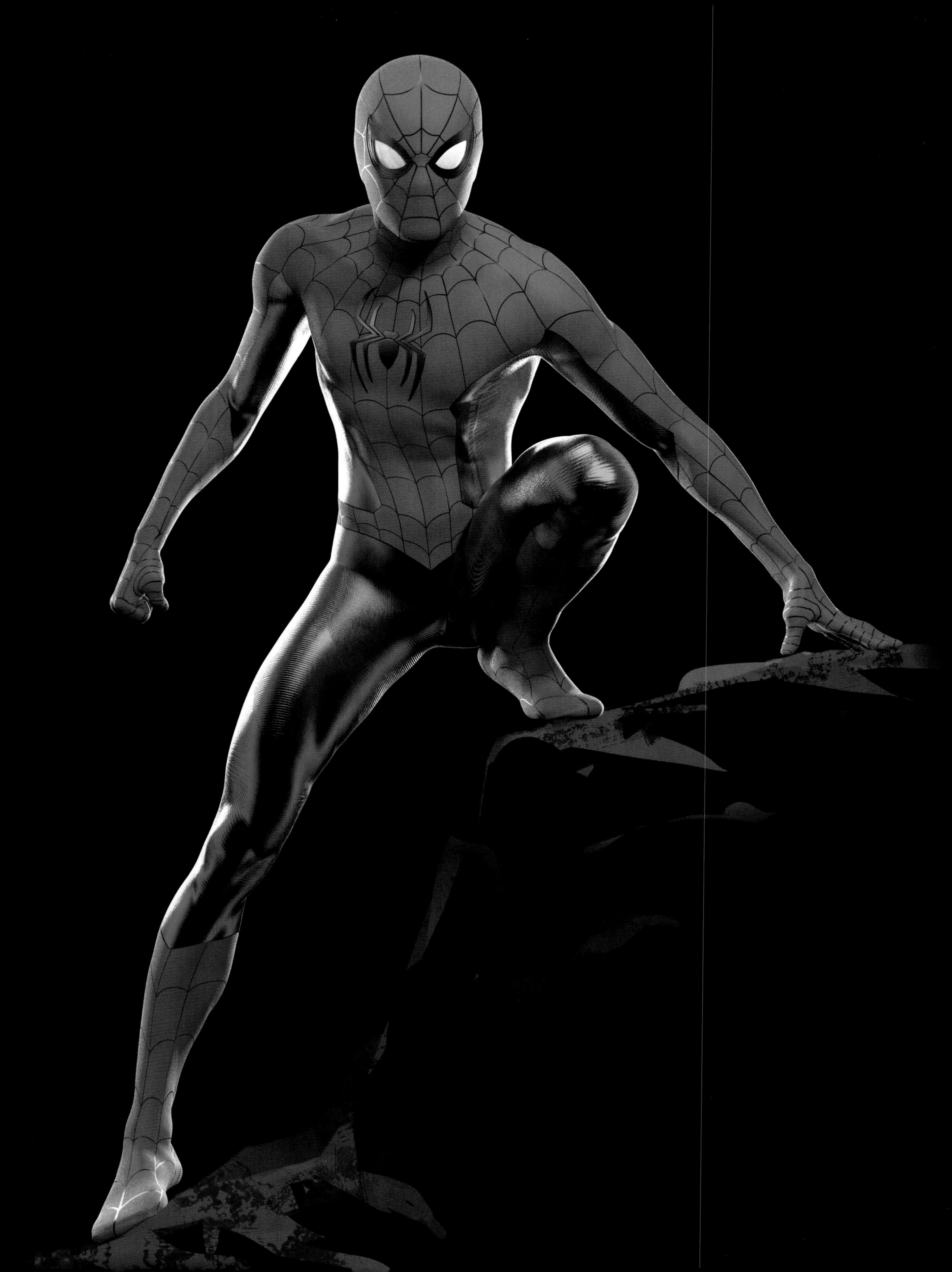

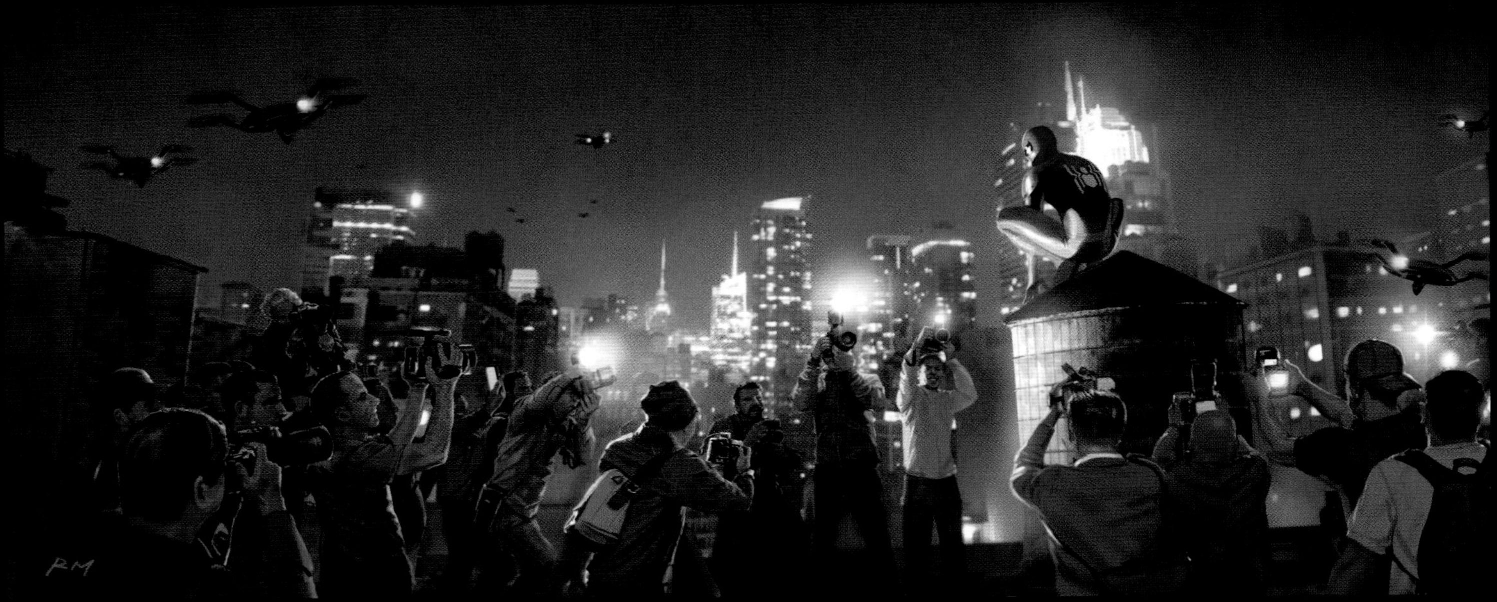
RM

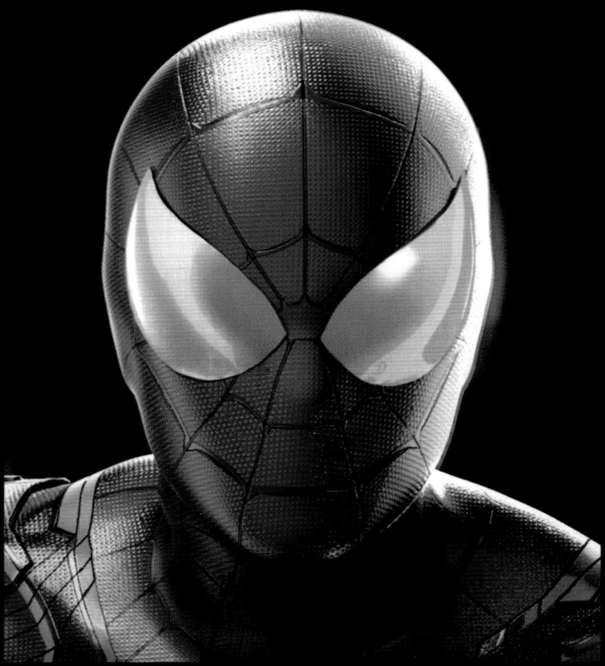

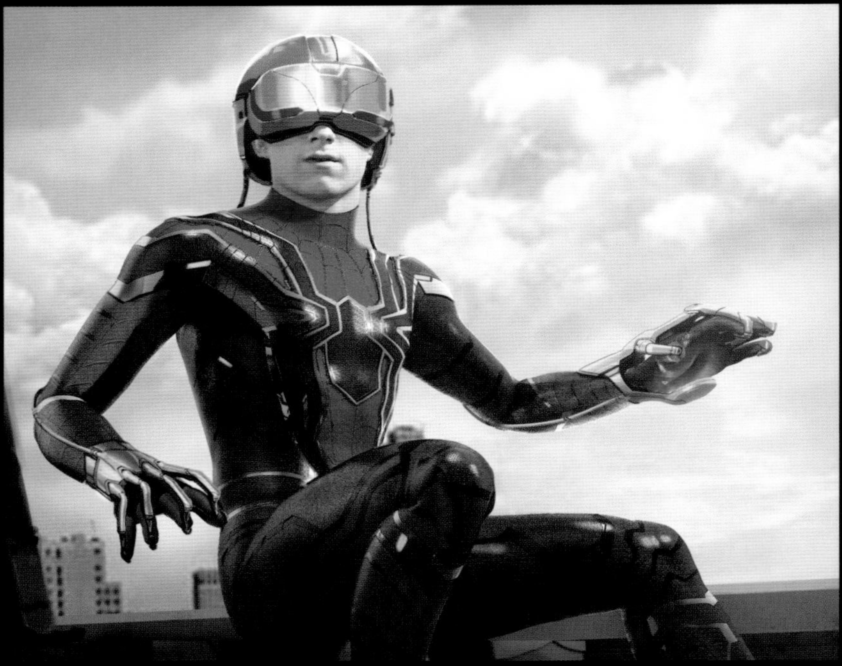

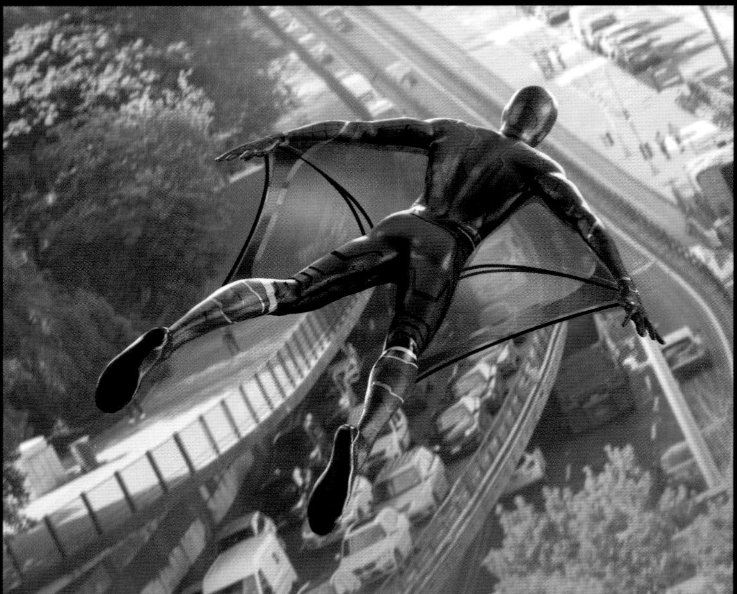

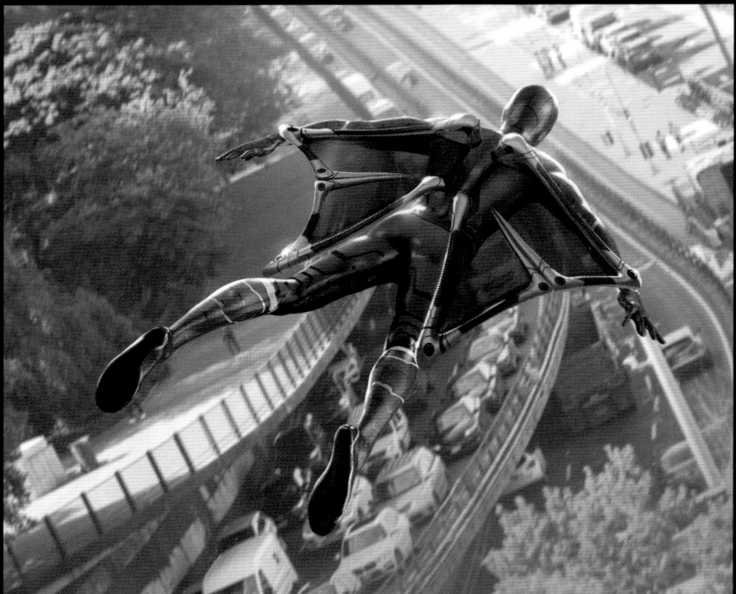

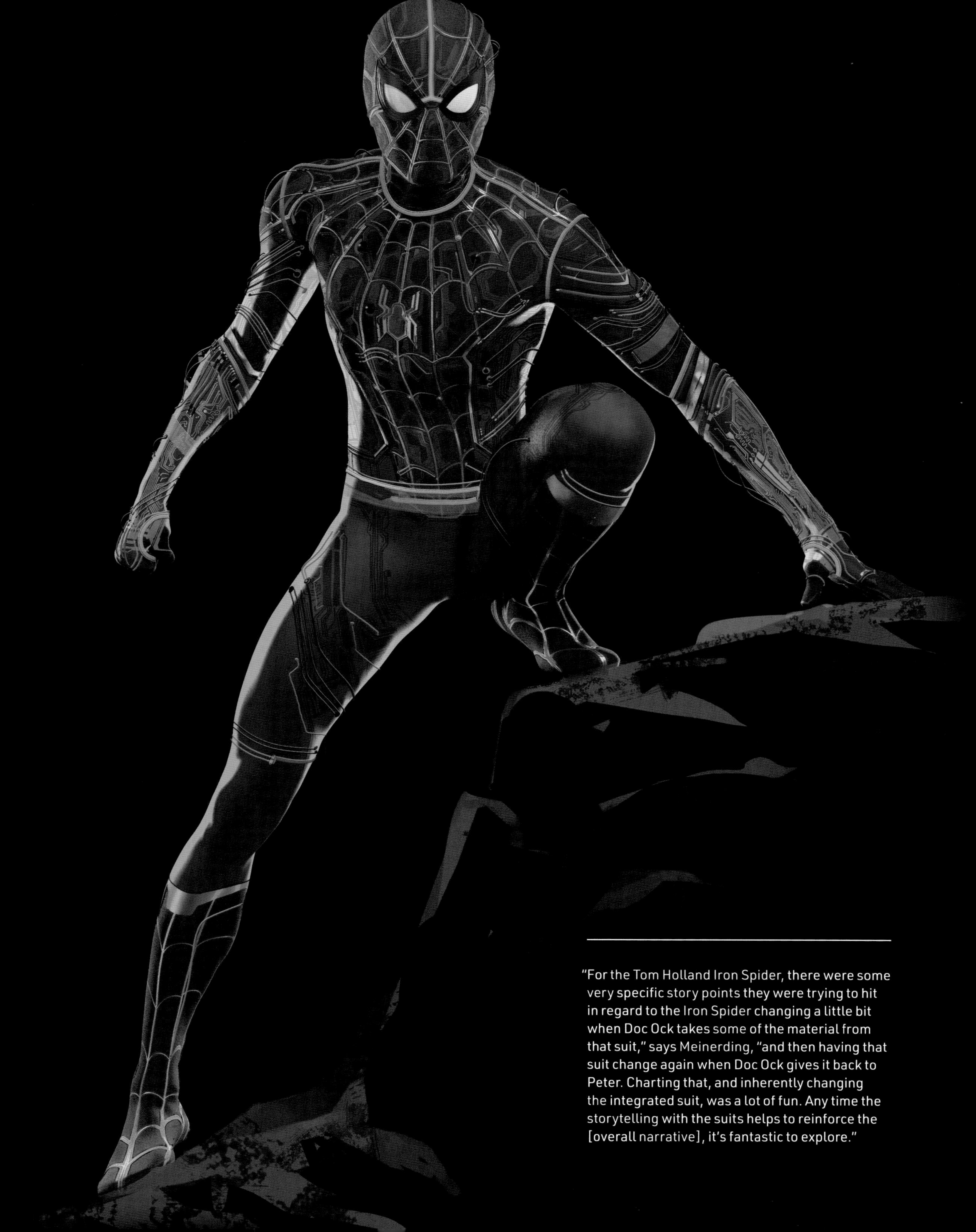

"For the Tom Holland Iron Spider, there were some very specific story points they were trying to hit in regard to the Iron Spider changing a little bit when Doc Ock takes some of the material from that suit," says Meinerding, "and then having that suit change again when Doc Ock gives it back to Peter. Charting that, and inherently changing the integrated suit, was a lot of fun. Any time the storytelling with the suits helps to reinforce the [overall narrative], it's fantastic to explore."

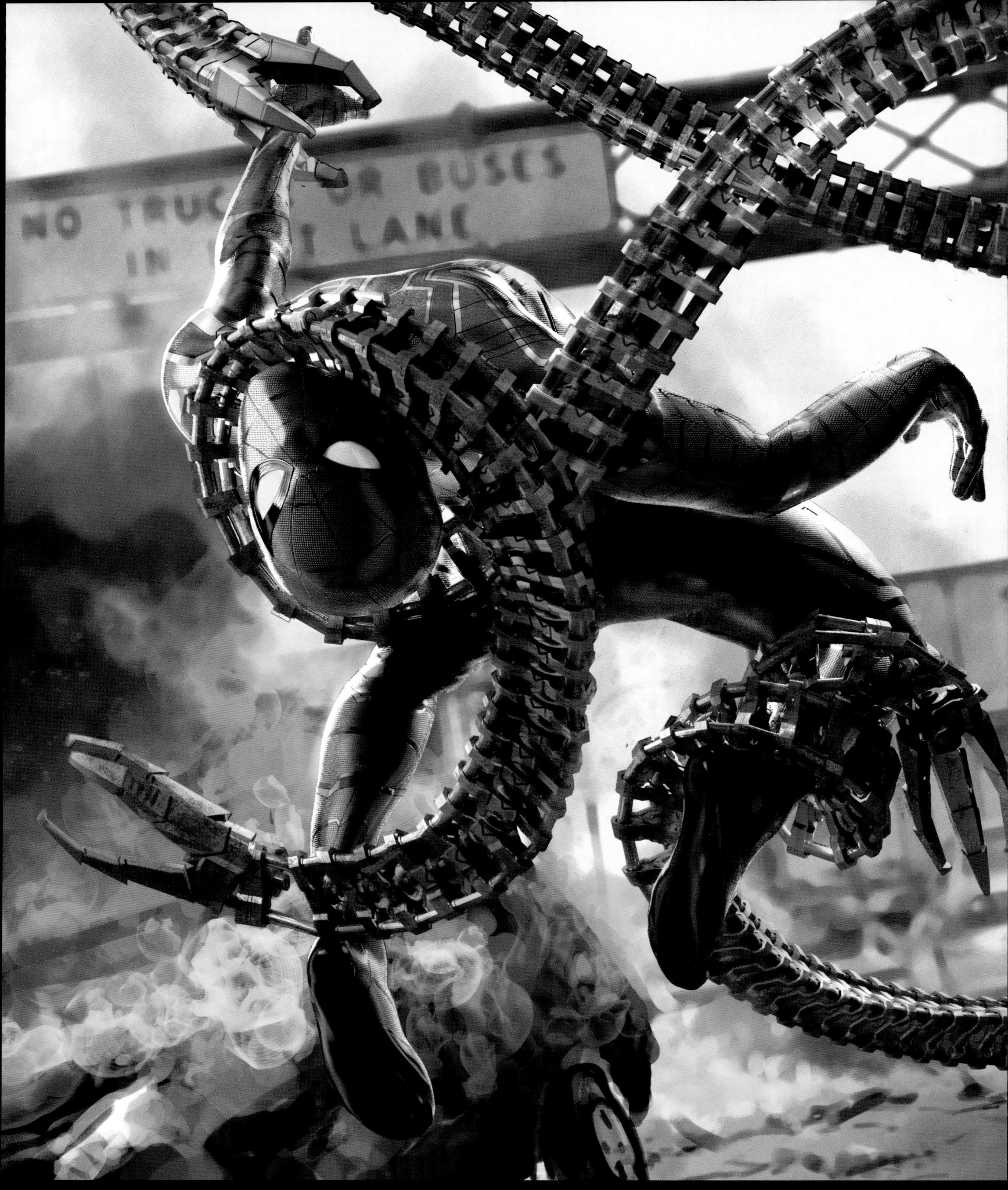
OR BUSES
LANE

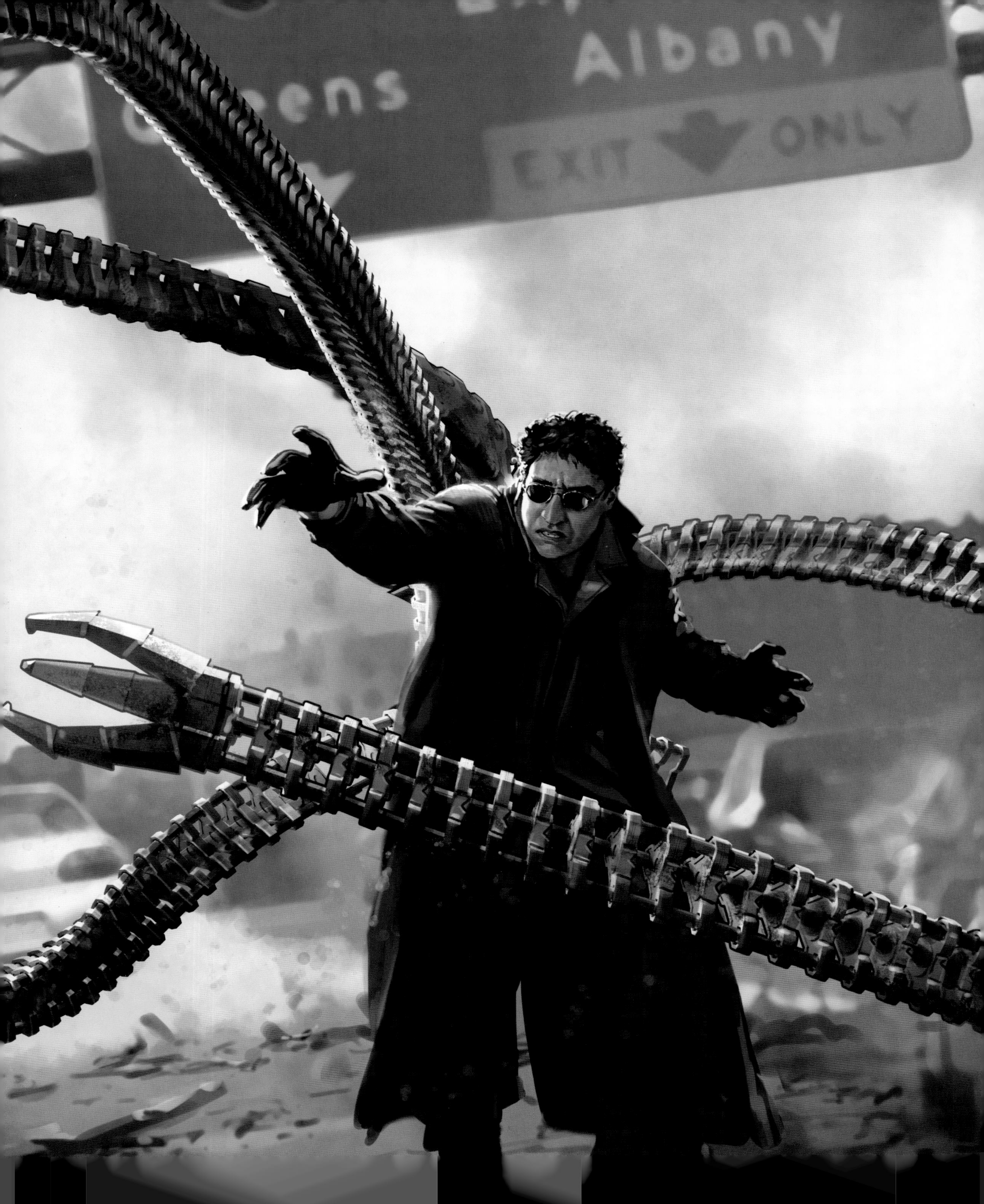
Albany
EXIT ONLY

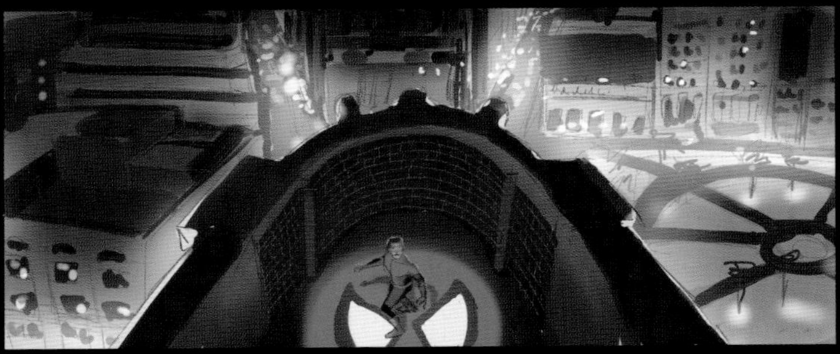

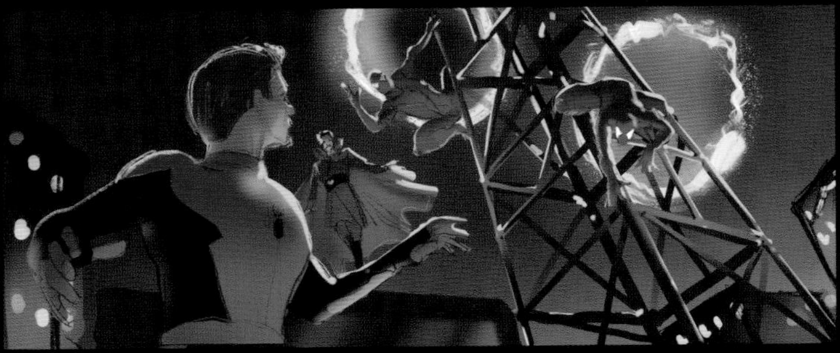

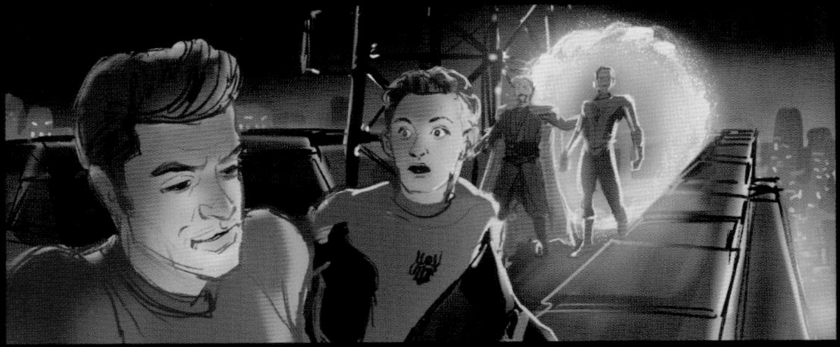

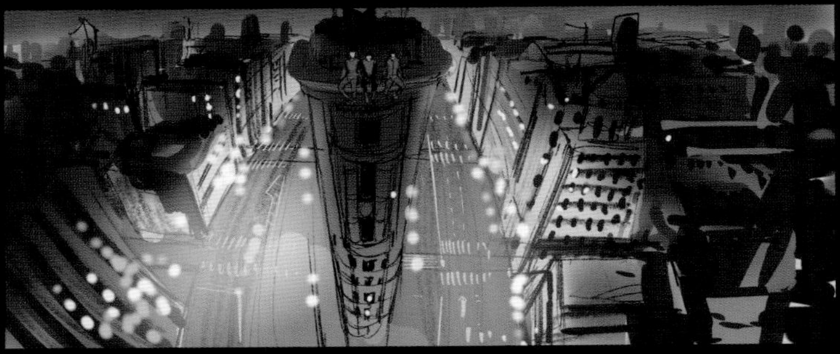

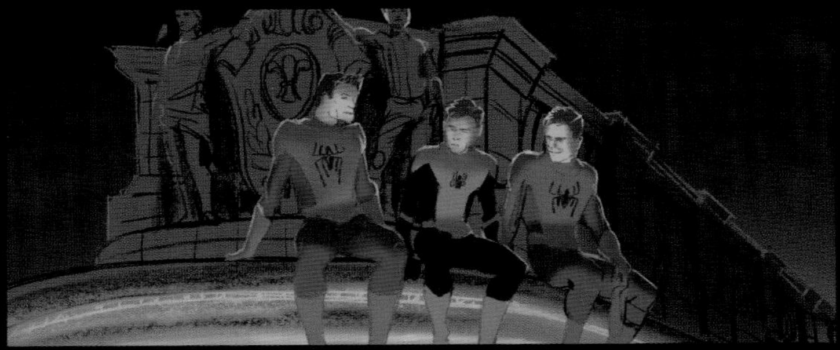

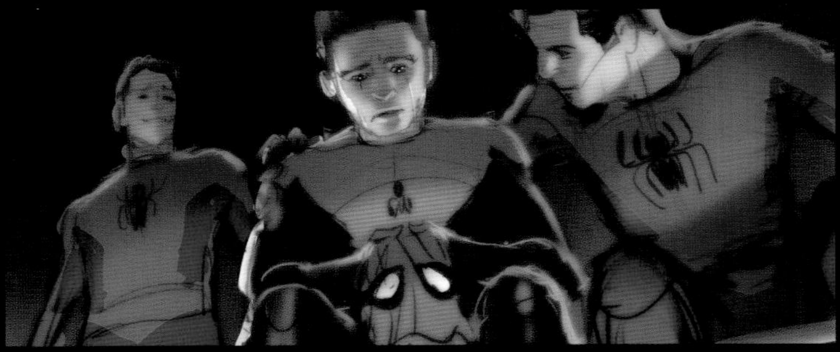

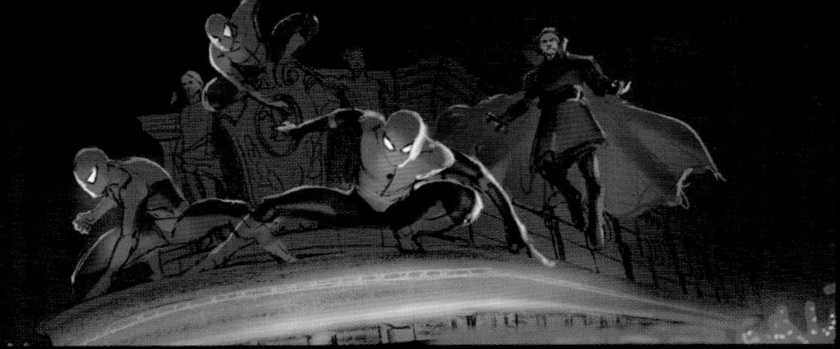

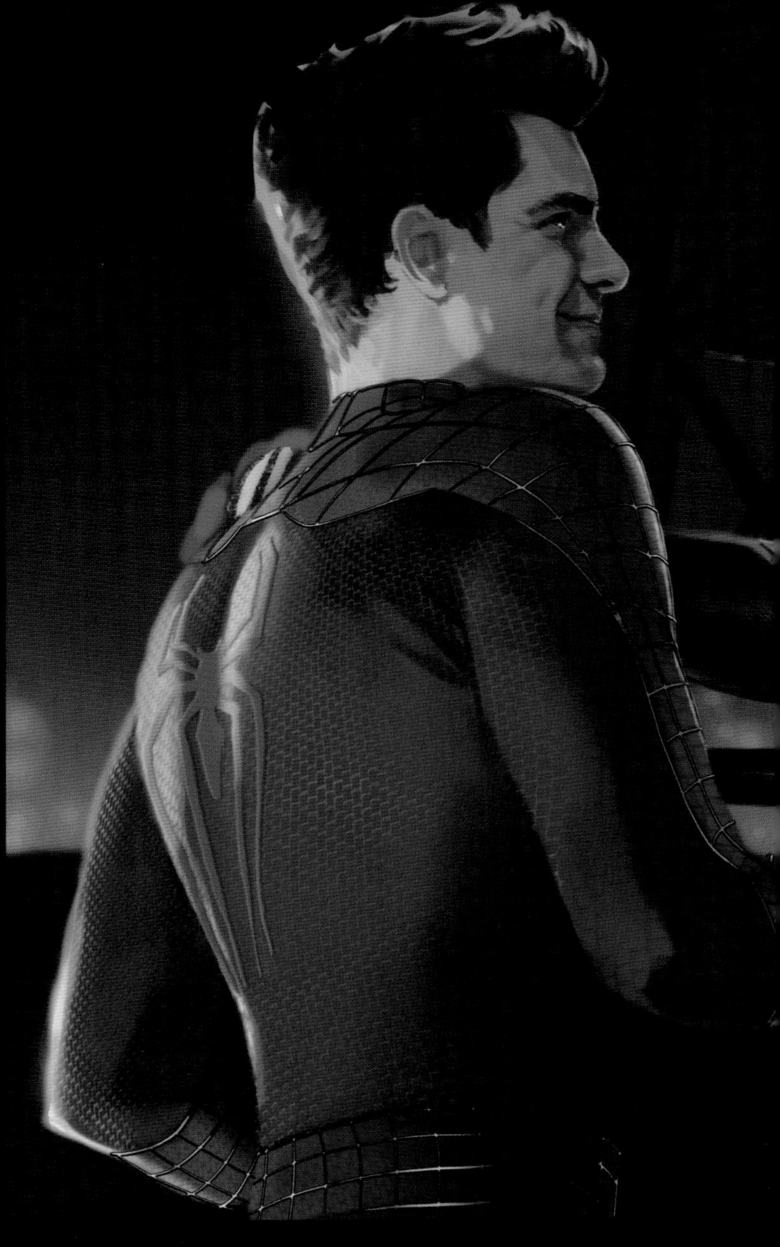

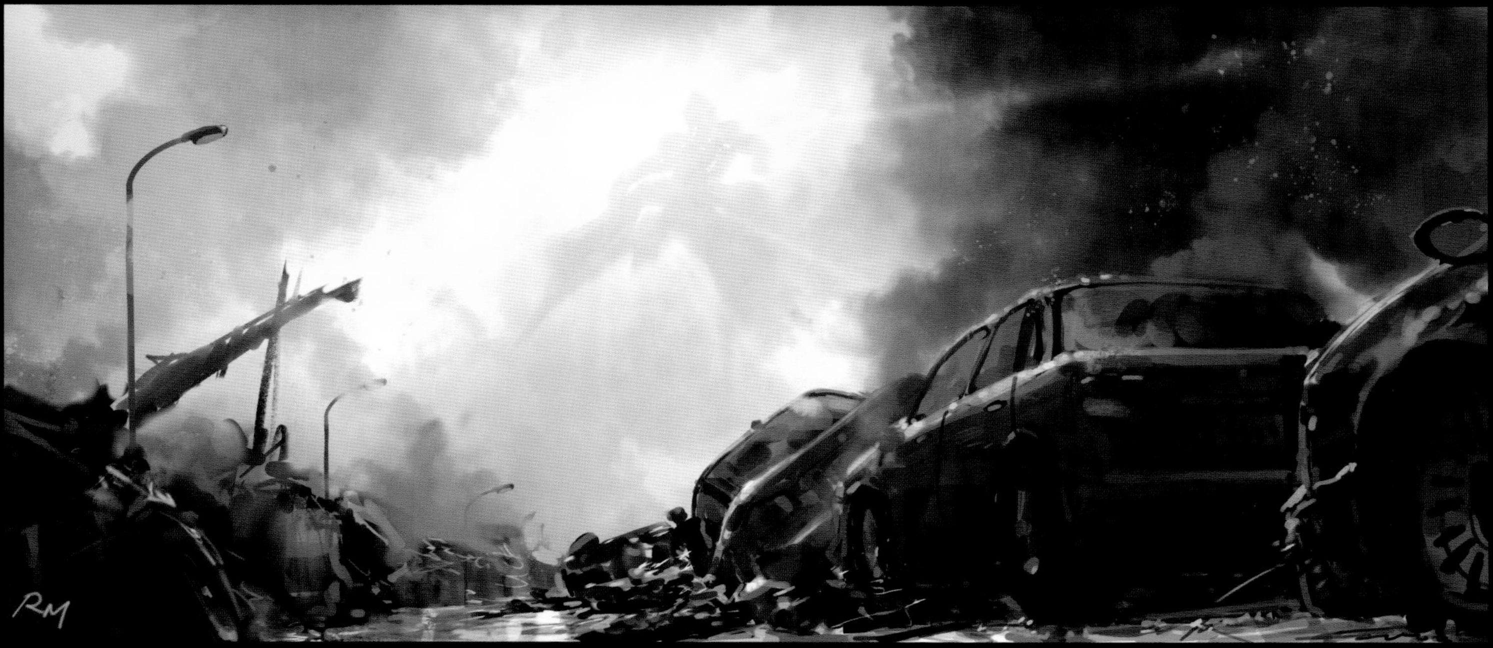
RM

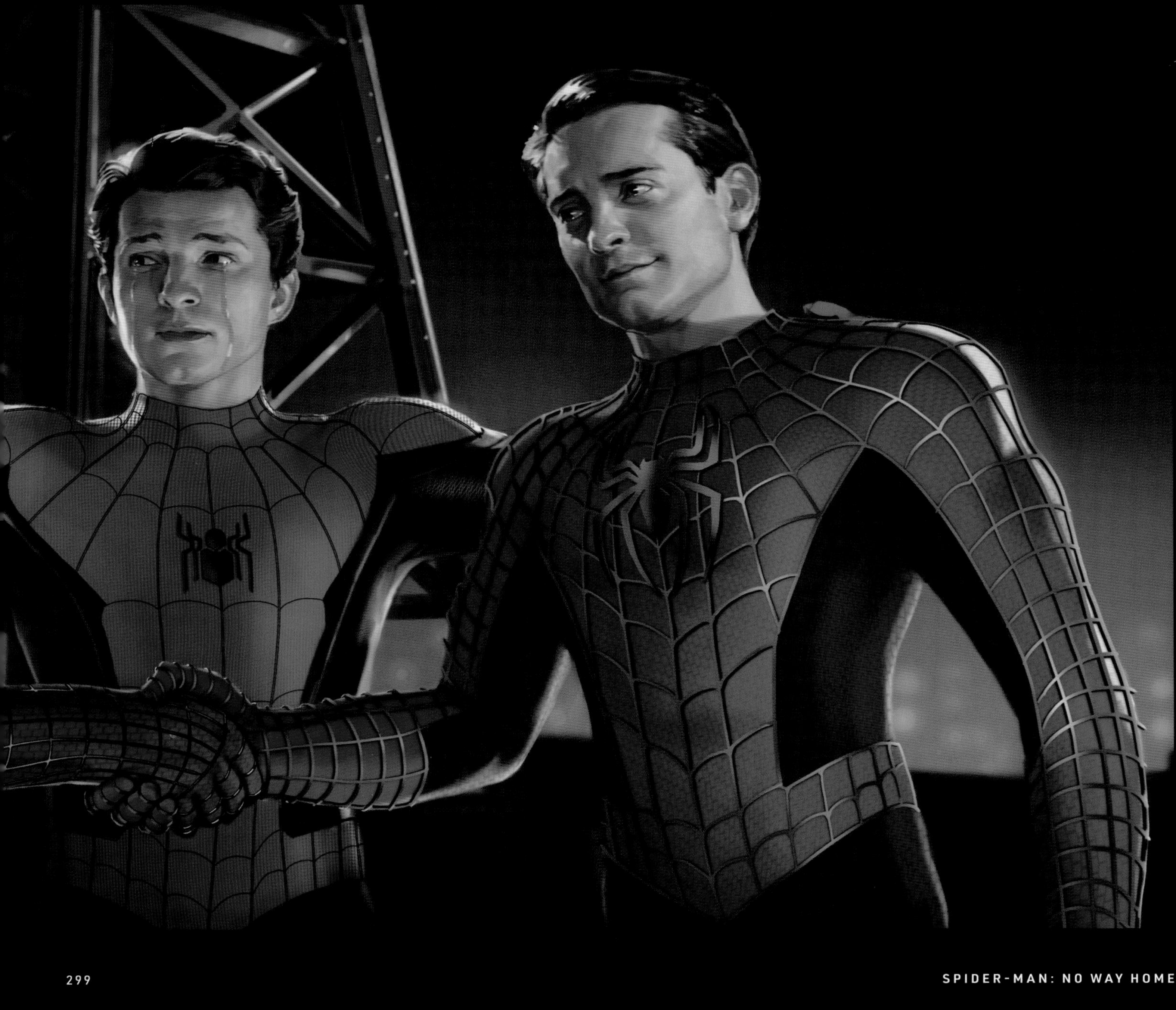

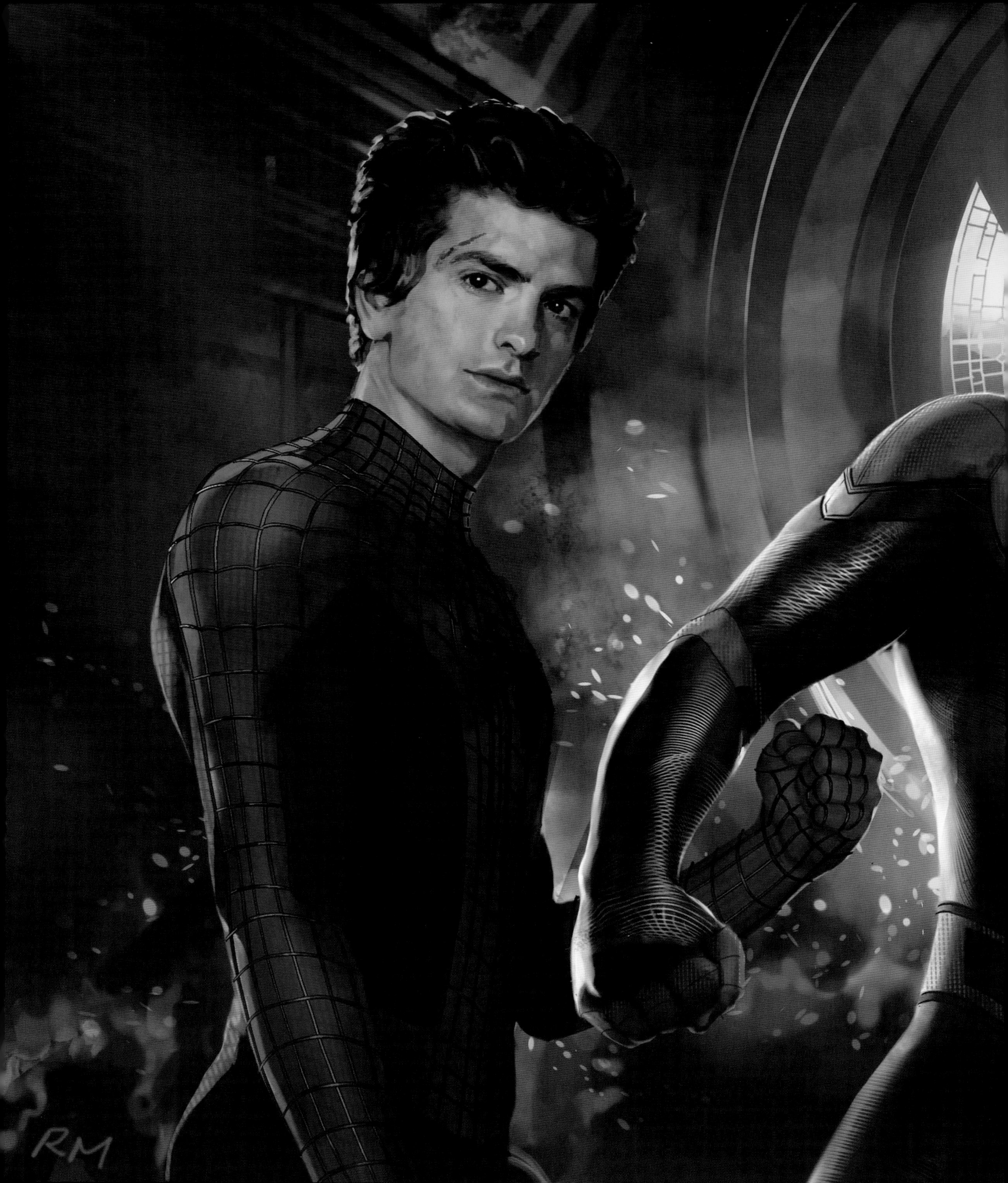
RM

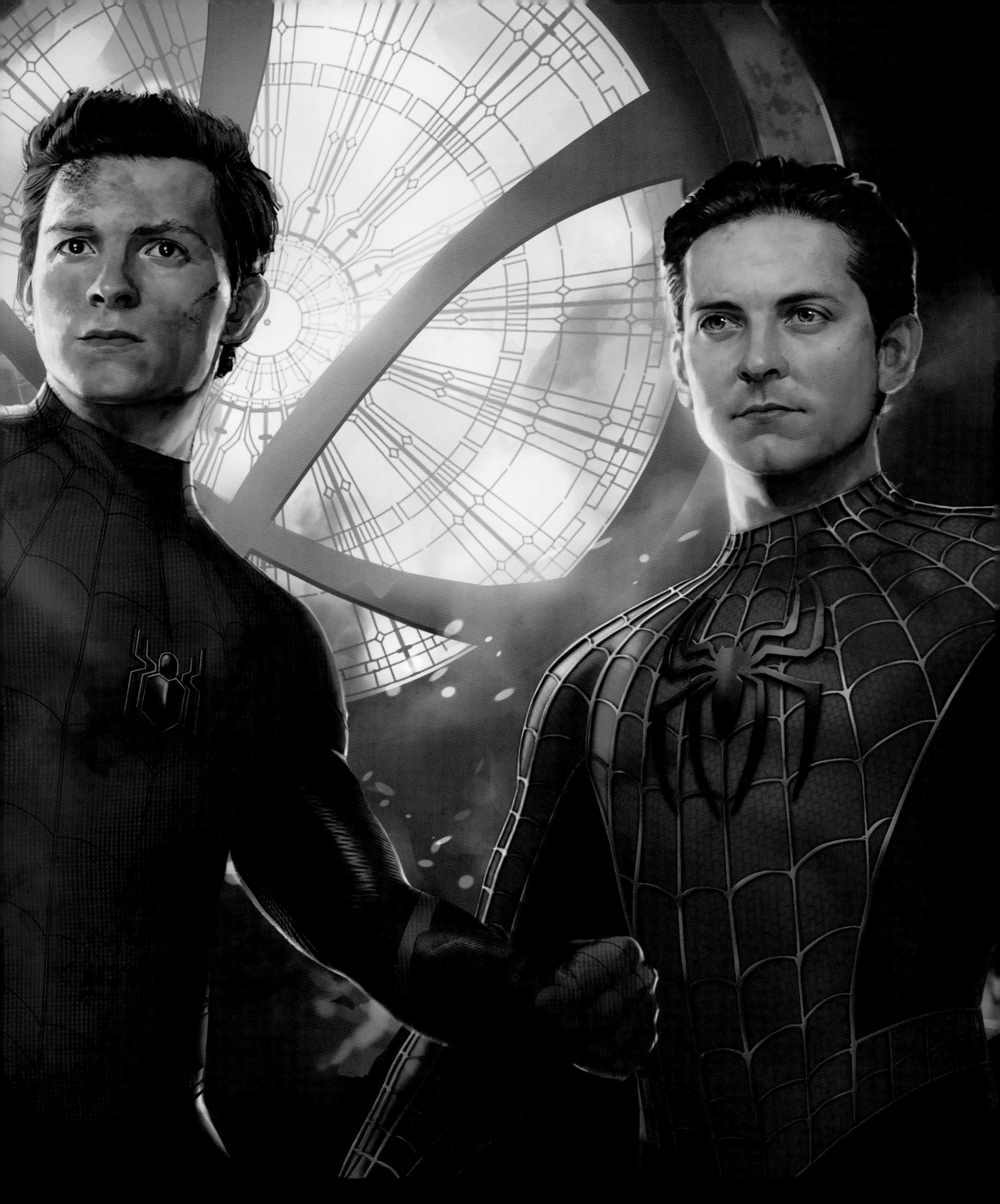

"Doing frames of the three Spider-Men together was incredibly fun, whether it's them with their masks off or them sort of posing at the Statue of Liberty," says Meinerding. The artist worked on Lady Liberty vis-dev very early on, but there were concerns it wasn't going to be an iconic enough set piece for the finale, simply because it had already been used that way at the end of *X-Men* (2000). "And especially if it was gonna have glowy energy around it and was gonna be set at night," he adds.

"We had worked a little bit on these before the pandemic lockdown, when I was doing more key frame stuff for the villain setups and some of the villains versus villains or a group shot of all the villains versus Peter," says Meinerding. "Phil Saunders, Josh Nizzi, and Adi Granov did amazing work bringing the Green Goblin to life. With Doc Ock, it was treated as more of a costume exercise, since he was literally coming in from *Spider-Man 2*. He's essentially wearing two overcoats, so there was an effort to try and make him fit within the MCU a little bit more."

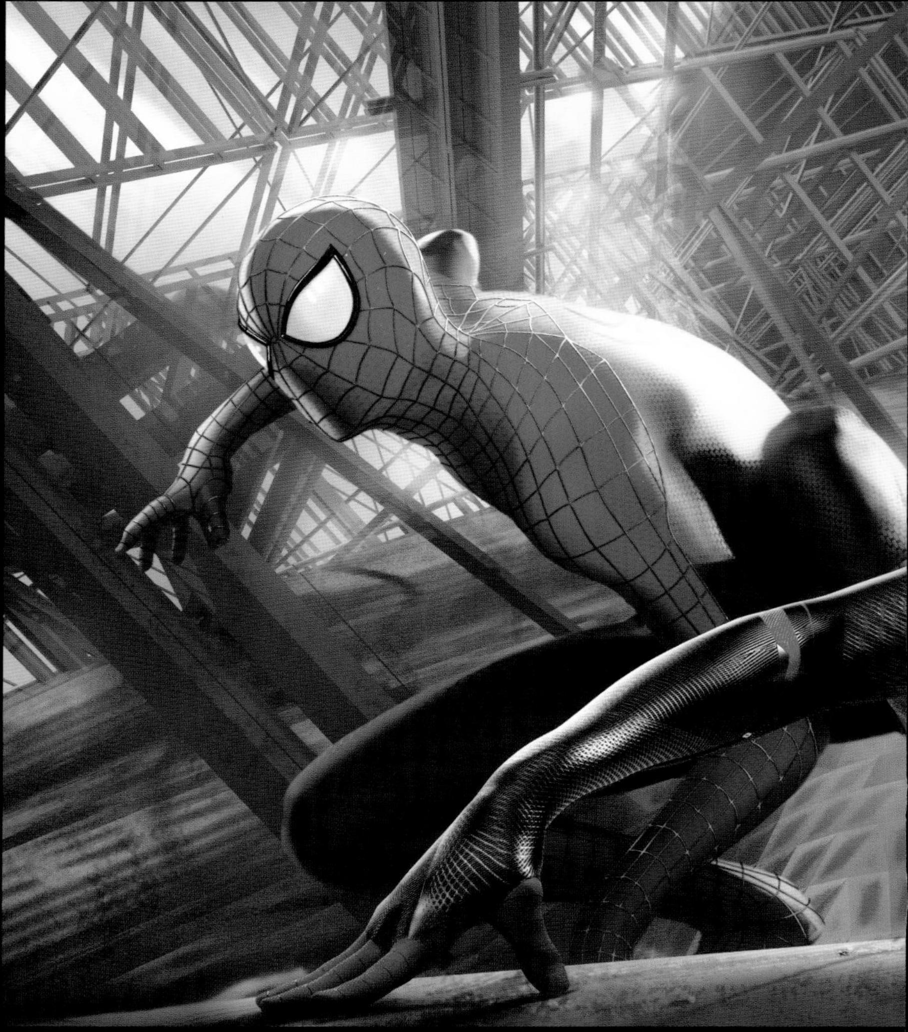

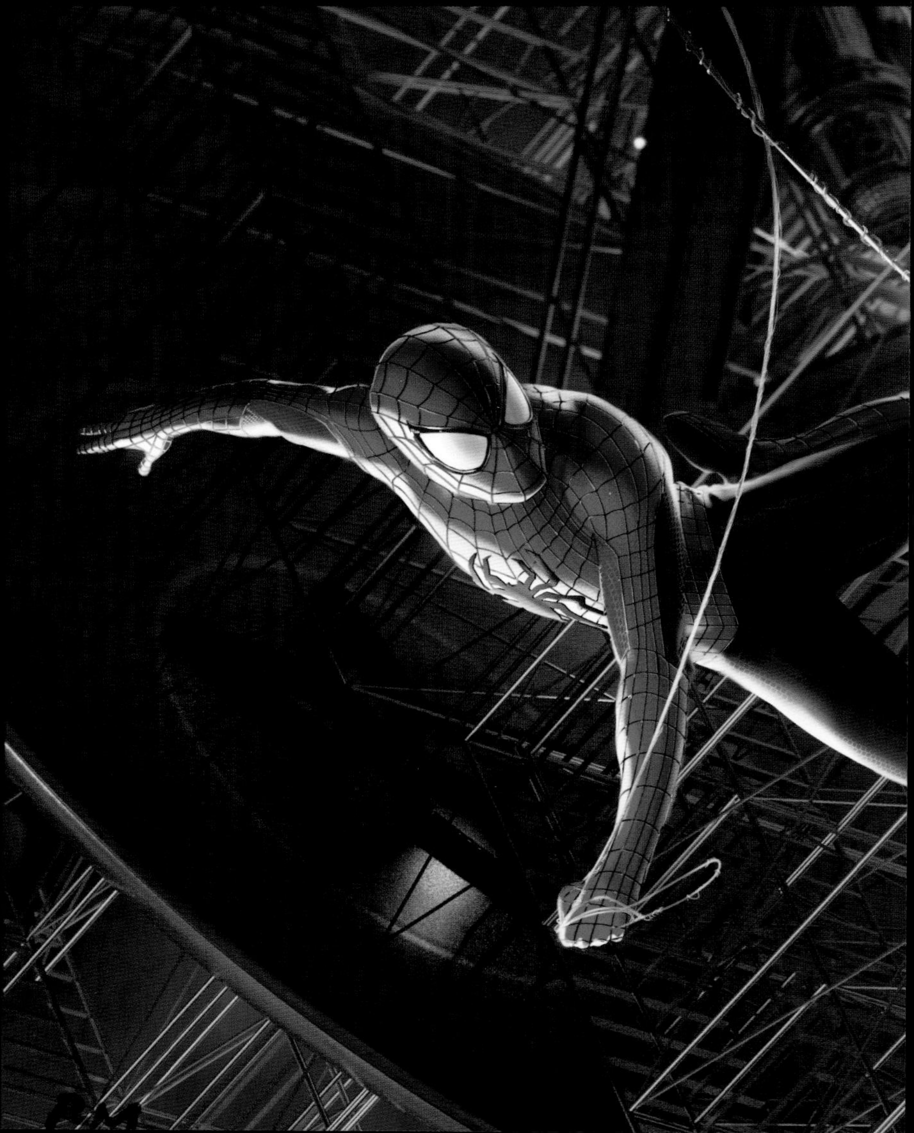

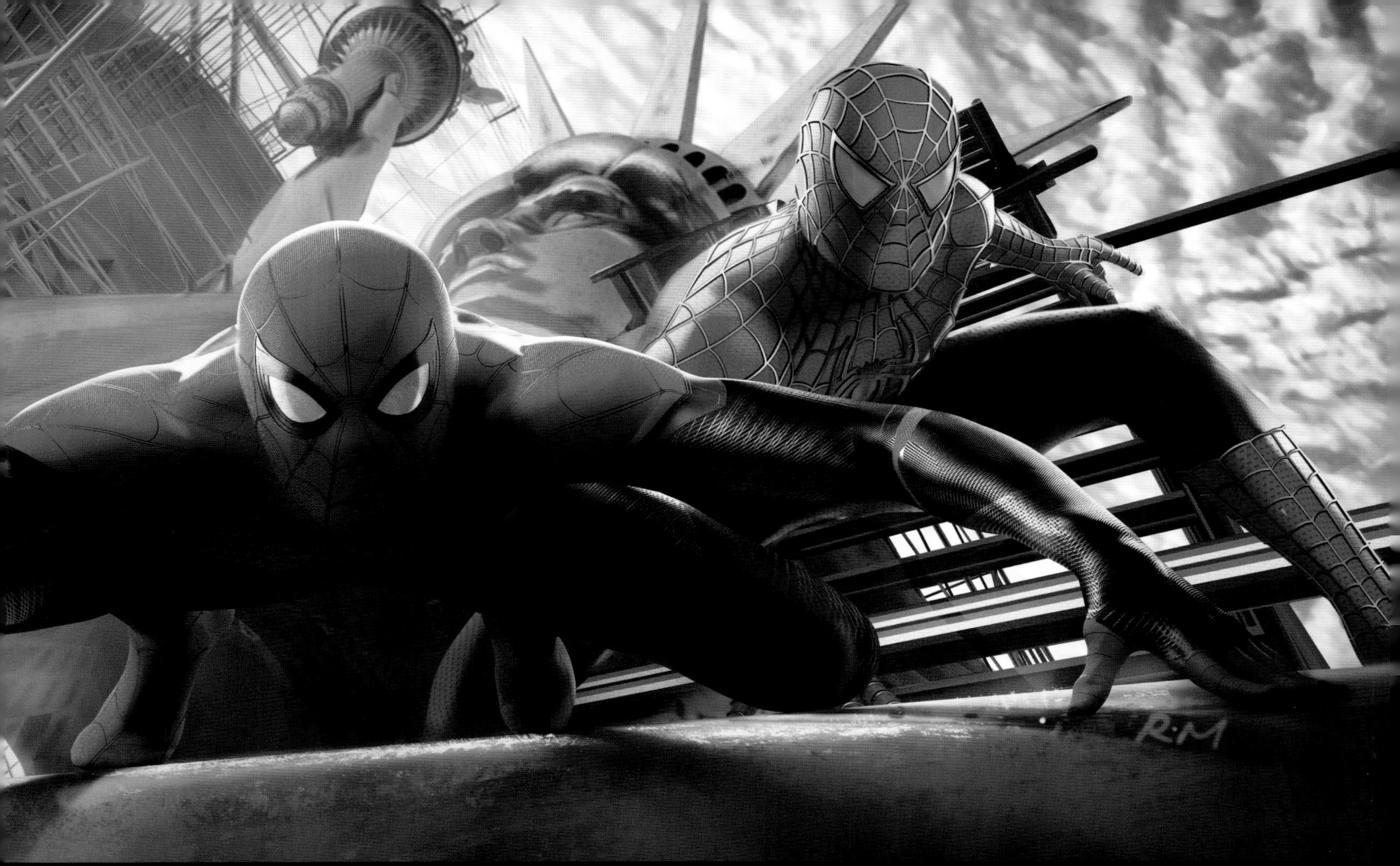
RM

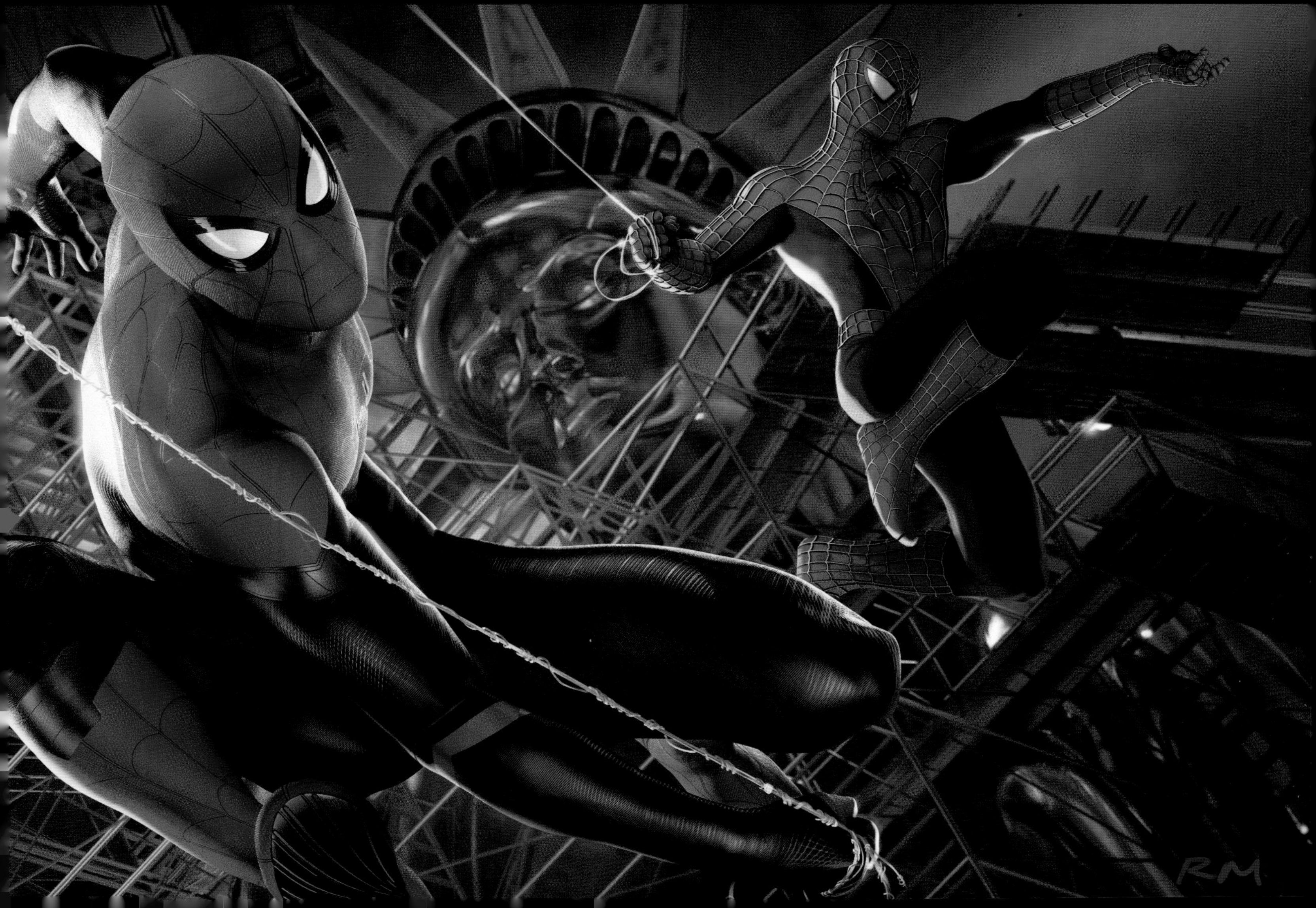
RM

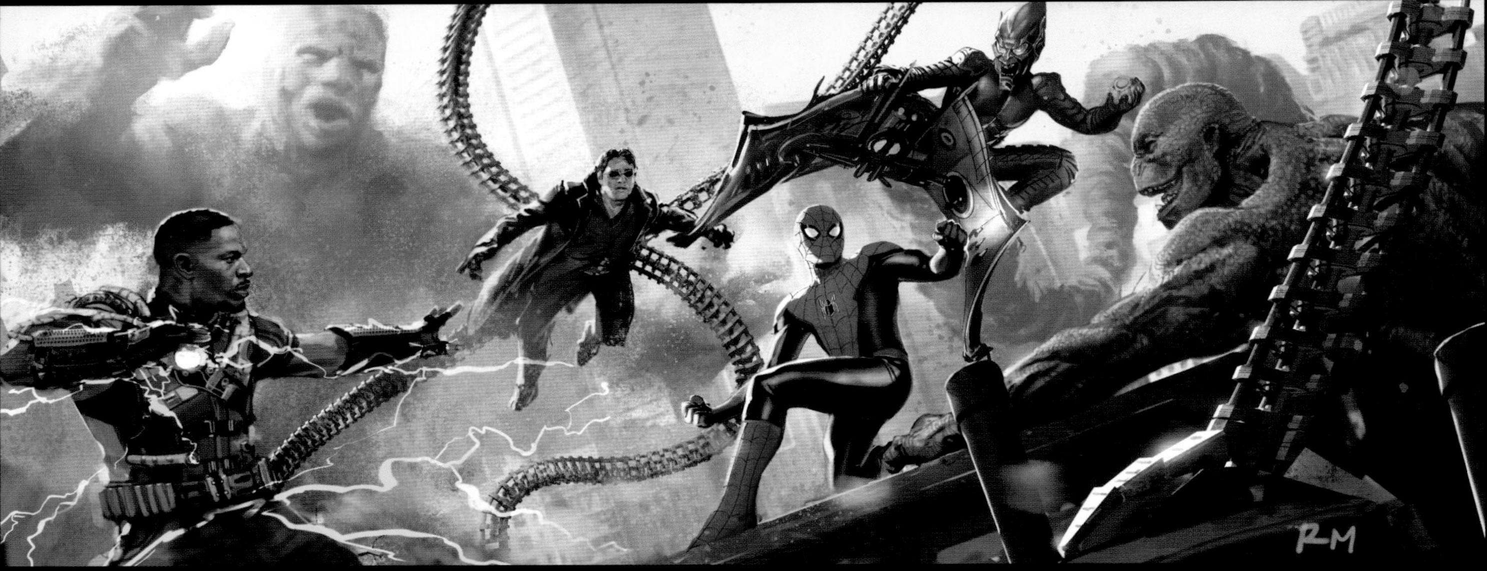
RM

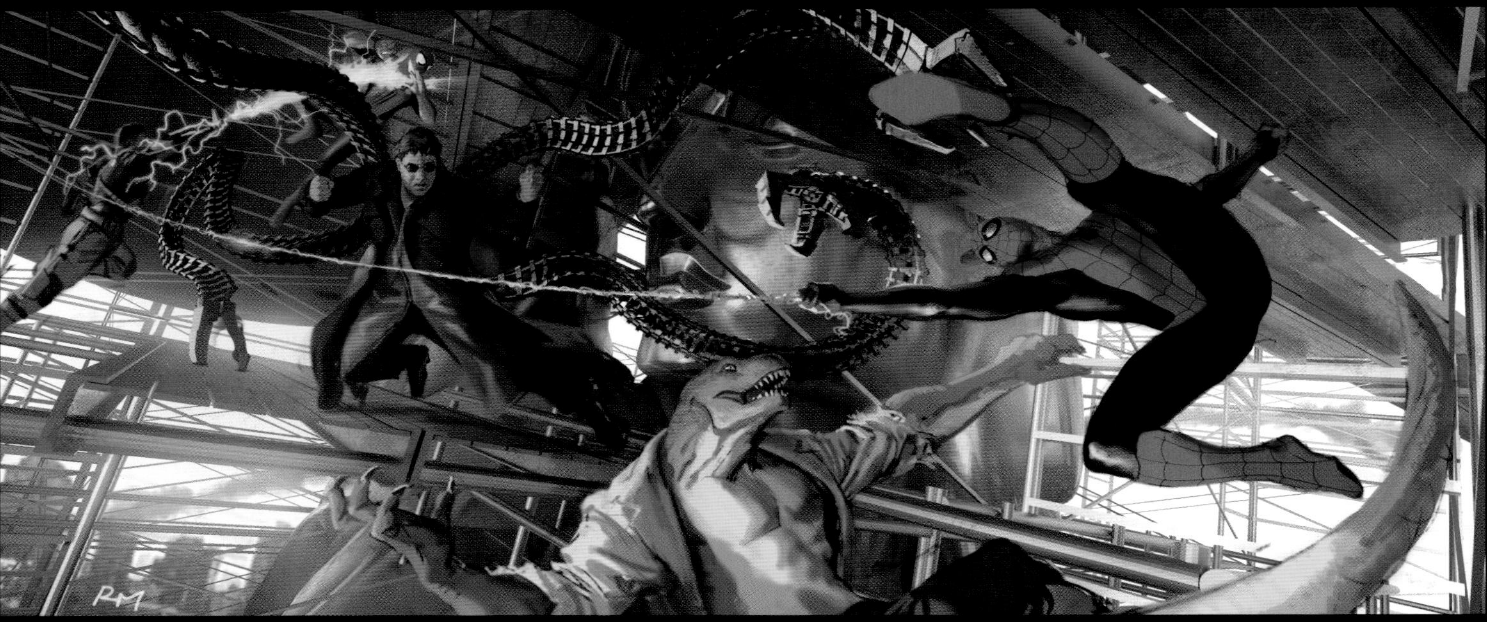
RM

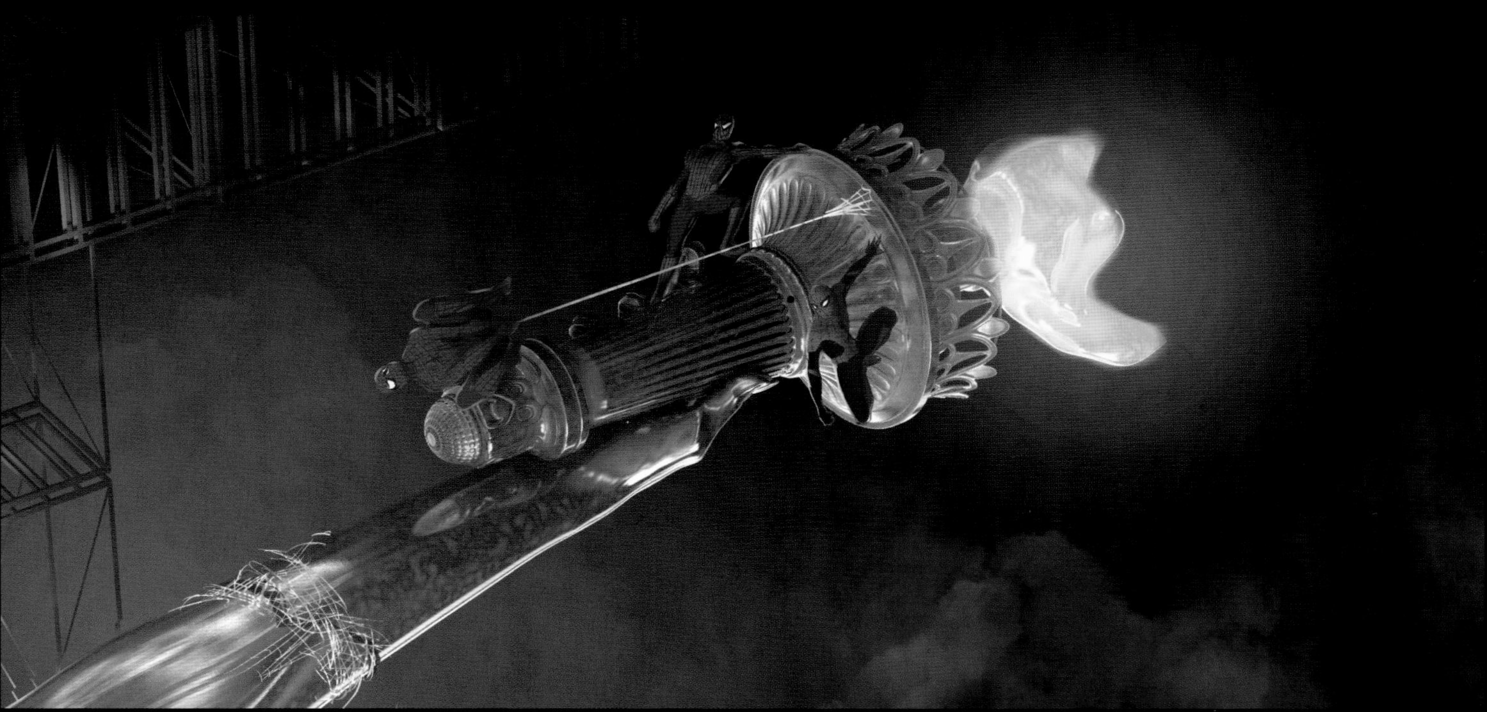

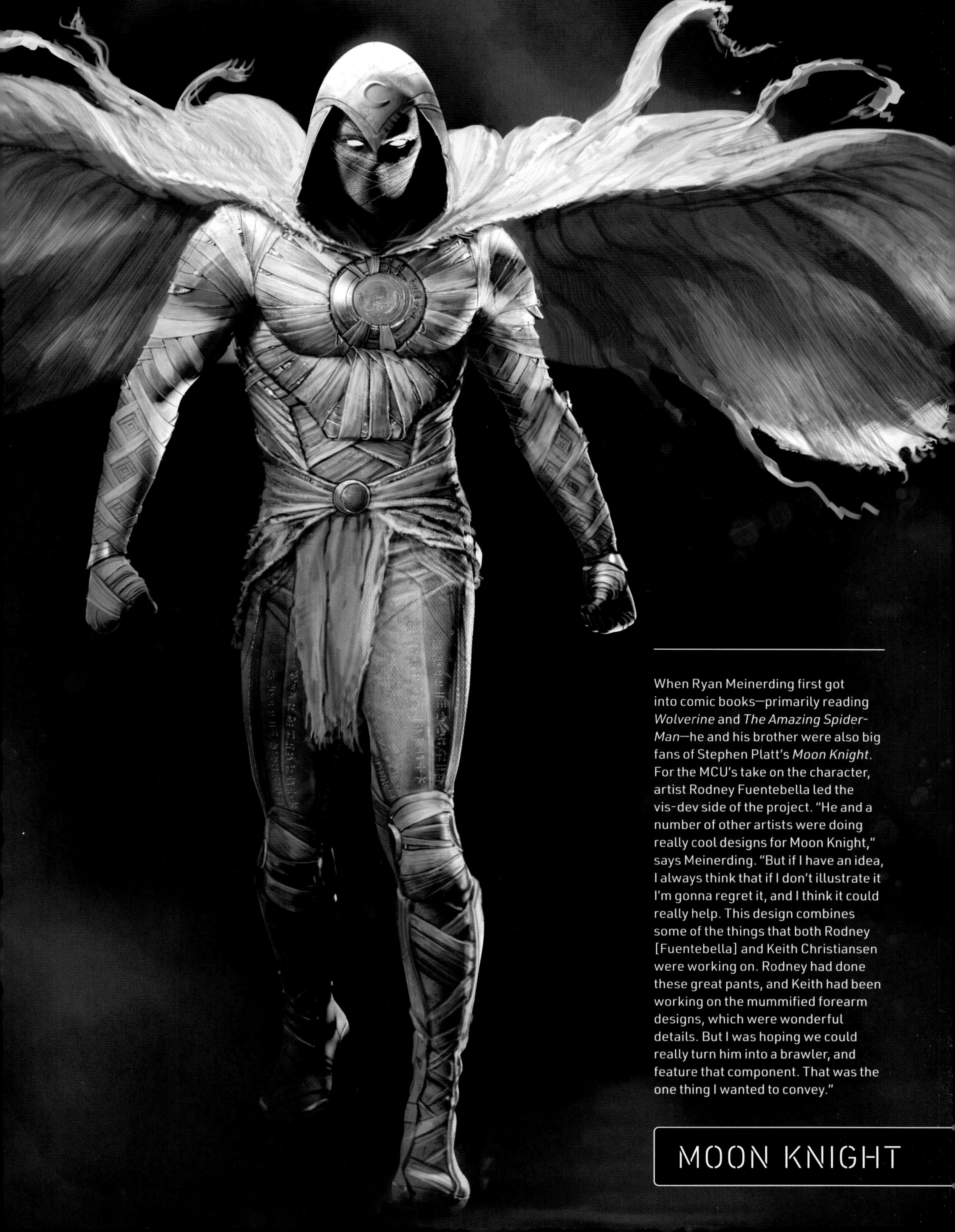

When Ryan Meinerding first got into comic books—primarily reading *Wolverine* and *The Amazing Spider-Man*—he and his brother were also big fans of Stephen Platt's *Moon Knight*. For the MCU's take on the character, artist Rodney Fuentebella led the vis-dev side of the project. "He and a number of other artists were doing really cool designs for Moon Knight," says Meinerding. "But if I have an idea, I always think that if I don't illustrate it I'm gonna regret it, and I think it could really help. This design combines some of the things that both Rodney [Fuentebella] and Keith Christiansen were working on. Rodney had done these great pants, and Keith had been working on the mummified forearm designs, which were wonderful details. But I was hoping we could really turn him into a brawler, and feature that component. That was the one thing I wanted to convey."

MOON KNIGHT

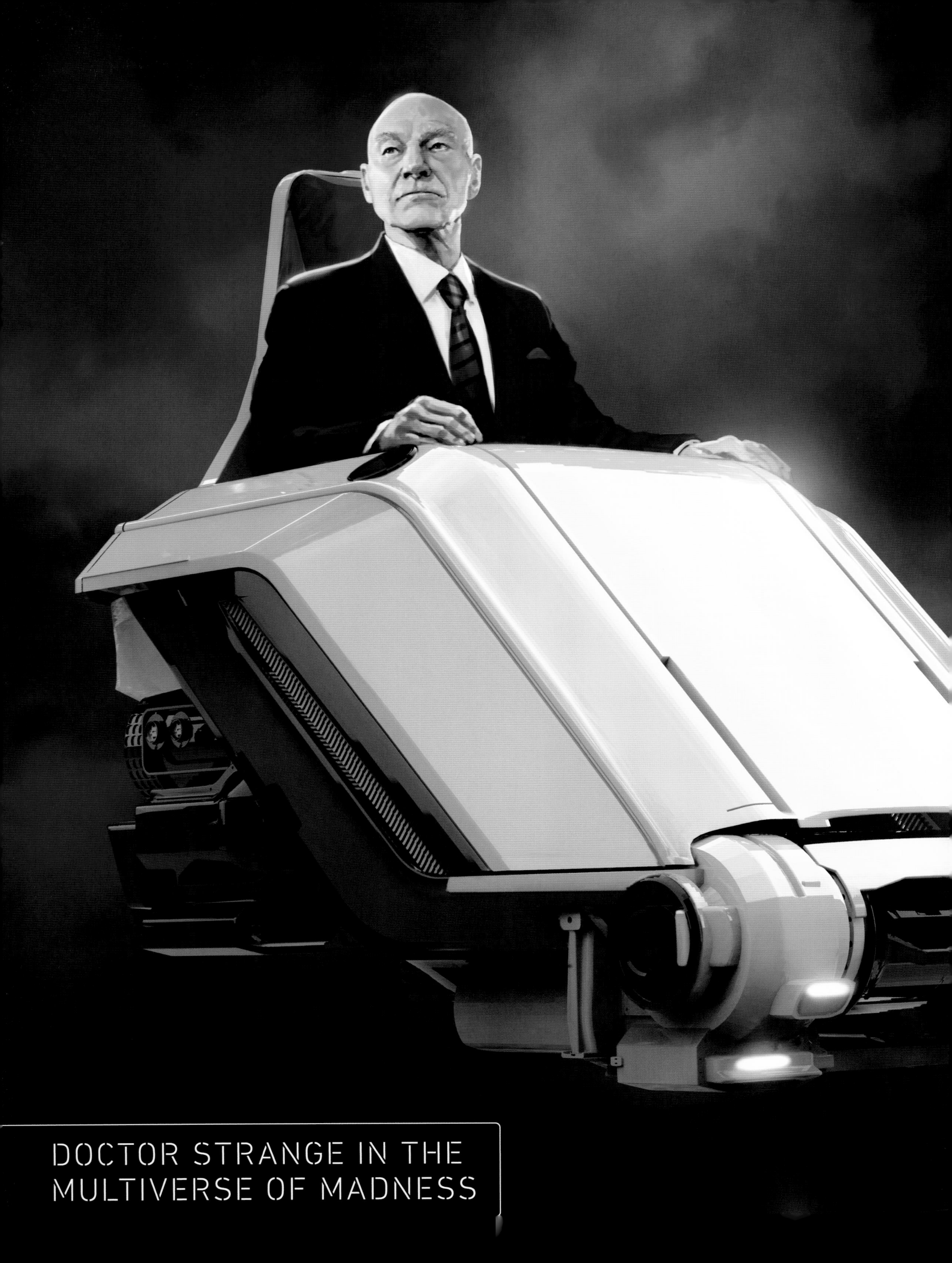

DOCTOR STRANGE IN THE
MULTIVERSE OF MADNESS

Ian Joyner led the vis-dev work on *Doctor Strange in the Multiverse of Madness*, with Ryan Meinerding overseeing what was being produced. "Ian suggested adding Professor X and Mr. Fantastic to the version of The Illuminati we meet in this film," says Meinerding. "When I heard they wanted to keep Charles Xavier's wheel-chair very close to the design of the hover chair from the 1990s *X-Men: The Animated Series*, I did one that was straight-up from the cartoon. But *Strange 2* production designer Charlie Wood's team ended up designing the final version. Then I rendered it and put it in with this painting of Patrick Stewart."

The announcement that a variant of Captain Peggy Carter would also serve on the board of The Illuminati was thrilling music to Meinerding's ears. But her design could not be a straight copy of the Captain Carter design from *What If...?* "That Captain Carter design is from an animated series where she has incredibly heroic proportions that are not based around normal human proportions," details Meinerding. "It's not based on Hayley [Atwell]'s body type. So what I was doing was actually trying to place her next to other characters to see how tall they wanted to make this live-action variant of Captain Carter. Do they want to make her taller than six feet? How augmented would her body be from the super soldier serum? And it's important that her design still read as Hayley, which I'm pleased it does."

The moment John Krasinski's casting of this Reed Richards/Mr. Fantastic variant was confirmed, Meinerding did multiple versions of his costume to find a different aesthetic than how the character had previously been seen on screen. "I was pitching that the black and the blue sections stretched at different rates," he notes. "The black parts wouldn't stretch as much, so when the blue pattern expanded, there would be some slippage underneath. It was more like mechanical plates separating in some ways."

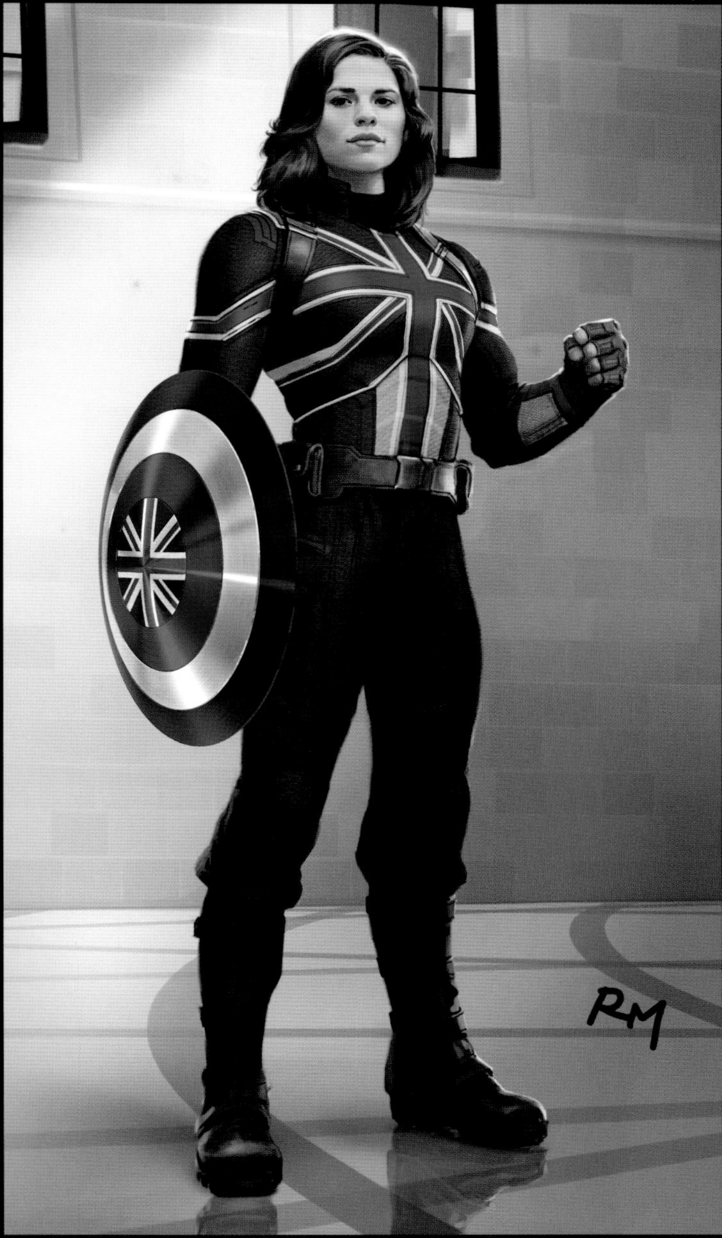
RM

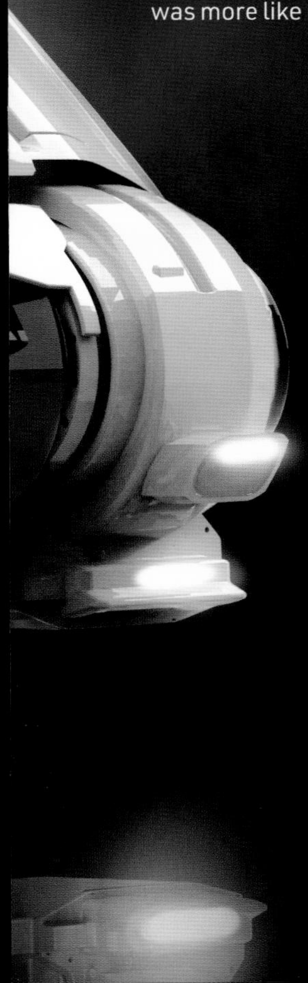

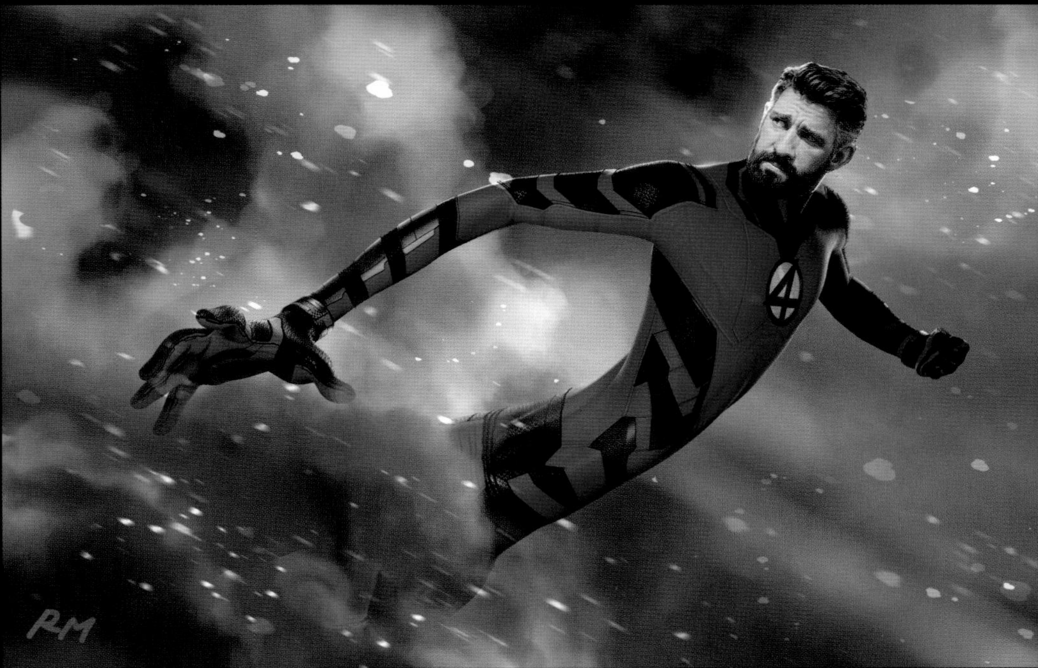
RM

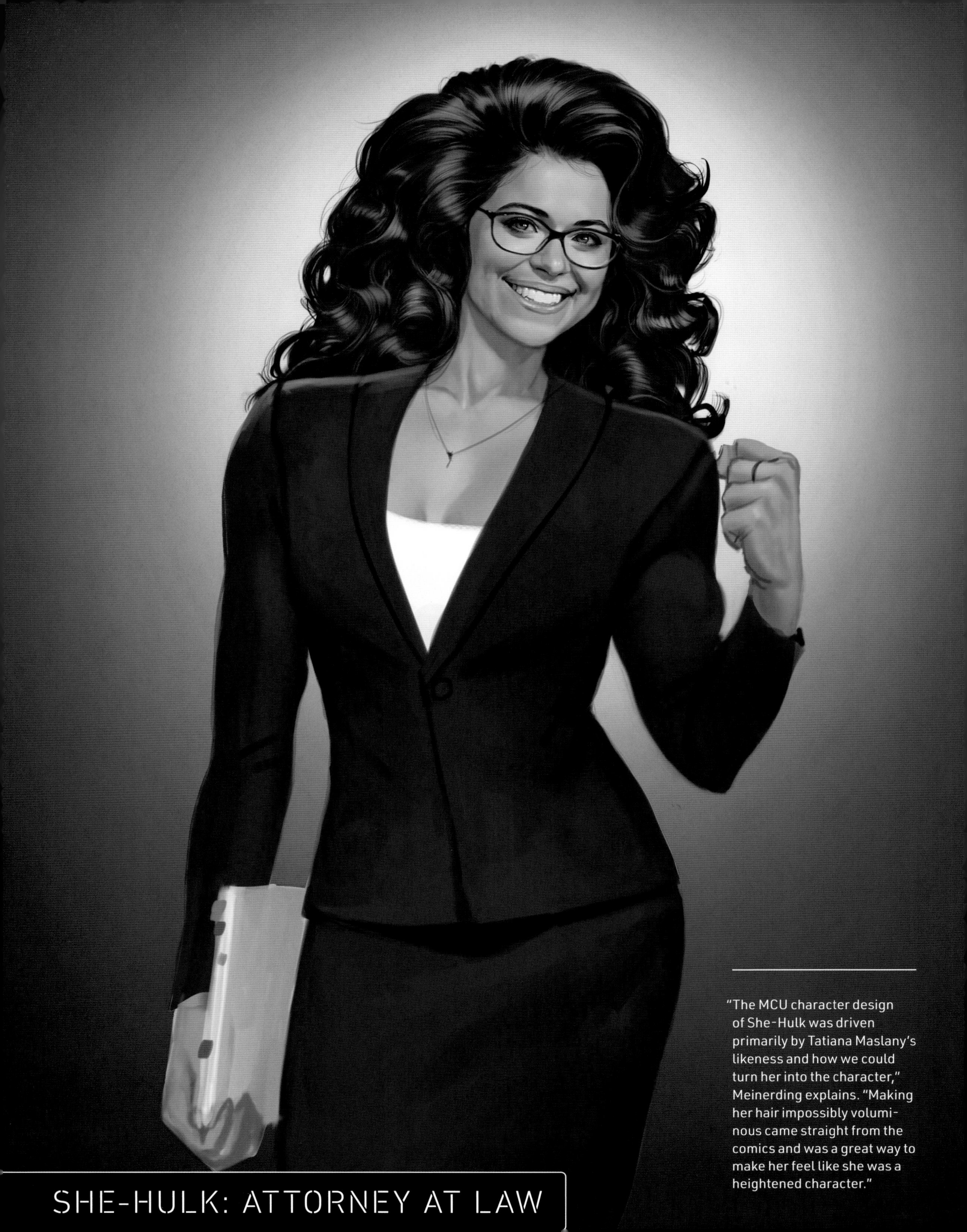

"The MCU character design of She-Hulk was driven primarily by Tatiana Maslany's likeness and how we could turn her into the character," Meinerding explains. "Making her hair impossibly voluminous came straight from the comics and was a great way to make her feel like she was a heightened character."

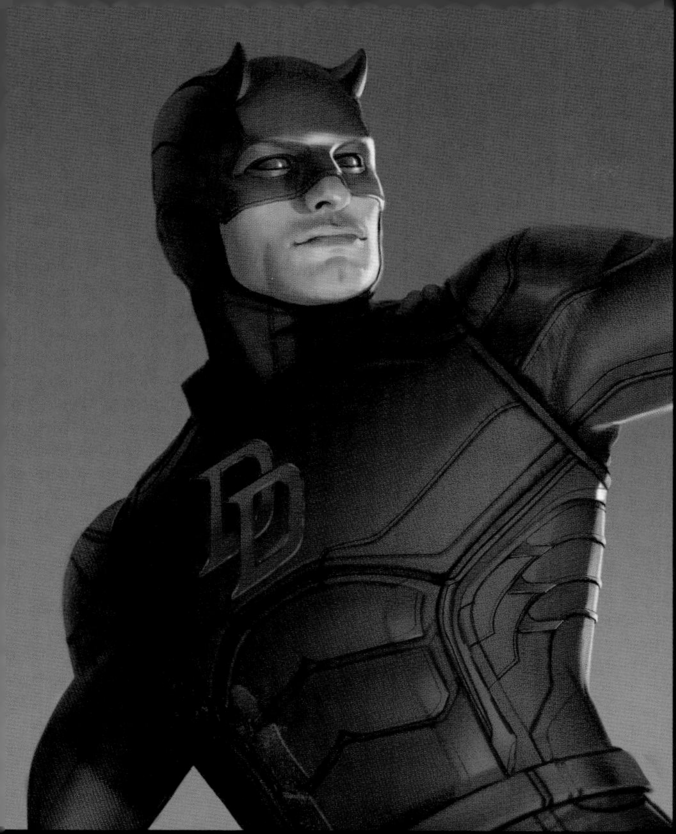

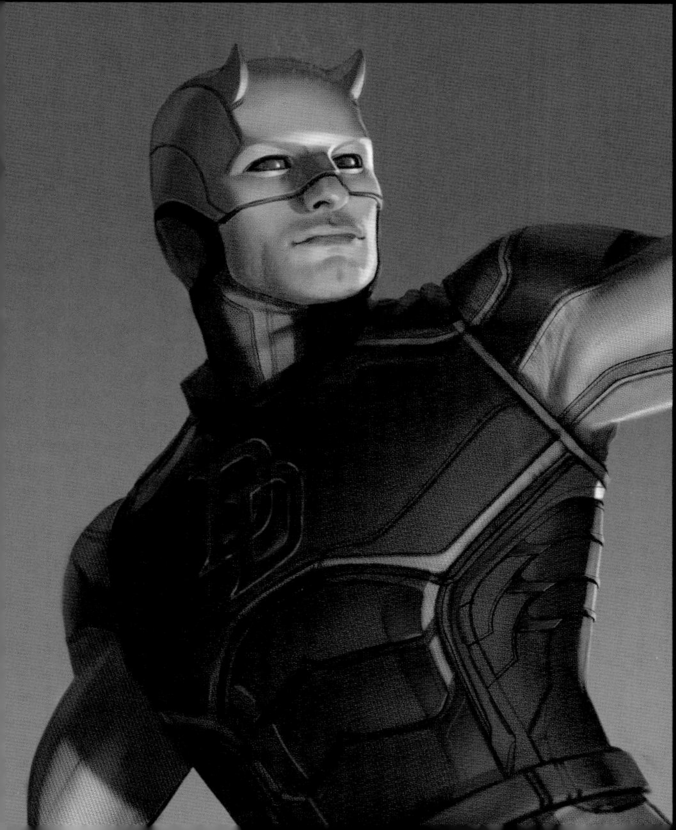

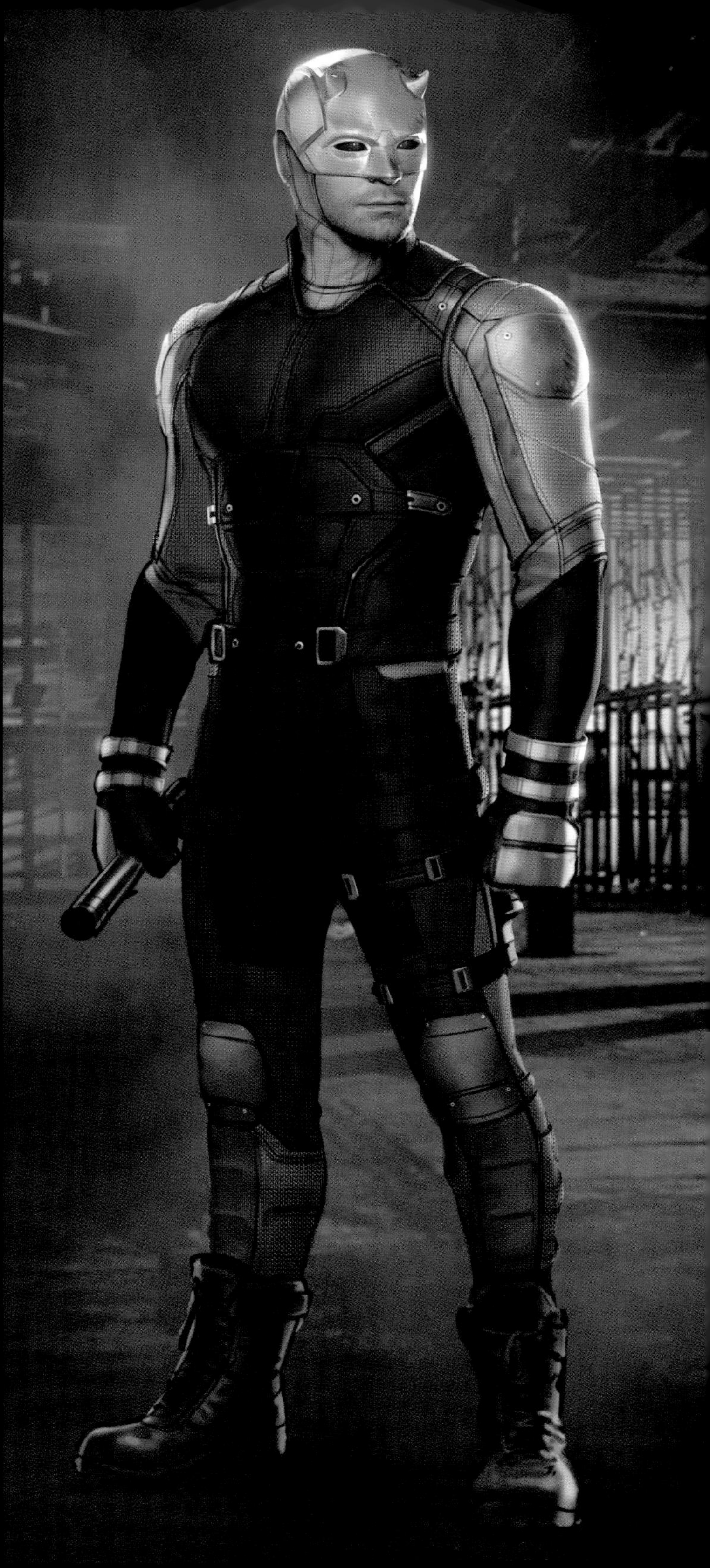

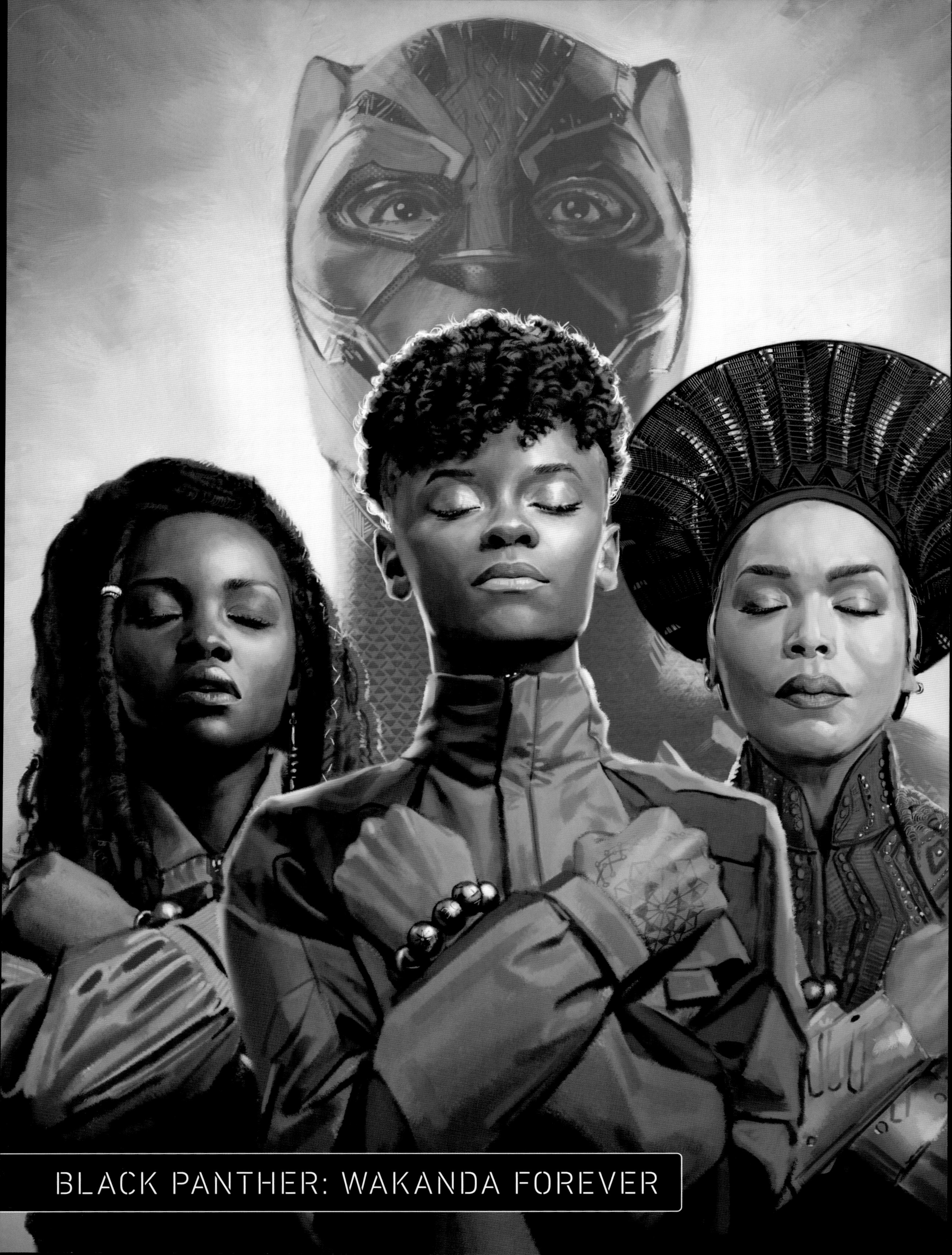

BLACK PANTHER: WAKANDA FOREVER

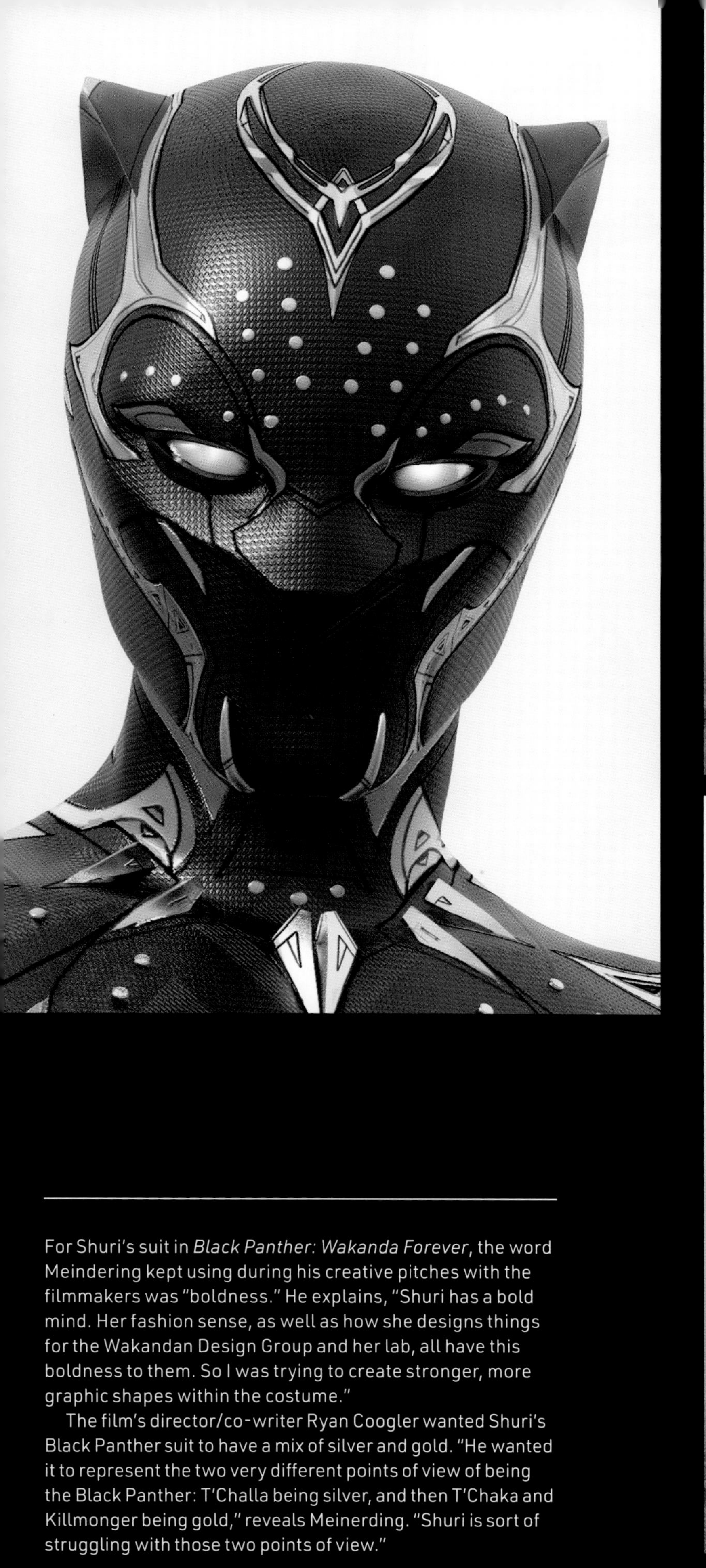

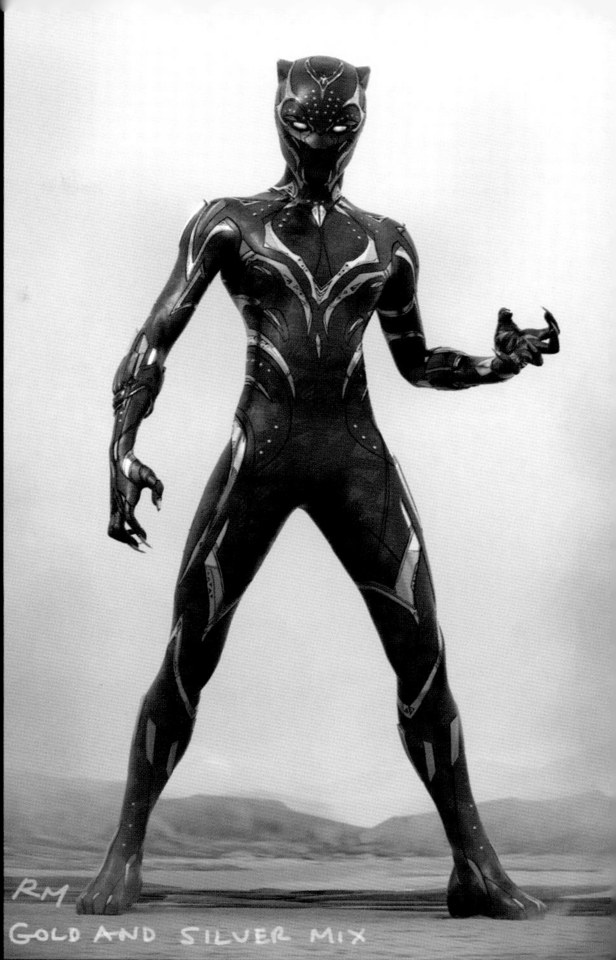
RM
GOLD AND SILVER MIX

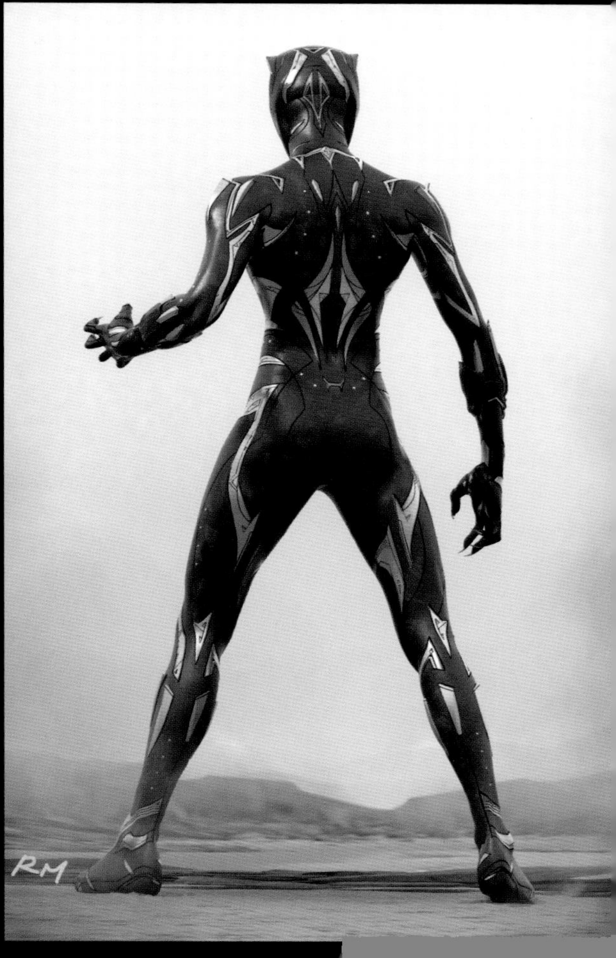
RM

For Shuri's suit in *Black Panther: Wakanda Forever*, the word Meindering kept using during his creative pitches with the filmmakers was "boldness." He explains, "Shuri has a bold mind. Her fashion sense, as well as how she designs things for the Wakandan Design Group and her lab, all have this boldness to them. So I was trying to create stronger, more graphic shapes within the costume."

The film's director/co-writer Ryan Coogler wanted Shuri's Black Panther suit to have a mix of silver and gold. "He wanted it to represent the two very different points of view of being the Black Panther: T'Challa being silver, and then T'Chaka and Killmonger being gold," reveals Meinerding. "Shuri is sort of struggling with those two points of view."

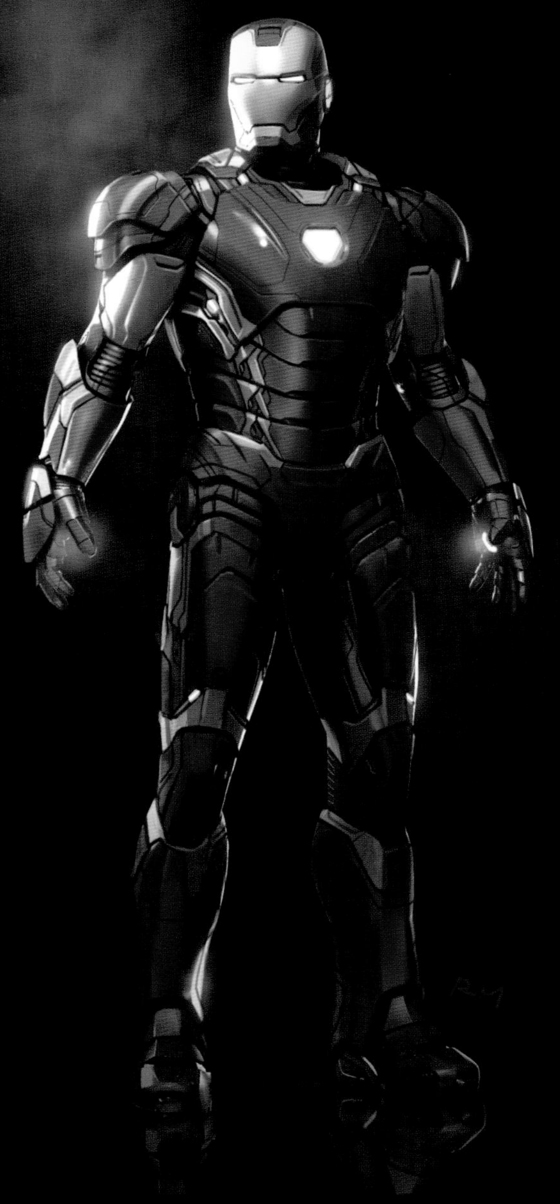

Ryan Meinerding has been involved with the visual development of the MCU's presence at Disney theme parks all the way back to the 2017 opening of the Iron Man Experience at Hong Kong Disneyland. Several years before this, and during the ride's development—when Marvel Studios was based in Manhattan Beach—Meinerding regularly drove up to visit the Walt Disney Imagineering team in Burbank to discuss their designs for the Hydra ride vehicle. Fast-forward to the development of Avengers Campus and, the artist says, "What the MCU does, both story-wise and visually, is very specific, and so, naturally, Kevin [Feige] wants some oversight—kind of an 'MCU eye' on things. He asks me to take a look at park projects and try and help. So I was involved from the very earliest stages. It has always been a joy to work with the Imagineering team." Meinerding's Visual Development department was heavily involved with WEB SLINGERS: A Spider-Man Adventure at Avengers Campus. "I designed the suit, we collaborated to design the ride vehicle, and Rodney Fuentebella designed the Spider-Bot and a number of the sets within the queue experience."

This Iron Man design was for an animatronic Mark XL-era suit that is part of the queue experience at Avengers Campus Disneyland Paris. "It was an interesting design experience because they needed the gaps and the plates to be wider for the animatronic's movement," details Meinerding. "Coming up with an Iron Man suit design that would work for that brief was a unique challenge."

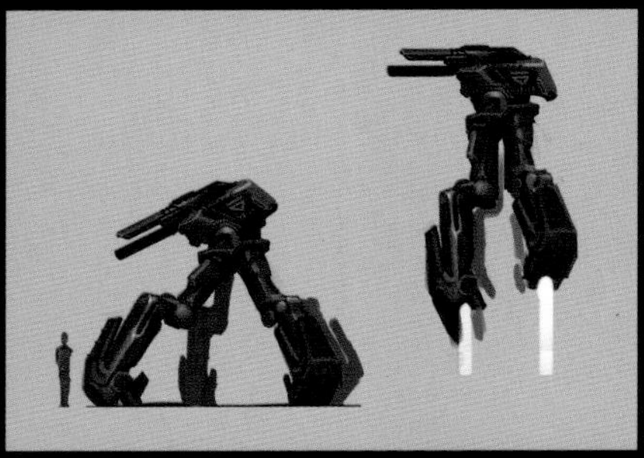

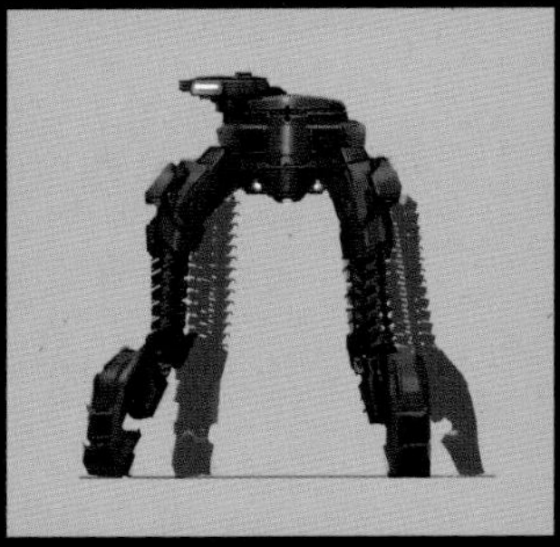

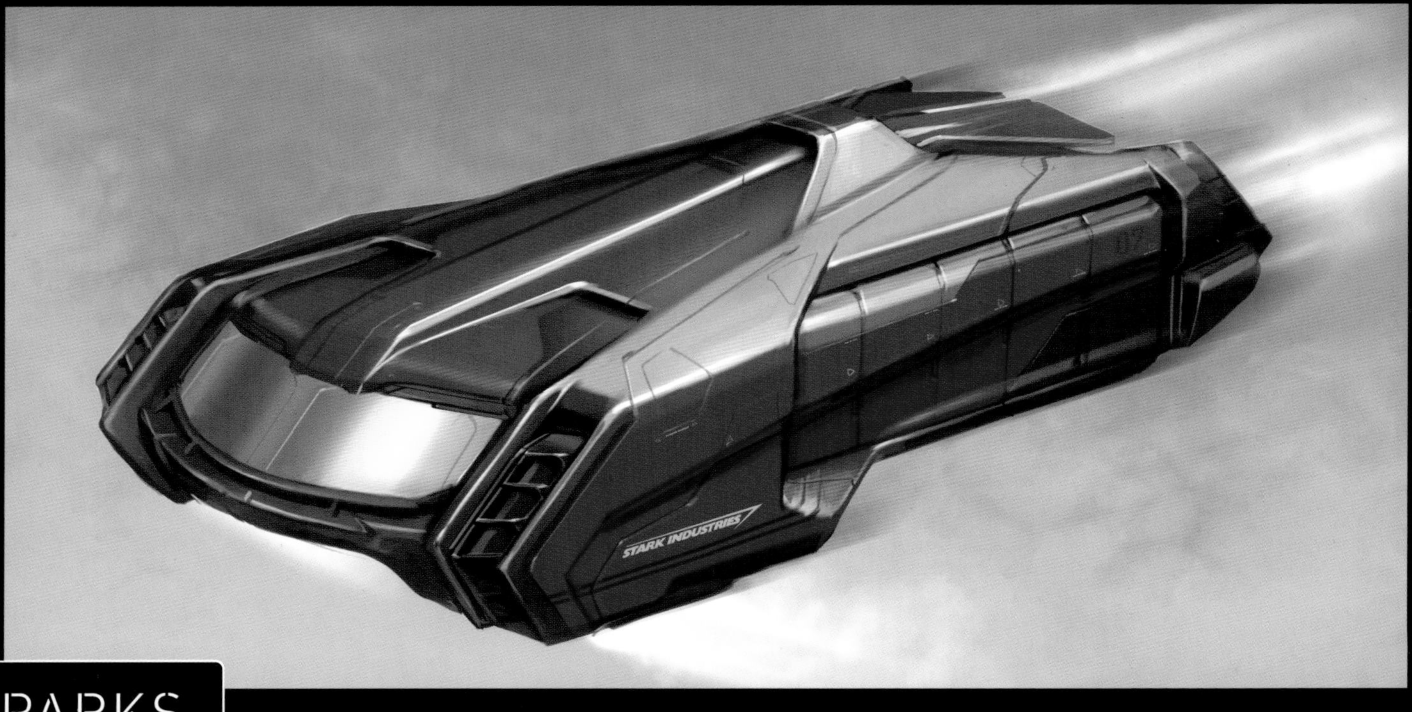
STARK INDUSTRIES

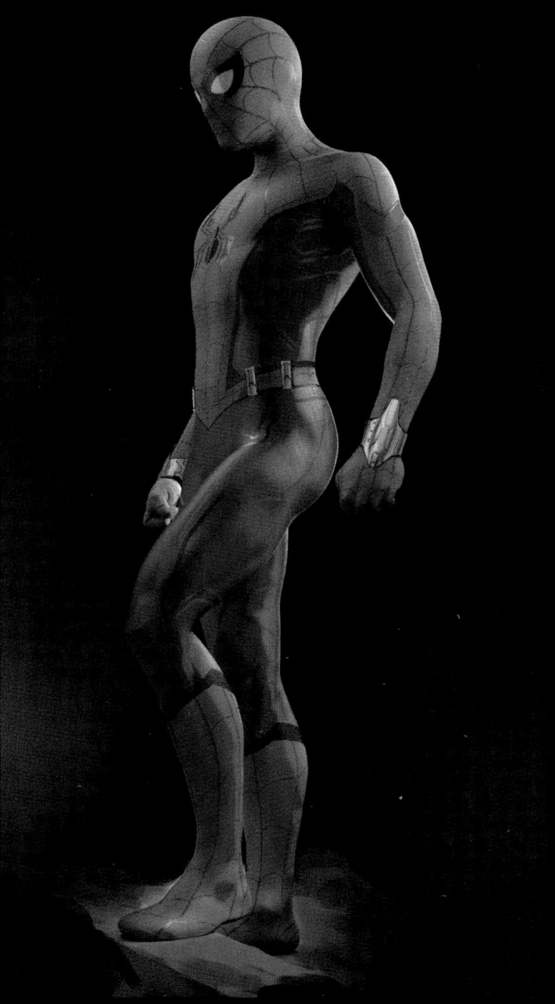

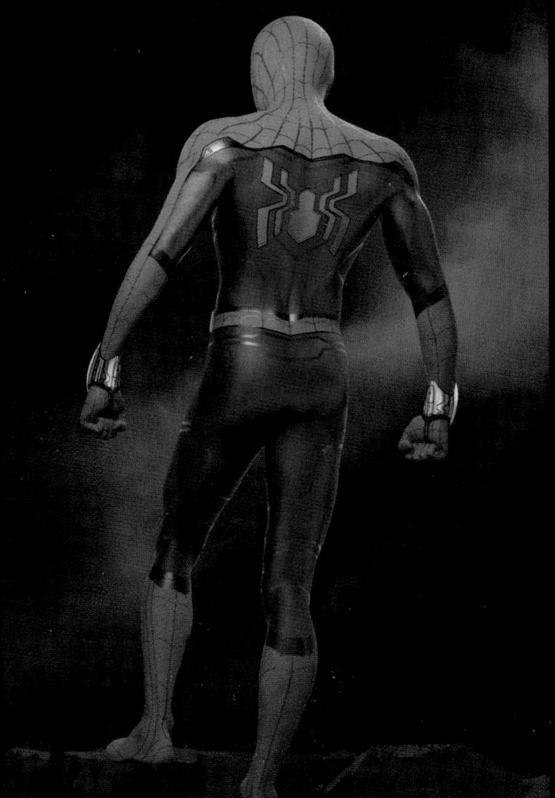
NEW LINES

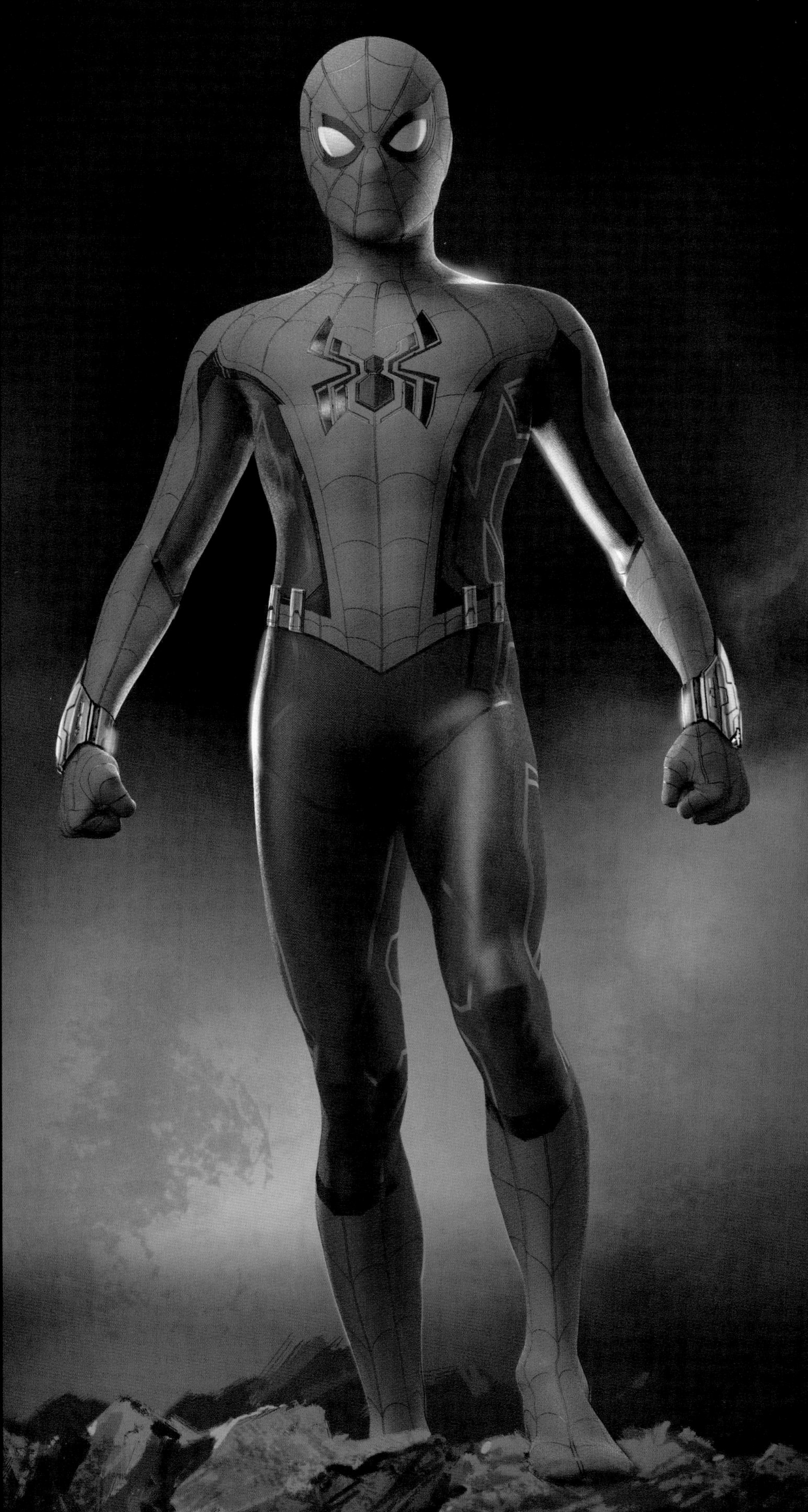

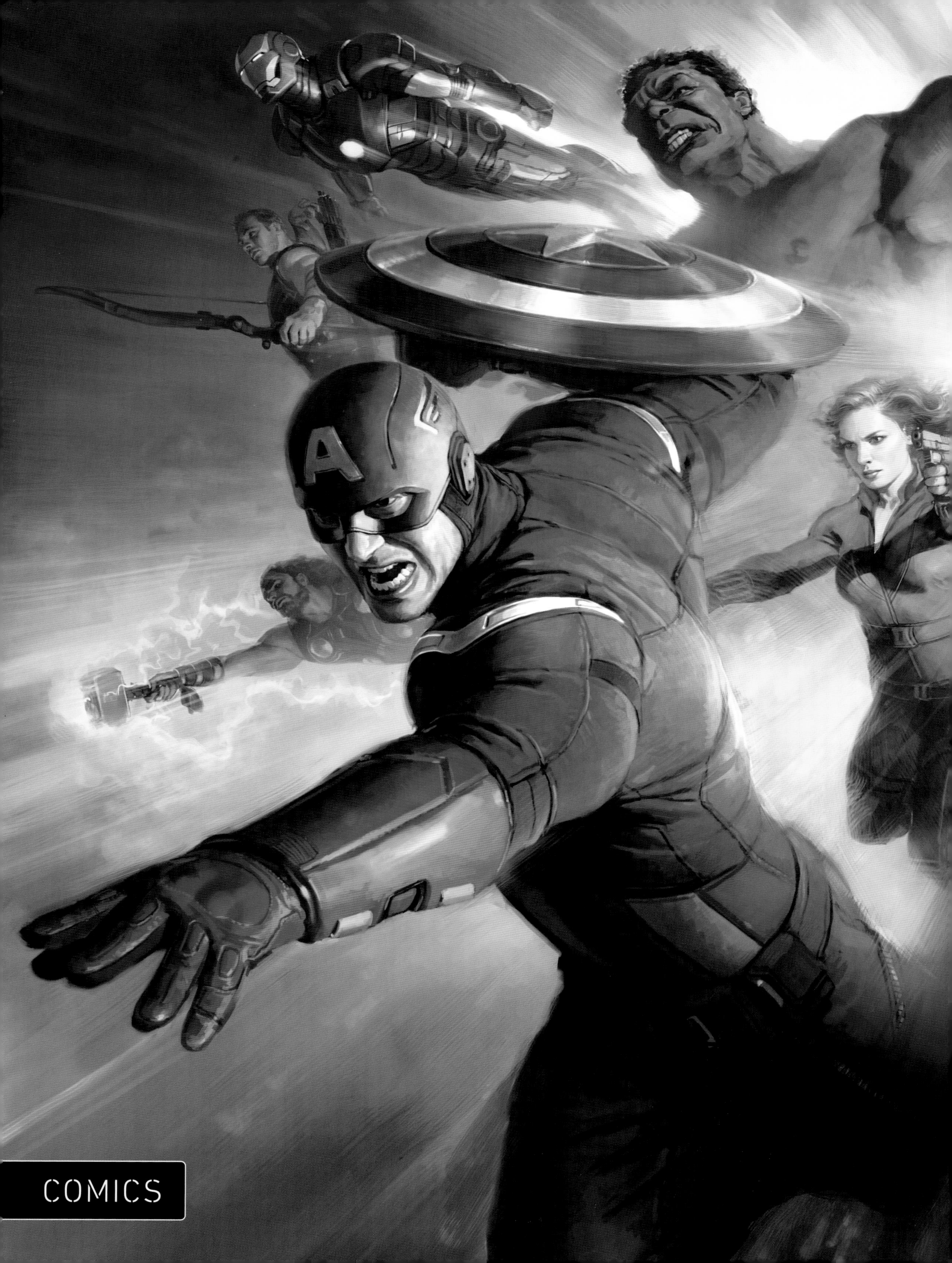

COMICS

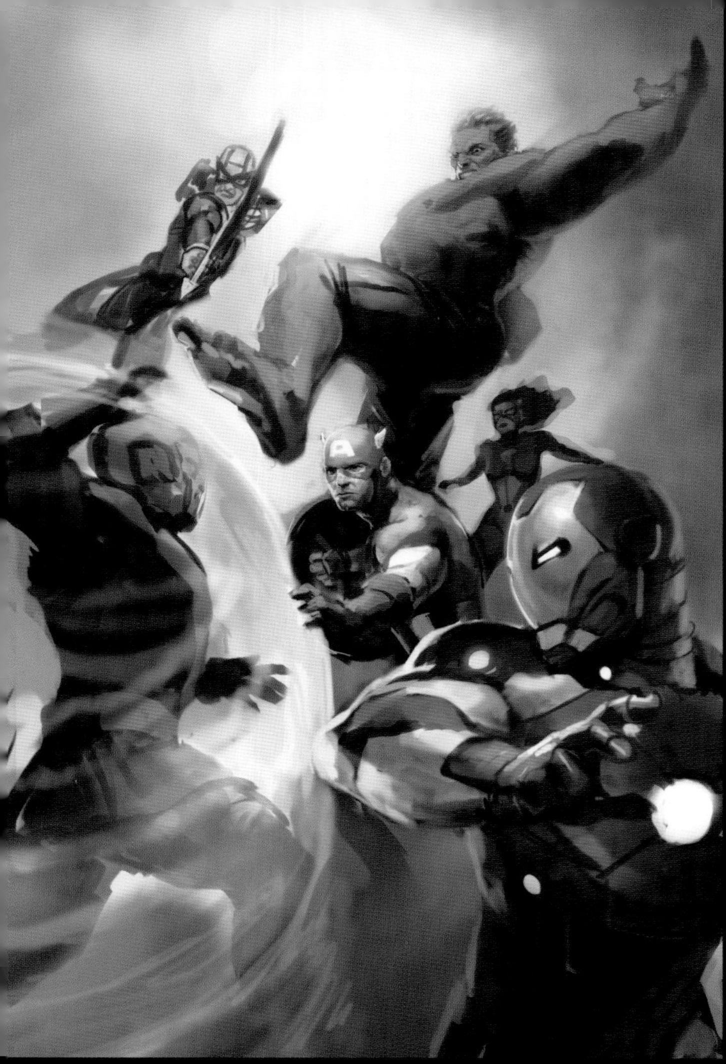

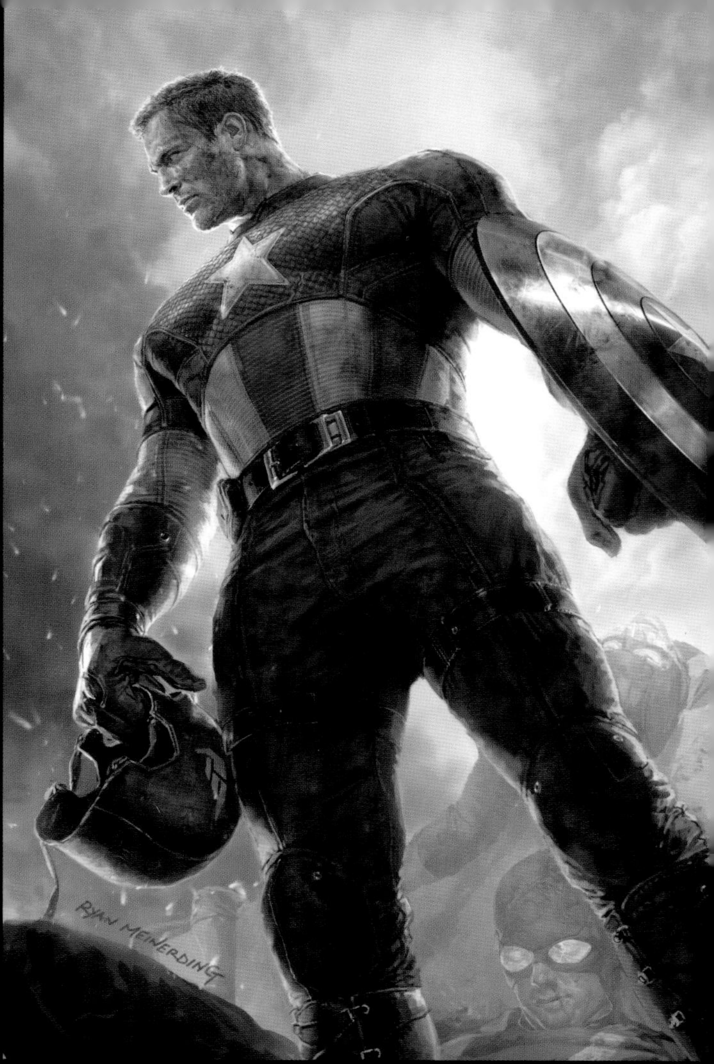
RYAN MEINERDING

"Covers are really about the visual punch, which is why they're fun to do," says Meinerding. "How can you make the character look iconic and amazing, and at the same time make people want to buy the book?"

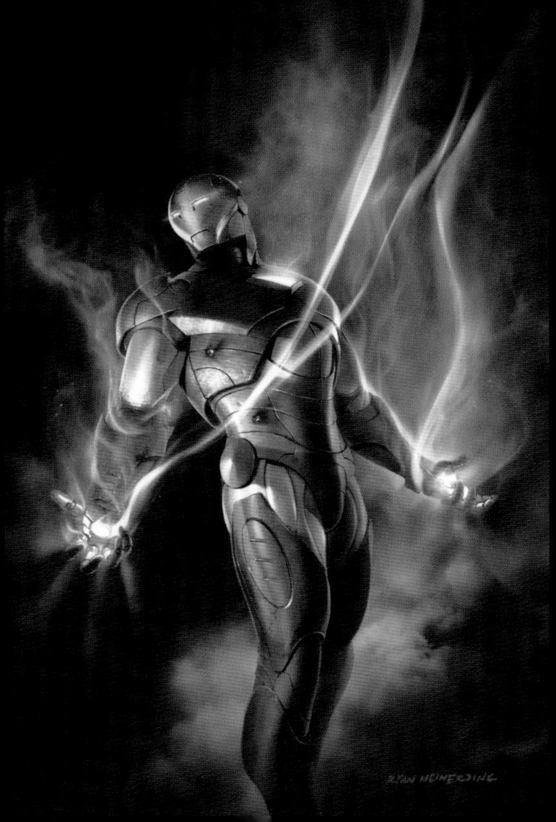

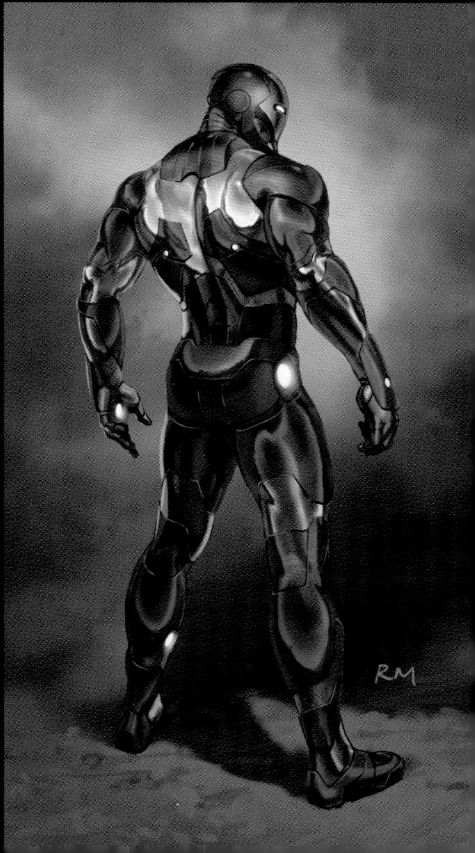
RM

OPPOSITE This team-up painting was displayed at the Marvel Studios art exhibition at Les Arts Ludiques Musée in Paris, France, which ran from March 22 through August 31, 2014.

THIS PAGE, CLOCKWISE FROM TOP LEFT Sketch of *The Avengers* (2010) #18; *Captain America* (2012) #1; *The Invincible Iron Man* (2010) #25; *The Invincible Iron Man* (2008) #5

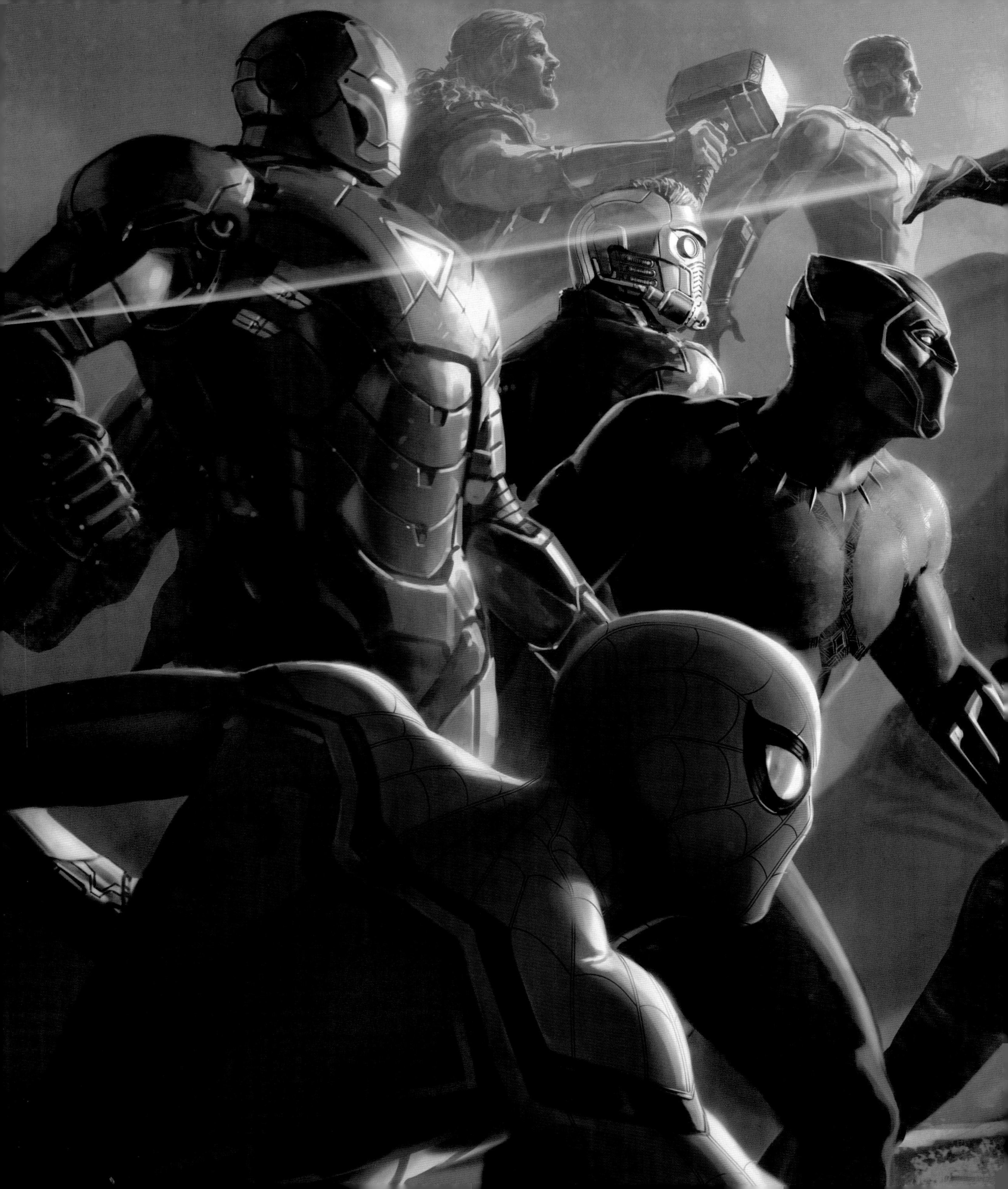

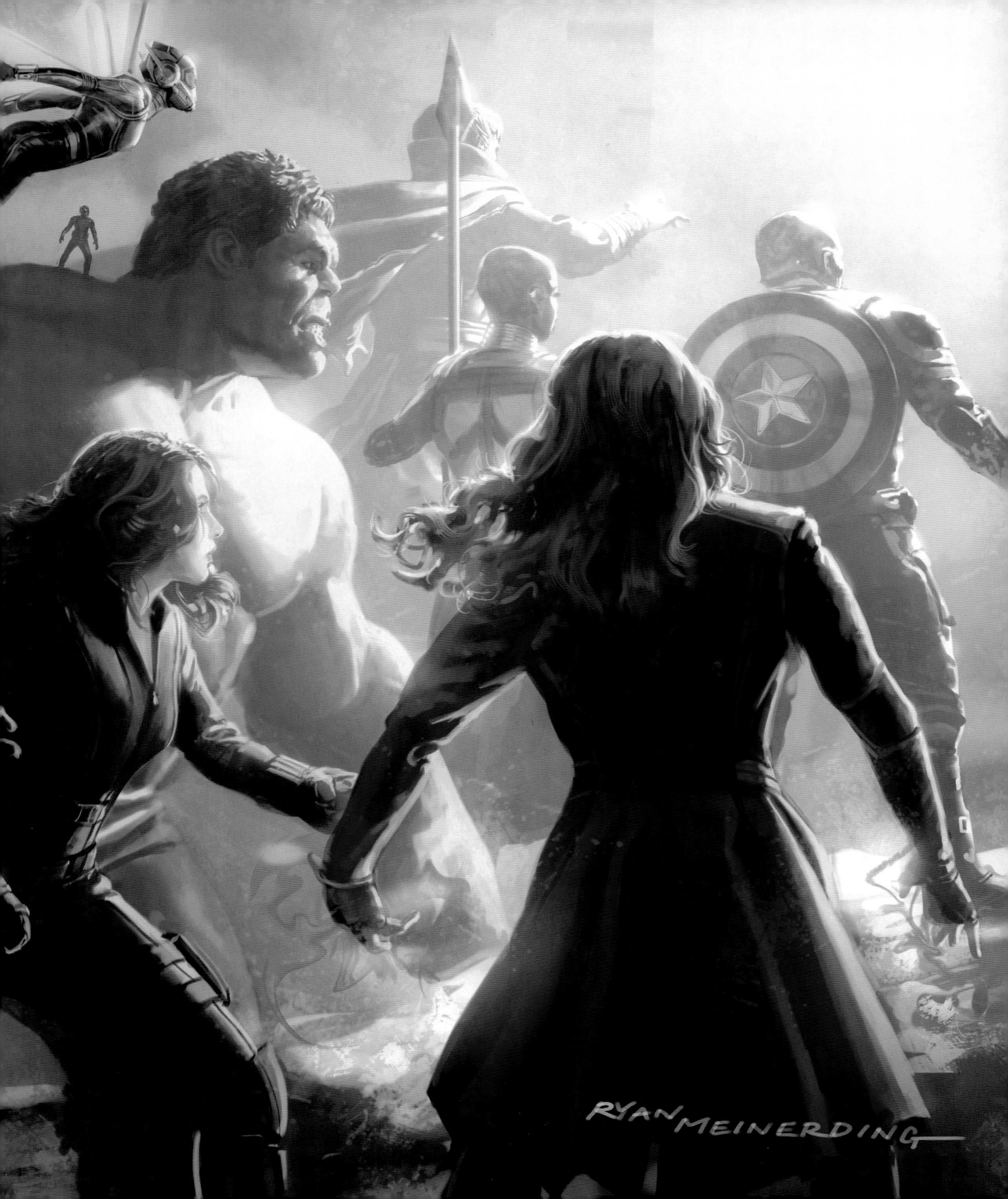
RYAN MEINERDING

OPPOSITE For the tribute to Spider-Man co-creator/artist Steve Ditko (who passed away in 2018), Meinerding notes, "The costume eyes that we had in the Tom Holland suit around this time were more geared toward the John Romita Sr.–style eye. I made sure the eye here matched the Ditko style more directly."

PAGE 320 Titled "I Love You 3,000" and created for D23 Expo 2019, this was Meinerding's celebration of Robert Downey Jr.'s Tony Stark journey from *Iron Man* to *Avengers: Endgame*. "And it was a chance to do sort of a sister piece to a poster I had done for the rerelease of *The Art of Iron Man* book, with a similar halo effect on both pieces," he explains. "It was a lot of fun to go back through all the appearances of Tony Stark/Iron Man in the MCU, choose iconic moments from his entire journey, and put them all together." Which also makes this the perfect image to end this celebration of Meinerding's artistic career with Marvel Studios during its first four phases. "I don't know if I could've written a script for the career that I wanted to have that would've allowed me to work on more things that engage and interest me and would be so well represented on screen," he says. "It's a crazy journey. It's a crazy career."

Thank you to Kevin and Lou for giving me a chance and trusting me for almost twenty years.

Thank you to my wife and kids for endlessly inspiring me and being more understanding about my working hours than I deserve. I love you.

Thank you to my parents for giving me a wonderful childhood and supporting creative aspirations I still can't believe you believed in.

Thank you to my brother for giving me a love of comics and for being my brother.

Thank you to Jon Favreau for seeing something in my work and opening so many doors for me.

Thank you to Iain McCaig for being my hero and good friend.

Thank you to my team—I couldn't have had a more amazing, more talented group of people to spend fifteen years working on movies with. Andy Park, Rodney Fuentebella, Jackson Sze, Ian Joyner, Jana Schirmer, Wes Burt, Naomi Baker, Ji Hye Lee, Mushk Rizvi, Joshua James Shaw, Adam Ross, and John Staub—I consider myself so lucky to work with all of you every day.

Thank you to Phil Saunders, Josh Nizzi, Adi Granov, Karla Ortiz, and the many artists who have shared their brilliant creativity and skill on this MCU journey over the years.

Thank you to all the amazing teachers I've been lucky enough to learn from—Ty Palmer, Paul Down, Dallas Good, and Richard Keyes, to name a few.

Thank you to Sam Ballard and Sam Vinzon, AJ Vargas, Holly Myer, and Kelly Burroughs for helping me get everything together for this book.

Thank you to Tara and Paul for talking through my years at Marvel Studios and writing this amazing book. You are awesome people, incredible collaborators, and wonderful writers.

Thank you to all of the Marvel comic artists whose work I'm fortunate enough to reference every day.

Thank you to the teams at Marvel Studios, Marvel Publishing, and Abrams for all of the help in bringing this book to life.

— Ryan Meinerding

Tara Bennett is a *New York Times* bestselling author and entertainment journalist. As an author or co-author, she's written more than 30 official movie and TV companion books, including: *The Art of Avatar: The Way of Water*; *The Story of Marvel Studios: The Making of the Marvel Cinematic Universe*; *Sons of Anarchy: The Official Collector's Edition*; *Outlander: The Series* official guides; *The Official Making of Big Trouble in Little China*; *Fringe: September's Notebook* (an Amazon Best Book of 2013); and many more. Tara is also the US editor for *SFX Magazine*, a contributing writer for Syfy Wire, NBC Insider, IGN, Paste, and others, and is a member of the TCA.

Paul Terry is a bestselling author, producer, and music artist. He concept-created/wrote the award-winning book series *The X-Files: The Official Archives*. Terry also co-authored (with Tara Bennett) *The Story of Marvel Studios: The Making of the Marvel Cinematic Universe*, *Fringe: September's Notebook*, and many more official film/TV companions. As a composer, Paul's scores include the multi-award-winning feature documentary *Sidney & Friends* (which he also executive produced), *Dave Stevens: Drawn to Perfection*, and NBCUniversal's *Behind the Panel*. Under the alias of Aptøsrs, his albums include *Elders* (mixed by Adam Noble). His other solo project, Cellarscape, includes the Independent Music Award-nominated album *The Act of Letting Go*.

Special thanks to Ryan Meinerding, Kevin Feige, Louis D'Esposito, Kristy Amornkul, Sarah Beers, Kelly Burroughs, Capri Ciulla, Erika Denton, Samantha Douglas, Jennifer Giandalone, Nigel Goodwin, Eli Holmes, Daryn Houston, Holly Myer, Ryan Potter, Jacqueline Ryan-Rudolph, Samantha Vinzon, Jeff Willis, and Jennifer Wojnar.

MARVEL PUBLISHING
VP, PRODUCTION AND SPECIAL PROJECTS Jeff Youngquist
EDITOR, SPECIAL PROJECTS Sarah Singer
MANAGER, LICENSED PUBLISHING Jeremy West
VP, LICENSED PUBLISHING Sven Larsen
SVP PRINT, SALES & MARKETING David Gabriel
EDITOR IN CHIEF C.B. Cebulski

ABRAMS BOOKS
EDITOR Connor Leonard
DESIGNER Liam Flanagan
MANAGING EDITOR Jan Hughes
PRODUCTION MANAGER Kathleen Gaffney

TRANSCRIBER Lori Dean Arias
PROOFREADER Erin Slonaker

Library of Congress Control Number: 2018958274

ISBN: 978-1-4197-3864-7

Limited edition ISBN: 978-1-4197-7854-4

MARVEL

Published in 2024 by Abrams, an imprint of ABRAMS.

Printed and bound in China
10 9 8 7 6 5 4 3 2 1

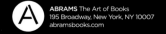

ABRAMS The Art of Books
195 Broadway, New York, NY 10007
abramsbooks.com